The Cambridge Handbook of Creativity and Emotions

The Cambridge Handbook of Creativity and Emotions provides a state-of-the-art review of research on the role of emotions in creativity. This volume presents the insights and perspectives of 60 creativity scholars from 13 countries who span multiple disciplines, including developmental, social, and personality psychology; industrial and organizational psychology; neuroscience; education; art therapy; and sociology. It discusses affective processes – emotion states, traits, and emotion abilities – in relation to the creative process, person, and product, as well as two major contexts for expression of creativity: school, and work. It is a go-to source for scholars who need to enhance their understanding of a specific topic relating to creativity and emotion, and it provides students and researchers with a comprehensive introduction to creativity and emotion broadly.

ZORANA IVCEVIC is a Senior Research Scientist at Yale University, USA. She has published more than 70 articles and book chapters and her work has been featured in the *Harvard Business Review*, ArtNet, *US News*, *Education Week*, *El Pais*, and others. She received the Award for Excellence in Research from the Mensa Education and Research Foundation, and the Berlyne Award for Outstanding Early Career Achievement from the American Psychological Association.

JESSICA HOFFMANN is a Research Scientist at Yale University and Director of Adolescent Initiatives at the Yale Center for Emotional Intelligence, USA. She is the co-creator of two social-emotional learning approaches (RULER & inspirED), used worldwide by over 3,000 schools, and co-editor of *The Cambridge Handbook of Lifespan Development of Creativity* (2021).

JAMES C. KAUFMAN is a Professor of Educational Psychology at the Neag School of Education at University of Connecticut, USA. He is the author/editor of more than 50 books, including *The Cambridge Handbook of Creativity* and the forthcoming *The Creativity Advantage*, and more than 400 papers.

Cambridge Handbooks in Psychology

The Cambridge Handbook of Creativity and Emotions

Edited by

Zorana Ivcevic
Yale University

Jessica D. Hoffmann
Yale University

James C. Kaufman
University of Connecticut

CAMBRIDGE
UNIVERSITY PRESS

Shaftesbury Road, Cambridge CB2 8EA, United Kingdom

One Liberty Plaza, 20th Floor, New York, NY 10006, USA

477 Williamstown Road, Port Melbourne, VIC 3207, Australia

314 321, 3rd Floor, Plot 3, Splendor Forum, Jasola District Centre,
New Delhi – 110025, India

103 Penang Road, #05–06/07, Visioncrest Commercial, Singapore 238467

Cambridge University Press is part of Cambridge University Press & Assessment,
a department of the University of Cambridge.

We share the University's mission to contribute to society through the pursuit of
education, learning and research at the highest international levels of excellence.

www.cambridge.org
Information on this title: www.cambridge.org/9781316515952

DOI: 10.1017/9781009031240

First published 2023

A catalogue record for this publication is available from the British Library.

Library of Congress Cataloging-in-Publication Data
Names: Ivcevic, Zorana, editor. | Hoffmann, Jessica D., editor. | Kaufman, James
    C., editor.
Title: The Cambridge handbook of creativity and emotions / edited by Zorana Ivcevic, Yale
    University, Connecticut, Jessica D. Hoffmann, Yale University, Connecticut, James
    C. Kaufman, University of Connecticut
Description: Cambridge, United Kingdom ; New York, NY : Cambridge University Press,
    2023. | Includes bibliographical references and index.
Identifiers: LCCN 2022029329 (print) | LCCN 2022029330 (ebook) | ISBN 9781316515952
    (hardback) | ISBN 9781009013086 (paperback) | ISBN 9781009031240 (epub)
Subjects: LCSH: Creative ability. | Emotions.
Classification: LCC BF408 .C17328 2023 (print) | LCC BF408 (ebook) |
    DDC 153.3/5–dc23/eng/20220705
LC record available at https://lccn.loc.gov/2022029329
LC ebook record available at https://lccn.loc.gov/2022029330

ISBN 978-1-316-51595-2 Hardback
ISBN 978-1-009-01308-6 Paperback

Dedications

For my husband, Jamie Pringle, and son, Alex Pringle, who are my loves and my models of creativity

– ZI

For my husband, Aaron, and sons, Asher and Finley, who bring me endless joy, love, and creative inspiration

– JDH

For Vlad Glăveanu,

A brilliant scholar who has become not only a treasured collaborator but one of my very favorite people in the world

– JCK

Contents

Figures

Tables

Contributors
(Alphabetical)

RODRIGO ALDAY, University Adolfo Ibáñez

ROSS C. ANDERSON, Inflexion and Oregon Research Institute

NEAL M. ASHKANASY, The University of Queensland

KIM N. AWA, University of Arkansas

MATTHIJS BAAS, University of Amsterdam

RONALD A. BEGHETTO, Arizona State University

MARION BOTELLA, Université de Paris & Université Gustave Eiffel

EVANGELIA G. CHRYSIKOU, Drexel University

SHANE CONNELLY, University of Oklahoma

KATHERINE N. COTTER, University of Pennsylvania

RODICA IOANA DAMIAN, University of Houston

ELIF GIZEM DEMIRAG BURAK, Koç University

JENNIFER E. DRAKE, Brooklyn College and City University of New York

JOSEPH I. EISMAN, Temple University

KYLE EMICH, University of Delaware

POLINA ERMOSHKINA, Case Western Reserve University

MARIE FORGEARD, William James College and McLean Hospital/Harvard Medical School

DOMINIK GOŁĄB, Université Catholique de Louvain

THALIA R. GOLDSTEIN, George Mason University

ELIANA GROSSMAN, City University of New York

MICHAEL HANCHETT HANSON, Columbia University

JESSICA D. HOFFMANN, Yale University

MOLLY HOLINGER, Miami University

JENNIFER RUTH HOYDEN, Columbia University

KENT HUBERT, University of Arkansas

MIGUEL IBACETA, University of Manchester

ZORANA IVCEVIC, Yale University

DOROTA M. JANKOWSKA, The Maria Grzegorzewska University

EVA KAHANA, Case Western Reserve University

STEPHANIE J. KANE, University of Arkansas

HANSIKA KAPOOR, Monk Prayogshala and University of Connecticut

MACIEJ KARWOWSKI, University of Wroclaw

JEN KATZ-BUONINCONTRO, Drexel University

JAMES C. KAUFMAN, University of Connecticut

SHOSHI KEISARI, University of Haifa

ALEXANDRA E. KELLY, Drexel University

IZABELA LEBUDA, University of Wroclaw

SHENGJIE LIN, Yale University

TINGSHU LIU, University of Houston

LI LU, West Chester University

HECTOR MADRID, University Adolfo Ibáñez

URVI MANGE, Monk Prayogshala and Carl Von Ossietzky Universität Oldenburg

SEAN MCFARLAND, Yale University

MEAGAN MILLIER, University of Nebraska at Omaha

HOD ORKIBI, University of Haifa

MALCOLM PATTERSON, University of Sheffield

RONI REITER-PALMON, University of Nebraska at Omaha

SANDRA W. RUSS, Case Western Reserve University

ANNETTE C. SCHMIDT, Arizona State University

EVA SPECKER, University of Vienna

CARL E. STEVENS, Jr., University of Arkansas

MEGAN G. STUTESMAN, George Mason University

CHRISTA L. TAYLOR, University Catholique de Louvain

PABLO P. L. TINIO, Montclair State University

MARCH L. TO, University of Western Australia

RADEK TRNKA, Palacky University Olomouc and Prague College of Psychosocial Studies

JOSHUA D. UPSHAW, University of Arkansas

INDRE V. VISKONTAS, University of San Francisco

DARYA L. ZABELINA, University of Arkansas

ALEKSANDRA ZIELIŃSKA, University of Wroclaw

Acknowledgments

The authors would like to thank their editor, Stephen Acerra, and Rowan Groat at Cambridge University Press for their hard work and guidance in helping this book become a reality. Zorana and Jessica would like to thank Marc Brackett for countless conversations about emotions and how they matter. This Handbook was made possible with the support by Fundación Botín (Emotions, Creativity and the Arts grant to Zorana Ivcevic).

Creativity and Emotions

Introduction

Zorana Ivcevic, James C. Kaufman, Jessica D. Hoffmann, and Shengjie Lin

What are we talking about when discussing creativity and emotions? When we say that creative idea generation is more successful in positive energized moods (Baas et al., 2008), when we describe artists as emotionally sensitive (Feist, 1998), and when we say that emotion regulation ability mediates the relationship between creative potential and observed creativity (Ivcevic & Brackett, 2015), we are discussing different aspects of creativity and different aspects of the affective process. These examples point to the need for specification that creativity scholars have recommended for years (Baer, 1998; Glăveanu et al., 2020). In describing the relationship between creativity and emotions, there isn't a simple answer. Rather, we are putting together a puzzle in which each piece has its particular place. Although the topic of emotions is regularly discussed in major edited volumes on creativity, these chapters are by necessity limited. This volume aims to give a broad overview of the diverse questions examined by creativity scholars in relation to affective processes.

Because we take an expansive approach to the study of both creativity and emotions, we need to start with definitions of basic concepts. First, what is creativity? The standard definition of creativity (Runco & Jaeger, 2012) includes two parts: originality and effectiveness (sometimes referred to as appropriateness, usefulness, or meaningfulness). These criteria can be applied to creative thinking (original and effective ideas), self-concept (perceiving oneself as original and effective), or behavior (acting in ways that are both original and effective). Each of these aspects of creativity has different attributes. For instance, creative thinking is most often examined in terms of idea generation (and even more specifically, divergent thinking), but it also includes problem finding, convergent creative thinking, and idea evaluation (Barbot et al., 2016; Mumford et al., 1991). Self-concept of creativity includes constructs such as creative self-efficacy (Farmer & Tierney, 2017), attitudes toward creativity (Ivcevic & Hoffmann, 2021), and creative personality (Gough, 1979). And creative behavior is variously studied as the frequency of different creativity-relevant activities (Diedrich et al., 2018), level of creative achievement (Carson et al., 2005), observations by relevant others (supervisors, peers, or teachers; Grohman et al., 2017; Zhou & George, 2001), or actual creative products

This chapter was made possible with the support by the Botin Foundation (Emotions, Creativity and the Arts grant to Zorana Ivcevic).

(Amabile, 1996). Finally, although it is not fully clear to what extent creativity-relevant attributes and processes are domain-general or domain-specific, creativity visible in behavior and achievement is expressed in specific domains – people write novels, create sculptures, develop choreographies, found new enterprises, invent new gadgets, or test scientific theories (Kaufman et al., 2017). Creativity is studied in reference to a specific domain of work (e.g., creativity in screenplay writing, Bourgeois-Bougrine et al., 2014), embedded within a domain of work, but assumed as relatively domain-general (creativity at work, across multiple industries and roles; Amabile et al., 2005), or as domain-general (Silvia et al., 2021).

In defining affective processes, we can distinguish affective states, affective traits, and emotion abilities. Affective states are physiological and psychological experiences evoked by internal or external events and their appraisals, from relatively brief emotions to longer and more diffuse moods (Ellsworth & Scherer, 2003). Affective states vary along dimensions of hedonic tone or valence (from more intensely negative/unpleasant to neutral to more intensely positive/pleasant) and activation or arousal (ranging from low to high; Barrett, 2006). Thus, four distinct groups of affective states can be distinguished: positive activated (e.g., happy, delighted), positive deactivated (e.g., serene, satisfied), negative activated (e.g., angry, apprehensive), and negative deactivated (e.g., gloomy, bored). In addition, motivational aspects of affective experiences can be described as prevention- or promotion-oriented (Higgins, 2006; Klenk et al., 2011). While emotions and moods are relatively short-lasting, typical affect experienced across time and situations (e.g., usual way of feeling) describes emotion traits, either broad ones (e.g., positive or negative trait affect; Watson & Clark, 1997; Widiger, 2009) or those pertaining to a specific emotion (e.g., trait curiosity; Kashdan & Steger, 2007).

Research on emotion and cognition points to a hybrid construct of emotion abilities – capacities to think and reason about and with emotions and to solve emotion-related problems (Mayer et al., 2008; Salovey & Mayer, 1990). These abilities are based on the view of emotions as conveying information (Martin et al., 1993; Schwarz, 2012), which can be used to guide thinking and problem solving, as well as the intrinsic property of the affective experiences to include an aspect of emotion regulation (Kappas, 2011; Mayer & Salovey, 1995). Two sets of emotion abilities have been studied in relation to creativity – emotional intelligence and emotional creativity. Emotional intelligence encompasses the abilities to accurately perceive emotions in oneself and others, use emotions to inform thinking and problem solving, understand the nature and the typical course of emotions, and effectively regulate emotions toward either hedonic or instrumental goals (Mayer et al., 2016). Emotional creativity is the ability to experience novel, yet appropriate and authentic, combinations of emotions (Averill & Thomas-Knowles, 1991). These abilities are theoretically and empirically distinct (Ivcevic et al., 2007). Both sets of abilities can be studied using performance-based tests that require solving of emotion-related problems using either convergent (in the case of emotional intelligence) or divergent thinking processes (in the case of emotional creativity). In addition to being assessed as abilities, both emotional intelligence and emotional creativity can be assessed as self-perceived traits (Averill, 1999; Wong & Law, 2002). Assessed as traits, emotional intelligence and emotional creativity are self-concept attributes akin to self-efficacy – self-perception or belief that one is able to solve emotion-related problems.

This volume is organized in five sections. The first section focuses on methodological issues. Baas (Chapter 1) reviews issues in experimental research in the study of creativity and emotions. This method has most commonly employed mood induction techniques to gain experimental control over the experienced affective states. Although much has been learned from these studies about creative idea generation, mood induction produces short-lasting effects, making it suitable for a limited scope of questions. Once researchers become interested in creative thinking and behavior directed at tasks lasting more than a few minutes, the experimental techniques cease to be helpful. That is where case study methods (Hanchett Hanson et al., Chapter 2), observational methods (Katz-Buonincontro, Chapter 3), and experience sampling and daily diary methods (Cotter, Chapter 4) offer promise of nuanced understanding of real-world creativity. The experience sampling and daily diary methods are capable of capturing creativity as it is occurring, examining within-person variability in affective processes and creative behavior, and addressing the influence of environment on creative behavior. Case studies (via evolving systems or participatory approaches) and observational methods (via structured observation or naturalistic observation) can be a source of hypotheses that can be tested using assessments in everyday environments.

We use the broad, yet useful distinction among the study of the creative process(es), the creative person, and creative products, and consider applied issues in the study of creativity and emotions in the contexts of school and work (Rhodes, 1961). We start with the consideration of affect in the creative process with the review of research on affective states in creativity (primarily creative thinking; Madrid et al., Chapter 5). Next, the neuroscience research on creative thinking and emotions is reviewed (Chrysikou et al., Chapter 6) and emerging research on the role of affect in relation to attentional processes relevant for both convergent and divergent creative thinking is considered, on the spectrum from mindfulness to mind wandering (Kane et al., Chapter 7). Forgeard (Chapter 8) describes research about the motivation, including intrinsic and intellectual, emotional, and prosocial motives for creativity, which reinforces the overlap between motivation and emotions and their influence on creativity. Two subsequent chapters relevant to emotion abilities discuss the coping with uncertainty and difference in creativity (Liu & Damian, Chapter 9) and the role of emotional intelligence abilities (and how they can be taught and learned) for creativity (Hoffmann & McFarland, Chapter 10). The final chapter in this section discusses the role of emotions in the creative process across domains of creativity (i.e., artistic, scientific, design, writing, musical, and culinary; Botella, Chapter 11).

In discussing the creative person, we start with the traditional question of how emotion traits relate to different aspects of creativity, from the decision to engage in creative work to self-perceived creativity to creative behavior to performance in specific creativity domains (Ivcevic, Chapter 12). Although the creative person has been primarily studied in relation to individual differences in personality traits, an understanding of other attributes describing creative individuals is necessary to complete the picture. Taylor (Chapter 13) discusses the surprisingly understudied topic of gender differences in the study of creativity and emotions, followed by two chapters that examine age as it relates to creativity and emotion: Russ (Chapter 14) reviews research on pretend play as a form of childhood creativity and affective processes at its core, and Ermoshkina and Kahana (Chapter 15) examine emotion regulation and creativity in relation to everyday challenges of aging. Because creativity does not happen in a social vacuum, and individual creators interact with others in their domain (coworkers, collaborators, and gate-keepers) as well as their audiences, Lebuda and colleagues (Chapter 16) discuss the emerging area of research on interpersonal relationships (e.g., parent–child, sibling, mentor–mentee), social emotions (e.g., embarrassment, gratitude, and shame), and their role in creativity.

In considering creativity as a product, the authors review research on emotions themselves as creative products as well as research on affective consequences of engagement in creative activities. Trnka (Chapter 17) reviews scholarship on emotional creativity – a set of abilities and traits describing original, authentic, and effective emotional experience; here, emotions are in themselves a creative product. Kapoor and Mange (Chapter 18) discuss dark creativity, which is defined by its emotion-related features (intent and/or actual harm), as well as how it is predicted by emotion-related states and traits. Although much work treats creativity as an outcome, when it is treated as a predictor, it is related to affective outcomes (Forgeard & Kaufman, 2016). Tinio and Specker (Chapter 19) present a model describing emotional effects of art on the audience and how these effects relate to emotions artists intended to express. Three chapters examine emotion-related benefits of creativity. Grossman and Drake (Chapter 20) focus on affect associated with participation in everyday activities that are artistic in nature (e.g., visual arts, music) and non-artistic (e.g., cooking, gardening); Holinger and Kaufman (Chapter 21) present a model of how everyday creativity creates a pathway to psychological well-being, especially purpose and meaning; and Orkibi and Keisari (Chapter 22) describe the therapeutic process of Creative Arts Therapies (CAT) and propose a new model to describe the role of creativity in the effectiveness of CAT to improve emotional well-being. Finally, instead of examining outcomes of emotional experiences (and well-being), Stutesman and Goldstein (Chapter 23) discuss engagement with the arts (visual art, theatre, dance, music, and multimodal art) as a vehicle for developing emotion abilities, such as theory of mind and emotion regulation.

The last major section of the Handbook grapples with applications of research on creativity and emotions in the context of school and work. Anderson (Chapter 24) focuses on affective states of anxiety and fear of failure in the creative process and discusses how to increase creativity by managing, or even leveraging, these states among children and adolescents. Karwowski (Chapter 25) examines peer and classroom climate influence on affective experiences and creative self-concept as they relate to creativity at school. Beghetto and Schmidt (Chapter 26) present a model describing potential pathways from creative curricular experiences to creative expression and development and the role of uncertainty (with the emotional reactions it engenders) in this process.

Creativity at work is examined on multiple levels. Emich and Lu (Chapter 27) discuss organizational affective climate and its consequences for individual creativity. They propose a new definition of affective climate: the affective state that forms among members of a collective in response to their shared experience. Madrid et al. (Chapter 28) focus on group affective tone and its relationship to creativity at work and proposes a model describing broaden and build and social integration processes as mediators between group affective tone and group creativity. Reiter-Palmon and Millier (Chapter 29) emphasize a single key dimension of emotional climate – psychological safety – and discuss the mechanisms through which it exerts influence on creative behavior of both individuals and teams. Connelly and Demirag Burak (Chapter 30) review research on leadership; leaders have an outsized influence on both employees' experience of work and the way they can perform their job (through providing creativity-relevant resources and supports). Finally, Ashkanasy and To (Chapter 31) present an integrative model depicting the role of emotions in creativity at work. They posit that creativity in organizations needs to be examined at (1) the within-person level (intraindividual variation through time), (2) the level of interindividual differences in creativity-relevant attributes, (3) interpersonal level, (4) team or group level, and (5) the level of organizational culture or climate.

The concluding chapter looks back at what we have learned across the five parts of the Handbook and chapters by 31 contributor teams and aims to both connect the dots and look ahead. This chapter builds on findings and proposals in this Handbook and the Editors' own work and presents a theoretical model of affective processes across different aspects of creativity. Here, the goal is primarily to stimulate new research that examines the role of affective experiences, traits, and emotion abilities in the prediction of creative beliefs and intentions, engagement in long-term creative behavior, and production of creative outcomes.

It may seem folly to construct a book centered on the interrelationships between two constructs that are multifaceted and nuanced yet also widely perceived as being "soft" and difficult to study. As you read the chapters that follow and the conclusion that aims to integrate them into a unifying model, we hope that you come to the same conclusion that we have reached: There is an astounding array of high-quality research on creativity and affective processes, with unlimited possibilities for continued work.

References

Amabile, T. M. (1996). *Creativity in Context: Update to the Social Psychology of Creativity.* Westview Press.

Amabile, T. M., Barsade, S. G., Mueller, J. S., & Staw, B. M. (2005). Affect and creativity at work. *Administrative Science Quarterly, 50*(2), 367–403. https://doi.org/10.2189/asqu.2005.50.3.367

Averill, J. R. (1999). Individual differences in emotional creativity: Structure and correlates. *Journal of Personality, 67*(2), 331–371. https://doi.org/10.1111/1467-6494.00058

Averill, J. R., & Thomas-Knowles, C. (1991). Emotional creativity. In K. T. Strongman (Ed.), *International Review of Studies on Emotion* (vol. 1, pp. 269–299). Wiley.

Baas, M., De Dreu, C. K. W., & Nijstad, B. A. (2008). A meta-analysis of 25 years of mood-creativity research: Hedonic tone, activation, or regulatory focus? *Psychological Bulletin, 134*(6), 779–806. https://doi.org/10.1037/a0012815

Baer, J. (1998). The case for domain specificity in creativity. *Creativity Research Journal, 11*, 173–177. https://doi.org/10.1207/s15326934crj1102_7

Barbot, B., Besançon, M., & Lubart, T. (2016). The generality-specificity of creativity: Exploring the structure of creative potential with EPoC. *Learning and Individual Differences, 52*, 178–187. https://doi.org/10.1016/j.lindif.2016.06.005

Barrett, L. F. (2006). Solving the emotion paradox: Categorization and the experience of emotion. *Personality and Social Psychology Review, 10*(1), 20–46. https://doi.org/10.1207/s15327957pspr1001_2

Bourgeois-Bougrine, S., Glăveanu, V., Botella, M., et al. (2014). The creativity maze: Exploring creativity in screenplay writing. *Psychology of Aesthetics, Creativity, and the Arts, 8*(4), 384–399. https://doi.org/10.1037/a0037839

Carson, S. H., Peterson, J. B., & Higgins, D. M. (2005). Reliability, validity, and factor structure of the Creative Achievement Questionnaire. *Creativity Research Journal, 17*(1), 37–50. https://doi.org/10.1207/s15326934crj1701_4

Diedrich, J., Jauk, E., Silvia, P. J., et al. (2018). Assessment of real-life creativity: The Inventory of Creative Activities and Achievements (ICAA). *Psychology of Aesthetics, Creativity, and the Arts, 12*(3), 304–316. https://doi.org/10.1037/aca0000137

Ellsworth, P. C., & Scherer, K. R. (2003). Appraisal processes in emotion. In R. J. Davidson, K. R. Scherer, & H. H. Goldsmith (Eds.), *Handbook of Affective Sciences* (pp. 572–595). Oxford University Press.

Farmer, S. M., & Tierney, P. (2017). Considering creative self-efficacy: Its current state and ideas for future inquiry. In M. Karwowski & J. C. Kaufman (Eds.), *The Creative Self: Effect of Beliefs, Self-Efficacy, Mindset, and Identity* (pp. 23–47). Elsevier Academic Press. https://doi.org/10.1016/B978-0-12-809790-8.00002-9

Feist, G. J. (1998). A meta-analysis of personality in scientific and artistic creativity. *Personality and Social Psychology Review, 2*(4), 290–309. https://doi.org/10.1207/s15327957pspr0204_5

Forgeard, M. J., & Kaufman, J. C. (2016). Who cares about imagination, creativity, and innovation, and why? A review. *Psychology of Aesthetics, Creativity, and the Arts, 10*, 250–269. https://doi.org/10.1037/aca0000042

Glăveanu, V. P., Hanson, M. H., Baer, J., et al. (2020). Advancing creativity theory and research: A socio-cultural manifesto. *Journal of Creative Behavior, 54*(3), 741–745. https://doi.org/10.1002/jocb.395

Gough, H. G. (1979). A creative personality scale for the Adjective Check List. *Journal of Personality and Social Psychology, 37*(8), 1398–1405. https://doi.org/10.1037/0022-3514.37.8.1398

Grohman, M. G., Ivcevic, Z., Silvia, P., & Kaufman, S. B. (2017). The role of passion and persistence in creativity. *Psychology of Aesthetics, Creativity, and the Arts, 11*(4), 376–385. https://doi.org/10.1037/aca0000121

Higgins, E. T. (2006). Value from hedonic experience and engagement. *Psychological Review, 113*(3), 439–460. https://doi.org/10.1037/0033-295X.113.3.439

Ivcevic, Z., & Brackett, M. A. (2015). Predicting creativity: Interactive effects of openness to experience and emotion regulation ability. *Psychology of Aesthetics, Creativity, and the Arts, 9*(4), 480–487. https://doi.org/10.1037/a0039826

Ivcevic, Z., Brackett, M. A., & Mayer, J. D. (2007). Emotional intelligence and emotional creativity. *Journal of Personality, 75*(2), 199–236. https://doi.org/10.1111/j.1467-6494.2007.00437.x

Ivcevic, Z., & Hoffmann, J. D. (2021). The creativity dare: Attitudes toward creativity and prediction of creative behavior in school. *The Journal of Creative Behavior.* https://doi.org/10.1002/jocb.527

Kappas, A. (2011). Emotion and regulation are one!. *Emotion Review, 3*(1), 17–25. https://doi.org/10.1177/1754073910380971

Kashdan, T. B., & Steger, M. F. (2007). Curiosity and pathways to well-being and meaning in life: Traits, states, and everyday behaviors. *Motivation and Emotion, 31*(3), 159–173. https://doi.org/10.1007/s11031-007-9068-7

Kaufman, J. C., Glăveanu, V. P., & Baer, J. (2017). *The Cambridge Handbook of Creativity across Domains.* Cambridge University Press.

Klenk, M. M., Strauman, T. J., & Higgins, E. T. (2011). Regulatory focus and anxiety: A self-regulatory model of GAD-depression comorbidity. *Personality and Individual Differences, 50*(7), 935–943. https://doi.org/10.1016/j.paid.2010.12.003

Martin, L. L., Ward, D. W., Achee, J. W., & Wyer, R. S. (1993). Mood as input: People have to interpret the motivational implications of their moods. *Journal of Personality and Social Psychology, 64*(3), 317–326. https://doi.org/10.1037/0022-3514.64.3.317

Mayer, J. D., Caruso, D. R., & Salovey, P. (2016). The ability model of emotional intelligence: Principles and updates. *Emotion Review, 8*(4), 290–300. https://doi.org/10.1177/1754073916639667

Mayer, J. D., Roberts, R. D., & Barsade, S. G. (2008). Human abilities: Emotional intelligence. *Annual Review of Psychology, 59*(1), 507–536. https://doi.org/10.1146/annurev.psych.59.103006.093646

Mayer, J. D., & Salovey, P. (1995). Emotional intelligence and the construction and regulation of feelings. *Applied and Preventive Psychology, 4*(3), 197–208. https://doi.org/10.1016/s0962-1849(05)80058-7

Mumford, M. D., Mobley, M. F., Uhlman, C. E., Reiter-Palmon, R., & Doares, L. (1991). Process analytic models of creative thought. *Creativity Research Journal, 4*, 91–122. https://doi.org/10.1080/10400419109534380

Rhodes, M. (1961). An analysis of creativity. *Phi Delta Kappan, 42*, 305–311.

Runco, M. A., & Jaeger, G. J. (2012). The standard definition of creativity. *Creativity Research Journal, 24*(1), 92–96. https://doi.org/10.1080/10400419.2012.650092

Salovey, P., & Mayer, J. D. (1990). Emotional intelligence. *Imagination, Cognition, and Personality, 9*, 185–211. https://doi.org/10.2190/DUGG-P24E-52WK-6CDG

Schwarz, N. (2012). Feelings-as-information theory. In P. A. M. Van Lange, A. Kruglanski, & E. T. Higgins (Eds.), *Handbook of Theories of Social Psychology* (pp. 289–308). Sage.

Silvia, P. J., Rodriguez, R. M., Beaty, R. E., et al. (2021). Measuring everyday creativity: A Rasch model analysis of the Biographical Inventory of Creative Behaviors (BICB) scale. *Thinking Skills and Creativity, 39*, 100797. https://doi.org/10.1016/j.tsc.2021.100797

Watson, D., & Clark, L. A. (1997). Extraversion and its positive emotional core. In R. Hogan, J. A. Johnson, & S. R. Briggs (Eds.), *Handbook of Personality Psychology* (pp. 767–793). Academic Press. https://doi.org/10.1016/B978–012134645-4/50030-5

Widiger, T. A. (2009). Neuroticism. In M. R. Leary & R. H. Hoyle (Eds.), *Handbook of Individual Differences in Social Behavior* (pp. 129–146). Guilford Press.

Wong, C.-S., & Law, K. S. (2002). The effects of leader and follower emotional intelligence on performance and attitude: An exploratory study. *The Leadership Quarterly, 13*(3), 243–274. https://doi.org/10.1016/S1048–9843(02)00099-1

Zhou, J., & George, J. M. (2001). When job dissatisfaction leads to creativity: Encouraging the expression of voice. *Academy of Management Journal, 44*(4), 682–696. https://doi.org/10.2307/3069410

PART I

Methods in the Study of Creativity and Emotions

1 Experimental Methods in the Study of Emotions and Creativity

Matthijs Baas

Introduction

Affective states, including mood, emotion, and general affect, are among the most widely studied predictors of creativity (Baas et al., 2008; Davis, 2009; Isen, 2000; Ivcevic & Hoffmann, 2019). Within this burgeoning field of discovery, experimental research designs play a crucial role. Experimental research designs enable researchers to better understand the link between affective states and creativity as well as make causal inferences. In order to study the influence of affective states on creativity, the researcher first has to bring a respondent into an intended emotional state, after which the respondent performs a suitable creativity task. For instance, before respondents perform a creativity task, they may first watch a clip from a sad movie to become relatively sad (Kaufmann & Vosburg, 2002), receive an unexpected bag of candy to elicit positive affect (Isen et al., 1987), or recollect and reexperience an event that made them feel anxious (De Dreu et al., 2008). Although less common, it is also possible to study the reversed link: the influence of the act of creative thinking on experienced affective states. Here, the researcher first has to induce creative thinking in respondents, after which respondents rate how they feel.

Importantly, there are a multitude of affect-elicitation procedures, affect-rating instruments, and creativity tasks, each having its own strengths and limitations. Which ones should a researcher use? For instance, should a researcher elicit affective states with film clips, music, or the recollection of emotional memories? In addition, there are general experimental design characteristics to consider. For instance, should researchers implement their mood-manipulation check before or after their measurement of creativity? How long can a researcher allow for the creativity task to be performed before the manipulation of the emotional state wears off? Answering these questions, this chapter provides an overview of affect-elicitation procedures along with examples of experiments and general experimental design considerations. This chapter's aim is to assist researchers in making informed decisions in designing their experiments to study the link between affective states and creativity. Before turning to the possible affect-elicitation procedures, this chapter first briefly addresses the terms *mood*, *emotion*, and *affect*.

Mood, Emotion, and General Affect

Mood, emotion, and general affect are often, but incorrectly, used interchangeably when referring to affective phenomena. These affective phenomena are specified in the affect literature. *General affect* refers to subjective feelings and is used as an umbrella term for all affective phenomena, including moods and emotions (Frijda, 1993). Compared to moods, emotions are more strongly directed toward a specific target, which could be a person, an event, or an object (Frijda, 1993; Joseph et al., 2020). For example, someone is sad because of the loss of a dear person. Another person is fearful because of heavy turbulence during a flight. This direction toward a specific target is lacking in moods: people in a sad mood are just generally gloomy and not necessarily sad about anything or anyone in particular. In addition, moods tend to be more enduring and less intense than emotions (Frijda, 1993; Roseman et al., 1994), although exceptions to this rule are possible: for instance, the sadness that is experienced during clinical depression can be overwhelmingly intense.

In interpreting the effects of affective states on creativity, researchers can use broad categories such as positive and negative affect. For instance, in early work on the influence of affective states and creativity, the general consensus was that positive affective states enhanced people's creativity (e.g., Ashby et al., 1999; Isen, 2000). However, specific affective states within these broader categories may not predict creativity in the same way. In fact, although relieved and happy moods are both positive, only happy moods lead to more creativity (Baas et al., 2011a; De Dreu et al., 2008; Gilet & Jallais, 2011). This insight has inspired researchers to move beyond valence and focus on the effects on creativity of specific affective states to draw conclusions about the causal role of anger (Baas et al., 2011b), boredom (Gasper & Middlewood, 2014), surprise (Filipowicz, 2006), and social anxiety (Byron et al., 2010).

Researchers can also interpret the effect of affective states on creativity in terms of their underlying dimensions. According to the dimensional approach to affective states, specific affective states vary on a number of dimensions (Baas et al., 2008; Frijda, 1993; Lerner & Keltner, 2000; Russell & Barrett, 1999). For instance, specific affective states differ not only in valence, but also in terms of activation level (Russell & Barrett, 1999). *Activation level*, or *arousal*, refers to the level of engagement of motivational systems to mobilize energy to sustain attention and effort toward goal-related activities (Baas et al., 2011a). The specific affective states happiness, relief, and calmness are all positive in valence, but happiness is activating, whereas relief and calmness are deactivating. Similarly, anger, anxiety, sadness, and depressed mood are all negative in valence, but anger and anxiety are activating, whereas sadness and depressed mood are deactivating. Accordingly, a researcher may decide to elicit a range of specific affective states that vary systematically along dimensions such as valence and activation level, to be able to interpret any effects on creativity in terms of (interactions between) these different dimensions. In fact, De Dreu and colleagues (2008) had participants recall a happy, joyful, calm, relaxed, sad, depressed, angry, or anxious event from their lives, after which they completed a standardized creativity task. The results showed that happy, joyful, angry, and anxious moods led to more creativity than calm, relaxed, sad, and depressed moods. Moreover, effects of happy and joyful moods were explained by increased flexible thinking, whereas effects of angry and anxious moods were explained by more effortful and systematic thinking. Based on these findings, the authors concluded that activation level is the crucial affect dimension that determines the level of creativity, whereas valence determines the process that supports creative outcomes.

When a researcher is interested in the effects on creativity of specific affective states or their underlying affective dimensions, it is crucial that specific affective states can be reliably elicited in experiments. Fortunately, this can be done (for overviews, see Brenner 2000; Gerrards-Hesse et al., 1994; Joseph et al., 2020; Martin 1990). In fact, there is a great variety of affect-elicitation procedures that a researcher can choose from. The next section describes these different procedures and their capacity to elicit specific affective states.

Experimental Paradigms for the Influence of Affective States on Creativity

Affect-Elicitation Procedures

There is a variety of affect-elicitation procedures (AEPs; also referred to as emotion-elicitation or mood-induction procedures; Brenner 2000, Joseph et al., 2020; Martin 1990). This section describes the most commonly used AEPs in experiments on affect and creativity (also see Table 1.1). Each AEP will be evaluated in terms of the range of affective states it can induce and the strength of its impact on specific affective feelings.

Autobiographical Recall

Many studies use autobiographical recall to induce specific affective states. In this AEP, participants are instructed to recollect and reexperience an autobiographical event or situation involving a specific affective state (Joseph et al., 2020). Sometimes, the participants are also asked to write down the event and describe how they felt. For instance, in their study on the influence of specific moods on creativity, Baas and colleagues (2011b) asked respondents to retrieve, write down, and reexperience a personal event in which they felt particularly angry (or, in another condition, sad); in the mood-neutral condition, participants were asked to describe the route they took to the psychology department. Afterward, respondents had 4 minutes to generate creative solutions to preserve and improve the environment.

The rationale behind this procedure is that rather than confronting respondents with emotionally charged stimuli, respondents themselves draw on their

Table 1.1 *Most commonly used affect-elicitation procedures in affect-creativity research*

Autobiographical recall	• Respondents are instructed to recall and reexperience a personal situation or event that involves a specific affective state. • Respondents may also be instructed to describe the event or situation and experienced feelings.
Velten (1968)	• Respondents read or hear 60 self-referential affective statements and are asked to feel the suggested affective state.
Film clips	• Respondents watch a film clip that involves a specific affective state.
Music and sounds	• Participants listen to music or sounds that involve a specific affective state.
Jokes/cartoons	• Respondents read/hear jokes or cartoons.
Gift	• Respondents receive an unexpected gift.
Feedback	• Respondents receive (false) positive or negative feedback about their task performance (e.g., ability test, essay on a personally relevant topic).
Public performance	• Respondents perform tasks in (anticipation of) a publicly challenging situation.
Body posture/facial expression	• Respondents are instructed to contract specific facial muscles or maintain a specific body posture that represents a particular affective state.

Note. There are other affect elicitation procedures as well (for an overview, see Joseph et al., 2020).

memory to retrieve personally significant emotional events (Izard & Ackerman, 2000). Indeed, this method has been highly effective in inducing affective states, with a strong average effect size of $d = 1.21$ (Joseph et al., 2020). This method is also highly versatile and has been used in creativity research to produce a range of specific affective states, including happiness, joy, relief, calmness, anger, anxiety, sadness, depressed mood, and emotional ambivalence (Baas et al., 2011b; De Dreu et al., 2008, Fong, 2006). In other research areas, other affective states have also been targeted with this procedure, including regret and disappointment (Zeelenberg & Pieters 2004).

Autobiographical recall is a relatively simple technique that is highly versatile in producing a range of specific affective states. The downside is that the experimenter has no control over the content of the emotionally charged events that respondents have in mind. When asked to recollect and relive a sad event, one person may think of the loss of a dear friend, whereas another person may think of a negative evaluation by a teacher. This content may have unintended consequences for creative thinking.

Velten

The Velten (1968) procedure consists of a list of 60 self-referential statements that are either positive, negative, or neutral. For instance, in the positive affect condition, respondents read statements, such as "This is great . . . I really do feel good. I am elated about things!" In the negative affect condition, they could read a statement such as "All of the unhappiness of my past life is taking possession of me." Usually, participants are instructed to try to feel the mood described by the statement. In the neutral affective condition, participants read factual statements with no direct emotional reference, for example, "Utah is the Beehive State." Although the original Velten procedure focused on happy and sad affective states, other versions were developed with statements that target anxiety or anger (e.g., Carter et al., 2002). The Velten procedure has also been used in mood-creativity research (Clapham, 2000–2001).

The Velten procedure has been highly effective in inducing affective states, with a strong average effect size of $d = 1.09$ (Joseph et al., 2020). An advantage of the Velten procedure is that researchers can standardize the presentation of the statements, although the number of statements and the exact instructions vary across studies (Kenealy, 1986). A disadvantage is the presence of demand characteristics, cues in the experimental setting that suggest to the participant the experimental hypotheses (Polivy & Doyle, 1980).

Film Clips

In this AEP, respondents watch a film clip, typically a brief excerpt of a movie, that involves a specific affective state (see Rottenberg et al., 2007, for an overview). For instance, in their study on mood and creativity, Fernández-Abascal and Díaz (2013) first had all participants watch a neutral movie clip, after which half watched a brief excerpt from the comedy *When Harry Met Sally* (happy mood condition) and the other half watched a brief excerpt from the movie *The Champ* (sad mood condition). Hereafter, respondents completed the Torrance Test of Creative Thinking (TTCT) figural (Torrance, 1966).

As vivid and emotionally charged mediums, it is not surprising that movie clips are highly effective in inducing affective states, with a strong average effect size of $d = 1.38$ (Joseph et al., 2020). There is a variety of brief film clips that usually take less than 5 minutes and that target various specific affective states, including happiness, amusement, anger, disgust, fear, sadness, surprise, and emotional ambivalence (Rottenberg et al., 2007). However, prior experiences with the films may influence participants' responses to the movie clips (Gross, 1998). In addition, although each movie clip can be pretested and standardized, it may be more difficult to standardize movie clips across different affective states. This is because films often differ from one another in multiple characteristics that may influence creative thinking (e.g., complexity of dialogue, colors used, background music).

Music and Sounds

In this class of AEPs, participants listen to music or sounds that involve a specific affective state. For instance, in a study by Ritter and Ferguson (2017), participants listened to calm (an excerpt from Saint-Saens' "The Swan" from *Carnaval des Animaux*), happy (an excerpt from Vivaldi's "Spring" concerto from *The Four Seasons*), sad (an excerpt from Barber's *Adagio for Strings*), or anxious music (an excerpt from Holst's *The Planets*: "Mars, Bringer of War"). Respondents listened to this music before and during a set of standardized creativity tests; in the control condition, participants completed the tests in silence. As Ritter and Ferguson did, researchers may decide to play the musical pieces while participants perform the creativity task. There is a variety of music excerpts that target multiple specific affective states, including happiness, calmness, anxiety, and sadness. Although sounds have not often been used in creativity research (see Topolinski & Deutsch, 2012, for an exception), research suggests that naturally occurring sounds (e.g., screams, erotica, bombs) reliably influence valence and arousal ratings (these sounds are part of the International Affective Digitized Sound [IADS] system; Bradley & Lang, 2000).

Although less powerful than the previously discussed AEPs, music and sounds are effective in inducing affective states, with a strong average effect size of $d = 0.74$ (Joseph et al., 2020). The advantage of music is that it can be played during the performance of a creativity task and can be easily combined with other AEPs (also see below). The main disadvantage is that personal preferences and prior experiences with the music pieces may greatly influence participants' responses to the music.

Jokes/Cartoons

In this AEP, respondents read cartoons or read or hear jokes. In a study by Ziv (1976) half of the respondents listened to jokes that were made by a famous comedian and subsequently performed the TTCT; those in the control condition only performed the TTCT. Usually, cartoons and jokes are used to induce a positive affective state. With a small to medium effect size ($d = 0.31$), the effect of jokes/cartoons on affective states is much smaller than those of the other AEPs (Joseph et al., 2020). In addition, cartoons and jokes are restricted to positive affect and do not target other specific affective feelings.

Gifts

In her seminal work on positive affect and creativity, Alice Isen presented an unexpected gift to participants to induce positive affect. For instance, participants received a transparent plastic bag tied with a red ribbon that contained five miniature chocolate bars and four hard candies. Thereafter, respondents performed the Remote Associates Test (RAT; Estrada et al., 1994) or the Duncker Candle task (Isen et al., 1987). Although it is assumed that participants are in a positive mood when they receive an unexpected gift, this AEP did not influence affect ratings (Isen et al., 1987), nor is it part of the standard AEPs (Joseph et al., 2020). Also, although this AEP could potentially involve intentionally disappointing or nasty gifts that could evoke negative affective states, current work using this AEP is restricted to positive affect.

Feedback

In this AEP, respondents perform a task (e.g., ability test, essay on a personally relevant topic) and respondents then receive (false) positive or negative feedback about their task performance (Brenner, 2000; Joseph et al., 2020). For instance, Fodor and Carver (2000) had engineering and science students generate a solution for an engineering problem for 20 minutes. Their solutions were evaluated by the experimenter who took 10 minutes for the evaluation to enhance the credibility of the procedure. The experimenter then gave participants preprogrammed feedback that was either positive (e.g., "The solution you proposed shows evidence of achievement. It looks good relative to the standards of comparison the manual provides") or negative (e.g., "The solution you proposed shows little evidence of achievement. It does not measure high against the standards of comparison the manual provides"); the respondents in the control condition just sat for 10 minutes. Thereafter, participants received another engineering problem and took 25 minutes to generate a solution, which was rated for creativity and complexity.

Participants who receive positive feedback experience positive affect, whereas participants who receive negative feedback experience negative affect (Nummenmaa & Niemi, 2004). Although less powerful than some previously discussed AEPs, feedback is effective in inducing affective states, with a strong average effect size of $d = 0.83$ (Joseph et al., 2020). The ecological validity of the task can be improved when the task is connected to meaningful situations in which people typically experience success and failure. Potential downsides of this AEP are that the variety of induced affective states is restricted and that other factors, such as self-efficacy, are manipulated as well (Hutchinson et al., 2008).

Public Performance

In another class of AEPs, respondents perform tasks in (anticipation of) a publicly challenging situation. For instance, they give a public speech or perform a difficult task in front of an audience, after which they perform a creativity task. Alternatively, respondents anticipate an evaluation of their creative performance by others. For example, in Shalley's (1995) study, participants generated solutions for complex problems that were presented by a human resource director of a steel company. In the expected-evaluation condition, they were told that the quantity and creativity of their responses on this task would be compared to all the other participants and evaluated by experts; there was no mention of this in the control condition.

With medium effect sizes ranging between $d = 0.39$ and $d = 0.68$, the effect of challenging public situations on affective states is smaller than some of the other AEPs (Joseph et al., 2020). Moreover, although challenging public situations influence affective states, they are also interpreted as operationalizations of extrinsic versus intrinsic motivation (Baer, 1997) or social evaluative stress (Byron et al., 2010).

Body Posture/Facial Expression

In another class of AEPs, respondents are instructed to maintain a specific body posture or contract specific facial muscles that represent a particular affective state. An example stems from Friedman and Förster (2002) where participants flexed their arms by lightly pressing the palm of their right hand upward against the bottom of a table, a bodily state associated with implicit positive affective cues and approach motivation. In another experimental condition, participants extended their arms by lightly pressing the palm of their right hand downward against the top of a table, a bodily state associated with implicit negative affective cues and avoidance motivation (Friedman & Förster, 2010). While maintaining this position, participants performed three creative insight problems (Friedman & Förster, 2002, Study 1) or took 1 minute to generate creative uses for a brick (Friedman & Förster, 2002, Study 2). It is important to note that later work revealed that arm tension and flexion effects on creativity depend on whether the left or right hand is used to perform the posture (Cretenet & Dru, 2009).

Modifying people's facial expression represents another example of this AEP. Here, participants are instructed to contract and relax specific facial muscles to produce a frown or a smile, thereby inducing a negative or positive emotional state (Gerrards-Hesse et al. 1994). Attempts to elicit more specific affective feelings using facial expression have also been successful. To elicit fear, Duclos and colleagues (1989) instructed participants to raise their eyebrows, to open their eyes wide, to move their whole head back, so that their chin would tuck in a little bit, and to let their mouth relax and hang open a little. Such detailed instructions were also provided to elicit anger, disgust, and sadness. The results showed that participants reported feelings that matched the specific facial expression.

With a medium effect size of $d = 0.66$, the effect of facial expression and body posture on affective states is smaller than some of the previously discussed AEPs (Joseph et al., 2020). However, stronger effects occur when matching combinations of facial expressions and bodily postures are used (Flack et al., 1999). The advantage, particularly of using body postures where no explicit reference to emotion is being made, is that demand characteristics are minimized. However, this class of AEP has also been criticized for producing inconsistent results and for the uncertainty about whether specific emotional feelings are activated or simply related cognitions (Frijda, 1986).

Combination of Affect Elicitation Procedures

To increase their effectiveness, different AEPs can also be combined (Gerrards-Hesse et al. 1994; Joseph et al., 2020). For instance, in a study by Akinola and Mendes (2008), feedback was applied in a publicly challenging situation. Participants prepared and delivered a speech followed by a question-and-answer (Q&A) period in a mock job interview. The speech and Q&A were done either alone in a room (low evaluation condition) or in front of two evaluators (high evaluation condition). Moreover, participants in the high evaluation conditions received scripted and timed nonverbal and verbal feedback by the evaluators that was either positive (e.g., nodding and smiling, while saying, "You are very self-assured and authentic, really great job") or negative (e.g., shaking heads, frowning, while saying, "I felt that you could be much clearer and more articulate"; Akinola & Mendes, 2008, pp. 1679–1680). After the speech and Q&A, participants were asked to make a collage with presented craft materials.

Music can also quite easily be used in combination with other AEPs. For instance, Siemer (2001) combined an autobiographical recollection with musical fragments of the corresponding affective state. Meta-analytic findings show that this addition of music only slightly increases the effect of autobiographical recollection from $d = 1.21$ to $d = 1.43$ (Joseph et al., 2020). However, the effects may linger longer as a musical piece sustains a particular affective state while participants perform a subsequent creativity task. Overall, with a medium effect size of $d = 1.20$, the effect of combined AEPs is strong, but not necessarily stronger than some of the single AEPs (Joseph et al., 2020).

New Possibilities

Although not part of the standard AEPs yet, technological developments have resulted in new methods to elicit specific affective feelings in an engaging and realistic manner. From these new methods, virtual reality stands out as the most promising, which allows a participant to interact with objects and individuals within a simulated and controlled environment that is presented in three-dimensional computer graphics (Loomis et al., 1999). Indeed, a study by Felnhofer and colleagues (2015) shows that five different virtual park scenarios each elicited a specific affective state: joy, sadness, boredom, anger, and anxiety. Other affective feelings, such as awe, have also been successfully induced using virtual reality (Chirico et al., 2018). Although promising as a powerful AEP, disadvantages are that virtual reality requires expensive tools and technology and specialized computer skills for programming experiments.

Can Negative Affective States Be Reliably Induced?

The AEPs discussed in the preceding paragraphs reliably influence specific negative affective states when comparing the degree of negative affect in different negative affect conditions against different positive and neutral affect conditions or baseline. It is a relative effect that does not necessarily imply that people feel negative affect to a large degree. Indeed, people more strongly experience positive affect than negative affect at baseline, with negative affect ratings prior to the administration of an AEP ranging between 1.32 and 1.46 on a 5-point Likert scale (Joseph et al., 2020). After a negative AEP, the level of negative affect ratings increases compared to baseline. However, with a score of

1.91 on a 5-point scale, the intensity of experienced negative affect remains mild at best and well below the mid-point of the scale. The degree of positive affect ratings reduces after a negative AEP, but is, with an average level of 2.37, still greater than the degree of experienced negative affect (Joseph et al., 2020). This suggests that negative AEPs are successful in inducing a negative affective state only in relative but not in absolute terms.

General Methodological Considerations

Ethical Considerations

From an ethical perspective, it is even desirable that the degree of AEP-induced negative affect that respondents experience is relatively mild. It is unethical to let respondents experience very intense negative affective states. However, even if the respondent's negative affect is relatively mild, researchers should provide participants with clear informed consent and debriefing procedures and may want to implement a mood repair/reset AEP after the main study is done. The researcher may simply use one of the more effective positive AEPs that were discussed in the previous section.

Temporal Characteristics

In most experiments on the effect of affective states on creativity, creativity is assessed after the elicitation of the affective state occurred (music is a noteworthy exception that can be played during the performance of the creativity task). How long the affective state persists before it wears off therefore has direct consequences for the performance on a creativity task and affect ratings on the mood manipulation check. For instance, Baas and colleagues (2011b) discovered that people who recollected and reexperienced an angry rather than sad emotional event showed an initial peak in creativity that decreased more rapidly over time. One explanation for this pattern of findings is that an angry mood may dissipate more quickly than a sad mood.

There is little systematic research on how long elicited affective states last as a function of the chosen AEP and specific affective state involved (Joseph et al., 2020). For naturally occurring emotional events, Verduyn and colleagues (2009) showed that the intensity of emotional experiences peaks initially and then decreases over time. They also showed that the higher the emotional intensity at onset, the longer it takes before the emotional intensity returned to baseline. This suggests that stronger AEPs last longer. However, often AEPs are less intense than naturally occurring emotional events. In a study by Boyes and colleagues (2020), participants watched an amusing or sad movie clip and then rated the intensity of amusement and sadness each minute during a 5-minute interval. The results showed that emotional ratings peaked directly following the film clip, after which the intensity linearly decreased over time, approaching baseline after 5 minutes. In another study by Kuijsters et al. (2016), respondents watched sad or anxious movie clips. Respondents then reported every 2 minutes how pleasant they felt during an 8-minute interval. Again, the results showed that pleasantness ratings showed a negative peak directly following the film clip, after which the intensity of these ratings linearly decreased over time, approaching baseline after 6 minutes.

From this research, it follows that the effects of AEPs on experienced affect quickly wear off. However, to make things more complicated, the effects of the affect elicitation on creativity may last well beyond the point where reported experienced affective feelings have returned to baseline. For instance, Tan and Qu (2015) showed that the superior creative perform-ance in a positive affective state lasted 20 minutes. Although the temporal dynamics of effects of affective states on creativity deserve more attention, both empirically and theoretically, the general advice to creativity research-ers is to limit the duration of their creativity task. By implication, AEPs are not suited to study the role of affective states in the unfolding of creative production over days, months, or years (e.g., writing a play, inventing something).

When and How to Measure the Manipulation Check?

Related to the temporal dynamics of affective experience following the AEP is the question of when to implement the manipulation check in the experimental design. Since affective experiences peak directly following the AEP, it makes sense to administer the manipulation check directly following the AEP. However, the measurement of experienced affect may interfere with people's emotional experience, and it takes longer before the creativity task begins (while the dissipation of the intensity of emotional experience progresses). Therefore, most researchers administer the manipulation check after the creativity task is completed. Usually, this involves participants rating how much they felt a number of specific feeling states (e.g., lively, sad, tired, grouchy, nervous) on a Likert scale. Because the passage of time and the mere act of doing the creativity task influences experienced affect, researchers often ask participants in retrospect how they felt as a consequence of the AEP.

Measuring Creativity

In an experimental study with creativity as the dependent variable, a researcher should look for instruments that enable the measurement of state-level variance in creativity. To give an all-too-obvious example, it does not make sense to expect an incidental mood induction to influence variance in responses on the creative achievements questionnaire (Carson et al., 2005) that involves concrete and recognized creative achievements in different domains that take months or years to arise. Instead, the researcher should be looking for well-known creativ-ity tests or tasks that do not take much time. For instance, participants may spend 8 minutes to brainstorm about possible ways to improve the quality of teaching in the psychology department (De Dreu et al., 2008) or 10 minutes solving the Duncker's candle task (Isen et al., 1987).

Cover Story

Researchers should minimize demand characteristics in their experiment to prevent hypothesis guessing by participants. For instance, based on cues in the experimental setting, respondents may guess that the research is about mood effects on creativity and, out of social desirability, are motivated to behave according to what they guess is the intended purpose or hypothesis of the study. AEPs differ in their demand characteristics, as discussed above. However, it is the whole experimental setup that truly determines the level of demand. To minimize demand effects, researchers should construct a credible and internally consistent cover story: the narrative for the experiment in which the administration of the AEP and creativity task are logically introduced and connected in a meaningful context but that at the same time prevents participants from guessing the true purpose of the experiment (see Harmon-Jones et al., 2007, for a more detailed discussion, which also involves guidelines for neutral and consistent experimenter behavior). To give an example, in their study on mood and creativity, De Dreu and colleagues (2008) told participants that they would participate in two different and independent studies; the first was an autobiographical memory task (the task used to manipulate specific moods) and the other was a brainstorming task about possible ways to improve the quality of teaching in the psychology department (the task to assess creativity).

Experimental Design: Within or between Subjects

In experiments on affective states and creativity, AEPs are usually administered in a between-subjects design, whereby the respondent is only exposed to one level of the independent variable, be it sadness, anger, or another mood. Although less common, AEPs can also be administered in within-subjects designs whereby each respondent is exposed to each level of the independent variable. For instance, in their study on mood and performance on the RAT, Rowe et al. (2007) had each participant perform the RAT in each of three affective states: sad, happy, and neutral. Happy and sad moods were induced with appropriate classical music pieces, and a neutral mood was induced by reading a collection of basic facts about Canada; the order of induced moods was counterbalanced between participants. The big advantage of within-subjects designs is that the same participant is exposed to each level of the independent variable, which reduces unwanted variance between different levels of the independent variable. However, it is challenging to implement within-subjects designs in affect-creativity research. For instance, the repeated measurement of creativity can result in test effects, and effects of the different affective states may well carry over and contaminate subsequent affect elicitations. In addition, research suggests that shifts in affective feelings may be particularly conducive to creative thinking (Bledow et al., 2013).

Suitable Research Questions

The final methodological consideration discussed here pertains to the type of research questions that are (not) suited for using experimental methods.

Experimental methods are particularly suited for explanatory research questions that focus on establishing causal relationships (e.g., How or why do specific affective states influence creative performance?; Does listening to fearful music lead to more creativity than listening to sad music?; Robson & McCartan, 2016). This makes experimental methods less suited for descriptive research questions that aim to determine the nature, magnitude, change, or development of psychological differences between individuals (e.g., How do individual differences in positive affectivity relate to [the development of] creative ability?; How do fluctuations in daily moods predict people's creativity?). This notwithstanding, it would be perfectly possible to combine experimental methods with individual differences research taking a person-by-situation approach. For instance, Leung et al. (2014) asked whether the relation between personality and creativity depended on situation-induced emotional events. The authors discovered that people scoring high on neuroticism were more creative if they recalled a trait-consistent (i.e., worry) rather than trait-inconsistent (i.e., happy) emotional event. In addition, because the impact of AEPs on affective experience is limited in strength and duration, there are practical constraints in the type of explanatory research questions that can be answered. As explained above, AEPs are not suited to study the influence of affective states on how creative achievement unfolds over an extended time.

Conclusion

Which methods should a researcher use to effectively induce specific affective states? This obviously depends on the research question. For instance, when a researcher wants to compare the impact of many different affective states, many AEPs are unsuitable because they fail to produce a variety of specific affective states. Here, music, film clips, and autobiographical recall may work much better. In addition, researchers must find a suitable creativity task, craft a logical and coherent cover story to minimize demand effects, and decide whether to use a within- or between-subjects design. Each procedure has its shortcomings, and it can be recommended to use different affect-elicitation procedures that complement one another within a series of studies.

Experimental Paradigms for the Influence of Creative Thinking on Affective States

Creativity is most commonly used as the dependent variable (Snyder et al., 2019). Although rare, it is also possible to study the reverse link: the influence of creativity on experienced affective states. Here, the researcher first has to induce creative thinking in respondents or present participants with stimuli that vary in creativity, after which the respondents rate how they feel. The challenge is often to create a suitable comparison condition. For instance, Chermahini and Hommel (2012) gave participants 5 minutes to generate as many possible uses for a cup as they could (divergent thinking condition) or solve 30 RAT items (convergent-thinking condition). Participants rated their current mood with the mood inventory by Phillips and colleagues (2002) before and after the experimental task. In their study, Chermahini and Hommel could therefore compare how performing a divergent-thinking task altered momentary mood as compared to performing a convergent-thinking task. Because a suitable neutral control task was missing in their experimental design, no comparisons with control conditions could be made.

In another study employing a within-subjects design, participants were presented with unpleasant pictures (e.g., someone vomiting, an attacking animal). Each picture was accompanied with an appraisal that was either creative ("Although she just threw up, she has great joy in her heart because she will finally have a baby"), ordinary ("While the vomit is a mess, fortunately, this is nothing serious, and she will get better after some rest"), or objective ("The toilet is blocked by unidentified yellow objects, and the water cannot go down because of black objects floating in it"). Respondents then indicated their emotional valence associated with the processing of the target picture (Wu et al., 2019).

The study of creativity as the independent variable is relatively uncharted territory, whether affective experience is the dependent variable or another variable. The challenge here is to develop materials that are similar in terms of possible confounding factors, such as difficulty, interest, and clarity while being different in the key variable of interest: creativity. This will require extensive pretesting. Once experimental paradigms with creativity as the independent variable become more developed, researchers can share and use a set of valid experimental procedures, much like the set of AEPs discussed earlier (see Table 1.1).

Conclusion

Creativity researchers often use experiments to better understand the relation between emotion and creativity and draw causal conclusions. Whether one is interested in the effect of affective states on creativity or the effect of creativity on emotional experience, researchers should consider methodological and practical requirements while designing their experiments. Assisting these researchers in their endeavors, this chapter has provided the main methodological and practical guidelines for designing experimental research into the relation between emotion and creativity.

References

Akinola, M., & Mendes, W. B. (2008). The dark side of creativity: Biological vulnerability and negative emotions lead to greater artistic creativity. *Personality and Social Psychology Bulletin, 34*(12), 1677–1686. https://doi.org/10.1177/0146167208323933

Ashby, F. G., Isen, A. M., & Turken, A. U. (1999). A neuropsychological theory of positive affect and its influence on cognition. *Psychological Review, 106*, 529-550. https://doi.org/10.1037/0033-295X.106.3.529

Baas, M., De Dreu, C. K. W., & Nijstad, B. A. (2008). A meta-analysis of 25 years of research on mood and creativity: Hedonic tone, activation, or regulatory focus? *Psychological Bulletin, 134*, 739–756. https://doi.org/10.1037/a0012815

Baas, M., De Dreu, C. K. W., & Nijstad, B. A. (2011a). When prevention promotes creativity: The role of mood, regulatory focus, and regulatory closure. *Journal of Personality and Social Psychology, 100*, 794–809. https://doi.org/10.1037/a0022981

Baas, M., De Dreu, C. K. W., & Nijstad, B. A. (2011b). Creative production by angry people peaks early on, decreases over time, and is relatively unstructured. *Journal of Experimental Social Psychology, 47*, 1107–1115. https://doi.org/10.1016/j.jesp.2011.05.009

Baer, J. (1997). Gender differences in the effects of anticipated evaluation on creativity. *Creativity Research Journal, 10*(1), 25–31. https://doi.org/10.1207/s15326934crj1001_3

Bledow, R., Rosing, K., & Frese, M. (2013). A dynamic perspective on affect and creativity. *Academy of Management Journal, 56*(2), 432–450. https://doi.org/10.5465/amj.2010.0894

Boyes, M. E., Clarke, P. J., & Hasking, P. A. (2020). Relationships between dispositional and experimentally elicited emotional reactivity, intensity, and perseveration. *Personality and Individual Differences, 152*, 109573. 10.1016/j.paid.2019.109573

Bradley, M. M., & Lang, P. J. (2000). Affective reactions to acoustic stimuli. *Psychophysiology, 37*, 204–215. https://doi.org/10.1111/1469-8986.3720204

Brenner, E. (2000). Mood induction in children: Methodological issues and clinical implications. *Review of General Psychology, 4*, 264–283. https://doi.org/10.1037/1089-2680.4.3.264

Byron, K., Khazanchi, S., & Nazarian, D. (2010). The relationship between stressors and creativity: A meta-analysis examining competing theoretical models. *Journal of Applied Psychology, 95*(1), 201. https://doi.org/10.1037/a0017868

Carson, S. H., Peterson, J. B., & Higgins, D.M. (2005). Reliability, validity, and factor structure of the creative achievement questionnaire. *Creativity Research Journal, 17*(1), 37–50. https://doi.org/10.1207/s15326934crj1701_4

Carter, L. E., McNeil, D. W., Vowles, K. E., et al. (2002). Effects of emotion on pain reports, tolerance and physiology. *Pain Research and Management, 7*(1), 21–30. https://doi.org/10.1155/2002/426193

Chermahini, S. A., & Hommel, B. (2012). Creative mood swings: divergent and convergent thinking affect mood in opposite ways. *Psychological Research, 76*(5), 634–640. https://doi.org/10.1007/s00426–011-0358-z

Chirico, A., Ferrise, F., Cordella, L., & Gaggioli, A. (2018). Designing awe in virtual reality: An experimental study. *Frontiers in Psychology, 8*, 2351. https://doi.org/10.3389/fpsyg.2017.02351

Clapham, M.M. (2000–2001). The effects of affect manipulation and information exposure on divergent thinking. *Creativity Research Journal, 13*, 335–350. https://doi.org/10.1207/S15326934CRJ1334_11

Cretenet, J., & Dru, V. (2009). Influence of peripheral and motivational cues on rigid–flexible functioning: Perceptual, behavioral, and cognitive aspects. *Journal of*

Experimental Psychology: General, 138(2), 201–217. https://doi.org/10.1037/a0015379

Davis, M. A. (2009). Understanding the relationship between mood and creativity: A meta-analysis. *Organizational Behavior and Human Decision Processes, 108* (1), 25–38. https://doi.org/10.1016/j.obhdp.2008.04.001

De Dreu, C. K. W., Baas, M., & Nijstad, B. A. (2008). Hedonic tone and activation in the mood-creativity link: Towards a dual pathway to creativity model. *Journal of Personality and Social Psychology, 94*, 739–756. https://doi.org/10.1037/0022-3514.94.5.739

Duclos, S. E., Laird, J. D., Schneider, E., et al. (1989). Emotion-specific effects of facial expressions and postures on emotional experience. *Journal of Personality and Social Psychology, 57*, 100–108. https://doi.org/10.1037/0022-3514.57.1.100

Estrada, C. A., Isen, A. M., & Young, M. J. (1994). Positive affect improves creative problem solving and influences reported source of practice satisfaction in physicians. *Motivation and Emotion, 18*(4), 285–299. https://doi.org/10.1007/BF02856470

Felnhofer, A., Kothgassner, O. D., Schmidt, M., et al. (2015). Is virtual reality emotionally arousing? Investigating five emotion inducing virtual park scenarios. *International Journal of Human-Computer Studies, 82*, 48–56. https://doi.org/10.1016/j.ijhcs.2015.05.004

Fernández-Abascal, E. G., & Díaz, M. D. M. (2013). Affective induction and creative thinking. *Creativity Research Journal, 25*(2), 213–221. https://doi.org/10.1080/10400419.2013.783759

Filipowicz, A. (2006). From positive affect to creativity: The surprising role of surprise. *Creativity Research Journal, 18*(2), 141–152. https://doi.org/10.1207/s15326934crj1802_2

Flack, W. F., Jr., Laird, J. D., & Cavallaro, L. A. (1999). Separate and combined effects of facial expressions and bodily postures on emotional feelings. *European Journal of Social Psychology, 29*, 203–217. https://doi.org/10.1002/(SICI)1099-0992(199903/05)29:2/3<203::AID-EJSP924>3.0.CO;2-8

Fodor, E. M., & Carver, R. A. (2000). Achievement and power motives, performance feedback, and creativity. *Journal of Research in Personality, 34*(4), 380–396. https://doi.org/10.1006/jrpe.2000.2289

Fong, C. T. (2006). The effects of emotional ambivalence on creativity. *Academy of Management Journal, 49*(5), 1016–1030. https://doi.org/10.5465/amj.2006.22798182

Friedman, R. S., & Förster, J. (2002). The influence of approach and avoidance motor actions on creative cognition. *Journal of Experimental Social Psychology, 38*, 41–55. https://doi.org/10.1006/jesp.2001.1488

Friedman, R. S., & Förster, J. (2010). Implicit affective cues and attentional tuning: An integrative review. *Psychological Bulletin, 136*, 875–893. https://doi.org/10.1037/a0020495

Frijda, N. H. (1986). *The Emotions*. Cambridge University Press.

Frijda, N. H. (1993). Moods, emotion episodes, and emotions. In M. Lewis & J. M. Haviland (Eds.), *Handbook of Emotions* (pp. 381–403). Guilford Press.

Gasper, K., & Middlewood, B. L. (2014). Approaching novel thoughts: Understanding why elation and boredom promote associative thought more than distress and relaxation. *Journal of Experimental Social Psychology, 52*, 50–57. https://doi.org/10.1016/j.jesp.2013.12.007

Gerrards-Hesse, A., Spies, K., & Hesse, F. W. (1994). Experimental inductions of emotional states and their effectiveness: A review. *British Journal of Psychology, 85*, 55–78. https://doi.org/10.1111/j.2044-8295.1994.tb02508.x

Gilet, A. L., & Jallais, C. (2011). Valence, arousal and word associations. *Cognition and Emotion, 25*(4), 740–746. https://doi.org/10.1080/02699931.2010.500480

Gross, J. J. (1998). The emerging field of emotion regulation: An integrative review. *Review of General Psychology, 2*(3), 271–299. https://doi.org/10.1037/1089-2680.2.3.271

Harmon-Jones, E., Amodio, D. M., & Zinner, L. (2007). Social psychological methods of emotion elicitation. In J. J. B. Allen & J. A. Coan (Eds.), *The Handbook of Emotion Elicitation and Assessment*. Oxford University Press.

Hutchinson, J. C., Sherman, T., Martinovic, N., & Tenenbaum, G. (2008). The effect of manipulated self-efficacy on perceived and sustained effort. *Journal of Applied Sport Psychology, 20*(4), 457–472. https://doi.org/10.1080/10413200802351151

Isen, A. M. (2000). Positive affect and decision making. In M. Lewis & J. M. Haviland-Jones (Eds.), *Handbook of Emotions* (2nd ed., pp. 417–435). Guilford Press.

Isen, A. M., Daubman, K. A., & Nowicki, G. P. (1987). Positive affect facilitates creative problem solving. *Journal of Personality and Social Psychology, 52*, 1122–1131. https://doi.org/10.1037/0022-3514.52.6.1122

Ivcevic, Z., & Hoffmann, J. D. (2019). Emotions and creativity: From process to person and product. In J. C. Kaufman & R. S. Sternberg (Eds.), *Cambridge Handbook of Creativity* (pp. 273–295). Cambridge University Press.

Izard, C. E., & Ackerman, B. P. (2000). Motivational, organizational, and regulatory functions of discrete emotions. In M. Lewis & J. M. Haviland-Jones (Eds.), *Handbook of Emotions* (2nd ed., pp. 253–264). Guilford Press.

Joseph, D. L., Chan, M. Y., Heintzelman, S. J., Tay, L., Diener, E., & Scotney, V. S. (2020). The manipulation of affect: A meta-analysis of affect induction procedures. *Psychological Bulletin, 146*(4), 355. https://doi.org/10.1037/bul0000224

Kaufmann, G., & Vosburg, S. K. (2002). The effects of mood on early and late idea production. *Creativity Research Journal, 14*(3-4), 317–330. https://doi.org/10.1207/S15326934CRJ1434_3

Kenealy, P. M. (1986). The Velten mood induction procedure: A methodological review. *Motivation and Emotion, 10*, 315–335. https://doi.org/10.1007/BF00992107

Kuijsters, A., Redi, J., de Ruyter, B., & Heynderickx, I. (2016). Inducing sadness and anxiousness through visual media: Measurement techniques and persistence. *Frontiers in Psychology, 7*, 1141. https://doi.org/10.3389/fpsyg.2016.01141

Lerner, J. S., & Keltner, D. (2000). Beyond valence: Toward a model of emotion-specific influences on judgment and choice. *Cognition and Emotion, 14*, 473–493. https://doi.org/10.1080/026999300402763

Leung, A. K.-y., Liou, S., Qiu, L., et al. (2014). The role of instrumental emotion regulation in the emotions–creativity link: How worries render individuals with high neuroticism more creative. *Emotion, 14*(5), 846–856. https://doi.org/10.1037/a0036965

Loomis, J. M., Blascovich, J. J., & Beall, A. C. (1999). Immersive virtual environment technology as a basic research tool in psychology. *Behavior Research Methods, Instruments, and Computers, 31*, 557–564. https://doi.org/10.3758/BF03200735

Martin, M. (1990). On the induction of mood. *Clinical Psychology Review, 10*, 669–697. https://doi.org/10.1016/0272-7358(90)90075-L

Nummenmaa, L., & Niemi, P. (2004). Inducing affective states with success-failure manipulations: A meta-analysis. *Emotion, 4*, 207–214. https://doi.org/10.1037/1528-3542.4.2.207

Phillips, L. H., Bull, R., Adams, E., & Fraser, L. (2002). Positive mood and executive function: Evidence from Stroop and fluency tasks. *Emotion, 2*(1), 12–22. https://doi.org/10.1037/1528-3542.2.1.12

Polivy, J., & Doyle, C. (1980). Laboratory induction of mood states through the reading of self-referent mood statements: Affective changes or demand characteristics? *Journal of Abnormal Psychology, 89*, 286–290. https://doi.org/10.1037/0021-843X.89.2.286

Ritter, S. M., & Ferguson, S. (2017). Happy creativity: Listening to happy music facilitates divergent thinking. *PloSone, 12*(9), e0182210. https://doi.org/10.1371/journal.pone.0182210

Robson, C., & McCartan, K. (2016). *Real World Research* (4th ed.). Wiley

Roseman, I. J., Wiest, C., & Swartz, T. S. (1994). Phenomenology, behaviors, and goals differentiate discrete emotions. *Journal of Personality and Social Psychology, 67*(2), 206. https://doi.org/10.1037/0022-3514.67.2.206

Rottenberg, J., Ray, R. R., & Gross, J. J. (2007). Emotion elicitation using films. In J. J. B. Allen & J. A. Coan (Eds.), *The Handbook of Emotion Elicitation and Assessment*. Oxford University Press.

Rowe, G., Hirsh, J. B., & Anderson, A. K. (2007). Positive affect increases the breadth of attentional selection. *Proceedings of the National Academy of Sciences, 104*(1), 383–388. https://doi.org/10.1073/pnas.0605198104

Russell, J. A., & Barrett, L. F. (1999). Core affect, prototypical emotional episodes, and other things called emotion: Dissecting the elephant. *Journal of Personality and Social Psychology, 76*(5), 805–819. https://doi.org/10.1037/0022-3514.76.5.805

Shalley, C. E. (1995). Effects of coaction, expected evaluation, and goal setting on creativity and productivity. *Academy of Management Journal, 38*(2), 483–503. https://doi.org/10.5465/256689

Siemer, M. (2001). Mood-specific effects on appraisal and emotion judgments. *Cognition and Emotion, 15*, 453–485. https://doi.org/10.1080/02699930126083

Snyder, H. T., Hammond, J. A., Grohman, M. G., & Katz-Buonincontro, J. (2019). Creativity measurement in undergraduate students from 1984–2013: A systematic review. *Psychology of Aesthetics, Creativity, and the Arts, 13*(2), 133–143. https://doi.org/10.1037/aca0000228

Tan, C. S., & Qu, L. (2015). Stability of the positive mood effect on creativity when task switching, practice effect, and test item differences are taken into consideration. *The Journal of Creative Behavior, 49*(2), 94–110. https://doi.org/10.1002/jocb.56

Topolinski, S., & Deutsch, R. (2012). Phasic affective modulation of creativity. *Experimental Psychology, 59*, 302–310. https://doi.org/10.1027/1618-3169/a000159

Torrance, E. P. (1966). *Torrance Tests of Creative Thinking*. Personnel Press.

Velten, E. (1968). A laboratory task for induction of mood states. *Behaviour Research and Therapy, 6*, 473–482. https://doi.org/10.1016/0005-7967(68)90028-4

Verduyn, P., Van Mechelen, I., Tuerlinckx, F., Meers, K., & Van Coillie, H. (2009). Intensity profiles of emotional experience over time. *Cognition and Emotion, 23*(7), 1427–1443. https://doi.org/10.1080/02699930902949031

Wu, X., Guo, T., Tan, T., et al. (2019). Superior emotional regulating effects of creative cognitive reappraisal. *Neuroimage, 200,* 540–551. https://doi.org/10.1016/j.neuroimage.2019.06.061

Zeelenberg, M., & Pieters, R. (2004). Beyond valence in customer dissatisfaction: A review and new findings on behavioral responses to regret and disappointment in failed services. *Journal of Business Research, 57,* 445–455. https://doi.org/10.1016/S0148–2963(02)00278-3

Ziv, A. (1976). Facilitating effects of humor on creativity. *Journal of Educational Psychology, 68*(3), 318–322. https://doi.org/10.1037/0022-0663.68.3.318

2 Affect, Complexity, and the Case Study Method

Michael Hanchett Hanson, Joseph I. Eisman, and Jennifer Ruth Hoyden

Case study research directly addresses a core concern regarding creative work: how people who live real, messy, and unpredictable lives contribute to dynamic changes in their worlds with new ideas and practices (Hanchett Hanson & Glăveanu, 2020; Wallace & Gruber, 1989). These investigations are not just important because of real-world relevance. In the broader field of creativity research, they also anchor, question, inform, and are informed by other methodologies.

This chapter focuses on data that, without careful consideration, can be "seen but not noticed" in case studies as well as other methods: affect (Löfgren, 1981, p. 26). Like any aspect of case study research, here researchers must actively work to be conscious of their methods, the available data, their own positionalities and assumptions, and their insights. The particular challenge of affect is that, although it pervades all human experience, relevant data are often not available and, when they are, can be difficult to interpret.

Below we clarify our terms, introduce a brief history of the constructs of affect and creativity, and review considerations of data sources. We then discuss approaches to case studies, with emphasis on the evolving systems approach, developed specifically to study creative development and its application in the participatory framework (e.g., Gruber & Davis, 1988; Hanchett Hanson, 2005). The main body of the chapter offers five guiding questions to assist researchers in framing case research to recognize and utilize affect data.

Affect and Creativity

Terms

There are different ways to conceive the construct of affect and related concepts. For example, *affect* has been used as an umbrella term that includes

The authors wish to express gratitude to past and current members of the Participatory Creativity Lab, especially Alex Wojcik for his contributions to an earlier sketch of this chapter. In addition, Joseph Eisman thanks Ilya Lyashevsky, PhD, and Joshua Sterling Friedman for their rich discussions during the development of this chapter.

Michael Hanchett Hanson orcid.org/0000-0003-3213-3345
Joseph I. Eisman orcid.org/0000-0002-4171-913X
Jennifer Ruth Hoyden orcid.org/0000-0002-6095-0732

mood and emotion; *mood* to indicate a sustained and long-term affective state; and *emotion* to describe a short-term experience (Gilet & Jallais, 2012). *Feeling* is then an embodied awareness of an experience (Damasio, 2000). Another way to approach the topic is to differentiate between *emotion states*, which include moods, and *emotion abilities*, such as self-regulation and strategic uses of emotions (Ivcevic & Hoffmann, 2019). The various distinctions can be useful in different research contexts, but, for the claims that case studies can make, a relatively streamlined set of terms is most useful. Except in longitudinal cases (repeated measures), available data seldom distinguishes short-term emotions and longer-term moods. We will use *emotion states* in reference to short-term emotions and longer-term moods. We will use *affect* as an umbrella term to include any of the related concepts, and *affective system* to discuss the dynamics of a person's or group's overall affect, including emotion states and feelings. Here, the use of *system* to describe affect is meant to reinforce that emotions, moods, and feelings have complex dynamics.

Parallel Histories

Research on affect has evolved considerably over more than 100 years. Barrett and Lindquist (2008) have described how early theorists tended to view affect as originating either in the body (e.g., Ekman, 1972; Laird, 1984) or the mind (e.g., Frijda, 1986; McDougall, 1908; Titchner, 1921; Wundt, 1897). In the next wave of research, scholars developed dual body-and-mind theories (emergence from interaction, e.g., Duffy, 1934; Schacter & Singer, 1962). Many theories have described emotions as *basic*, universal experiences that are hardwired into the brain (e.g., Ekman, 1972). However, more recent research has shown significant variability in the physical expression of *emotion categories* (Siegel et al., 2018) and has begun to embrace a relational and sociocultural approach, which suggests emotional categories are socially constructed (Barrett, 2006, 2017).

Creativity research in psychology has followed a similar path. The construct of creativity gained prominence in American psychology in the middle of the twentieth century (Guilford, 1950; Hanchett Hanson, 2015; Weisberg, 2006). A primary focus, which endured for decades, was identification of traits, locating creativity entirely within the individual. A growing number of contemporary theories in psychology now understand creativity as socially and materially distributed over many people, objects, and time (Clapp, 2016; Csikszentmihalyi, 1999; Glăveanu, 2010; Glăveanu et al., 2020; Hanchett Hanson, 2015; Hanchett Hanson et al., 2021; Sawyer, 2012). These theories situate the person within dynamic systems that influence the work, eschewing the creative genius model and acknowledging relational forces.

The parallel histories of our understanding of affect and creativity reflect a recognition of people's engagement in socially mediated meaning-making processes. Here, we focus on how case studies can examine emotion states and larger affective systems as part of creative work, with implications for attention, motivation, and the responses the work arouses.

Data Sources

Researchers have sought to identify and/or measure emotion states and creativity using a variety of tools, attending to different aspects of experience. Common measures include artifact assessment and evaluation; brain and somatic measures; observations by others; self-reports; interviews; and surveys. Each supports different goals, yields different results, aligns with different paradigmatic stances, and is accepted by different audiences. Each also has limitations. For example, artifacts and observations require inferences, while self-report surveys may not provide detailed descriptions of an emotion state. All may include biases. Neuroscience has been criticized for being reductive and using contrived stimuli (Zaki & Ochsner, 2012). The concern here is validity and rigor: What do the data actually tell us?

Any of these measures could conceivably be part of a case study. For studies of the development of people who have completed creative work, the most common data are artifact analysis, observations, and self-reports. Here, the measures confront the same limitations as when used in other methods, but in case study methodology, triangulation between different types of data is a matter of course for any important finding (Stake, 1995).

When using these data sources, developmental case studies address two important factors that other methods generally do not: time frame and dynamic complexity. A developmental approach can situate the probabilities identified in experiments, surveys, psychometrics, and historiometrics in specific contexts and time frames; analyze both how and when those probable outcomes occur, and raise caveats to consider. Additionally, in real life, emotion states may not be experienced separately or one-at-a-time (Frijda, 1988; Lane & Schwartz, 1987). They form dynamic systems. Different emotion states interact with each other and with the social and material world. Those emotion states can also interact with, and come from, knowledge and goals related to creative work: affect is part of and encompasses creative work (cf. Immordino-Yang & Damasio, 2007).

Case Studies of Creativity

Dialogue with Other Methods

As mentioned above, case research should work in dialogue with other methods. Case studies often precede other methods in pilot research. More generally – and less widely recognized – serious case research continues to complement and inform other methods by linking them to real-world examples. While many methodologies in psychology work toward predicting *what* is likely to happen, case study work examines *how* things happen in order to consider *why* (Gruber, 1989; Stake, 1995; Yin, 2018). Whereas psychological research typically seeks to isolate variables and predict their impact on generalized populations, case research seeks to understand complex patterns in specific instances (Gruber, 1989; Stake, 1995).

Well-conducted case study research, like experimental research, is difficult. Ideally, a conversation among methodologies emerges, involving many researchers over time. Because a case study should always situate the questions it poses within the matrix of existing research, the researchers need to be current on other lines of inquiry – an added layer of work. Although the challenges are daunting, we have no equivalent alternative for the crucial role case studies play in understanding real-world conditions. It is, therefore, imperative that case research be conducted and conducted well. To do so, researchers should be sensitive to affective data.

Approaches and Forms

There are several approaches to case study research (Yazan, 2015). Because cases look at complex relationships, they are necessarily in-depth analyses that include multiple data sources. Cases are generally presented in a mix of qualitative narrative, schematized, and quantitative formats, ranging from long chapter to whole book formats. (The case examples used later in this chapter are brief summaries of much longer analyses.)

Case research may be used to investigate intrinsic concerns (interests of scholars in the specific person, time, or policy examined), instrumental concerns (the case as an example of more general issues, such as how emotion states can influence motivation), or both. In relation to creativity, case studies can be conducted on the work of specific people (e.g., Hanchett Hanson et al., 2021; Wallace & Gruber, 1989; Weisberg, 2006); on the development of ideas across history, which Clapp (2016) has called "biographies of ideas"; on the conditions of particular places or times, like Schorske's (1980) analysis of the social and intellectual dynamics of *fin de siècle* Vienna; or on a particular situation, like a specific school program (Clapp, 2016; Stake, 1995). Cases about places and times tend to be more historiographic in focus; cases of situations, more sociological; biographies of ideas, historiographic or sociological; and cases of specific people's work, psychological and sociocultural. All look at complex dynamics of change over some defined period of time, and affect is always a factor.

Of its various forms, case study method is uniquely suited to focus on individuals, the application for which it may be best known. Even in biographies of ideas or analyses of places and times, portraits of the development and roles of the individuals involved are usually crucial to the analysis. Case research does not have to reflect an individualist ideology. The experiences of specific people can be examined as part of their social and material milieux. However, much of the available data will be found at the level of individual experience, even though the affective system extends beyond the individual to immediate social and material interactions, to group dynamics, and to sociohistorical conditions. By situating individuals in larger sociohistorical dynamics, we can discover the unique contributions of the case subject, as well as the dynamics of a larger cast of players. Each of those players is a hub who experiences, transforms, and relays affect.

The rest of the discussion focuses on cases of people doing creative work, but many of the principles discussed apply to case work generally. (For an overview of case study methodology in creativity, specifically, see Hanchett Hanson & Glăveanu, 2020.)

The Evolving Systems Approach and the Participatory Framework

An approach to case research designed specifically to study the development of creativity is *evolving systems* developed by Howard Gruber and his associates (Gruber, 1981; Gruber & Davis, 1988; Hanchett Hanson, 2005; Wallace & Gruber, 1989). Gruber saw creativity as a form of work, a complex, purpose-driven behavior, and creative development as a systemic emergence of a unique point of view. The point of view was both expressed by and developed through the creative work – a feedback system (Hanchett Hanson & Glăveanu, 2020; Wallace & Gruber, 1989). A person's point of view is, thus, an evolving system working within and through broader natural, social, and material dynamics. This system is composed of loosely coupled subsystems, including purpose, knowledge, and – crucial to the current discussion – affect.

The case study method complements this view of development in its concern for complex dynamics. The questions asked of any evolving systems case involve how people recognize and organize resources to do the creative work (Hanchett Hanson & Glăveanu, 2020). For affect, the organization may depend on learning, consciously or unconsciously, how emotion states can influence inspiration, maintain motivation, overcome obstacles, convey ideas, and so on. Note that this approach is very much in keeping with the idea of emotional abilities that develop dynamically over time and may transfer from one project or task to another (Ivcevic & Hoffmann, 2019).

Gruber's approach has been one of the foundational elements of today's distributed and participatory views of creativity (e.g., Clapp, 2016; Glăveanu, 2014; Glăveanu et al., 2020; Hanchett Hanson, 2015). The participatory framework follows Gruber's view of creative work as a dynamic and purposeful behavior that emerges, nonlinearly, over time and augments evolving systems by elaborating on the embodied, social, and material interactions that are part of creative work. Both the evolving systems and the participatory framework have recognized affect as crucial to creative work and pervasive throughout personal and social systems (Gruber, 1989; Hanchett Hanson et al., 2021). The researcher, therefore, should be concerned about affect.

Case Research and Affect in Practice: Guiding Questions

To facilitate careful consideration of affect within case research, we propose the following questions as tools to maintain the standards of that research:

1. Philosophical stance: What are your ontological assumptions?
2. The intersection of subject, focus, and data: What can the case do?
3. Pragmatics: How does affect function in the case?
4. Dynamics: What are the patterns?
5. Insight, inference, and bias: What is the role of the researcher?

Philosophical Stance: What Are Your Ontological Assumptions?

There are choices for how to think about emotion states. One ontological controversy is whether or not – or to what extent – emotion states are hard-wired and universal versus socially constructed. Here, the assumption will be that emotion states are socially constructed – the development of, motivations for, labeling of, expression of, and interpretation of people's emotion states are embedded in the social discourse of their time and place. Love, anger, fear, and so on have different meanings, values, and conventions of expression in different historical and social contexts. Emotion states also relate to each other and to ideas in complex ways, shifting in different contexts. Desire for another person may be called love and linked to arousal of joy in one context and called sin and linked to fear in another.

Another, sometimes related, ontological issue is the origin of emotion states. Are they inherently unidirectional, (a) emerging from the body or the mind of the person or (b) caused by events in the world? Alternatively, are emotion states (c) complexly related, emerging directly from interactions between people and their worlds or (d) complex systems that may be dominated by different dynamics at different times for different people? Here, options (c) and (d) are the same theory but with pragmatic differences for researchers. They both agree that person–world interactions are always at play. Complex systems, however, can vary dramatically in the relation of input to output (Fieguth, 2017). A case may consider psychopathologies, such as neuroses, in which internal feelings are being projected onto the world. The focus of the case is then on internal sources of emotion states. Or the case may focus on a period in which dramatic circumstances overwhelm a person's affective system, directing how the person engages the world, at least temporarily. For example: war. There, the impact of external forces is the focus. Both of these extreme examples concern person–world interactions in wide view, but the context from which emotion states develop has swung dramatically. As an ontological stance, option (d) – complexity that may be dominated by different dynamics at different times for different people – reminds researchers that, although the interactions of person–world are always relevant, the emotion states do not necessarily center on some form of equilibrium between the two. Again, the two examples of psychopathology and external crisis given here are extremes. More subtle projections onto, and dissociations from, the world may be present in any case of creative work and may, indeed, be near the heart of the work.

For theorists believing that affect is not socially constructed or that it is always unidirectional in either interior/exterior or mind/body dichotomies, experiments may serve their goals more efficiently. Because case study research is set up to look at complexity and specific contexts, it is better leveraged for views of affect as complexly emergent and constructed and, therefore, context dependent.

The Intersection of Subject, Focus, and Data: What Can the Case Do?

Assuming that the researcher is approaching affect as complexly emergent from a wide range of possible dynamics, any case study takes form in a tension among the subject of the case (e.g., a specific person's development), the focus of the case (e.g., specific shifts in motivation over a defined period of time), and the available data for the case.

For example, Gruber's (1981) groundbreaking case on Charles Darwin's discovery of natural selection was chosen by Gruber primarily because Darwin kept extraordinarily detailed notebooks on his work. Those data allowed Gruber to trace the winding road of observations and theories that Darwin took in coming to his discovery. The content of the notebooks could also be triangulated to Darwin's letters, published works, and actions. Fear was important to a particular issue for this case as both a negative and positive motivational factor. Darwin wrote up a quick sketch of his theory of natural selection shortly after his insight in 1838 but did not publish it for another 20 years. At that point he had written a long summary of the theory and was in the process of writing a much longer work that would have further delayed publication, and that few people would probably have read. He only wrote the shorter and highly accessible *On the Origin of Species* under external pressure because the younger naturalist Alfred Russel Wallace had come to the same insight and was ready to publish it. Why did Darwin delay so long? Gruber concluded that fear of negative reception was a key driving factor. He triangulated Darwin's comments about possible reception of the idea in his notes and letters; dreams about persecution, reported in the notebooks when he came to the insight; direct experiences of seeing others persecuted for advocating materialist beliefs while Darwin was in college, documented from historical records; and the actions themselves.

Note the narrow conclusion serving the needs of the case: linking motivation for a specific set of actions to a particular emotion state (fear), not Darwin's entire affective system nor even how his mood could have interacted with the fear. (He was chronically ill during the period of the insight.) The data on those larger questions might not have been strong enough to make a case.

Other cases support and need different levels of analysis concerning affect. For example, a case looking at material actors focused on craftsperson Elizabeth Zimmermann, who revolutionized knitting in America during the mid-to-late twentieth century. She promoted and expanded on techniques that she had learned as a girl in England to liberate American knitters to make their own designs, rather than always working from patterns (see Hanchett Hanson et al., 2021). Based on her extensive writing, her videotapes, accounts from her children, and her actions, two long-term patterns of her affective system are evident: an intense enjoyment of the embodied practice of knitting and a consistent reaction to obstacles as motivation to action. She had loved knitting and identified with the practice from the time she was a young child and throughout her adolescence. Her books and videos detail her experience of knitting as a powerful engagement of thought and feeling. In contrast, her project to liberate other knitters emerged over time, largely in reaction to a series of obstacles others put in her way, such as editors rewriting her patterns, readers being unable to obtain her preferred yarns, and a craft guild refusing to acknowledge knitting. In response to each obstacle, she expanded her entrepreneurial enterprises and her commitment to an emerging purpose. There is not sufficient data to say what mix of anger, mirth, sadness, excitement, or other specific emotion states she experienced in responding to each obstacle, but there are data to support that her overall affective system increasingly tied her practice of knitting to the liberation of other knitters and her response to obstacles.

The key point of these examples is that the examination of affect in any case can be narrow or broad. It should also serve the focus of the case and must be possible given existing data.

Pragmatics: How Does Affect Function in the Case?

The examples above look at different ways that affect functions within the two cases. Of particular interest for creativity studies is the relationship of affect to attention and to motivation. For example, emotion states can cue attention to salient features in internal and external environments, altering arousal, interest, actions, and self-beliefs about work. These functions align with a number of specific theories of affect (Clore et al., 1994; Clore et al., 2001; Fredrickson, 2004; Glăveanu & Womersley, 2021; Jaber & Hammer, 2016; Schwartz & Clore, 1983).

Researchers investigating motivation have come to some similar conclusions on how emotion states and motivations interact, but often with different emphases and/or terminology. Different approaches to motivation research have looked at the effects of prospective and retrospective appraisals of control over tasks (Pekrun, 2006); beliefs concerning causes of a task outcome (Weiner, 1986); the association of emotion states with approach and avoidance behaviors (Elliot, 2005); and role identity within complex dynamics of beliefs, perceptions, goals, and actions (Kaplan & Garner, 2017).

For example, motivation theories have looked a good deal at perceptions of control, suggesting the need to consider how Darwin's motivations may have related to his value of control. A lack of control over public reaction inhibited him from publishing, and then he switched to action in the face of losing control over the theory to Wallace. In both cases, he feared losing control. Another issue suggested by motivation concepts is role identity. Both the fear of public response and the reaction to being scooped by the younger and less well-known

Wallace may be linked to Darwin's well-established identity as a leading British scientist from a family of famous scientists.

In this methodological dialogue, the Darwin case does not advance one perspective on emotion states or motivation over others, but provides an example of how various functions of emotion states can overlap in real-world experience. Instead of stopping at the conclusion that fear was a motivating factor for Darwin's hesitation to publish, issues like control, identity, expectancy for success, value of the creative work, and more can be considered. The analysis is raised from a unidirectional description of fear motivating action to a consideration of multiple aspects of the larger affective system.

Dynamics: What Are the Patterns?

Whether looking at specific emotion states within the affective system, as in the Darwin case, or longer-term consistencies in behavior, as previously described in relation to the Zimmermann case, identifying patterns is key to understanding creative development and the systemic complexity of the work (Gruber, 1989; Stake, 1995).

Feedback loops are part of such patterns. Returning to the Zimmermann case, not only do the data show a mix of positive emotion states associated with knitting and an energized response to obstacles, the case also shows how certain obstacles provided feedback loops leading to more knitting and new initiatives over extended periods of time. When the Wisconsin Designer Craftsmen Association (WDC) refused to grant Zimmermann membership because they did not consider knitting a craft, she proceeded to lobby for this recognition of her craft with new entries into WDC exhibitions *for 15 years*. This ongoing confrontation required that Zimmermann produce her highest quality work repeatedly, maintaining her standards and pushing her ingenuity – a loop of more and more production at ever-higher quality and gradual steps of greater recognition within the guild, resulting in work that enriched her commercial patterns and reputation as well. Once Zimmermann was awarded the highest level of membership, she stopped producing entries for the guild entirely. The engaging aspect of the relationship seemed to be the battle, not the victory. Her achievement coincided with the publication of her first book, solidifying her status as an authority within the larger knitting world. This is an example of the function of a nemesis in an affective system. In the methodological dialogue, the nemesis dynamic that the case reveals raises questions for further study that could involve surveys, interviews, and experiments, including game-based simulations.

Insight, Inference, and Bias: What Is the Role of the Researcher?

In any type of research, the perspective of the researcher can be crucial (Stake, 1995). For example, awareness of positionality and social power dynamics can help avoid procedures that might bias findings or the interpretation of the findings from an experiment. Because case studies accommodate complexity, and the focus can shift with new findings that emerge during the course of the research, the intuitions, curiosity, and insights of the researcher are particularly important.

All perspectives, though, come with limits, and interpretation of affect data can be influenced by personal perspectives that may be irrelevant or overly simplified. Researchers must guard against presuming their own perspectives to be universal or "correct" in some objective sense that can lead to misinterpretation of the functions of the affective systems within the case. All kinds of affective experience may take on different meaning to different people and is sensitive to context (Barrett, 2006, 2012). These concerns call for specific, practical steps for case study research.

First, as noted above, researchers need to reflect on their own potential biases. Here, humility about the particularity of one's own experience of affect and curiosity about the possibilities of very different experiences are key.

Second, triangulation to multiple data sources is needed for any major claims about a subject's affective system. This may include self-reports, observations of others, patterns of behavior across contexts, or content analysis of works – all looking for disconfirming as well as confirming evidence. For content analysis, triangulation to other data in the case, as well as to supported theories about interpretation of affect within the medium of the work, can be important (e.g., interpretation of color, form, pitch, key, metaphor – construct validity). Then, correlation of multiple coders can provide further validation, as can member checking, when possible (input from the subject of the case). In conducting content analysis in general, though, the researcher must, again, be on the lookout for hidden universalizing assumptions that might not apply to the specific context. (We see here how the ontological stance concerning affect runs as a current throughout work on the topic.) The significance of colors or language, for example, cannot be simply extracted from their specific context, without justification, and interpreted through theories on their contemporary affective associations. In-depth consideration of the context – the reason we use case studies – always comes first.

Third, elaborating on that last point, study the details of the context. Pay attention to evidence for how different types of affect were viewed at the time or about how activities that might be associated today with positive or negative affect were viewed then. For example, curiosity was considered a sin in early medieval Europe, particularly among monastic communities (Bruce, 2019). The positive interpretation we have today of the heightened sense of excitement and anticipation associated with curiosity would not likely transfer directly onto the monastic settings where extraordinary works were done during that time.

Fourth, the juxtapositions of the researchers' and other scholars' conflicting interpretations of affect within the case can, and usually should, be part of the case discussion – keeping in mind the value of raising questions as a function of case studies in the larger field of research.

An example of these points is the case of Fritz Haber, a groundbreaking, energetic, and patriotic chemist with a controversial legacy. Haber was born in 1868 in the wake of the German Enlightenment and was socialized and guided by the Prussian maxim *Deo-Litteris-Patriae* (for God, for Science, and for the Fatherland), which favored collective work in service of the state (Dunikowska & Turko, 2011; Popper, 2012). Haber worked with his father in the family business producing paints and other chemical products before going to university to become a full-time professional chemist. There, he was exposed to a philosophy of science that may have strongly influenced his "rational temper" (Stern, 1963, p. 88). The Habers were an assimilated Jewish family, but, after graduation, Haber became a *Kultur-Protestantismus*, a Culture-Protestant, giving him more freedom to participate in society (Stern, 2012).

In his late 20s, as a full-time chemist, Haber entered the race to save the world by stabilizing the world food supply. In 1911, having worked on the question for 17 years, Haber formulated a process fixing atmospheric nitrogen to hydrogen, for which he later won a Nobel Prize (Witschi, 2000b). Applied to large-scale production by Carl Bosch, his contribution enabled the Haber–Bosch process to increase crop yield worldwide. Today's world population would not exist without the nitrogen-rich fertilizer Haber made possible (Huxtable, 2002). This high-profile success also made Haber a member of the social elite.

During World War I, Haber was quick to support the German war effort. Throughout the war, he and his team produced around 900 million tons of nitrates used for explosives and developed poisonous chlorine gas (Huxtable, 2002). In late April of 1915, Haber and his colleagues released approximately 180 tons of chlorine gas on French and Algerian soldiers (Huxtable, 2002; Witschi, 2000b). While some German military officers did not see the tactical advantage of Haber's gas (Witschi, 2000b), the German Minister of War congratulated Haber in a letter, saying, "You put your broad knowledge and your energy unrestrainedly in the service of the fatherland . . . . You were able to mobilize German chemistry . . . . Your brilliant success will remain . . . unforgotten" (in Stern, 1999, p. 126).

Haber's enthusiastic development of chemical warfare brought further strain to his already stressed marriage to the accomplished chemist Clara Immerwahr and may have contributed to Clara's suicide (Huxtable, 2002; Manchester, 2002). On May 2, 1915, she shot herself with Haber's army pistol (Huxtable, 2002). Hermann, their 13-year-old son, found Clara dying (Oyama, 2015). The day following his wife's suicide, Haber returned to the war front to prepare for another chemical attack, which was carried out against the Russian army on May 31, 1915 (Huxtable, 2002).

This summary of one aspect of the Haber case outlines some of the evidence that national identity played a central role in Haber's affective system. Service to and recognition within the national leadership guided much of his work, evidenced by his extraordinarily consistent actions and descriptions of his patriotic commitment (e.g., Haber, 1933; Witschi, 2000b). Details of how other emotion states and values were organized in the system are not as clear, though.

Was his immediate return to work a reaction to his wife's suicide – and, if so, was it an expression of apathy about or anger toward her and/or a defense against sadness, hurt, guilt, or complex feelings *per se*? Additionally – or alternatively – was it a circumstance of the professional and personal pressure he was under to support the war effort? He did not undergo any form of therapy for which notes might be available.

Another aspect of the Haber case is legacy, and, here again, the researcher's perspective can come into play. Posterity has tended to treat Haber's legacy as brilliant, emphasizing the Haber–Bosch process (e.g., Oyama, 2015); inhumane, emphasizing the introduction of gas warfare (e.g., Harrison, 1992); or "complex" (Witschi, 2000a, p. 1). Beyond recounting the controversies, the case analysis may also contribute to the views of legacy. In addition to good, bad, or complex, another possibility, raised by his case, is that Haber was consistent in his motivations. He was a man for whom interpersonal relationships were difficult but who repeatedly tried to combine his expertise in chemistry, his identification with his nation, and the needs of humanity. From the beginning of World War I, bringing the conflict to a quick end had been a goal and motivation for both sides (Shaw, 1914/1931; Tuchman, 1962). By the spring of 1915, when the Germans first used chlorine gas, the conflict had already lasted longer than expected, with hundreds of thousands of men dying on both sides in "battles" that dragged on for days or even months (Fussell, 1975/2000). Bringing the war to a swift and decisive end would have been a key theme for the military milieu in which Haber was working, framed as both patriotism and humanitarianism.

There are multiple, plausible interpretations that could be presented. Depending on the triangulated data, one or another interpretation may be argued as a hypothesis, or all interpretations may be simply posed as questions to be explored in other research. In any case, the researchers should not jump to conclusions based on their own experience or assumptions.

Conclusion

Affect can make things both messy and rich for case research. The crucial functions of emotion, mood, feeling, and other affective constructs that inform how we understand one another and evaluate our worlds can be a source of insight for researchers, defining specific issues to investigate, but those same instincts also pose a minefield of traps. Affect is, however, an aspect of cases that stands to illuminate more than it confounds. Ignoring it can skew or impoverish the analysis. Case studies address two important factors that other methods generally do not: time frame and dynamic complexity. Since affect permeates all aspects of creative work over time, it is particularly important to the unique contributions of case studies.

There are a number of approaches to case studies. This chapter has listed several and focused on the evolving systems approach and the related participatory framework, which uses systems theory and has been designed specifically for analysis of creative development. In some cases, a single emotion state may be important to a case, but in these approaches, affect is still conceived as a subsystem, linked to a person's overall evolving point of view.

In practice, researching affect within a case requires consideration of a number of issues that have been grouped here under five guiding questions:

1. *Philosophical stance: What are your ontological assumptions?* Because case research looks at systemic complexity of specific situations, the method fits some views of affect better than others, specifically views that see affect as socially constructed or complex fit better than those that see emotions or moods as hard-wired or unidirectional. Even for the more reductive views of affect, however, cases can provide examples and raise questions about development of internal mechanisms or external influences over time.

2. *The intersection of subject, focus, and data: What can the case do?* These factors define the constraints in which the case will develop. The extent of available, compelling, triangulated data determines what can be said about the affective system of a given person. As the summaries of the Darwin and Zimmermann cases illustrate, the level of analysis can vary according to the focus of the case and available data – for example, a specific emotion in relation to the initial delay and subsequent rush to publish in the Darwin example or a consistent pattern of affect over the course of long-term work in Zimmermann's responses to obstacles.

3. *Pragmatics: How does affect function in the case?* Different theories of the motivational functions of affect provide lenses through which to consider an affective system and the available data about it. For example, theories focusing on relations between motivation and control suggest examining the case data concerning Darwin's fear of publishing in relation to control. In turn, the Darwin case can then raise questions about the assumptions concerning fear.

4. *Dynamics: What are the patterns?* A reminder: look for amplifying and/or stabilizing feedback loops and relations of the person in question to varying aspects of the context from immediate to societal and historical. Examination of systemic patterns distinguishes the case study method, and it should be used for its strengths.

5. *Insight, inference, and bias: What is the role of the researcher?* Affect can work in case research in many of the ways it does in everyday life – evoking empathy for another's situation but also, potentially, blocking insight into the differences between the subject's and the researcher's perspectives. To counter the worst difficulties of misinterpretation or to avoid missing the value of the case through misapplied examples of how emotion states can work, researchers should (a) be aware of their own positionalities and potential biases; (b) insist on multiple data sources for any important conclusion, search for disconfirming evidence, and member check when possible – triangulate, triangulate, triangulate; (c) keep asking questions about the subject's context even beyond what might seem immediately necessary;

and (d) remember that part of the case value may be in laying out possible interpretations even when there are not sufficient data to argue for one interpretation over the others.

Ultimately, the case researcher will need to come to the work with a paradoxical thick-skinned humility, convinced of the value of the work for the larger research discourse even when others are skeptical but also aware that to do the work well is to question each step. Applying this method to considerations of affect ups the ante because affect is inseparable from human experience, including creative work, but data and their interpretation can be so challenging.

References

Barrett, L. F. (2006). Solving the emotion paradox: Categorization and the experience of emotion. *Personality and Social Psychology Review, 10*(1), 20–46. http://doi.org/10.1207/s15327957pspr1001_2

Barrett, L. F. (2012). Emotions are real. *Emotion, 12*(3), 413–429. https://doi.org/10.1037/a0027555

Barrett, L. F. (2017). *How Emotions Are Made: The Secret Life of the Brain.* Houghton-Mifflin-Harcourt.

Barrett, L. F., & Lindquist, K. A. (2008). The embodiment of emotion. In G. R. Semin & E. R. Smith (Eds.), *Embodied Grounding: Social, Cognitive, Affective, and Neuroscientific Approaches* (pp. 237–262). Cambridge University Press. https://doi.org/10.1017/CBO9780511805837.011

Bruce, S. G. (2019). Curiosity killed the monk: The history of early medieval vice. *Journal of Medieval Monastic Studies, 8,* 73–94. https://doi.org/10.1484/J.JMMS.5.117960

Clapp, E. P. (2016). *Participatory Creativity: Introducing Access and Equity to the Creative Classroom.* Routledge. https://doi.org/10.4324/9781315671512

Clore, G. L., Schwarz, N., & Conway, M. (1994). Affective causes and consequences of social information processing. In R. S. Wyer & T. Srull (Eds.), *The Handbook of Social Cognition* (2nd ed., pp. 323–417). Erlbaum.

Clore, G. L., Wyer, R. S., Dienes, B., et al. (2001). Affective feelings as feedback: Some cognitive consequences. In L. L. Martin & G. L. Clore (Eds.), *Theories of Mood and Cognition: A User's Guidebook* (pp. 27–62). Erlbaum.

Csikszentmihalyi, M. (1999). Implications of a systems perspective for the study of creativity. In R. J. Sternberg (Ed.), *Handbook of Creativity* (pp. 313–335). Cambridge University Press.

Damasio, A. (2000). *The Feeling of What Happens: Body and Emotion in the Making of Consciousness.* Mariner Books.

Duffy, E. (1934). Is emotion a mere term of convenience? *Psychological Review, 41*(1), 103–104. https://doi.org/10.1037/h0075951

Dunikowska, M., & Turko, L. (2011). Fritz Haber: The damned scientist. *Angewandte Chemie International Edition, 50*(43), 10050–10062.

Ekman, P. (1972). Universal and cultural differences in facial expressions of emotions. In J. K. Cole (Ed.), *Nebraska Symposium on Motivation* (vol. 19, pp. 207–283). University of Nebraska Press.

Elliot, A. J. (2005). A conceptual history of the achievement goal construct. In A. J. Elliot & C. S. Dweck (Eds.), *Handbook of Competence and Motivation* (pp. 52–72). Guilford Press.

Fieguth, P. (2017). *An Introduction to Complex Systems: Society, Ecology, and Nonlinear Dynamics.* Springer. https://doi.org/10.1007/978-3-319-44606-6

Fredrickson, B. L. (2004). The broaden-and-build theory of positive emotions. *Philosophical Transactions of the Royal Society of London, B Series, 359* (1449), 1367–1378. https://doi.org/10.1098/rstb.2004.1512

Frijda, N. H. (1986). *The Emotions.* Cambridge University Press.

Frijda, N. H. (1988). The law of emotion. *American Psychologist, 43*(5), 349–358. https://doi.org/10.1037/0003-066X.43.5.349

Fussell, P. (2000). *The Great War and Modern Memory.* Oxford University Press. (Original published in 1975)

Glăveanu, V. P. (2010). Creativity as cultural participation. *Journal for the Theory of Social Behaviour, 41*(1), 48–67. https://doi.org/10.1111/j.1468-5914.2010.00445.x

Glăveanu, V. P. (2014). *Distributed Creativity: Thinking Outside the Box of the Creative Individual.* Springer.

Glăveanu, V. P., & Womersley, G. (2021). Affective mobilities: Migration, emotion and (im)possibility. *Mobilities, 16*(1), 1–15. https://doi.org/10.1080/17450101.2021.1920337

Glăveanu, V. P., Hanchett Hanson, M., Baer, J., et al. (2020), Advancing creativity theory and research: A socio-cultural manifesto. *Journal of Creative Behavior, 54*(3), 741–745. https://doi.org/10.1002/jocb.395

Gilet, A.-L., & Jallais, C. (2012). Mood's influence on semantic memory: Valence or arousal? In S. Masmoudi, D. Y. Dai, & A. Naceur (Eds.), *Attention, Representation, and Human Performance: Integration of Cognition, Emotion, and Motivation* (pp. 77–91). Psychology Press.

Gruber, H. E. (1981). *Darwin on Man: A Psychological Study of Scientific Creativity* (2nd ed.). University of Chicago Press.

Gruber, H. E. (1989). The evolving systems approach to creative work. In D. B. Wallace & H. E. Gruber (Eds.), *Creative People at Work* (pp. 3–24). Oxford University Press.

Gruber, H. E., & Davis, S. N. (1988). Inching our way up Mount Olympus: The evolving systems approach to creative thinking. In R.J. Sternberg (Ed.), *The Nature of Creativity: Contemporary Psychological Perspectives* (pp. 243–270). Cambridge University Press.

Guilford, J. P. (1950). Creativity. *American Psychologist, 5*(9), 444–454. https://doi.org/10.1037/h0063487

Haber, F. (1933). Correspondence. Fritz Haber. Haber Collection, Rep. 13, 911. Archives of the Max Planck Society, Berlin, Germany.

Hanchett Hanson, M. (2005). Irony and conflict: Lessons from Shaw's wartime journey. In D. B. Wallace (Ed.), *Education, Art and Morality: Creative Journeys* (pp. 19–44). Kluwer Academic Press.

Hanchett Hanson, M. (2015). *Worldmaking: Psychology and the Ideology of Creativity.* Palgrave Macmillan.

Hanchett Hanson, M., Amato, A., Durani, A., et al. (2021). *Improvised Educations: Case Studies for Understanding Impact and Implications.* Routledge.

Hanchett Hanson, M., & Glăveanu, V. (2020). The importance of case studies and the evolving systems. In V. Dörfler & M. Stierand (Eds.), *Handbook of Research Methods on Creativity* (pp.195–208). Edward Elgar. https://doi.org/10.4337/9781786439659.00023

Harrison, T. (1992). *Square Rounds*. Faber and Faber.

Huxtable, R. J. (2002). Reflections: Fritz Haber and the ambiguity of ethics. *Proceedings of the Western Pharmacology Society, 45*, 1–3.

Immordino-Yang, M. H., & Damasio, A. (2007). We feel, therefore we learn: The relevance of affective and social neuroscience to education. *Mind, Body, and Education, 1*(1), 3–10. https://doi.org/10.1111/j.1751-228X.2007.00004.x

Ivcevic, Z., & Hoffmann, J. (2019). Emotions and creativity: From process to person and product. In J. C. Kaufman & R.J. Sternberg (Eds.), *The Cambridge Handbook of Creativity* (2nd ed., pp. 273–295). Cambridge University Press.

Jaber, L. Z., & Hammer, D. (2016). Learning to feel like a scientist. *Science Education, 100*(2), 189–220. https://doi.org/10.1002/sce.21202

Kaplan, A., & Garner, J. K. (2017). A complex dynamic systems perspective on identity and its development: The dynamic systems model of role identity. *Developmental Psychology, 53*(11), 2036–2051. http://doi.org/10.1037/dev0000339

Laird, J. D. (1984). The real role of facial response in the experience of emotion: A reply to Tourangeau and Ellsworth, and others. *Journal of Personality and Social Psychology, 47*(4), 909-917. https://doi.org/10.1037/0022-3514.47.4.909

Lane, R. D., & Schwartz, G. E. (1987). Levels of emotional awareness: A cognitive-developmental theory and its application to psychopathology. *The American Journal of Psychiatry, 144*(2), 133–143.

Löfgren, O. (1981). On the anatomy of culture: The problem of home blindness. *Ethnologia Europaea, 12*(1), 26–46. http://doi.org/10.16995/EE.1860

Manchester, K. L. (2002). Man of destiny: The life and work of Fritz Haber. *Endeavour, 26*(2), 64–69. http://doi.org/10.1016/s0160–9327(02)01420-5

McDougall, W. (1908). *An Introduction to Social Psychology*. Methuen.

Oyama, H. T. (2015). Setsuro Tamaru and Fritz Haber: Links between Japan and Germany in science and technology. *The Chemical Record, 15*(2), 535–549. https://doi.org/10.1002/tcr.201402086

Pekrun, R. (2006). The control-value theory of achievement emotions: Assumptions, corollaries, and implications for educational research and practice. *Educational Psychology Review, 18*, 315–341. https://doi.org/10.1007/s10648–006-9029-9

Popper, K. (2012). *The Open Society and Its Enemies*. Routledge.

Sawyer, K. (2012). *Explaining Creativity: The Science of Human Innovation*. Oxford University Press.

Schacter, S., & Singer, J. E. (1962). Cognitive, social, and physiological determinants of emotional state. *Psychological Review, 69*(5), 379–399. https://doi.org/10.1037/h0046234

Schorske, C. E. (1980). *Fin-de-Siècle Vienna: Politics and Culture*. Vintage.

Schwarz, N., & Clore, G. L. (1983). Mood, misattribution, and judgments of well-being: Informative and directive functions of affective states. *Journal of Personality and Social Psychology, 45*(3), 513–523. https://doi.org/10.1037/0022-3514.45.3.513

Shaw, G. B. (1931). Commonsense about the war. In, *What I Really Wrote about the War* (pp. 19–96). Brentano. (Original published in 1914)

Siegel, E. H., Sands, M. K., Van den Noortgate, W., et al. (2018). Emotion fingerprints or emotion populations? A meta-analytic investigation of autonomic features of emotion categories. *Psychological Bulletin*, *144*(4), 343–393. http://doi.org/10.1037/bul0000128

Stake, R. E. (1995). *The Art of Case Study Research*. SAGE Publications.

Stern, F. (1999). *Einstein's German World*. Princeton University Press.

Stern, F. (2012). Fritz Haber: Flawed greatness of person and country. *Angewandte Chemie International Edition*, *51*(1), 50–56. https://doi.org/10.1002/anie.201107900

Stern, R. A. (1963). Fritz Haber: Personal recollections. *The Leo Baeck Institute Yearbook*, *8*(1), 70–102. https://doi.org/10.1093/leobaeck/8.1.70

Titchner, E. B. (1921). *A Textbook of Psychology*. Macmillan.

Tuchman, B. (1962). *The Guns of AUGUST*. Macmillan.

Wallace, D. B., & Gruber, H. E. (Eds.). (1989). *Creative People at Work: Twelve Cognitive Case Studies*. Oxford University Press.

Weiner, B. (1986). *An Attributional Theory of Motivation and Emotion*. Springer.

Weisberg, R. J. (2006). *Creativity: Understanding Innovation in Problem Solving, Science, Invention and the Arts*. John Wiley & Sons.

Witschi, H. (2000a). Fritz Haber: 1868–1934. *Toxicological Sciences*, *55*(1), 1–2. https://doi.org/10.1093/toxsci/55.1.1

Witschi, H. (2000b). Fritz Haber: December 9, 1868 – January 29, 1934. *Toxicology*, *149*(1), 3–15. https://doi.org/10.1016/s0300–483x(00)00227-4

Wundt, W. M. (1897). *Outlines of Psychology*. Engelmann.

Yazan, B. (2015). Three approaches to case study methods in education: Yin, Merriam, and Stake. *The Qualitative Report*, *20*(2), 134–152. https://doi.org/10.46743/2160-3715/2015.2102

Yin, R. K. (2018). *Case Study Research and Applications: Design and Methods*. Sage.

Zaki, J., & Ochsner, K. (2012). The neuroscience of empathy: Progress, pitfalls and promise. *Nature Neuroscience*, *15*(5), 675–680. https://doi.org/10.1038/nn.3085

3 Observational Methods in the Study of Creativity and Emotions

Jen Katz-Buonincontro

Our lives are infused with *emotion*, intrasubjective feelings based on appraisals of events (Lazarus, 1991), and *creativity*, thinking and solving problems in new ways deemed useful, appropriate or authentic (Sundararajan & Averill, 2007). For example, a child might play excitedly while building a sandcastle, a teacher might help students learn math creatively with manipulatives to help break through their math anxiety, or a therapist might help a group of cancer patients cope with pain through musical vocalization. All these examples involve the centrality of *emotion* (excitement; anxiety; pain) in an *activity* (building; learning; managing pain) that uses *creativity* (transforming sand into a castle; using manipulatives to learn math other than rote memorization; managing pain through musical vocalization to complement traditional treatment). In these examples, a *person* (e.g., child; teacher; student; therapist, patient) *interacts with objects* (e.g., sand; manipulative; microphone) and/or *other people* (e.g., children; students; patients). Given this, one could also argue that all these examples allude to other constructs, like "play" (example 1), "teaching" (example 2), and "therapy" (example 3).

How, then, would a researcher make sense of these activities as specific instances of creativity and of emotion, as opposed to examples of other research constructs? And how would these instances be properly captured and treated as data to submit to analysis? Observational methods are one way to capture either creativity or emotion, or both. The nuanced affordances of both structured and naturalistic observation on creativity and emotion are considerable, but they are underutilized compared to other creativity and emotion research methods. To help researchers understand and use observational methods, this chapter will compare the strengths and weaknesses of structured versus naturalistic observation and offer qualitative and quantitative design and implementation strategies for conducting rigorous observations using published examples of creativity and emotion studies.

To begin, I examine the benefits of observation from the perspective of quantitative, qualitative, and mixed methods research traditions. Next, I will offer tips for planning, designing, and implementing observation studies of creativity and emotions: identifying definitions of creativity and emotion that can be adequately operationalized for the purposes of observation, developing observation protocols, clarifying the observer role, and addressing validity, reliability, and principles of generalizability and transferability. Quantitative, qualitative, and mixed methods observation protocols are described. The observation settings used in these studies include theatrical performance (quantitative), creative engagement in science-based instruction (mixed methods), and empathy development in leaders' creative problem solving using improvisational theatre (qualitative). In the conclusion, I discuss the importance of the contribution of observation to the continued growth of the field of creativity studies and emotion research.

What Is Observation, Why Use It, and What Are the Challenges?

What is observation? Observation is the purposeful act of watching people engaged in activities to represent these activities in words (field notes) or numbers (instances). The goal of observation studies is to generate meaningful data that cannot be obtained through other forms of data collection (e.g., surveys, assessments, interviews). In the social sciences, there are two general research approaches to observation: quantitative and qualitative. Isolating, selecting, and rating nonverbal, spatial, and linguistic behaviors constitute *structured quantitative observational methods* (also called laboratory observation). Interrogating the nature of the socially constructed interactions and cultural dimensions of activities is the objective of *naturalistic observations*, either direct, passive, or participant. Once collected and analyzed, observation data can help us understand how and why people act in certain ways in parallel or similar situations and therefore advance psychological, behavioral, and social sciences.

Why use observation? For some researchers, understanding human behavior would be incomplete without observation. Researchers use observation to make sense of how issues like emotion and creativity operate and unfold in people's behaviors and activities. Unlike other data collection methods such as intervention, survey, interview, or focus group, observational methods carve out time and space for focusing attention on people engaged in creative thinking or problem-solving activities. During data collection, we draw on our visual acuity and senses to notice, wonder about, and describe activities, thereby going beyond regular, fleeting observations of daily life to produce substantial data-based inferences. Empirical observational methods harness our own natural perceptive qualities to generate objective inferences about emotion and creativity.

What are the challenges to observing creativity and emotions? Good research examines complex and knotty questions but communicates the data in as straightforward and clear a way as possible. As alluded to in the introduction, it can be tricky to research creativity and emotion for many reasons, particularly using observational methods. Here are four central observation challenges:

Observation Challenge #1: Variability and Unpredictability of Creativity

Many definitions, theories, and models of creativity exist. In addition, creativity has what some scholars refer to as "unpredictable elements" (Shaw, 1994).

Cultural differences in the recognition of creativity also influences the orientation toward authenticity as a key criterion of creativity versus the emphasis on novelty in creativity, for example (Sundararajan & Averill, 2007). This means that we first need to establish consensus about which aspects of creativity to observe. In addition to the question of *what* to observe, researchers might not be able to figure out *when* to observe creativity, or how to set up the right experiment to elicit the type of creative thinking or problem solving we aim to assess and measure. This implies that the design phase of a study is critically important for anticipating what kind of settings lend themselves to observing creativity and emotion or choosing what kind of conditions are optimal for an experiment. Classroom observation studies, for example, might focus on instruction and curriculum aimed to encourage creativity, but there are many issues that affect the suitability of the classroom for observation (discussed later in the chapter).

Observation Challenge #2: Elusiveness of Emotions

Though it is now more acceptable and common to study emotion than in decades past, some researchers remain skeptical about whether it's possible to empirically study emotional qualities of life. Researchers debate the range of emotions and whether certain emotions reflect or pair with specific aspects of life more than other aspects. One such debate is the distinction between emotion states versus moods: Emotions are considered to be more fleeting, whereas moods states are defined as longer periods of time (Ekman, 2022). The stability of emotions remains another issue of debate. Last, cultural views of emotion and its appropriateness as a category to research is still not considered appropriate in many contexts. Many organizations feel that it might be important to promote creativity, for example, and therefore might allow researchers to study creativity as a form of workforce productivity. However, studying emotions in the workplace or in schools, for instance, can appear off-putting at best, disruptive, or even challenging the status quo of workplace culture and normativity.

Observation Challenge #3: Capturing Intrasubjective Reality

Is it possible to capture intrasubjective reality, especially when people go through hundreds of experiences a day that they may or may not experience at the conscious level? This issue is especially important to wrestle with when observing creativity or thinking in novel ways or feeling excited. How can we be certain that participants are aware of their emotions and creative experiences (Rogers, 1964) when acting on their feelings and thoughts (self-report data via questionnaires, surveys, assessments, and interviews)? This becomes a key question for the observer because the researcher might infer acts as creative, somewhat creative, or not creative, but we cannot know if the person or group of people actually think they are acting creatively. Therefore, this issue raises the specter of whether what we observe is the same as what people experience. Some emotion researchers suggest that people are not conscious of what they feel because their attention is directed toward immediate stimuli, they might deny their feelings, or they might experience them in an unconscious mode (Lewis, 2008).

Observation Challenge #4: Interpreting Observed Behavior

Given the issues above that pinpoint the possible differences between intrasubjective feeling and acting aligned with that feeling, how can we be sure that we are correctly interpreting emotion and creativity during an observation? This fourth challenge is a key issue in research. It gets at the heart of consistency in observer training, observation protocol development, and the coding process. Most research processes not only strive for consistency but also aim for consensus when rendering interpretations during the coding and rating processes. Variability is accepted when it enriches the interpretation of qualitative data, but not quantitative data. Therefore, research teams collecting and analyzing observation data at multiple sites or across several participants would need to discuss, clarify, and make clear the aims for interpreting observed behavior.

Taken together, these four observation challenges set the stage for exploring observational methods more deeply. The following section lays out the choices for selecting either structured or naturalistic observation, with key methodological considerations.

Types of Observation

What type of observation is most suitable for a creativity or emotion study, research problem, and research questions? Oftentimes we are constrained by access to specific sites, but when researchers are able to design their studies from the ground up, there are many choices. The purpose of this section is to walk the reader through structured and naturalistic observation.

Observational Science

Observation is the foundation of science and the scientific method. The verb *to observe* derives from the Latin words *ob* "in front of, before" and *servare* "to watch, keep safe." This definition helps us to understand the pivotal role of observation in the scientific process. That is, scientific observers try to position themselves *in front of what they observe*. This implies the need to anticipate, prepare for, and systematically approach how we observe objects, people, and places. As early as the 1500s, references were made to "paying attention to . . . something being observed" (Daston, 2021). From there, observation formed the basis of modern science, used in a variety of fields (Daston, 2021) and subsequently was adapted to the social sciences, namely, sociology, where observation methods, observer roles, and data collection strategies were formalized and further differentiated (see Gold, 1958).

Through observation, the researcher can situate themselves in proximity to other people (participants) and gain experiential knowledge of what a person or group of people are experiencing. Thus, the act of observation affords experiential knowledge unlike the type of observation used in the physical sciences. That is because social scientists observing other people can relate to their experiences and imagine themselves experiencing what another person thinks and feels. Overall, naturalistic observation with observers as participants is used more common in education than in psychology, where observations occur as part of the experiment. Qualitative observation research is used in ethnographic research, action research, and grounded theory studies (McKechnie, 2008). Observation as a social science method is used sparingly in creativity research.

Structured Observation

The benefits of structured and naturalistic observation differ. Observations can be structured in settings like classrooms, or instituted in controlled laboratory settings, face-to-face or online. Structured observation allows for precise quantification of in vivo qualities of creative and emotional expression that cannot be captured via other empirical means such as assessments, tests, surveys, interviews, or focus groups. Structured observation also provides direct documentation of behavioral change over time. Systematic coding of observed creative behavior using the consensual assessment technique, used widely in creativity research following Amabile (1982), is a predominant method. Measurement reactivity is a key consideration in structured observations: this refers to how people react to being observed and whether their behavior is significantly altered by the presence of the observer and the knowledge of being observed (Graziano & Raulin, 2013). Unobtrusive measures capitalize on obtaining behavior as natural as possible in order not to influence or alter that behavior, as opposed to asking people to participate in certain activities or providing people with incentives.

Naturalistic Observation

Naturalistic or field observation, on the other hand, allows for immersion in social situations that in turn allows the researcher to oscillate one's view across individuals, groups, and types of activities. That is, changing attention from one person to another provides a gestalt, or totality, that is not afforded in other research methods. In addition, this kind of observation exposes researchers to new and unplanned phenomena in field settings that can expand researcher awareness or "funds of impressions" (Becker & Geer, 1957). Direct versus passive versus participant observation of creative activities also affords different views. Qualitative observational methods in the study of creativity and emotions capitalize on the extralinguistic, expressive, temporal, and embodied qualities of human behavior. Extralinguistic qualities are important because they emphasize the emotional tone of human behavior, as opposed to just the outcomes. For the study of emotion, this is exceptionally important.

Trying Observation

The prospect of observation is exciting but daunting. At the institutional level, students are often dissuaded from pursuing observation for research due to the time intensive design, complicated human subjects protocol approval process with minors, and confusion about how to triangulate observation with other data sources. Creativity researchers often use experimental research to determine causal effects of certain interventions with multiple conditions, or surveys to capture creative experience, which are entered as independent variables in regression models. Therefore, observation is not frequently used. However, because creativity and emotion exist in many daily activities, it is imperative that the field capitalize on the affordances of observational methods.

Design Strategies for Observing Creativity and Emotion

Though observation may appear daunting at first blush, several design strategies can help address the considerations and challenges of observing. Designing an observation study relies on clear construct selection and operationalization of creativity and emotion anchored in a theoretical framework. Key strategies for working in the field include establishing or changing the observation setting to best suit observation aims. To do this requires great flexibility and willingness to travel to observation sites, craft unobtrusive observation studies on existing activities, or develop careful experimental settings designed specifically to elicit creative responses to certain stimuli. The setting description is critical, especially if naturalistic. Building a theoretical framework and rationale that purposefully integrate emotions and creativity is a key first step.

Building a Theoretical Framework That Integrates Emotions and Creativity

Observation studies of creativity and emotion can be grounded in larger topical areas within early childhood, developmental studies (Vygotsky, Piaget, etc.), cognitive psychology, or management and leadership (e.g., Zhou, 2003), for example. Within each of these fields, the challenge is to zero in on the subfield and forge an appropriate theoretical framework. Theoretical frameworks clearly link definitions and anchor or situate a study within the larger landscape of a theory or several theories. Because few observation studies exist on creativity and emotion, the theoretical framework will likely review both past research on creativity and past research on emotion and propose a way to conjoin these areas for the purposes of observation. For example, the expressive qualities of creative improvisation and emergent creativity (Sawyer, 2012) within a group of people might lend itself well to observation.

The theoretical framework might use one dominant theory or fuse together past streams or strands of research to show what's been studied in the past,

Figure 3.1 *Rationale linked to theoretical framework as the basis for observational study.*

demonstrate how the observation study will address gaps in past research, and help to move the field forward. For example, in one observational study on leaders solving school problems in new ways through improvisational theatre, I could not find a theory or body of research about how leaders use emotions to solve problems effectively, so I selected the nexuses of *emotion management* and *creative problem solving* as the background literature for examining ways to improve leadership skills for addressing workplace conflicts. One of the weaknesses of observation studies on creativity in education is the lack of clarity of theoretical frameworks and the conceptual ambiguity of creativity to include terms like *imagination* (Katz-Buonincontro et al., 2020) (Figure 3.1).

Rationale Building

To build this integrated theoretical framework, a rationale must link these areas in a logical way. I first considered the research problem of why emotional aspects of problem solving are not addressed much in leadership development. Then, I addressed the stereotype of leaders exhibiting masculine traits of acting competent and not needing assistance in the area of further leadership development. For instance, in popular culture, emotional, affectionate, and creative attributes have been ascribed more frequently to women than to men. One possible explanation is that because women are the primary caregivers for babies and are prevalent in the early childhood and elementary-level teaching workforce, they are probably associated more with caretaking and nurturing than men. This fosters an association between emotional labor and women's professional educational experience.

In addition to the gendered associations with emotion, affection, caring, and empathy, the Cartesian legacy of the mind–body split pervades the approach to management and administration of schools. That is, rationality and cognitive processes are considered as separate from emotion and affect, implying that one can control or switch off emotions. As a result, emotions are not viewed or discussed as an essential element of daily activity and behavior in schools and are thus not worthy of empirical investigation.

Construct Selection and Operationalization of Creativity and Emotion

Several strategies can help offset the complexity of planning controlled or field observations of creativity and emotions. In addition to building a theoretical framework that purposefully integrates emotions and creativity and builds a clear rationale, it's important to assess the potential fit of observation for a study or grant project. Though it might seem obvious, not all projects work well with observation because researchers either need to plan creative activities (structured observation) or need access to activities and groups that will engage in creative behavior (naturalistic observation). To unpack the appropriateness of observation for a study, it's important to construct research questions that specifically aim to observe emotions and creative behavior. For example:

- When students participate in project-based learning activities, what emotions emerge during each stage of creative problem solving?
- How does a school leader develop empathy to solve problems through improvisational theatre role-playing?

These research questions can be either quantitative or qualitative depending on the measures, observation setting, and research design. Like other basic research questions, they are relatively simple, indicating some type of relationship between *emotions* and *creativity*. In the case of these questions, the interest is in how emotions and creativity overlap. But other researchers examine aspects like the novelty or appropriateness of a creatively experienced and expressed emotion, for example (see Sundararajan & Averill, 2007).

In addition to research questions focusing on observation, it's critical to explore and select an appropriate definition, theory, or model that lends itself to operationalization in an observation. Creativity definitions that align well with the method of observation stress the *interactional* and/or *temporal* nature of creativity focusing on concepts like improvisation and emergence (Sawyer, 2012). The dynamism of these interactions is quite difficult to capture through retrospective reporting in surveys or retrospective recollection in interviews.

Emotion expressions such as the *embodied* nature of creativity focusing on gestures and body language are relevant to observation. Emotional qualities of observed creative thought, expression, and behavior focus on the *valence* of affective tone (negative, positive, neutral) (Zhou, 2003) and other motivational variables (Hennessy, 2019). *Group interactions* that accentuate emotions in how people present themselves in a recursive manner (Stets & Turner, 2008) emphasizing the exchange of emotional communication would also be appropriate for investigation through observation. Table 3.1 outlines several observable qualities of creativity and emotion that can be considered when selecting what to observe in a study.

Observation Settings

How do researchers find out about potential observation settings? For instance, a researcher might learn about a regular session, institute, or class that could serve as a potential setting that is accessible and conducive to observation. The rationale for sampling the setting is critical. Within the setting, it's also important to select or sample specific creative and emotional activities appropriate for

Table 3.1 *Observable qualities of creativity and emotion*

Construct		Qualities				
	Multimodal	Expressive	Extralinguistic	Temporal	Individual	Group
Creativity	Which modes of creative thinking and behaving including the body are part of the observation? What makes creative behavior different from other types of "normal" behavior?	How do people choose to share their ideas and react to problems when presented to them?	What kind of tone or facial or other body expression affects creative thinking/problem solving?	Are the observed activities time-bound?	Individual creativity: What are the situations and conditions of the observed activities?	Group creativity: How do people interact together to solve problems and work in teams?
Emotion	How does body language and posturing support or impede emotional expression?	How do people convey emotion through expressive mediums like dance, acting, painting, or music?	What kind of tone or facial or other body expression characterizes emotion?	How do emotions change throughout the course of an episode, instance, or specific activity?	Individual emotion expression: How do people characterize, rate, or perceive their emotions in creative activities?	Group emotional exchanges: What emotions facilitate group creativity processes?

and amenable to the act of observation, such as group activities in which the explicit goal is to develop a new service or product (e.g., a specific series of team meetings), projects that require hands-on making (e.g., a robotics project), developmental activities (e.g., imaginary play), or art forms stressing the creative process (e.g., dance and theatre). Example observation settings include role-playing situations, group projects, special events and performances, meetings, and communal art activities.

For one observational study, I chose to videotape and observe people interacting in improvisational theatre (Katz-Buonincontro, 2008). These types of settings can reveal thoughts and feelings that might not be obvious or apparent to the researcher through conventional research methods like interviews. Videotaping observations is key, as they allow the researcher to rewind and observe group interactions multiple times, therefore leading to more valid interpretations. Arts-based research methods focus on studying the psychological aspects of learning in and through the arts. Complex emotional reactions are not uncommon in arts such as improvisational theatre that uses role-playing: First, there are several levels of emotional states in terms of a person's production of the art: for example, an artist might feel frustrated when facing the constraints of lack of time or lack of material resources near the beginning of a project, but feel relieved and elated when the project is completed. As well, another person's response to the artwork can be quite different from what was intended and vary across people. Last, then the social context of multiple reactions to both the original work of art and people's responses to it provides an excellent example of a setting suitable to observation.

Setting Liaison and Site Access

It's easy to get excited about doing an observation without knowing how to get started. That's where *liaisons* can be really helpful. Typically, there's a person who knows the group of people you want to observe or is responsible for running the very activity you'd like to observe. As researchers prepare and plan studies, which typically includes drafting a human subjects protocol, think about identifying a liaison. It's not uncommon to contact someone up front before the research project begins to explore the possibility of observing. This is an important first step in establishing potential access. If you have not yet established access to where you'd like to observe people, then you can suggest working with the site to provide them with something useful (remuneration, data report, instruction, etc.) as well as create a contingency plan. Oftentimes researchers rely too heavily on one site without exploring other backup sites.

Observer Roles

Observer roles vary along a continuum of passivity to participation. As a researcher, you have a choice as to the degree of participation in the observation setting, observation activities, and the relationship to those being observed.

Passive or Nonparticipant

Researchers adopting a passive or nonparticipant role in observation typically do so because of bias issues. Keeping oneself removed from the activity being observed allows researchers to refrain from interrupting or acting in an obtrusive manner that would potentially alter the normal course of observation activities or distract participants. For example, classroom observations using a passive or nonparticipant strategy would rely on someone other than the teacher or person participating in the learning activities. This helps reduce the possibility that observation notes reflect anything but the moment at hand, excluding the history of the participants or the influence of the relationship between teacher and learner, for example. In this case, the observer has several choices: *Complete Separation*: using a one-way mirror to watch activities from another room, or *Separation from Activity*: using the same location as the activities but refraining from interacting with participants. In either case, the observer can use electronic means for taking notes or using a handwritten protocol.

Active or Participant

An active or participant observer role can provide a real sense of what's going on, but also challenging when attempting to faithfully record data. The primary benefit to this strategy is that participant observers get the opportunity to experience almost exactly what other subjects/participants are experiencing. For example, if the observation focuses on improv role-playing, then the observer gets to do role-playing. This also helps equalize the power across the researcher and the participants and establish a collaborative relationship. The drawback is conveying the authenticity of the experience as it happens. Participant observers struggle with how to record notes that are fresh, using electronic means or jotting down notes on sticky notes or paper or using audio or video recordings.

In one participant observation study examining improv (Katz-Buonincontro, 2008), I attended a leadership institute with programming for 8–10 hours per day. I took observation field notes during the sessions and recorded my thoughts as memos postparticipant observation. Because most of the improv role-plays were spontaneous in nature, it was fun but also challenging to anticipate when the improv role-playing would take place. In addition, some of the improv sessions were quite short and did not go deeply into problem solving. Therefore, I had to narrow my focus on which improv role-plays elicited creative problem solving the most. The videotaping required placing microphones on five people. I videotaped one improv role-play session that involved a lot of interaction with leadership students, as opposed to other role-plays that focused on the professional actors and the leadership facilitator. This videotape included two different scenarios, each with a different school leader's problem as its focus.

Switching Roles

Sometimes observers switch between active/participant to nonparticipant roles and vice versa (Creswell, 2003). For example, a quantitative observational study of managers' team creativity might start with the researcher participating in management training to get a sense of the techniques used for teaching creativity. Then, the researcher might return some time afterward to see how managers implement the creativity strategies that they learned with their team members. Whichever role is selected, the most important aspect is to notify the site liaison and participant about the planned switch far ahead of time so that participants are not surprised. In past studies, I've switched from between-participant observer doing improv theatre alongside leadership students to being a passive observer watching others interact and engage in improv. This kind of switching allows for different experiences. With an MFA in visual arts, I was aware of the complexity of the artistic process, which aided my awareness of the nuances of communication during the improv role-playing discussions and acting. This has been described as an empathetic relationship with research participants in the artistic process. Feelings like empathy can enhance the understanding of research participants' experiences as opposed to producing bias, thus enhancing the validity of qualitative findings.

Crafting Protocols for Observing Creativity and Emotion

One of the most important steps in the observation of creativity and emotions is crafting an observation protocol that carefully reflects the construct. In this section, I describe qualitative, quantitative, and mixed methods approaches to observation protocol development.

Quantitative Protocols

Quantitative protocols for examining both creativity and emotion look at these variables individually and then examine their relationships. For example, in one current study, colleagues Vida Manalang and Dr. Lila Chrysikou and I examine the extent to which emotion states and emotion expression relate to creativity outcomes in the area of theatrical performance in non-actors versus actors. To do so, we developed an online experiment and crafted a standard observation protocol for experts to observe and then rate recorded theatre monologues.

Though acting is known as a historical form of art dating back to ancient Greece (384–322 BCE) (Konijn, 1997), acting as a domain of creativity (Sawyer, 2012) has received comparatively less attention than other artistic domains like the visual arts and music and literature (Oatley & Johnson-Laird, 1987). Several theories of art explicitly pinpoint emotion, for example, "satisfying emotional qualities" as a key element of creativity (Dewey, 1934,

p. 599) and as a source of intrinsic motivation for creative performance (Hennessy et al., 2015). The most prominently studied example of theatre creativity is the phenomenon of improvisational theatre, a form that is noted for its quick, collaborative, and spontaneous nature (Sawyer, 2012). But improv is a less frequently used form of theatre than classical theatre. Few studies examine the role of emotion states and expressivity in the creative process of theatre monologues.

In the study, participants complete self-reported surveys on emotional regulation and creativity using an online survey platform. These surveys include the Beliefs About Creativity Scale (BACS; Hass et al., 2016), Creative Achievement Questionnaire (CAQ; Carson et al., 2003), Positive and Negative Affect Scale (PANAS; Watson et al., 1988), Interpersonal Reactivity Index (IRI; Davis, 1983), Emotional Regulation Questionnaire (ERQ; Gross & John, 2003), and the Neuroticism-Extraversion-Openness Five Factor Inventory (NEO-FFI; Costa & McCrae, 1988). After completing the surveys, the participants complete a theatrical text interpretation exercise. First, participants read a piece of theatrical text and identify which emotions are present in the text. Next, participants record a video of themselves performing the theatrical text and upload their video to the online platform.

Experts in the area of theatre, including faculty who teach theatre at the college level, produce creativity and emotion ratings. We developed an observation protocol for creativity in theatre using the definitions provided by the national theatre standards in education so that raters can produce domain-specific judgments of creativity of the videos (see Table 3.2). This technique has been used by teams of other researchers (Phonemthibsayads et al., 2019). The consensual assessment technique (Amabile, 1982) is being used to assess levels of novelty/originality, emotional expressivity, and overall theatrical performance when observing the videotaped performances.

Qualitative Protocols

While qualitative protocols address similar issues, they are not as concerned with isolating and paring down levels and types of emotion and creativity. Philosophically, creativity and emotion are viewed as integrated, co-occurring, and possibly reinforcing each other. Because this view is more about socially reinforced cognition, it's challenging to parse how emotions emerge during creative problem-solving phases. Therefore, qualitative researchers using this approach first describe what they see in a narrative fashion, and then organize the field notes into a framework to make sense of the behaviors and activities.

The qualitative standard of thick description and verisimilitude, or *truth value*, guide the crafting of observation protocols. For example, Table 3.3 outlines how to develop a qualitative observation protocol pairing creativity and emotions based on the principle of thick description, which is the use of detailed, accurate, and verifiable notes. Anthropologist Clifford Geertz (1973) developed the term *thick description* as a principle of rigor. Geertz defined thick

Table 3.2 *Observation protocol used to rate theatrical creativity, emotional expressivity, and overall performance quality, developed by Katz-Buonincontro, Manalang, and Chrysikou*

	0	1	2	3
Novelty & originality	Performer rarely, exhibits new, unexpected, and/or interesting choices and tactics in their interpretation of the text.	Performer infrequently exhibits new, unexpected, and/or interesting choices and tactics in their interpretation of the text.	Performer frequently exhibits new, unexpected, and/or interesting choices and tactics in their interpretation of the text.	Performer consistently exhibits new, unexpected, and/or interesting choices and tactics in their interpretation of the text.
Emotional expressivity	Performer is rarely emotionally believable.	Performer is infrequently emotionally believable.	Performer is frequently emotionally believable.	Performer is consistently and believably expressing emotions.
	Choices and/or tactics to prompt reaction from implied scene partners are not evident.	Choices and/or tactics prompt some reaction from implied scene partners.	Choices and tactics prompt identifiable reaction from implied scene partners.	Choices and tactics prompt intuitive reactions from implied scene partners.
	Vocal performance is limited and the use of tone, tempo, pitch, and inflection to communicate the character's emotion and subtext is rare.	Vocal performance is inconsistent and the use of tone, tempo, pitch, and inflection to communicate the character's emotion and subtext is sometimes evident.	Vocal performance is usually varied and the use of tone, tempo, pitch, and inflection to communicate character's emotion and subtext is frequent.	Vocal performance is appropriately varied and the use of tone, tempo, pitch, and inflection to communicate character's emotion and subtext is consistent.
Overall performance quality	Concentration and commitment to moment-to-moment choices are limited or absent. Integration of voice, body, and emotion choices rarely create a	Concentration and commitment to moment-to-moment choices are inconsistently sustained. Integration of voice, body, and emotion choices sometimes create	Concentration and commitment to moment-to-moment choices are sustained throughout most of the performance. Integration of voice, body, and	Concentration and commitment to moment-to-moment choices are sustained throughout the performance. Integration of voice, body, and emotions choices

Table 3.2 (*cont.*)

0	1	2	3
believable character/ relationship that tells a story.	a believable character/ relationship that tells a story.	emotion choices frequently create a believable character/ relationship that tells a story.	create a believable character/ relationship that tells a story.
Acting technique, mastery, and talents are rarely showcased.	Acting technique, mastery, and talents are showcased frequently.	Acting technique, mastery, and talents are showcased evidently.	Acting technique, mastery, and talent are showcased consistently and purposefully.

description as accurate, inclusive of both thoughts and emotions, articulating the motivations of individuals, providing verisimilitude or truth-like statements and thick interpretation. The opposite of thick description is thin or surface-like data that do not expose the underlying feelings and motivations associated with people's activities.

Table 3.3 pairs the principle of thick description (Geertz, 1973) with principles of creativity (Sawyer, 2012). Taken together, they form a potentially powerful combination for producing in-depth observations of group creativity. The first area focuses on watching for the emergence of group creativity in the observation site. The second area attempts to pinpoint what emotions pair with the thought expressed in the group interactions. The third area looks for ways that each person chooses to interact with another person or object to either support, enhance, or suppress creative expression. The fourth area focuses on truth-like in vivo statements that are representative of creative thinking or problem solving. In vivo statements are excerpts or clips of speech that channel readers' attention to certain key events or processes in observation. Finally, the fifth area examines the gestalt, or entirety of the group, for evidence of creativity. This means thinking about how the group functions as a whole, across individual actors or agents.

Mixed Methods Protocols

Though it is more common to use either quantitative or qualitative observation protocols to observe creativity and emotions, mixed methods observation approaches are becoming more prevalent. Convergent mixed methods designs allow researchers to draw attention to simultaneously occurring aspects within a data set (Morse, 1991). For example, in one study with colleagues Anderson

Table 3.3 *Qualitative observation protocol checklist pairing the principle of thick description with creativity and emotions principles*

Thick description principle (Geertz, 1973)	Creativity principle (Sawyer, 2012)	Thin to thick rating 1 (thin), 2 (thick)
Area #1 Accurate description	How do we ensure taking notes that are as close as possible to emergent group creativity in the observation site?	Thin ratings describe the group setting, whereas thick ratings would describe the interactions between and among the group members.
Area #2 Thoughts & emotions	What emotions pair with the thoughts expressed?	Thin ratings give a global description of the group near the end of the activity, whereas thick ratings would discuss the transformation and evolution of emotions as they progress or change over time.
Area #3 Assigning motivations of individuals	How are individuals supporting, enhancing, suppressing creativity in the group (e.g., Collaborative Emergence)?	Thin ratings look at individuals in the group, whereas thick ratings look at the summative collaborative emergence of group creativity that shows the difference between individual and team or group creativity.
Area #4 Verisimilitude	What truth-like statements can we provide to represent actual creative thinking or problem solving?	Thin ratings describe the group without quotes, whereas thick ratings give in vivo or actual quotes and even provide clips of people talking or debating back and forth.
Area #5 Thick interpretation	How do we interpret group creativity as accurately as possible?	Thin ratings provide logistical information without including member checking with group members as to creative experience.

and Manalang (Katz-Buonincontro et al., 2020), we examined the qualitative process of creative engagement in theatre-based instruction as well as the salience or prevalence of the intensity and the frequency of the creative engagement indicators. We looked at videos of teachers teaching various scientific topics through the technique of tableaux vivant, a process for demonstrating a concept through body movement.

For the design, we selected what is called the convergence data-transformation variant (Creswell & Plano Clark, 2018, p. 73), meaning that the qualitative data are first collected and analyzed. Next, the qualitative data are quantified. Many mixed methods studies privilege quantitative data, but we decided to make sure all data had equivalent status (Creamer, 2018).

The qualitative transcription, coding, and analysis of the videos occurred first. Qualitative analytical procedures were used to segment the video content into indicators and codes (Strauss, 1987). This is a time-consuming process to carefully make note of multimodality (see Table 3.1), or the full range of verbal and bodily gestures expressed in the videos. We used the codes relating to the four creative engagement indicators: creative resources, autonomy, belonging, and competency. Essentially, coding attempts to pare down a concept to its smallest unit (Lincoln & Guba, 1985). In addition, each code is mutually exclusive (Merriam, 2009). To help ensure consistency in the application or labeling of codes, we then compared the coded transcription passages to each other.

Some would argue that a qualitative analysis is sufficient in observational studies. However, quantitative analysis offers more precision. We used a type of intensity coding (Saldana) to code the videos using a Likert scale (0 = no evidence, 1 = minimal evidence, 2 = moderate evidence, 3 = strong evidence).

As I stated earlier in my qualitative observation studies of improv theatre, multiple viewings of the videos are a critical part of understanding the context of multimodal expression for both qualitative and quantitative coding. In this study, interpersonal interactions, movements, gestures, and facial expressions were coded using the Likert scale. For example, evidence of high engagement including collaboration, discussion, or looking at each other multiple times warranted a rating of "3." We summed the codes within each small group. The last step was averaging these sums and comparing across classes using nonparametric tests of analysis of variance.

Other researchers such as Cheung (2012) use descriptive statistics to summarize the number of episodes or instances of creativity, but using inferential statistics, when appropriate, allows for comparisons of classroom-based data sets. Convergent mixed methods designs typically represent qualitative codes as dichotomous variables indicating the absence (0) or presence (1) of a code (Creswell & Plano Clark, 2018). To build on this method, we analyzed the strength of the presence of the codes using a Likert scale of 0 (absence) to 1 (minimal prevalence [of creative engagement]), 2 (moderate prevalence), or 3 (strong prevalence). Examining the strength of the presence of the codes helps enhance the validity, or accuracy, by indicating the nuances of how creative engagement varied.

Merging the qualitative and quantitative analyses centered on comparing what we called qualitative mechanisms of creativity with the prevalence of creativity (Qualitative Mechanisms of Creative Engagement with Quantitative Prevalence of Creative Engagement). Among the findings, we found that students' individual gestures needed to be reinforced by their team for high levels of creative engagement. In addition to merging analyses, one can triangulate by comparing teachers' stated beliefs versus observed pedagogies (Cheung, 2012) and variations across classroom creative practices (Cheung, 2017). As a result, teaching dilemmas emerge such as teacher-directed versus child-centered teaching (Leung, 2020). Such stated gaps in teaching drive instructional improvements, for example.

Visual Materials and Maps

Visual materials such as video clips (Albar & Southcott, 2021), photographs, pictures, or maps can be used as supporting materials in creativity observations to illustrate obstacles and affordances to creativity. Some examples are performances, drawings, or collages created by people in an activity. Visual images such as photo voice are a self-representational research method used to allow participants the freedom to capture their own visual images of their daily lives, instead of researchers collecting photographs (Weber, 2008). This technique places the power of describing phenomenological aspects of creativity in the hands of the study participants.

Geographical maps can be helpful tools for delimiting the types of communities, spaces, or areas observed. Charts and diagrams can be useful for explicating the physical layout of the observation space, including the seating or placement of objects, layout of a building, or how people purposefully arrange a space to promote creativity in a setting, for example. This might include how spaces are designed to either control or facilitate porous boundaries between people. Architectural choices such as cubicles, glass walls, and whiteboards affect the access to resources for facilitating creative work across groups.

Conclusion

Observational methods in creativity and emotion provide a window into human feeling and behavior like no other research method. Drawing on visual acuity and perception, observers can cast a wide-ranging gaze on lived experience for understanding emotional aspects of creative behavior that cannot be captured through other research methods. Though underutilized in the field of creativity, structured and naturalistic observations offer unique opportunities for social scientists to understand how people use emotion in creative processes by pinpointing key emotional blocks and facilitators and other qualities of emotional expressivity.

Four main challenges to observation are (1) multiple if not competing definitions of creativity, (2) the elusiveness of emotions, (3) the nature of intersubjective reality and experience, and (4) figuring out how to make sound and fair inferences about observations. To offset these challenges, researchers should purposefully integrate theories relevant to the field within which the researcher is attempting to make a contribution. Interactional, emergent, and temporal (like planned or spontaneous improvisational theatre) creative activities lend themselves well to observation. Theoretical frameworks that purposefully integrate emotion and creativity provide a clear and justified structure before designing an experiment or field study. Multimodal, expressive, and extralinguistic properties of emotion can be captured through videotape and audio, which also help for making sound inferences by repeatedly playing back and reviewing the observations. This helps to ensure validity and reliability in the process of coding and analyzing observation data.

Three observation approaches of creativity and emotions were covered in the chapter. Quantitative observation protocols clearly partition aspects of creativity and emotion into specific categories relative to the domain of study. Multiple expert raters blind to the condition or type of participant use the protocols. Qualitative observation protocols, on the other hand, use the principle of thick description to engage in deep inquiry and provide rich narrative descriptions of individual or group creativity, which can be later subjected to coding. Mixed methods observation protocols attempt to draw attention to the prevalence and salience of quantitative indicators of creativity while also highlighting process and conditions of creativity. The scarcity of research in this area implies there are many more options waiting to be discovered and developed.

References

Albar, S. B. & Southcott, J. E. (2021). Problem and project-based learning through an investigation lesson: Significant gains in creative thinking behavior within the Australian foundation (prepatory) classroom, *Thinking Skills & Creativity, 41*, 1–19. https://doi.org/10.3390/educsci12010058

Amabile, T. M. (1982). Social psychology of creativity: A consensual assessment technique. *Journal of Personality and Social Psychology, 43*(5), 997–1013. https://doi.org/10.1037/0022-3514.43.5.997

Becker, H. S. & Geer, B. (1957). Participant observation and interviewing: A comparison. *Human Organization*, 28–32.

Carson, S., Peterson, J. B, & Higgins, D. (2003). Decreased latent inhibition is associated with increased creative achievement in high-functioning individuals. *Journal of Personality and Social Psychology, 85*, 499–506. https://doi.org/10.1037/0022-3514.85.3.499

Cheung, R. H. P. (2012). Teaching for creativity: Examining the beliefs of early childhood teachers and their influence on teaching practices. *Australasian Journal of Early Childhood, 37*(3), 43–51. https://doi.org.ezproxy2.library.drexel.edu/10.1177/183693911203700307

Cheung, R. H. P. (2017). Teacher-directed versus child-centred: the challenge of promoting screativity in Chinese preschool classrooms. *Pedagogy, Culture & Society, 25*(1), 73–86. https://doi.org/10.1080/14681366.2016.1217253

Costa, P. T., Jr., & McCrae, R. R. (1988). From catalog to classification: Murray's needs and the Five-Factor Model. *Journal of Personality and Social Psychology, 55*, 258–265. https://doi.org/10.1037/0022-3514.55.2.258

Creamer, E. G. (2018). *An Introduction to Fully Integrated Mixed Methods Research.* Sage.

Creswell, J. W. (2003). *Research Design: Qualitative, Quantitative, and Mixed Methods Approaches* (2nd ed.). Sage.

Creswell, J. W., & Plano Clark, V. L. (2018). *Designing and Conducting Mixed Methods Research* (3rd ed.). Sage.

Daston, L. (2021). *The History of Scientific Observation*. Max Planck Institute for the History of Science.

Davis, M. H. (1980). A multidimensional approach to individual differences in empathy. *JSAS Catalog of Selected Documents in Psychology, 10*, 85. https://www.uv.es/friasnav/Davis_1980.pdf

Dewey, J. (1934). *Art as Experience*. Capricorn Books.

Ekman, P. (2022). Mood versus emotion: Differences and traits. https://www.paulekman.com/blog/mood-vs-emotion-difference-between-mood-emotion/

Geertz, C. (1973). *The Interpretation of Cultures*. Basic Books.

Gold, R. (1958). Roles in sociological field observation. *Social Forces, 36*, 217–223. https://doi.org/10.2307/2573808

Graziano, A. M., & Raulin, M. L. (2013). *Research Methods: A Process of Inquiry*. Pearson.

Gross, J. J., & John, O. P. (2003). Individual differences in two emotion regulation processes: Implications for affect, relationships, and well-being. *Journal of Personality and Social Psychology, 85*, 348–362.

Hass, R. W., Katz-Buonincontro, J., & Reiter-Palmon, R. (2016). Disentangling creative mindsets from creative self-efficacy and creative identity: Do people hold fixed and growth theories of creativity? *Psychology of Aesthetics, Creativity, and the Arts, 10*(4), 436–446. https://doi.org/10.1037/aca0000081

Hennessy, B. A. (2019). Motivation and creativity. In J. C. Kaufman & R. J. Sternberg, (Eds.) *The Cambridge Handbook of Creativity* (2nd ed., pp. 374–395). Cambridge University Press.

Hennessey, B., Moran, S., Altringer, B., & Amabile, T. M. (2015). Extrinsic and intrinsic motivation. In C. L. Cooper, P. C. Flood, & Y. Freeney (Eds.), *Wiley Encyclopedia of Management.*, vol. 11, *Organizational Behavior* (3rd ed.). Wiley. https://doi.org/10.1002/9781118785317.weom110098

Katz-Buonincontro, J. (2008). Fanning the firs of conflict versus leading with empathy: Understanding the aesthetic learning "tipping point" in improvisational theatre role-playing. *Canadian Review of Art Education: Research and Issues.*

Katz-Buonincontro, J., Anderson, R., & Manalang, V. (2020). Understanding the mechanisms and prevalence of creative engagement in theatre-based instruction. *Methods in Psychology, 2.* https://doi.org/10.1016/j.metip.2019.100013

Konijn, E. (1997). *Acting Emotions*. Amsterdam University Press.

Lazarus, R. S. (1991). *Emotion and Adaptation*. Oxford University Press.

Leung, S. K. Y. (2020). Teachers' belief-and-practice gap in implementing early visual arts curriculum in Hong Kong. *Journal of Curriculum Studies, 52*(6), 857–869. https://doi.org/10.1080/00220272.2020.1795271

Lewis, M. (2008). The emergence of human emotions. In M. Lewis, J. M. Haviland-Jones, & L. F. Barrett (Eds.), *Handbook of Emotions* (pp. 304–319). Guilford Press.

Lincoln, Y. S., & Guba, E. G. (1985). *Naturalistic Inquiry*. Sage.

McKechnie, L. E. F. (2008). Observation. In L. Givens (Ed.), *Handbook of Qualitative Research Methods* (pp. 573–575). Sage.

Merriam, S. B. (2009). *Qualitative Research: A Guide to Design and Implementation*. Wiley.

Morse, J. M. (1991). Approaches to qualitative and quantitative methodological triangulation. *Nursing Research, 40*(2), 120–123.

Oatley, K., & Johnson-Laird, P. N. (1987). Towards a cognitive theory of emotions. *Cognition and Emotion, 1*(1), 29–50. https://doi.org/10.1080/02699938708408362

Phonethibsavads, A., Peppler, K. A., & Bender, S. M. (2019). Utilizing the consensual assessment technique to compare creativity in drama spaces. *Creativity – Theories, Research, Applications, 6*(1), 4–19. https://doi.org/10.1515/ctra-2019-0001

Rogers, C. (1964), Toward a science of the person. In T. W. Wann (Ed.) *Behaviorism and Phenomenology: Contrasting Bases for Modern Psychology* (pp. 109–132). University of Chicago Press.

Sawyer, R. K. (2012). *Explaining Creativity: The Science of Human Innovation* (2nd ed.). Oxford University Press.

Shaw, M. P. (1994). Affective components of scientific creativity. In M. P. Shaw & M. Runco (Eds.), *Creativity and Affect* (pp. 3–43). Ablex Publishing.

Stets, J. E., & Turner, J. H. (2008). The sociology of emotions. In M. Lewis, J. M. Haviland-Jones, & L. F. Barrett, (Eds.), *Handbook of Emotions* (pp. 32–46). Guilford Press.

Strauss, A. L. (1987). *Qualitative Analysis for Social Scientists.* Cambridge University Press.

Sundararajan, L., & Averill, J. R. (2007). Creativity in the everyday: Culture, self, and emotions. In R. Richards (Ed.), *Everyday Creativity and New Views of Human Nature: Psychological, Social, and Spiritual Perspectives* (pp. 195–220). American Psychological Association.

Watson, D., Clark, L. A., & Tellegen, A. (1988). Development and validation of brief measures of positive and negative affect: The PANAS scales. *Journal of Personality and Social Psychology, 54*(6), 1063–1070. https://doi.org/10.1037/0022-3514.54.6.1063

Weber, S. (2008). Visual images in research. In J. G. Knowles & A. L. Cole (Eds.), *Handbook of the Arts in Qualitative Research* (pp. 41–54). Sage.

Zhou, J. (2003). When the presence of creative coworkers is related to creativity: Role of supervisor close monitoring, developmental feedback, and creative personality. *Journal of Applied Psychology, 88*(3), 413-422. https://doi.org/10.1037/0021-9010.88.3.413

4 Assessing Creativity and Affect in Everyday Environments

Experience-Sampling and Daily Diary Methods

Katherine N. Cotter

Many factors contribute to creativity – the qualities creative people tend to possess, the originality of a particular product or work, the processes engaged in the midst of creative activities or when working on a creative product, and the environments and contexts people tend to be creative in (Rhodes, 1961). Likewise, creativity exists in a variety of magnitudes, from the widely recognized creators, such as Leonardo da Vinci and Sylvia Plath, to the people who just shared their first "knock-knock" joke. Everyone is capable of being creative and engaging in creative activities, but there is a wide range of expertise, experiences, and contexts that informs the ways in which people pursue creativity.

This chapter focuses on creativity and affect in everyday environments – the ways in which people are creative, use their imagination, and engage with the arts in their everyday lives and idiosyncratic environments. Here I provide a brief overview of the forms of creativity commonly studied in everyday environments and discuss how researchers have commonly approached the assessment of creativity and affect in everyday environments (i.e., daily diary and experience-sampling methods), including what topics are best suited for these methods, the advantages and disadvantages of these methods, and some guidelines for best practices. I close this chapter with a brief discussion of exemplar studies examining creativity and affect situated in people's everyday environments.

Varieties of Creativity

One perspective on everyday creativity focuses on the nature of creative engagement. A helpful way to conceptualize the nature of creative engagement is the Four C model of creativity (Kaufman & Beghetto, 2009). This framework

The author of this chapter is a member of a National Endowment for the Arts Research Lab, supported in part by an award from the National Endowment for the Arts (Award#: 1862782-38-C-20). The opinions expressed are those of the author and do not necessarily represent the views of the National Endowment for the Arts Office of Research & Analysis or the National Endowment for the Arts. The National Endowment for the Arts does not guarantee the accuracy or completeness of the information included in this material and is not responsible for any consequences of its use. This chapter was also made possible through the support of a grant from Templeton Religion Trust. The opinions expressed in this chapter are those of the author and do not necessarily reflect the views of Templeton Religion Trust.

allows for organization of creative acts, from small personal "a-ha" moments to major innovations, inventions, and works of art. *Big-C* creativity describes the people and accomplishments that define or revolutionize a field – figures such as Albert Einstein and Leonardo da Vinci would be considered Big-C creators. Similarly, *Pro-c* creativity also involves significant achievements in a domain, often by those working professionally in the domain (e.g., Meryl Streep and Lady Gaga), but the work does not rise to the level of Big-C creativity. Big-C and Pro-c levels of creativity require specialized expertise within a domain and accomplishments are widely recognized as being creative.

On the other hand, *little-c* and *mini-c*, which can be collectively referred to as "everyday creativity" (Richards, 2007), represent the creative activities, pursuits, and experiences of the general population. Everyday creativity describes the acts that nonexperts can and do readily engage in. *Little-c* creativity refers to products that are novel and appropriate; however, these products do not need to represent advances to the domain. Little-c creative products represent something novel to the creator, even though they may be similar to other products from the domain at large (Weisberg, 2006). This form of creativity can take many forms, from tweaking a chili recipe or using ultrastrength hairspray to fix your knitting needles, to writing a poem or trying out a new cross stich design. *Mini-c* creativity represents "novel and personally meaningful interpretation of experiences, actions, and events" (Beghetto & Kaufman, 2007, p. 73). This form of creativity, like little-c creativity, emphasizes the novelty of the creator rather than novelty to the field. Mini-c creativity captures the individual insights and imagination inherent in everyday life – as we have new ideas, use different perspectives, or change up our routine, we're showing creativity (Tanggaard, 2015). This conceptualization of everyday creativity suggests that creativity may be more integral to our lives than we may often think.

Creativity and Affect in Everyday Environments

When thinking about creativity within our typical environments assessed using ecological methods, research has most often focused on everyday creativity (i.e., little-c and mini-c) but an increasing number of studies have examined Pro-c creativity. Ecological methods emphasize capturing creativity as it is occurring in the everyday environments in which it occurs. The environment is a central component to the ecological approach to creativity – our environments shape when or how creativity emerges (Glăveanu, 2010; Tanggaard, 2015) and may be specifically chosen or designed to aid in creative pursuits (Allport, 1958). Understanding where creativity happens is essential to understanding the creative process and what role affect plays in this process.

What Is Ecological Assessment?

There are many methodological approaches that can inform our knowledge of the ecology of creativity. We may seek to observe little-c and mini-c as they happen in the classroom (Beghetto & Kaufman, 2017), query acting instructors about the creative development of their students (Stutesman et al., 2022), or interview screenplay writers about factors that influence the creative process at different stages of screenplay writing (Bourgeois-Bougrine et al., 2014). Although researchers have used a range of techniques to study creativity in everyday life (see Richards, 2007), ecological momentary assessment (EMA) techniques have been frequently and fruitfully applied (Cotter & Silvia, 2019).

EMA techniques have three central principles: natural environments, real-time (or near-time) data collection, and intensive repeated assessment over time (Silvia & Cotter, 2021). One of the largest motivators of EMA approaches is to better understand the range of environments people enter in their everyday lives and to examine how people navigate these environments. With EMA techniques, assessments are occurring in people's idiosyncratic environments, meaning that each participant will be entering unique environments that they would typically enter in their lives. When we conduct research in the lab, participants are asked to complete questionnaires and tasks in an environment dissimilar to the other, more familiar environments they will enter that day (Reis, 2012). These unfamiliar and often artificial contexts undoubtably influence people's ability to be creative and their emotional state and do not resemble the environments in which they prefer to engage in creative practices. EMA helps to address this limitation.

A second quality of EMA techniques is the focus on real-time or near-time data collection, meaning that we are measuring a phenomenon as it is happening or close to when it is happening (Schwarz, 2012). In measuring experiences close to when they happen, we can reduce recall biases and are also able to capture fleeting or subtle experiences that people may have difficulty retrospectively reporting on (Schooler, 2002), such as what song is playing in our mind (Cotter & Silvia, 2017), or factors that fluctuate frequently, such as our emotional state (Miner et al., 2005). When these experiences are interrupted with an EMA prompt, people can relatively easily take a moment to reflect on and label their experiences.

Finally, a hallmark of EMA techniques is its repeated assessment schedule. Many research designs use repeated assessments, such as pre–post designs or years-long longitudinal studies, but EMA studies do this on a more intensive and shorter schedule (Bolger & Laurenceau, 2013). People may be sent dozens of surveys across a few weeks or months to understand the heterogeneity of experiences or how a certain experience fluctuates within a person across time. By collecting multiple responses over the course of days or weeks, we can study change over short time courses and generate a rich data set that provides a large sample of a person's thoughts and experiences. In the study of creativity, researchers have tended to use either *daily diaries* or *experience-sampling*, here referred to collectively as *daily life methods* (Silvia & Cotter, 2021).

Daily Diaries. Daily diary approaches are one of the most common forms of EMA (Gunthert & Wenze, 2012). In this design, participants complete one survey per day and reflect on how they felt overall that day, what activities they engaged in, and other factors of interest. In most cases, people will complete the survey in the evening or right before bed (e.g., Benedek et al., 2017; Karwowski et al., 2017), but sometimes the diaries might be completed at the end of a workday if the interest is in creativity in the workplace (e.g., Bormann, 2020; Petrou et al., 2019) or at a different time relevant to the topic of interest (e.g., at the end of the school day to understand creativity by teachers in the classroom). Generally, the questions in daily diaries focus on factors that will be salient and remembered at the end of the day – such as whether you did something creative (e.g., Karwowski et al., 2017) or worked on a particular project (e.g., Benedek et al., 2017) that day. Because people are completing a survey only once per day, daily diary studies will typically last for weeks or months (Silvia & Cotter, 2021).

Experience-Sampling Methods. Experience-sampling approaches, on the other hand, repeatedly samples people's thoughts, feelings, and environments throughout a day. This approach will signal people multiple times per day for several days and ask them to report what they were doing when they were signalled, how they feel at that moment, and the qualities of their environment, such as whether it is familiar or if they're with other people. In many cases, these studies will ask about fleeting qualities or experiences that may be poorly recalled at a later time, such as whether someone was imagining music in their mind (Cotter et al., 2019b) or if they were mind-wandering (Seli et al., 2018). A staple of experience-sampling studies is the inclusion of items related to people's emotional states – given the frequent fluctuation of emotional states experienced over the course of a day (e.g., Miner et al., 2005), experience-sampling methods are particularly useful for understanding how emotion is associated with a variety of constructs. Because people are completing many surveys per day, the surveys tend to be shorter than daily diaries, and experience-sampling studies tend to last for a couple weeks or less rather than for months (Silvia & Cotter, 2021).

Why Use Daily Life Methods?

There are many reasons why daily life techniques have been increasingly used by creativity researchers. First, daily life designs allow us to capture creativity as it is occurring. Many survey methods require people to reflect on their past behaviors, such as in activity list measures (e.g., Biographical Inventory of Creative Behaviors, Batey, 2007) in which people check off which activities they have engaged in, or to pool and summarize past experiences to report on their typical attitudes, feelings, or processes. When we're asked to retrospect on experiences that change and fluctuate, there are likely some aspects, such as shifts in emotion, that are not recalled as accurately (Reis, 2012; Schwarz, 2012), and research indicates that daily life and retrospective reports diverge for a variety of constructs (e.g., activities in daily life, Sonnenberg et al., 2012; musical imagery, Cotter & Silvia, 2017; quality of life, Maes et al., 2015). These divergences may be more pronounced for infrequent activities or activities occurring on variable schedules, such as time spent engaging in leisure activities

(Sonnenberg et al., 2012). It's likely that similar differences exist for retrospective and daily life reports of creative activities.

Second, not all experiences are created equal – when we use retrospective measures we cannot capture the ways in which instances of the same experience, such as imagining music, vary. Retrospective reports ask us to pool our heterogeneous experiences to provide a single response; the repeated assessment of daily life methods allows us to capture this within-person variability (Cotter et al., 2019a; Schwarz, 2012; Silvia et al., 2017). With this repeated assessment, we are also able to understand which qualities tend to be more stable across multiple instances and which factors tend to be more variable.

Finally, daily life designs allow us to capture the environments in which creativity is occurring. The cornerstone of ecological approaches to creativity is studying it when and where it is happening. Lab studies have many virtues, but they cannot tell us about environmental influences on creative processes (Hennessey, 2015). Bringing people into the lab to ask about their creativity in everyday life will miss certain aspects of the creative process, such as how quiet or loud their environment tends to be (Silvia et al., under review) or how often they're around others when being creative (Karwowski et al., 2017).

One virtue of daily life methods is the ability to track changes over time or how a single project evolves. For example, Benedek et al. (2017) examined participants in an international art competition as they created their film or video submission to the competition. For two weeks, participants completed daily diaries about their progress – their progress toward a finished submission, their personal experience working on the submission, their feelings about their work on the project, and behaviors related to their work on the project. Progress toward a completed submission was predicted by enjoying the work, low levels of anxiety related to the work, and deliberately engaging with the details of the project. The quality of the finished submission was associated with past artistic achievement and lower levels of agreeableness (Benedek et al., 2017). This type of study, in which there is a clearly identifiable creative project, is an excellent application of daily life methods to better understand how a creative project unfolds, changes, and finishes.

How Should I Design a Daily Life Project?

Although there are many pieces that go into designing any study, a daily life study often has more moving parts than a typical lab study. Here I provide some factors to consider when thinking about launching a daily life study to study creativity and emotion. In general, these methods are best suited to study everyday (i.e., little-c or mini-c) creativity in a variety of samples or Pro-c creativity, which has commonly been studied in the workplace, in well-defined samples (e.g., musicians, scientists). The recommendations and guidelines listed below have been drawn from Cotter and Silvia (2019) and Silvia and Cotter (2021).

Choosing a Topic. Daily life methods are increasingly being used to study creativity and affect, but not all research topics and questions are suited for study with daily life methods. Because one of the motivating factors of daily life research is examining how things change or fluctuate over time, it's important to think about whether the topic you're interested in will vary across the study period. If people are primarily giving the same answers, there won't be much variability within person and a daily life approach doesn't make much sense. To help make this determination, consider who will be in your sample and the likely base rate for the experience of interest is for that sample. For instance, if you're interested in examining how emotional experiences change during different stages of the composition of a song, a sample of undergraduate psychology students will very rarely say they're composing music when asked. A sample of graduate students studying music, however, are much more likely to say they're working on a composition at different points of the study. Alternatively, experiences with a high base rate, such as if a sample of music students listened to music that day, will also provide data with little within-person variability. In the study of creativity and emotion, making sure that the creativity-related constructs are likely to vary is the most important; people's emotions will naturally vary across the study period.

Choosing a Design. Once an appropriate topic and research question are identified, the next decisions are about the fundamental design elements. First, which design – daily diary or experience-sampling – makes the most sense? Likely when identifying your topic, you are leaning toward one design over the other, but one way to make this decision is to consider whether the main creativity variables are something you expect to regularly fluctuate within a single day (e.g., whether they think their current activity is creative) or between days (e.g., whether they worked on a specific creative project). For within-day fluctuations, experience-sampling will work best, and for between-day fluctuations, daily diaries will work best.

After the overall design is selected, there are some other design parameters that will need to be specified. If using daily diaries, people will complete one survey per day, but when does access to the survey start and end each day? You will also need to decide how long the survey will be. Generally, diaries around 15 minutes long will provide rich data about the day without being too burdensome for participants.

If using experience-sampling, people are completing multiple surveys per day, so it's important to balance how long each survey is with how many surveys are sent each day. If survey take a minute to complete, frequent surveys are OK; if the survey takes 5 minutes, only a few surveys each day is appropriate. It's a delicate balance to find the right survey length and number of surveys per day. One way to test this is to be your own participant for a few days – if you're annoyed by how much time you're spending on the surveys, shortening the surveys or reducing the number sent per day is a good idea.

For experience-sampling studies, you'll also want to decide on the timing of the surveys sent each day. There are three main survey signalling schemes: event-contingent, fixed-interval, and random-interval. In event-contingent signalling, the survey is always available to participants, and they complete a survey whenever the focal event occurs – some days they may complete no surveys and other days they may complete many. This scheme works best when the focal event is easily identifiable and memorable. In fixed-interval signalling, people are sent surveys at the same time each day. These surveys are predictable for participants, but it's possible that they will change their behavior in anticipation of a survey (e.g., take an early break from their work to be able to complete the survey). And in random-interval signalling, people are sent surveys at different times of the day, and these times will vary from day to day and between participants. Usually the surveys will also be constrained not to occur right after each other (e.g., making each survey at least 30 minutes apart).

Developing Items. After the design elements have been outlined comes crafting the survey itself. Because the surveys used in daily life studies are much shorter than the ones used in the lab, each item is going to do some heavy lifting. Generally, preestablished measures that you may use in the lab aren't appropriate for daily life. To put together a survey, a good place to start is to identify what constructs you hope to capture and see if other daily work has studied those constructs. It's very common for surveys to be published alongside daily life studies, so using preexisting items that have worked well in past daily life research can be a great starting point.

For the items unique to your study, generate a pool of potential items, some of which may be adaptations from traditional lab scales, and discuss whether each makes sense in a daily life context. A lot of this has to do with how items are framed – in the lab, we may ask, "How often do you do something creative?" but this won't work in daily life. A better item would be, "Are you doing something creative right now?" or "Did you do something creative today?" Likewise, "I usually feel happy" doesn't make sense in daily life but "Right now I feel happy" will be a good item.

Collecting Data. Collecting daily life data can be a complex and time-consuming process. Because data collection is outside the lab, it's important to set clear expectations with participants and to provide clear instructions about what participants can expect. Make sure to tell participants how many surveys they will receive per day, when they can expect to receive the surveys, and what happens if they miss a survey. People are unlikely to contact you once they've started the study, so provide many opportunities for them to ask questions. One way to solicit questions is to allow participants to complete a practice survey that presents all questions they'll see outside the lab to make sure they understand the questions, know how to use any technology employed in the study, and to verify devices are working properly.

Another major component of daily life data collection is making sure people keep participating across the study. Monitoring response rates and compliance with study instructions and scheduling email check-ins with participants can go a long way. One way to encourage compliance and to frame the check-ins can be through the use of escalating incentives as people complete more surveys. For example, for every 10 surveys completed, people receive additional pay-ment or people who complete a certain percentage of surveys are entered into a raffle for additional compensation. These techniques may nudge participants to complete more surveys, especially as the study periods drags on.

Data Analysis. Data analysis for daily life studies is complex, and this chapter won't cover all of the intricacies. The big aspect to keep in mind for data analysis is that all observations are nested, meaning that individual survey responses are grouped by the participant who provided the response. This means that individual responses are not independent and traditional regression techniques cannot be used. Multilevel models (i.e., hierarchical linear models) will be your friend (and potentially also your enemy). These modelling techniques account for variation within a participant and between different participants. Even though your study was designed to send 20 surveys to participants doesn't mean each participant will provide you with 20 responses – multilevel models are able to handle this type of missingness and differences in observations. There are many great resources that outline using these types of models with daily life data (e.g., Bolger & Laurenceau, 2013; Nezlek, 2012).

Although the exact models used will vary from study to study, when reporting on daily life data there are a few pieces that are necessary to include. Intraclass correlations provide us with an index of how much variability in a construct can be attributed to between-person factors. These statistics range from 0 to 1, with higher numbers indicating a greater proportion of the variability can be attributed to between-person differences. There is also a strong tradition of including ample information on descriptive statistics and correlations. Because data are nested, there will be descriptive information and correlations available for both the within-person and between-person levels. Even if description was not a motivating factor for the study, it is expected to include a short summary of this information within the text in addition to providing full information within tables.

What Have We Learned about Creativity and Affect Using Daily Life Methods?

Researchers have used a variety of methodologies to study mini-c and little-c forms of everyday creativity. Here, I focus on work that has used daily life methods to study creativity in everyday environments. Daily life methods are being increasingly used in creativity research, and a small but mighty collection of studies has emerged.

Creative Engagement in Daily Life

A major tradition in research of creativity in daily life is to describe the nature of these experiences – How often are people doing something creative? Who tends to engage in creative activities more frequently? What sorts of activities do people view as creative?

People are quite often creative in their everyday lives. In experience-sampling studies in which people are asked whether they are doing something creative at that moment report being engaged in creativity around 20% of the time in undergraduate student samples (Ivcevic et al., under review; Silvia et al., 2014) and around 33% of the time in middle-aged adult samples (Karwowski et al., 2017). In daily diary studies in which people are asked whether they engaged in creative activity at some point during the day, they report being "a little" creative on most days (Conner & Silvia, 2015) or having creative days during 43% of the study days (Karwowski et al., 2017). But it's important to note the wide range in frequency of creative engagement – in some cases, people report never engaging in creative activities during the study period, and in other cases, people indicate almost constant engagement in creative pursuits. The widespread occurrence of self-reported engagement in creative activities in everyday life makes it a fruitful topic for study with daily life methods.

But who tends to be more creative in their everyday lives? A common individual difference studied in creativity is personality. Openness to experience is the personality trait most consistently linked with creativity (Oleynick et al., 2017) – this relationship also holds for creativity in everyday life. People higher in openness to experience self-report more frequent creative engagement in daily life (Conner & Silvia, 2015; Karwowski et al., 2017; Silvia et al., 2014), and there is some evidence that other personality traits (higher conscientiousness, higher agreeableness, and lower neuroticism) are also associated with everyday creativity (Karwowski et al., 2017).

When people say they're being creative, what do they mean? Many studies ask whether someone was engaged in a creative activity at that moment (e.g., Karwowski et al., 2017, Study 1; Silvia et al., 2014) or at some point that day (e.g., Conner & Silvia, 2015), but this doesn't tell us what types of activities people view as creative. Karwowski et al. (2017, Study 2) provided participants with a list of possible creative activities that participants could endorse engaging in, but this approach does not encompass the full range of creative activities. Silvia et al. (under review) used a different approach and asked people to report what they were doing at the time of the signal and whether they considered that activity creative. These open-ended activity reports were then coded and categorized, enabling a more complete picture of the variety of creative activities people engage in. Over the course of a week, people, on average, engaged in three different types of creative activities and tended to engage in these different activities in relatively equal proportions. This may suggest that people tend more toward deeply engaging in a few domains rather than broadly engaging in a range of creative activities.

Everyday Creativity and Well-Being

In addition to understanding how often people are creative in everyday life, who tends to pursue creativity more frequently, or the variety of creative activities people engage in, research has also explored how creative engagement impacts us. A frequently examined area has been how creative engagement is related to different indices of well-being. Because creativity is often regarded as a positive trait and the field of positive psychology views creativity and creative engagement as an important piece of flourishing in life (e.g., Seligman & Csikszentmihalyi, 2000), it is unsurprising that many researchers seek to understand how creativity may impact our well-being.

A common emphasis in this thread of research is on subjective states associated with well-being, including emotion and feelings of flourishing (i.e., feeling a sense of purpose, engagement, and social connection). Several studies have examined the associations between creative engagement and emotional states. In general, positive emotions, particularly higher activation positive emotions, are associated with greater creative engagement (Conner & Silvia, 2015; Silvia et al., 2014), and negative emotions are associated with lower levels of creativity (Conner & Silvia, 2015). Taking this line of inquiry a step further, Conner et al. (2018) examined whether creativity on one day influenced well-being (i.e., positive and negative affect, flourishing) on the subsequent day. They found that creativity on day one predicted greater positive affect and higher flourishing on day two, even after controlling for creative engagement on day two.

Other research has examined flow states and creativity. Flow is a state during which people completely absorbed and engaged in what they are doing (Csikszentmihalyi, 1990), a construct that has often been associated with creativity (e.g., Csikszentmihalyi, 1996; Perry, 1999). In fact, many of the early studies using experience-sampling methods were pioneered during the study of flow states (e.g., Csikszentmihalyi, 1975; Csikszentmihalyi & Figurski, 1982; Csikszentmihalyi & LeFevre, 1989). Fullagar and Kelloway (2009) examined flow in architecture students when working on projects in their studio. In their experience-sampling design, they found that flow more closely resembles a state construct rather than a trait construct, as most of the variability in flow was at the within-person level. Further, projects that encouraged high levels of autonomy and use of a range of skill sets were associated with more frequent flow states as were active, positive emotions.

Researchers have also examined how the three components of self-determination theory (Ryan & Deci, 2000) – autonomy, competence, and environmental mastery – contribute to our understanding of creativity and well-being. Koehler and Neubauer (2020) examined how engagement in a particular creative activity – music making – relates to need satisfaction and positive and negative affect. Using a 10-day daily diary design, a sample of musicians was asked whether they actively made music that day and the degree to which their needs for autonomy, competence, and environmental mastery were met that day. People also indicated how often they felt a range of positive and negative affective states during that day. Koehler and Neubauer (2020) found that people actively made music on approximately half of the study days and also found that engaging in making music was associated with greater positive affect and need satisfaction and lower negative affect and need dissatisfaction. But the relationship between music making and positive affect was mediated by the three self-determination theory components – engaging in music making aided in fulfilling the needs for autonomy, competence, and environmental mastery, which in turn bolstered positive affect (Koehler & Neubauer, 2020). There was not a significant mediation effect for negative affect.

Given the consistent association between well-being and creativity, it is unsurprising researchers have also started using daily life methods to implement creativity interventions. In one such creativity intervention, Zielinksa et al. (2022) developed and assessed a *wise intervention* (Harackiewicz & Priniski, 2018) to increase people's everyday creative engagement. Wise interventions contend that people's beliefs and values are vital in shaping their behaviors, reactions, and outcomes – a wise intervention thus seeks to change behaviors, reactions, and outcomes through targeting and changing how people think or feel (Walton & Wilson, 2018). In this creativity wise intervention (Zielinksa et al., in press), participants were given eight prompts to follow (e.g., reflecting on why creativity is important, watching advertisements and noting how they are surprising and original). These prompts were designed to bring greater awareness to creativity and to cultivate the belief that they can be creative. To assess this intervention, Zielinska et al. (in press) had participants complete 16 daily diaries – 8 days when they received the intervention prompts and 8 days when they did not receive any prompts. On the days when people received prompts, they reported feeling more creative and engaging in more creative activities that day than on days they did not receive these prompts. Further, on days during which participants felt higher levels of positive active emotions, they also reported greater levels of creativity, whereas experiencing passive negative emotions was associated with reduced reports of creativity. This work suggests that daily life methods can be effective in implementing creativity interventions and that relatively simple prompts can increase creative engagement.

Creativity and Affect in the Workplace

In addition to describing and examining people's everyday creativity across many contexts and environments, daily life methods can also help us to understand creativity within a particular context through assessing how context-specific environmental and individual factors relate to creativity. A frequently studied example of this is creativity in the workplace. An early workplace study using daily life methods (Miner et al., 2005) used experience-sampling to examine the interrelations between mood and positive and negative workplace events, finding robust links between workplace events and mood. Given the consistent relationship between engaging in creativity and experiencing positive moods in everyday life, it's unsurprising that researchers have sought to examine creativity and emotion in the workplace.

Multiple studies have examined the role of emotions in creativity at work. A classic study by Amabile and colleagues (2005) examined the dynamics of the creativity and emotion relationship in the workplace using a multiweek daily diary design. In their approach, the researchers used daily self-report ratings of affect, researcher-coded measures of daily creative thought based on participant narratives, and monthly peer reports of participant creativity. Amabile et al. (2005) found that positive affect and creativity were positively related but that negative affect and creativity were not related. Further, they found evidence that the nature of this relationship is complex – in some instances positive affect predates creativity; in others, it is a consequence. Using a different approach, Chi et al. (2021) used a daily diary design to examine the time course of the relation between emotion and changes in creativity during work. Testing the lagged effects of the prior day's emotional experiences on the subsequent day's creativity (controlling for the prior day's creativity and current day's emotional experiences), they found that experiencing both positive (e.g., excited, inspired) and negative (e.g., angry, anxious) activated emotions the day before were associated with greater reported creativity on the current day.

Although most research has emphasized the distinction between positive and negative affect, researchers are increasingly examining how the level of activation of emotional experiences, in addition to valence, relates to creativity at work. Using experience-sampling methods, To et al. (2012) examined both valence and activation of emotions and their association with creative engagement when working on a long-term project requiring creativity. Higher activation positive and negative emotions were reported when engaging in creativity, with a stronger relation with high-activation positive emotion. Conversely, low activation emotions – positive or negative – were related to less engagement in creativity. In a sample of entrepreneurs, Williamson et al. (2019) also found that high-activation emotions were important for work-related creativity. In a 10-day experience-sampling study, entrepreneurs reported on their innovative behavior, mood, and sleep quality each day. Unsurprisingly, better sleep quality was associated with more innovative behavior; however, this relationship was mediated by emotional experiences – high-activation positive emotions mediated the relationship between sleep quality and innovative behavior, but negative emotions did not mediate this relationship. This suggests that the relationship between sleep quality and innovative behavior can largely be attributed to people who have better sleep quality subsequently experiencing more positive emotion (Williamson et al., 2019). But these relationships between emotion and creativity can differ due to individual characteristics. For instance, one experience-sampling study noted that for younger employees it was more common for creativity to co-occur with negative affect, whereas older employees typically engaged in creativity when experiencing positive emotions (Volmer et al., 2018).

Conclusion

In this chapter, I discussed two methods of assessing creativity and emotion in everyday environments – daily diaries and experience-sampling methods. Given the increased prevalence of daily life methods, I provided an overview of a few lines of inquiry that have become popular within everyday creativity research – describing the nature of creative engagement in everyday life, everyday creativity and well-being, and creativity in the workplace. The use of these methods will likely continue to increase, and I believe that fully exploring the environmental and contextual factors influencing creativity will bring the field new and exciting insights on how, when, and why people tap into their creativity and pursue creative hobbies and how these creative pursuits impact and interact with our emotional experiences.

References

Allport, G. W. (1958). What units shall we employ? In G. Lindzey (Ed.), *Assessment of Human Motives* (pp. 239–260). Holt, Rinehart, & Winston.

Amabile, T. M., Barsade, S. G., Mueller, J. S., & Shaw, B. M. (2005). Affect and creativity at work. *Administrative Science Quarterly, 50*, 367–403. http://dx.doi.org/10.2189/asqu.2005.50.3.367

Batey, M. (2007). *A Psychometric Investigation of Everyday Creativity.* Unpublished doctoral dissertation. University College, London.

Beghetto, R. A., & Kaufman, J. C. (2007). Toward a broader conception of creativity: A case for "mini-c" creativity. *Psychology of Aesthetics, Creativity, and the Arts, 1*, 13–79. http://dx.doi.org/10.1037/1931-3896.1.2.73

Beghetto, R. A., & Kaufman, J. C. (Eds). (2017). *Nurturing Creativity in the Classroom* (2nd ed.) Cambridge University Press.

Benedek, M., Jauk, E., Kerschenbaur, K., Anderwald, R., & Grond, L. (2017). Creating art: An experience sampling study in the domain of moving image art. *Psychology of Aesthetics, Creativity, and the Arts, 11*(3), 325–334. http://dx.doi.org/10.1037/aca0000102

Bolger, N., & Laurenceau, J. P. (2013). *Intensive Longitudinal Methods: An Introduction to Diary and Experience Sampling Research.* Guilford Press.

Bormann, K. C. (2020). Turning daily time pressure into a creative day: The interactionist roles of employee neuroticism and time pressure dispersion. *Applied Psychology, 69*(3), 589–615. http://dx.doi.org/10.1111/apps.12183

Bourgeois-Bougrine, S., Glaveanu, V., Botella, M., et al. (2014). The creativity maze: Exploring creativity in screenplay writing. *Psychology of Aesthetics, Creativity, and the Arts, 8*(4), 384–399. http://dx.doi.org/10.1037/a0037839

Chi, N. W., Liao, H. H., & Chien, W. L. (2021). Having a creative day: A daily diary study of the interplay between daily activating moods and physical work environment on daily creativity. *Journal of Creative Behavior, 55*(3), 752–768. https://doi.org/10.1002/jocb.488

Conner, T. S., DeYoung, C. G., & Silvia, P. J. (2018). Everyday creative activity as a path to flourishing. *Journal of Positive Psychology, 13*(2), 181–189. http://dx.doi.org/10.1080/17439760.2016.1257049

Conner, T. S., & Silvia, P. J. (2015). Creative days: A daily diary study of emotion, personality, and everyday creativity. *Psychology of Aesthetics, Creativity, and the Arts, 9*(4), 463–470. http://dx.doi.org/10.1037/aca0000022

Cotter, K. N., Christensen, A. P., & Silvia, P. J. (2019a). Creativity's role in everyday life. In J. C. Kaufman & R. J. Sternberg (Eds.), *Cambridge Handbook of Creativity* (2nd ed., pp. 640–652). Cambridge University Press.

Cotter, K. N., Christensen, A. P., & Silvia, P. J. (2019b). Understanding inner music: A dimensional approach to musical imagery. *Psychology Aesthetics, Creativity, and the Arts, 13*(4), 489–503. http://dx.doi.org/10.1037/aca0000195

Cotter, K. N., & Silvia, P. J. (2017). Measuring mental music: Comparing retrospective and experience sampling methods for assessing musical imagery. *Psychology of Aesthetics, Creativity, and the Arts, 11*(3), 335–343. http://dx.doi.org/10.1037/aca0000124

Cotter, K. N., & Silvia, P. J. (2019). Ecological assessment in research on aesthetics, creativity, and the arts: Basic concepts, common questions, and gentle warnings. *Psychology of Aesthetics, Creativity, and the Arts, 13*(2), 211–217. http://dx.doi.org/10.1037/aca0000218

Csikszentmihalyi, M. (1975). *Beyond Boredom and Anxiety: The Experience of Play in Work and Games.* Jossey-Bass.

Csikszentmihalyi, M. (1990). *Flow: The Psychology of Optimal Experience.* Harper & Row.

Csikszentmihalyi, M. (1996). *Creativity: Flow and the Psychology of Discovery and Invention.* HarperCollins.

Csikszentmihalyi, M., & Figurski, T. J. (1982). Self-awareness and aversive experience in everyday life. *Journal of Personality, 50,* 15–28. http://dx.doi.org/10.1111/j.1467-6494.1982.tb00742.x

Csikszentmihalyi, M., & LeFevre, J. (1989). Optimal experience in work and leisure. *Journal of Personality and Social Psychology, 56,* 815–822. http://dx.doi.org/10.1037/0022-3514.56.5.815

Fullagar, C. J., & Kelloway, E. K. (2009). "Flow" at work: An experience sampling approach. *Journal of Occupational and Organizational Psychology, 82,* 595–615. http://dx.doi.org/10.1348/096317908X357903

Glăveanu, V. P. (2010). Paradigms in the study of creativity: Introducing the perspective of cultural psychology. *New Ideas in Psychology, 28,* 79–93. http://dx.doi.org/10.1016/j.newideapsych.2009.07.007

Gunthert, K. C., & Wenze, S. J. (2012). Daily diary methods. In M. R. Mehl & T. S. Conner (Eds.), *Handbook of Research Methods for Study Daily Life* (pp. 144–159). Guilford Press.

Harackiewicz, J. M., & Priniski, S. J. (2018). Improving student outcomes in higher education: The science of targeted intervention. *Annual Review of Psychology, 69,* 409–435. http://dx.doi.org/10.1146/annurev-psych-122216-011725

Hennessey, B. A. (2015). Creative behavior, motivation, environment and culture: The building of a systems model. *Journal of Creative Behavior, 49*(3), 194–210. http://dx.doi.org/10.1002/jocb.97

Ivcevic, Z., Cotter, K. N., Ranjan, A., Nusbaum, E. C., & Silvia, P. J. (under review). Self-regulation for creativity: Assessing the process between having ideas and doing something with them.

Karwowski, M., Lebuda, I., Szumski, S., & Firkowska-Mankiewicz, A. (2017). From moment-to-moment to day-to-day: Experience sampling and diary investigations in adults' everyday creativity. *Psychology of Aesthetics, Creativity, and the Arts, 11*(3), 309–324. http://dx.doi.org/10.1037/aca0000127

Kaufman, J. C., & Beghetto, R. A. (2009). Beyond big and little: The Four C model of creativity. *Review of General Psychology, 13,* 1–12. http://dx.doi.org/10.1037/a0013688

Koehler, F., & Neubauer, A. B. (2020). From music making to affective well-being in everyday life: The mediating role of need satisfaction. *Psychology of Aesthetics, Creativity, and the Arts, 14*(4), 493–505. http://dx.doi.org/10.1037/aca0000261

Maes, I. H. L., Delespaul, P. A. E. G., Peters, M. L., et al. (2015). Measuring health-related quality of life by experiences: The experience sampling method. *Value in Health, 18*(1), 44–51. http://dx.doi.org/10.1016/j.jval.2014.10.003

Miner, A. G., Glomb, T. M., & Hulin, C. (2005). Experience sampling mood and its correlates at work. *Journal of Occupational and Organizational Psychology, 78*, 171–193. http://dx.doi.org/10.1348/096317905X40105

Nezlek, J. B. (2012). *Multilevel Modeling for Social and Personality Psychology*. Sage.

Oleynick, V. C., DeYoung, C. G., Hyde, E., et al. (2017). Openness/intellect: The core of the creative personality. In G. J. Feist, R. Reiter-Palmon, & J. C. Kaufman (Eds.), *The Cambridge Handbook of Creativity and Personality Research* (pp. 9–27). Cambridge University Press. https://doi.org/10.1017/9781316228036.002

Perry, S. K. (1999). *Writing in Flow: Keys to Enhanced Creativity*. Writer's Digest Books.

Petrou, P., Bakker, A. B., & Bezemer, K. (2019). Creativity under task conflict: The role of proactively increasing job resources. *Journal of Occupational and Organizational Psychology, 92*, 305–329. http://dx.doi.org/10.1111/joop.12250

Reis, H. T. (2012). Why researchers should think "real world": A conceptual rationale. In M. R. Mehl & T. S. Conner (Eds.), *Handbook of Research Methods for Studying Daily Life* (pp. 3–21). Guilford Press.

Rhodes, M. (1961). An analysis of creativity. *The Phi Delta Kappan, 42*(7), 305–310.

Richards, R. (2007). Everyday creativity: Our hidden potential. In R. Richards (Ed.), *Everyday Creativity and New Views of Human Nature* (pp. 25–53). APA.

Ryan, R. M., & Deci, E. L. (2000). Self-determination theory and the facilitation of intrinsic motivation, social development, and well-being. *American Psychologist, 55*, 68–78. http://dx.doi.org/10.1037/0003-066X.55.1.68

Schooler, J. W. (2002). Re-representing consciousness: Dissociations between experience and meta-consciousness. *Trends in Cognitive Sciences, 6*(8), 339–344. https://doi.org/10.1016/S1364-6613(02)01949-6

Schwarz, N. (2012). Why researchers should think "real-time": A cognitive rationale. In M. R. Mehl & T. S. Conner (Eds.), *Handbook of Research Methods for Studying Daily Life* (pp. 22–42). Guilford Press.

Seli, P., Kane, M. J., Smallwood, J., et al. (2018). Mind-wandering as a natural kind: A family-resemblances view. *Trends in Cognitive Sciences, 22*(6), 479–490. http://dx.doi.org/10.1016/j.tics.2018.03.010

Seligman, M. E. P., & Csikszentmihalyi, M. (2000). Positive psychology: An introduction. *American Psychologist, 55*(1), 5–14. http://dx.doi.org/10.1037/0003-066X.55.1.5

Silvia, P. J., Beaty, R. E., Nusbaum, E. C., et al. (2014). Everyday creativity in daily life: An experience-sampling study of "little c" creativity. *Psychology of Aesthetics, Creativity, and the Arts, 8*(3), 183–188. http://dx.doi.org/10.1037/a0035722

Silvia, P. J., & Cotter, K. N. (2021). *Measuring Daily life: A Guide Experience Sampling and Daily Diary Methods*. American Psychological Association.

Silvia, P. J., Cotter, K. N., & Christensen, A. P. (2017). The creative self in context: Experience sampling and the ecology of everyday creativity. In M. Karwowski & J. C. Kaufman (Eds.), *Creativity and the Self* (pp. 275–288). Elsevier.

Silvia, P. J., Cotter, K. N., & Christensen, A. P. (under review). In search of creative omnivores: An experience sampling study of the variety and diversity of everyday creative activities.

Sonnenberg, B., Riediger, M., Wrzus, C., & Wagner, G. G. (2012). Measuring time use in surveys – Concordance of survey and experience sampling methods. *Social Science Research, 41*, 1037–1052.

Stutesman, M. G., Havens, J., & Goldstein, T. R. (2022). Developing creativity and other 21st century skills through theatre classes. *Translational Issues in Psychological Science, 8*(1), 24–46. https://doi.org/10.1037/tps0000288.

Tanggaard, L. (2015). The creative pathways of everyday life. *Journal of Creative Behavior, 43*(3), 181–193. http://dx.doi.org/10.1002/jocb.95

To, M. L., Fisher, C. D., Ashkanasy, N. M., & Rowe, P. A. (2012). Within-person relationships between mood and creativity. *Journal of Applied Psychology, 97* (3), 599–612. http://dx.doi.org/10.1037/a0026097

Volmer, J., Richter, S., & Syrek, C. J. (2018). Creative at each age: Age-related differences in drivers of workplace creativity from an experience sampling study. *Journal of Creative Behavior, 53*(4), 531–545. http://dx.doi.org/10.1002/jocb.233

Walton, G. M., & Wilson, T. D. (2018). Wise interventions: Psychological remedies for social and personal problems. *Psychological Review, 125*, 617–655. http://dx.doi.org/10.1037/rev0000115

Weisberg, R. W. (2006). *Creativity: Understanding Innovation in Problem Solving, Science, Invention, and the Arts.* Wiley.

Williamson, A. J., Battisti, M., Leatherbee, M., & Gish, J. J. (2019). Rest, zest, and my innovative best: Sleep and mood as drivers of entrepreneurs' innovative behavior. *Entrepreneurship Theory and Practice., 43*(3), 582–610. http://dx.doi.org/10.1177/1042258718798630

Zielinska, A., Lebuda, I., & Karwowski, M. (2022). Simple yet wise? Students' creative engagement benefits from a daily intervention. *Translational Issues in Psychological Science, 8*(1), 6–23. https://doi.org/10.1037/tps0000289.

PART II

The Development of Creativity

5 Affective States and Creativity

Hector Madrid, Malcolm Patterson, and Miguel Ibaceta

Creativity is a complex endeavor. It involves identifying problems and envisioning new opportunities in the environment, leading to the generation of novel ideas. As such, creativity conveys problem identification together with the generation, selection, promotion, and implementation of ideas (Amabile, 1988). These psychological processes demand a series of cognitive and behavioral processes profoundly influenced by affective states (Madrid & Patterson, 2018).

This chapter reviews the literature in this area, identifying theoretical approaches to understanding why and how affect is related to creativity, and discussing the body of empirical research derived from these theories.

Affective States

Affect is an umbrella construct referring to the experience of discrete emotions and moods. Emotions are psychological reactions toward specific stimuli or events, which are episodic and intense, limited to seconds or minutes, interrupting and influencing our immediate thinking and behavior (Ekman, 1992; Frijda, 1994). For example, when confronting a hazardous event, we tend to experience fear and, as a result, our thinking narrows around the source of risk, and the behavioral tendency is to remove ourselves from the situation. In turn, moods are long-lasting psychological states with an unclear origin, experienced over hours, days, and even weeks (Watson, 2000). Moods are mild states that are often not intense enough to influence our conscious thinking and behavior; however, they have substantial effects on cognitive and behavioral processes outside our awareness (Forgas, 1995; Schwarz & Clore, 2003). For example, moods are associated with perception, attention, memory, information processing, and motivation over time. Research on creativity has mostly adopted the notion of moods to study whether and how affect is associated with creative performance, such that, in this chapter, we use the concepts of affect, affective states, and moods interchangeably.

The most used framework to structurally describe affective states is the Positive and Negative Model of Affect (Watson et al., 1999). According to this, positive and negative affect are independent dimensions in which the diverse possible affective experiences in the psychological realm are classified. Thus, positive affect, for example, refers to states of enthusiasm, excitement, and inspiration, while negative affect involves states such as nervousness, distress, and guilt. Because positive and negative affect are independent dimensions, they can coexist, such that, for example, an individual may feel enthusiastic and nervous over the same time frame. This is the case when we receive a promotion at work to a position with greater responsibilities, which leads us to feel enthusiastic due to the new challenges involved and, at the same time, nervous because of the additional expectations for our job.

Furthermore, affective activation is another parameter that defines affective states. This refers to the energy expenditure involved in the affective experience, such that there are positive feelings high in activation (e.g., enthusiasm) and low in activation (e.g., comfort). The same applies to negative affect, in which case high-activated negative affect is expressed in, for example, nervousness, whereas low-activated negative affect in despondency. The interplay between affective valence and activation offers a finer-grained understanding of the affective experience and how it influences other constructs of interest, such as creativity.

Research on affect and creativity has primarily drawn on the definitions and conceptualizations of affect described above. Consequently, we present theoretical and empirical developments in this area organized by the experience of positive and negative affect, acknowledging also differences in affective activation, based on our scoping literature review summarized in Table 5.1. This method offers an overview of the available research from which we mapped existing studies and identified opportunities for future research.

Positive Affect and Creativity

The more robust finding from studies on the creativity literature indicates that the production of novel and useful ideas is a function of positive affect (Baas et al., 2008; Davis, 2009). This means that when feeling enthusiastic, joyful, and inspired, individuals are prone to think in an unconventional way and generate novel ideas to solve problems or take advantage of new opportunities to reach desired goals. This effect was initially observed by Isen and her associates, who in a series of experiments manipulated the affective states of participants and then measured their creativity using activities demanding divergent thinking (Isen et al., 1987). The rationale for this effect is that positive feelings enhance cognitive flexibility leading to atypical associations among knowledge to solve problems.

The insight that positive affective states are associated with cognitive flexibility was one of the roots of the development of Broaden-and-Build Theory (Fredrickson, 2001). This conceptual framework theorizes that positive affect expands psychological resources and participates in constructing new ones, which have diverse implications for an individual's well-being and performance. Thus, positive feelings are associated with psychological resources expressed in flexible, open, and divergent thinking (Clore et al., 2001; Kaufmann, 2003;

Table 5.1 *Studies conducted in the field of affect and creativity*

Reference	Affective valence	Type of effect	Theoretical background	Research methods	Main results
Isen et al. (1987)	Positive	Main	Not specified	Experimental	• Positive affect is positively related to creativity.
George & Zhou (2002)	Positive Negative	Moderation	Affect-as-Information Mood-as-Input	Survey cross-sectional	• Positive affect is negatively related to creativity when perceived recognition and rewards for creative performance, and clarity of feelings are high rather than low. • Negative affect is positively related to creativity when perceived recognition for creative performance and rewards, and clarity of feelings are high rather than low.
Madjar et al. (2002)	Positive	Mediation	Not specified	Survey cross-sectional	• Positive affect mediates the positive relationship between support for creativity and creativity.
Amabile et al. (2005)	Positive	Main	Broaden-and-Build theory	Survey daily diary study	• Positive affect is positively related to creativity.
Filipowicz (2006)	Positive	Mediation	Affect-as-Information	Experimental	• Surprise mediates the positive relationship between positive affect and creativity.
Fong (2006)	Ambivalence	Main	Broaden-and-Build theory Affect-as-Information	Experimental	• Affective ambivalence is positively related to creativity.
George & Zhou (2007)	Positive Negative	Moderation	Dual-Ttuning Model	Survey cross-sectional	• Negative affect is positively related to creativity when both positive affect and supervisor developmental feedback are high. • Negative affect is positively related to creativity when both positive affect and supervisor interactional justice are high.

89

Table 5.1 (*cont.*)

Reference	Affective valence	Type of effect	Theoretical background	Research methods	Main results
					• Negative affect is positively related to creativity when both positive affect and trust in supervisor are high.
De Dreu et al. (2008)	Positive Negative	Main	Dual Pathway Model	Experimental	• High-activated positive affect is positively related to creativity. • High-activated negative affect is positively related to creativity.
Baas et al. (2008)	Positive Negative	Main	Dual Pathway Model	Meta-analysis	• High-activated positive affect is positively related to creativity. • High-activated negative affect is negatively related to creativity.
Davis (2009)	Positive	Main	Mood-as-Input	Meta-analysis	• Positive affect, compared to negative affect, is positively related to creativity.
Rasulzada & Dackert (2009)	Positive	Main	Not specified	Survey cross-sectional	• Positive affect is positively related to creativity.
Zaman (2010)	Positive	Main	Not specified	Survey cross-sectional	• Positive affect is positively related to perceived expected creativity.
To et al. (2011)	Positive Negative	Main Moderation	Dual Pathway Model	Survey experience sampling	• High-activated positive affect is related to creative process engagement. • High-activated negative affect is related to creative process engagement. • Learning goal orientation moderates the relationship between high-activated positive affect and creative process engagement, such that this relationship occurs when learning goal orientation is high but not when it is low.
Binnewies & Woernlein (2011)	Positive	Main	Activation theory	Survey daily diary study	• Positive affect is positively related to creativity.

Study	Affect	Relationship	Theory	Method	Findings
Chermahini & Hommel (2012)	Positive Negative	Reverse	Reciprocity hypothesis	Experimental	• Divergent thinking is positively related to positive affect. • Convergent thinking is negatively related to positive affect.
Rego et al. (2012a)	Positive	Mediation	Broaden-and-Build theory	Survey cross-sectional	• Positive affect mediates the positive relationship between optimism and creativity.
Rego et al. (2012b)	Positive	Mediation	Broaden-and-Build theory	Survey cross-sectional	• Positive affect mediates the positive relationship between self-efficacy and creativity. • Positive affect mediates the positive relationship between hope and creativity.
Bledow et al. (2013)	Positive Negative	Moderation	Affective-Shift Model	Survey diary study (study 1) Experimental (study 2)	• Negative affect at time 1 moderates the positive relationship between positive affect and creativity at time 2, such that this relationship is stronger when negative affect at time 1 is high rather than low.
Madrid et al. (2014)	Positive	Main Mediation Moderation	Broaden-and-Build theory	Survey weekly diary study	• High-activated positive affect is positively related to creativity. • High-activated positive affect mediates the positive relationship between support for innovation and creativity. • Openness to experience moderates the positive relationship between positive affect and creativity, such that this relationship is stronger when openness is high rather than low.
Gasper and Middlewood (2014)	Positive Negative	Main	Broaden-and-Build theory	Experimental	• Approach-oriented affect is positively related to creativity.

91

Table 5.1 (*cont.*)

Reference	Affective valence	Type of effect	Theoretical background	Research methods	Main results
Parke et al. (2014)	Positive	Moderation	Affective information processing theory	Survey cross-sectional	• Emotional intelligence moderates the positive relationship between positive affect and creativity, such that this relationship occurs when emotion facilitation is high rather than low.
Silvia et al. (2014)	Positive	Main	Not specified	Survey experience sampling	• Positive affect is positively related to everyday creativity.
Conner & Silvia (2015)	Positive	Main Moderation	Not specified	Survey daily diary study	• High-activated positive affect is positively related to creativity. • Openness to experience moderates the positive relationship between high-activated positive affect and creativity, such that this relationship is stronger when openness is high rather than low.
To et al. (2015)	Negative	Moderation	Dual Pathway Model	Survey experience sampling	• Psychological empowerment moderates the positive relationship between high-activated negative affect and creative process engagement, such that this relationship is stronger when empowerment is high rather than low. • Psychological empowerment and learning goal orientation moderate the positive relationship between high-activated negative affect and creative process engagement, such that this relationship is stronger when both empowerment and learning goal orientation are high rather than low.

Study	Direction	Effect type	Theoretical model	Method	Findings
Tang et al. (2016)	Positive	Moderation	Affect infusion Model	Survey cross-sectional	• Problem clarity moderates the positive relationship between positive affect and creativity, such that this relationship is stronger when problem clarity is low rather than high.
Tavares (2016)	Positive	Reverse	Not specified	Survey two-waves	• Creativity is positively related to positive affect over time through the experience of meaningfulness.
Intasao & Hao (2018)	Positive	Mediation	Dual Pathway Model	Survey cross-sectional	• Positive affect mediates the positive relationship between self-efficacy and creativity.
Madrid & Patterson (2019)	Positive	Mediation	Affect-as-Information	Survey cross-sectional	• Positive affect mediates the positive relationship between time control and creativity. • Problem-solving demands moderate the mediation between time control, positive affect and creativity, such that the positive relationship between time control and positive affect is stronger when problem-solving demands are high rather low.
Mastria et al. (2019)	Positive Negative	Main	Hedonic-tone hypothesis	Experimental	• Positive affect is positively related to evaluation of creative ideas.
Han et al. (2019)	Positive Negative	Main	Not specified	Survey experience sampling Day reconstruction method	• High-activated positive affect is positively related to creativity. • Low-activated negative affect is negatively related to creativity.

Table 5.1 (*cont.*)

Reference	Affective valence	Type of effect	Theoretical background	Research methods	Main results
Zhang et al. (2020)	Positive Negative	Moderation	Broaden-and-Build theory	Survey experience sampling	• Trait creativity moderates the positive relationship between positive affect and creativity, such that this relationship is stronger when trait creativity is high rather than low. • Trait creativity moderates the positive relationship between negative affect and creativity, such that this relationship occurs when trait creativity is high but not low.
Hwang & Choi (2020)	Positive Negative	Main	Affect-as-Information	Survey cross-sectional	• High-activated positive affect is positively related to creativity. • High-activated negative affect is positively related to creativity. • Low-activated positive affect is negatively related to creativity. • Low-activated negative affect is not related to creativity.
J. Du et al. (2021)	Positive	Mediation	Broaden-and-Build theory	Survey cross-sectional	• Psychological safety mediates the positive relationship between positive affect and creativity.
Park et al. (2021)	Positive	Mediation	Broaden-and-Build theory	Survey experience sampling	• Positive affect mediates the positive relationship between affect stability and creativity.
Y. Du et al. (2021)	Positive Negative	Mediation	Dual Pathway Model	Survey cross-sectional	• Rumination and reflection mediate the positive relationship between negative affect and creativity.
Xu et al. (2021)	Negative	Main Mediation	Dual Pathway Model	Survey cross-sectional	• Depression is positively related to creativity.

94

Schwarz, 2002; Schwarz & Clore, 2003), all of which are the rudiments of, for example, creative performance. Based on these assumptions, Amabile et al. (2005) conducted a comprehensive and large-scale longitudinal study in an organizational setting, showing that positive affect is positively correlated to creative thinking and the production of novel solutions to problems in the workplace. More specifically, positive affect and creativity were positively linked at the same point in time and even over days. This study was the beginning of a body of research replicating the same results, using diverse methodologies based on cross-sectional, longitudinal, and diary study designs (Binnewies & Woernlein, 2011; Gasper & Middlewood, 2014; Intasao & Hao, 2018; Mastria et al., 2019; Rasulzada & Dackert, 2009; Rego et al., 2012a, 2012b; Silvia et al., 2014; Zaman et al., 2010).

Expanding the previous stream of research, the studies of De Dreu and colleagues propose that not all forms of positive affect are associated with creative outcomes. They developed the Dual Pathway Model to affect and creativity, proposing that understanding the influence of affect on creative performance should account for both valence and activation (De Dreu et al., 2008). Thus, there are positive states high in energy expenditure but also states low in activation. Based on this conceptualization, various studies, including a meta-analysis, have shown that creativity is a function of high-activated positive affect, such as enthusiasm, but not low-activated positive feelings, like tranquility (Baas et al., 2008; Conner & Silvia, 2015; De Dreu et al., 2008; Han et al., 2019; Hwang & Choi, 2020; Madrid et al., 2014; Madrid & Patterson, 2019; To et al., 2011). The association between affective activation and working memory functioning and psychological engagement (Bledow et al., 2013; Nijstad et al., 2010) help to explain these results. Working memory manages content about memories, information processing, and planning courses of action, while psychological engagement entails the level of involvement and persistence individuals bring to performing tasks. Low levels of activation could imply neglection of information in working memory, and reduced cognitive engagement, whereas moderate to high levels of affective energy are associated with optimal psychological performance in terms of, for example, alertness, information processing, and motivation.

While studies support a reliable link between positive affect and creativity, whether the strength of this relationship varies according to the action of other third variables is also a consideration. In this regard, diverse individual differences have been hypothesized as playing a moderation role. From the personality perspective, Zhang et al. (2020) adopted the notion of trait creativity to describe the stable dispositions of individuals to think divergently. They argued that the effect of positive affect on state creativity, namely, the contingent production of novel and valuable ideas, would be dependent on this trait because of the synergetic process between flexible information processing associated with both personality and positive affective experience. This was supported in their empirical study. Along the same lines, but adopting the Big-5 model of personality, openness to experience is another potential trait relevant to the relationship between positive feelings and novel idea generation, promotion, and implementation. The moderating function of openness to experience is likely because this is a trait with experiential meaning, such that it intensifies the experience and consequences of emotions and moods for cognition and behavior (McCrae & Costa, 1997). In addition, openness to experience enhances individuals' motivation and disposition to be involved in novel activities, a core rudiment of creative performance. All these processes along with cognitive flexibility and psychological willingness associated with positive affect can lead to greater creativity. The moderating effect of openness to experience has received support from two studies examining associations between high-activated positive affect and weekly work-related creativity (Madrid et al., 2014) and daily context-free creativity (Conner & Silvia, 2015).

Another set of individual differences relevant to the relationship between positive affect and creativity focus on goal orientation and emotional intelligence. In general, goal orientation is an individual difference comprising self-regulation in mastering the achievement of desired goals (DeShon & Gillespie, 2005). Specifically, learning goal orientation involves the willingness to engage in challenging tasks and beliefs that effort leads to appropriate performance and obstacles can be surpassed (VandeWalle, 1997). To et al. (2011) supported this argument, finding that the positive effect of high-activated positive feelings on creative performance occurs when individuals are characterized by high, but not low, learning goal orientation. They argue that this effect is due to positive affect facilitating cognitive flexibility and involvement, which are boosted by the motivational dispositions embedded in this form of goal regulation. In turn, considering the moderating role of emotional intelligence, the evidence suggests that positive affect is primarily related to creativity when abilities of emotion facilitation characterize individuals (Parke et al., 2014). The latter denotes differences in how effective the use of affect is for motivational and performance purposes. Thus, individuals skilled in emotion facilitation use positive affect to focus on solving problems and developing a novel solution, together with effectively managing their attention and effort. In contrast, the ineffective use of positive affect may lead to distraction and, therefore, poorer performance.

Some progress has been made in understanding how the performance context influences the relationship between affect and creativity. For example, Tang et al. (2016) expected that the clarity of the problem confronted by individuals should influence the strength of the positive affect–creativity relationship. They observed that this relationship is stronger when the problem managed is uncertain and weakly specified (low clarity), which is explained by affective infusion processes (Forgas, 1995). The latter entails that the influence (infusion) of affect on cognition and behavior varies according to the level of task complexity. Thus, when the task is complex in terms of, for example, uncertainty, such as the case of a problem demanding creativity, affect should have stronger effects on performance, such as creative outcomes. In a more complex configuration, contextual conditions and individual differences can interact to explain conditions under which positive affect is positively related to creativity. In this regard, George and Zhou (2002) postulated that the affective influence on creativity, in terms of direction and magnitude, is context-dependent and determined by the level of individuals' awareness about their feelings. Thus, there could be the case in which, for example, positive affect would be negatively, rather than positively, related to creative performance under certain circumstances. Accordingly, in an organizational context, they showed that the latter effect could occur in a context of recognition and rewards for creativity, interacting with individual differences in clarity of feelings (Salovey et al., 1995). This situation is likely because high recognition and rewards signal to individuals that expected performance has been reached; thus, no additional creative effort is needed (cf., Carver & Scheier, 1990; Martin & Stoner, 1996); yet this informational process only influences creative behavior if individuals are aware of their positive feelings.

Scholars have also proposed that positive affect should be a psychological mechanism that mediates the indirect effects of individual differences and contextual conditions on creative performance. In the first case, Rego and colleagues, using a series of survey studies with retail workers, observed that positive affect mediates the association of optimism, hope, and self-efficacy with creativity (Rego et al., 2012a, 2012b). According to their theorization, positive affect is a signal of psychological reward stemming from, for example, the perception of successful goal pursuit. Because optimism, hope, and self-efficacy are personal resources to deal effectively with challenges (Luthans et al., 2007), their expression should be linked to a self-perception of individual effectiveness, which is conducive to positive affect. This was supported by two samples of retail employees rated in terms of their creative behavior by their supervisors at work. Consistent with these results, Intasao and Hao (2018) also supported that positive affect mediates the positive relationship between self-efficacy and creativity, measured with a divergent thinking task in a sample of secondary school students.

Using an innovative approach, the construct of trait affective spins/emotional stability has recently been examined as individual factors impacting creative performance through positive affect. Affective spin is the degree of variation in the experience of diverse affective states over time (positive, negative, or both), such that when it is high, there is greater variation in the feelings experienced (Beal & Ghandour, 2011). The opposite applies to low affective spin, which has been labeled as affective stability. Higher levels of affective spins are associated with greater efforts of emotion regulation to reduce affective variation; however, this process is taxing and depletes cognitive and emotional resources, affecting individual performance and well-being (Richels et al., 2020; Uy et al., 2017). In contrast, high emotional stability (low spins) helps conserve and effectively manage the available psychological resources. Based on these premises, Park and colleagues (2021) proposed and found support for positive affect as a mechanism connecting affect stability and creativity, such that greater stability enhanced positive affect, and therefore increased creativity in the workplace. This effect is theoretically plausible if positive affect is considered a psychological resource that is conserved when emotional stability is high but depleted when affective spins dominate.

Positive affect has also been conceptualized as a mediator between contextual conditions and individuals' creativity, supported by theories of affect-as-information. According to the latter, affect conveys information about the contextual conditions under which individuals are performing, influencing cognition and behavior (Martin & Stoner, 1996; Schwarz & Clore, 1983). Thus, affect signals about the presence of contextual opportunities to satisfy psychological needs or alternatively threats to well-being. Consistent with this rationale, Madjar et al. (2002) showed that positive affect is a mediator between an organizational context that supports, fosters, and motivates creativity and employees' creative performance at work. Madrid et al. (2014), using an interactionist approach, expanded on the above findings, showing that the mediation between support for innovation, positive affect, and the generation, promotion, and implementation of novel ideas is dependent on individuals' openness to experience. These results rely on the integration of affect-as-information theories and cognitive appraisal theory (Lazarus & Folkman, 1984), arguing that positive affect should be a function of the encounter between both organizational and employee interests in working with novel ideas. As such, the stronger relationship between support for innovation and positive affect occurs for individuals characterized by high openness to experience.

In a further study, Madrid and Patterson (2019) use a similar theoretical rationale to posit that time control and problem-solving demands lead to the implementation of novel ideas through the experience of positive feelings, integrating affect-as-information and self-determination theories. Specifically, they reasoned that when positive feelings are experienced, individuals inferred the presence of contextual conditions satisfying basic psychological needs. In this connection, self-determination theory provides the conceptualization of basic psychological needs participating in the informational process associated with time control and problem-solving demands in terms of the needs of autonomy and mastery (Deci et al., 2017). Time control is about opportunities to manage and make decisions about one's own schedule and pace of time (Wall et al., 1996), which should satisfy the psychological need for autonomy. In turn, problem-solving demand reflects a challenging set of requirements from the job, expressed in working with uncertainty, complex problems, and the need for a wide array of skills and knowledge (Wall et al., 1990). This job demand is typically associated with negative affect (e.g., distress, anxiety, tension); however, positive affect is also a possible outcome of the same contextual condition because it should satisfy the psychological need for mastery. In the study reported by Madrid and Patterson, the interaction effect between time control and problem-solving demands on positive affect theoretically suggests that higher levels positive affect are experienced when individuals feel autonomous and competent because of the perception of a work context associated with individual agency and involving challenge, which in turn is associated with implementation of novel ideas.

In this section we reviewed the extant research examining the relationship between positive affect and creativity. A weight of research, both theoretical and empirical, has been undertaken, showing that positive feelings are potentially a strong precursor of creativity, acting as main, interaction and mediation effects. In the next section, we will present and discuss research on the role of negative affect in creative performance.

Negative Affect and Creativity

Whereas we have robust evidence showing a positive and pervasive relationship between positive affect and creative performance, our knowledge about whether negative affect is associated with the same outcome is less straightforward. It could be expected that negative affect is negatively related to creativity because of the information processing and motivational correlates of displeasing feelings. This type of affect is generally associated with narrowing cognition, expressed in closer attentional focus and convergent thinking (George & Zhou, 2007; Nijstad et al., 2010). All the above should not be helpful for creative thinking and the production of novel ideas. Nevertheless, most empirical studies have shown the absence of a main effect of negative feelings on creativity outcomes (Madrid & Patterson, 2018). Instead, the relationship between these constructs appears complex.

Ambiguous results on the influence of negative feelings on creativity, sometimes null, positive, or negative associations, suggests the possible presence of more intricate psychological processes linking negative affect and creativity. For example, a possible explanation for these mixed results is that other third variables, acting as boundary conditions, might be participating here. George and Zhou (2002) addressed this possibility by examining whether recognition and rewards for creativity, together with clarity of feelings were moderators in the relationship between negative affect and creativity. They drew their theorization from the Mood-as-Input model (Martin & Stoner, 1996), which proposes that the consequences of affective states are not predetermined but depend on, for example, the context in which they are experienced. In general, negative affect involves information signaling unsatisfactory progress toward desired goals, such that the tendency is then to invest more effort and dedication. However, this motivational process occurs if the context provides cues highlighting that the goal is highly valuable and efforts to achieve it are rewarded. In George and Zhou's model, this context is given by perceptions that creative outcomes are desirable and efforts to achieve them are symbolically rewarded by means of recognition of one's competencies and creativity capabilities. Thus, recognition and rewards for creativity is the first moderator for a positive relationship between negative affect and creativity. However, according to George and Zhou's model, a second moderator at the individual level, clarity of feelings, is needed to reinforce this effect. Clarity of feelings involves awareness and understanding about one's own affective experience (Salovey et al., 1995). Only if individuals are clear about their experience of negative affect, then negative feelings could lead to individuals investing effort and persistence in creative performance under a context of recognition and rewards for creativity. George and Zhou's (2002) study provided empirical support consistent with this theorizing. More recently, To et al. (2015) explored a similar rationale arguing that negative affect can result in increased creativity through boosted cognitive effort and persistence but this effect is aided, first, by the individual differences in self-regulation of learning goal orientation. This trait tendency conveys a propensity to experience intrinsic motivation and pursue task mastery when faced with a problem signal (i.e., negative affect) (DeShon & Gillespie, 2005; VandeWalle, 1997). Then, this process should be even more heightened if individuals are empowered; namely, they can take initiative and personal control over the task at hand and the context in which it is performed (Spreitzer, 1995). To and colleagues supported these proposals in their daily diary study conducted over a week.

In a more detailed theoretical work, the dual pathway model to affect and creativity provides an advance in our understanding of the relationship between affect and creativity. As introduced in the previous sections, this model holds that *both* affective valence and activation need to be accounted for in this relationship when considering the main effects of positive and negative feelings (De Dreu et al., 2008; Nijstad et al., 2010). In the case of the direct effect of high-activated negative affect on creativity, this is likely to occur because negative affective valence is associated with narrowing cognition that helps problem identification, such as the case of a closer attentional focus and convergent thinking. In turn, activation provides alertness, motivation, and persistence to develop a novel solution to the problem identified and confronted. De Dreu et al. (2008) supported these proposals in a series of laboratory studies, showing that high-activated negative affect is positively related to various indices of creative performance, as was found in the more recent studies of To et al. (2011) and Hwang and Choi (2020).

George and Zhou (2007) make a step further in their dual-tuning model of affect and creativity. This proposes that understanding creative performance requires accounting for an *interaction* process between positive and negative feelings, and not just considering the main direct effects on creativity outcomes. More specifically, there is a joint function between negative and positive affect in which the first participates in creative problem identification, while the second in creative ideation. Because problem identification involves delineating issues to be addressed, this is aided by negative affect due to its narrowing cognition correlates, manifested in focused attention and convergent thinking (Kaufmann, 2003; Schwarz & Clore, 2003). In turn, novel ideas generated in response to the problem faced are fostered by, as discussed in the previous sections, cognitive flexibility, open attentional focus, and divergent thinking facilitated by positive affect. Notwithstanding, this dual-tuning process is only given in a context of support for creativity, where individuals perceive that there is learning orientation and recognition when showing a willingness to solve problems in an unconventional way. This is the case, for example, when in an organizational context, work supervisors trust, treat fairly and provide developmental feedback to employees. Notably, the joint function of positive and negative affect is possible because, as described at the beginning of the chapter, both are conceptualized as independent dimensions of the affect construct, such that they can coexist over the same period (Watson, 2000).

Another complementary approach is the Affective-Shift Model (Bledow et al., 2013), which also posits that creativity results from both positive and negative affect, but not in the static fashion described in the dual-tuning model. The affective shift model explicitly acknowledges that creative performance is given by a longitudinal and dynamic process started by problem identification and followed by creative ideation. At the beginning of the process, discontinuities and issues emerging in the environment lead to the experience of negative affect, which, due to its informational function, cues individuals to the presence of problems to be solved. The same negative feelings are associated with cognitive engagement, problem-solving orientation, and controlled thinking based on bottom-up information processing to clearly identify and delineate the problem confronted (Baumann & Kuhl, 2002; Gasper, 2003; Spering et al., 2005). Specifically, negative affect narrows attention to threatening elements, leading individuals to examine issues in an analytical, isolated, and sequential way. As a result, the basics for generating novel ideas are built, and possible courses of action to solve the problem start to be incubated. Then, beginning with the stage of novel idea generation, negative affect should steadily decrease and, in parallel, positive affect should increase to provide the broadened cognition needed for creative ideation, such as the case of top-down information processing and divergent thinking (Baumann & Kuhl, 2005; Derryberry & Tucker, 1994). Thus, the affective shift is a longitudinal process of swapping the valence of the affective experience, which as a result modifies the cognitive mindset conducive to the effectiveness of the diverse stages of creativity.

In this section, we reviewed the research on negative affect and creativity. In contrast to positive affect, the relationship between negative feelings and creative performance is less straightforward, involving greater complexity and elaborated psychological processes. Theory and concomitant evidence show that negative affective is dependent on other variables, at the individual and contextual level, to be conducive to creativity; otherwise, the relationship between these constructs becomes null and sometimes negative.

Thus far, we have concentrated on extant research conducted in the affect and creativity literatures. Building on this, in the next section we identify gaps in our understanding and present opportunities for future research in affect and creativity

Future Research

Research on affect and creativity is extensive, with the weight of theoretical and empirical work devoted to understanding the association of the affective experience with creative performance. Nevertheless, as with any field of knowledge, there are a series of opportunities to continue expanding this stream of research, some of which are presented below.

Robustness of the Relationship between Negative Affect and Creativity. There is little doubt that positive affect is a strong driver of creative performance, but the same cannot be said about negative affect. In general, studies have shown an ambiguous relationship between negative feelings and creativity, which is null in most cases. The exception is the studies showing that boundary conditions at the individual and context level could facilitate a positive relationship between high-activated negative feelings and creativity. This positive effect has been observed in studies based on the dual-tuning model, the dual pathway model, and the affective-shift model of affect and creativity, however there are only a handful of emerging studies supporting these models (Bledow et al., 2013; De Dreu et al., 2008; George & Zhou, 2007). As such, much more evidence is still needed to determine the robustness and generalizability of their proposals.

Affective Ambivalence. There are complex affective states that cannot be classified as positive or negative only but mixed in terms of their valence. Thus, in some circumstances, individuals can feel positive and negative at the same time (Larsen et al., 2001). In a seminal study, Fong (2006) postulated that affective ambivalence provides individuals information about the presence of an unusual environment. As a result, this ambivalence facilitates the recognition of unconventional associations between concepts and objects in the given context, leading to the construction of creative outcomes. Affective ambivalence and mixed emotions have become a focus of interest in psychology, but research on these affective experiences and creativity are still scarce. It is important not to confuse the dual-tuning and dual pathway models of affect and creativity as frameworks dealing with affective ambivalence. This is because the latter is a *meta* experience in which positive and negative affect is lived as a whole; instead, dual models understand the effects of positive and negative feelings in an independent or interactive fashion. Since daily life is experienced not only by clearly positive or negative events but also by ambiguous situations, creativity might be somehow influenced by affect emerging from these situations.

Creativity Causing Affect over Time. Almost all the studies in this field of knowledge assume that affect is a cause of creativity but not the other way around. Amabile et al. (2005) were one of the first proposing that creativity could be an affective event itself that engenders affective reactions and states over time. However, in the study conducted with her colleagues, their results were not supportive of this assertion because whereas positive affect and creativity were correlated at the same point in time, creativity did not predict positive affect over the days that the study was conducted. In another study in an organizational context, Tavares argued and supported that creative performance could lead to positive affect over a long-lasting lifespan described by a couple of months, but this effect was indirect through the experience of having a meaningful job (2016). Thus, whether creativity might cause positive feelings remains ambiguous. To the best of our knowledge, the impact of creativity on negative affect has not been studied thus far.

Affect Regulation. Studies about affect and creativity have concentrated on the affective experience itself and its relationship with creative outcomes. Nevertheless, other relevant affective variables and processes have received limited attention, this is especially the case for affect regulation. The latter comprises a series of behavioral strategies to elicit or change one's own affective experience by selecting and modifying the performing environment, cognitively reappraising and deploying attention from affective events, and modulating the feelings that remain from affective situations (Gross, 2015). Conducting research on affect regulation would be informative about, for example, how creativity emerges from affect associated with distressful situations. Another interesting possibility is the application of affect regulation to the affective-shift process proposed by Bledow et al. (2013). According to the latter, the optimal level of creativity occurs when there is a switch between a negative and positive affective experience, which might occur as a result of individuals' actions of affect regulation.

Final Remarks

This chapter aimed to provide a comprehensive description and discussion of the literatures that constitute our knowledge base on whether and how affective states are related to creativity. The review of the literature informs us about a vast number of theoretical and empirical studies providing evidence that affect is related to creative performance. Specifically, studies are robust in showing that positive affect, high in activation, is a substantive driver of diverse forms of creativity in diverse contexts, including research laboratories and applied environments such as work organizations. In contrast, studies about negative affect are less conclusive because its influence on creativity seems to be given in very specific situations along with the influence of individual differences. Thus, the negative affect-creativity relationship is an elusive and less clear-cut phenomenon. Finally, research on this field of research is far from complete. There are still interesting opportunities for further theoretical and empirical studies to forward our understanding of how, when, and why affective states are related to creative outcomes.

References

Amabile, T. M. (1988). A model of creativity and innovation in organizations. *Research in Organizational Behavior, 10,* 123–167.

Amabile, T. M., Barsade, S. G., Mueller, J. S., & Staw, B. M. (2005). Affect and creativity at work. *Administrative Science Quarterly, 50*(3), 367–403.

Baas, M., De Dreu, C. K. W., & Nijstad, B. A. (2008). A meta-analysis of 25 years of mood-creativity research: Hedonic tone, activation, or regulatory focus? *Psychological Bulletin, 134*(6), 779–806. https://doi.org/10.1037/a0012815

Baumann, N., & Kuhl, J. (2002). Intuition, affect, and personality: Unconscious coherence judgments and self-regulation of negative affect. *Journal of Personality and Social Psychology, 83*(5), 1213–1223. https://doi.org/10.1037/0022-3514.83.5.1213

Baumann, N., & Kuhl, J. (2005). Positive affect and flexibility: Overcoming the precedence of global over local processing of visual information. *Motivation and Emotion, 29*(2), 123–134. https://doi.org/10.1007/s11031–005-7957-1

Beal, D. J., & Ghandour, L. (2011). Stability, change, and the stability of change in daily workplace affect. *Journal of Organizational Behavior, 32*(4). https://doi.org/10.1002/job.713

Binnewies, C., & Woernlein, S. C. (2011). What makes a creative day? A diary study on the interplay between affect, job stressors, and job control. *Journal of Organizational Behavior, 32*(4), 589–607. https://doi.org/10.1002/job.731

Bledow, R., Rosing, K., & Frese, M. (2013). A dynamic perspective on affect and creativity. *Academy of Management Journal, 56*(2), 432–450. https://doi.org/10.5465/amj.2010.0894

Carver, C. S., & Scheier, M. F. (1990). Origins and functions of positive and negative affect: A control-process view. *Psychological Review, 97*(1), 19–35. https://doi.org/10.1037/0033-295X.97.1.19

Chermahini, S. A., & Hommel, B. (2012). Creative mood swings: Divergent and convergent thinking affect mood in opposite ways. *Psychological Research, 76*(5), 634–640. https://doi.org/10.1007/s00426–011-0358-z

Clore, G. L., Gaspar, K., & Garvin, E. (2001). Affect as information. In J. P. Forgas (Ed.), *Handbook of Affect and Social Cognition* (pp. 121–144). Erlbaum.

Conner, T. S., & Silvia, P. J. (2015). Creative days: A daily diary study of emotion, personality, and everyday creativity. *Psychology of Aesthetics, Creativity, and the Arts, 9*(4), 463–470. https://doi.org/10.1037/aca0000022

Davis, M. A. (2009). Understanding the relationship between mood and creativity: A meta-analysis. *Organizational Behavior and Human Decision Processes, 108*(1), 25–38. https://doi.org/10.1016/j.obhdp.2008.04.001

De Dreu, C. K. W., Baas, M., & Nijstad, B. A. (2008). Hedonic tone and activation level in the mood-creativity link: Toward a dual pathway to creativity model. *Journal of Personality and Social Psychology, 94*(5), 739–756. https://doi.org/10.1037/0022-3514.94.5.739

Deci, E. L., Olafsen, A. H., & Ryan, R. M. (2017). Self-determination theory in work organizations: The state of a science. *Annual Review of Organizational Psychology and Organizational Behavior, 4*(1), 19–43. https://doi.org/10.1146/annurev-orgpsych-032516-113108

Derryberry, D., & Tucker, D. M. (1994). *Motivating the Focus of Attention*. Academic Press.

DeShon, R. P., & Gillespie, J. Z. (2005). A motivated action theory account of goal orientation. *Journal of Applied Psychology, 90*, 1096–1127. https://doi.org/10.1037/0021-9010.90.6.1096

Du, J., Ma, E., Cabrera, V., & Jiao, M. (2021). Keep your mood up: A multilevel investigation of hospitality employees' positive affect and individual creativity. *Journal of Hospitality and Tourism Management, 48*(550), 451–459. https://doi.org/10.1016/j.jhtm.2021.07.004

Du, Y., Yang, Y., Wang, X., et al. (2021). A positive role of negative mood on creativity: The opportunity in the crisis of the COVID-19 epidemic. *Frontiers in Psychology, 11*(January), 1–14. https://doi.org/10.3389/fpsyg.2020.600837

Ekman, P. (1992). An argument for basic emotions. *Cognition & Emotion, 6*, 169–200.

Filipowicz, A. (2006). From positive affect to creativity: The surprising role of surprise. *Creativity Research Journal, 18*, 141–152. https://doi.org/10.1207/s15326934crj1802_2

Fong, C. T. (2006). The effects of emotional ambivalence on creativity. *Academy of Management Journal, 49*(5), 1016–1030. https://doi.org/10.5465/AMJ.2006.22798182

Forgas, J. P. (1995). Mood and judgment: The Affect Infusion Model (AIM). *Psychological Bulletin, 116*, 39–66. https://doi.org/10.1037/0033-2909.117.1.39

Fredrickson, B. L. (2001). The role of positive emotions in positive psychology: The broaden-and-build theory of positive emotions. *American Psychologist, 56*, 218–226. https://doi.org/10.1037/0003-066X.56.3.218

Frijda, N. H. (1994). Varietes of affect: Emotions and episodes, moods and sentiments. In P. Ekman & R. J. Davidson (Eds.), *The Nature of Emotion. Fundamental Questions* (pp. 59–67). Oxford University Press.

Gasper, K. (2003). When necessity is the mother of invention: Mood and problem solving. *Journal of Experimental Social Psychology, 39*(3), 248–262. https://doi.org/10.1016/S0022–1031(03)00023-4

Gasper, K., & Middlewood, B. L. (2014). Approaching novel thoughts: Understanding why elation and boredom promote associative thought more than distress and relaxation. *Journal of Experimental Social Psychology, 52*, 50–57. https://doi.org/10.1016/j.jesp.2013.12.007

George, J. M., & Zhou, J. (2002). Understanding when bad moods foster creativity and good ones don't: The role of context and clarity of feelings. *Journal of Applied Psychology, 87*(4), 687. https://doi.org/10.1037/0021-9010.87.4.687

George, J. M., & Zhou, J. (2007). Dual tuning in a supportive context: Joint contributions of positive mood, negative mood, and supervisory behaviors to employee creativity. *Academy of Management Journal, 50*, 605–622. https://doi.org/10.5465/AMJ.2007.25525934

Gross, J. J. (2015). Emotion regulation: Current status and future prospects. *Psychological Inquiry, 26*(1), 1–26. https://doi.org/10.1080/1047840X.2014.940781

Han, W., Feng, X., Zhang, M., Peng, K., & Zhang, D. (2019). Mood states and everyday creativity: Employing an experience sampling method and a day reconstruction method. *Frontiers in Psychology, 10*, 1698. https://doi.org/10.3389/fpsyg.2019.01698

Hwang, T. J., & Choi, J. N. (2020). Different moods lead to different creativity: Mediating roles of ambiguity tolerance and team identification. *Creativity Research Journal, 32*(2), 161–173. https://doi.org/10.1080/10400419.2020.1751542

Intasao, N., & Hao, N. (2018). Beliefs about creativity influence creative performance: The mediation effects of flexibility and positive affect. *Frontiers in Psychology, 9*(1810), 1–17. https://doi.org/10.3389/fpsyg.2018.01810

Isen, A. M., Daubman, K. A., & Nowicki, G. P. (1987). Positive affect facilitates creative problem solving. *Journal of Personality and Social Psychology, 52*(6), 1122–1131. https://doi.org/10.1037//0022-3514.52.6.1122

Kaufmann, G. (2003). The effect of mood on creativity in the innovative process. In L. Shavinina (Ed.), *The International Handbook on Innovation* (pp. 191–203). Elsevier Science.

Larsen, J. T., McGraw, A. P., & Cacioppo, J. T. (2001). Can people feel happy and sad at the same time? *Journal of Personality and Social Psychology, 81*, 684–696. https://doi.org/10.1037/0022-3514.81.4.684

Lazarus, R. S., & Folkman, S. (1984). *Stress, Appraisal and Coping.* Springer.

Luthans, F., Youssef, C. M., & Avolio, B. J. (2007). *Psychological Capital. Developing the Human Competitive Edge.* Oxford University Press.

Madjar, N., Oldham, G. R., & Pratt, M. G. (2002). There's no place like home? The contributions of work and nonwork creativity support to employees' creative performance. *Academy of Management Journal, 45*, 757–767. https://doi.org/10.2307/3069309

Madrid, H. P., & Patterson, M. G. (2018). Affect and creativity. In R. Reiter-Palmon & J. C. Kaufmann (Eds.), *Individual Creativity in the Workplace.* Elsevier.

Madrid, H. P., & Patterson, M. G. (2019). How and for whom time control matter for innovation? The role of positive affect and problem-solving demands. *Applied Psychology, 69*(1), 93–119. https://doi.org/10.1111/apps.12194

Madrid, H. P., Patterson, M. G., Birdi, K. S., Leiva, P. I., & Kausel, E. E. (2014). The role of weekly high-activated positive mood, context, and personality in innovative work behavior: A multilevel and interactional model. *Journal of Organizational Behavior, 35*(2), 234–256. https://doi.org/10.1002/job.1867

Martin, L. L., & Stoner, P. (1996). Mood as input: What we think about how we feel determines how we think. In L. L. Martin & A. Tesser (Eds.), *Striving and Feeling: Interactions among Goals, Affect, and Self-Regulation* (pp. 279–301). Erlbaum.

Mastria, S., Agnoli, S., & Corazza, G. E. (2019). How does emotion influence the creativity evaluation of exogenous alternative ideas? *PLoS ONE, 14*(7), 1–16. https://doi.org/10.1371/journal.pone.0219298

McCrae, R. R., & Costa, P. T. (1997). Conceptions and correlates of openness to experience. In R. Hogan, J. Johnson, & S. Briggs (Eds.), *Handbook of Personality Psychology* (pp. 825–847). Academic Press.

Nijstad, B. A., De Dreu, C. K. W., Rietzschel, E. F., & Baas, M. (2010). The dual pathway to creativity model: Creative ideation as a function of flexibility and persistence. *European Review of Social Psychology, 21*, 34–77. https://doi.org/10.1080/10463281003765323

Park, I. J., Choi, J. N., & Wu, K. (2021). Affect stability and employee creativity: the roles of work-related positive affect and knowledge sharing. *European Journal of Work and Organizational Psychology*, *31*(3), 331–340. https://doi.org/10 .1080/1359432X.2021.1953990

Parke, M. R., Seo, M.-G., & Sherf, E. N. (2014). Regulating and facilitating: The role of emotional intelligence in maintaining and using positive affect for creativity. *Journal of Applied Psychology, 100*(3), 917–934. https://doi.org/10.1037/a0038452

Rasulzada, F., & Dackert, I. (2009). Organizational creativity and innovation in relation to psychological well-being and organizational factors. *Creativity Research Journal, 21*(2–3), 191–198. https://doi.org/10.1080/10400410902855283

Rego, A., Sousa, F., Marques, C., & Cunha, M. P. (2012a). Optimism predicting employees' creativity: The mediating role of positive affect and the positivity ratio. *European Journal of Work and Organizational Psychology, 21*(2), 244–270. https://doi.org/10.1080/1359432X.2010.550679

Rego, A., Sousa, F., Marques, C., & Cunha, M. P. E. (2012b). Retail employees' self-efficacy and hope predicting their positive affect and creativity. *European Journal of Work and Organizational Psychology, 21*(6), 923–945. https://doi .org/10.1080/1359432x.2011.610891

Richels, K. A., Day, E. A., Jorgensen, A. G., & Huck, J. T. (2020). Keeping calm and carrying on: Relating affect spin and pulse to complex skill acquisition and adaptive performance. *Frontiers in Psychology, 11*, 337. https://doi.org/10 .3389/fpsyg.2020.00377

Salovey, P., Mayer, J. D., Goldman, S. L., Turvey, C., & Palfai, T. P. (1995). Emotional attention, clarity, and repair: Exploring emotional intelligence using the Trait Meta-Mood Scale. In J. W. Pennebaker (Ed.), *Emotion, Disclosure, and Health* (pp. 125–154). American Psychological Association. https://doi.org/10.1037/ 10182-006

Schwarz, N. (2002). Situated cognition and the wisdom of feelings: Cognitive tuning. In L. Feldman Barrett & P. Salovey (Eds.), *The Wisdom in Feelings* (pp. 144–166). Guilford Press.

Schwarz, N., & Clore, G. L. (1983). Mood, misattribution, and judgments of well-being: Informative and directive functions of affective states. *Journal of Personality and Social Psychology, 45*(3), 513–523. https://doi.org/10.1037/0022-3514.45.3 .513

Schwarz, N., & Clore, G. L. (2003). Mood as information: 20 years later. *Psychological Inquiry, 14*(3–4), 296–303. https://doi.org/10.1207/s15327965pli1403&4_20

Silvia, P. J., Beaty, R. E., Nusbaum, E. C., et al. (2014). Everyday creativity in daily life: An experience-sampling study of "little c" creativity. *Psychology of Aesthetics, Creativity, and the Arts, 8*(2), 183–188. https://doi.org/10.1037/a0035722

Spering, M., Wagener, D., & Funke, J. (2005). The role of emotions in complex problem-solving. *Cognition & Emotion, 19*(8), 1252–1261. https://doi.org/10 .1080/02699930500304886

Spreitzer, G. M. (1995). Psychological empowerment in the workplace: Dimensions, measurement, and validation. *Academy of Management Journal, 38*, 1442–1465.

Tang, C., Li, Q., & Kaufman, J. C. (2016). Problem clarity as a moderator between trait affect and self-perceived creativity. *Journal of Creative Behavior, 52*(3), 267–279. https://doi.org/10.1002/jocb.152

Tavares, S. M. (2016). How does creativity at work influence employee's positive affect at work? *European Journal of Work and Organizational Psychology*, *25*(4), 525–539. https://doi.org/10.1080/1359432X.2016.1186012

To, M. L., Fisher, C. D., & Ashkanasy, N. M. (2015). Unleashing angst: Negative mood, learning goal orientation, psychological empowerment and creative behaviour. *Human Relations*, *68*(10), 1601–1622. https://doi.org/10.1177/0018726714562235

To, M. L., Fisher, C. D., Ashkanasy, N. M., & Rowe, P. A. (2011). Within-person relationships between mood and creativity. *Journal of Applied Psychology*, *97* (3), 599–612. https://doi.org/10.1037/a0026097

Uy, M. A., Sun, S., & Foo, M. D. (2017). Affect spin, entrepreneurs' well-being, and venture goal progress: The moderating role of goal orientation. *Journal of Business Venturing*, *32*(4), 443–460. https://doi.org/https://doi.org/10.1016/j.jbusvent.2016.12.001

VandeWalle, D. (1997). Development and validation of a work domain goal orientation instrument. *Educational and Psychological Measurement*, *57*, 995–1015. https://doi.org/10.1177/0013164497057006009

Wall, T. D., Corbett, J. M., Clegg, C. W., Jackson, P. R., & Martin, R. (1990). Advanced manufacturing technology and work design: Towards a theoretical framework. *Journal of Organizational Behavior*, *11*(3), 201–219. https://doi.org/10.1002/job.4030110304

Wall, T. D., Jackson, P. R., Mullarkey, S., & Parker, S. K. (1996). The demands-control model of job strain: A more specific test. *Journal of Occupational and Organizational Psychology*, *69*, 153–166. http://dx.doi.org/10.1111/j.2044-8325.1996.tb00607.x

Watson, D. (2000). *Mood and Temperament*. Guilford Press.

Watson, D., Wiese, D., Vaidya, J., & Tellegen, A. (1999). The two general activation systems of affect: Structural findings, evolutionary considerations, and psychobiological evidence. *Journal of Personality and Social Psychology*, *76*(5), 820–838. https://doi.org/10.1037/0022-3514.76.5.820

Xu, Y., Shao, J., Zeng, W., et al. (2021). Depression and creativity during COVID-19: Psychological resilience as a mediator and deliberate rumination as a moderator. *Frontiers in Psychology*, *12*(May), 1–13. https://doi.org/10.3389/fpsyg.2021.665961

Zaman, M., Rajan, M. A., & Dai, Q. Z. (2010). Experiencing flow with instant messaging and its facilitating role on creative behaviors. *Computers in Human Behavior*, *26*(5), 1009–1018. https://doi.org/10.1016/j.chb.2010.03.001

Zhang, M., Wang, F., & Zhang, D. (2020). Individual differences in trait creativity moderate the state-level mood-creativity relationship. *PLoS ONE*, *15*, 1–15. https://doi.org/10.1371/journal.pone.0236987

6 The Neuroscience of Creativity and Emotions

Evangelia G. Chrysikou, Alexandra E. Kelly, and
Indre V. Viskontas

Introduction

Creativity is multifaceted and the processes it encompasses differ from one domain to another: the brain networks supporting musical improvisation, for example, are not the same as those that underlie design thinking. Yet there are certain aspects of creative behaviors that are more common across domains, such as novel idea generation (Runco & Jaeger, 2012; Sawyer, 2006), which characterizes many different forms of creativity. Therefore, there is no one brain basis of creativity: instead, neuroscientists interested in the topic choose specific tasks or stages to query, with the goal of mapping out networks of brain activity that support each form or step in the creative process, and then combining these findings to build a comprehensive model of the creative brain more generally.

The neuroscience of creativity has grown significantly over the past several years, with key findings pointing toward extensive involvement and interactions of and between large-scale brain networks supporting creative thinking (Saggar et al., 2021). At the same time, substantially more theoretical and empirical work is needed to detail how specific aspects of creative cognition are enabled by distinct patterns of neural activity (Abraham, 2019; Jung & Vartanian, 2018). One aspect of creative ideation, for example, that has received relatively limited attention among neuroscientists is how emotional processes – and the neural systems underlying them – shape creativity and influence the brain activity that accompanies it (Khalil et al., 2019). Extensive behavioral work (some featured in this volume) has highlighted the significance of affective states, motivational factors, and reward processes for creative idea or product generation (Ashby et al. 1999; Baas et al., 2008; Costa et al., 2020; De Dreu et al., 2008; Hwang & Choi, 2020; Kao & Chiou, 2020; Isen & Baron, 1991; Mumford, 2003; Strasbaugh & Connelly, 2021; To et al., 2012, 2015; Van Kleef et al., 2010; Yang & Hung, 2015). Similarly, an independent line of research has discussed the contributions of different neurotransmitter systems as the potential backdrop for creative thinking (e.g., Beversdorf, 2018). Yet, participants' emotional states and neuromodulatory characteristics are not typically

Evangelia G. Chrysikou is supported in part by the National Science Foundation (grant# DRL-2100137).

recorded or incorporated in neuroscientific studies of creativity that have, thus far, prioritized measurement of the neural processes supporting creative cognition at the cortical or subcortical level (e.g., Beaty et al., 2015, 2016; Zabelina & Andrews-Hanna, 2016).

In this chapter, we review findings underscoring the critical interactions between cognitive and emotional neuromodulatory mechanisms during creative thinking, including the potential impact of mood, stress, and reward processes on known neurocognitive components of creative ideation such as attention, memory, and cognitive control. We further examine whether and under what circumstances such interactions can have positive or negative consequences for creativity. Last, we discuss how emotional task content may impact the generation of the creative product on the part of the creator. Across these domains, we synthesize this literature and propose a framework for future research that integrates brain function at the neurochemical, neuroanatomical, and systems levels with emotional aspects of creative thinking.

Cognitive and Emotional Neuromodulatory Mechanisms of Creative Thinking

The Cognitive Neuroscience of Creativity

A significant proportion of recent work on the neural bases of creative thinking has examined the contributions of large-scale neural systems and their interactions during creative cognition. Spontaneous fluctuations of neural activity have been shown to correlate either positively or negatively across regions of the brain that are functionally related, and these coordinated patterns of activity are interpreted as reflecting the brain's intrinsic functional organization (e.g., Greicius et al., 2004; Seeley et al., 2007). Such neural fluctuations appear to be organized depending on either the nature of the cognitive tasks performed or, conversely, in their absence. Task-based and resting-state functional connectivity studies have revealed consistent patterns of activation across several areas within the prefrontal and parietal cortices, that have been shown to support attention and cognitive control functions. This large-scale network has been collectively discussed as the brain's *executive control network* (ECN; Seeley et al., 2007). Equally, resting state functional connectivity studies have identified a different set of regions that show coherent patterns of neural activity in the absence of specific tasks. These regions span across the medial prefrontal cortex, posterior cingulate cortex, bilateral inferior parietal lobule, and bilateral medial temporal lobe structures, and are collectively known as the brain's *default mode network* (DMN; Andrews-Hanna et al., 2014; Buckner et al., 2008; Raichle, 2015). Activity in the DMN and ECN tends to be negatively correlated, such that increases in ECN activation during cognitively demanding tasks that require focused attention and cognitive control, are accompanied by deactivation in the DMN (e.g., Fox et al., 2005; Raichle et al., 2001).

An early framework on how the brain's intrinsic functional architecture may support creative cognition proposed that creative ideation is the result of complex interactions between ECN and DMN regions (Jung et al., 2013; see also Jung et al., 2010). Patterns of activity within these networks are ostensibly aligned with a two-stage model of creative generation that entails a "blind variation" generative process, followed by a "selective retention" evaluative process of the generated ideas (cf. Simonton, 1999, 2010). Activity in DMN regions is thought to reflect the former generative process, whereas activity in ECN regions is thought to reflect the latter evaluative process. Negotiating the switch between the prioritization of activity within DMN or ECN regions may occur as a result of the engagement of the brain's salience network, which includes bilateral insular cortex and the anterior cingulate (Chand et al., 2017; Goulden et al., 2014; Sridharan et al., 2008). The salience network is hypothesized to detect and bring to the forefront stimuli of particular behavioral relevance for the task at hand, supporting the selection of specific ideas for further evaluation (cf. Bendetowicz et al., 2018; Chrysikou, 2018, 2019; Jung, 2013; Zabelina & Andrews-Hanna, 2016).

Subsequent empirical work, however, has shown that higher creative performance is associated with increased resting-state functional connectivity between the inferior frontal cortex and DMN regions. Such connectivity is indicative of cooperative interactions between ECN and DMN for creative cognition, relative to the frequently antagonistic relationship observed between them for other cognitive tasks (Beaty et al., 2014; 2015). In support of the potentially mediating role of the salience network, connectivity between DMN and salience regions has been associated with performance earlier in a creative generation task, whereas performance later in the task was marked by increased connectivity between DMN and ECN regions (Beaty et al., 2015). Other work has also revealed that the originality of the ideas produced was associated with increased connectivity between the ventral anterior cingulate and posterior (occipito-temporal) regions (Mayseless et al., 2015). Potentially reflective of the regulatory role of regions within the ECN in creative generation, a recent study has shown that ECN areas and, prominently, prefrontal cortex, may unidirectionally control DMN regions, including the temporal and parietal cortices, during creative idea generation (Vartanian et al., 2018). Overall, a considerable body of recent work on the neural bases of creative thinking has linked the generation of original ideas with complex interactions between these large-scale neural networks (e.g., Beaty et al., 2018; Chen et al., 2014; Feng et al., 2019; Gao et al., 2017; Shi et al., 2018; Sun et al., 2019).

The majority of the work discussed above has employed variations of divergent thinking tasks – primarily the Alternative Uses Task (AUT; Christensen & Guilford, 1958) – as measures of creative thinking, scoring participant responses in the dimensions of fluency, originality, and flexibility. Across studies, self-reported measures of lifetime creativity achievements (e.g., the Creative Achievement Questionnaire; Carson et al., 2005) have also been collected, as well as measures of personality and intelligence – albeit the inclusion of such measures varies widely among investigations (e.g., Beaty et al., 2016; Kenett et al., 2018). Notably, however, the potential impact of emotional or affective factors in determining the engagement of different neural networks in creative ideation has been insufficiently explored.

It is worth noting that a strict distinction between emotional and cognitive brain activity is no longer supported by the broader affective neuroscience literature. Instead, affective neuroscientists have proposed that emotions are constructed in a way that mirrors many other types of cognition, pulling meaning from sensations and interpreting contexts in terms of an emotional valence (Barrett, 2017). This approach recognizes that, just like the creative process, emotional experiences are variable and therefore have different neural signatures. Because emotions are constructed moment to moment, highly influenced by external and internal contexts, they interact with environmental and other factors during the creative process. This complexity is reflected in the paucity of neuroscientific studies examining the interplay between creativity and emotion.

There are multiple ways in which emotional variation may impact the neurocognitive processes that support creative thinking: mood, stress, or reward-based affective states may significantly influence spontaneous or task-based fluctuations in neural activity across ECN, DMN, and salience networks. Additionally, affective content may guide creative generation for certain artistic domains or impact the evaluation of certain creative products. We review some of these factors next.

Mood, Intrinsic Brain Functional Organization, and Creativity

Since the early days of creativity research, a large proportion of behavioral studies has examined the effects of various affective states on creative performance, demonstrating the impact that these states have on creativity. This work has focused on both temporary affective states that tend to be context-specific, and more enduring emotional predispositions, typically in the context of long-term psychopathology. Such investigations have further distinguished moods on the dimensions of valence (positive vs. negative moods), as well as activation (activating vs. deactivating moods). Although this body of work is substantial, it includes many different methodological approaches, such as those investigating specific mood states (e.g., negative vs. neutral moods) while excluding other states. Additionally, these methods have focused on selective aspects of creative performance (e.g., fluency but not flexibility or vice versa). This variability in methodology represents, in part, the shift in theoretical framing of emotions from primarily reactive to actively constructed.

Partially due to this methodological variability and the framing shift, the results of this work are inconsistent and difficult to reconcile, with some studies showing that positive moods can promote creativity (Ashby et al., 1999; Lyubomirsky et al., 2005), while others find that it can diminish it (e.g., Kaufmann & Vosburg, 1997). Similarly, some studies have shown that negative moods can enhance creative performance (e.g., Carlsson et al., 2000; Clapham, 2001; Costa et al., 2020; De Dreu et al., 2008; Huang & Choi, 2020; Kao & Chiou, 2020; Strasbaugh & Connelly, 2021; To et al., 2012, 2015; Van Kleef et al., 2010; Yang & Hung, 2015), or impede it (e.g., Vosburg, 1998), or have no effect on creative generation (e.g., Verhaeghen et al., 2005). Bringing together this disparate literature, an influential meta-analysis of the impact of positive and negative moods on creative task performance has shown that positive *activating* moods (e.g., happiness) enhanced creative performance relative to positive *de-activating* moods (e.g., relaxation). In contrast, negative deactivating moods (e.g., sadness) did not affect creativity, whereas negative activating moods (e.g., anxiety) were associated with decreases in creative performance – although the limited negative mood repertoire included in this analysis would require additional empirical examination to confirm the replicability of these findings (Bass et al., 2008).

How do such variations in mood influence the neural mechanisms implicated in creative thinking? This question has received very little attention in the empirical creativity neuroscience literature. To our knowledge, there is currently no published experimental neuroscience study of creativity that has recorded, controlled for, or explicitly manipulated participants' mood to investigate the impact of mood changes on the neural processes supporting creative thinking, such as large-scale network connectivity. Several affective neuroscience investigations not involving creativity tasks have revealed that mood is a powerful determinant of neural intrinsic macro-scale network engagement and dynamic neural activity pattern shifts across the brain. High positive affect has been shown to correlate positively with hippocampal volume (e.g., Dennison et al., 2015) and higher trait positive affect has been linked to lower amygdala activity during negative emotion regulation (e.g., Sanchez et al., 2015). Increased positive affect has also been linked to lower functional connectivity across the brain (Rohr et al., 2013). Consistent with this finding, a recent neuroimaging study employed a resting-state connectivity approach to investigate how positive and negative moods influenced intrinsic connectivity between salience, emotional, and DMN regions (Qi et al., 2021). The results showed that increased positive affect was related to decreased connectivity within salience (bilateral anterior insula) and emotion (nucleus accumbens) regions, as well as decreased connectivity between emotion (right amygdala) and DMN (right middle temporal gyrus) regions. Similarly, Provenzano and colleagues (2019) have shown that negative mood induction increased the efficiency of the salience network but decreased the efficiently of the ECN in an emotional Stroop task, with this neural modulation fully mediating the effects of mood induction on participants' reaction times to negative words. Greater negative and positive mood states recorded continuously in daily life have also been associated with increased resting state functional connectivity between posterior cingulate and both medial prefrontal as well as precuneus regions of the DMN (Ismaylova et al., 2018).

Overall, these findings suggest that such transient shifts in network organization may account for how affect contributes to our interactions with the environment and could be critical to understand in the context of creativity tasks. For example, a recent study has documented the impact of emotion–cognition interactivity on work performance, with affective states influencing work performance through their effects on the attentional and regulatory resources dedicated to the task at hand (Weiss & Merlo, 2020). What's more, evidence from a large sample from the Human Connectome Project suggests that cognitive abilities and affective experience share a genetic relationship influencing local brain structure, with significant phenotypic correlation at the behavioral level between fluid cognition and affective trait scores (Kraljevic et al., 2021). Furthermore, cortical thickness in the left superior frontal cortex showed a significant phenotypic relationship with both cognitive and affective characteristics and supported the convergence of both cognition and emotion in morphological features of left superior cortex. These results point to the possibility of overlapping neural mechanisms supporting cognitive and affective regulation that could be critical for understanding the neural mechanisms enabling creativity. Overlapping affective states and fluctuating attentional resources can impact creative performance through their effects on the large-scale neural network interactivity that has been shown to underlie creative idea production.

Stress and Its Impact on Creative Performance: Possible Neurocognitive Mechanisms

Stress has been generally described as an adaptive physical response to environmental challenges that allows an organism to increase alertness, attentiveness, and efficiency in addressing unexpected circumstances (Noack et al., 2019). Prolonged exposure to such conditions, however, may result in increased inefficiency of these responses, with significant negative consequences for physical and mental health, as exhaustion sets in (Gianaros & Wager, 2015). Stress resulting from physical threats (e.g., Herman, 2011) tends to be less commonly experienced in our modern environment than stress arising from perceived threats to our self-esteem or social status (Dickerson & Kemeny, 2004). Neurally, the stress response is initiated in the context of one's interpretation of a situation as stressful. Increases in activity in the amygdala and the medial prefrontal cortex through the stria terminalis give rise to two responses: a fast autonomic response mediated by the sympathetic nervous system and adrenal catecholamine (epinephrine [adrenaline], norepinephrine [noradrenaline], and dopamine) secretions that result in physiological markers in support of fight-or-flight behavior (e.g., increased heart rate, respiration, and blood pressure); and a slower hypothalamus-pituitary-adrenal (HPA) response mediated by the synthesis and secretion of cortisol from the adrenal cortex (Beversdorf, 2018). Cortisol has varying effects throughout the nervous system, including the regulation of the HPA axis, which is further modulated by increased neural signals from the medial prefrontal cortex, the anterior cingulate cortex, the hippocampus, and the amygdala (Herman, 2011; Herman et al., 2005).

Noradrenergic system antagonists, specifically drugs that block the noradrenergic system via action on β-adrenergic receptors (e.g., propranolol), have been successful in treating excessive stress responses to common performance-related stressors in individuals prone to anxiety (e.g., Lader, 1988; Laverdue & Boulenger, 1991). An interesting line of research has leveraged these findings to examine whether pharmacological modulation of the noradrenergic system may mitigate the potentially negative effects of stress on creative thinking. In one such investigation, participants exposed to a psychosocial stressor who were treated with propranolol were spared from reductions in performance in a verbal problem-solving task requiring flexible semantic associations (Alexander et al., 2007). Other studies, however, have shown that the benefits of propranolol for creativity extend beyond stress manipulations, thus supporting the view that noradrenergic system antagonists' effects on creative thinking are likely mediated by their widespread influence on cognitive functions related to creativity such as working memory, attention, or cognitive and affective regulation (e.g., Beversdorf et al., 1999, 2002; Heilman et al., 2003; see Beversdorf, 2019 for a review).

The majority of studies examining the relationship between creativity and stress have focused on the potential impact of evaluative (i.e., social) kinds of stressors on the cognitive processes related to creativity. Byron and colleagues (2010) performed a meta-analysis of 76 studies exploring the relationship between creativity and stressors and revealed a pattern of results suggestive of a curvilinear relationship, with non-evaluative (i.e., nonsocial) stressors promoting creative performance whereas highly evaluative (i.e., social) stressors – particularly when considered uncontrollable – impeding creative performance. Individual differences in trait anxiety may further function as a significant moderator of these effects: for participants low in trait anxiety, stressors were shown to increase performance, whereas for those high in trait anxiety the opposite relationship was observed, albeit it was not statistically significant. One potential interpretation of these findings is that stressors require attention and limit the pool of cognitive resources one has available for creative ideation. Narrow attentional focus in the presence of stressors may result in simpler cognitive strategies, which are hypothesized to restrict creative ideas to more common and easily accessible solutions. Alternatively, moderate stressors may increase arousal, which in turn increases one's motivation, attentional focus, and persistence toward problem solving.

In line with the hypothesized effects of stress on attentional and inhibitory mechanisms, Duan and colleagues (2019) showed that cognitive inhibition, measured by the Flanker task was modulated by participants' trait anxiety and the presence of acute social stressors, induced by the Trier Social Stress test. For participants low on trait anxiety, the presence of the stressor decreased performance on the Flanker task, but increased fluency on the AUT. In contrast, for individuals high on trait anxiety, the presence of the stressor decreased performance across both tasks. All participants regardless of trait anxiety status showed increased performance on the Remote Associates Test (RAT) following the stressor. A subsequent study including a no-stress control condition, revealed that stress reduced divergent thinking performance as captured by less flexibility and variety of solutions on the AUT, but improved accuracy and reaction times on the RAT (Duan et al., 2020).

The curvilinear relationship between stress and creativity might be a function of the effects of cortisol: cortisol can improve attentional focus in moderation, but in higher concentrations it can induce a negative mood state that could be detrimental for creative performance (Yeh et al., 2015). Individual differences in vulnerability to perceived threat and its consequences on mood may also influence responses to stressful situations. For example, Akinola and Mendes (2008) measured participants' baseline levels of the adrenal steroid dehydroepiandrosterone-sulfate (DHEAS), low levels of which have been associated with depression, and then exposed participants to either social rejection, or social approval on the Trier Social Stress test, or to a nonsocial situation. Following this exposure, participants completed an artistic creativity task that was evaluated by expert raters using various creativity metrics. Participants in the social rejection situation produced more creative artistic products; however, this effect was more pronounced for those lower in baseline DHEAS. Taken together, these results point to a potentially complex interaction among trait and situational factors, as well as biological predispositions to affective vulnerabilities, that mitigate the relationship between acute stress and creativity (see also Akinola et al., 2019).

Although several measures have been developed and standardized for acute stress induction in cognitive and affective neuroscience studies, only one investigation thus far has incorporated direct measurements of brain function during creative performance under stress. Psychosocial stress induced by the Montreal Imaging Stress task (Dedovic et al., 2009) was associated with reduced upper-frequency alpha band activity, as well as reduced alpha synchronization. These neural markers of stress were associated behaviorally with significant reductions in originality scores on the AUT (Wang et al., 2019). Although stress has been shown to elicit large-scale neural network reconfiguration (e.g., Hermans et al., 2011), to our knowledge, no investigation has yet leveraged acute stress manipulations for the study of creativity using functional neuroimaging. Regarding local regional engagement, prior work with psychosocial stressor tasks has shown both activations and deactivations of limbic and paralimbic regions, including the anterior cingulate cortex, insula, hippocampus, amygdala, and ventral striatum (see Noack et al., 2019 for a review). The variability in these results depends on individual differences in responsiveness to the stressors, with participants determined as responders showing primarily deactivations across these neural regions, whereas participants determined as non-responders showing activation within regions of the DMN and salience networks, including the insula and medial prefrontal cortex. Given these findings, it stands to reason that psychosocial stress, overall, could result in reductions in activity within the DMN, thus potentially impeding the generative process of creative thinking. For those who experience subthreshold responses to stress, however, increases in activity in salience and DMN regions could support creative ideation by highlighting potential responses of increased behavioral significance (cf. Vartanian et al., 2020). Future studies are needed to carefully examine the combined effects of stress-induction manipulations or pharmacological modulation of noradrenergic system function on ECN, DMN, and salience network activity and connectivity during tasks that tap on different aspects of creative thinking.

Neural Mechanisms of Motivation and Reward and Creative Thinking

A growing body of research over the past decade has examined the potential role of reward processing neurocircuitry and neurotransmission for different aspects of creative thinking. Functional neuroimaging studies of creative cognition have shown both contributions of the ECN mainly supported by dorsal and ventral prefrontal cortex regions, but also the ventral striatum (e.g., Abraham et al., 2012). Extensive connectivity and dopaminergic modulation of both prefrontal cortex and the striatum have been proposed to underlie cognitive flexibility (e.g., Alexander et al., 1986; Aston-Jones & Cohen, 2005; Cools et al., 2007) related to creative performance (e.g., Chrysikou et al., 2014). Many aspects of creative thinking have been linked to this system, which has been shown to functionally differentiate striatal and prefrontal dopamine contributions. Behavioral flexibility can facilitate creative idea generation and has been associated with moderate levels of striatal dopamine. In contrast, persistence toward finding a solution has been associated with moderate levels of prefrontal dopamine. An optimal balance between these two systems might support an optimal balance between flexibility and persistence underlying creative thinking (Khalil et al., 2019).

Overall, modulation of the fronto-striatal circuitry has been linked to the neurotransmitter dopamine. Dopamine originates subcortically in the substantia nigra and ventral tegmental area and projects extensively throughout the brain. With respect to the fronto-striatal network of interest for creative cognition, the nigro-striatal pathway regulates dopamine in the ventral striatum and supports switching and other aspects of cognitive flexibility. In contrast, the mesocortical pathway originates in the ventral tegmental area and projects to the prefrontal cortex and has been generally associated with maintaining and acting upon task goals (e.g., Alexander et al., 1986). Interestingly, the two pathways appear to function antagonistically, with increased dopaminergic activity in the one associated with decreased dopaminergic activity in the other and vice versa (Nijstad et al., 2010). Studies have shown that drugs that influence D1 receptors, abundant in the mesocortical pathway and the prefrontal cortex, can promote working memory and cognitive control, whereas drugs that influence D2 receptors may benefit cognitive flexibility (Boot et al., 2017). Under this model, different studies have either used dopamine agonists or antagonists to investigate their effects on creative performance, or focused on genetic and behavioral indicators of dopamine receptor prevalence in the mesocortical or nigrostriatal pathways, or examined creative performance in patients afflicted by dopaminergic system abnormalities. Overall, these studies have shown an inverted U-shaped curvilinear relationship between striatal dopamine and cognitive flexibility, as well as prefrontal dopamine and the fluency and originality aspects of common behavioral tasks (see Beversdorf, 2018, and Boot et al., 2017, for detailed reviews).

How is the dopaminergic system influenced by the participants' mood or other affective factors during creative thinking? To our knowledge, only one study has experimentally examined this question: Chermahini and Hommel (2012) collected measures of mood and performance on the AUT, along with eye-blink rates – shown previously to be a reliable clinical marker of individual dopamine levels – before and after inducing a positive or negative mood via an established mental imagination procedure. In line with the prediction that positive mood increases dopamine levels (e.g., Ashby et al., 1999; Dreisbach & Goschke, 2004), positive mood induction increased eye-blink rates, but only for those individuals with below-median rates at baseline; interestingly, these individuals showed increased flexibility on the AUT. These results suggest that mood-boosting interventions might facilitate creative flexibility for individuals with lower endogenous dopamine levels, but might not be strong enough to impact creative cognition for individuals with average or greater levels. It's possible that low dopamine levels signal low motivation, and that a positive mood can increase motivation via this dopamine pathway, or that the intervention is not strong enough to move the dopamine needle in people whose baseline dopamine levels are near or above the median.

Activity fluctuations in the dopaminergic system that may impact cognitive flexibility or goal directedness in creative ideation can also be attributed to the intrinsically rewarding aspects of creative behavior itself (e.g., finding a successful solution to a hard problem) or reward-related personality traits related to creativity. For example, a recent study examined whether oxytocin – a neuropeptide that has been implicated in many behaviors including creativity and that converges with mesolimbic dopaminergic pathways – is associated with reward-based personality traits. Using a multilocus genetic profile approach, four oxytocin receptor genes were shown to be significantly associated with reward behaviors that may be supportive of evolutionarily important aspects of cognition such as creativity (Davis et al., 2019). In the context of prior work that has revealed certain personality traits (e.g., openness to experience) to predict reliably efficiency of default mode network connectivity (Beaty et al., 2016), future work is invited to examine how situational or trait factors (e.g., mood, personality) may interact and modulate the dopaminergic system with consequences for large-scale network connectivity and creative behavior.

Affective Stimuli and the Neural Systems Supporting Creativity

Very few creativity neuroscience studies have explicitly employed affective stimuli to examine their effects on the neurocognitive mechanisms enabling creative thinking. Among them, Fink and colleagues (2011) used a within-subjects design to examine the potential of cognitive or affective stimulation to improve creative ideation as measured by the AUT. In the cognitive stimulation condition, participants were exposed to other people's ideas, whereas in the affective stimulation condition, they were asked to complete the task while exposed to emotionally contagious sound clips; there was also a no-stimulation control condition. Electroencephalogram (EEG) measurements were used to characterize brain activity. Right prefrontal alpha synchronization as measured by EEG was associated with creative ideation and was more prominent in both stimulation conditions relative to the no stimulation condition. No differences, however, were observed between cognitive and affective stimulation conditions. These results support the conclusion that either type of stimulation may positively impact creativity by an overall increase in participants' internal awareness that can make certain ideas more salient than they would have been in the absence of stimulation (Fink et al., 2011).

Similarly, an interesting recent study examined the neural responses associated with creative problem solving relevant to real-life contexts (Perchtold et al., 2018). While undergoing functional magnetic resonance imaging (fMRI), participants were asked to generate creative ideas in an emotional relative to a nonemotional task. For the emotional task, they were asked to generate alternative appraisals of anger-evoking events, whereas for the nonemotional task they were asked to perform the AUT. Both tasks elicited significant activity in left prefrontal cortex suggestive of inhibition, shifting, or controlled memory retrieval. The affective creativity task also led to the recruitment of the right superior frontal gyrus and core hubs of the DMN that have been shown to support social cognition. These results highlight the potential importance of task content in network-selective engagement that could be important for creative thought.

One of the very few neuroscience studies that has examined directly the relationship between creativity and emotion focused on emotion as a motivator for musical improvisation (McPherson et al., 2016). While undergoing fMRI, professional pianists were presented with positive, negative, and neutral emotional images and they were asked to improvise music reflective of the emotional content of the image cues. The results showed that the emotional stimuli modulated activity throughout the brain and induced widespread deactivation in the dorsolateral prefrontal cortex, angular gyrus, and the precuneus. These reductions in activity were more prominent following the positive emotional content cues; in addition, the emotional task affected connectivity of areas within the limbic and paralimbic system such as the left amygdala and left anterior insula. These effects were not observed when the participants were simply viewing the emotional images. These findings parallel the results of a recent fMRI study involving the generation of humorous ideas; humorous ideation was associated with a combined decrease in prefrontal activity along with an increase in amygdala activity; the reverse was observed for nonhumorous ideas. This pattern of results is suggestive of emotion regulation mechanisms implicated in the generation of content with affective signatures which have been previously reported to characterize emotion dysregulation in various forms of psychopathology (Bitsch et al., 2021). Together, these findings suggest that emotional intent in the creation of artistic pieces is strongly influenced by context, with affective content having particularly marked effects on creative production.

The influence of the affective task context on creative ideation might also be indirect. For example, listening to music can influence arousal and mood, which in turn can affect cognitive abilities implicated in creative cognition. In line with this prediction, Eskine and colleagues (2020) examined the relationship between music, mood, semantic knowledge, and creative cognition and found that listening to music was associated with greater creativity, as was semantic memory retrieval. Creative performance, however, in this case, was not significantly correlated with mood alone. Therefore, it's possible that the influence of mood is mitigated by other features of the context, and further study is warranted to tease apart the unique contributions of contextual factors, including affect, on creative performance.

Conclusion: A Framework toward Cognitive–Emotional Interactions in Creative Thinking

In this chapter we reviewed and synthesized literature highlighting the potential impact of neuromodulatory mechanisms related to emotional processing for different aspects of creativity. Overall, overlapping affective states may result in variations in cognitive processes underlying creativity, such as attention, memory, and cognitive control. Given that both creative cognition and emotional experiences are highly variable and influenced by internal and external environmental contexts, it should come as no surprise that there is no single region, network, or other measure of brain function or structure that drives their interplay. From the behavioral work, however, it is clear that a complete understanding of the neuroscience of creativity must include emotional factors, such as mood states, stress, and motivation.

We propose that such emotional factors influence large-scale neural network interactivity underlying creative ideation. The potentially powerful effects of mood or stress on creativity are hypothesized to rely on complex interactions among trait, personality, situational factors, biological predispositions to affective vulnerabilities, and the effects of such variation on dopaminergic system reactivity.

Although most previous research has emphasized, overall, how emotion influences aspects of attentional control or cognitive regulation during creative performance, future work should build on these findings by exploring in more depth cognitive–affective interactions pertaining to memory content and retrieval mechanisms supported by ECN, DMN, and salience network activity (see Figure 6.1). For example, the dorsomedial prefrontal cortex – an area

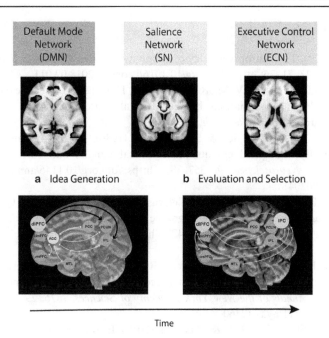

Figure 6.1 *Connectivity between three large-scale brain networks is linked to creative cognition. Higher creative performance is characterized by (a) connectivity between default mode network (DMN) and salience network (SN) regions as well as unidirectional influence of executive control network (ECN) on DMN regions during idea generation and (b) increased connectivity between DMN and ECN regions during later stages. dlPFC = dorsolateral prefrontal cortex, ACC = anterior cingulate cortex, dmPFC = dorsomedial prefrontal cortex, vmPFC = ventromedial prefrontal cortex, MTL = medial temporal lobe, PCC = posterior cingulate cortex, PCUN = precuneus, IPL = inferior parietal lobule.* Color image provided for online, electronic version of the chapter.

within the DMN that has been shown to cross-cut socio-affective and cognitive domains – plays a key role in distinguishing emotional memories depending on their affective tone and framing (Kensinger & Ford, 2021). Emotional memories are more likely to be remembered, and emotion has been shown to improve memory for imagined future events for healthy individuals, but not individuals with high anxiety (Montijn et al., 2021).

Future research that leverages established cognitive paradigms, along with stress or mood-induction manipulations, or pharmacological modulation of noradrenergic and dopaminergic system function should examine systematically how each manipulation independently and combined affects ECN, DMN, and salience network activity and connectivity during tasks that capture different aspects of creative thinking. Such efforts can reveal the precise (and possibly person-specific) circumstances under which emotion-related variables can promote or hinder creative thought.

References

Abraham, A. (2019). The neuropsychology of creativity. *Current Opinion in Behavioral Sciences, 27*, 71–76. https://doi.org/10.1016/j.cobeha.2018.09.011

Abraham, A., Beudt, S., Ott, D. V. M., & von Cramon, D. R. (2012). Creative cognition and the brain: Dissociations between frontal, parietal-temporal and basal ganglia groups. *Brain Research, 1482*, 55–70.

Alexander, G. E., DeLong, M. R., & Strick, P. L., (1986). Parallel organisation of functionally segregated circuits linking basal ganglia and cortex. *Annual Review of Neuroscience, 9*, 357–381. https://doi.org/10.1146/annurev.ne.09 .030186.002041

Alexander, J. K., Hillier, A., Smith, R. M., Tivarus, M. E., & Beversdorf, D. Q. (2007). Beta-adrenergic modulation of cognitive flexibility during stress. *Journal of Cognitive Neuroscience, 19*, 468–478. https://doi.org/10.1162/jocn.2007.19.3 .468

Andrews-Hanna, J. R., Smallwood, J., & Spreng, R. N. (2014). The default network and self-generated thought: Component processes, dynamic control, and clinical relevance. *Annals of the New York Academy of Sciences, 1316*, 29–52. https://doi.org/10.1111/nyas.12360

Akinola, M., Kapadia, C., Lu, G. J., & Malia, M. (2019). Incorporating physiology into creativity research and practice: The effects of bodily stress responses on creativity in organizations. *Academy of Management, Perspectives 33*(2), 163-184. https://doi.org/10.5465/amp.2017.0094

Akinola, M., & Mendes, W. B. (2008). The dark side of creativity: Biological vulnerability and negative emotions lead to greater artistic creativity. *Personality & Social Psychology Bulletin, 34*(12), 1677–1686. https://doi.org/10.1177/ 0146167208323933

Ashby, F. G., Isen, A. M., & Turken, A. U. (1999). A neuropsychological theory of positive affect and its influence on cognition. *Psychological Review, 106*, 529–550. https://doi.org/10.1037/0033-295X.106.3.529

Aston-Jones, G., & Cohen, J. D., (2005). An integrative theory of locus coeruleusnor-epinephrine function: Adaptive gain and optimal performance. *Annual Review of Neuroscience, 28*, 403–450. https://doi.org/10.1146/annurev.neuro.28.061604 .135709

Baas, M., Dreu, C. K. W. D., & Nijstad, B. A. (2008). A meta-analysis of 25 years of mood–creativity research: Hedonic tone, activation, or regulatory focus? *Psychological Bulletin, 134*(6), 779–806. https://doi.org/10.1037/a0012815

Barrett, L. F. (2017). *How Emotions Are Made: The Secret Life of the Brain*. Houghton Mifflin Harcourt.

Beaty, R. E., Benedek, M., Kaufman, S. B., & Silvia, P. J. (2015). Default and executive network coupling supports creative idea production. *Scientific Reports*, 1–14. http://doi.org/10.1038/srep10964

Beaty, R. E., Benedek, M., Wilkins, R. W., Jauk, E., Fink, A., Silvia, P. J., et al. (2014). Creativity and the default network: A functional connectivity analysis of the creative brain at rest. *Neuropsychologia, 64*, 92–98. http://doi.org/10.1016/j .neuropsychologia.2014.09.019

Beaty, R. E., Benedek, M., Silvia, P. J., & Schacter, D. L. (2016). Creative cognition and brain network dynamics. *Trends in Cognitive Sciences, 20*, 87–95. https://doi .org/10.1016/j.tics.2015.10.004

Beaty, R. E., Kenett, Y. N., Christensen, A. P., et al. (2018). Robust prediction of individual creative ability from brain functional connectivity. *Proceedings of the National Academy of Sciences, 115*(5), 1087–1092. https://doi.org/10.1073/pnas.1713532115

Bendetowicz, D., Urbanski, M., Garcin, B., et al. (2018). Two critical brain networks for generation and combination of remote associations. *Brain, 141*, 217–233. https://doi.org/10.1093/brain/awx294

Beversdorf, D. Q. (2018). Stress, pharmacology, and creativity. In R. E. Jung & O. Vartanian (Eds.), *The Cambridge Handbook of the Neuroscience of Creativity* (pp. 207–258). Cambridge University Press. https://doi.org/10.1017/9781316556238.018

Beversdorf, D. Q. (2019). Neuropsychopharmacological regulation of performance on creativity-related tasks *Current Opinion Behavioral Sciences, 27*, 55–63. https://doi.org/10.1016/j.cobeha.2018.09.010)

Beversdorf, D. Q., Hughes, J. D., Steinberg, B. A., Lewis, L. D., & Heilman, K. M. (1999). Noradrenergic modulation of cognitive flexibility in problem solving. *Neuroreport, 10*(13), 2763–2767. https://doi.org/10.1097/00001756-199909090-00012

Beversdorf, D. Q., White, D. M., Chever, D. C., Hughes, J. D., & Bornstein, R. A. (2002). Central beta-adrenergic modulation of cognitive flexibility. *Neuroreport, 13*(18), 2505–2507. https://doi.org/10.1097/00001756-200212200-00025

Bitsch, F., Berger, P., Fink, A., et al. (2021). Antagonism between brain regions relevant for cognitive control and emotional memory facilitates the generation of humorous ideas. *Scientific Reports*, 1–12. https://doi.org/10.1038/s41598-021-89843-8

Boot, N., Baas, M., van Gaal, S., Cools, R., & De Dreu, C. K. W. (2017). Creative cognition and dopaminergic modulation of fronto-striatal networks: Integrative review and research agenda. *Neuroscience and Biobehavioral Reviews, 78*, 13–23. https://doi.org/.1016/j.neubiorev.2017.04.007

Buckner, R. L., Andrews-Hanna, J. R., & Schacter, D. L. (2008). The brain's default network: Anatomy, function, and relevance to disease. *Annals of the New York Academy of Sciences, 1124*, 1–38. https://doi.org/10.1196/annals.1440.011

Byron, K., Khazanchi, S., & Nazarian, D. (2010). The relationship between stressors and creativity: A meta-analysis examining competing theoretical models. *Journal of Applied Psychology, 95*(1), 201–212. https://doi.org/10.1037/a0017868

Carson, S. H., Peterson, J. B., Higgins, D. M. (2005). Reliability, validity, and factor structure of the Creative Achievement Questionnaire. *Creativity Research Journal, 17*, 37–50. https://doi.org/10.1207/s15326934crj1701_4

Carlsson, I., Wendt, P. E., & Risberg, J. (2000). On the neurobiology of creativity. Differences in frontal activity between high and low creative subjects. *Neuropsychologia, 38*, 873–885. https://doi.org/10.1016/S0028-3932(99)00128-1

Chand, G. B., Wu, J., Hajjar, I., & Qiu, D. (2017). Interactions of the salience network and its subsystems with the default-mode and the central-executive networks in normal aging and mild cognitive impairment. *Brain Connectivity, 7*(7), 401–412. https://doi.org/10.1089/brain.2017.0509

Chen, Q., Yang, W., Li, W., et al. (2014). Association of creative achievement with cognitive flexibility by a combined voxel-based morphometry and resting-state functional connectivity study. *NeuroImage*, *102*, 474–483. doi:10.1016/j.neuroimage.2014.08.008

Chermahini, S. A., & Hommel, B. (2012). More creative through positive mood? Not everyone! *Frontiers in Human Neuroscience*, *6*, 1–7. https://doi.org/10.3389/fnhum.2012.00319

Christensen, P. R., Guilford, J. P. (1958). *Creativity/Fluency Scales*. Sheridan Supply.

Chrysikou, E. G. (2018). The costs and benefits of cognitive control for creativity. In O. Vartanian & R. E. Jung (Eds.), *The Cambridge Handbook of the Neuroscience of Creativity* (pp. 299–317). Cambridge University Press. https://doi.org/10.1017/9781316556238.018

Chrysikou, E. G. (2019). Creativity in and out of (cognitive) control. *Current Opinion in Behavioral Sciences*, *27*, 94–99. https://doi.org/10.1016/j.cobeha.2018.09.014

Chrysikou, E. G., Weber, M., & Thompson-Schill, S. L. (2014). A matched filter hypothesis for cognitive control. *Neuropsychologia, 62,* 341–355. https://doi.org/10.1016/j.neuropsychologia.2013.10.021

Clapham, M. M. (2001). The effects of affect manipulation and information exposure on divergent thinking. *Creativity Research Journal*, *13*, 335–350. https://doi.org/10.1207/S15326934CRJ1334_11

Cools, R., Sheridan, M., Jacobs, E., & D'Esposito, M. (2007). Impulsive personality predicts dopamine-dependent changes in frontostriatal activity during component processes of working memory. *Journal of Neuroscience*, *27*, 5506–5514. https://doi.org/10.1523/JNEUROSCI.0601-07.2007

Costa, C. G., Zhou, Q., & Ferreira, A. I. (2020). State and trait anger predicting creative process engagement – The role of emotion regulation. *The Journal of Creative Behavior, 54*(1), 5–19. https://doi.org/10.1002/jocb.236

Davis, C., Zai, C. C., Adams, N., Bonder, R., & Kennedy, J. L. (2019). Oxytocin and its association with reward-based personality traits: A multilocus genetic profile (MLGP) approach. *Personality and Individual Differences*, *138*, 231–236. https://doi.org/10.1016/j.paid.2018.09.002

Dennison, M., Whittle, S., Yucel, M., et al. (2015). Trait positive affect is associated with hippocampal volume and change in caudate volume across adolescence. *Cognitive, Affective, & Behavioral Neuroscience*, *15*(1), 80–94. https://doi.org/10.3758/s13415–0140319-2.

Dedovic, K., Rexroth, M., Wolff, E., et al. (2009). Neural correlates of processing stressful information: An event-related fMRI study. *Brain Research, 1293*, 49–60. https://doi.org/10.1016/j.brainres.2009.06.044

De Dreu, C. K. W., Baas, M., & Nijstad, B. A. (2008). Hedonic tone and activation level in the mood-creativity link: Toward a dual pathway to creativity model. *Journal of Personality and Social Psychology*, *94*(5), 739–756. https://doi.org/10.1037/0022-3514.94.5.739

Dickerson, S. S., & Kemeny, M. E. (2004). Acute stressors and cortisol responses: A theoretical integration and synthesis of laboratory research. *Psychological Bulletin, 130*, 355–391. https://doi.org/10.1037/0033-2909.130.3.355

Dreisbach, G., Goschke, T. (2004). How positive affect modulates cognitive control: Reduced perseveration at the cost of increased distractibility. *Journal of Experimental Psychology: Learning, Memory, & Cognition*, *30*, 343–353. https://doi.org/10.1037/0278-7393.30.2.343

Duan, H., Wang, X., Hu, W., & Kounios, J. (2020). Effects of acute stress on divergent and convergent problem-solving. *Thinking & Reasoning, 26*(1), 1–19. https://doi.org/10.1080/13546783.2019.1572539

Duan, H., Wang, X., Wang, Z., et al. (2019). Acute stress shapes creative cognition in trait anxiety. *Frontiers in Psychology, 10*, 1517. https://doi.org/10.3389/fpsyg.2019.01517

Eskine, K. E., Anderson, A. E., Sullivan, M., Golob, E. J. (2020). Effects of music listening on creative cognition and semantic memory retrieval. *Psychology of Music, 48*, 513–528. https://doi.org/10.1177/0305735618810792

Feng, Q., He, L., Yang, W., et al. (2019). Verbal creativity is correlated with the dynamic reconfiguration of brain networks in the resting state. *Frontiers in Psychology, 10*, 894. https://doi.org/10.3389/fpsyg.2019.00894

Fink, A., Schwab, D., & Papousek, I. (2011). Sensitivity of EEG upper alpha activity to cognitive and affective creativity interventions. *International Journal of Psychophysiology, 82*(3), 233–239. https://doi.org/10.1016/j.ijpsycho.2011.09.003

Fox, M. D., Snyder, A. Z., Vincent, J. L., et al. 2005). The human brain is intrinsically organized into dynamic, anticorrelated functional networks. *Proceedings of the National Academy of Sciences of the United States of America, 102*(27), 9673–9678. https://doi.org/10.1073/pnas.0504136102

Gao, Z., Zhang, D., Liang, A., et al. (2017). Exploring the associations between intrinsic brain connectivity and creative ability using functional connectivity strength and connectome analysis. *Brain Connectivity, 7*(9), 590–601. https://doi.org/10.1089/brain.2017.0510

Gianaros, P. J., & Wager, T. D. (2015) Brain-body pathways linking psycho-logical stress and physical health. *Current Directions in Psychological Science, 24*, 313–321. https ://doi.org/10.1177/09637 21415 58147 6

Goulden, N., Khusnulina, A., Davis, N. J., et al. (2014). The salience network is responsible for switching between the default mode network and the central executive network: Replication from DCM. *Neuroimage, 99*, 180–190. https://doi.org/10.1016/j.neuroimage.2014.05.052

Greicius, M. D., Srivastava, G., Reiss, A. L., & Menon, V. (2004). Default-mode network activity distinguishes Alzheimer's disease from healthy aging: evidence from functional MRI. *Proceedings of the National Academy of Sciences of the United States of America, 101*, 4637–4642. https://doi.org/10.1073/pnas.0308627101

Herman, J. P. (2011). Central nervous-system regulation of the hypotha-lamic–pituit-ary–adrenal axis stress response. In C. D. Conrad (Ed.), *The Handbook of Stress: Neuropsychological Effects on the Brain* (pp. 29–46). Wiley.

Herman, J. P., Ostrander, M. M., Mueller, N. K., & Figueiredo, H. (2005). Limbic system mechanisms of stress regulation: Hypothalamo–pituitary–adrenocortical axis. *Progress in Neuro-Psychopharmacology & Biological Psychiatry, 29*, 1201–1213. https://doi.org/10.1016/j.pnpbp.2005.08.006

Hermans, E. J., Van Marle, H. J. F., Ossewaarde, L., et al. (2011). Stress-related noradrenergic activity prompts large-scale neural network reconfiguration. *Science, 334*, 1151–1153. https://doi.org/10.1126/science.1209603

Heilman, K. M., Nadeau, S. E., & Beversdorf, D. Q. (2003). Creative innovation: possible brain mechanisms. *Neurocase, 9*, 369–379. https://doi.org/10.1076/neur.9.5.369.16553

Hwang, T. J., & Choi, J. N. (2020). Different moods lead to different creativity: Mediating roles of ambiguity tolerance and team identification. *Creativity Research Journal, 32*(2), 161–173. https://doi.org/10.1080/10400419.2020.1751542

Isen, A. M., & Baron, R. A. (1991). Positive affect as a factor in organizational behavior. *Research in Organizational Behavior, 13*, 1–53.

Ismaylova, E., Sante, J. D., Gouin, J.-P., et al. (2018). Associations between daily mood states and brain gray matter volume, resting-state functional connectivity and task-based activity in healthy adults. *Frontiers in Human Neuroscience, 12*, 168. https://doi.org/10.3389/fnhum.2018.00168

Jung, R. E., Mead, B. S., Carrasco, J., & Flores, R. A. (2013). The structure of creative cognition in the human brain. *Frontiers in Human Neuroscience, 7*, 330. https://doi.org/10.3389/fnhum.2013.00330

Jung, R. E., Segall, J. M., Jeremy Bockholt, H., et al. (2010). Neuroanatomy of creativity. *Human Brain Mapping, 31*, 398–409. https://doi-org/10.1002/hbm.20874

Jung, R. E., & Vartanian, O. (Eds.). (2018). *The Cambridge Handbook of the Neuroscience of Creativity.* Cambridge University Press.

Kao, C. C., & Chiou, W. B. (2020). The moderating role of agreeableness in the relationship between experiencing anger and creative performance. *The Journal of Creative Behavior, 54*(4), 964–974. https://doi.org/10.1002/jocb.425

Kensinger, E. A., & Ford, J. H. (2021). Guiding the emotion in emotional memories: The role of the dorsomedial prefrontal cortex. *Current Directions in Psychological Science, 30*(2), 111–119. https://doi.org/10.1177/0963721421990081

Kraljevic, N. K., Schaare, H. L., Eickhoff, S. B., et al. (2021). Behavioral, anatomical and heritable convergence of affect and cognition in superior frontal cortex. *NeuroImage, 243*, 118561. https://doi.org/10.1016/j.neuroimage.2021.118561

Kaufmann, G., & Vosburg, S. K. (1997). "Paradoxical" mood effects on creative problem-solving. *Cognition and Emotion, 11*, 151–170. https://doi.org/10.1080/026999397379971

Kenett, Y. N., Medaglia, J. D., Beaty, R. E., et al. (2018). Driving the brain towards creativity and intelligence: A network control theory analysis. *Neuropsychologia*, 1–12. https://doi.org/10.1016/j.neuropsychologia.2018.01.001

Khalil, R., Goode, B., & Karim, A. A. (2019). The link between creativity, cognition, and creative drives and underlying neural mechanisms. *Frontiers in Neural Circuits, 13*, 18. https://doi.org/10.3389/fncir.2019.00018

Lader, M. (1988). Beta-adrenergic antagonists in neuropsychiatry: An update. *Journal of Clinical Psychiatry, 49*, 213–223. https://europepmc.org/article/med/2897959

Laverdue, B., & Boulenger, J. P. (1991). Medications beta-bloquantes et anxiete. Un interet therapeutique certain. [Beta-blocking drugs and anxiety. A proven therapeutic value.] *L'Encephale, 17*, 481–492. https://europepmc.org/article/med/1686251

Lyubomirsky, S., King, L., & Diener, E. (2005). The benefits of frequent positive affect: Does happiness lead to success? *Psychological Bulletin, 131*, 803–855. https://doi.org/10.1037/0033-2909.131.6.803

Mayseless, N., Eran, A., & Shamay-Tsoory, S. G. (2015). Generating original ideas: The neural underpinning of originality. *NeuroImage, 116*(C), 232–239. http://doi.org/10.1016/j.neuroimage.2015.05.030

McPherson, M. J., Barrett, F. S., Lopez-Gonzalez, M., Jiradejvong, P., & Limb, C. J. (2016). Emotional intent modulates the neural substrates of creativity: An fMRI study of emotionally targeted improvisation in jazz musicians. *Scientific Reports*, *6*(1), 18460. https://doi.org/10.1038/srep18460

Montijn, N. D., Gerritsen, L., & Engelhard, I. M. (2021). Forgetting the future: Emotion improves memory for imagined future events in healthy individuals but not individuals with anxiety. *Psychological Science*, 1–11. https://doi.org/10.1177/0956797620972491

Mumford, M. D. (2003). Where have we been, where are we going? Taking stock in creativity research. *Creativity Research Journal*, *15*, 107–120. https://doi.org/10.1080/10400419.2003.9651403

Nijstad, B. A., De Dreu, C. K. W., Rietzschel, E. F., & Baas, M., (2010). The dual pathway to creativity model: Creative ideation as a function of flexibility and persistence. *European Review of Social Psychology*, *21*, 34–77. https://doi.org/10.1080/10463281003765323

Noack, H., Nolte, L., Nieratschker, V., Habel, U., & Derntl, B. (2019). Imaging stress: An overview of stress induction methods in the MR scanner. *Journal of Neural Transmission*, *126*(9), 1187–1202. https://doi.org/10.1007/s00702-018-01965-y

Perchtold, C. M., Papousek, I., Koschutnig, K., et al. (2018). Affective creativity meets classic creativity in the scanner. *Human Brain Mapping*, *39*(1), 393–406. https://doi.org/10.1002/hbm.23851

Provenzano, J., Verduyn, P., Daniels, N., Fossati, P., & Kuppens, P. (2019). Mood congruency effects are mediated by shifts in salience and central executive network efficiency. *Social Cognitive and Affective Neuroscience*, *14*(9), 987–995. https://doi.org/10.1093/scan/nsz065

Qi, D., Lam, C. L. M., Wong, J. J., Chang, D. H. F., & Lee, T. M. C. (2021). Positive affect is inversely related to the salience and emotion network's connectivity. *Brain Imaging and Behavior*, *15*(4), 2031–2039. https://doi.org/10.1007/s11682-020-00397-1

Raichle, M. E. (2015). The brain's default mode network. *Annual Review of Neuroscience*, *38*, 433–447. https://doi.org/10.1146/annurev-neuro-071013-014030

Raichle, M. E., MacLeod, A. M., Snyder, A. Z., et al. (2001). A default mode of brain function. *Proceedings of the National Academy of Sciences of the United States of America*, *98*(2), 676–682. https://doi.org/10.1073/pnas.98.2.676

Rohr, C. S., Okon-Singer, H., Craddock, R. C., Villringer, A., & Margulies, D. S. (2013). Affect and the brain's functional organization: A resting-state connectivity approach. *PLoS ONE*, *8*(7), e68015. https://doi.org/10.1371/journal.pone.0068015.

Runco, M. A., & Jaeger, G. J. (2012). The standard definition of creativity. *Creativity Research Journal*, *24*(1), 92–96. https://doi.org/10.1080/10400419.2012.650092

Sanchez, T. A., Mocaiber, I., Erthal, F. S., et al. (2015). Amygdala responses to unpleasant pictures are influenced by task demands and positive affect trait. *Frontiers in Human Neuroscience*, *9*, 107. https://doi.org/10.3389/fnhum.2015.00107

Saggar, M., Volle, E., Uddin, L. Q., Chrysikou, E. G., & Green, A. E. (2021). Creativity and the brain: An editorial introduction to the special issue on the neuroscience of creativity. *NeuroImage*, *231*, 117836. https://doi.org/10.1016/j.neuroimage.2021.117836.

Sawyer, R. K. (2006). *Explaining Creativity: The Science of Human Innovation*. Oxford University Press.

Seeley, W. W., Menon, V., Schatzberg, A. F., et al. (2007). Dissociable intrinsic connectivity networks for salience processing and executive control. *Journal of Neuroscience, 27*, 2349–2356. http://doi.org/10.1523/JNEUROSCI.5587-06.2007

Shi, L., Sun, J., Xia, Y., et al. (2018). Large-scale brain network connectivity underlying creativity in resting-state and task fMRI: Cooperation between default network and frontal-parietal network. *Biological Psychology, 135*, 102–111. https://doi.org/10.1016/j.biopsycho.2018.03.005

Simonton, D. K. (1999). Creativity as blind variation and selective retention: Is the creative process Darwinian? *Psychological Inquiry, 10*, 309–328. https://www.jstor.org/stable/1449455

Simonton, D. K. (2010). Creative thought as blind-variation and selective-retention: Combinatorial models of exceptional creativity. *Physics of Life Reviews, 7*, 156–179. https:/doi.org/10.1016/j.plrev.2010.02.002

Sridharan, D., Levitin, D. J., & Menon, V. (2008). A critical role for the right fronto-insular cortex in switching between central-executive and default-mode networks. *Proceedings of the National Academy of Sciences of the United States of America, 105*(34), 12569–12574. https://doi.org/10.1073/pnas.0800005105

Strasbaugh, K., & Connelly, S. (2021). The influence of anger and anxiety on idea generation: Taking a closer look at integral and incidental emotion effects. *Psychology of Aesthetics, Creativity, and the Arts*. Advance online publication. https://doi.org/10.1037/aca0000400

Sun, J., Liu, Z., Rolls, E. T., et al. (2019). Verbal creativity correlates with the temporal variability of brain networks during the resting state. *Cerebral Cortex, 29*(3), 1047–1058. https://doi.org/10.1093/cercor/bhy010

To, M. L., Fisher, C. D., & Ashkanasy, N. M. (2015). Unleashing angst: Negative mood, learning goal orientation, psychological empowerment and creative behaviour. *Human Relations, 68*(10), 1601–1622. https://doi.org/10.1177/0018726714562235

To, M. L., Fisher, C. D., Ashkanasy, N. M., & Rowe, P. A. (2012). Within-person relationships between mood and creativity. *Journal of Applied Psychology, 97*(3), 599–612. https://doi.org/10.1037/a0026097

Van Kleef, G. A., Anastasopoulou, C., & Nijstad, B. A. (2010). Can expressions of anger enhance creativity? A test of the emotions as social information (EASI) model. *Journal of Experimental Social Psychology, 46*(6), 1042–1048. https://doi.org/10.1016/j.jesp.2010.05.015

Vartanian, O., Beatty, E. L., Smith, I., et al. (2018). One-way traffic: The inferior frontal gyrus controls brain activation in the middle temporal gyrus and inferior parietal lobule during divergent thinking. *Neuropsychologia, 118*, 68–78. https://doi.org/10.1016/j.neuropsychologia.2018.02.024

Vartanian, O., Saint, S. A., Herz, N., & Suedfeld, P. (2020). The creative brain under stress: Considerations for performance in extreme environments. *Frontiers in Psychology, 11*, 585969. https://doi.org.10.3389/fpsyg.2020.585969

Verhaeghen, P., Joormann, J., & Khan, R. (2005). Why we sing the blues: The relation between self-reflective rumination, mood, and creativity. *Emotion, 5*, 226–232. https://doi.org/10.1037/1528-3542.5.2.226

Vosburg, S. K. (1998). The effects of positive and negative mood on divergent-thinking performance. *Creativity Research Journal, 11*, 165–172. https://doi.org/10.1207/s15326934crj1102_6

Weiss, H. M. W., & Merlo, K. L. (2020). Affect, attention, and episodic performance. *Current Directions in Psychological Science*, 1–7. https://doi.org/10.1177/0963721420949496

Wang, X., Duan, H., Kan, Y., et al. (2019). The creative thinking cognitive process influenced by acute stress in humans: an electroencephalography study. *Stress, 22*(4), 472–481. https://doi.org/10.1080/10253890.2019.1604665

Yang, J.-S., & Hung, H. V. (2015). Emotions as constraining and facilitating factors for creativity: Companionate love and anger. *Creativity and Innovation Management, 24*(2), 217–230. https://doi.org/10.1111/caim.12089

Yeh, Y., Lai, G.-J., Lin, C. F., Lin, C.-W., & Sun, H.-C. (2015). How stress influences creativity in game-based situations: Analysis of stress hormones, negative emotions, and working memory. *Computers & Education, 81*, 143–153. https://doi.org/10.1016/j.compedu.2014.09.011

Zabelina, D. L., & Andrews-Hanna, J. R. (2016). Dynamic network interactions supporting internally-oriented cognition. *Current Opinion in Neurobiology, 40*, 86–93. https://doi.org/10.1016/j.conb.2016.06.014

7 Attention, Affect, and Creativity, from Mindfulness to Mind-Wandering

Stephanie J. Kane, Kim N. Awa, Joshua D. Upshaw, Kent Hubert, Carl E. Stevens Jr., Darya L. Zabelina

Introduction

Our ability to imagine and create unique works of art, literature, music, and innumerable other artifacts, could be considered as the defining aspect of our species. Being human is characterized by an innate cognitive capacity for observation, reflection, and creation for the purpose of promoting richness in our lives. By thinking creatively, we can solve challenges in innovative ways, thus allowing us to adapt to a continually changing world.

The psychological construct of creativity is defined as the ability to develop something unique and contextually useful (Guilford, 1967). This very broad description includes everything from works of art to new scientific theories. What is considered unique and useful can vary broadly, so even with these guidelines in hand, creative works can still be difficult to analyze experimentally. Despite this challenge, creativity researchers have developed numerous methods to address this issue.

Historically, experimental tasks investigating creative cognition have primarily focused on two types of creative thinking: convergent and divergent thinking. Convergent thinking is the ability to decide on a single best creative solution to a problem (Mednick, 1962). In contrast, divergent thinking involves the exploration of multiple possible creative solutions to open-ended problems (Guilford, 1967). Another way to measure creativity is by assessing actual creative achievements, as opposed to in-lab tests of creative ability (e.g., Carson et al., 2005). All of these methods are discussed in subsequent sections.

Given the somewhat nebulous nature of creativity, a useful way to understand how it fits into the fields of psychology and neuroscience is to investigate its relationships to other well-known domains within those broader areas of research. Specifically, we will look at creativity in relation to, and through the lenses of, (1) attention, (2) emotion, and (3) mindfulness. Then we will attempt to tie these domains together to paint a relatively comprehensive picture of the psychology

This research was supported in part by the Office of Naval Research grant #N00014–21-1-2213 to DLZ. Correspondence concerning this book chapter should be addressed to Darya L. Zabelina, Department of Psychological Science, 480 Campus Drive, Fayetteville, AR 72701. Ph: 479-575-5813. Email: dlzabeli@uark.edu.

and neuroscience of the creative brain. Finally, we will look at the leading edge of creativity research and entertain a few ideas about its possible future.

Attention and Creativity

Thinking creatively and producing creative works involves a dynamically balanced system of cognitive processes that concurrently support and influence each other (for overview, see Abraham, 2018). To a large degree, harnessing one's creative abilities requires the recruitment of a multifaceted system of attentional processes. For instance, being creative may require one to recognize potential solutions and disregard distracting information – a cognitive process known as selective, or focused, attention (Posner, 1988). In contrast, people with higher levels of leaky, or diffused, attention may more easily generate and recognize potential solutions by allowing a greater amount of information into their awareness (Carson, 2011). Creative thinking and attention are inextricably linked and, importantly, attentional capacities vary between individuals and across multiple subtypes of attention (e.g., focused, diffused, flexible; Zabelina, 2018). When empirically investigating creative cognition, attentional processes need to be thoughtfully considered in a broader context. This section discusses prior work investigating the connections between attention and creativity.

Who Says You Can't Teach an Old RAT New Tricks? The Role of Convergent Thinking

Research on convergent thinking has found it to be supported by a narrow attentional scope during semantic knowledge retrieval (Mendelsohn, 1974). Tasks assessing convergent thinking tend to be oriented more toward a specific goal than divergent thinking tasks, and performance on these tasks is therefore supported by greater focused attention (Colzato et al., 2012). For example, during the Remote Associates Task (RAT; Mednick, 1962) participants are provided a list of seemingly semantically unrelated words, such as *pine, crab, sauce*, and asked to provide the single best linking word – in this case, *apple*. People are said to converge on answers in one of two ways: creative insight – a sudden '*Aha!*' or '*eureka*' moment – or via analysis – a deliberate, trial-and-error approach (Kounios & Beeman, 2009).

Prior EEG studies have demonstrated that solving problems with creative insight or analysis is linked with distinct patterns of neural activation (Kounios & Beeman, 2009). For example, Jung-Beeman and colleagues (2004) found that immediately before a creative insight emerged into consciousness, there was an increase in alpha-band activity, followed by a burst of gamma activity. Greater alpha activity is suggested to reflect higher levels of internally directed attention, while gamma is considered to indicate higher levels of focused attention when engaging with external sensory information (Tallon-Baudry & Bertrand, 1999).

Two Roads Diverged in a Wood: De"Frost"ing Our Attention

In contrast to converging on a single solution in convergent thinking tasks, a divergent thinking task typically presents a problem and asks people to generate many possible creative solutions to that problem (Guilford, 1950). For example, in the Torrance Test of Creative Thinking (Goff & Torrance, 2002), participants are provided incomplete figure drawings and are asked to complete them within a short amount of time. Participants are given little guidance and are not given a clear goal. Those who draw more unique and complex figures are considered to have greater divergent thinking ability. Multiple theories exist about which type of attention is most beneficial for divergent thinking. Some work shows that divergent thinking is linked with greater flexibility of attention (Zabelina et al., 2016). Similarly, people with better divergent thinking abilities are considered to be more likely to filter out "irrelevant" sensory stimuli, as assessed with the P50 event-related potential (ERP; Zabelina et al., 2015).

Like convergent thinking, divergent thinking is associated with increased alpha activity in frontal and parietal regions (Benedek et al., 2011). One study found people who generated more remote (i.e., creative) ideas on a divergent thinking task had an increased ability to sustain alpha synchronization in temporo-parietal brain regions (Camarda et al., 2018). Another EEG study found that more creative people, determined by their ability to generate more unique image captions, demonstrated greater functional connectivity between mid-frontal and occipital cortices (Wokke et al., 2018). This suggests that creative people may have an enhanced capacity for long-range neural communication.

Everyday I'm Shuffling (My Creativity): Real-World Creativity and Attentional Shifting

Experimental tasks designed to assess creative cognition (i.e., divergent and convergent thinking tasks) are one strategy for measuring creative thinking ability. Another strategy to gauge the extent of one's creativity involves assessing lifetime creative accomplishments. Better known as "real-world" creative achievement, this method assesses an individual's achievements across multiple domains of creative pursuits (e.g., visual arts, comedy, science, architecture). Example measures include the Creative Achievement Questionnaire (Carson, et al., 2005) and the Inventory of Creative Activities and Achievements (Diedrich et al., 2018).

Higher levels of "real-world" creative accomplishments have been associated with defocused or leaky attention (Zabelina et al., 2016). This form of attention may afford one a perceptual "open-mindedness" (Feist, 1999). It could indeed be useful for creative inspiration, yet it is also linked with a decreased ability to disregard irrelevant information (Carson et al, 2003). Leaky attention can come with potential costs, such as increased distractibility, attentional disorders, and other forms of psychopathology (Carson, 2011). Findings from electrophysiological studies have also reported that people with more real-world creative achievements show an increased tendency for "leaky attention." (Zabelina et al., 2015). Specifically, people with more real-world creative achievement demonstrated greater engagement of neural resources underlying early sensory processes when presented with "irrelevant" auditory stimuli on a sensory gating task, as assessed with a P50 ERP.

Not the Unused Gym Equipment: Stair-Stepping Our Way into a Creative Future

An important, yet less understood, aspect of the relationship between attention and creativity is the dynamic interplay of various forms of attention during different stages of the creative process (Zabelina, 2018). Diffuse attention may be the most relevant form of attention during the idea-generation stage of the creative process when there is no clear solution to a problem. Diffuse attention may reduce the fixedness of more common ideas, allowing more creative solutions to emerge. Focused attention may be more relevant during the idea implementation stage of the creative process. Flexible attention may be the most important attentional capacity needed to generate creative ideas and subsequently follow through with a creative production.

Although it seems that all forms of attention play some role in the creative process, we also need to explore how a lack of attention relates to creativity. According to the meaning-and-attentional-components model, the feeling of boredom can range from high to low arousal, but the outcome may feel similar – a disinterest and disengagement of attention in continuing goal-directed behavior (Westgate, 2020). The cognitive resources required to engage in activities that elicit boredom may feel taxing, but Gasper and Middlewood (2014) found that people who felt boredom (and elation) performed better on associative thought tasks, in comparison to those who felt distressed or relaxed. Boredom as an attentional resource then acts in a feedback loop to modify our goal-oriented behaviors (Tam et al., 2021).

Attention, and even a lack thereof, in combination with our emotions paints a broader picture of how our internally directed systems influence our creative cognition. Naturally, we then should explore the way in which our valence, activation, and regulation fold into our creative behaviors and shape the creative person.

Emotions and Creativity

So far, we have seen how our attention and ability to connect information are extremely dynamic; our cognitive resources are both benefited and disadvantaged depending on the context of our goals. How then do our emotions emerge as an additional moderator in who the creative person is? In a critical examination of the stereotypes of stand-up comedians, Lintott (2020) stated that a comedian is seen as an "intelligent narcissist ... stymied by severe social anxiety and introversion, with a desperate and insatiable need for attention and validation fueled by past neglect, abandonment, or loneliness ..." (p. 200). The belief of the role of emotion, or, more stereotypically, an imbalance of emotion, seems to saturate our society. Even past research has examined the relationships between mood disorders, creativity, and the history behind these beliefs (Dietrich, 2014; Jamison et al., 1980). Is the prevalence of this trope based on fragments of truth? Benedek and colleagues (2021) found that despite the advancement of empirical evidence denouncing many commonly held beliefs about creativity, around 50% of people still endorse certain creativity-related myths (e.g., children are more creative than adults and creative accomplishments result from sudden inspiration).

The myth of the creative person as being aloof, a touch mad, or a rare bird may seem alluring, but what does that mean for someone who wishes to deepen their creativity? Under these trait-typic assumptions, are people expected to surface their emotional turmoil to generate and externalize more original ideas or products? Is being happy a kiss of death to the creative person and their process? In this section, we examine the current research on the emotion-creativity link and review how context can shape the types of emotional processing we use in everyday creativity. Lastly, we review potential reasons why emotions act as moderators for creative thinking.

Understanding and Defining Emotions

The link between emotions and creativity can be examined using three broad dimensions: valence, activation, and regulation. Much like valence, which can be understood on a positive and negative dimension, activation levels categorize emotions as either activating or deactivating. Emotions such as boredom, calmness, and depression are categorized as deactivating states of emotion, whereas excitement, nervousness, and alertness are activating states (Russell, 1980). It is through an interrelated system of activating/deactivating physiological arousal and our cognitive interpretations of the context that we experience a particular emotion (Posner et al., 2005).

While activation and valence account for our physiological state and cognitive appraisal, these dimensions fail to account for the motivations of our actions. The third dimension, regulation, allows researchers to better understand how emotions determine the desirability of an action based on two-dimensional subscales: prevention and promotion (Higgins, 1997). Under this model, promotion is understood as self-regulation toward a desired goal or outcome, whereas prevention focuses on regulatory systems that aid in the avoidance of undesirable end-states. When we factor in the relationship between our motivational systems and affect, we can paint a fuller picture of aids to creativity. This approach goes beyond simply finding associations between emotions and creativity. Rather, by incorporating self-regulatory models in the exploration of the creative process, we can utilize our emotions as tools to aid in our own creativity.

Walking on Sunshine: The Role of Positive Emotions

Baas and colleagues (2008) conducted a meta-analysis categorizing 66 reports of mood and creativity research on three broad scales: hedonic tone, activation level, and regulatory focus. They found that positive moods were associated with more enhanced creativity, compared to mood-neutral states. Support for the role of positive emotions in creativity was also found in daily diary studies (Amabile et al., 2005; Conner & Silvia, 2015; Silvia et al., 2014; To et al., 2012). The researchers found that those who felt high activation and positive affect (e.g., excitement) reported more daily creativity.

Similarly, Benedek and colleagues (2019) found that enjoyment and expression are the strongest motivations for overall everyday creativity, but those motivations may not be so straightforward. The same study found that people reported having different motivations for pursuing tasks in their free time and that their motivations were associated with creative domain types. For example, they found that people who engaged in visual arts reported being strongly motivated by expression, whereas those who engaged in music and literature were strongly motivated by coping. They went on to suggest that emotions and everyday creative behavior may be bidirectional – the variability in motivation to pursue various creative activities suggests that the activities themselves may be ways of seeking out positive emotions.

Our emotional states not only facilitate ideation and act as motivators for pursuing creative activities, they also nourish positive affect (Conner et al., 2018). Those who engaged in creative pursuits on day one reported feeling more energetic, enthusiastic, and excited (high activation positive affect) the following day. Although there were emotional carry-over effects, future engagement in creative activities was not related to emotional states. High-activation positive affect seems to the be main ingredient in everyday creativity (Baas et al., 2008; De Dreu et al., 2008; Han et al., 2019), but can it really be that straightforward that enhanced creativity merely requires being in a highly active and positive mood? In a five-day experience sampling study, Zhang and colleagues (2020) found differences in flexibility and originality scores for students: People in positive mood states had higher flexibility scores, whereas people in negative mood states had higher originality scores. One's ability to think creatively seems to depend on the interplay between mood and the context of the task at hand.

Adding Fuel to the Creative Fire: The Importance of Context and Affect

Dumas and Dunbar (2016) found that people performed comparatively worse on divergent thinking tasks when they were told to take inhibiting perspectives (e.g., take the perspective of a rigid librarian vs an eccentric poet). Divergent thinking scores both improved and diminished in the presence of stereotypic manipulation, which suggests that the malleability of divergent thinking may depend heavily on the cognitive framing of the task (Zuo et al., 2019).

Friedman and colleagues (2007) found that participants who were positively induced produced more ideas when the framing of the alternative uses task was fun and silly. On the other hand, those who were induced negatively demonstrated higher fluency when the task was framed as being serious. The study shows us that goal-oriented behaviors are elicited from negative and positive emotions that are compatible with the interpretation of the task. Incompatible moods may then be beneficial if the participant reframes the task as requiring more deliberate processing (Isen, 2001). In another study comparing the effects of divergent and convergent thinking tasks on mood, researchers found that divergent thinking resulted in more positive mood, while convergent thinking resulted in more negative mood (Chermahini & Hommel, 2012). Likewise, Hirt and colleagues (2008) found that happy participants performed better on idea-tion tasks and exhibited greater cognitive flexibility.

These findings suggest that different creativity tasks rely on contrasting types of cognitive control. Depending on the desired end-state, our emotions then act as a resource for us to achieve those goals. For example, being in a positive state may help us generate more ideas while writing a draft, whereas being in a negative state could help us be more critical in editing down content in a manuscript. We need to remember that both positive and negative states of emotion are in a delicate dance with each other, shifting and adapting based on our end goals and the context of those goals.

Cognitive Benefits: The Power of Positivity Compels You

The benefits of positive states of emotion include enhanced cognitive flexibility (De Dreu et al., 2011), broader thought–action repertoires (Sugawara & Sugie, 2021), enhanced problem solving and decision making (Isen, 2001), and better global processing (Baas et al., 2008). Our ability to approach problems can be understood through Higgins' (1997) proposal that promotion-focused end-states combine with emotions that aid in the motivations toward those goals. The activation of promotion and prevention systems through our emotions indicate our success (or lack thereof) toward desired end-states. For example, happiness is categorized as a pleasant, promotion-based emotion that acts as a cognitive green light for our course of action. If we are having fun with a task, we have more incentive to continue and thus improve creative performance.

Time Flies When You're Feeling ... Sad?

If positive emotions are found to aid in cognitive flexibility and on divergent thinking tasks, surely all we need in order to think of as many creative ways to use a brick as possible is to be in a good mood, right? Kaufmann and Vosburg (2002) found that positive moods led to a higher number of ideas in the early stages of creativity tasks, but negative mood (in addition to the control group) led to higher number of ideas later in production. Likewise, Lai and colleagues (2021) examined affective shifting and found that the people who ended the task in the positive affect condition had a decrease in creative ideation over time. The inverse was found for those ending in the negative affect condition, such that their creative ideation performance actually increased over time. Depending on the direction of our affective shifts, ideating would then have a suite of returns; the downside to this is we do not deliberately pick and choose our emotions to use at our convenience. Manipulating mood in the lab aids our understanding of the bidirectional relationship between creative cognition and our emotions, but this does not give insight into how our emotional intensities influence those cognitive processes.

To and colleagues (2012) found that not only were high-activating positive moods associated with creative process engagement, but so were high-activating negative moods. Highly activating states of positive and negative arousal promote creative performance via cognitive flexibility and the persistence to continuously work on a task (De Dreu et al., 2008). Unfortunately, persistence as a cognitive resource is typically underestimated and therefore, underutilized (Lucas & Nordgren, 2015). Highly activating negative states like anger and fear signal that the problem at hand requires more attention and analytical processing. Deactivating positive states like relief, on the other hand, signal the problem is resolved. The internal pressure that negative moods elicit may, ironically, motivate us to work more decisively toward a goal.

Although negative states of arousal facilitate more critical evaluations of moderately creative ideas, this could hurt one's ability during creative ideation. In other words, if ideas are evaluated more harshly in comparison to when our mood is positive or neutral, we might dismiss novel, workable ideas. Interestingly, non-creative ideas were judged more liberally when people were in a positive state, which could potentially hurt one's ability to determine whether an idea is appropriate or novel (Mastria et al., 2019).

On creative insight and ideation tasks, prevention-focused states (e.g., fear) were found to boost creativity only when the goal was unfulfilled (Baas et al., 2011). When people have a high trait learning orientation, negative emotions (such as fear and anxiety) actually enhance creative engagement (To et al., 2015). These negative emotions reduce our reliance on pre-existing schemas of information, allowing for more critical problem solving (Forgas, 2013). Sadness, although a promotion-focused and deactivating emotion, has been found to be unrelated to enhanced creativity (Baas et al., 2008). Further, being relaxed – a positive, deactivating, and prevention-focused emotion – is not related to enhanced or inhibited creativity (Baas et al., 2008). Though manipulating mood in experimental design yields varying results for creativity, we need to better understand the broad spectrum of everyday emotions and embrace the benefits that these naturally occurring states provide.

Live, Laugh, Love Your Shifting Emotions: The Highs and Lows

As reviewed above, agreement on which affective states are the most beneficial to creativity, and why, is not clear. Perhaps, instead of asking ourselves which emotions are best suited for creative behavior, we should focus on the reciprocal relationship range of emotions and our actions. While there is overwhelming evidence for the benefits of positive affect in creative cognition, negative affective states can have their benefits as well, such as higher accuracy with memory recall (Storbeck & Clore, 2011); better emotional and cognitive conflict processing (Zinchenko et al., 2017); and improved adaptability to goal unfulfillment (Forgas, 2013). Our negative moods motivate our regulatory systems to work toward a desired end-state by investing more attention and effort into the problem. Even during the first year of the COVID-19 outbreak, researchers found associations between negative mood and an increase in emotional and cognitive creativity (Du et al., 2021). Though negative mood has typically been associated with inhibited ideation, the mediating role of rumination during the pandemic seemed to actually aid in creative ideation (Zeng et al., 2021). Those who tend to ruminate may express more openness to ideas, which could result in enhanced creativity. Though rumination is associated with clinical psychopathology (Smith & Alloy, 2009), perhaps we don't necessarily have to embrace the trope of being a tortured artist to garner the benefits of more open ideation. Researchers found that mindfulness-based interventions were associated with less recurring rumination (Blanke et al., 2020), meaning that mindfulness as an emotion-regulation strategy could help us find the balance in regulating emotional states that aid in our creativity without hindering our well-being.

Mindfulness and Creativity

It Takes Two to Tango: Mindfulness and Creativity

The contemporary Westernized description of mindfulness emerged through the creation of Mindfulness-Based Stress Reduction (MBSR) programs developed by American professor and meditation teacher Jon Kabat-Zinn. He defines mindfulness as "paying attention in a particular way: on purpose, in the present moment, and nonjudgmentally" (Kabat-Zinn, 1994, p. 4). In practice, mindful attention and present moment awareness is said to be cultivated through Buddhist meditation techniques (Bishop et al., 2004). Shapiro and colleagues (2006) describe meditation as the "scaffolding" by which mindfulness is reached. To create an operational definition of mindfulness, Baer and colleagues (2006) examined five existing mindfulness self-report questionnaires and identified five clear facets that empirically describe mindfulness. The subsequent measure was named the Five Facet Mindfulness Questionnaire (FFMQ). These five facets are nonreactivity, observing, acting with awareness, describing, and nonjudging.

The relationship between mindfulness and creativity has shown inconsistencies in prior literature. Some of these inconsistencies may be related to the type of mindfulness under investigation (e.g., open-monitoring meditation, focused attention meditation) and the five facets that underlie meditation. Focused attention (FA) meditation requires one to have a sustained focus on a chosen object, thought, or item. Anything that might distract from that focus should be disregarded, and attention must be redirected back to the chosen object (Colzato et al., 2012). There are three regulatory practices that arise during FA meditation: the monitoring of attention to identify distracters, the full disengagement from distracters, and the redirection of attention back to the focal object (Lutz et al., 2008). Beginning meditators must engage these regulatory practices frequently, while practiced meditators can identify distracters with ease, making attention on the focal object less effortful.

While FA meditation requires a focal point, open-monitoring (OM) meditation has no explicit focus on one object. In OM meditation, the mind can observe experiences as they arise without focusing on one particular thing (Lutz et al., 2008). Open-monitoring meditation is said to involve a reflexive awareness of the mind, and, with practice, leads to a less reactive interpretation of one's inner experiences (Lutz et al., 2008).

Divergent thinking has been shown to be enhanced following OM meditation. In a study of experienced meditators, the Alternate Uses Task (AUT) was given after both OM and FM meditation. AUT fluency, flexibility, and originality were significantly improved following OM meditation (versus FA meditation and baseline; Colzato et al., 2012). In an additional study, experienced meditators were given the AUT and a creative drawing task following mindfulness meditation and concentrative meditation (the authors conceptualize mindfulness meditation as OM meditation). The researchers found that meditation significantly increased AUT performance in both conditions, while the creative drawing task showed no effects (Müller et al., 2016). Both studies have the limitations of only using experienced meditators as their sample population, a low sample size, and a lack of randomization to groups, which means conclusions should be interpreted cautiously.

The different skills, or facets, that comprise mindfulness meditation may be differentially related to creative performance. For instance, the mindfulness skill *observe* (to notice, or attend to internal stimuli such as emotions and bodily sensations as well as the external environment, such as sounds and smells) was shown to be consistently associated with enhanced creativity (Baas et al., 2014). In the same study, the mindfulness skills *describe* (the ability to verbally describe or label experiences) and *act with awareness* (the ability to provide undivided attention and focus with full awareness) either did not predict creative performance or were associated with reduced creativity. In another study, the mindfulness component *acting with awareness* was found to enhance creative idea generation at the group level, rather than at the individual level (Baas et al., 2020). Considering these interesting and varied results, more nuanced studies are needed to begin untangling the mechanisms by which mindfulness impacts creative cognition.

A Penny for Your (Wandering) Thoughts? Linking Mind-Wandering and Creativity

The field of mind-wandering (MW) has exploded over the past decade, leading to a difficulty in defining this unique phenomenon. It has been described as involving freely moving, unconstrained thoughts, and stimulus- and task-independent thinking (Christoff et al., 2016). Though not an exhaustive list, common descriptions for MW have included spontaneous thoughts, absent-mindedness, zoning out, and daydreaming. Despite efforts to settle on a universal definition, MW is generally thought of as an attentional shift from the external environment to one's internal thought processes (Smallwood & Schooler, 2015). Mind-wandering is estimated to occupy a substantial portion of the waking day – on average 30–50% (Christoff et al., 2016) – and has been shown to be associated with various cognitive processes, including creativity (Baird et al., 2012; Smallwood & Schooler, 2015). For example, during an investigation of resting-state functional magnetic resonance imaging (fMRI), divergent thinking was shown to be supported by brain regions associated with cognitive control, and with brain regions related to spontaneous processes, such as MW (Beaty et al., 2014). In addition, a task-based fMRI study investigating the evaluative and generative modes of creative thought found that the evaluative phase (estimating the usefulness of the generated novel ideas) was jointly associated with MW and executive control brain regions (Ellamil et al., 2012). These studies point to a relationship between disparate brain networks that underlie both creative thinking and MW, which may also indicate a trait-level relationship between the two.

In examining the impact of MW on creativity, it is important to consider the type of creativity (e.g., divergent and convergent creativity, and real-world creative achievement), task demands, and the intentionality of MW (e.g., deliberate or spontaneous types). The following sections describe the MW–creativity link in relation to the type of creative thought, how demanding a task is, and the intentionality of MW.

Mind-wandering is theorized to support creativity by allowing for free, unconstrained thought processes. This may permit the formation of novel associations, and it may be particularly useful during tests of divergent thinking where individuals are asked to come up with as many new and unusual uses for an object as they can. Experimental evidence for this relationship stems from a seminal paper by Baird and colleagues (2012). The authors varied the task demands during an incubation period (i.e., the temporary shift away from an unsolved problem) to understand the relationship between MW and divergent thinking. They found enhanced problem solving for previously encountered problems during the incubation period in the undemanding task group (versus a demanding task, rest, or no break condition). The authors concluded that allowing the mind to wander, or incubate, during low-demand external tasks may improve creative problem solving. The findings from Baird et al. (2012) were not replicated in a more recent study by Murray and colleagues (2021). Murray et al. suggest that this failure to replicate stems from the operationalization of mind-wandering as task-unrelated thought and that different MW measures might better capture this relationship.

Problem solving is an integral part of creativity. Mind-wandering was found to enhance convergent thinking when researchers used experience sampling probes during a sustained attention to response task (SART) prior to completing the RAT (Leszczynski et al., 2017). The authors found that mind-wandering during the SART prolonged reaction times, which replicated previous findings of MW impacting the SART. At the same time, they found that MW increased the number of creative insights on the RAT. In another task in which experience sampling probes were embedded within the SART during an incubation period, participants completed number-reduction tasks that had a hidden rule; if the rule was found, the problem was considered to be solved (Tan et al., 2015). Participants who solved the problem following the incubation period reported significantly more episodes of MW during the SART. These studies point to the idea that MW may facilitate creative performance on previously seen problems when task demands are low.

A number of studies have investigated the role of MW or daydreaming in real-world creative thinking. In a daily diary study, physicists and professional writers were asked to report on their most creative idea, the contents of their thoughts, what they were doing, and the quality of the idea (Gable et al., 2019). Results indicated that roughly 20% of creative ideas arose during task independent MW, and these ideas were more likely to aid in overcoming an impasse in the individual's work. In another daily diary study, artists provided daily reflections on their work as they created a short film (Benedek et al., 2017). The authors reported that ideas for their work spontaneously arose when they were occupied doing tasks outside of working on the film (i.e., task independent MW) approximately every second day.

The studies investigating the role of MW in real-world creativity also bring up an important distinction in the intentionality of MW episodes. That is, MW episodes can be further described by a deliberate, goal-directed form, and by a spontaneous form that arises outside of cognitive control. Given that MW is not a unitary construct and that creative cognition is a dynamic process, making the distinction between spontaneous and deliberate MW can only serve to give new insight into the organization of the creative process.

Mind-Wandering, Mindfulness, and Creativity: Chicken Soup Ingredients for the Creative Soul

Given the variety of facets that comprise mindfulness, the differing characteristics of MW, and the dynamic nature of creativity, there are many avenues of research to expound upon. For example, Agnoli and colleagues (2018) explored the interactive roles of spontaneous and deliberate MW along with the components of mindfulness on creative thinking. While deliberate MW was a positive predictor of creative performance, spontaneous MW was a negative predictor. Interaction effects between the mindfulness component *acting with awareness* and MW predicted originality in the divergent thinking task, while the mindfulness facet *describe* and spontaneous MW produced the lowest originality scores (Agnoli et al., 2018). In the past, mindfulness and MW have been described as opposing processes, but considering the most recent literature showing their joint relationship in the creative process, it appears that they may not be on opposite ends of the spectrum after all. They may have overlapping functions, or it could be the case that engagement in one construct may produce benefits in the other. Either way, unraveling this relationship is a fruitful area for future research.

Discussion

The role of creativity in humankind is monumental. The production of novel inventions, services, and even the generation of concepts and theories, have erected and altered entire civilizations – the world, in fact. On an individual level, creative cognition is a complex phenomenon that can be difficult to harness. It is likely that a large number of transformative ideas have never taken shape outside the minds in which they were born. Given the various layers of complexity that can prevent ideas from developing to fruition, examining the key components of the creative process will provide a more holistic understanding of the workings of the creative brain.

The previous sections highlighted the roles of attention, emotion, and mindfulness/mind-wandering in creativity. Across these three broad factors, it seems that the more a psychological factor serves remoteness of associations (broad or leaky attention; positive mood; open-monitoring meditation and mind-wandering), the more it benefits divergent thinking. Convergent thinking, on the other hand, is a different beast. This construct of creativity seems to be related to narrower attention and elevated mood, in addition to having inconsistent ties with focused attention meditation.

Creativity is also thought to be bolstered by mind-wandering through incubation periods. Stories about Einstein's ground-breaking insights while working an unstimulating job in a patent office come to mind. It is possible that the loose, inwardly directed attention of MW provides an environment in which far-flung, unconventional shreds of information can emerge together in consciousness and be combined. But this begs the question: Why do people mind-wander? Perhaps Einstein's insights were an escape from boredom. After all, mind-wandering is thought to be a by-product of boredom (Mann & Cadman, 2014), and in this way, it's a stepping-stone to more stimulating thoughts, experiences, and emotions.

In the section on emotion, we discussed the overly romanticized view of elevated creativity as being primarily for individuals who are a bit "mad," "tortured," or otherwise unstable. The bidirectional relationship between emotion and creativity allows us the flexibility and malleability to regulate our emotions and aid in problem solving; however, creativity can be hindered if we fixate on perceived novelty. It is not enough to just "feel happy" to get the best results; rather, we need to recognize the cognitive benefits of our day-to-day affective shifting and take advantage of those times when we aren't feeling our best.

Very few of the connections among these three factors – notwithstanding their subfactors – and creativity are straightforward, isolated, or easy to assess. But that challenge is part of the fun of studying something so delightfully intricate.

References

Abraham, A. (2018). *The Neuroscience of Creativity* (Cambridge Fundamentals of Neuroscience in Psychology). Cambridge University Press. https://doi.org/10.1017/9781316816981

Agnoli, S., Vanucci, M., Pelagatti, C., & Corazza, G. E. (2018). Exploring the link between mind wandering, mindfulness, and creativity: A multidimensional approach. *Creativity Research Journal, 30*(1), 41–53. https://doi.org/10.1080/10400419.2018.1411423

Amabile, T. M., Barsade, S. G., Mueller, J. S., & Staw, B. M. (2005). Affect and creativity at work. *Administrative Science Quarterly, 50*(3), 367–403. https://doi.org/10.2189/asqu.2005.50.3.367

Baas, M., De Dreu, C. K. W., & Nijstad, B. A. (2008). A meta-analysis of 25 years of mood-creativity research: Hedonic tone, activation, or regulatory focus? *Psychological Bulletin, 134*(6), 779–806. https://doi.org/10.1037/a0012815

Baas, M., De Dreu, C. K. W., & Nijstad, B. A. (2011). When prevention promotes creativity: the role of mood, regulatory focus, and regulatory closure. *Journal of Personality and Social Psychology, 100*(5), 794–809. https://doi.org/10.1037/a0022981

Baas, M., Nevicka, B., & Ten Velden, F. S. (2014). Specific mindfulness skills differentially predict creative performance. *Personality and Social Psychology Bulletin, 40*(9), 1092–1106. https://doi.org/10.1177/0146167214535813

Baas, M., Nevicka, B., & Ten Velden, F. S. (2020). When paying attention pays off: The mindfulness skill act with awareness promotes creative idea generation in groups. *European Journal of Work and Organizational Psychology, 29*(4), 619–632. https://doi.org/10.1080/1359432X.2020.1727889

Baer, R. A., Smith, G. T., Hopkins, J., Krietemeyer, J., & Toney, L. (2006). Using self-report assessment methods to explore facets of mindfulness. *Assessment, 13*(1), 27–45. https://doi.org/10.1177/1073191105283504

Baird, B., Smallwood, J., Mrazek, M. D., et al. (2012). Inspired by distraction: Mind wandering facilitates creative incubation. *Psychological Science, 23*(10), 1117–1122. https://doi.org/10.1177/0956797612446024

Beaty, R. E., Benedek, M., Wilkins, R. W., et al. (2014). Creativity and the default network: A functional connectivity analysis of the creative brain at rest. *Neuropsychologia, 64*, 92–98. https://doi.org/10.1016/j.neuropsychologia.2014.09.019

Benedek, M., Bergner, S., Könen, T., Fink, A., & Neubauer, A. C. (2011). EEG alpha synchronization is related to top-down processing in convergent and divergent thinking. *Neuropsychologia, 49*(12), 3505–3511. https://doi.org/10.1016/j.neuropsychologia.2011.09.004

Benedek, M., Bruckdorfer, R., & Jauk, E. (2019). Motives for creativity: Exploring the what and why of everyday creativity. *The Journal of Creative Behavior, 54*(3), 610–625. https://doi.org/10.1002/jocb.396

Benedek, M., Jauk, E., Kerschenbauer, K., Anderwald, R., & Grond, L. (2017). Creating art: An experience sampling study in the domain of moving image art. *Psychology of Aesthetics, Creativity, and the Arts, 11*(3), 325–334. https://doi.org/10.1037/aca0000102

Benedek, M., Karstendiek, M., Ceh, S. M., et al. (2021). Creativity myths: Prevalence and correlates of misconceptions on creativity. *Personality and Individual Differences, 182*, 111068. https://doi.org/10.1016/j.paid.2021.111068

Bishop, S. R., Lau, M., Shapiro, S., et al. (2004). Mindfulness: A proposed operational definition. *Clinical Psychology: Science and Practice, 11*, 230–241. https://doi.org/10.1093/clipsy.bph077

Blanke, Schmidt, M. J., Riediger, M., & Brose, A. (2020). Thinking mindfully: How mindfulness relates to rumination and reflection in daily life. *Emotion, 20*(8), 1369–1381. https://doi.org/10.1037/emo0000659

Camarda, A., Salvia, É., Vidal, J., et al. (2018). Neural basis of functional fixedness during creative idea generation: An EEG study. *Neuropsychologia, 118*, 4–12. https://doi.org/10.1016/j.neuropsychologia.2018.03.009

Carson, S. H. (2011). Creativity and psychopathology: A shared vulnerability model. *The Canadian Journal of Psychiatry, 56*, 144–153. https://doi.org/10.1177/070674371105600304

Carson, S. H., Peterson, J. B., & Higgins, D. M. (2003). Decreased latent inhibition is associated with increased creative achievement in high-functioning individuals. *Journal of Personality and Social Psychology, 85*, 499–506. https://doi.org/10.1037/0022-3514.85.3.499

Carson, S. H., Peterson, J. B., & Higgins, D. M. (2005). Reliability, validity, and factor structure of the creative achievement questionnaire. *Creativity Research Journal, 17*(1), 37–50. https://doi.org/10.1207/s15326934crj1701_4

Chermahini, S. A., & Hommel, B. (2012). More creative through positive mood? Not everyone! *Frontiers in Human Neuroscience, 6*, 319. https://doi.org/10.3389/fnhum.2012.00319

Christoff, K., Irving, Z. C., Fox, K. C. R., Spreng, R. N., & Andrews-Hanna, J. R. (2016). Mind-wandering as spontaneous thought: A dynamic framework. *Nature Reviews Neuroscience, 17*(11), 718–731. https://doi.org/10.1038/nrn.2016.113

Colzato, L. S., Ozturk, A., & Hommel, B. (2012). Meditate to create: The impact of focused-attention and open-monitoring training on convergent and divergent thinking. *Frontiers in Psychology, 3*. https://doi.org/10.3389/fpsyg.2012.00116

Conner, T. S., & Silvia, P. J. (2015). Creative days: A daily diary study of emotion, personality, and everyday creativity. *Psychology of Aesthetics, Creativity, and the Arts, 9*(4), 463–470. https://doi.org/10.1037/aca0000022

Conner, T. S., DeYoung, C. G., & Silvia, P. J. (2018). Everyday creative activity as a path to flourishing. *The Journal of Positive Psychology, 13*(2), 181–189. https://doi.org/10.1080/17439760.2016.1257049

De Dreu, C. K. W., Baas, M., & Nijstad, B. A. (2008). Hedonic tone and activation level in the mood-creativity link: Toward a dual pathway to creativity model. *Journal of Personality and Social Psychology, 94*(5), 739–756. https://doi.org/10.1037/0022-3514.94.5.739

De Dreu, C. K. W., Nijstad, B. A., & Baas, M. (2011). Behavioral activation links to creativity because of increased cognitive flexibility. *Social Psychological & Personality Science, 2*(1), 72–80. https://doi.org/10.1177/1948550610381789

Diedrich, J., Jauk, E., Silvia, P. J., et al. (2018). Assessment of real-life creativity: The Inventory of Creative Activities and Achievements (ICAA). *Psychology of Aesthetics, Creativity, and the Arts, 12*(3), 304. https://doi.org/10.1037/aca0000137

Dietrich, A. (2014). The mythconception of the mad genius. *Frontiers in Psychology, 5*, 79–79. https://doi.org/10.3389/fpsyg.2014.00079

Du, Y., Yang, Y., Wang, X., et al. (2021). A positive role of negative mood on creativity: The opportunity in the crisis of the COVID-19 epidemic. *Frontiers in Psychology, 11*, 600837–600837. https://doi.org/10.3389/fpsyg.2020.600837

Dumas, D., & Dunbar, K. N. (2016). The creative stereotype effect. *PLoS ONE, 11*(2), e0142567–e0142567. https://doi.org/10.1371/journal.pone.0142567

Ellamil, M., Dobson, C., Beeman, M., & Christoff, K. (2012). Evaluative and generative modes of thought during the creative process. *Neuroimage, 59*(2), 1783–1794. https://doi.org/10.1016/j.neuroimage.2011.08.008

Feist, G. J. (1999). The influence of personality on artistic and scientific creativity. In R. J. Sternberg (Ed.), *Handbook of Creativity* (pp. 273–296). Cambridge University Press.

Forgas, J. P. (2013). Don't worry, be sad! On the cognitive, motivational, and interpersonal benefits of negative mood. *Current Directions in Psychological Science, 22*(3), 225–232. https://doi.org/10.1177/0963721412474458

Friedman, R. S., Förster, J., & Denzler, M. (2007). Interactive effects of mood and task framing on creative generation. *Creativity Research Journal, 19*(2–3), 141–162. https://doi.org/10.1080/10400410701397206

Gable, S. L., Hopper, E. A., & Schooler, J. W. (2019). When the muses strike: Creative ideas of physicists and writers routinely occur during mind wandering. *Psychological Science, 30*(3), 396–404. https://doi.org/10.1177/0956797618820626

Gasper, K., & Middlewood, B. L. (2014). Approaching novel thoughts: Understanding why elation and boredom promote associative thought more than distress and relaxation. *Journal of Experimental Social Psychology, 52*, 50–57. https://doi.org/10.1016/j.jesp.2013.12.007

Goff, K., & Torrance, E. P. (2002). Abbreviated Torrance Test for Adults. *Scholastic Testing Service.*

Guilford, J. P. (1967). Creativity: Yesterday, today, and tomorrow. *The Journal of Creative Behavior, 1*(1), 3–14. https://doi.org/10.1002/j.2162-6057.1967.tb00002.x

Guilford, J. P. (1950). Creativity. *American Psychologist, 5*, 444–454. https://doi.org/10.1037/h0063487

Han, W., Feng, X., Zhang, M., Peng, K., & Zhang, D. (2019). Mood states and everyday creativity: Employing an experience sampling method and a day reconstruction method. *Frontiers in Psychology, 10*, 1698–1698. https://doi.org/10.3389/fpsyg.2019.01698

Higgins, E. T. (1997). Beyond pleasure and pain. *The American Psychologist, 52*(12), 1280– 1300. https://doi.org/10.1037/0003-066X.52.12.1280

Hirt, E. R., Devers, E. E., & McCrea, S. M. (2008). I want to be creative: Exploring the role of hedonic contingency theory in the positive mood-cognitive flexibility link. *Journal of Personality and Social Psychology, 94*(2), 214–230. https://doi.org/10.1037/0022-3514.94.2.94.2.214

Isen, A. M. (2001). An influence of positive affect on decision making in complex situations: Theoretical issues with practical implications. *Journal of Consumer Psychology, 11*(2), 75–85. https://doi.org/10.1207/153276601750408311

Jamison, K. R., Gerner, R. H., Hammen, C., & Padesky, C. (1980). Clouds and silver linings: positive experiences associated with primary affective disorders. *The American Journal of Psychiatry, 137*(2), 198–202. https://doi.org/10.1176/ajp.137.2.198

Jung-Beeman, M., Bowden, E. M., Haberman, J., et al. (2004). Neural activity when people solve verbal problems with insight. *PLoS Biology, 2*(4), e97. https://doi.org/10.1371/journal.pbio.0020097

Kabat-Zinn, J. (1994). *Wherever You Go There You Are: Mindfulness Meditation in Everyday Life*. Hachette Books.

Kaufmann, G., & Vosburg, S. K. (2002). The effects of mood on early and late idea production. *Creativity Research Journal, 14*(3–4), 317–330. https://doi.org/10.1207/S15326934CRJ1434_3

Kounios, J., & Beeman, M. (2009). The Aha! moment: The cognitive neuroscience of insight. *Current Directions in Psychological Science, 18*(4), 210–216. https://doi.org/10.1111/j.1467-8721.2009.01638.x

Lai, Y., Peng, S., Huang, P., & Chen, H. (2021). The impact of affective states and affective shifts on creative ideation and evaluation. *The Journal of Creative Behavior, 55*(1), 130–144. https://doi.org/10.1002/jocb.440

Leszczynski, M., Chaieb, L., Reber, T. P., et al. (2017). Mind wandering simultaneously prolongs reactions and promotes creative incubation. *Scientific Reports, 7*(1), 10197. https://doi.org/10.1038/s41598-017-10616-3

Lintott, S. (2020). Stand-up comedy and mental health: Critiquing the troubled stand-up stereotype. In P. A. Oppliger & E. Shouse (Eds.), *The Dark Side of Stand-Up Comedy* (pp. 197–222). Springer International. https://doi.org/10.1007/978-3-030-37214-9_10

Lucas, B. J., & Nordgren, L. F. (2015). People underestimate the value of persistence for creative performance. *Journal of Personality and Social Psychology, 109*(2), 232–243. https://doi.org/10.1037/pspa0000030

Lutz, A., Slagter, H. A., Dunne, J. D., & Davidson, R. J. (2008). Attention regulation and monitoring in meditation. *Trends in Cognitive Sciences, 12*(4), 163–169. https://doi.org/10.1016/j.tics.2008.01.005

Mann, S., & Cadman, R. (2014). Does being bored make us more creative? *Creativity Research Journal, 26*(2), 165–173. https://doi.org/10.1080/10400419.2014.901073

Mastria, S., Agnoli, S., & Corazza, G. E. (2019). How does emotion influence the creativity evaluation of exogenous alternative ideas? *PLoS ONE, 14*(7), e0219298–e0219298. https://doi.org/10.1371/journal.pone.0219298

Mednick, S. (1962). The associative basis of the creative process. *Psychological Review, 69*(3), 220–232. https://doi.org/10.1037/h0048850

Mendelsohn, G. A. (1974). Associative and attentional processes in creative performance. *Journal of Personality, 44*(2), 341–369. https://doi.org/10.1111/j.1467-6494.1976.tb00127.x

Müller, B. C. N., Gerasimova, A., & Ritter, S. M. (2016). Concentrative meditation influences creativity by increasing cognitive flexibility. *Psychology of Aesthetics, Creativity, and the Arts, 10*(3), 278–286. https://doi.org/10.1037/a0040335

Murray, S., Liang, N., Brosowsky, N., & Seli, P. (2021). What are the benefits of mind wandering to creativity? *Psychology of Aesthetics, Creativity, and the Arts.* https://doi.org/10.1037/aca0000420

Posner, M. I. (1988). Structures and functions of selective attention. In T. Boll & B. Bryant (Eds.), *Master Lectures in Clinical Neuropsychology and Brain Function: Research, Measurement, and Practice* (pp. 171–202). American Psychological Association. https://doi.org/10.1037/10063-005

Posner, J., Russell, J. A., & Peterson, B. S. (2005). The circumplex model of affect: An integrative approach to affective neuroscience, cognitive development, and psychopathology. *Development and Psychopathology, 17*(3), 715–734. https://doi.org/10.1017/S0954579405050340

Russell, J. A. (1980). A circumplex model of affect. *Journal of Personality and Social Psychology, 39*(6), 1161–1178. https://doi.org/10.1037/h0077714

Shapiro, S. L., Carlson, L. E., Astin, J. A., & Freedman, B. (2006). Mechanisms of mindfulness. *Journal of Clinical Psychology, 62*(3), 373–386. https://doi.org/10.1002/jclp.20237

Silvia, P. J., Beaty, R. E., Nusbaum, E. C., et al. (2014). Everyday creativity in daily life: An experience-sampling study of "little c" creativity. *Psychology of Aesthetics, Creativity, and the Arts, 8*(2), 183. https://doi.org/10.1037/a0035722

Smallwood, J., & Schooler, J. W. (2015). The science of mind wandering: Empirically navigating the stream of consciousness. *Annual Review of Psychology, 66*(1), 487–518. https://doi.org/10.1146/annurev-psych-010814-015331

Smith, J. M., & Alloy, L. B. (2009). A roadmap to rumination: A review of the definition, assessment, and conceptualization of this multifaceted construct. *Clinical Psychology Review, 29*(2), 116–128. https://doi.org/10.1016/j.cpr.2008.10.003

Storbeck, J., & Clore, G. L. (2011). Affect influences false memories at encoding: Evidence from recognition data. *Emotion, 11*(4), 981–989. https://doi.org/10.1037/a0022754

Sugawara, D., & Sugie, M. (2021). The effect of positive emotions with different arousal levels on thought-action repertoires. *Japanese Psychological Research, 63*(3), 211–218. https://doi.org/10.1111/jpr.12300

Tallon-Baudry, C., & Bertrand, O. (1999). Oscillatory gamma activity in humans and its role in object representation. *Trends in Cognitive Sciences, 3*(4), 151–162. https://doi.org/10.1016/S1364-6613(99)01299-1

Tam, K. Y. Y., van Tilburg, W. A. P., Chan, C. S., Igou, E. R., & Lau, H. (2021). Attention drifting in and out: The boredom feedback model. *Personality and Social Psychology Review, 25*(3), 251–272. https://doi.org/10.1177/10888683211010297

Tan, T., Zou, H., Chen, C., & Luo, J. (2015). Mind wandering and the incubation effect in insight problem solving. *Creativity Research Journal, 27*(4), 375–382. https://doi.org/10.1080/10400419.2015.1088290

To, M. L., Fisher, C. D., Ashkanasy, N. M., & Rowe, P. A. (2012). Within-person relationships between mood and creativity. *Journal of Applied Psychology, 97*(3), 599–612. https://doi.org/10.1037/a0026097

To, M. L., Fisher, C. D., & Ashkanasy, N. M. (2015). Unleashing angst: Negative mood, learning goal orientation, psychological empowerment and creative behaviour. *Human Relations, 68*(10), 1601–1622. https://doi.org/10.1177/0018726714562235

Westgate, E. C. (2020). Why boredom is interesting. *Current Directions in Psychological Science, 29*(1), 33–40. https://doi.org/10.1177/0963721419884309

Wokke, M. E., Padding, L., & Ridderinkhof, K. R. (2018). Creative minds are out of control: Mid frontal theta and creative thinking. *BioRxiv*, 370494. https://doi.org/10.1101/370494

Zabelina, D. L. (2018). Attention and creativity. In R. E. Jung & O. Vartanian (Eds.), *The Cambridge Handbook of the Neuroscience of Creativity* (pp. 161–179). Cambridge University Press. https://doi.org/10.1017/9781316556238.010

Zabelina, D. L., O'Leary, D., Pornpattananangkul, N., Nusslock, R., & Beeman, M. (2015). Creativity and sensory gating indexed by the P50: Selective versus leaky sensory gating in divergent thinkers and creative achievers. *Neuropsychologia, 69*, 77–84. https://doi.org/10.1016/j.neuropsychologia.2015.01.034

Zabelina, D., Saporta, A., & Beeman, M. (2016). Flexible or leaky attention in creative people? Distinct patterns of attention for different types of creative thinking. *Memory & Cognition, 44*, 488–494.

Zeng, W., Zeng, Y., Xu, Y., et al. (2021). The influence of post-traumatic growth on college students' creativity during the COVID-19 pandemic: The mediating role of general self-efficacy and the moderating role of deliberate rumination. *Frontiers in Psychology, 12*, 665973–665973. https://doi.org/10.3389/fpsyg.2021.665973

Zhang, M., Wang, F., Zhang, D., & Trujillo, C. A. (2020). Individual differences in trait creativity moderate the state-level mood-creativity relationship. *PLoS ONE, 15*(8), e0236987–e0236987. https://doi.org/10.1371/journal.pone.0236987

Zinchenko, A., Obermeier, C., Kanske, P., et al. (2017). The influence of negative emotion on cognitive and emotional control remains intact in aging. *Frontiers in Aging Neuroscience, 9*, 349–349. https://doi.org/10.3389/fnagi.2017.00349

Zuo, B., Wen, F., Wang, M., & Wang, Y. (2019). The mediating role of cognitive flexibility in the influence of counter-stereotypes on creativity. *Frontiers in Psychology, 10*, Article 105. https://doi.org/10.3389/fpsyg.2019.00105

8 Motivations, Emotions, and Creativity

Marie Forgeard

Although much research has investigated the cognitive processes explaining how creative individuals generate and implement novel and useful ideas (Sternberg & Lubart, 1999), understanding *why* they decide to do so, that is, their motivations, has also yielded important insights into determinants of creativity (Amabile, 1996). Understanding the role motivations play is especially important because these are often the starting point of the creative process and may guide cognition (Forgeard & Mecklenburg, 2013; Ruscio et al., 1998). Motivations have been described as "the forces that drive and direct behavior" and encompass beliefs, emotions, and action tendencies geared toward accomplishing specific goals (Dweck, 2017, p. 697). Motivations are therefore inherently linked to affective states (Izard, 1993), and a comprehensive understanding of the role played by motivations in creativity requires an examination of relationships between their cognitive and affective aspects. Importantly, studying motivations can help shed light not just on what creators think and accomplish, but also on how they feel and what benefits they may anticipate and/or derive from creative work (Forgeard & Kaufman, 2016). To date, three separate lines of research have proposed different but complementary frameworks to describe and classify the various motives that drive creative behavior.

Three Frameworks for Understanding the Role of Motivations in Creativity

The three frameworks presented here characterize motivations for creativity at three different levels, going from broad to specific (see Figure 8.1). The first, broadest and best known framework describes whether creators are driven by factors that are internal or external (i.e., intrinsic or extrinsic) to the creative process (Amabile, 1996). The second (Forgeard, 2022)

Correspondence concerning this chapter should be addressed to Marie Forgeard, Department of Clinical Psychology, William James College, 1 Wells Avenue, Newton MA 02459. Email: marie_forgeard@williamjames.edu. Some of the research described in this chapter was made possible through the support of grant # 24365 from the John Templeton Foundation. The opinions expressed in this publication are those of the author and do not necessarily reflect the views of the John Templeton Foundation.

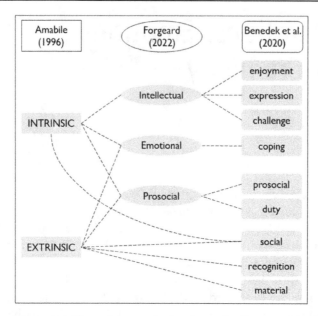

Figure 8.1 *Three frameworks for the study of motivations driving creativity.*

and third (Benedek et al., 2020) frameworks provide specific information about the phenomenology or content of motivations, describing ways in which intrinsic and extrinsic motives take conscious form. In addition to considering whether creators are motivated by intrinsic or extrinsic factors, these frameworks also examine the intended beneficiaries of creative work – the creator themselves, and/ or members of the audience (see also Forgeard & Mecklenburg, 2013).

Amabile (1996). Much of the research examining effects of intrinsic versus extrinsic motivations on creativity stems from the pioneering work of Amabile and colleagues (for reviews see Amabile, 1996, 2021; Amabile & Pillemer, 2012). According to Amabile's componential conceptualization of creativity (1983, 1996), three main components together shape the creative process: *domain-relevant skills* (e.g., knowing specific artistic techniques or scientific methods), *creativity-relevant processes* (e.g., being able to generate novel and useful ideas), and *task motivation* (e.g., having specific reasons for wanting to engage in creative behavior). When intrinsically motivated, individuals are driven to engage in creative work for its own sake – in other words, they hope to derive benefits from the act of creation itself; when extrinsically motivated, individuals are engaged in creative work in order to attain external goals or fulfill external constraints (Hennessey et al., 2015). As will become clear from the other frameworks described below, both intrinsic and extrinsic motivations can take many forms; the great parsimony of this broad framework is therefore one of its appealing features, as it allows researchers and practitioners to distinguish between the many reasons people create according to a central feature – whether creators hope to derive benefits from the creative process itself, or whether they hope this process will give rise to desirable external consequences.

As explained above, two recent lines of research have provided motivational accounts that are more specific in nature, but still consistent with previous research on intrinsic and extrinsic motivations (and therefore intend to complement rather than replace this previous framework). First, Forgeard (2022) conducted two studies examining conscious motivations in the arts and sciences. In the first study, a qualitative investigation using semistructured interviews, professional artists and scientists reported on self- and other-oriented motives driving their work. Findings from this study formed the basis for the development of a self-report scale of creative motivations, which was subsequently validated in a second study using a sample of graduate students training in artistic and scientific disciplines. Results of this project showed that artists' and scientists' motivations for their work fell into three main categories: *intellectual* (i.e., wanting intellectual stimulation and challenge), *emotional* (i.e., wanting to address emotional difficulties), and *prosocial* (i.e., wanting to contribute to the lives of others). Intellectual motivations are generally intrinsic in nature, as rewards are found in the cognitive stimulation provided by creative work itself. Similarly, emotional motivations are generally intrinsic, as therapeutic benefits occur during creative work. Extrinsic emotional motivations (e.g., hoping that extrinsic outcomes such as rewards or recognition may bring emotional benefits) are theoretically possible, though were not reported by participants in Forgeard's (2022) study. Finally, prosocial motivations can be either intrinsic or extrinsic in nature. Unlike intellectual and emotional motivations, the intended beneficiaries of the work are other people rather than the creator themselves (Forgeard & Mecklenburg, 2013). Admittedly, most prosocial motivations are likely extrinsic in nature, focusing on the rewards provided by changing the lives of others for the better. However, such motivations are likely synergistic with intrinsic motivation and reinforce (rather than detract from) the creator's intrinsic interest in their work (Amabile, 1993; Auger & Woodman, 2016; Grant, 2008). Some prosocial motives could also be considered intrinsic in nature if rewards are found in interpersonal processes inherent to creative work, such as through mentoring and collaborating with junior colleagues (Forgeard & Mecklenburg, 2013).

Second, Benedek et al. (2020) proposed another, still more specific framework including nine motives based on the work of Bruckdorfer (2017). *Enjoyment* (i.e., seeking positive affect), *expression* (i.e., wanting to express oneself), and *challenge* (i.e., wanting to challenge oneself) motives are all intrinsic. These also align with intellectual and/or emotional motivations depending on the specific nature of relevant goals, as Benedek et al. (2020) mentioned the relevance of both thoughts and feelings for these three motives. In other words, individuals may create in order to experience enjoyment through intellectually satisfying pursuits and/or through emotionally pleasurable activities. When creating for the purpose of self-expression, individuals may seek to communicate their thoughts and/or feelings. Finally, when driven by the desire to challenge themselves, individuals may want to do so by tackling intellectually and/or emotionally difficult problems. *Coping* motives (i.e., wanting to manage negative emotions) are intrinsic in nature and closely resemble emotional motivations. *Prosocial* motives align with those described by Forgeard (2022). *Duty*-related motives are extrinsic and likely prosocial (i.e., seeking to fulfill one's responsibilities for the greater good of the group). Finally, *social* motives (i.e., wanting to spend time with others) are intrinsic when accomplished through the creative process (e.g., enjoying the act of collaboration on creative work) but extrinsic when attained in other ways (e.g., wanting to make new friends). *Recognition* (i.e., seeking approval from others) and *material* motives (i.e., expecting tangible financial or similar rewards) are both extrinsic in nature.

The three empirically based frameworks presented here complement each other well, providing different levels of specificity to describe motivations and how these relate to creativity. It is worth highlighting that the parsimony of Amabile's (1996) framework makes sense given the original roots of this model in social psychology and the goal of studying how situations affect creativity in educational and occupational settings. In contrast, the specificity of the other two frameworks is more in line with an individual differences or personality psychology approach to the study of motivations. For the purpose of organization, the present chapter is structured according to Forgeard's (2022) framework but still refers to other related research to provide a comprehensive review of the topic at hand. In addition, this chapter highlights relationships between cognitive and affective components of motivations considered. Much of what has been written on the role of motivations for creativity has focused on their cognitive (e.g., setting goals) and/or behavioral (e.g., taking action) aspects. The emotional underpinnings of motivations are, however, important to understand in order to give a full account of the forces that enable and sustain (or impede) creativity over time and provide a full picture of the creative experience. To do so, this chapter considers both short-term emotions experienced during the creative process, as well as the potential longer-term effects of creative work on the creators themselves. Whenever relevant, this chapter also considers the potential effects of creative work on audience members.

Intrinsic and Intellectual Motivations

To date, the most robust finding pertaining to the role of motivation in creativity is that intrinsic motivation, defined as pursuing an activity for its own sake, enhances creativity (Amabile, 1996; Collins & Amabile, 1999). Intrinsically motivated creators generate and implement their ideas because of the inherent satisfaction they find in the process of creation itself. Intrinsic motivation ensures that creators remain focused on the task at hand; in contrast, introducing external motivators can decrease creativity by taking attention away from the creative process and by providing a more salient reason than interest for pursuing goals, leading individuals to discount their intrinsic interest in the task at hand (Amabile, 1996; Hennessey et al., 2015). This idea is in line with Csikszentmihalyi's (1996) notion of creative work as an autotelic experience – the reward is the work itself. Early studies, for example, showed that expecting to be evaluated led to lower creativity in samples of college students generating artistic products such as collages or poems (e.g., Amabile, 1979; Amabile et al., 1990). Expected rewards have also been found to sometimes impede creativity in a variety of domains (e.g., Amabile, 1982; Amabile et al., 1986; Hennessey, 1989; Joussemet & Koestner, 1999), though this depends on their specific nature. Rewards that constrain the creative process impede creativity, whereas rewards that provide useful information and/or support the creator's interest, autonomy, and competence are helpful (Amabile, 1996; Byron & Khazanchi, 2012; Eisenberger & Selbst, 1994). Potential negative effects can therefore be prevented or reversed either through the use of appropriate extrinsic motivators, or by training or "immunizing" individuals to anticipate and withstand the challenges posed by certain extrinsic factors (Hennessey et al., 1989; Hennessey & Zbikowski, 1993). Overall, a meta-analysis of 15 projects (comprising 26 samples) conducted on this topic between 1990 and 2010 confirmed that intrinsic motivation is significantly and moderately associated with the creativity of products (e.g., ideas, solutions, or objects) generated by study participants (de Jesus et al., 2013). This association was not moderated by sample type (college students vs. employees); however, cross-sectional studies yielded stronger results than studies that used causality-oriented designs (de Jesus et al., 2013).

One of the key features of intrinsic motivation is, by definition, the satisfaction and therefore positive affect associated with creating. Not surprisingly, then, intrinsic motivation has empirically been found to be associated with positive affect and higher levels of satisfaction with products generated (Amabile, 1996; Hennessey, 1999; Stańko-Kaczmarek, 2012). More broadly, positive affect helps create a virtual cycle or progress loop feeding the creative process (Amabile et al., 2005; Amabile & Kramer, 2011). Consistent with this, enjoyment is the most commonly reported motivator for engaging in everyday creative behavior, defined as day-to-day creative activities that take place during leisure time (Benedek et al., 2020). Everyday creativity has also been referred to as "little-c" creativity and stands in contrast to "Big-C" exceptional creative achievements or "Pro-c" creative accomplishments occurring in professional contexts (Kaufman & Beghetto, 2009). In keeping with the idea that little-c creativity may be motivated by the search for enjoyment, engagement in everyday creative behaviors is associated with the experience of positive affect in everyday life (Conner et al., 2018) and with well-being (Richards, 2007).

Rather than try to determine whether intrinsic motivation generates positive affect or positive affect generates intrinsic motivation, it may be more useful to think of them as different facets of the same experience, one in which the creator is immersed in the pleasurable act of creation. Over the longer term, engaging in intrinsically rewarding creative behavior may help foster well-being by fulfilling basic psychological needs of autonomy, competence, and relatedness (Ryan & Deci, 2000a, 2000b). This hypothesis is consistent with findings indicating that intrinsic motivation in general is associated with higher levels of self-efficacy (Prabhu et al., 2008) and life satisfaction (del Mar Salinas-Jiménez et al., 2010), among other aspects of well-being.

Another way in which creators have described the intrinsic rewards of the creative process is by emphasizing the intellectual satisfaction they derive from this activity. In Forgeard's (2022) qualitative study of professional artists and scientists, participants reported wanting to "feed [their] intellectual curiosity," to "be surprised and learn new things," to "explore and understand something [they] are interested in," and to experience "a sense of accomplishment." One mathematician commented: "I don't actually believe in the afterlife, but if there is one, I hope they let me do math!" Several participants also added that intrinsic interest in one's work stemmed from the desire to "challenge and test" themselves. Thus, although intrinsic motivation may be associated with pleasure and excitement, it may also entail working through some level of difficulty and negative affect to experience satisfaction. One novelist explained:

> It's so exciting for me to sit down and try to solve all of the insoluble problems that a particular piece of fiction poses. It feels like the most complicated and thrilling kind of game at times, especially when I'm working on something longer and trying to figure out questions of character, motivation, and narrative development.

Similarly, another mathematician noted:

> You find something interesting – usually, to me, one component of being interesting is that it has to be challenging. If it's too easy, that's not interesting. So one component is challenge, the little boy's challenge, and you have a certain response of having to prove oneself.

These reports are in line with Csikszentmihalyi's (1996) description of eminent creators' finding flow, satisfaction, and creative inspiration in pursuing ever-increasing challenges. In keeping with this, Forgeard (2022) also found that intellectual motivation was indirectly associated with greater creative achievement through longer hours worked in a sample of graduate students in the arts and sciences. Intellectual motivation was also indirectly associated with some aspects of well-being through greater consideration of one's audience, though the exact nature of findings differed according to the domain considered.

Emotional Motivations

In addition to the intellectual motivations described above, artists and scientists in Forgeard's (2022) study also endorsed emotional motivations, defined as the desire to address emotional difficulties. Although past research has documented higher-than-average rates of such difficulties in individuals involved in specific creative domains such as the arts (e.g., Taylor, 2017; Young et al., 2013), little research to date has examined this question using a motivational lens. Yet, the idea that creators would use their work to address emotional challenges is not surprising given the large body of research showing that engaging in artistic activities has therapeutic benefits (e.g., Dalebroux et al., 2008; De Petrillo & Winner, 2005; Drake et al., 2016) and that creators in artistic fields have higher-than-average rates of mood disorders (e.g., Andreasen, 1987; Carson, 2019; Kyaga, 2014). This research largely consists of studies examining the effectiveness of art therapy (for reviews, see Malchiodi, 2012; Maujean et al., 2014; Orkibi & Keisari, this volume); although empirical support mostly comes from uncontrolled studies, art therapy may be useful for variety of concerns including depression (e.g., Thyme et al., 2007), anxiety (e.g., Abbing et al., 2018), schizophrenia (e.g., Richardson et al., 2007), or posttraumatic stress (e.g., Schouten et al., 2015), among others. Most of the research suggesting that creators may be driven by the desire to address their own difficulties therefore surrounds creative work in the arts only. A motivational explanation could therefore (at least in part) account for the link between mental illness and artistic creativity, an understudied hypothesis for an otherwise popular idea (Forgeard & Elstein, 2014). Little research has looked at the existence of emotional motivations in science and other creative domains outside of the arts.

The very existence of emotional motivations, by definition, suggests that the experience of negative emotions can give rise to the desire to generate novel and useful ideas and/or products. Professional artists and scientists in Forgeard's (2022) study described creating in order to feel good both "physically and mentally," to "express and manage [their] emotions," "to help deal with difficult personal experiences," and "to escape into an imaginary world," and because it functions as a "spiritual or religious practice." Thus, although the driving force behind this motivation might be a negative emotional state, the hope is that engaging in creative work will provide relief. One novelist explained:

> I think it was a mode of escape. I was kind of escaping my life and escaping all of the things that were happening. this novel was an expression of that. I didn't know that at the time, but it was. It served a purpose.

Prosocial Motivations

Creative individuals may often be motivated by the desire to meaningfully contribute to the lives of others (Forgeard & Mecklenburg, 2013; Liu et al., 2016). This is not surprising given that creative products are often (though not always) designed for others to interact with (Csikszentmihalyi, 1999). In addition, past research on values has shown that creative individuals score high on universalism and therefore have a large moral circle (Dollinger et al., 2007). Although most prosocial motivations are likely extrinsic in nature, these motivations may still benefit creativity by synergistically helping reinforce the creator's intrinsic interest for their work, by providing useful information for the creative process, and/or by supporting the creator's autonomy and competence (Amabile, 1993, 1996; Byron & Khazanchi, 2012; Eisenberger & Selbst, 1994).

Grant and Berry (2011) produced convincing evidence that prosocial motivation may help creators better understand the viewpoints of the intended beneficiaries of their work, and in doing so generate more creative ideas (but see Bechtold et al., 2010; Van Damme et al., 2019 for mixed findings in the context of groups). In their series of studies, prosocial motivation predicted employee creativity as rated by supervisors. Going beyond correlational evidence, Grant and Berry (2011) also demonstrated that experimentally inducing prosocial motivation led to generating more creative solutions for a problem, and that this effect was explained by better perspective-taking (i.e., enhanced ability to understand what audience members might benefit from). Other experimental research suggests that thinking about other people during the creative process helps by increasing psychological distance, which is associated with a more holistic and abstract reasoning style (Förster et al., 2004, 2009; Polman & Emich, 2011). In a recent study, Shukla and Kark (2020) also found that prosocial motivation may help persevere through challenges such as being discouraged by a supervisor to pursue an idea.

Prosocial motives may represent a wide range of goals. Professional artists and scientists in Forgeard's (2022) study reported three subtypes of prosocial motives. First, creators explained creating in order to establish a sense of *connection* among others. For example, they explained wanting to "foster a sense of kinship and connection between people," to "make sure that certain important experiences or facts are not forgotten," or "to make other people feel validated in some way." Second, creators reported wanting to help others see the world through different *perspectives*. They described seeking to "reach people that would otherwise not have been exposed to particular ideas," wanting people "to think in a more nuanced way about the world," hoping for others "to have a more accurate and rich understanding of reality," or "to respect and appreciate experiences that are unlike their own." Third, creators reported wanting to promote tangible *changes* in the lives of others. These creators explained wanting to "contribute to fairness and justice in the world," trying to "put into action important political or social ideals," and hoping to have "positive and concrete repercussions on the lives of others." One visual artist commented:

> Whatever I do should have some kind of a social, cultural, political, or environmental impact. I care too much about responsibility. As a creative and critical practitioner, how would I make people respond to certain things? How can I make them think about certain things in a different way? And more importantly, how can I enable them to transform their situation?

Little research has examined the type of emotional experiences that are associated with prosocial motivation during the creative process. The specific affective experiences associated with prosocial motivations are likely to be complex. In the short-term, freely pursuing prosocial motives appears to be associated with positive affect; pursuing prosocial motives out of obligation is not, though this depends on the culture considered (Gebauer et al., 2008; Gherghel et al., 2020). In the longer run, one might speculate that prosocial motivation could be associated with greater well-being by helping creators cultivate a sense of meaning in life and connection with others (Kaufman, 2018). Related, the pursuit of prosocial motives may be associated with a desire for generativity (McAdams & de St Aubin, 1992; McAdams et al., 1993), defined as the desire to contribute to the well-being of the next generation through one's actions (here, creative work), though more research is needed to substantiate this hypothesis (see also Kaufman, 2018). Related research examining the effects of prosocial behavior more generally (e.g., helping others) have shown positive effects for well-being (e.g., Curry et al., 2018; Layous et al., 2012; Weinstein & Ryan, 2010).

With prosocial motives, the issue of the emotions experienced by the audience or other beneficiaries is also of high interest. At first glance, creators may often be motivated by a desire to please their audience and inspire positive emotions in them. One visual artist in Forgeard's (2022) study described the experience of a viewer as follows:

> She had come to have breakfast with the painting every morning. It was the sunshine in her life. No matter what the weather was outside, this yellow was her morning wake-up. So she had experienced it, lived with it, and became involved, engaged with it. And this, to me, is exactly what it's about.

However, creators may also often seek to benefit audience members by challenging them in ways that may not always be enjoyable, and that they may not even always recognize as beneficial. Silvia (2012), for example, noted that artists often want to inspire a range of emotions (positive, negative, or ambivalent) in their audience in the hopes that this experience might be of value (see also Forgeard & Mecklenburg, 2013).

One novelist in Forgeard's (2022) study stated:

> We look for moments that are actually uncomfortable because that's the moment in which you really have to think, you have to feel, you have to put all of yourself into it so that you yourself have to be a little bit transformed. Otherwise, how could it be transforming for anyone else? And the only moments of transformation are those that are discomforting and awkward and embarrassing and whatever – shocking, surprising ...

Scientists may also seek to advance their work and benefit others by challenging them. A psychologist interviewed in Forgeard's (2022) study explained:

> When I was developing my dissertation, one of the questions I got asked is, "who's going to be mad about this, when this gets published?" And I think like that now. I think "who's going to be mad, or whose mind is going to be changed?" I think some people are pretty good at publishing in their own little domain and they never tip the boat, and they were successful at that, and that's totally a valid approach to science. But I'm often thinking, "who's going to be really mad, or who's going to be shocked, or who's going to be upset?" And I think that's a good sign if it's people who are really influential, because I think, maybe now they get the chance to say something interesting.

Creativity researchers would benefit from working with experts in empirical aesthetics to jointly study the emotional processes experienced by creators and their audience (and how these interact). In particular, Tinio's (2013) mirror model proposes that the process of aesthetic reception mirrors the process of art creation, as early stages of appreciation correspond to the late stages of creation (e.g., attention to superficial features). Relevant research integrating scholarship on the motivations of creators and the ways in which these are (or are not) accomplished through the experiences of audience members may be especially fruitful to provide a more comprehensive account of determinants and outcomes of creativity in the real world.

Future Directions for Research

The study of relationships between motivations, emotions, and creativity is at an exciting time. Past research has already described the types of goals and aspirations that drive creative work at varying levels of specificity. Future research on this topic will be aided by the recent development of empirically validated tools to measure creative motivations. Amabile et al.'s (1994) Work Preference Inventory (WPI) as well as Taylor and Kaufman's (2021)'s Creative Trait Motivation Scales (CTCM) are two useful instruments for capturing the degree to which individuals are motivated by intrinsic versus extrinsic factors. More specific motivations can be captured using Benedek et al.'s (2020) 18-item Motives for Creativity (MoCS) scale or Forgeard's (2022) 38-item scale of creative motivations[1]. Yet, much remains to be understood about how specific motivations relate to various emotional experiences. Examining in greater detail how motivations relate to emotions may be valuable for several reasons: (a) to provide a more comprehensive and accurate description of motivational states, which by definition include an affective component (Dweck, 2017); (b) to help facilitate creativity by setting up the conditions necessary to experience particular emotions; and (c) to anticipate and identify possible obstacles and what might be done to address them. Overall, the literature suggests that both positive and negative emotions can be an integral part of creative motivations. For both, however, there is intentionality in the function of the emotion and the associated behavior: for example, creators enjoy the positive affect associated with their work; or they may understand the value of experiencing negative states by challenging themselves in order to produce a work that will fulfill important goals. Not surprisingly, then, the creative process is often described as a complex experience in which different emotions coexist (Moss & Wilson, 2014).

One variable that will need to be studied in greater depth in the future in order to provide a more accurate picture of relationships between motivations, emotions, and creativity is culture. Most of the research described in this chapter was conducted in Western samples. Yet, motivations likely have different effects for creators operating in different cultural contexts in which certain goals may have

---

[1] A briefer version of this scale is also available upon request.

different meanings and be more or less valued by the group. Culture may also influence the emotional experiences associated with pursuing specific motivations. For example, previous scholarship has noted that prosocial reasons for creating may be more salient in Eastern cultures (Kaufman, 2009; Niu & Sternberg, 2002, 2006). In one study mentioned above, pursuing prosocial motives out of obligation was associated with positive affect in Japanese culture, but not in Romanian or American (U.S.) culture (Gherghel et al., 2020).

Finally, and importantly, the nature of the motives driving creative work is likely to differ in important ways based on the creative domains considered. Potential differences were not emphasized in the present chapter not only because of the relative lack of research on this topic, but also because there is some degree of commonality in creative processes reported across fields (Feldman et al., 1994; Kemp, 2005; Root-Bernstein, 1996; Root-Bernstein & Root-Bernstein, 2004). Although taking a big-picture view of the role of motivations for creativity across domains is a valuable first step, more research is needed to compare findings across domains. In Forgeard's (2022) second study, graduate students in the arts endorsed significantly higher levels of *all* motivations (intellectual, emotional, prosocial) than graduate students in the sciences. Findings were therefore not specific to one type of motivation. More research is needed to investigate why artists reported higher levels of all motivations, including whether differences in affect intensity (i.e., the tendency for artists to experience stronger emotions; e.g., Botella et al., 2015; Sheldon, 1994) may explain these findings. Related, in Benedek et al.'s (2020) study of everyday creativity, engagement in three artistic domains (visual arts, literature, music) was associated with expression and coping motives. Engaging in handicrafts and creative cooking related to prosocial and recognition motives. It is possible that the degree to which the final product is meant to be shared with others could determine the degree to which particular motives are relevant.

These early findings may pave the way for future investigations of domain-specific motives guiding creative behavior. To comprehensively study this topic, relevant scholarship should strive to examine the role of specific types of motivations for creativity in different domains, and at different levels (little-c, Pro-c, Big-C). Current challenges experienced on a global scale may also lead to important developments in the study of creativity in specific areas. Of note, emerging research on creativity in social entrepreneurship (i.e., the pursuit of solutions to important social, cultural, or environmental issues such as climate change, COVID-19, or societal inequalities) may be especially conducive to studying whether and when prosocial motivations can fuel creativity, and in turn produce more sustainable, healthier, and fair societies (Kaufman, 2017; Peredo & McLean, 2006).

Conclusion

A growing body of research suggests that a wide range of motivations drive creative behavior. These motivations are associated with a complex range of emotions. Continuing to study the role of motivations in guiding the creative process may be especially valuable as relevant insights could help refine applied interventions aimed at increasing creativity. To date, most interventions included in creativity-training programs focus on cognitive strategies aimed at enhancing idea-generation processes (Bi et al., 2020; Scott et al., 2004; Valgeirsdottir & Onarheim, 2017). Experimental studies looking at effects of intrinsic motivation on creativity have, however, shown that targeting motivation can also be fruitful (Amabile, 1996). Future work designing and testing interventions to aid creators may benefit from examining the effects of more specific types of motives as well. In doing so, they should also help creators recognize the emotions associated with specific motivational orientations, and what role these emotions might play in their work. This is an especially important and exciting mission for future research because motivations ultimately relate not only to how people feel during the moment of creation, but also to how they make meaning of their work and derive benefits over the long run.

References

Abbing, A., Ponstein, A., van Hooren, S., et al. (2018). The effectiveness of art therapy for anxiety in adults: A systematic review of randomised and non-randomised controlled trials. *PLoS ONE, 13*, e0208716. https://doi.org/10.1371/journal.pone.0208716

Amabile, T. (1982). Children's artistic creativity: Detrimental effects of competition in a field setting. *Personality and Social Psychology Bulletin, 8*, 573–578. https://doi.org/10.1177/0146167282083027

Amabile, T. M. (1979). Effects of external evaluation on artistic creativity. *Journal of Personality and Social Psychology, 37*, 221–233. https://doi.org/10.1037/0022-3514.37.2.221

Amabile, T. M. (1983). Social psychology of creativity: A componential conceptualization. *Journal of Personality and Social Psychology, 45*, 357–377. https://doi.org/10.1037/0022-3514.45.2.357

Amabile, T. M. (1993). Motivational synergy: Toward new conceptualizations of intrinsic and extrinsic motivation in the workplace. *Human Resource Management Review, 3*, 185–201. https://doi.org/10.1016/1053-4822(93)90012-S

Amabile, T. M. (1996). *Creativity in Context*. Westview Press.

Amabile, T. M. (2021). A labor of love: Reflections on a research career, with love. In R. Reiter-Palmon, C. M. Fisher, J. S. Mueller (Eds.), *Creativity at Work: A Festschrift in Honor of Teresa Amabile* (pp. 225–242). Palgrave Macmillan.

Amabile, T. M., Barsade, S. G., Mueller, J. S., & Staw, B. M. (2005). Affect and creativity at work. *Administrative Science Quarterly, 50*, 367–403. https://doi.org/10.2189/asqu.2005.50.3.367

Amabile, T. M., Goldfarb, P., & Brackfield, S. C. (1990). Social influences on creativity: Evaluation, coaction, and surveillance. *Creativity Research Journal, 3*, 6–21. https://doi.org/10.1080/10400419009534330

Amabile, T. M., Hennessey, B. A., & Grossman, B. S. (1986). Social influences on creativity: The effects of contracted-for reward. *Journal of Personality and Social Psychology, 50*, 14–23. https://doi.org/10.1037/0022-3514.50.1.14

Amabile, T. M., Hill, K. G., Hennessey, B. A., & Tighe, E. M. (1994). The Work Preference Inventory: Assessing intrinsic and extrinsic motivational orientations. *Journal of Personality and Social Psychology, 66*, 950–967. https://doi.org/10.1037/0022-3514.66.5.950

Amabile, T. M., & Kramer, S. J. (2011). The power of small wins. *Harvard Business Review, 89*, 70–80. https://doi.org/10.1037/a0013688

Amabile, T. M., & Pillemer, J. (2012). Perspectives on the social psychology of creativity. *The Journal of Creative Behavior, 46*, 3–15. https://doi.org/10.1002/jocb.001

Andreasen, N. C. (1987). Creativity and mental illness: prevalence rates in writers and their first-degree relatives. *The American Journal of Psychiatry, 144*, 1288–1292. https://doi.org/10.1176/ajp.144.10.1288

Auger, P., & Woodman, R. W. (2016). Creativity and intrinsic motivation: Exploring a complex relationship. *The Journal of Applied Behavioral Science, 52*, 342–366. https://doi.org/10.1177/0021886316656973

Bechtold, M. N., De Dreu, C. K. W., Nijstad, B. A., & Choi, H.-S. (2010). Motivated information processing, social tuning, and group creativity. *Journal of Personality and Social Psychology, 99*, 622–637. https://doi.org/10.1037/a0019386

Benedek, M., Bruckdorfer, R., & Jauk, E. (2020). Motives for creativity: Exploring the what and why of everyday creativity. *The Journal of Creative Behavior, 54*, 610–625. https://doi.org/10.1002/jocb.396

Bi, H., Mi, S., Lu, S., & Hu, X. (2020). Meta-analysis of interventions and their effectiveness in students' scientific creativity. *Thinking Skills and Creativity, 38*, 100750. https://doi.org/10.1016/j.tsc.2020.100750

Botella, M., Zenasni, F., & Lubart, T. (2015). Alexithymia and affect intensity of fine artists. *The Journal of Creative Behavior, 49*(1), 1–12. https://doi.org/10.1002/jocb.54

Bruckdorfer, R. (2017). *Challenge, Joy, or Health – The Common Artist's Wealth?* Unpublished Master's thesis. University of Graz, Austria.

Byron, K., & Khazanchi, S. (2012). Rewards and creative performance: A meta-analytic test of theoretically derived hypotheses. *Psychological Bulletin, 138*, 809–830. https://doi.org/10.1037/a0027652

Carson, S. H. (2019). Creativity and mental illness. In J. C. Kaufman & R. J. Sternberg (Eds.), *The Cambridge Handbook of Creativity* (pp. 296–318). Cambridge University Press.

Collins, M. A., & Amabile, T. M. (1999). Motivation and creativity. In R. J. Sternberg (Ed.), *Handbook of Creativity* (pp. 297–312). Cambridge University Press.

Conner, T. S., DeYoung, C. G., & Silvia, P. J. (2018). Everyday creative activity as a path to flourishing. *The Journal of Positive Psychology, 13*, 181–189. https://doi.org/10.1080/17439760.2016.1257049

Csikszentmihalyi, M. (1996). *Creativity: Flow and the Psychology of Discovery and Invention.* HarperCollins.

Csikszentmihalyi, M. (1999). Implications of a systems perspective for the study of creativity. In R. J. Sternberg (Ed.), *Handbook of Creativity* (pp. 313–335). Cambridge University Press.

Curry, O. S., Rowland, L. A., Van Lissa, C. J., et al. (2018). Happy to help? A systematic review and meta-analysis of the effects of performing acts of kindness on the well-being of the actor. *Journal of Experimental Social Psychology, 76*, 320–329. https://doi.org/10.1016/j.jesp.2018.02.014

Dalebroux, A., Goldstein, T. R., & Winner, E. (2008). Short-term mood repair through art-making: Positive emotion is more effective than venting. *Motivation and Emotion, 32*, 288–s295. https://doi.org./10.1007/s11031–008-9105-1

de Jesus, S. N., Rus, C. L., Lens, W., & Imaginário, S. (2013). Intrinsic motivation and creativity related to product: A meta-analysis of the studies published between 1990–2010. *Creativity Research Journal, 25*, 80–84. https://doi.org/10.1080/10400419.2013.752235

De Petrillo, L., & Winner, E. (2005). Does art improve mood? A test of a key assumption underlying art therapy. *Art Therapy: Journal of the American Art Therapy Association, 22*, 205–212. https://doi.org/10.1080/07421656.2005.10129521

del Mar Salinas-Jiménez, M., Artés, J., & Salinas-Jiménez, J. (2010). Income, motivation, and satisfaction with life: An empirical analysis. *Journal of Happiness Studies, 11*, 779–793. https://doi.org/10.1007/s10902–010-9185-y

Dollinger, S. J., Burke, P. A., & Gump, N. W. (2007). Creativity and values. *Creativity Research Journal, 19*, 91–103. https://doi.org/10.1080/10400410701395028

Drake, J. E., Hastedt, I., & James, C. (2016). Drawing to distract: Examining the psychological benefits of drawing over time. *Psychology of Aesthetics, Creativity, and the Arts, 10*, 325–331. https://doi.org/10.1037/aca0000064

Dweck, C. S. (2017). From needs to goals and representations: Foundations for a unified theory of motivation, personality, and development. *Psychological Review, 124*, 689–719. https://doi.org/10.1037/rev0000082

Eisenberger, R., & Selbst, M. (1994). Does reward increase or decrease creativity? *Journal of Personality and Social Psychology, 66*, 1116–1127. https://doi.org/10.1037/0022-3514.66.6.1116

Feldman, D. H., Csikszentmihalyi, M., & Gardner, H. (1994). *Changing the World: A Framework for the Study of Creativity*. Praeger/Greenwood.

Forgeard, M. (2022). Prosocial motivation and creativity in the arts and sciences: Qualitative and quantitative evidence. *Psychology of Aesthetics, Creativity, and the Arts*. Advance Online Publication.

Forgeard, M. J., & Elstein, J. G. (2014). Advancing the clinical science of creativity. *Frontiers in Psychology, 5*, 30–-33. https://doi.org/10.3389/fpsyg.2014.00613

Forgeard, M. J., & Kaufman, J. C. (2016). Who cares about imagination, creativity, and innovation, and why? A review. *Psychology of Aesthetics, Creativity, and the Arts, 10*, 250–269. https://doi.org/10.1037/aca0000042

Forgeard, M. J. C., & Mecklenburg, A. C. (2013). The two dimensions of motivation and a reciprocal model of the creative process. *Review of General Psychology, 17*, 255–266. https://doi.org/10.1037/a0032104

Förster, J., Epstude, K., & Özelsel, A. (2009). Why love has wings and sex has not: How reminders of love and sex influence creative and analytic thinking. *Personality and Social Psychology Bulletin, 35*, 1479–1491. https://doi.org/10.1177/0146167209342755

Förster, J., Friedman, R. S., & Liberman, N. (2004). Temporal construal effects on abstract and concrete thinking: consequences for insight and creative cognition. *Journal of Personality and Social Psychology, 87,* 177–189. https://doi.org/10.1037/0022-3514.87.2.177

Gebauer, J. E., Riketta, M., Broemer, P., & Maio, G. R. (2008). Pleasure and pressure based prosocial motivation: Divergent relations to subjective well-being. *Journal of Research in Personality, 42,* 399–420. https://doi.org/10.1016/j.jrp.2007.07.002

Gherghel, C., Nastas, D., Hashimoto, T., Takai, J., & Cargile, A. C. (2020). Culture, morality, and the effect of prosocial behavior motivation on positive affect. *Ethics & Behavior, 30,* 126–149. https://doi.org/10.1080/10508422.2019.1651651

Grant, A. M. (2008). Does intrinsic motivation fuel the prosocial fire? Motivational synergy in predicting persistence, performance, and productivity. *Journal of Applied Psychology, 93,* 48–58. https://doi.org/10.1037/0021-9010.93.1.48

Grant, A. M., & Berry, J. (2011). The necessity of others is the mother of invention: Intrinsic and prosocial motivations, perspective-taking, and creativity. *Academy of Management Journal, 54,* 73–96. https://doi.org/10.5465/amj.2011.59215085

Hennessey, B. A. (1989). The effect of extrinsic constraints on children's creativity while using a computer. *Creativity Research Journal, 2,* 151–168. https://doi.org/10.1080/10400418909534312

Hennessey, B. A. (1999). Intrinsic motivation, affect and creativity. In S. W. Russ (Ed.), *Affect, Creative Experience and Psychological Adjustment* (pp. 77–90). Taylor and Francis.

Hennessey, B. A., Amabile, T. M., & Martinage, M. (1989). Immunizing children against the negative effects of reward. *Contemporary Educational Psychology, 14,* 212–227. https://doi.org/10.1016/0361-476X(89)90011-8

Hennessey, B., Moran, S., Altringer, B., & Amabile, T. M. (2015). Extrinsic and intrinsic motivation. In C. L. Cooper, P. C. Flood, and Y. Freeney (Eds.), *Wiley Encyclopedia of Management* (vol. 11, pp. 1–4). Wiley. https://doi.org/10.1002/9781118785317.weom110098

Hennessey, B. A., & Zbikowski, S. M. (1993). Immunizing children against the negative effects of reward: A further examination of intrinsic motivation training techniques. *Creativity Research Journal, 6,* 297–307. https://doi.org/10.1080/10400419309534485

Izard, C. E. (1993). Four systems for emotion activation: Cognitive and noncognitive processes. *Psychological Review, 100,* 68–90. https://doi.org/10.1037/0033-295X.100.1.68

Joussemet, M., & Koestner, R. (1999). Effect of expected rewards on children's creativity. *Creativity Research Journal, 12,* 231–239. https://doi.org/10.1207/s15326934crj1204_1

Kaufman, J. C. (2009). *Creativity 101.* Springer.

Kaufman, J. C. (2017). Looking forward: The potential of creativity for social justice and equity (and other exciting outcomes). *The Journal of Creative Behavior, 51,* 305–307. https://doi.org/10.1002/jocb.195

Kaufman, J. C. (2018). Finding meaning with creativity in the past, present, and future. *Perspectives on Psychological Science, 13,* 734–749. https://doi.org/10.1177/1745691618771981

Kaufman, J. C., & Beghetto, R. A. (2009). Beyond big and little: The Four C model of creativity. *Review of General Psychology, 13*, 1–12. https://doi.org/10.1037/a0013688

Kemp, M. (2005). From science in art to the art of science. *Nature, 434*, 308–309. https://doi.org/ 10.1038/434308a

Kyaga, S. (2014). *Creativity and Mental Illness: The Mad Genius in Question.* Springer.

Layous, K., Nelson, S. K., Oberle, E., Schonert-Reichl, K. A., & Lyubomirsky, S. (2012). Kindness counts: Prompting prosocial behavior in preadolescents boosts peer acceptance and well-being. *PLoS ONE, 7*, e51380. https://doi.org/10.1371/journal.pone.0051380

Liu, D., Jiang, K., Shalley, C. E., Keem, S., & Zhou, J. (2016). Motivational mechanisms of employee creativity: A meta-analytic examination and theoretical extension of the creativity literature. *Organizational Behavior and Human Decision Processes, 137*, 236–263. https://doi.org/10.1016/j.obhdp.2016.08.001

Malchiodi, C. (2012). *Handbook of Art Therapy* (2nd ed.). Guilford Press.

Maujean, A., Pepping, C. A., & Kendall, E. (2014). A systematic review of randomized controlled studies of art therapy. *Art Therapy: Journal of the American Art Therapy Association, 31*, 37–44. https://doi.org/10.1080/07421656.2014.873696

McAdams, D. P., & de St Aubin, E. D. (1992). A theory of generativity and its assessment through self-report, behavioral acts, and narrative themes in autobiography. *Journal of Personality and Social Psychology, 62*, 1003–1015. https://doi.org./10.1037/0022-3514.62.6.1003

McAdams, D. P., de St Aubin, E. D., & Logan, R. L. (1993). Generativity among young, midlife, and older adults. *Psychology and Aging, 8*, 221–230. https://doi.org/10.1037/0882-7974.8.2.221

Moss, S. A., & Wilson, S. G. (2014). Ambivalent emotional states: The underlying source of all creativity? *The International Journal of Creativity and Problem Solving, 24*, 75-100.

Niu, W., & Sternberg, R. J. (2002). Contemporary studies on the concept of creativity: The East and the West. *Journal of Creative Behavior, 36*, 269–288. https://doi.org/10.1002/j.2162-6057.2002.tb01069.x

Niu, W., & Sternberg, X. (2006). The philosophical roots of western and eastern conceptions of creativity. *Journal of Theoretical and Philosophical Psychology, 26*, 1001–1021. https://doi.org/10.1037/h0091265

Peredo, A. M., & McLean, M. (2006). Social entrepreneurship: A critical review of the concept. *Journal of World Business, 41*, 56–65. https://doi.org/10.1016/j.jwb.2005.10.007

Polman, E., & Emich, K. J. (2011). Decisions for others are more creative than decisions for the self. *Personality and Social Psychology Bulletin, 37*, 492–501. https://doi.org/10.1177/0146167211398362

Prabhu, V., Sutton, C., & Sauser, W. (2008). Creativity and certain personality traits: Understanding the mediating effect of intrinsic motivation. *Creativity Research Journal, 20*, 53–66. https://doi.org/10.1080/10400410701841955

Richards, R. E. (2007). *Everyday Creativity and New Views of Human Nature: Psychological, Social, and Spiritual Perspectives.* American Psychological Association.

Richardson, P., Jones, K., Evans, C., Stevens, P., & Rowe, A. (2007). Exploratory RCT of art therapy as an adjunctive treatment in schizophrenia. *Journal of Mental Health, 16*, 483–491. https://doi.org/10.1080/09638230701483111

Root-Bernstein, R. S. (1996). The sciences and arts share a common creative aesthetic. In A. I. Tauber (Ed.), *The Elusive Synthesis: Aesthetics and Science* (pp. 49–82). Springer.

Root-Bernstein, R., & Root-Bernstein, M. (2004). Artistic scientists and scientific artists: The link between polymathy and creativity. In R. J. Sternberg, E. L. Grigorenko, & J. L. Singer (Eds.), *Creativity: From Potential to Realization* (pp. 127–151). American Psychological Association.

Ruscio, J., Whitney, D. M., & Amabile, T. M. (1998). Looking inside the fishbowl of creativity: Verbal and behavioral predictors of creative performance. *Creativity Research Journal, 11*, 243–263. https://doi.org/10.1207/s15326934crj1103_4

Ryan, R. M., & Deci, E. L. (2000a). Self-determination theory and the facilitation of intrinsic motivation, social development, and well-being. *American Psychologist, 55*, 68–78. https://doi.org/10.1037/0003-066X.55.1.68

Ryan, R. M., & Deci, E. L. (2000b). Intrinsic and extrinsic motivations: Classic defin itions and new directions. *Contemporary Educational Psychology, 25*, 54–67. https://doi.org/10.1006/ceps.1999.1020

Schouten, K. A., de Niet, G. J., Knipscheer, J. W., Kleber, R. J., & Hutschemaekers, G. J. (2015). The effectiveness of art therapy in the treatment of traumatized adults: A systematic review on art therapy and trauma. *Trauma, Violence, & Abuse, 16*, 220–228. https://doi.org/10.1177/1524838014555032

Scott, G., Leritz, L. E., & Mumford, M. D. (2004). The effectiveness of creativity training: A quantitative review. *Creativity Research Journal, 16*, 361–388. https://doi.org/10.1080/10400410409534549

Sheldon, K. M. (1994). Emotionality differences between artists and scientists. *Journal of Research in Personality, 28*, 481–491. https://doi.org/10.1006/jrpe.1994.1034

Shukla, J., & Kark, R. (2020). Now you do it, now you don't: The mixed blessing of creative deviance as a prosocial behavior. *Frontiers in Psychology, 11*, 313. https://doi.org/10.3389/fpsyg.2020.00313

Silvia, P. J. (2012). Human emotions and aesthetic experience: An overview of empirical aesthetics. In A. P. Shimamura & S. E. Palmer (Eds.), *Aesthetic Science: Connecting Minds, Brains, and Experience* (pp. 250–275). Oxford University Press.

Stańko-Kaczmarek, M. (2012). The effect of intrinsic motivation on the affect and evaluation of the creative process among fine arts students. *Creativity Research Journal, 24*, 304–310. https://doi.org/10.1080/10400419.2012.730003

Sternberg, R. J., & Lubart, T. I. (1999). The concept of creativity: Prospects and paradigms. In R. J. Sternberg (Ed.), *Handbook of Creativity* (pp. 3–15). Cambridge University Press.

Taylor, C. L. (2017). Creativity and mood disorder: A systematic review and meta-analysis. *Perspectives on Psychological Science, 12*, 1040–1076. https://doi.org/10.1177/1745691617699653

Taylor, C. L., & Kaufman, J. C. (2021). The creative trait motivation scales. *Thinking Skills and Creativity, 39*, 100763. https://doi.org/10.1016/j.tsc.2020.100763

Tinio, P. P. (2013). From artistic creation to aesthetic reception: The mirror model of art. *Psychology of Aesthetics, Creativity, and the Arts, 7*, 265–275. https://doi.org/10.1037/a0030872

Thyme, K. E., Sundin, E. C., Stahlberg, G., et al. (2007). The outcome of short-term psychodynamic art therapy compared to short-term psychodynamic verbal therapy for depressed women. *Psychoanalytic Psychotherapy, 21*, 250–264. https://doi.org/10.1080/02668730701535610

Valgeirsdottir, D., & Onarheim, B. (2017). Studying creativity training programs: A methodological analysis. *Creativity and Innovation Management, 26*, 430–439. https://doi.org/10.1111/caim.12245

Van Damme, M. J., Anseel, F., Duyck, W., & Rietzschel, E. F. (2019). Strategies to improve selection of creative ideas: An experimental test of epistemic and social motivation in groups. *Creativity and Innovation Management, 28*, 61–71. https://doi.org/10.1111/caim.12306

Weinstein, N., & Ryan, R. M. (2010). When helping helps: Autonomous motivation for prosocial behavior and its influence on well-being for the helper and recipient. *Journal of Personality and Social Psychology, 98*, 222–244. https://doi.org/10.1037/a0016984

Young, L. N., Winner, E., & Cordes, S. (2013). Heightened incidence of depressive symptoms in adolescents involved in the arts. *Psychology of Aesthetics, Creativity, and the Arts, 7*, 197–202. https://doi.org/10.1037/a0030468

9 Managing Difference and Uncertainty and Creativity

Tingshu Liu and Rodica Ioana Damian

Across history and culture, being *different* has taken on different values. For example, Confucius promoted *zhong yong*, that is, going along with the majority and exhibiting oneself as neither too good nor too bad, because standing out might trigger scrutiny and hostility. Similarly, Aristotle's *doctrine of the mean* stated that every virtue is a mean between the extremes of excess and deficiency. In contrast, some cultures are more encouraging of standing out and even associate being different with discovery, reflected in popular quotes such as "The person who follows the crowd will usually go no further than the crowd; the person who walks alone is likely to find himself in places no one has ever seen before."[1] Thus, *being different* has been imbued with both a negative (inadequacy or ostracism) and a positive (being outstanding) value. Similarly, *uncertainty* has taken both a negative (unstable adverse environment) and a positive value (flexibility). Threading the fine line between negativity and positivity when managing difference and uncertainty might require breaking old cognitive schemas and problem-solving modes and coming up with new ones to survive and thrive (Beghetto, 2019). This process is reminiscent of the creative process, where creativity is defined as generating novel and useful ideas and products that are recognizable by others (e.g., Csikszentmihályi, 1996; Runco & Jaeger, 2012; Simonton, 1994). Therefore, the process of managing difference and uncertainty might inform and enhance the creative process.

Diversifying experiences, defined as "unusual and unexpected events or situations that push people outside the realm of normality" (Damian, 2017, p. 102), include a wide range of experiences, both negative and positive, which reflect difference and uncertainty. In this chapter, we argue that successfully managing diversifying experiences at the individual level may foster creativity. Thus, we use the diversifying experiences and creativity framework to present theoretical arguments and empirical evidence that illustrate the link between managing uncertainty/difference and creativity. First, we present empirical evidence for the link between four broad categories of diversifying experiences and creativity: psychopathology, adversity, enrichment, and diversity. Second, we discuss

---

[1] The quote is attributed to Albert Einstein on GoodReads at www.goodreads.com/quotes/1286532-the-person-who-follows-the-crowd-will-usually-go-no, but the attribution is questioned on Quote Investigator at https://quoteinvestigator.com/tag/francis-phillip-wernig/. Regardless of the origin of the quote, it captures our point.

the possible mechanism of managing such experiences (at the individual level) in a way that fosters creativity. Third, we discuss future directions.

Empirical Evidence

Psychopathology

The *mad genius* idea has long been an intriguing topic in the field, from Aristotle's famous claim that "no great genius has existed without a strain of madness" to the modern research on creativity and mental disorders (Kaufman, 2014). Because, by definition, mental illness implies disruptions in intra- or interpersonal functioning, it brings about feelings of uncertainty and being different. Although the uncertainty and difference may pose problems, some have argued that they might also provide those involved with a chance or ability to think outside of the box. Indeed, when analyzing biographical data from 1,005 eminent creators, Ludwig (1992) found positive links between creative achievement and two types of psychopathologies: depression and anxiety. Post (1994) investigated biographies of 291 male eminent creators and found that artists and writers were more likely to be diagnosed with mental disorders compared to the general population; in a follow-up study, Post (1996) analyzed the biographies of 100 famous male writers and found a high prevalence of mental disorders among these writers (82%). However, these studies were criticized because of their heavy reliance on biographical data and lack of valid, meaningful control groups (Taylor, 2017).

Shifting the focus from psychopathology rates in eminent creators to rates of creativity in patients with mental illness, Kyaga and colleagues (2011) analyzed about 300,000 Swedish citizens diagnosed with schizophrenia, bipolar disorder, or unipolar depression and compared their occupations with a control group. The results showed that people with bipolar disorder were more likely to be in scientific and artistic professions compared to the control group, and people with schizophrenia were more likely to have artistic occupations. A follow-up study (Kyaga et el., 2012), with more types of mental disorders included, replicated the effect for bipolar disorder, but did not support a link between creative occupations and other types of mental disorders (although their oper-ationalization of creative occupations was biased toward the arts and eminent creativity). Another study (Parnas et al., 2019) examined over 10,000 university researchers in Denmark, who were deemed the more creative group. They compared these researchers and their relatives to a control group with similar education levels and found that researchers were *less* likely to be diagnosed with mental disorders, but their relatives were *more* likely to be so diagnosed. Although these studies used large samples and comparison groups to ensure generalizability, they were limited to studying professional creativity and they did not obtain first-hand data from the participants. These studies also received criticism that psychopathology and creativity were not both viewed as continuous variables (Simonton, 2014a); in other words, either psychopathology or creativity was treated dichotomously, simplifying the construct to people with or without mental disorders, or people with or without creativity. This dichotomization might have biased the observed associations due to the loss of variability in the data.

To address the above issues, Acar and Sen (2013) meta-analyzed 268 effect sizes reflecting the associations between creativity (which included measures of divergent and convergent thinking, creative personality, and self-reports of creativity; notably, the creativity measurement type did not moderate the meta-analytic estimates of the association between creativity and psychopathology) and schizophrenia tendency. They found that some subtypes of schizophrenia tendencies (i.e., positive, impulsive, and unspecified) had a positive association with creativity, whereas other subtypes (i.e., negative and disorganized) had a negative associations. In another meta-analysis, Baas et al. (2016) found that bipolar disorder was positively associated with creativity, whereas depressive mood was negatively associated with creativity. Damian and Simonton (2015) also found mental illness to be positively correlated with creative achievement in African American eminent artists, but the effect was diminished when developmental adversity was controlled; and as in the majority culture sample, eminent African American artists had significantly higher mental illness rates than creators in other domains.

Although prior research found some positive associations between psychopathology and creativity, humanistic and positive psychologists have a different point of view, where creativity is considered an important pathway to self-actualization (Maslow, 1970) and flourishing (Conner et al., 2018), and a result of cumulated optimal functioning (Csikszentmihályi, 1996) and mental health (Seligman & Csikszentmihályi, 2000). Indeed, numerous empirical studies have linked creativity and/or creative behaviors with positive emotions, physical and subjective well-being, and an optimal functioning experience (e.g., Cohen, 2006; Conner & Silvia, 2015; Conner et al., 2018; Karwowski et al., 2017; MacDonald et al., 2006; Pannells & Claxton, 2008; Tan et al., 2019). For example, Conner and colleagues (2018) did a daily diary study on 658 people and found that day-level creativity predicted next-day positive emotions. Also, Tan and colleagues (2019) found a positive relationship between creativity and happiness consistently across their three studies.

Overall, the empirical evidence on psychopathology and creativity has produced mixed findings, with both positive and negative associations. But why would this be the case? In a recent review, Simonton (2019) pointed out that there are several issues that complicate matters in the literature and lead to the mixed results and persistent debate. First, prior studies differ in the specific hypotheses they tested (e.g., incidence rates, correlations), and, as it turns out, studies with different approaches tend to generate different effect sizes, as suggested by a meta-analysis on mood disorder and creativity (Taylor, 2017).

Specifically, when studies focus on rates of mood disorders among eminent creators, the effects tend to be larger and indicative of a positive link between psychopathology and creativity; however, when studies focus on rates of creativity among people with mood disorders, the levels do not differ from the general population. Furthermore, when studies examine the link between continuous measures of mood disorder and creativity, they observe a small positive association. In sum, the question asked, and the method used render different conclusions. Second, prior studies differ in the populations they study (eminent creative geniuses vs. noneminent creators or general population). Indeed, prior research (Simonton, 2014b) has found that everyday creative people are more mentally *healthy* than the general population, whereas eminent creative geniuses are more mentally *ill* than other creators. Because these two seemingly contradictory statements can be simultaneously true, research on the two forms of creativity has produced mixed results.

A third reason for the mixed results might be the type of mental disorder studied. Prior work has supported the idea that only certain *types* of psychopathologies may be related to creativity (Acar et al., 2018; Baas et al., 2016; Furnham et al., 2008; Kyaga et al., 2011, 2012; Ludwig, 1992). Fourth, it is possible that psychopathology is related to creativity but only in *some* (not all) *domains* of creative endeavor (Damian & Simonton, 2015; Ludwig, 1992; Post, 1994). In line with this hypothesis, Simonton (2014a) revealed different association patterns between creativity and psychopathology across different domains of creativity; specifically, he found positive linear patterns for artists and writers (where more psychopathology was associated with more creativity), and inverted U-shape patterns for scientists, composers, and thinkers (where creativity peaked at moderate levels of psychopathology). Fifth, findings may differ based on the specific quantitative assessments (i.e., how creativity and psychopathology are measured). Sixth, findings may be shaped by the theoretical framework that drove the study in the first place, and there is no shortage of theories that attempt to explain the link between psychopathology and creativity. Indeed, beyond the developmental antecedent mechanism that this chapter focuses on (under the diversifying experience theory), other explanatory mechanisms have included convergent cognitive processes (Abraham, 2014), neurological mechanisms (de Souza et al., 2014), personality traits (Baas et al., 2016), genetic contributions (Kozbelt et al., 2014), evolutionary foundations (Jung, 2014), and various combinations of these factors (Bilder & Knudsen, 2014; Lindell, 2014). Last, publication bias is likely an issue in this field (Taylor, 2017), especially given strong feelings on both sides of the "mad genius" debate, which means that many null findings might have remained tucked away in the proverbial file drawer leading to overestimated published effects (see Open Science Collaboration, 2015).

In sum, empirical evidence suggests that psychopathology may foster creativity under specific circumstances, but the field needs a broad integrative theory that can further specify the conditions under which this happens and the most effective ways to manage psychopathology and turn it into creativity.

Adversity

"That which does not kill me makes me stronger" (Nietzsche, 1889) is a persistent belief across many cultures. Anecdotal evidence suggests that some people see their lives spiral into disaster following adversity, whereas others rise like a phoenix from the ashes. The notion of character growth from adversity has found support in research on posttraumatic growth (Tedeschi & Calhoun, 2004). There is considerable evidence that people report experiencing some positive change after traumatic events (Helgeson et al., 2006; Sawyer et al., 2010; Stanton et al., 2006) and that the phenomenon is relatively common (58–83% of survivors reporting positive changes; Affleck et al., 1991; McMillen et al., 1997; Sears et al., 2003). However, most previous studies on posttraumatic growth have had several limitations: (a) they used cross-sectional designs or retrospective self-perceived assessments of change, although we now have extensive evidence that perceived change does not correlate significantly with actual change (e.g., Boals et al., 2019; Frazier et al., 2009; Owenz & Fowers, 2018; Yanez et al., 2011); (b) they did not assess growth in specific traits, but used broad character measures (e.g., as measured by the Post Traumatic Growth Inventory or PTGI; Tedeschi & Calhoun, 1996); (c) they used positively biased scales, such as the PTGI, which only allows for retrospective *positive* changes; and (d) they did not investigate underlying developmental processes (Jayawickreme et al., 2021; Damian & Roberts, 2014; Jayawickreme & Blackie, 2014). Not surprisingly, the few high-quality prospective longitudinal studies available found that posttraumatic growth in character was far rarer and more nuanced than previously implied by cross-sectional work, with more boundary conditions (Jayawickreme et al., 2021). More important, there is very little research available on *creativity* as the main outcome of interest following growth, and we are not aware of any longitudinal studies conducted on the general population that have evaluated changes in creativity or creative achievement following trauma. Thus, in reviewing the literature on adversity and creativity, we are limited to work done on historical samples of eminent creators, a few cross-sectional studies including retrospective reports of trauma and creativity, and some experimental studies that may not have addressed the question at hand in an ecologically valid manner.

Previous research showed that a great number of eminent creators had experienced adversities throughout their life spans, such as familial instability, trauma, serious disease/disability, and other negative life experiences (Damian, 2017). Csikszentmihályi (1996) mentioned missing fathers as a recurring theme for creative genius. Indeed, orphanhood rates were found to exceed the normal range for the eminent creator population (Albert 1971; Roe, 1953), and this pattern was especially true for artistic creativity compared to scientific creativity (Berry, 1981). Supporting this prior work, Damian and Simonton (2015) found that eminent African American creators who went through developmental adversities such as early parental death, minority status, or poverty had higher levels of eminence and creative achievement. Although the evidence from studies of eminent creators seems robust, it does not directly speak to the effects that might be observed in the general population. It is indeed possible that the effects observed are due to selection effects which may have inflated the correlation between adversity and creativity, whereby the personal resources and characteristics that made people more likely to become eminent were the same characteristics that helped them overcome trauma, and the eminent samples are missing all the thousands of people who experienced adversity but did not become eminent.

To solve this generalizability issue, we need general population samples. The issue is that research on general population samples has been limited to cross-sectional studies including retrospective trauma measures. For example, evidence from a self-report cross-sectional study (Forgeard, 2013) found that people who reported greater posttraumatic growth also reported themselves to be more creative. Another survey study (Orkibi & Ram-Vlasov, 2019) found that Israeli adults who experienced more traumatic events, including being exposed to wars, performed better on a creativity task. More recently, studies have found that self-reported retrospective posttraumatic growth in the context of the COVID-19 pandemic was positively associated with self-reported creativity (Zeng et al., 2021; Zhai et al., 2021); self-reported creativity was also positively associated with ruminating on the pandemic itself (Wang et al., 2021), and self-reported motivation for engaging in creativity, as well as creative activity engagement, were both positively related to perceived impact of COVID-19 (Tang et al., 2021). Nevertheless, these studies provided only preliminary evidence because change in creativity was not assessed as a function of trauma. Experimental studies have also tried to test the link between adversity and creativity, but it is questionable to what extent "adversity" manipulated in the lab is ecologically valid. For example, an experimental study (Kim et al., 2013) found that students who were socially rejected performed better in a subsequential creative task (when primed with self- vs. collective pronouns). Bastian and colleagues (2018) also found that simply sharing traumatic experiences within a team boosted team creativity via increasing the supportive interactions within the team. Moreover, a longitudinal cross-lagged panel conducted during the COVID-19 pandemic found that thinking about death was related to self-reported creativity (though the study did not have any pre-pandemic measures; Takeuchi et al., 2021). Thus, there is some limited evidence supporting a positive link between adversity and creativity, but this link might be limited to eminent creators as the general population data are scarce and suffers from methodological issues like the broader research on posttraumatic growth.

Moreover, there is some evidence for null effects or even a *negative* link between adversity and creativity. Barrett and colleagues (2014) studied 91 scientists' biographies and did not find any significant relationship between their academic adversity and scientific creative achievement. Mumford and colleagues (2005) studied 499 scientists' obituaries and found that higher- (vs. lower-) achieving scientists had gone through *less* adversity in their early lives.

Furthermore, children who suffered separation from their parent(s) in childhood in China were found to display lower levels of intelligence and creativity compared to children who grew up with both parents (Liu & Shi, 2004; Shi et al., 2012).

Besides the methodological issues and mixed empirical findings, there is also the question of causal direction. That is, even if adversity and creativity were positively related, is it the case that overcoming adversity fosters creativity, or is creativity a necessary coping mechanism in overcoming adversity? Indeed, some have suggested that engagement in creative activities might buffer people from the harms of adversity (Metzl & Morrell, 2008). For example, Stephenson and Rosen (2015) found that writing narratives helped reduce college students' anxiety and depression. A qualitative study (Puvimanasinghe et al., 2019) found that engaging in expressive creative activities played an important role in helping refugees recover from psychological distress and trauma. Tang and colleagues (2021) found that engaging in creative activities was positively related to well-being during the pandemic.

Enrichment

Another category of experiences that seem to be related to creativity are those that can be considered enriching with regard to knowledge and ideas. Examples include schooling, mentoring, hobbies, reading, and peripheral training.

In Csikszentmihályi's (2014) systems model of creativity theory, a good understanding of the rules/knowledge of a specific domain is a necessary element for the development of creativity in this domain. For example, if a person did not play an instrument and knew nothing about music theory, it would be extremely difficult for them to write a new symphony. Contrary to the myth that prior knowledge is an impediment to creativity, it seems that enough formal education or training is necessary for it, especially in science and fields that require advanced knowledge/skill (Mayer, 2006; Mumford et al., 2005; Simonton 1986). Mumford and colleagues (2005) studied 499 scientists from multiple domains and found that compared to low-achieving scientists, high-achieving ones tended to have a good education, early domain exposure, and a mentor(s) early in their career. Nevertheless, there is also some evidence for an inverted U-shape relationship between years of formal schooling and creative achievement (see Simonton, 1994), meaning that not just too little, but also too much education, especially in more artistic domains, might hamper creativity. This is probably because formal schooling does not directly correspond to the level of domain knowledge necessary for creativity (Beghetto & Plucker, 2006).

Indeed, formal education is not the only path to enrichment. Some geniuses did not get an extensive formal education, but they still obtained enough knowledge via home-schooling or self-learning and made magnificent creative achievements. Examples that easily come to mind are Bill Gates, Thomas Edison, and Michael Faraday. An important way to make up for a lack of formal education is non-picky, extensive reading (Simonton, 1984) because it provides knowledge in multiple domains and enables the readers to make interdisciplinary connections and integrate the material. Other ways that complement formal education include peripheral training that provides knowledge from helpful adjacent domains and having a larger (and presumably more complex) academic social network (Simonton, 1984, 1992).

The above studies are limited to studies of eminent creators, but the idea that education is related to creativity has received support in a representative U..S sample ($n = 3,763$), where educational attainment was strongly and positively correlated ($r = 45$) with occupational creativity (i.e., the level of creativity required by people's jobs; Damian & Spengler, 2020).

Diversity

Studies of creative geniuses have shown that cultural diversity is highly characteristic of this population. One study found that 20% of twentieth-century eminent personalities were either first- or second-generation immigrants (Goertzel et al., 1978). Another study found that 25% of highly eminent scientists were second-generation immigrants (Eiduson, 1962). Moreover, an economic study conducted in the United States over 10 years (Peri, 2012) showed that, although foreign-born immigrants represented only 13% of the U.S. population, they accounted for 30% of all the patents granted, and for 25% of all the U.S. Nobel laureates. Further supporting the idea that cultural diversity is relevant for creativity, prior research has shown that eminent creators tend to have experienced extensive traveling (including traveling and living abroad) and that their families showed high geographical mobility (Simonton, 2004).

Research on the general population has also brought support for a positive link between cultural diversity and creativity. For example, Tadmor and colleagues (2012) showed that bicultural people (i.e., people who identify as belonging to two different cultures) were more creative to the extent to which they were able to better integrate their diverse cultural backgrounds (see also Saad et al., 2013; but, for null effects, see Forthmann and colleagues, 2018). Beyond a bicultural background, research has shown that having lived in a foreign country for a significant amount of time was linked to more creative thinking and cognitive flexibility (Lee et al., 2012; Leung et al., 2008; Maddux & Galinsky, 2009; Xu & Pang, 2020). Furthermore, Fee and Gray (2012) showed in a longitudinal study that people who had lived abroad had increased cognitive flexibility and creativity, relative to both other people who had not lived abroad, and to their own pre-departure scores.

Beyond diverse life experiences at the individual level, researchers have also investigated the effect of the diverse constitution of a group on team-level creativity. Specifically, studies found that when group membership was more diverse, both demographically (e.g., gender, age, ethnicity) and ideologically (e.g., from different company departments or various educational backgrounds), groups exhibited better team-level creativity and performance, presumably due to the increased heterogeneity of perspectives and ideas (Bell et al., 2011; Page, 2007). When team members were from different *cultural* backgrounds, group creativity was also higher (Stahl et al., 2010). However, other research suggested that cultural diversity may also harm team creativity due to a lack of common understanding, good communication, or conflict among group members (Paletz et al., 2014; Schimmelpfennig et al., 2021; van Knippenberg & Schippers, 2007). Indeed, experimental studies showed that diverse groups outperformed homogeneous groups only when group members were able to value group diversity or take other members' perspectives (Hoever et al., 2012; Homan et al., 2007). Thus, to prevent performance losses and enhance creativity, diverse teams must be provided with plenty of resources to ensure cooperation and effective communication (Schimmelpfennig et al., 2021).

Managing Difference and Uncertainty

So far, we have proposed that difference and uncertainty are well captured by several types of diversifying experiences, including psychopathology, adversity, enrichment, and diversity. We have also presented empirical evidence for links between various types of diversifying experiences and creativity. But one question remains: How might one get from diversifying experiences to creativity? In other words, how can one *manage* diversifying experiences (reflective of uncertainty and difference) and be set onto a path of creativity?

The Diversifying Experience Model (Gocłowska et al., 2018) provides an integrative framework from which to analyze the relation between diversifying experiences and creativity, and better understand how *managing* uncertainty and difference might be crucial to the underlying mechanisms that foster creativity. As mentioned before, diversifying experiences are defined as highly unusual and unexpected events or situations that push individuals outside the realm of "normality," and require them to adopt new ways of thinking and new perspectives (Damian & Simonton, 2014; Ritter et al., 2012). Diversifying experiences, including psychopathology, adversity, enrichment, and diversity can all be demanding due to the uncertainty and difference they introduce, so they are likely to require people to cognitively "adapt" or "accommodate" to their new circumstances (Crisp & Turner, 2011; Damian & Simonton, 2014; Gocłowska et al., 2018). This process may involve reconsidering strategies, values, and perspectives, and embracing new ones (Damian & Simonton, 2014; Tadmor et al., 2012). Prior research and theory proposed that the extent to which people can adapt or accommodate might depend on the intensity of the diversifying experiences and the available coping resources (Damian & Simonton, 2014; Gocłowska et al., 2018; Godart et al., 2015; Simonton, 2014a). The Diversifying Experience Model integrated and formalized prior thought and findings, proposing three key (testable) hypotheses on how managing diversifying experiences (uncertainty and difference) might foster creativity: (a) *managing intensity*; (b) *managing appraisal*, and (c) *managing adaptive resources*.

Regarding intensity, a curvilinear function might best characterize the link between diversifying experiences and creativity; that is, at lower levels, increments in diversifying experiences might foster creativity, but past a certain threshold of intensity, they might become detrimental. Indeed, a study of expatriate fashion designers (Godart et al., 2015) found a curvilinear link between cultural diversity and creativity, where creativity increased at low-to-moderate levels of diversity (years spent abroad, number of countries visited, distance between countries), but began to decrease at higher levels. The curvilinear link was also supported for adversity (abusive supervision) and creativity in the workplace among the general population (Lee et al., 2013) and for psychopathology and creativity among eminent figures (Simonton, 2014b), such that in both cases, mild levels of the diversifying experience were most conducive to creativity and high levels were detrimental. We are not aware of any research that specifically addressed ways of managing the objective intensity of diversifying experiences, and that is perhaps because each type of experience might have its own quirks. Furthermore, some types of experiences are more definitive and less amenable to intensity management (e.g., death of a loved one), but in this case, the "management" of the experience might be falling more under appraisals and adaptive resources, that is, the subjective experience of the event rather than the more "objective" intensity of the event. When attempting to characterize life experiences, it becomes apparent that there is a lack of dimensional life event taxonomies in the field (but see Luhmann et al., 2021 for a recent attempt to address this gap).

Regarding appraisal, challenge versus threat appraisals (Lazarus & Folkman, 1984) might explain the effects of diversifying experiences on creativity. Specifically, medium-intensity diversifying experiences might be linked with more challenge appraisals, greater cognitive accommodation, and more creativity, whereas more intense diversifying experiences, or those that exceed people's coping abilities, might be linked with more threat appraisals, lower cognitive accommodation, and less creativity. We are not aware of any research to date that has tested the proposed mediating role of challenge versus threat appraisals for the link between diversifying experiences and creativity, but prior work on appraisal and creativity does not deny the possibility. For instance, prior research found that challenge appraisals are associated with an approach motivation, positive affect, and a focus on gains and opportunities (Lazarus & Folkman, 1984; Schneider et al., 2009; Tomaka et al., 1997), all of which are known to benefit creative thinking (Baas et al., 2008). In contrast, threat appraisals tend to be associated with a narrow focus and an increased adherence to existing cognitive frameworks and decreased creativity (Jonas et al., 2014; Leung & Chiu, 2010.

Regarding adaptive resources, the model argues that adaptive resources available should moderate the effect of diversifying experiences on challenge and threat appraisals, and on creativity. These adaptive resources may include personality variables, cognitive abilities, coping skills, social resources, material resources, and more. Indeed, prior cross-sectional work on adversity and various outcomes has shown the moderating effects of personality traits such as high conscientiousness and emotional stability (Hengartner et al., 2017; Luchetti et al., 2016), cognitive abilities (Carson et al., 2003; Carson, 2011), social support (Ogińeska-Bulik, 2005; Prati & Pietrantoni, 2010), problem-focused coping skills (doing something to alter the source of the stress), and emotion-focused coping skills (managing the emotional distress associated with the situation) (Sattler et al., 2014; Yang & Ha, 2019). Despite this evidence from cross-sectional work, we are not aware of any longitudinal studies that have looked at moderators, and especially none that had creativity as the outcome of interest.

Notably, the Diversifying Experience Model, with its three different aspects related to managing diversifying experiences, allows room for the mixed results observed so far in the literature. Indeed, this model highlights the importance of understanding individual-level developmental processes and mechanisms.

Future Directions

We propose that one approach to learning more about facilitating creativity by managing difference and uncertainty at the individual level is to conduct high-quality longitudinal studies that track people's diversifying experiences and creativity across time. In an ideal world, we would have systematic tests, across multiple different samples, of different types of diversifying experiences and their possible co-development with creativity across the life span. These studies would need to consider a multitude of boundary conditions, such as different creative domains, different types of diversifying experiences, different types of populations, different types of measurement. Ideally, these studies will attempt not just to track the co-development of diversifying experiences and creativity, but also investigate the possible underlying mechanisms as laid out by the Diversifying Experience and Creativity model.

There are several challenges that this type of research faces: (a) obtaining sufficient samples (over a long enough time span) of people who will encounter, prospectively, the diversifying experience studied (or a combination of diversifying experiences); (b) measuring creativity using tools that are sensitive enough to record change over the span of the study, following the diversifying experiences; (c) measuring creativity in a way that can apply to the general population and/or conducting longitudinal studies of creativity within specific achievement domains (e.g., science, arts); and (d) better understanding causality (do diversifying experiences cause creativity or is creativity necessary to cope with diversifying experiences?). Ideally, the field will also adopt transparent and reproducible scientific practices.

Conclusion

We proposed that diversifying experiences are characterized by uncertainty and difference and reviewed empirical evidence for the link between four broad types of diversifying experiences (psychopathology, adversity, enrichment, and diversity) and creativity. We found mixed results, which pointed to the need of a more refined theoretical model. We proposed that the Diversifying Experience and Creativity model (Gocłowska et al., 2018) might be a good candidate for better explaining underlying mechanisms and boundary conditions, as well as the mixed results. Carefully designed longitudinal studies might help with the quest for understanding when, for whom, and how managing difference and uncertainty might foster creativity.

References

Abraham, A. (2014). Neurocognitive mechanisms underlying creative thinking: Indications from studies of mental illness. In J. C. Kaufman (Ed.), *Creativity and Mental Illness* (pp. 79–101). Cambridge University Press.

Acar, S., Chen, X., & Cayirdag, N. (2018). Schizophrenia and creativity: A meta-analytic review. *Schizophrenia Research, 195*, 23–31. https://doi.org/10.1016/j.schres.2017.08.036

Acar, S., & Sen, S. (2013). A multilevel meta-analysis of the relationship between creativity and schizotypy. *Psychology of Aesthetics, Creativity, and the Arts, 7*, 214–228. https://doi.org/10.1037/a0031975

Affleck, G., Tennen, H., & Rowe, J. (1991). *Infants in Crisis: How Parents Cope with Newborn Intensive Care and Its Aftermath*. Springer-Verlag.

Albert, R. S. (1971). Cognitive development and parental loss among the gifted, the exceptionally gifted and the creative. *Psychological Reports, 29*, 19–26. https://doi.org/10.2466/pr0.1971.29.1.19

Baas, M., De Dreu, C. K., & Nijstad, B. A. (2008). A meta-analysis of 25 years of mood-creativity research: Hedonic tone, activation, or regulatory focus? *Psychological Bulletin, 134*, 779–806. https://doi.org/10.1037/a0012815

Baas, M., Nijstad, B. A., Boot, N. C., & De Dreu, C. K. (2016). Mad genius revisited: Vulnerability to psychopathology, biobehavioral approach-avoidance, and creativity. *Psychological Bulletin, 142*, 668–692. https://doi.org/10.1037/bul0000049

Barrett, J. D., Vessey, W. B., Griffith, J. A., Mracek, D., & Mumford, M. D. (2014). Predicting scientific creativity: The role of adversity, collaborations, and work strategies. *Creativity Research Journal, 26*, 39–52. https://doi.org/10.1080/10400419.2014.873660

Bastian, B., Jetten, J., Thai, H. A., & Steffens, N. K. (2018). Shared adversity increases team creativity through fostering supportive interaction. *Frontiers in Psychology, 9*, 2309. https://doi.org/10.3389/fpsyg.2018.02309

Beghetto, R. A. (2019). Structured uncertainty: How creativity thrives under constraints and uncertainty. In C. A. Mullen (Ed.), *Creativity under Duress in Education? Resistive Theories, Practices, and Action* (pp. 27–40). Springer. 10.1007/978-3-319-90272-2_2

Beghetto, R. A., & Plucker, J. A. (2006). The relationship among schooling, learning, and creativity: "All roads lead to creativity" or "you can't get there from here"? In J. C. Kaufman & J. Baer (Eds.), *Creativity and Reason in Cognitive*

Development (pp. 316–332). Cambridge University Press. https://doi.org/10.1017/CBO9780511606915.019

Bell, S. T., Villado, A. J., Lukasik, M. A., Belau, L., & Briggs, A. L. (2011). Getting specific about demographic diversity variable and team performance relationships: A meta-analysis. *Journal of Management, 37*, 709–743. https://doi.org/10.1177/0149206310365001

Berry, C. (1981). The Nobel scientists and the origin of scientific achievement. *British Journal of Sociology, 32*, 381–391. https://doi.org/589284

Bilder, R. M., & Knudsen, K. S. (2014). Creative cognition and systems biology on the edge of chaos. *Frontiers in Psychology, 5*, 1104. http://dx.doi.org/10.3389/fpsyg.2014.01104.

Boals, A., Bedford, L. A., & Callahan, J. L. (2019). Perceptions of change after a trauma and perceived posttraumatic growth: A prospective examination. *Behavioral Sciences, 9*, 10. https://doi.org/10.3390/bs9010010

Carson, S. H. (2011). Creativity and psychopathology: A shared vulnerability model. *The Canadian Journal of Psychiatry, 56*, 144–153. https://doi.org/10.1177/070674371105600304

Carson, S. H., Peterson, J. B., & Higgins, D. M. (2003). Decreased latent inhibition is associated with increased creative achievement in high-functioning individuals. *Journal of Personality and Social Psychology, 85*, 499–506.

Cohen, G. (2006). Research on creativity and aging: The positive impact of the arts on health and illness. *Generations, 30*, 7–15.

Conner, T. S., DeYoung, C. G., & Silvia, P. J. (2018). Everyday creative activity as a path to flourishing. *The Journal of Positive Psychology, 13*, 181–189. https://doi.org/10.1080/17439760.2016.1257049

Conner, T. S., & Silvia, P. J. (2015). Creative days: a daily diary study of emotion, personality, and everyday creativity. *Psychology of Aesthetics, Creativity, and the Arts, 9*, 463–470. https://doi.org/10.1037/aca0000022

Crisp, R. J., & Turner, R. N. (2011). Cognitive adaptation to the experience of social and cultural diversity. *Psychological Bulletin, 137*, 242–266. https://doi.org/10.1037/a0021840

Csikszentmihályi, M. (1996). *Creativity: Flow and the Psychology of Discovery and Invention*. Collins.

Csikszentmihályi, M. (2014). *The Systems Model of Creativity: The Collected Works of Mihaly Csikszentmihalyi*. Springer. https://doi.org/10.1007/978-94-017-9085-7

Damian, R. L. (2017). Where do diversifying experiences fit in the study of personality, creativity, and career success? In G. J. Feist, R. Reiter-Palmon, & J. C. Kaufman (Eds.), *The Cambridge Handbook of Creativity and Personality Research* (pp. 102–123). Cambridge University Press. https://doi.org/10.1017/9781316228036.007

Damian, R. I., & Roberts, B. W. (2014). Integrating post-traumatic growth into a broader model of life experiences and personality change: Commentary on Jayawickreme and Blackie. *European Journal of Personality, 28*, 334–336.

Damian, R. I., & Simonton, D. K. (2014). Diversifying experiences in the development of genius and their impact on creative cognition. In D. K. Simonton (Ed.), *The Wiley Handbook of Genius* (pp. 375–393). Wiley Blackwell. https://doi.org/10.1002/9781118367377.ch18

Damian, R. I., & Simonton, D. K. (2015). Psychopathology, adversity, and creativity: Diversifying experiences in the development of eminent African Americans. *Journal of Personality and Social Psychology, 108*, 623–636. https://doi.org/10.1037/pspi0000011

Damian, R. I., & Spengler, M. (2020). Negligible effects of birth order on selection into scientific and artistic careers, creativity, and status attainment. *European Journal of Personality*. https://doi.org/10.1177/0890207020969010

de Souza, L. C., Guimarães, H. C., Teixeira, A. L., et al. (2014). Frontal lobe neurology and the creative mind. *Frontiers in Psychology, 5*, 761. http://dx.doi.org/10.3389/fpsyg.2014.00761

Eiduson, B. (1962). *Scientists: Their Psychological World*. Basic Books.

Fee, A., & Gray, S. J. (2012). The expatriate-creativity hypothesis: A longitudinal field test. *Human Relations, 65*, 1515–1538. https://doi.org/10.1177/0018726712454900

Forgeard, M. J. (2013). Perceiving benefits after adversity: The relationship between self-reported posttraumatic growth and creativity. *Psychology of Aesthetics, Creativity, and the Arts, 7*, 245–264. https://doi.org/10.1037/a0031223

Forthmann, B., Regehr, S., Seidel, J., et al. (2018). Revisiting the interactive effect of multicultural experience and openness to experience on divergent thinking. *International Journal of Intercultural Relations, 63*, 135–143. https://doi.org/10.1016/j.ijintrel.2017.10.002

Frazier, P., Tennen, H., Gavian, M., et al. (2009). Does self-reported posttraumatic growth reflect genuine positive change? *Psychological Science, 20*, 912–919. https://doi.org/10.1111/j.1467-9280.2009.02381.x

Furnham, A., Batey, M., Anand, K., & Manfield, J. (2008). Personality, hypomania, intelligence and creativity. *Personality and Individual Differences, 44*, 1060–1069. https://doi.org/10.1016/j.paid.2007.10.035

Godart, F. C., Maddux, W. W., Shipilov, A. V., & Galinsky, A. D. (2015). Fashion with a foreign flair: Professional experiences abroad facilitate the creative innovations of organizations. *Academy of Management Journal, 58*, 195–220. https://doi.org/10.5465/amj.2012.0575

Gocłowska, M. A., Damian, R. I., & Mor, S. (2018). The diversifying experience model: Taking a broader conceptual view of the multiculturalism–creativity link. *Journal of Cross-Cultural Psychology, 49*, 303–322. https://doi.org/10.1177/0022022116650258

Goertzel, M. G., Goertzel, V., & Goertzel, T. G. (1978). *300 Eminent Personalities: A Psychosocial Analysis of the Famous*. Jossey-Bass.

Helgeson, V. S., Reynolds, K. A., & Tomich, P. L. (2006). A meta-analytic review of benefit finding and growth. *Journal of Consulting and Clinical Psychology, 74*, 797–816. https://doi.org/10.1037/0022-006X.74.5.797

Hengartner, M. P., van der Linden, D., Bohleber, L., & von Wyl, A. (2017). Big five personality traits and the general factor of personality as moderators of stress and coping reactions following an emergency alarm on a Swiss University Campus. *Stress and Health, 33*, 35–44. https://doi.org/10.1002/smi.2671

Hoever, I. J., van Knippenberg, D., vanGinkel, W. P., & Barkema, H. G. (2012). Fostering team creativity: Perspective taking as key to unlocking diversity's potential. *Journal of Applied Psychology, 97*, 982–996. https://doi.org/10.1037/a0029159

Homan, A. C., van Knippenberg, D., Van Kleef, G. A., & De Dreu, C. K. W. (2007). Bridging faultlines by valuing diversity: The effects of diversity beliefs on information elaboration and performance in diverse work groups. *Journal of Applied Psychology*, *92*, 1189–1199. https://doi.org/10.1037/0021-9010.92.5.1189

Jayawickreme, E., & Blackie, L. E. (2014). Post-traumatic growth as positive personality change: Evidence, controversies and future directions. *European Journal of Personality*, *28*, 312–331. https://doi.org/10.1002/per.1963

Jayawickreme, E., Infurna, F. J., Alajak, K., et al. (2021). Post-traumatic growth as positive personality change: Challenges, opportunities, and recommendations. *Journal of Personality*, *89*, 145–165. https://doi.org/10.1111/jopy.12591

Jonas, E., McGregor, I., Klackl, J., et al. (2014). Threat and defense: From anxiety to approach. *Advances in Experimental Social Psychology*, *49*, 219–286. https://doi.org/10.1016/B978-0-12-800052-6.00004-4

Jung, R. E. (2014). Evolution, creativity, intelligence, and madness: "Here Be Dragons." *Frontiers in Psychology*, *5*, 784. http://dx.doi.org/10.3389/fpsyg.2014.0078

Karwowski, M., Lebuda, I., Szumski, G., & Firkowska-Mankiewicz, A. (2017). From moment-to-moment to day-to-day: Experience sampling and diary investigations in adults' everyday creativity. *Psychology of Aesthetics, Creativity, and the Arts*, *11*, 309–324. https://doi.org/10.1037/aca0000127

Kaufman, J. C. (Ed.) (2014). *Creativity and Mental Illness*. Cambridge University Press.

Kim, S. H., Vincent, L. C., & Goncalo, J. A. (2013). Outside advantage: Can social rejection fuel creative thought? *Journal of Experimental Psychology: General*, *142*, 605–611. https://doi.org/10.1037/a0029728

Kozbelt, A., Kaufman, S. B., Walder, D. J., Ospina, L. H., & Kim, J. U. (2014). The evolutionary genetics of the creativity-psychosis connection. In J. C. Kaufman (Ed.), *Creativity and Mental Illness* (pp. 102–132). Cambridge University Press. https://doi.org/10.1017/CBO9781139128902.009

Kyaga, S., Landén, M., Boman, M., et al. (2012). Mental illness, suicide and creativity: 40-year prospective total population study. *Journal of Psychiatric Research*, *47*, 83–90. https://doi.org/10.1016/j.jpsychires.2012.09.010

Kyaga, S., Lichtenstein, P., Boman, M., et al. (2011). Creativity and mental disorder: family study of 300 000 people with severe mental disorder. *The British Journal of Psychiatry*, *199*, 373–379. https://doi.org/10.1192/bjp.bp.110.085316

Lazarus, R. S., & Folkman, S. (1984). *Stress, Appraisal, and Coping*. Springer.

Lee, C. S., Therriault, D. J., & Linderholm, T. (2012). On the cognitive benefits of cultural experience: Exploring the relationship between studying abroad and creative thinking. *Applied Cognitive Psychology*, *26*, 768-778. https://doi.org/10.1002/acp.2857

Lee, S., Yun, S., & Srivastava, A. (2013). Evidence for a curvilinear relationship between abusive supervision and creativity in South Korea. *The Leadership Quarterly*, *24*, 724–731. https://doi.org/10.1016/j.leaqua.2013.07.002

Leung, A. K. Y., & Chiu, C. Y. (2010). Multicultural experience, idea receptiveness, and creativity. *Journal of Cross-Cultural Psychology*, *41*, 723–741. https://doi.org/10.1177/0022022110361707

Leung, A. K. Y., Maddux, W. W., Galinsky, A. D., & Chiu, C. Y. (2008). Multicultural experience enhances creativity: the when and how. *American Psychologist*, *63*, 169–181. https://doi.org/10.1037/0003-066X.63.3.169

Lindell, A. K. (2014). On the interrelation between reduced lateralization, schizotypy, and creativity. *Frontiers in Psychology*, *5*, 813. http://dx.doi.org/10.3389/fpsyg.2014.00813

Liu, G., & Shi, J. (2004). Development and education of rural children's creative thinking. *Chinese Journal of Special Education*, *44*, 76–79.

Luchetti, M., Terracciano, A., Stephan, Y., & Sutin, A. R. (2016). Personality and cognitive decline in older adults: Data from a longitudinal sample and meta-analysis. *Journals of Gerontology Series B: Psychological Sciences and Social Sciences*, *71*, 591–601. https://doi.org/10.1093/geronb/gbu184

Ludwig, A. M. (1992). Creative achievement and psychopathology: Comparison among professions. *American Journal of Psychotherapy*, *46*, 330–354.

Luhmann, M., Fassbender, I., Alcock, M., & Haehner, P. (2021). A dimensional taxonomy of perceived characteristics of major life events. *Journal of Personality and Social Psychology*, *121*, 633–668. https://doi.org/10.1037/pspp0000291

MacDonald, R., Byrne, C., & Carlton, L. (2006). Creativity and flow in musical composition: An empirical investigation. *Psychology of Music*, *34*, 292–306. https://doi.org/10.1177/0305735606064838

Maddux, W. W., & Galinsky, A. D. (2009). Cultural borders and mental barriers: The relationship between living abroad and creativity. *Journal of Personality and Social Psychology*, *96*, 1047–1061. https://doi.org/10.1037/a0014861

Maslow, A. H. (1970). *Motivation and Personality* (2nd ed.). Harper & Row.

Mayer, R. E. (2006). The role of domain knowledge in creative problem solving. In J. C. Kaufman & J. Baer (Eds.), *Creativity and Reason in Cognitive Development* (pp. 145–158). Cambridge University Press.

McMillen, J. C., Smith, E. M., & Fisher, R. H. (1997). Perceived benefit and mental health after three types of disaster. *Journal of Consulting and Clinical Psychology*, *65*, 733–739. https://doi.org/10.1037/0022-006X.65.5.733

Metzl, E. S., & Morrell, M. A. (2008). The role of creativity in models of resilience: Theoretical exploration and practical applications. *Journal of Creativity in Mental Health*, *3*, 303–318. https://doi.org/10.1080/15401380802385228

Mumford, M. D., Connelly, M. S., Scott, G., et al. (2005). Career experiences and scientific performance: A study of social, physical, life, and health sciences. *Creativity Research Journal*, *17*, 105–129. https://doi.org/10.1080/10400419.2005.9651474

Nietzsche, F. (1889). *Götzen-Dämmerung, oder, Wie man mit dem Hammer philosophiert* [Twilight of the Idols, or, How to Philosophize with a Hammer]. C.G. Naumann.

Ogińska-Bulik, N. (2005). The role of personal and social resources in preventing adverse health outcomes in employees of uniformed professions. *International Journal of Occupational Medicine and Environmental Health*, *18*, 233–240.

Open Science Collaboration. (2015). Estimating the reproducibility of psychological science. *Science*, *349*, aac4716. https://doi.org/10.1126/science.aac4716

Orkibi, H., & Ram-Vlasov, N. (2019). Linking trauma to posttraumatic growth and mental health through emotional and cognitive creativity. *Psychology of Aesthetics, Creativity, and the Arts*, *13*, 416–430. https://doi.org/10.1037/aca0000193

Owenz, M., & Fowers, B. J. (2018). Perceived post-traumatic growth may not reflect actual positive change: A short-term prospective study of relationship dissolution. *Journal of Social and Personal Relationships*, *36*, 3098–3116. https://doi.org/10.1177/0265407518811662

Page, S. E. (2007). *Difference: How the Power of Diversity Creates Better Groups, Firms, Schools, and Societies.* Princeton University Press.

Paletz, S. B., Miron-Spektor, E., & Lin, C. C. (2014). A cultural lens on interpersonal conflict and creativity in multicultural environments. *Psychology of Aesthetics, Creativity, and the Arts*, *8*, 237–252. https://doi.org/10.1037/a0035927

Pannells, T. C., & Claxton, A. F. (2008). Happiness, creative ideation, and locus of control. *Creativity Research Journal*, *20*, 67–71. https://doi.org/10.1080/10400410701842029

Parnas, J., Sandsten, K. E., Vestergaard, C. H., & Nordgaard, J. (2019). Schizophrenia and bipolar illness in the relatives of university scientists: An epidemiological report on the creativity-psychopathology relationship. *Frontiers in Psychiatry*, *10*, 175. https://doi.org/10.3389/fpsyt.2019.00175

Peri, G. (2012). The effect of immigration on productivity: Evidence from US states. *Review of Economics and Statistics*, *94*, 348–358. https://doi.org/10.1162/REST_a_00137

Post, F. (1994). Creativity and psychopathology a study of 291 world-famous men. *The British Journal of Psychiatry*, *165*, 22–34. https://doi.org/10.1192/bjp.165.1.22

Post, F. (1996). Verbal creativity, depression and alcoholism. *The British Journal of Psychiatry*, *168*, 545–555. https://doi.org/10.1192/bjp.168.5.545

Prati, G., & Pietrantoni, L. (2010). The relation of perceived and received social support to mental health among first responders: A meta-analytic review. *Journal of Community Psychology*, *38*, 403–417. https://doi.org/10.1002/jcop.20371

Puvimanasinghe, T., Denson, L. A., Augoustinos, M., & Somasundaram, D. (2019). Flexibility, creativity and responsiveness in trauma counselling: Working with refugees and asylum-seekers. *Australian Community Psychologist*, *30*, 10–29.

Ritter, S. M., Damian, R. I., Simonton, D. K., et al. (2012). Diversifying experiences enhance cognitive flexibility. *Journal of Experimental Social Psychology*, *48*, 961–964. https://doi.org/10.1016/j.jesp.2012.02.009

Roe, A. (1953). *The Making of a Scientist.* Dodd, Mead.

Runco, M. A., & Jaeger, G. J. (2012) The standard definition of creativity. *Creativity Research Journal*, *24*, 92–96. https://doi.org/10.1080/10400419.2012.650092

Saad, C. S., Damian, R. I., Benet-Martínez, V., Moons, W. G., & Robins, R. W. (2013). Multiculturalism and creativity: Effects of cultural context, bicultural identity, and ideational fluency. *Social Psychological and Personality Science*, *4*, 369–375. https://doi.org/10.1177/1948550612456560

Sattler, D. N., Boyd, B., & Kirsch, J. (2014). Trauma-exposed firefighters: Relationships among posttraumatic growth, posttraumatic stress, resource availability, coping and critical incident stress debriefing experience. *Stress and Health*, *30*, 356–365. https://doi.org/10.1002/smi.2608

Sawyer, A., Ayers, S., & Field, A. P. (2010). Posttraumatic growth and adjustment among individuals with cancer or HIV/AIDS: A meta-analysis. *Clinical Psychology Review*, *30*, 436–447. https://doi.org/10.1016/j.cpr.2010.02.004

Schimmelpfennig, R., Razek, L., Schnell, E., & Muthukrishna, M. (2021). Paradox of diversity in the collective brain. *Philosophical Transactions of the Royal Society B*, *377*, 20200316. https://doi.org/10.1098/rstb.2020.0316

Schneider, T. R., Rivers, S. E., & Lyons, J. B. (2009). The biobehavioral model of persuasion: Generating challenge appraisals to promote health 1. *Journal of Applied Social Psychology, 39*, 1928–1952. https://doi.org/10.1111/j.1559-1816.2009.00510.x

Sears, S. R., Stanton, A. L., & Danoff-Burg, S. (2003). The yellow brick road and the emerald city: Benefit finding, positive reappraisal coping and posttraumatic growth in women with early-stage breast cancer. *Health Psychology, 22*, 487–497. https://doi.org/10.1037/0278-6133.22.5.487

Seligman, M., & Csikszentmihályi, M. (2000). Positive psychology. *American Psychologist, 55*, 5–14. 10.1037//0003-066X.55.1.5

Shi, B., Qian, M., Lu, Y., Plucker, J. A., & Lin, C. (2012). The relationship between migration and Chinese children's divergent thinking. *Psychology of Aesthetics, Creativity, and the Arts, 6*, 106–111. https://doi.org/10.1037/a0028023

Simonton, D. K. (1984). Artistic creativity and interpersonal relationships across and within generations. *Journal of Personality and Social Psychology, 46*, 1273–1286. https://doi.org/10.1037/0022-3514.46.6.1273

Simonton, D. K. (1986). Biographical typicality, eminence, and achievement style. *Journal of Creative Behavior, 20*, 14–22. https://doi.org/10.1002/j.2162-6057.1986.tb00413.x

Simonton, D. K. (1992). The social context of career success and course for 2,026 scientists and inventors. *Personality and Social Psychology Bulletin, 18*, 452–463. https://doi.org/10.1177/0146167292184009

Simonton, D. K. (1994). *Greatness: Who Makes History and Why*. Guilford Press.

Simonton, D. K. (2004). *Creativity in Science: Chance, Logic, Genius, and Zeitgeist*. Cambridge University Press.

Simonton, D. K. (2014a). More method in the mad-genius controversy: A historiometric study of 204 historic creators. *Psychology of Aesthetics, Creativity, and the Arts, 8*, 53–61. https://doi.org/10.1037/a0035367

Simonton, D. K. (2014b). The mad-genius paradox: Can creative people be more mentally healthy but highly creative people more mentally ill? *Perspectives on Psychological Science, 9*, 470–480. https://doi.org/10.1177/1745691614543973

Simonton, D. K. (2019). Creativity and psychopathology: The tenacious mad-genius controversy updated. *Current Opinion in Behavioral Sciences, 27*, 17–21. https://doi.org/10.1016/j.cobeha.2018.07.006

Stahl, G. K., Maznevski, M. L., Voigt, A., & Jonsen, K. (2010). Unraveling the effects of cultural diversity in teams: A meta-analysis of research on multicultural work groups. *Journal of International Business Studies, 41*, 690–709. https://doi.org/10.1057/jibs.2009.85

Stanton, A. L., Bower, J. E., & Low, C. A. (2006). Posttraumatic growth after cancer. In L. G. Calhoun & R. G. Tedeschi (Eds.), *Handbook of Posttraumatic Growth: Research & Practice* (pp. 138–175). Erlbaum.

Stephenson, K., & Rosen, D. H. (2015). Haiku and healing: An empirical study of poetry writing as therapeutic and creative intervention. *Empirical Studies of the Arts, 33*, 36–60. https://doi.org/10.1177/0276237415569981

Tadmor, C. T., Galinsky, A. D., & Maddux, W. W. (2012). Getting the most out of living abroad: Biculturalism and integrative complexity as key drivers of creative and professional success. *Journal of Personality and Social Psychology, 103*, 520–542. https://doi.org/10.1037/a0029360

Takeuchi, R., Guo, N., Teschner, R. S., & Kautz, J. (2021). Reflecting on death amidst COVID-19 and individual creativity: Cross-lagged panel data analysis using four-wave longitudinal data. *Journal of Applied Psychology*, *106*, 1156–1168. https://doi.org/10.1037/apl0000949

Tan, C. S., Tan, S. A., Mohd Hashim, I. H., et al. (2019). Problem-solving ability and stress mediate the relationship between creativity and happiness. *Creativity Research Journal*, *31*, 15–25. https://doi.org/10.1080/10400419.2019.1568155

Tang, M., Hofreiter, S., Reiter-Palmon, R., Bai, X., & Murugavel, V. (2021). Creativity as a means to well-being in times of COVID-19 pandemic: Results of a cross-cultural study. *Frontiers in Psychology*, *12*, 265. https://doi.org/10.3389/fpsyg.2021.601389

Taylor, C. L. (2017). Creativity and mood disorder: A systematic review and meta-analysis. *Perspectives on Psychological Science*, *12*, 1040–1076. https://doi.org/10.1177/1745691617699653

Tedeschi, R. G., & Calhoun, L. G. (1996). The Posttraumatic Growth Inventory: Measuring the positive legacy of trauma. *Journal of Traumatic Stress*, *9*, 455–471. https://doi.org/10.1007/BF02103658

Tedeschi, R. G., & Calhoun, L. G. (2004). Posttraumatic growth: Conceptual foundations and empirical evidence. *Psychological Inquiry*, *15*, 1–18. https://doi.org/10.1207/s15327965pli1501_01

Tomaka, J., Blascovich, J., Kibler, J., & Ernst, J. M. (1997). Cognitive and physiological antecedents of threat and challenge appraisal. *Journal of Personality and Social Psychology*, *73*, 63–72. https://doi.org/10.1037/0022-3514.73.1.63

van Knippenberg, D., & Schippers, M. C. (2007). Work group diversity. Annual Review *Psychology*, *58*, 515-541. https://doi.org/10.1146/annurev.psych.58.110405.085546

Wang, Q., Zhao, X., Yuan, Y., & Shi, B. (2021). The relationship between creativity and intrusive rumination among Chinese teenagers during the COVID-19 pandemic: Emotional resilience as a moderator. *Frontiers in Psychology*, *11*, 601104. https://doi.org/10.3389/fpsyg.2020.601104

Xu, X., & Pang, W. (2020). Reading thousands of books and traveling thousands of miles: Diversity of life experience mediates the relationship between family SES and creativity. *Scandinavian Journal of Psychology*, *61*, 177–182. https://doi.org/10.1111/sjop.12591

Yanez, B. R., Stanton, A. L., Hoyt, M. A., Tennen, H., & Lechner, S. (2011). Understanding perceptions of benefit following adversity: How do distinct assessments of growth relate to coping and adjustment to stressful events? *Journal of Social and Clinical Psychology*, *30*, 699–721. https://doi.org/10.1521/jscp.2011.30.7.699

Yang, S. K., & Ha, Y. (2019). Predicting posttraumatic growth among firefighters: The role of deliberate rumination and problem-focused coping. *International Journal of Environmental Research and Public Health*, *16*, 3879. https://doi.org/10.3390/ijerph16203879

Zeng, W., Zeng, Y., Xu, Y., et al. (2021). The influence of post-traumatic growth on college students' creativity during the COVID-19 pandemic: the mediating role of general self-efficacy and the moderating role of deliberate rumination. *Frontiers in Psychology*, *12*, 665973. https://doi.org/10.3389/fpsyg.2021.665973

Zhai, H. K., Li, Q., Hu, Y. X., et al. (2021). Emotional creativity improves posttraumatic growth and mental health during the COVID-19 pandemic. *Frontiers in Psychology*, *12*, 600798. https://doi.org/10.3389/fpsyg.2021.600798

10 Creativity and Emotional Intelligence

A Complementary Pairing

Jessica D. Hoffmann and Sean McFarland

Are emotionally intelligent people more creative? Are creative people more emotionally intelligent? The short answer is, it depends on who you ask. We know that emotions are part of the creative process from the enhancing effects of pleasant emotions in laboratory studies of divergent thinking to the deep immersion in emotions of successful method acting. We also know that in between the emotions and the creative product is a person – a person with a personality and a set of skills, living in a particular context – and we know that how the person interprets, channels, and manages their emotions is important for their creativity. Yet, how we conceptualize and understand the relationship between a person's emotional abilities and their creativity vary widely by how we define these two constructs. In this chapter, we first describe prominent models of emotional intelligence (EI) and creativity and then review what evidence exists for the connection between the two. We next describe our own conceptualization of EI and creative achievement grounded in ability and actual performance, concluding with examples of training programs and educational initiatives that can support both the development of EI and creative abilities.

Models of Emotional Intelligence

The term *emotional intelligence* was first coined in 1990 and defined as "the ability to monitor one's own and others' feelings and emotions, to discriminate among them, and to use this information to guide one's thinking and actions" (Salovey & Mayer, 1990, p. 189). The idea reflected a more modern view of emotions as information and as experiences that can support cognition and decision making rather than hinder them. In 1995, EI was popularized by Daniel Goleman in his book, *Emotional Intelligence*: *Why It Can Matter More than IQ,* which brought the importance of social and emotional skills to the workforce. Over the next 27 years, both the basic construct of EI as well as its myriad benefits and potential predictive qualities have been investigated. Over this time, two major models have emerged.

First is the ability model of emotional intelligence. The construct, first introduced in 1990, refined in 1997, and since updated by Mayer and colleagues (2016), considers EI to be a set of skills, or a collection of four branches:

perception, appraisal, and expression (Branch I); emotional facilitation of thinking (Branch II); understanding and analyzing emotions (Branch III); and the regulation of emotions (Branch IV; Mayer et al., 2016; Neubauer & Freudenthaler, 2005). An advantage of ability models is that it is easy to imagine how the listed sets of skills within each branch could be learned (and taught) over time, leaving room for individual growth beyond one's natural talents.

The ability model is partial to performance-based assessments such as the Mayer-Salovey-Caruso Emotional Intelligence Test (MSCEIT; Mayer et al., 2003). The MSCEIT includes subtests such as emotion recognition using pictures of faces, emotion vocabulary, and selecting effective emotion-regulation strategies in response to vignettes. Similar to a test of cognitive intelligence, the MSCEIT measures EI based on the quality of one's answers according to either the number of respondents who selected each item (consensus criterion), or based on the judgments of the members of the International Society for Research on Emotions (expert criterion; Mayer et al., 2003). Higher scores on the MSCEIT have been found to predict leadership effectiveness, satisfaction with social relationships, and academic success (Brackett & Mayer, 2003; Kerr et al., 2006; Lopes et al., 2003).

The second of the theoretical approaches to EI is the mixed models, and most notably the trait model of EI (Bar-On, 1997). Whereas the ability model considers EI as a collection of various learned competencies, the trait model views EI as a broad label for a series of desirable, noncognitive, personality characteristics that predict adaptive social and emotional outcomes. These include intrapersonal attributes (self-regard, emotional self-awareness, and assertiveness), interpersonal skills (empathy and interpersonal relationships), adaptability (problem solving, reality testing, and flexibility), and stress management (stress tolerance and impulse control; Bar-On, 1997; Neubauer & Freudenthaler, 2005). According to Bar-On (2004), these competencies can be facilitated by different variables, such as self-actualization, independence, happiness, and optimism. Other notable mixed models of EI include Schutte and colleagues' (1998) model that stemmed from their created self-report measure, and the four cornerstone model of EI (Cooper & Sawaf, 1998) and six seconds model of EI (Freedman et al., 2005), both of which primarily consider the theoretical application of EI in social interactions rather than the theoretical conceptualization of what it means to be emotionally intelligent (Kewalramani et al., 2015).

The most widely adopted scale of the trait model of EI is Bar-On's own Emotional Quotient-Inventory (EQ-i; 1997). The EQ-i is a 133-item self-report measure administered to determine an individual's EI grounded in the competencies and facilitators that Bar-On names in his trait model. Scores on the EQ-i have been found to be correlated to various personality factors, self-monitoring ability, and life satisfaction (Livingstone & Day, 2005). However, research has found little to no correlation between how people perform on an ability test of EI and their self-report (Brackett et al., 2006), calling into question whether people are reliable reporters of their EI abilities and/or the ecological validity of existing EI ability tests.

As we explore how EI is related to creativity in the following sections, it will be important to consider which model of EI the researchers used, and thus which measures were administered.

Definitions of Creativity

Like EI, creativity is also a construct with multiple valid conceptualizations, and consequently, various measurement approaches. To start, *creative* – the adjective – can refer to a person: someone who has a particular set of traits, such as the personality trait of openness to experience or a tolerance for ambiguity, which can be measured by personality inventories. *Creative* can also refer to the person's behavior – someone who performs or produces things that are new and useful. Checklists of creative behaviors or creative achievements, such as the Creative Achievement Questionnaire (CAQ; Carson et al., 2005), or the Creative Behavior Questionnaire: Digital (CBQD; Hoffmann et al., 2016), are one way of determining frequency of creative behavior and level of creative achievement. Yet, such measures inevitably are not an exhaustive list of possible creative behaviors. Other options are self-reports of creative ability (e.g., the Kaufman Domains of Creativity Scale, K-DOCS; Kaufman, 2012; McKay et al., 2017), on which people are asked to rate their creativity, or creative potential, compared to others of similar life experience and age. As with EI, there are questions about how closely tied a person's perceptions of their creativity are to their actual creativity. For example, men tend to rate themselves more highly than women on scientific creativity, which may be a reflection of a stereotype rather than a true difference in ability (Miroshnik et al., 2021).

Creative can also refer to the product(s) the person produces: something that is new or original, and useful or relevant to a situation or problem (Stein, 1953). In the laboratory, studies may ask participants to produce something creative following a specific prompt. Most commonly used are tests of divergent thinking (e.g., Alternate Uses Test; Wallach & Kogan, 1965), which ask participants to generate ideas such as uses for a newspaper, and the responses can be rated by experts to determine those that are more or less creative in nature. These more performance-based measures too have their own issues, most notably their ecological validity. Idea generation in the lab for some hypothetical problem is quite different from generating creative ideas in real life, and even more removed from whether a person is likely to actually act upon them. In fact, some argue that divergent thinking is not a measure of creativity per se, but an estimate of creative potential (Runco & Acar, 2012).

The conceptualizations of creativity described here are nowhere near a complete list. There may be nearly as many models of creativity as there are creativity researchers. Of note, *creativity* can also be thought of and studied as a process (e.g., Rhodes, 1961). Within industrial organizational psychology, the term *creativity* is sometimes reduced to represent only the idea-generation stage, and the term *innovation* is used for the idea-implementation stage (Anderson et al., 2014). In other spheres, insights and "aha" moments are used to describe creative inspiration, leading to creativity assessments that go in completely the opposite direction from divergent thinking, instead asking people to employ convergent thinking to arrive at a single correct solution (e.g., the Remote Associates Test; Mednick & Mednick, 1971). Additional challenges in the measurement of creativity abound as creative talents can be extremely domain specific (Baer, 2012), and whether something is deemed creative must account for the social and material context in which it is received (Glăveanu, 2013, 2015).

Summary

In the end, both EI and creativity are dynamic constructs. Whether a person, behavior, or process is viewed as emotionally intelligent depends on the context, the audience, and the person's goal, just as is true for creativity. Both creativity and EI have documented gaps between knowledge and skill and whether that is translated into behavior in a moment, and both have gaps between people's self-perceptions and their achievement as judged by others. Finally, both EI and creativity must be viewed through a developmental lens; an impressive feat of emotion regulation for a 5-year-old is different from what we expect of an adult, just as is true for creative thinking and production. As we ask how EI and creativity are connected, we must be careful to consider the definitions used, the measures selected, and the samples studied.

Connecting Creativity and Emotional Intelligence

What do we know about the connection between creativity and EI so far? In 2019, Xu and colleagues completed a meta-analysis of 75 studies to compile the evidence to-date on the relationship between EI and creativity. Overall, the authors reported a moderate association between EI and creativity ($r = .32$, p < .001). However, this relationship was significantly moderated by the type of EI measure and creativity measure used, such that a stronger relationship was found for trait EI and creative behavior or creative personality, and was significantly weaker when using EI ability or creativity performance tests such as divergent thinking or remote associations.

Xu and colleagues (2019) also reported a number of moderators of the EI and creativity relationship, including culture (i.e., East Asian samples yielded higher EI and creativity correlations), as well as gender and employment status. For gender, the researchers found that the relationship between EI and creativity was stronger in males than in females. For employment status, the authors found that employees exhibited a stronger relationship between EI and creativity than did students. When considering findings on the relationship between EI and creativity, it seems one must consider the type of EI measure deployed, the type of creativity measure deployed, and the potential demographic moderators listed above. Further examination of studies contained in this meta-analysis better clarify the relationship.

A 2018 study conducted by Tu and colleagues tested the relationship between trait EI (measured by subjective reports) and creativity (measured by both a subjective report and an objective test). Participants for this study included 281 undergraduate students in a gifted program at a top university in Beijing, China. The authors found a significant effect such that trait EI was correlated with a subjective report of creative behavior ($r = .47, p < .01$). There was also a smaller significant correlation between trait EI and an objective test of divergent thinking ($r = .15, p < .01$). It is important to note that some of these results may be explained in Xu and colleagues' (2019) findings that East Asian samples had a significantly higher correlation between EI and creativity ($r = .48, p < .01$) than other cultural samples. While both sets of analyses by Tu and colleagues showed significant correlations, the correlation coefficient between trait EI and the divergent thinking test is small enough that it may be explained by this cultural bias. Also of note is that these students studied creativity improvement as part of their program and were likely familiar with creativity constructs and measures before their participation.

Another study that illustrates the meta-analysis findings of Xu and colleagues (2019) is a study by Ivcevic and colleagues (2007). Here, the researchers tested and replicated the correlation between ability EI and both objective tests and a subjective report of trait and ability model emotional creativity, as well as ability model cognitive creativity and self-reported creative behavior. The sample consisted of undergraduate psychology students at the University of New Hampshire in both the initial study and replication study. Results in the initial study showed a low negative correlation between ability EI and both the subjective report measure of creativity and the objective tests of creativity. Similar findings appeared in the replication sample of the study. We can see this pattern in findings continuing across various studies. In studies conducted by Neubauer and colleagues (2018) and Parke and colleagues (2015) on the direct link between ability EI and creativity, both reported findings supporting the null hypothesis despite utilizing different methods of measuring ability EI and creativity. Of note, Parke and colleagues did find evidence for the moderating effect of emotion-regulation ability on the relationship between the processing requirements of a particular job and a worker's positive affect, as well as a moderating effect of emotion facilitation skills (i.e., using emotions to facilitate thought) on the relationship between positive affect and creativity. These indirect ways in which specific emotional intelligence skills can support creativity are discussed more in depth in later sections.

Conversely, in studies by Tajpour and colleagues (2018) and Furnham (2016) on the relationship between trait EI and creativity, the relationship was seemingly moderated by the type of measurement for creativity such that there was a stronger correlation when measuring cumulative creative behavior or lifetime accomplishment rather than performance on short, divergent thinking tasks. These findings support those of Xu and colleagues (2019) such that, when considering the ability model of EI and either subjective reports or objective tests of creativity, the two constructs are predominantly independent of each other. Ivcevic et al. (2007) make the case for why this might be, writing that "in order to obtain a high score on the test of EI, one has to conform to a criterion of correctness ... which may impose constraints on originality ... ability to use emotions in unconventional ways (i.e., creating in negative rather than positive moods) is not captured by tests of EI" (p. 206).

Emotional Intelligence Abilities in Support of Creative Goals

Hoffmann et al. (2021) proposed a model of the intersection between creativity, personality, and emotions in which they wrote, "if emotions are fuel for creativity ... certain personality traits, such as openness to experience, are akin to turbocharging the engine, lowering the threshold for creative thought and creative behavior" (p. 152). Here we dare to extend the metaphor further to include the skill of the driver. They may be brave, motivated, and behind the wheel of a fast car, but can they shift, steer, overcome setbacks, and persist to the finish line? From here, we focus on EI abilities and make the case that while there may not be a one-to-one correlation between greater EI and creative behavior, emotional abilities can certainly enable greater creativity in more subtle, yet influential, ways. Moreover, engaging in creative tasks can support the development of EI abilities.

Self-Awareness

A vast body of research on the role of emotion states in the creative process exists, much citing the role of pleasant and activating emotions in enhanced performance on tests of creative thinking (Baas et al., 2008), and others showing that unpleasant emotions can also support creative ideas (e.g., Akinola & Mendes, 2008; Friedman et al., 2007; Kaufmann & Vosburg, 2002). The dual pathway model (De Dreu et al., 2008) explains how both pleasant and unpleasant moods might support creative thinking. Essentially, pleasant moods enhance creativity through increasing cognitive flexibility and broad thinking, while unpleasant moods might signal that the problem is not yet solved and more work is needed, or might be the motivation to solve a problem creatively (after all, necessity is the mother of invention). This model is in line with the feelings-as-information theory (Schwarz, 1990, 2001, 2012) and mood-as-input model (Martin et al., 1993), which posit that people attend to their feelings and use them as a source of information. However, for any of these feelings to have their hypothesized impact on creativity, the person must be aware of their emotion state, and able to accurately identify what they are feeling and why they are feeling it.

In a study of the potential benefits of negative moods on creativity in the workplace, George and Zhou (2002) specifically looked at the moderating effect of *clarity of feelings* – awareness and understanding about one's own affective experience (Salovey et al., 1995). The authors ascribed to the mood-as-input model, which holds that in contexts where creativity is the objective, and workers have autonomy to determine the adequacy of their creative efforts, employees will use their emotions as information about their job performance. In their study of employees at a large helicopter manufacturer, they found that both high recognition and reward for creativity and clarity of feelings moderated the relationship between unpleasant moods and greater worker creativity. In other words, when workers were self-aware of their unpleasant affect, and were in a context where creativity would be recognized and rewarded, then their negative affect led to greater worker creative performance.

Using Emotions to Facilitate Creative Thought

Another skill within the EI construct is the ability to use emotions to facilitate thinking (Mayer et al., 2001; Mayer & Salovey, 1997). *Using emotions* refers to the act of channeling emotional information to support thinking, reasoning, and decision-making. As with the other components of EI, using emotions is a skill with individual variation. Whereas excitement might lead some to launch a creative project, others might find that excitement distracting. In the context of creativity, emotions can be skillfully applied to specifically support the creative thinking process. There are many avenues by which creators might use emotions. Emotions might serve as the impetus for a project (e.g., a photographer who sees an awe-inspiring sunset and captures the image on film). Alternatively, emotions might be used to guide the creative process (e.g., a painter halfway through a mural whose displeasure at the likely outcome signals a need to completely change course on the project). Still others might use emotions to enhance task performance (e.g., a writer who knows they write best in the morning and saves editing for the evening when they are lower energy).

Interviews with creators support this notion of using emotions. Brace and Johns-Putra (2010) summarize their study of writers: "moved by the affective qualities of a landscape, sound, place, conversation, troubled relationship or emotion, these writers sought to make it real . . ." (p. 404). In another study of 100 artists, including dancers, creative writers, paintings, and graphic designers, among others, each was asked to describe the role of emotions throughout their creative process (Hoffmann & Russ, 2016). The answers were analyzed for mention of EI skills, and the theme of using emotions to facilitate thinking arose repeatedly. In one case a painter wrote, "Sadness allows the colors of the painting to create mood. Happiness helps hold the painting together and keeps the composition flowing." A writer expressed a similar sentiment, noting, "As I write, the emotion is something to use, not feel. Later, when I edit, I can call up the emotions and gauge whether I've 'used' them well (not too much or too little)."

Another way to think about using emotions to facilitate creative production is to consider how one might take advantage of mood congruence – the enhancing relationships between a particular mood and a particular task. For example, in his book *When: The Scientific Secrets of Perfect Timing*, Daniel Pink (2018) describes how for many there is a natural daily rhythm to their moods. This is also described as a person's chronotype – their personal sleep patterns and preference for different activities at different times of the day. Kühnel et al. (2022) applied this concept to creativity, hypothesizing that alignment between a person's chronotype and the time of day would improve creativity (measured by divergent thinking and a work-related creativity survey). In three studies, with a diverse set of workers from a range of industries, they found that they called a *synchrony effect*, that early chronotypes (i.e., morning people, who have peak energy in the morning) tended to be more creative in the morning, while late chronotypes (i.e., evening people, whose energy peaks later in the day) tended to be more creative in the late afternoon. Given these findings, an emotionally intelligent worker, therefore, with the autonomy to do so, might use this information and self-awareness of their own chronotype to their benefit.

A study by Cohen and Andrade (2004) demonstrates that, at some level, people are aware that certain moods will best facilitate upcoming tasks. In their study, participants were told that they would be completing either an analytic task or an imaginative one, and were then offered the option to listen to happy or sad music before beginning. The authors found that people tended to choose the music that would put them in the mood most congruent with their anticipated task (i.e., those expecting to do analytic work chose sad music, while those expecting a creative task chose happy music). These results speak not only to mood congruence, but also to the fact that people may purposefully put themselves into a necessary mood, rather than simply take the moods as they come. In other words, they might match the mood to the task, rather than the task to the mood – through emotion regulation.

Emotion-Regulation Ability

Emotion regulation refers to "the processes by which individuals influence which emotions they have, when they have them, and how they experience and express these emotions" (Gross, 1998, p. 275). Effective emotion regulation can support creativity in numerous ways, from decreasing unhelpful emotions (e.g., stage fright), or intentionally generating helpful ones (e.g., generating pleasantness prior to brainstorming), to down-regulating excitement when it is time to focus and execute, or decreasing feelings of frustration to persevere through creative setbacks.

Discussion of emotion regulation in the service of creativity has a long history; Freud (1958/1925) proposed that strong emotions led to creativity through sublimation (e.g., expressing one's aggressive or otherwise socially unacceptable thoughts and feelings through art). Pine and Holt (1960) wrote of adaptive regression as a pathway to creativity – a take on Kris' (1952) regression in the service of the ego – describing the "at least partially controlled use of primitive, nonlogical, and drive dominated modes of thinking" (p. 370). Artist interviews reveal evidence of such purposeful, (temporary) regression (Hoffmann & Russ, 2016). One artist stated, "Initially, I worked on impulse, letting my excitement drive the process," and another stated, "Anger helps create strong striking lines in the painting." A choreographer described an early stage of creating a new piece in which she turned off the lights, closed her eyes, and let the music flow through her.

More contemporary pathways by which emotion regulation might support creativity have also been articulated. For example, at its simplest, a person with greater emotion regulation might more successfully maintain or increase the frequency of their positive moods, which could then enhance creative thinking. We can also consider the link between emotion regulation and creativity through the lens of the "affective shift" research, in which "high creativity results if a person experiences an episode of negative affect that is followed by a decrease in negative affect and an increase in positive affect" (Bledow et al., 2013, p. 432). Such a shift, starting from a place of unpleasantness, and shifting to pleasantness, need not be happenstance, but rather could be due to a person's active, intentional emotion regulation.

Empirical research has also demonstrated an association between those with greater emotion-regulation ability and creativity. For example, children who demonstrated greater imagination in pretend play and higher performance on divergent thinking tests were also rated by their parents as having higher emotion-regulation abilities (Hoffmann & Russ, 2012). Ivcevic and Brackett (2015) added to this body of work, reporting findings that in adolescents high on openness to experience, emotion-regulation ability predicted peer nominations of creativity. In other words, emotion regulation served as a bridge between creative potential and creative achievement. We also see the reverse: that poor emotion regulation is associated with lower creative performance. For example, Butcher and Niec (2005) found that poor emotion regulation mediated the relationship between disruptive behavior and lower creative achievement as measured both by parent reports and divergent thinking tests.

Emotional Intelligence and Creativity Training

A benefit of conceptualizing EI as a set of abilities is that we can more easily adopt a growth mindset. Rather than treating EI as a stable trait – something you either have or you don't – we can delineate a clear set of skills that can be learned, practiced, and developed. Mayer and Salovey (1997) listed four skills: recognizing emotions, using emotions to facilitate thought, understanding emotions, and regulating emotions. Goleman (2001) proposed a different set, making a self–other distinction, and a recognizing versus regulating distinction, leading to four abilities: (a) recognition of emotions in self; (b) recognition of emotions in others; (c) regulation of emotions in self; and (d) regulation of emotions in others. Zeidner et al. (2006) summarize, "EI has been defined as: the competence to identify, monitor, and express emotions; to label, differentiate, and understand the complex nature, antecedents, and consequences of emotions; to assimilate emotions in thought and strategically use emotions to achieve one's adaptive goals; and to effectively regulate positive and negative emotions, both in self and others" (p. 101).

Despite the lack of consensus, we can acknowledge that a benefit of clearly and somewhat narrowly defining EI is that it allows us to more easily imagine how a person might get better at it. We can learn to decode microexpressions accurately in others' faces. We can read more great literature and develop a larger repertoire of emotion words with which to communicate the nuances of our inner experience. Indeed, research shows that EI skills can be improved through training and practice (Greenberg et al., 1995; Rivers et al., 2013).

In parallel, research has increasingly recognized that creativity is for everyone, and not merely for a gifted, eminent few (Kaufman & Beghetto, 2009). Research, in turn, has also demonstrated that creativity skills can be improved through training and practice. Scott and colleagues (2004) conducted a meta-analysis of 70 creativity training studies, and found significant effects across populations studied, settings, and various kinds of creativity (divergent thinking, problem solving, performance, and attitudes and behavior). The authors do note that the most successful training programs were those that focused on developing participants' cognitive skills by providing people with specific strategies such as heuristics for generating ideas or combining disparate concepts, and then opportunities for realistic practice. A review specifically examining creative problem-solving tools that have been used to enhance problem finding and idea generation found additional supporting evidence that certain techniques are effective, though many caveats remain regarding context, creativity measurement, and individual differences (Vernon et al., 2016).

These findings are compelling; however, they leave open the question of what impact EI training might have if combined with creativity training. Engaging with art and other creative disciplines, especially in the context of creativity training, could lead to the added benefit of developing EI skills as well. For example, learning to reduce anxiety through taking deep breaths before a ballet performance is an emotion-regulation skill that dancers can use when faced with other high-pressure situations in the future. At a minimum, talking about the emotional content of artwork is a great way to help those unpracticed in discussing feelings to get started while maintaining some psychological distance. Given the potential complementary benefits of EI and creativity skills, several lines of research have begun examining simultaneous training in both. We next describe several such programs, their theoretical underpinnings, strategies for developing EI and creativity skills simultaneously, and their outcomes.

Creativity and Emotion Skills through Play

Goldstein and Lerner (2018) point out that while there are a multitude of social and emotional learning programs available, most for young children do involve elements of creative engagement, whether that be play, puppet shows, or reading fiction. Yet, the unique contribution of the creative elements in the development of emotional skills has not been determined. In an effort to determine the specific benefit of dramatic play on emotional control, the authors conducted a randomized trial with three groups: a dramatic play group, a block-building group (to control for physical activity and group interaction without the fantasy element), and a story-time group (to control for their being a story with characters without the physical activity element), and found that for the dramatic play group only, there were improvements in emotional-control skills.

Other studies have specifically aimed at enhancing creativity skills (including the requisite emotion skills). For one, research conducted by Sandra Russ and colleagues has explored the facilitation of pretend play skills, both cognitive (e.g., organization of a narrative, inclusion of imaginative elements) and emotional (e.g., positive and negative affect expression). In an intervention aimed at enhancing children's imagination during play, Moore and Russ (2008) found that individual play sessions between a child and facilitator led not only to gains in children's imagination during play, but also to changes in emotion expression, leading the authors to conclude, "cognitive play skills may have a stronger impact on affective processes than anticipated" (p. 427). Additional work on Russ' play intervention has since been done, most recently with groups of preschoolers (Fehr et al., 2021), and in a sample of children diagnosed with Prader–Willi syndrome using a telehealth model (Dimitropoulos et al., 2021).

Creativity and Emotion Skills through the Visual Arts

In a series of multiweek courses designed for the Botin Foundation, Hoffmann, Ivcevic, and colleagues tested the impact of combining EI and creativity training through engagement with the visual arts (see Hoffmann & Ivcevic, 2022, for a review). Hosted at the Botin Center's art center in Santander, Spain, children, adolescents, adults, and families were led through 6- to 8-session courses. For children, the course centered on art-observation and art-making based around an emotion-of-the-week (i.e., happiness, sadness, anger, fear, and calm). In a pilot test of children (ages 6–12), children reported greater understanding of how emotions could facilitate their thinking, agreed that their first idea was not always their most creative, and endorsed that they had learned new emotion vocabulary words, strategies to express themselves, and ways of identifying feelings in others (Ebert et al., 2015a). In an additional controlled experiment with 64 children, 9–12 years old, children enrolled in the course showed significantly improved emotions skills and a greater frequency of engaging in everyday creative behaviors compared to the control group (Hoffmann et al., 2020).

In the course for adults, participants engaged in intensive observation of artwork (up to 15 minutes) and were taught to notice and engage with their unpleasant and pleasant emotions as information for problem solving. A pilot study revealed that adult participants felt they had gained more ability to sustain attention with art, to use multiple perspectives to understand art, and to use imagination and visualization strategies. They also stated that they were leaving with more confidence in their creative problem-solving skills (Ebert et al., 2015b). Sixty-six adults were then recruited for a controlled experiment of the course, and were found to have more creative behaviors and more original responses when problem finding than those in the control condition (Hoffmann et al., 2018).

The successful implementation of courses for all ages that simultaneously taught EI and creativity demonstrated several important points. First, the simple demonstration that creativity skills and EI skills can be improved and can be addressed in a complementary fashion rather than one as the target and one as an outcome. Second, the visual arts were a viable medium for teaching EI as well as teaching creativity, making the case that art centers, galleries, and exhibition spaces play an active role in fostering a creative and emotionally intelligent citizenry (Ivcevic et al., 2016).

Creativity and Emotion Skills through Advocacy

In a school-based approach, Hoffmann and colleagues describe a youth empowerment social-emotional learning program built on a creative problem-solving framework and grounded in fostering EI skills: inspirED (Hoffmann et al., in press). Through inspirED, middle and high school students get training, coaching, and free resources to form a team at their school and launch a campaign or project to improve their school's climate (e.g., student connectedness, celebration of diversity, physical safety). InspirED follows four steps (acronym ABCD): *assess* your school climate, *brainstorm* project ideas, *commit and complete* your project, and *debrief* your impact. These stages map nicely onto general stages of creative problem solving (i.e., problem finding and/or problem construction; idea generation; idea evaluation and execution; and validation and reflection). The stages of inspirED also each incorporate EI skills (e.g., recognizing emotions in oneself and others, such as disappointment or frustration that signals an opportunity for change; using emotions to generate ideas; managing emotions to maintain motivation and persistence or to advocate for others to join the cause).

A cornerstone of inspirED is what is called the "emotions matter mindset" – an attitude that emotions are information, and thus both pleasant and unpleasant emotions have value. In the work context, George and Zhou (2007) note that the benefits of pleasant and unpleasant emotions for creativity are most evident when the context is supportive and both pleasant and unpleasant emotions are high – the dual tuning model. For inspirED, the same theory applies, though the context is school, and the supportive supervisors are the inspirED team: educator advocates and the inspirED coaches. Students are taught that unpleasant emotions signal opportunities to advocate for change (e.g., outrage at injustices), the need to persist (e.g., disappointment with little progress), or the need to switch tactics (e.g., frustration with a roadblock). Pleasant emotions help get a project started (e.g., excitement about a new idea), help generate bold, unconventional ideas (e.g., happiness that supports broad, flexible thinking), and keep people going when excitement starts to wane (e.g., optimism and anticipation of the positive outcome). Early data from a trial of inspirED indicate that students on inspirED teams do show an improved "emotions matter mindset" – an increase in their endorsement that both pleasant and unpleasant emotions are helpful – after completing just one round of the ABCD process (Hoffmann, 2021).

Creativity and Emotion Skills through Interval Training

In a randomized controlled trial of secondary students, Ruiz-Ariza and colleagues (2019) studied the effects that an increase in physical activity had on various factors of social-emotional well-being, including creativity and emotionality. Students were guided in completing structured cooperative high-intensity interval training (C-HIIT) over 2 weeks. C-HIIT is described as relatively short physical activity in small groups and at a high-intensity threshold, designed to reach an individual's target heart rate quickly. In both pre- and post-intervention, these participants were given a measure of creativity and emotional intelligence, and they also took a baseline measure of physical activity pre-intervention. Results showed a significant improvement in well-being and sociability in all students, as well as especially significant improvement in creativity among students who were considered inactive students from their self-reported physical activity prior to the intervention. The authors did note that students' measured body mass index (BMI) was a confounding variable; however, there is a growing body of literature criticizing BMI as an accurate method of measuring body fat percentage (e.g., Nuttall, 2015). Taking this into consideration, this study supports C-HIIT as a method of physical activity to promote both creativity and emotional intelligence in adolescents, especially in students who were previously not often engaged in physical activity. C-HIIT would be ideal for students who find themselves with the will to engage in more physical activity for its well-being benefits but lacking the time for a more extensive exercise routine.

Conclusion

In summary, there is no single answer to how creativity and EI are connected, but rather there are many – a variety of potential pathways by which EI might enhance creativity, or a person might possess traits connected to both constructs. Specifically within ability models and true creative performance, we have seen that those already predisposed to high creative potential are helped by having better emotion-regulation ability, and those who are aware of and can manage their emotions effectively may more easily navigate the emotional rollercoaster that is the creative process.

Not covered in this chapter are the additional ways in which other-oriented emotion skills are relevant to creativity. The comedian must have a sense of what the audience will find funny. The advertiser must know how to spark emotions in potential customers. The emotionally intelligent leader is one who can manage not only their own emotions but also those of their team members. This too is an important area for future research. Unsurprisingly, creativity and EI both make the top 10 list of skills sought by employers (World Economic Forum, 2018, 2020). The world increasingly needs a workforce that can collaborate and innovate, and EI and creativity will be increasingly necessary to meet this need.

Finally, we consider how creativity training might be enhanced by EI training and vice versa. This work is particularly interesting because much research in creativity training has proven to be domain specific and, in some cases, extremely specific (e.g., learning to write poetry well does not lead to better short storytelling). A focus on EI to support creativity incorporates skills that are relevant across creative tasks (e.g., handling frustrating setbacks, recovering from critique), and thus creativity training programs focused on emotion skills may have promise of generalization that other training programs have failed to demonstrate. This too is a direction for future research.

References

Akinola, M., & Mendes, W. B. (2008). The dark side of creativity: Biological vulnerability and negative emotions lead to greater artistic creativity. *Personality and Social Psychology Bulletin*, *34*(12), 1677–1686. https://doi.org/10.1177/0146167208323933

Anderson, N., Potočnik, K., & Zhou, J. (2014). Innovation and creativity in organizations: A state-of-the-science review, prospective commentary, and guiding framework. *Journal of Management*, *40*(5), 1297–1333. https://doi.org/10.1177/0149206314527128

Baas, M., De Dreu, C. K., & Nijstad, B. A. (2008). A meta-analysis of 25 years of mood-creativity research: Hedonic tone, activation, or regulatory focus? *Psychological Bulletin*, *134*(6), 779–806. https://doi.org/10.1037/a0012815

Baer, J. (2012). Domain specificity and the limits of creativity theory. *The Journal of Creative Behavior*, *46*(1), 16–29. https://doi.org/10.1002/jocb.002

Bar-On, R. (2004). The Bar-On Emotional Quotient Inventory (EQ-i): Rationale, description and summary of psychometric properties. In G. Geher (Ed.), *Measuring Emotional Intelligence: Common Ground and Controversy* (pp. 115–145). Nova Science.

Bar-On, R. (1997). *The Bar-On Emotional Quotient Inventory (BarOn EQ-i)*. Multi-Health Systems Inc.

Bledow, R., Rosing, K., & Frese, M. (2013). A dynamic perspective on affect and creativity. *Academy of Management Journal*, *56*(2), 432–450. https://doi.org/10.5465/amj.2010.0894

Brace, C., & Johns-Putra, A. (2010). Recovering inspiration in the spaces of creative writing. *Transactions of the Institute of British Geographers, 35*(3), 399–413. https://doi.org/10.1111/j.1475-5661.2010.00390.x

Brackett, M. A., & Mayer, J. D. (2003). Convergent, discriminant, and incremental validity of competing measures of emotional intelligence. *Personality and Social Psychology Bulletin, 29*(9), 1147–1158. https://doi.org/10.1177/0146167203254596

Brackett, M. A., Rivers, S. E., Shiffman, S., Lerner, N., & Salovey, P. (2006). Relating emotional abilities to social functioning: A comparison of self-report and performance measures of emotional intelligence. *Journal of Personality and Social Psychology, 91*(4), 780–795. https://doi.org/10.1037/0022-3514.91.4.780

Butcher, J. L., & Niec, L. N. (2005). Disruptive behaviors and creativity in childhood: The importance of affect regulation. *Creativity Research Journal, 17*(2–3), 181–193. https://doi.org/10.1080/10400419.2005.9651478

Carson, S. H., Peterson, J. B., & Higgins, D. M. (2005). Reliability, validity, and factor structure of the creative achievement questionnaire. *Creativity Research Journal, 17*(1), 37–50. https://doi.org/10.1207/s15326934crj1701_4

Cohen, J. B., & Andrade, E. B. (2004). Affective intuition and task-contingent affect regulation. *Journal of Consumer Research, 31*, 358–367. https://doi.org/10.1086/422114

Cooper, R. K., & Sawaf, A. (1998). *Executive EQ: Emotional Intelligence in Leadership and Organizations.* Grosset-Putnam.

De Dreu, C. K., Baas, M., & Nijstad, B. A. (2008). Hedonic tone and activation level in the mood-creativity link: Toward a dual pathway to creativity model. *Journal of Personality and Social Psychology, 94*(5), 739–756. https://doi.org/10.1037/0022-3514.94.5.739

Dimitropoulos, A., Zyga, O., Doernberg, E., & Russ, S. W. (2021). Show me what happens next: Preliminary efficacy of a remote play-based intervention for children with Prader-Willi syndrome. *Research in Developmental Disabilities, 108*, 103820. https://doi.org/10.1016/j.ridd.2020.103820

Ebert, M., Hoffmann, J. D., Ivcevic, Z., Phan, C., & Brackett, M. A. (2015a). Teaching emotion and creativity skills through art: A workshop for children. *International Journal of Creativity and Problem Solving, 25*(2), 23–35.

Ebert, M., Hoffmann, J. D., Ivcevic, Z., Phan, C., & Brackett, M. A. (2015b). Creativity, emotion and art: Development and initial evaluation of a workshop for professional adults. *International Journal of Creativity and Problem Solving, 25*(2), 47–59.

Fehr, K., Hoffmann, J. D., Ramasami, J., & Chambers, D. (2021). Feasibility of a group play intervention in early childhood. *Journal of Creativity, 31*. 100008. https://doi.org/10.10116/j.yjoc.2021.100008

Freedman, J., Ghini, M., & Fiedeldey-van Dijk, C. (2005). Emotional intelligence and performance. *Journal of Personal Relationships, 15*(4), 8–20.

Friedman, R. S., Förster, J., & Denzler, M. (2007). Interactive effects of mood and task framing on creative generation. *Creativity Research Journal, 19*(2–3), 141–162. https://doi.org/10.1080/10400410701397206

Freud, S. (1958). On creativity and the unconscious. In *Papers on Applied Psychoanalysis*, vol. 4, *Collected Works of Sigmund Freud*. Harper (original work published in 1925).

Furnham, A. (2016). The relationship between cognitive ability, emotional intelligence and creativity. *Psychology, 7*(2), 193–197. https://doi.org/10.4236/psych.2016.72021

George, J. M., & Zhou, J. (2002). Understanding when bad moods foster creativity and good ones don't: The role of context and clarity of feelings. *Journal of Applied Psychology, 87*(4), 687–697. https://doi.org/10.1037/0021-9010.87.4.687

George, J. M., & Zhou, J. (2007). Dual tuning in a supportive context: Joint contributions of positive mood, negative mood, and supervisory behaviors to employee creativity. *Academy of Management Journal, 50*(3), 605–622. https://doi.org/10.5465/amj.2007.25525934

Glăveanu, V. P. (2013). Rewriting the language of creativity: The Five A's framework. *Review of General Psychology, 17*(1), 69–81. https://doi.org/10.1037/a0029528

Glăveanu, V. P. (2015). Creativity as a sociocultural act. *The Journal of Creative Behavior, 49*(3), 165–180. https://doi.org/10.1002/jocb.94

Goldstein, T. R., & Lerner, M. D. (2018). Dramatic pretend play games uniquely improve emotional control in young children. *Developmental Science, 21*(4), e12603 https://doi.org/10.1111/desc.12603

Goleman, D. (1995). *Emotional intelligence: Why It Can Matter More than IQ.* Bantam.

Goleman, D. (2001). An EI-based theory of performance. In C. Cherniss & D. Goleman (Eds.), *The Emotionally Intelligent Workplace: How to Select for, Measure, and Improve Emotional Intelligence in Individuals, Groups, and Organizations* (pp. 27–44). Jossey-Bass.

Greenberg, M. T., Kusche, C. A., Cook, E. T., & Quamma, J. P. (1995). Promoting emotional competence in school-aged children: The effects of the PATHS curriculum. *Development and Psychopathology, 7*, 117–136.

Gross, J. J. (1998). The emerging field of emotion regulation: An integrative review. *Review of General Psychology, 2*(3), 271–299. https://doi.org/10.1037/1089-2680.2.3.271

Hoffmann, J. D. (2021, December). Creativity, collaboration, and compassion: Early findings of the inspirED program. Presentation at the Yale Child Study Center Research in Progress Meeting. [Virtual].

Hoffmann, J. D., McGarry, J. A., Baumsteiger, R., Seibyl, J., & Brackett, M. A. (in press). Emotional empowerment in high school life. In G. Misra & I. Misra (Eds.). *Emotions in Cultural Context.* Springer.

Hoffmann, J. D., & Ivcevic, Z. (2022). Creativity, emotions, and the arts courses: An art center at the center. In Z. Ivcevic (Ed.), *Creativity, Emotions, and the Arts: Research, Application, and Impact* (pp. 45–55). Fundacion Botin.

Hoffmann, J. D., Ivcevic, Z., & Brackett, M. (2016). Creativity in the age of technology: Measuring the digital creativity of millennials. *Creativity Research Journal, 28*(2), 149–153. https://doi.org/10.1080/10400419.2016.1162515

Hoffmann, J. D., Ivcevic, Z., & Feist, G. (2021). Personality, emotions, and creativity. In J. Kaufman & R. Sternberg (Eds.), *Creativity: An Introduction.* Cambridge University Press.

Hoffmann, J. D., Ivcevic, Z., & Maliakkal, N. (2018). Creative thinking strategies for life: A course for professional adults using art. *Journal of Creative Behavior, 54*, 293–310. https://doi.org/10.1002/jocb.366

Hoffmann, J. D., Ivecvic, Z., Maliakkal, N. (2020). Emotions, creativity, and the arts: Evaluating a course for children. *Empirical Studies of the Arts*, 1–26. https://doi.org/10.1177/0276237420907864

Hoffmann, J. D. & Russ, S. (2012). Pretend play, creativity and emotion regulation in children. *Psychology of Aesthetics Creativity and the Arts, 6,* 175–184. https://doi.org/10.1037/a0026299

Hoffmann, J. D. & Russ, S. W. (2016, August). Adaptive regression: Emotion ability for creativity? In E. Nusbaum (Chair), *Looking Back to Look Forward: Re-examining and Re-imagining Historical Ideas in Creativity Research.* Symposium conducted at the meeting of the American Psychological Association, Denver, CO.

Ivcevic, Z., & Brackett, M. A. (2015). Predicting creativity: Interactive effects of openness to experience and emotion regulation ability. *Psychology of Aesthetics, Creativity, and the Arts, 9*(4), 480–487. https://doi.org/10.1037/a0039826

Ivcevic, Z., Brackett, M. A., & Mayer, J. D. (2007). Emotional intelligence and emotional creativity. *Journal of Personality, 75*(2), 199–236. https://doi.org/10.1111/j.1467-6494.2007.00437.x

Ivcevic, Z., & Maliakkal, N. T. Botin Foundation. (2016). Teaching emotion and creativity skills through the arts. In E. M. Gokcigdem (Ed.), *Fostering Empathy through Museums* (pp. 1–19). Rowman & Littlefield.

Kaufman, J. C. (2012). Counting the muses: development of the Kaufman domains of creativity scale (K-DOCS). *Psychology of Aesthetics, Creativity, and the Arts, 6*(4), 298–308. https://doi.org/10.1037/a0029751

Kaufman, J. C., & Beghetto, R. A. (2009). Beyond big and little: The Four C model of creativity. *Review of General Psychology, 13*(1), 1–12. https://doi.org/10.1037/a0013688

Kaufmann, G., & Vosburg, S. K. (2002). The effects of mood on early and late idea production. *Creativity Research Journal, 14*(3–4), 317–330. https://doi.org/10.1207/s15326934crj1434_3

Kerr, R., Garvin, J., Heaton, N., & Boyle, E. (2006). Emotional intelligence and leadership effectiveness. *Leadership & Organization Development Journal, 27,* 265–279. https://doi.org/10.1108/01437730610666028

Kewalramani, S., Agrawal, M., & Rastogi, M. R. (2015). Models of emotional intelligence: Similarities and discrepancies. *Indian Journal of Positive Psychology, 6*(2), 178.

Kris, E. (1952). *Psychoanalytic Explorations in Art.* International Universities Press.

Kühnel, J., Bledow, R., & Kiefer, M. (2022). There is a time to be creative: The alignment between chronotype and time of day. *Academy of Management Journal, 65*(1), 218–247. https://doi.org/10.5465/amj.2019.0020

Livingstone, H. A., & Day, A. L. (2005). Comparing the construct and criterion-related validity of ability-based and mixed-model measures of emotional intelligence. *Educational and Psychological Measurement, 65*(5), 757–779. https://doi.org/10.1177/0013164405275663

Lopes, P. N., Salovey, P., & Straus, R. (2003). Emotional intelligence, personality, and the perceived quality of social relationships. *Personality and Individual Differences, 35*(3), 641–658. https://doi.org/10.1016/s0191–8869(02)00242-8

Martin, L. L., Ward, D. W., Achee, J. W., & Wyer, R. S. (1993). Mood as input: People have to interpret the motivational implications of their moods. *Journal of Personality and Social Psychology, 64*(3), 317–326. https://doi.org/10.1037/0022-3514.64.3.317

Mayer, J. D., Caruso, D. R., & Salovey, P. (2016). The ability model of emotional intelligence: Principles and updates. *Emotion Review, 8*(4), 290–300. https://doi .org/10.1177/1754073916639667

Mayer, J. D., & Salovey, P. (1997). What is emotional intelligence? In P. Salovey & D. Sluyter (Eds.), *Emotional Development and Emotional Intelligence: Implications for Educators* (pp. 3–31). Basic Books.

Mayer, J. D., Salovey, P., Caruso, D. R., & Sitarenios, G. (2001). Emotional intelligence as a standard intelligence. *Emotion, 1,* 232–242. https://doi.org/10.1037/1528-3542.1.3.232

Mayer, J. D., Salovey, P., Caruso, D. R., & Sitarenios, G. (2003). Measuring emotional intelligence with the MSCEIT V2. 0. *Emotion, 3*(1), 97–105. https://doi.org/10 .1037/1528-3542.3.1.97

McKay, A. S., Karwowski, M., & Kaufman, J. C. (2017). Measuring the muses: Validating the Kaufman domains of creativity scale (K-DOCS). *Psychology of Aesthetics, Creativity, and the Arts, 11*(2), 216–230. https://doi.org/10.1037/ aca0000074

Mednick, S. A., & Mednick, M. T. (1971). *Remote Associates Test.* Houghton Mifflin.

Miroshnik, K. G., Shcherbakova, O. V., & Kaufman, J. C. (2021). Kaufman Domains of Creativity Scale: Relationship to occupation and measurement invariance across gender. *Creativity Research Journal*, 1–19. https://doi.org/10.1080/ 10400419.2021.1953823

Moore, M., & Russ, S. W. (2008). Follow-up of a pretend play intervention: Effects on play, creativity, and emotional processes in children. *Creativity Research Journal, 20*(4), 427–436. https://doi.org/10.1080/10400410802391892

Neubauer, A. C., & Freudenthaler, H. H. (2005). Models of emotional intelligence. In R. Schulze & R. D. Roberts (Eds.), *Emotional Intelligence: An International Handbook* (pp. 31–50). Hogrefe & Huber.

Neubauer, A. C., Pribil, A., Wallner, A., & Hofer, G. (2018). The self–other knowledge asymmetry in cognitive intelligence, emotional intelligence, and creativity. *Heliyon, 4*(12), e01061. https://doi.org/10.1016/j.heliyon.2018 .e01061

Nuttall F. Q. (2015). Body mass index: Obesity, BMI, and health: A critical review. *Nutrition today, 50*(3), 117–128. https://doi.org/10.1097/NT.0000000000000092

Parke, M. R., Seo, M. G., & Sherf, E. N. (2015). Regulating and facilitating: The role of emotional intelligence in maintaining and using positive affect for creativity. *Journal of Applied Psychology, 100*(3), 917–934. https://doi.org/10.1037/ a0038452

Pine, F., & Holt, R. R. (1960). Creativity and primary process: A study of adaptive regression. *The Journal of Abnormal and Social Psychology, 61*(3), 370–379. https://doi.org/10.1037/h0048004

Pink, D. H. (2018). *When: The Scientific Secrets of Perfect Time.* Riverhead Books.

Rhodes, M. (1961). An analysis of creativity. *The Phi Delta Kappan, 42*(7), 305–310.

Rivers, S. E., Brackett, M. A., Reyes, M. R., Elbertson, N. A., & Salovey, P. (2013). Improving the social and emotional climate of classrooms: A clustered randomized controlled trial testing the RULER approach. *Prevention Science, 14* (1), 77–87. https://doi.org/10.1007/s11121–012-0305-2

Ruiz-Ariza, A., Suárez-Manzano, S., López-Serrano, S., & Martínez-López, E. J. (2019). The effect of cooperative high-intensity interval training on creativity and emotional intelligence in secondary school: A randomised controlled trial. *European Physical Education Review, 25*(2), 355–373.

Runco, M. A., & Acar, S. (2012). Divergent thinking as an indicator of creative potential. *Creativity Research Journal, 24*(1), 66–75. https://doi.org/10.1080/10400419.2012.652929

Salovey, P., & Mayer, J. D. (1990). Emotional intelligence. *Imagination, Cognition and Personality, 9*(3), 185–211. https://doi.org/10.2190/DUGG-P24E-52WK-6CDG

Salovey, P., Mayer, J. D., Goldman, S. L., Turvey, C., & Palfai, T. P. (1995). Emotional attention, clarity, and repair: Exploring emotional intelligence using the Trait Meta-Mood Scale. In J. W. Pennebaker (Ed.), *Emotion, Disclosure, and Health* (pp. 125–154). American Psychological Association.

Schutte, N. S., Malouff, J. M., Hall, L. E., et al. (1998). Development and validation of a measure of emotional intelligence. *Personality and Individual Differences, 25* (2), 167–177.

Schwarz, N. (1990). *Feelings as Information: Informational and Motivational Functions of Affective States*. Guilford Press.

Schwarz, N. (2001). Feelings as information. In L. L. Martin & G. L. Clore (Eds)., *Theories of Mood and Cognition: A User's Guidebook* (pp. 159–176). Erlbaum.

Schwarz, N. (2012). Feelings-as-information theory. In P. A. M. Van Lange, A. Kruglanski, & E. T. Higgins (Eds.), *Handbook of Theories of Social Psychology* (pp. 289–308). Sage.

Scott, G., Leritz, L. E., & Mumford, M. D. (2004). The effectiveness of creativity training: A quantitative review. *Creativity Research Journal, 16*(4), 361–388. https://doi.org/10.1207/s15326934crj1604_1

Stein, M. I. (1953). Creativity and culture. *The Journal of Psychology, 36*(2), 311–322.

Tajpour, M., Moradi, F., & Jalali, S. E. (2018). Studying the influence of emotional intelligence on the organizational innovation. *International Journal of Human Capital Urban Management, 3*(1), 45–52. https://doi.org/10.22034/ijhcum.2018.03.01.005

Tu, C., Guo, J., Hatcher, R. C., & Kaufman, J. C. (2018). The relationship between emotional intelligence and domain-specific and domain-general creativity. *The Journal of Creative Behavior, 54*(2), 337–349. https://doi.org/10.1002/jocb.369

Vernon, D., Hocking, I., & Tyler, T. C. (2016). An evidence-based review of creative problem solving tools: A practitioner's resource. *Human Resource Development Review, 15,* 230–259.

Wallach, M., & Kogan, N. (1965). *Modes of Thinking in Young Children*. Holt, Rinehart & Winston.

World Economic Forum. (2018). *The Future of Jobs Report*. World Economic Forum.

World Economic Forum. (2020). *The Future of Jobs Report*. World Economic Forum.

Xu, X., Liu, W., & Pang, W. (2019). Are emotionally intelligent people more creative? A meta-analysis of the emotional intelligence–creativity link. *Sustainability, 11* (21), 6123. https://doi.org/10.3390/su11216123

Zeidner, M., Matthews, G., & Roberts, R. D. (2006). Emotional intelligence, adaptation, and coping. In J. Ciarrochi, J. Forgas, & J. D. Mayer (Eds.), *Emotional Intelligence in Everyday Life: A Scientific Inquiry* (2nd ed., pp. 82–97). Psychology Press.

11 Emotions across the Creative Process and across Domains of Creativity

Marion Botella

Introduction: Emotions and the Creative Process

By definition, our emotions describe a transitory, short-term, and intense state (Ekman & Davidson, 1994) in response to a stimulus. For example, if we hear good news, we will immediately react intensely and positively to this stimulus. This state will have physiological, cognitive, and behavioral manifestations (Luminet, 2002; Scherer, 2000). To continue with the example of the good news, the physiological activation will be the acceleration of the heartbeat with the release of certain hormones such as dopamine and oxytocin; the cognitive activation will be the subjective experience of the individual feeling joy; and the behavioral activation will be jumping up and down and exploring the environment (Mikolajczak et al., 2009). If needed, it is possible to regulate an emotional state by directly interacting with the stimulus (Gross, 2007). Thus, the emotions designate a nonlinear phenomenon (Plutchik, 2001; Wei & Chen, 2019): emotions designate a dynamic phenomenon that, at the same time, comes from the environment and can act in return on this environment. There is therefore the emotion that we feel from a stimulus and the action that we will have on our environment because of this emotion.

By definition, the creative process describes the sequence of thoughts and actions that leads to idea that is both original and contextually appropriate (Lubart et al., 2015). Based on an analysis of the literature, Wallas (1926) was one of the first to propose a model of the creative process, in four stages: preparation (gather information), incubation (let the unconscious associate the ideas), illumination (sudden emergence of the idea in the consciousness) and verification (development of idea details). This process is "dynamic by its components itself, their organization, their combination, the successive interactions it maintains with the environment, the unfolding nature of a phenomenon over time and its cyclical nature" (Botella & Lubart, 2019, p. 272).

Thus, if we cross the definitions of emotions and the creative process, two dynamic phenomena, we understand that they will influence each other and vary over time. But how will emotions vary during the creative process?

Based on empirical evidence and a literature review, Russ (1993, 1999) is the first to propose a model which identifies five emotional processes involved in creativity: (a) access to thoughts with emotional content, which consists of recalling cognitive memories associated with emotions, (b) openness to a variety of emotions, which consists of tolerating intense emotions, (c) enjoyment of a challenge, which corresponds to the enjoyment of identifying a problem and working on it, (d) enjoyment of solving a problem, which corresponds to "deep pleasure and passion involved" (p. 13; Russ, 1993), and (e) the ability to control and regulate emotional processes cognitively. These emotional processes would also moderate motivation to perform the task. In this model, the activation of the affective system leads us to control our emotions so as not to let ourselves be overwhelmed and therefore activates our cognitive system. It is this cognitive system that would then contribute to creativity. Russ (1993) then proposes to superimpose these five affective processes on the four stages of Wallas' (1926) creative process. Thus, preparation would essentially mobilize the affective pleasure in challenge. Incubation would be the stage involving "*the major affective processes*" (Russ, 1993, p. 15). Indeed, incubation would involve thoughts with affective content and openness to the affective state itself, that is, the ability to experience and tolerate this affective state. Illumination would also mobilize these two emotional processes as well as the affective pleasure in problem solving. Finally, the last step of the creative process, verification, would mobilize the affective pleasure in problem solving as well the cognitive integration of the affective component.

Through this model of Russ (1993, 1999), we understand the complexity of linking two dynamic concepts that are emotions and the creative process. The emotional resonance model provides a complementary perspective (Lubart & Getz, 1997). According to this model, our memories are stored along with the emotions we felt during the event. These emotions are specific to each of us (idiosyncratic), meaning that we can feel very different emotions while experiencing the same situation. The memories are therefore stored differently from one individual to another. The principle of the emotional resonance model is simple: as soon as the memory is activated, the emotional profile associated with this memory is also activated. Then, the profile will propagate in the memory and activate memories that are stored with the same emotion. The authors call this the phenomenon of emotional resonance. The initial memory resonates with another memory through an emotional pathway and not a cognitive one. We can take for example the memory of a "cat." From a semantic point of view, the cat is in the category of animals and can activate a close concept, the concept "dog" for example. But we can also follow an emotional path. Imagine that the "cat" is associated with positive memories of a feeling of calm, relaxation, and well-being. We can then, by resonance, activate emotionally similar memories of calm, relaxation, and well-being and then activate the concept of "holiday," for example. Here, we see that emotional resonance allows us to associate ideas emotionally and not only cognitively. This emotional association allows one to activate memories and concepts that are cognitively very distant in the memory and therefore to propose ideas that are different from those proposed by someone else, increasing the probability that this idea is original and creative.

In this chapter, we lead a literature review to answer the question of how emotions vary across the creative process and we also discuss these emotional variations according to the creative domain. Indeed, the process is not completely different but not either completely similar in art, science, design, writing, or music (Glăveanu et al., 2013). There are other configurations of the domains of creativity where, for example, creative potential is expressed in the verbal or figurative domain (Barbot et al., 2016), or creativity at work (Amabile et al., 2005). These differences in configurations refer to the level of generalization-specialization of creativity. In this chapter, we focus on an intermediate level to explore similarities and differences in emotions across six domains more broadly (art, science, design, writing, music, and culinary) as they correspond to real domains of creativity. In order to review rich content, useful for future research, we focus on qualitative studies where experts in each domain were interviewed about their emotions during the process. We see how models of the creative process integrate emotions across these six domains of creativity.

Emotions in the Artistic Creative Process

When we think of creativity, we immediately think of art. It is indeed the prototypical domain of creativity (Schlewitt-Haynes et al., 2002; Stanko-Kaczmarek, 2012). Focusing on the link between emotions and creativity in art, Flanders (2004) proposes to reformulate the Romantic theory of art so that the creative process becomes "the personal exploration and authentic expression of the emotions" (p. 95). We can immediately recognize from this quote that the exploration and expression of emotions imply that emotions vary during the artistic process. Flanders (2004) illustrates his theory with Collingwood's (1938) *The Principles of Art* where the author explains that at the beginning of the artistic process, the emotion is not formed. Still being at an unconscious stage, unexpressed, undefined, the emotion represents a burden for the artist. The creative process will consist in exploring and expressing this emotion in a new language: art. The emotion, initially undefined, will be expressed in an artistic form and when the emotion takes its final form, that is to say at the end of the process, the artist will feel a positive aesthetic feeling.

To understand the variations of emotions in the process, it is essential to ask the first people involved: the artists themselves. Thus, Glăveanu et al. (2013) interviewed experts in several domains about their creative process and the emotions involved. We discuss the different domains in the following sections, but first let's start with the prototypical domain of creativity, the artistic domain. Analysis of the discourse of twelve established professional artists, with between 10 and 20 years of experience, identified six stages to the activity of creating art and associated emotions felt by the artists: (1) first, there is a period of emptiness that leads to a general idea or "vision" for a project, and this stage is often associated with excitement; (2) then, documentation and reflection allow gathering more information about the materials and technologies that could be used in this project; (3) the artists then start the first sketches to give a material form to the project; (4) there follows a more or less long period where the artists test forms and this stage is associated with different emotions which, most of the time, are positive; (5) from there, the artists create provisional objects; and (6) it often happens that a first object is followed by a series, which the artists associate with satisfaction and exhaustion. The artists specify that certain emotions such as satisfaction, happiness, frustration, or anger can facilitate their creative process while emotions such as fear or guilt can inhibit it (Botella et al., 2013).

To illustrate what the artists are saying, the oil painter Ying Xu (2016) described the emotions she felt while creating. She explains that her emotions vary throughout her process. For her, everything starts with creative impulses that give her a sense of joy and excitement but also anxiety related to the unpredictability of the process that is going to take place. Indeed, at this stage, she does not know yet what will happen, and this uncertainty can generate anxiety. The painter advises then to control her emotions, especially negative ones, and to relax. Xu (2016) considers that positive emotions are those that greatly facilitate the process.

To complete the interviews with the artists, it is also possible to invite them to fill out questionnaires. Using this method, St-Louis and Vallerand (2015) have shown that passionate artists experienced more moderate than a high level of activation of positive emotions during all the stages of the creative process and especially more in phase 1 of preparation. Moreover, artists globally felt fewer negative emotions than positive emotions. When they felt negative emotions, it was more frequently higher than moderate level of activation of negative emotions during all the stages of the creative process.

In addition to research that interrogates artists via interviews or question-naires, it is also possible to follow them directly when they create. For example, by observing the creative process of art students in the real context of creation, that is, in their art school, differences have been highlighted between the emotions felt at each stage of the creative process by the most creative students and the least creative students (Botella, 2018). The least creative art students begin by being disappointed when they define the project and reflect on it. We can then speculate that they are simply not motivated by their art school's project. The least creative students continue their process by feeling surprised when they research and combine their ideas. They are frustrated by the con-straints of the project, and they are also frustrated when they diverge, that is when they explore other possible responses to their project. Surprisingly, these uncreative students end the process feeling satisfaction when they finally con-verge on a solution and implement their idea. We can speculate whether they are relieved to finish a project they did not like. For their part, the most creative students feel satisfaction in documenting their project and are stressed and disappointed by the constraints but unlike the least creative students, they are not frustrated by constraints. The more creative students are then stressed when they have to combine the ideas and then frustrated and disappointed when they have to implement them. It is interesting to note that the two groups feel very different emotions at each stage of the process and that stress, which is an unpleasant emotion, has positive consequences here because the students are finally the most creative (Folkman, 2013; Lazarus & Folkman, 1984). We can speculate whether these creative students are stressed because they are involved and committed to the school's project. Finally, the only stage where both groups experience the same emotions is the stage of judgment of ideas which is experienced as a stressful moment. We understand that any evaluation, even if it is done by ourselves, is always a stressful step.

In the domain of artistic creativity, according to experts, positive emotions were present throughout the creative process, especially positive emotions with moderate intensity (St-Louis & Vallerand, 2015). However, concerning students, for the most creative students, positive emotions were mainly present at the beginning of the process and then, students experienced stress, an unpleasant emotion with positive consequence; however, for the least creative students, the process is unpleased and positive emotions only arrive at the end of the process (Botella, 2018). Therefore, it appears important in this domain to regulate negative emotions.

Emotions in the Scientific Creative Process

As much as we talk about creativity, we immediately think of art, and we do not always think of science as a creative domain. Continuing this naive reasoning, we could also wonder if there are emotions in science. Yet "a gifted man cannot handle bacteria or equations without taking fire from what he does and having his emotions engaged" (Bronowski, 1958, p. 59). This quote under-lines that to create, whatever the domain, emotions are important.

In 1989, Shaw interviewed eleven scientists and engineers to build a model of the creative process based on the cognitive stages of the process while superposing the affective stages. Thus, Shaw (1989, 1994) described the succession of thoughts (the cognitive component) and emotions (affective component) which jointly lead to an original and adapted production in the scientific domain. Based on the work of McNally (1982), Shaw identified six stages beginning with an immersion that corresponds to a learning phase. This is followed by the incubation stage, as previously described by Wallas (1926), which is an uncon-scious phase, such as when dreaming. These first two stages, immersion, and incubation, are linked by bipolar emotions going from negative emotions (overworked, burned out, bored ...) through neutral emotions (stimulated, puzzled, awed ...) toward positive emotions (obsessed[1], compelled, overexcited ...). The third step in the process is illumination "when the pieces of the puzzle fall into place" (Shaw, 1989, p. 288). This stage is associated with

---

[1] Shaw's model (1989) places "obsessed" in the positive pole. Later, St-Louis and Vallerand (2015) distinguish between harminiously passionate, individuals who are freely and passionately engaged in an activity; and obsessively passionate, individuals who feel an uncontrollable urge to engage in an activity. The results show that harminiously passionate individuals experience more positive emotions and are therefore more creative than obsessively passionate individuals.

unipolar emotions, that is, either negative emotions (frustrated, angry, feared, sad, depressed, shamed . . .) or positive emotions (orgasmic, free, walke-on-air, euphoric, alive, enchanted, . . .). In the illumination stage, therefore, there is no continuum between negative and positive emotions. It is all one or all the other. The fourth stage is called explanation and corresponds to the elaboration and the details brought to the idea. The fifth stage is the creative synthesis, involving the transformation of the idea into a material object. As stages 1 and 2, stages 4 and 5 are also linked by bipolar emotions. Scientists and engineers can then have emotions starting from negative emotions (anxious, bored, annoyed), through neutral emotions (resigned, energized, excited) to end the continuum with positive emotions (frenzied, compelled, powerful). Finally, the last step of the creative process consists in validating the production to start a new creative process. This validation can be done by oneself (personal validation) or by peers (collective validation). In the case of collective validation, the creator must accept the criticism. This acceptance is associated with unipolar emotions, that is, either negative emotions (shame, sadness, frustration, lost, attacked, self-depreciation . . .) or positive emotions (orgasmic, free, highly pleasant, unified, euphoric, enchanted . . .). This model of the cognitive and affective process has the advantage of describing the whole range of emotions felt by scientists when they create. We note here that a wide range of emotions can be experienced at each stage. Shaw (1989) specifies that the two stages associated with unipolar emotions, enlightenment and acceptance (in the case of collective validation) rarely trigger negative emotions.

In addition to interviewing artists, Glăveanu et al. (2013) also interviewed 12 science experts and identified six stages of scientific creation activity: (1) scientists begin by questioning a problem, having a discussion, or researching a topic; (2) then scientists experiment or test alternatives, and this stage is frustrating for them; (3) this is followed by positive emotions of euphoria and certitude when the idea suddenly emerges to consciousness with a "Eureka moment"; (4) scientists continue the process by modeling or proving a theory for example; (5) then they experiment, which for them is a step involving satisfaction and/or frustration; and (6) finally, the process ends with a reporting which is associated with the emotions of exhaustion and gratification.

By observing the creative process of science students working collaboratively on a project, Peilloux and Botella (2016) found that students experienced positive emotions at the beginning of the creative process (interested/curious, determined/decided, inspired/stimulated) then from the experimentation to the end of the project, the students felt negative emotions (hesitant/doubtful, anxious/nervous, stressed/overwhelmed). In the same vein, the first stages of the process are associated with satisfaction among the most creative engineering students (definition, inspiration, insight, association stages) and the last steps are stressful (finalization, finish) or even frustrating and disappointing (judgment) (Botella & Dalloubeix, 2020). As with art students, we note here that stress at the end of the project allows for more creativity. At this point, however, it is important to remember that emotion regulation is important. Too much stress can be "paralyzing" and "inhibit action" (Grebot, 2011, p. 8). In contrast, the least creative students start with frustration, continue with disappointment and they end with satisfaction and surprise in the judging and finalization stages of their project. Even though their work was not considered creative, we can hypothesize here that these uncreative students are just satisfied with finishing their project.

In this section we saw that professional scientists approach the creative process with negative emotions (frustration) and end up with positive emotions (exhaustion, gratification; Glăveanu et al., 2013). However, we also saw that this shift from negative to positive emotions was followed by the least creative students (Botella & Dalloubeix, 2020). Indeed, the most creative students follow the opposite emotional path, starting with feeling satisfaction and ending with frustration and disappointment. This finding raises questions about the emotions felt by experts and beginners in the creative process in science, suggesting that the emotional process may change with experience.

Emotions in the Design Creative Process

The field of design enables the creation of innovations on a societal scale (Bonnardel & Lubart, 2019). Thus, by interviewing twelve expert designers, Glăveanu et al. (2013) have identified six stages of creative activity in design associated with emotions: (1) designers start by having a general idea;, (2) then they research and during these first two stages, they feel the excitement, pressure or stress; (3) then the designers start the first drawings; (4) then they adapt the shape, feeling during these two steps the pleasure of working with different materials; (5) this work leads to the elaboration of a prototype; and (6) finally, the designers produce the final object which will either provoke a feeling of contentment or a feeling of deception.

In the domain of design, even the end user's emotions influence the designer's process (Desmet & Hekkert, 2009; Desmet & Schifferstein, 2012). Indeed, the emotions that the user of the object will feel represent an additional constraint that the designer must integrate from the beginning in his specifications to produce an object that will be accepted (Botella et al., in press; Ho, 2010). In the E-Wheel model, Ho (2010) explains that external factors (such as social, cultural, technological, and economical factors) will play on internal factors. Theses internal factors are availability of materials, thinking and communication skills, ability to process information, application of a strategy, and project management. Then, they will themselves influence the design production. The designer's emotions are at the junction of external and internal factors. Then, emotional changes will promote divergent thinking (Vosburg, 1998) and decision-making processes (Ho, 2010).

Thus, in the domain of design, we find that designers can engage in a creative process by feeling either positive or negative emotions and that the process ends with the same bipolarity (Glăveanu et al., 2013). The specificity of design is to integrate the emotions of the user of the object in the specifications and thus influence the creation process (Desmet & Hekkert, 2009; Desmet & Schifferstein, 2012).

Emotions in the (Script)writing Creative Process

In addition to the three domains most studied by creativity researchers: art, science, and design, we now focus on the domain of creative writing. By interviewing twelve experts in scriptwriting, Glăveanu et al. (2013) have identified six stages of creative activity in screenwriting by associating emotions: (1) screenwriters start with a general idea; (2) then they research; (3) then they write a lot and from there, the emotions of doubts, stress, anxiety, joy, and jubilation emerge until step 5; (4) then the writers revise and rewrite the script; (5) then they edit it; and (6) finally, the process ends with the final version of the script and the writers' satisfaction.

By exploring the interviews with these writers, it was possible to identify the emotions felt at each stage of the process (Bourgeois-Bougrine et al., 2014). In general, the scriptwriting process mobilizes pleasure (82% of the scriptwriters) and doubts (80%), constantly oscillating between jubilation (50%) and frustration (55%) and anxiety (55%). More specifically, the process begins with meetings with sponsors and the writers feel pleasure, desire, and interest in the project. The illumination stage, where the writer comes up with an idea, is associated with a feeling of jubilation (50%). Writing is then an exciting experience but when writers get stuck, the writing process becomes painful (80%). At the end of the writing process, feelings of relief, joy, and fatigue were reported. After the film has been screened, if the director changes of attitude and seem to forget the many meetings that led to the writing of the script, and so if the director seems to forget the writer, scriptwriter can then be disappointment.

Using the questionnaire method with 191 writers, Brand (1990) highlighted that emotions vary during the writing process. In particular, positive emotions increase, while negative emotions decrease, especially deactivating emotions such as boredom, confusion, loneliness. However, these negative deactivation emotions are quite rare. Negative activating emotions such as afraid, angry, anxious, disgusted, or frustrated, remain relatively stable throughout the writing process. Anxiety is the most important negative emotion for all writers, and at the end of the process, all writers feel a weakness, mostly accompanied by relief and satisfaction. With this large sample (191 writers), Brand (1990) was able to identify differences by type of writer and level of experience (college students, advanced expository students, professionals, English majors, pre- and in-service teachers of English, and student poets). Thus, writers, who are self-financed most of the time, feel better and perform better than overall. As for students, they experience more negative emotions during a required writing exercise. In addition, the more proficient students feel more positive emotions than the less proficient students, and at the end of the process, the positive emotions of the less proficient students increase to the level of those of the more proficient students. Students' emotions also vary according to the type of exercise requested by the teacher (students are more anxious about a free writing exercise but are more relieved after a structured writing exercise) and the place of writing (when writing at home, students are more anxious and stressed, and less confused but they are also more relieved and satisfied, at the end than when writing in class).

To summarize the emotions in the domain of creative writing, we find that the process can begin with both positive (jubilation) and negative emotions (frustration; Bourgeois-Bougrine et al., 2014) but positive emotions are dominant throughout (Brand, 1990). However, if the writing process is blocked then it becomes painful (Bourgeois-Bougrine et al., 2014).

Emotions in the Musical Creative Process

We could discuss whether music is included in the artistic domain or whether it is a separate domain. In this chapter, we devote a special section to it. Thus, by interviewing twelve experts in music composition, Glăveanu et al. (2013) have identified six stages of creative activity in music by associating emotions: (1) composers start with initial research and they feel excitement and restlessness;, (2) these emotions continue in the second phase where an idea or ideas emerge; (3) then composers organize their ideas and reflect; (4) then they write and rewrite their composition, which gives them joy, anxiety and "pain"; (5) this emotion continues in the next stage which consists of formulating a "draft"; and (6) finally, the process ends with the composers' production and performance where, depending on the result, they may feel satisfaction or dissatisfaction.

Based on the four-step model of the musical process (Chaffin et al., 2003) and adding a step of *artistic appropriation* (Héroux & Fortier, 2014), Héroux (2018) conducted a study combining questionnaires, observations, and interviews with nine professional musicians. Although she does not directly associate emotions with the stages of the music creation process, we can find in her article elements that refer to it for some musicians. Thus, the process of musical creation can be divided into five stages: (1) *scouting-it-out*, which consists in making a mental representation of the piece by noting or drawing sensations or emotions; (2) *artistic appropriation*, which consists in seeking and introducing one's personal touch to the piece, for example, by stimulating one's memories to feel an emotion that will help to play the part of the piece that corresponds to this emotion; (3) *section-by-section*, which consists of developing motor skills by exploring the piece using different expressive tools that include the fingering and the rhythmic feel; (4) *gray stage*, which consists in memorizing the piece and automating the movements to feel the music; and (5) *maintenance*, which consists of checking one's knowledge and finalizing details in preparation for playing the piece in front of an audience. Héroux (2018) states "get in the mood" to play the piece (p. 10).

In the domain of music, there are fewer studies linking emotions to the stages of the creative process. However, we find that emotions remain an essential element of the process, with a majority of positive emotions (Glăveanu et al., 2013) since it is essential to find the appropriate emotional tone to play (Héroux, 2018).

Emotions in the Culinary Creative Process

We finish the overview of creative domains by addressing another creative domain that has been emerging for several years: culinary creativity. Like music, we can wonder if this domain is part of art. Some authors refer to it as culinary art (Horng & Hu, 2008; Horng & Lee, 2009). However, creativity in cooking is still rarely studied, so we will discuss it separately from the artistic domain. There is new research on the creative process in cooking (Horng & Hu, 2008) but the emotions in this process are not yet systematically studied. The few authors who already address the link between emotions and cooking can provide us with some thoughts here.

Interviews with eighteen Michelin-starred chefs identified three main stages and some substages to the culinary creativity process (Madeira et al., 2021): (1) the inspiration moment (having as substages the inspiration, the idea, and the mental cooking) corresponds to an introspective process and a solitary pleasure; the chefs are focused on their own memories and experiences, and they are not yet thinking about the clients; (2) the teamwork moment (with conception, testing, final version, and training) consists of explaining the dish to the team, which can then be reworked with the sous-chef in particular; and (3) the moment of truth (with commercialization, client experience, and feedback), which consists of serving the dish to the clients and getting their feedback to rework it and return to the conception substage of the teamwork moment, if necessary.

We had already seen in the scientific domain the validation step (Shaw, 1989) that could initiate a new creative process if the critique was accepted by the designer. In the design domain, we had also underlined that the user's emotions can influence the designer's creative process (Desmet & Hekkert, 2009; Desmet & Schifferstein, 2012). In the culinary domain, we thus find here also the influence of clients' emotions on the creative process, intervening rather at the end of the process of creating a dish (Madeira et al., 2021). Moreover, researchers have collected 400 questionnaires from customers of Michelin-starred restaurants (Leong et al., 2020). Their results show that the aesthetic value of dishes (examples of items: "the food looks beautiful," "elegant," "like a piece of artwork") is the factor that has the strongest effect on clients' emotions compared to the value or rarity of products.

Although emotions in the process of culinary creativity are not yet systematically studied, the lines of inquiry discussed here highlight similarities with the domain of design by incorporating the emotions of the end-user, in this case, the client, which can influence the process (Leong et al., 2020; Madeira et al., 2021). However, unlike design, the client's emotions would intervene at the end of the process.

Conclusion: Emotions across the Creative Processes

We began this chapter with the definitions of emotions and the creative process, which are both dynamic phenomena. Thus, when we address the question of emotions in the creative process, especially according to the domain, we have observed that emotions vary. Nevertheless, we must underline the general tendency of all creators to feel positive emotions, which are indeed essential to creativity (see chapter "Emotion states and creativity"). Negative emotions are present in all domains, and it is these that highlight the greatest differences between domains: negative emotions can occur at the beginning or the end of the process, and depend on the level of expertise (expert/students), creativity (more or less creative), type of personality of the creators, or place.

In addition to these variables, it would also be interesting to take into account emotional variations according to the emotional traits of the creators. Contrary to the emotional states which are triggered by a stimulus, the emotional traits are specific to the individuals and characterize them. To take our initial example, the good news is a stimulus and will lead to an emotional state of joy. This transient state does not indicate whether or not we are joyful people in general. If we tend to be joyful in most events, then this corresponds to a trait that defines us: an emotional trait. In a study on the emotional state and trait of anger, Da Costa and colleagues (2018) showed that the emotional trait of anger had a stronger impact on engagement in the creative process than the emotional state of anger. Thus, individuals characterized by the emotional trait of anger will be more inclined to engage in the creative process than individuals occasionally experiencing anger. This effect is moderated by emotional regulation: the relationship between the anger trait and engagement in the creative process is stronger when individuals are less inclined to implement an emotion suppression strategy of not expressing their emotions. Thus, if individuals characterized by the emotional trait of anger do not try to suppress their emotions, they are all the more engaged in the creative process.

In addition to furthering research on emotions during the creative process and depending on the domain, we have shown that emotional processes are linked to motivation (Russ, 1993). It is therefore important to examine the motivation of creators for the task. In particular, we observed this with the less creative students who started their project feeling negative emotions and ended it feeling positive emotions, such as relief that the unpleasant project was finally over. We can maybe suppose that students who experience negative emotions are blocked, either because they cannot find the necessary motivation to create or because they cannot regulate their emotions. However, it would be enough to accept these negative emotions to create. Indeed, the emotional resonance model (Lubart & Getz, 1997) indicates that initial negative emotions could be used as leverage to propose distant and therefore creative associations of ideas. So if students are prepared to associate ideas with the negative emotions they experience, they may find remoted ideas.

In an attempt to support participants in understanding changes in their emotions over time, Donaghey and Magowan (2021) developed the methodology of "emotion curves." This methodology consists of asking participants to draw a curve in a defined space that represents their emotions during a creative project. Participants are instructed to use "any design, graphic or colour that

[they] feel reflect this process" (p. 5) to illustrate the variations in empathy, confidence, frustration, satisfaction, and joy. In addition, there are open-ended questions to specify which emotion was the most important, if any emotions are missing, what were the important changes and why, and a legend to their emotion curve. This methodology seems particularly interesting to support learners in understanding the emotional changes that occurred during the creative process.

More broadly, the Creative process Report Diary method (CRD, Botella et al., 2019) consists in inviting participants to rate both their creative activity during a learning session and also the factors involved. Here, the factors can, of course, be about emotions but more broadly these factors can cover the multi-variate approach to creativity by including cognitive, conative, emotional, and environmental factors (Lubart, 1999; Lubart et al., 2015; Sternberg & Lubart, 1991, 1995).

As we saw previously, Glăveanu and colleagues (2013) are the only ones to have directly confronted five creative domains through interviews. However, the topic of emotions was not central to their study. Emotions are either secondary in the comparison between the domains or they are studied in a specific domain. The fields need to be confronted more often, even two by two (and not only art and science). What are the similarities and differences between the emotions experienced by a musician and those experienced by a cook? What emotions differentiate a designer and a scriptwriter? A simple quantitative study could consist in cutting the creative process into several stages. Then ask experts in two or more fields to indicate which emotion(s) they experience at each stage. Such a study would allow objectifying the differences between the domains. The variables mentioned previously such as emotional traits, level of expertise, or ability to regulate emotions could be considered to examine these differences.

Moreover, the creative process is not always considered in its overall perspective. Indeed, some quantitative studies, which we have not discussed in this chapter, often focus on divergent, which is indeed one of the most important micro-processes of creativity (Botella et al., 2016), but they do not examine the process from beginning to end. The Design-Realization-Socialization model provides a more comprehensive overview of the creative process. Conceptualization corresponds to the generation of ideas (including divergent thinking, for example). Realization corresponds to the implementation of ideas. Finally, socialization refers to the use of the object. This simple three-step model allows considering the overall creative process from the beginning to the end.

To conclude, we have considered throughout this chapter that emotions and the creative process are closely related. This statement may lead us to propose a broader definition of the creative process by considering the sequence of thoughts, actions, and emotions that produces an idea that is both original and contextually appropriate

References

Amabile, T. M., Barsade, S. G., Mueller, J. S., & Staw, B. M. (2005). Affect and creativity at work. *Administrative Science Quarterly, 50*(3), 367–403. https://doi.org/10.2189/asqu.2005.50.3.367

Barbot, B., Besançon, M., & Lubart, T. (2016). The generality-specificity of creativity: Exploring the structure of creative potential with EPoC. *Learning and Individual Differences, 52*, 178–187. https://doi.org/10.1016/j.lindif.2016.06.005

Bonnardel, N., & Lubart, T. (2019). La créativité: approches et méthodes en psychologie et en ergonomie. RIMHE: Revue Interdisciplinaire Management. *Homme Entreprise, 4*, 79–98. https://doi.org/10.3917/rimhe.037.0079

Botella, M. (2018). The creative process in graphic art. In T. I. Lubart (Ed.), *The Creative Process: Perspectives from Multiple Domains* (pp. 59–88). Palgrave Macmillan.

Botella, M., & Dalloubeix, C. (2020, September). What is the path followed by the most creative engineering students? Communication presented to MIC Conference – Nuturing creative potential, Marooni Institut for Creativity, Bologna (Italy). Virtual conference.

Botella, M., & Lubart, T. I. (2019). From dynamic processes to a dynamic creative process. In R. Beghetto & G. Corazza (Eds.), *Dynamic Perspectives on Creativity: New Directions for Theory, Research, and Practice in Education* (pp. 261–278). Springer.

Botella, M., Glăveanu, V. P., Zenasni, F., et al. (2013). How artists create: Creative process and multivariate factors. *Learning and Individual Differences, 26*, 161–170. https://doi.org/10.1016/j.lindif.2013.02.008

Botella, M., Lockner, D., & Pavani, J.-B. (in press). Créativité et émotions. In N. Bonnardel, F. Girandola, E. Bonetto, & T. Lubart (Eds.), *Créativité en situations: Des théories aux applications* (pp. 99–112). Dunod.

Botella, M., Nelson, J., & Zenasni, F. (2016). Les macro et micro processus créatifs [The mirco and macro creative processes]. In I. Capron-Puozzo (Ed.), *Créativité et apprentissage [Creativity and Learning]* (pp. 33–46). De Boeck.

Botella, M., Nelson, J., & Zenasni, F. (2019). It is time to observe the creative process: How to use a Creative process Report Diary (CRD). *Journal of Creative Behavior, 53*(2), 211–221. https://doi.org/10.1002/jocb.172

Bourgeois-Bougrine, S., Glăveanu, V., Botella, M., et al. (2014). The creativity maze: Exploring creativity in screenplay writing. *Psychology of Aesthetics, Creativity, and the Arts, 8*(4), 384–399. https://doi.org/10.1037/a0037839

Brand, A. G. (1990). Writing and feelings: Checking our vital signs. *Rhetoric Review, 8* (2), 290–308.

Bronowski, J. (1958). The creative process. *Scientific American, 199*(3), 58–65.

Chaffin, R., Imreh, G., Lemieux, A. F., & Chen, C. (2003). "Seeing the big picture": Piano practice as expert problem solving. *Music Perception, 20*(4), 465–s490. https://doi.org/10.1525/mp.2003.20.4.465

Da Costa, C. G., Zhou, Q., & Ferreira, A. I. (2018). The impact of anger on creative process engagement: The role of social contexts. *Journal of Organizational Behavior, 39*(4), 495–506. https://doi.org/10.1002/job.2249

Desmet, P. M. A., & Hekkert, P. (2009). Special issue editorial: Design & emotion. *International Journal of Design, 3*(2), 1–6.

Desmet, P. M. A., & Schifferstein, H. (2012). Emotion research as input for product design. In J. Beckley, D. Paredes, K. Lopetcharat (Eds.), *Product Innovation Toolbox: A Field Guide to Consumer Understanding and Research* (pp. 149–175). John Wiley & Sons.

Donaghey, J., & Magowan, F. (2021). Emotion curves: Creativity and methodological "fit" or "commensurability." *International Review of Qualitative Research.* Online first. https://doi.org/10.1177/_1940_8447_2110_02768.

Ekman, P., & Davidson, R. J. (1994). Afterword: How are emotions distinguished from moods, temperament, and other relative affective constructs? In P. Ekman & R. J. Davidson (Eds.), *The Nature of Emotions: Fundamental Questions* (pp. 94–96). Oxford University Press.

Flanders, J. L. (2004). Creativity and emotion: Reformulating the Romantic theory of art. In B. Hardy-Vallée (Ed.), *Cognitio: Matter and Mind* (pp. 95–102.

Folkman, S. (2013). Stress: Appraisal and coping. In M. D. Gellman, & J. R. Turner (Eds.), *Encyclopedia of Behavioral Medicine* (pp. 1913–1915). Springer. https://doi.org/10.1007/978-1-4419-1005-9_215

Glăveanu, V. P., Lubart, T., Bonnardel, N., et al. (2013). Creativity as action: Findings from five creative domains. *Frontiers in Educational Psychology, 4*, 1–14. https://doi.org/10.3389/fpsyg.2013.00176

Grebot, E. (2011). *Stress et burnout au travail: Identifier, prévenir, guérir.* Editions Eyrolles.

Gross, J. J. (2007). *Handbook of Emotion Regulation.* Guilford Press.

Héroux, I. (2018). Creative processes in the shaping of a musical interpretation: A study of nine professional musicians. *Frontiers in Psychology, 9*, 665. https://doi.org/10.3389/fpsyg.2018.00665

Héroux, I., & Fortier, M.-S. (2014). Expérimentation d'une méthodologie pour expliciter le processus de création d'une interprétation musicale. *Cahiers Société Québécoise Recherche Musique, 15*, 67–79. https://doi.org/10.7202/1033796ar

Ho, A. G. (2010). Exploring the relationships between emotion and design process for designers today. In *DS 66-2: Proceedings of the 1st International Conference on Design Creativity (ICDC 2010).*

Horng, J. S., & Hu, M. L. (2008). The mystery in the kitchen: Culinary creativity. *Creativity Research Journal, 20*(2), 221–230. https://doi.org/10.1080/1040041080206016

Horng, J.-S., & Lee, Y.-C. (2009). What environmental factors influence creative culinary studies? *International Journal of Contemporary Hospitality Management, 21*, 100–117. https://doi.org/10.1108/09596110910930214

Lazarus, R. S., & Folkmann S. (1984). *Stress, Appraisal, and Coping.* Springer.

Leong, M. W. A., Yeh, S. S., Fan, Y. L., & Huan, T. C. (2020). The effect of cuisine creativity on customer emotions. *International Journal of Hospitality Management, 85*, 102346. https://doi.org/10.1016/j.ijhm.2019.102346

Lubart, T. I. (1999). Componential models. In M. A. Runco & S. R. Pritzker (Eds.), *Encyclopaedia of Creativity* (vol. 1, pp. 295–300). Academic Press.

Lubart, T. I., & Getz, I. (1997). Emotion, metaphor, and the creative process. *Creativity Research Journal, 10*(4), 285–301. https://doi.org/10.1207/s15326934crj1004_1

Lubart, T. I, Mouchiroud, C., Tordjman, S., & Zenasni, F. (2015). *La psychologie de la creativité [Psychology of Creativity]* (2nd ed.). Armand Colin.

Luminet, O. (2002). *Psychologie des émotions: Confrontation et évènement*. De Boeck University.

Madeira, A., Palrão, T., Mendes, A. S., & Ottenbacher, M. C. (2021). The culinary creative process of Michelin Star chefs. *Tourism Recreation Research*, 1–19. https://doi.org/10.1080/02508281.2021.1958170

McNally, C. (1982). *The Experience of Being Sensitive*. Unpublished doctoral dissertation, Center for Humanistic Studies, Detroit.

Mikolajczak, M., Quoidbach, J., Kotsou, I., & Nelis, D. (2009). *Les compétences émotionnelles*. Dunod.

Peilloux, A., & Botella, M. (2016). Ecological and dynamical study of the creative process and affects of scientific students working in groups. *Creativity Research Journal, 28*(2), 165–170. https://doi.org/10.1080/10400419.2016.1162549

Plutchik, R. (2001). The nature of emotions: Human emotions have deep evolutionary roots, a fact that may explain their complexity and provide tools for clinical practice. *American Scientist, 89*(4), 344–350.

Russ, S. W. (1993). *Affect and Creativity: The Role of Affect and Play in the Creative Process*. Routledge.

Russ, S. W. (1999). Emotion/Affect. In M. A. Runco & S. R. Pritzker (Eds.), *Encyclopaedia of Creativity* (vol. 1, pp. 659–668). Academic Press.

Scherer, K. R. (2000). Psychological models of emotion. In J. Blood (Ed.), *The Neuropsychology of Emotion* (pp. 92–120). Oxford University Press.

Schlewitt-Haynes, L. D., Earthman, M. S., & Burns, B. (2002). Seeing the world differently: An analysis of descriptions of visual experiences provided by visual artists and nonartists. *Creativity Research Journal, 14*, 361–372. https://doi.org/10.1207/S15326934CRJ1434_7

Shaw, M. P. (1989). The eureka process: A structure for the creative experience in science and engineering. *Creativity Research Journal, 2*(4), 286–298. https://doi.org/10.1080/10400418909534325

Shaw, M. P. (1994). Affective components of scientific creativity. M. P. Shaw & M. A. Runco (Eds.), *Creativity and Affect* (pp. 3–43). Ablex.

Stanko-Kaczmarek, M. (2012). The effect of intrinsic motivation on the affect and evaluation of the creative process among fine arts students. *Creativity Research Journal, 24*(4), 304–310. https://doi.org/10.1080/10400419.2012.730003

Sternberg, R. J., & Lubart, T. I. (1991). An investment theory of creativity and its development. *Human Development, 34*, 1–31. https://doi.org/10.1159/000277029

Sternberg, R. J., & Lubart, T. I. (1995). *Defying the Crowd: Cultivating Creativity in a Culture of Conformity*. Free Press.

St-Louis, A. C., & Vallerand, R. J. (2015). A successful creative process: The role of passion and emotions. *Creativity Research Journal, 27*(2), 175–187. https://doi.org/10.1080/10400419.2015.1030314

Vosburg, S. K. (1998). The effects of positive and negative mood on divergent-thinking performance. *Creativity Research Journal, 11*(2), 165–172. https://doi.org/10.1207/s15326934crj1102_6

Xu, Y. (2016). The emotion analysis during oil painting creation process. *Advances in Social Science, Education and Humanities Research*, 5, 37–40. https://doi.org/10.2991/icadce-16.2016.8

Wallas, G. (1926). *The Art of Thought*. Harcourt, Brace and Company.

Wei, Z., & Chen, J. (2019). The application of emotion creative strategy in advertising design. *Journal of Literature and Art Studies*, 9(10), 1088–1092. https://doi.org/10.17265/2159-5836/2019.10.012

PART III

Emotions and the Creative Person

12 Emotion Traits and Creativity

Zorana Ivcevic

Emotions matter for creativity. Emotion states, from nostalgia to interest to frustration, influence creative thinking (meta-analysis: Baas et al., 2008; review: Madrid, Patterson, & Ibaceta, this volume) and creative process engagement (To et al., 2012). By contrast with short-lasting emotion states, emotion traits are long-lasting individual difference variables that influence all aspects of creativity, from the decision to engage in creative work to the frequency of creative activity to communication of creative work to relevant audiences. While other articles have been written to provide a broad overview of the role of emotion-related variables (pertaining to emotion states, traits, and abilities) in creativity (Ivcevic & Hoffmann, 2019), this chapter examines in more depth the role of emotion traits in creativity.

The chapter is organized into six sections. The first section defines the approach to both creativity and personality traits adopted in this chapter, followed by a description of the model of how emotion-related traits influence different aspects of creativity. The following sections review research on the role of emotion traits across four aspects of creativity. The final section looks ahead to unanswered questions and directions for future research.

Defining Creativity and Emotion Traits

In an inspirational review of creativity studies, Mumford and Gustafson (1988) spoke of a creativity syndrome, which integrates the study of cognitive abilities and processes with individual difference variables, developmental, and social or environmental processes. A sweeping one-sentence definition of *creativity* (or the creativity syndrome) is provided by Plucker and colleagues (2004) as "the interaction among aptitude, process and environment by which an individual or group produces a perceptible product that is both novel and useful as defined within a social context" (p. 90). This definition points to the necessity for specification when discussing creativity; that is, when

Correspondence concerning this chapter should be addressed to Zorana Ivcevic, Yale Center for Emotional Intelligence, Yale University, 350 George St., New Haven, CT 06511. Email: zorana. ivcevic@yale.edu. Work on this chapter was made possible by Fundación Botín (Creativity, Emotion, and the Arts grant, PI Zorana Ivcevic).

we study creativity, we are usually studying specific aspects, such as aptitude (e.g., divergent thinking abilities; Barbot et al., 2016), creative process (e.g., problem finding or problem identification, Csikszentmihalyi, 1988), or creative environments (e.g., climate for creativity at work, Hunter et al., 2007). When we are not speaking of creativity in general, but specifying that a particular study examines creative idea generation or creative achievement, we are building conceptual clarity. The need for this specification is made empirically clear by findings that different aspects of the creativity syndrome are differentially predicted by important variables, such as personality traits (Puryear et al., 2017).

This chapter specifically refers to four aspects of the creativity syndrome: (1) the decision to be creative, (2) creative process engagement; (3) domain-specific performance; and (4) frequency of creative behavior and level of creative achievement. This is not meant to be an exhaustive or definitive list of aspects of the creative syndrome. Rather, this is an attempt to offer one conceptual systematization of the existing literature and invite a discussion in the field about its utility.

The first aspect of the creativity syndrome is largely internal to the person and involves ways of thinking, self-definition, and identity. Sternberg (2002) equated creativity with a decision. Creative behavior will not be likely without a desire to be creative or a decision to attempt being creative. Creativity measures pertaining to the decision to be creative include attitudes and values toward creativity (Ivcevic & Hoffmann, 2021; Noller, cited in Isaksen et al., 1994), creative self-efficacy (Farmer & Tierney, 2017), and intentions to engage or persist in creativity and innovation (Hoffmann et al., 2016; Moriano et al., 2012).

The other aspects of the creativity syndrome referred to in this chapter are largely external. Most often, creative behavior is demonstrated in a domain-specific way (Baer, 2010; Ivcevic & Mayer, 2009). Domain-relevant performance can be studied in terms of observable differences between domains (e.g., artists vs. scientists) or in terms of intra-domain performance differences (e.g., more or less creative scientists, Feist, 1998). Creative process engagement involves behaviors that are likely to result in creative performances or products (Zhang & Bartol, 2010), including problem identification, information processing, and idea generation. These aspects of the creativity syndrome are often studied in laboratory tasks (Barbot et al., 2016; Reiter-Palmon, 2017), but increasingly also in experience sampling studies (To et al., 2012, 2015). Finally, creative activities and achievements refer to creativity manifested in action and include criteria such as time spent on creative work (e.g., Amabile et al., 1994), self-reported activities and achievements (Carson et al., 2005; Diedrich et al., 2018), and ratings of creativity by knowledgeable others (e.g., George & Zhou, 2001; Ivcevic & Brackett, 2015). Creative activities and achievements can further be examined in terms of their level, as radical versus incremental (Madjar et al., 2011) or on a continuum from mini-c manifest in learning, everyday life little-c creativity to professional creativity with varying levels of achievement, to eminent or Big-C (Kaufman & Beghetto, 2009).

Having defined creativity, it is important to do the same with emotion traits. Personality traits are predispositions toward certain ways of feeling, thinking, and behaving (Matthews et al., 2003) that affect how people select situations or environments and lower the threshold for trait-related behavior, making trait-congruent behavior more likely (Roberts et al., 2008). For instance, openness to experiences is a tendency to be interested in a broad range of ideas, be open to diverse emotional experiences, be interested in aesthetic experiences, and act in unconventional ways and is a personality dimension that can be described as a predisposition for creativity (McCrae, 1996; Puryear et al., 2017).

The history of research on personality traits related to creativity mirrors research on personality more broadly, from the study of many traits to the study of broad trait dimensions to emerging work on functional divisions of personality traits. The many traits tradition employed instruments such as the California Personality Inventory or the Minnesota Multiphasic Personality Inventory (review: Barron & Harrington, 1981). The study of broad trait dimensions is most closely associated with the Big Five model, which employed factor-analytic techniques to reduce many traits into few based on their empirical covariation (Goldberg, 1990). Structurally, each Big Five trait dimension is composed of a small number of aspects (e.g., DeYoung et al., 2007; Soto & John, 2017), each includes a larger number of more specific traits that could be related to specific affective (e.g., openness to feelings), cognitive (e.g., openness to ideas), and behavioral components (e.g., openness to action; Costa & McCrae, 1995; DeYoung, 2015).

This chapter focuses specifically on emotion-related traits. This decision is based on emerging functional approaches to personality, which divide traits based on their role in personality. Mayer (2003) defined four areas of personality: the energy lattice includes emotional, motivational, and emotion-motivation interactions; the knowledge works refers to mental models of the self, the world, and reasoning mechanisms; the role player involves expressiveness, social roles and actions, and motor mechanisms; and executive consciousness describes awareness and self-control mechanisms. Similarly, Feist (2019) distinguished emotional-motivational, cognitive, social, and clinical traits. Here, a review of emotion-related traits is presented, acknowledging that they are closely related to motivational traits (e.g., trait passion includes the emotional desire to engage in an activity, as well as motivational component of long-term commitment to an activity).

This chapter is not an exhaustive review of emotion traits related to different aspects of the creativity syndrome. For example, there are emotional aspects in the dark triad traits – psychopathy, narcissism, and Machiavellianism – and emerging research points to these emotional aspects as related to creative activities, achievement, and creative idea generation (e.g., Sordia et al., 2020). The chapter focuses on traits that have been most consistently examined in relation to different aspects of creativity.

Figure 12.1 presents a proposed model depicting the relationship between emotion-related traits and different aspects of the creativity syndrome.

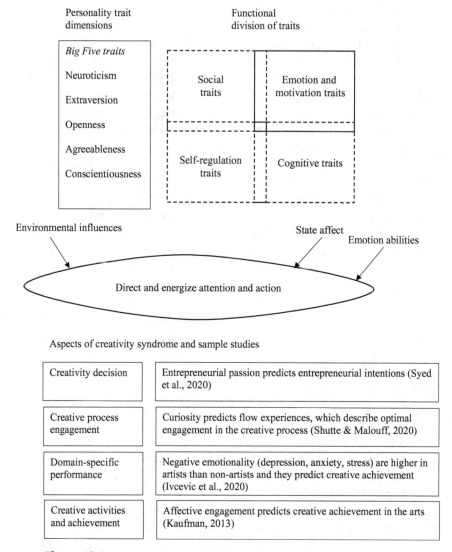

Figure 12.1 *Emotion traits and different aspects of the creativity syndrome.*

The model situates emotion-related traits in relation to other categories of traits and trait dimensions. Within the Big Five traits, neuroticism and extraversion can be considered primarily emotion-related. Emotion-related traits direct and energize attention and action. In doing so, they help form behavioral intentions, invigorate action, facilitate domain-relevant performance, and help maintain effort and persistence necessary for achievement. The following sections summarize research on key emotion-related traits in different aspects of the creativity syndrome.

Creativity Decision

When confronted with an open-ended problem or task, people face a decision whether to attempt being creative or take a relatively conventional or familiar approach. This is not a single decision made only at the beginning of the creative process, but it is a continual commitment to creativity. Creativity criteria in this category include creativity intentions, self-efficacy, creative self-perceptions, and creativity-relevant attitudes. Creativity intentions indicate that a specific decision about creative action has been made (Choi, 2004, 2012), creative self-efficacy is a motivating belief that one is able to be creative in thinking and action (Farmer & Tierney, 2017), creative self-perception includes endorsing general tendencies related to creative behavior (Ivcevic & Kaufman, 2013; McKay et al., 2017), and attitudes toward creativity are evaluations of creativity-relevant situations that direct behavior (Ivcevic & Hoffmann, 2021).

Self-perceptions of creativity have been a commonly studied outcome that is consistently related to positive emotionality. Self-perceptions of creativity are related to extraversion (Furnham & Bachtiar, 2008; Wolfradt & Pretz, 2001), as well as trait hypomania (Schuldberg, 2001). One proposed mechanism of how trait hypomanic mood facilitates creativity is through increased risk-taking and boldness (Lloyd-Evans et al., 2006). Furnham and colleagues (2008) found that trait hypomania had incremental validity over fluid intelligence in predicting creative self-perception. Moreover, trait hypomania was significant even after controlling for Big Five personality traits, suggesting that its qualities go beyond general positive emotionality assessed by extraversion. Similarly, creative self-perceptions are related to trait emotional intelligence, which describes a sense of efficacy to perceive, use, understand, and manage emotions (Xu et al., 2019).

Social psychological research shows that attitudes predict behavioral intentions (Eagly & Chaiken, 2007). Attitudes negatively evaluating creativity – anticipating negative social consequences for creativity and anxious risk aversion – are negatively related to extraversion and neuroticism, while the positive attitude of valuing creativity is positively related to extraversion (Ivcevic & Hoffmann, 2021). Silvia's (2017) theoretical analysis suggests that curiosity should be an emotion trait that creates a desire to learn for its own sake, as well as counteracting anxiety (which is related to avoidance motivation), and balancing enjoyment (which can motivate premature satisfaction and taking proven strategies that lead to known rewards). Thus, it is not surprising that curiosity is related to creative self-efficacy and creative identity (Karwowski, 2012). Moreover, creative self-efficacy mediates the relationship between trait curiosity and both imagination and performance on divergent thinking tasks (Puente-Díaz & Cavazos-Arroyo, 2017).

While curiosity energizes creativity-supportive behavior and creative self-concept, emotion traits that describe level of comfort or acceptance of uncertainty should lower the anxiety when facing open-ended tasks.

Willingness to take risks lowers the threshold of evaluating situations requiring creativity as desirable and worthy of potential costs they might have. Risk-taking is based on an individual appraisal of potential harm or benefit and risk magnitude (Weber et al., 2002), as well as ability to regulate risk-related emotions (Loewenstein et al., 2001). Tyagi and colleagues (2017) found that social risk-taking – taking risks to one's reputation, readiness to challenge social norms – is related to creative personality. Bonetto et al. (2020) showed that social risk-taking predicted creative self-efficacy, creative personal identity, and self-rating of creativity. Similarly, Beghetto et al. (2021) found that intellectual risk-taking – taking risks of learning new skills and trying new ideas – was related to creative confidence and that it moderated the relationship between creative confidence and creative behavior. When intellectual risk-taking was low, creative confidence did not predict creativity, but once a low threshold of intellectual risk-taking was reached, it strengthened the relationship between creative confidence and creative behavior ad achievement.

Most direct evidence about the creative decision comes from studies of creativity intentions. Creativity intention mediated the relationship between creativity-relevant motivations and skills and creative performance evaluated by course instructors in university students enrolled in an organizational behavior course (Choi, 2004). In a study of computer programmers, in addition to openness to experience, creativity intention was predicted positively by extraversion and negatively by neuroticism (Amin et al., 2020).

Furthermore, passion motivates creative decisions. Entrepreneurial passion predicts entrepreneurial intention in samples as diverse as students, academic researchers, homebrewers, and technology-based firms (Biraglia & Kadile, 2017; Campos, 2017; Huyghe et al., 2016; Turner & Gianiodis, 2018). Specifically, entrepreneurial passion is related to entrepreneurial intentions through innovativeness, and this effect is stronger in those higher in curiosity (Syed et al., 2020). Passion can also predict entrepreneurial intention both directly and through self-efficacy (Biraglia & Kadile, 2017).

Creativity decision is influenced by one's perceived ability to cope with emotional challenges during the creative process. Trait emotional intelligence describes one's self-perception of skills to perceive, use, understand, and manage emotions (Wong & Law, 2002). Trait emotional intelligence is related to creative personality (Guastello et al., 2004), as well as attitudes toward entrepreneurship and entrepreneurial intent in university students, and this relationship is mediated by students' self-ratings of creativity and proactive orientation (Li et al., 2020). Similarly, trait emotional intelligence is related to social entrepreneurship intentions both directly and through attitudes toward social entrepreneurship in university students (Tiwari et al., 2017).

Creative Process Engagement

Creative process engagement – behavior likely to lead to creative performance (Zhang & Bartol, 2010) – can be studied in either short-term or long-term tasks.

Laboratory studies tend to examine cognitive processes that are assumed to be a basis for creative work and achievement in everyday settings, while experience sampling and survey studies examine creative process engagement in long-term projects or ongoing creative work.

Research on the creative process has largely focused on understanding divergent thinking. When affective variables are examined, they tend to focus on emotion states, rather than traits. This decision is theoretically meaningful because prediction is most successful when predictors and outcomes are similar in breadth; therefore, short-lasting state affect will be most relevant for short-term tasks. A meta-analysis showed that both extraversion and neuroticism correlated with performance on divergent thinking tasks, although the effects were small (Puryear et al., 2017). Extraversion was more strongly related to fluency than to originality, flexibility, and elaboration. Neuroticism was positively related to flexibility and elaboration, but negatively with fluency.

Emerging research points to curiosity as a trait that increases information seeking early in the creative problem-solving process, which then predicts quality and originality of solutions. Furthermore, this relationship remains significant when controlling for constructs conceptually related to curiosity (epistemic openness to experience, need for cognition, and typical intellectual engagement; Hardy et al., 2017). Curiosity also predicts the likelihood of experiencing flow while working on a creative problem-solving task, which is related to creative performance (Schutte & Malouff, 2020).

Creative process engagement on longer-term tasks is related to extraversion, curiosity, and passion. Extraversion predicted self-reported creative process engagement at the end of an introductory course in organizational behavior – supplying new ideas and perspectives in class, raising interesting issues and challenging questions for discussion, and integrating ideas to offer creative solutions (Sung & Choi, 2009). Moreover, this relationship was stronger for students high in extrinsic motivation (i.e., those motivated to get a high grade). In a study of graduate students working on research projects, positive emotionality predicted creative process engagement, and this effect was stronger when problem clarity was low (Tang et al., 2018).

Although Chang and Shih (2019) theoretically proposed that curiosity facilitates engagement in different activities pertaining to creative process engagement, research is only emerging to support this proposal. For instance, curiosity predicts different attributes of creative process engagement, such as asking open-ended questions from those providing feedback to graphic designers participating in web-based T-shirt competitions (Harrison & Dossinger, 2017). Research is also examining the role of passion in creative process engagement. Harmonious passion predicted deliberate practice, which was in turn related to performing arts students' creativity rated by their instructors and program directors (Vallerand et al., 2007). Entrepreneurial passion predicted time spent engaging in entrepreneurial activities (Murnieks et al., 2014) and compulsive passion predicted both entrepreneurial persistence and performance (Feng & Chen, 2020).

Domain-Specific Performance

Emotion-related traits predict domain-specific behavior and performance. Feist (1998) conducted a meta-analysis of personality traits in artists and scientists. While emotion traits did not distinguish between scientists and non-scientists or more and less creative scientists, several emotion-related traits distinguished artists and non-artists – artists are less emotionally stable and less guilt-free or happy compared to non-artists. Similarly, traits related to negative emotionality have been found in studies comparing dancers and athletes (Thomson & Jaque, 2013), comparing visual arts students with music and psychology students (Haller & Courvoisier, 2010), and comparing advanced art students and science students (Sheldon, 1995). Furthermore, negative emotionality (measured as depression, anxiety, and stress) was higher in artists than non-artists and it predicted the level of creative achievement (Ivcevic et al., 2022).

Studies about the relationship between personality traits and vocational interests are also relevant (Barrick et al., 2003; Larson et al., 2002). Extraversion predicts enterprising interests, which are characteristic of creative occupations such as those of architects, entrepreneurs, and fashion designers. Wille and De Fruyt (2014) followed a sample of college graduates 15 years into their careers and found that the relationship between personality traits and occupational interests was reciprocal: personality traits influenced occupational choice, but were also influenced by these choices and vocational experiences. It may thus be that those who are more extraverted, for instance, are more likely to engage in everyday creative behavior (such as self-expressive creativity or interpersonal creativity, Ivcevic, 2007) or entrepreneurial creativity (Lee & Tsang, 2001; Zhao et al., 2010), and that performance in these activities that benefit from positive and high-energy traits in turn strengthens extraversion.

Frequency of Behavior and Achievement

Beside openness to experience, which is the strongest personality predictor of creative behavior and achievement, a recent meta-analysis points to extraversion as a significant predictor of creative behavior and achievement (Puryear et al., 2017). This finding is further supported by studies explicitly measuring trait positive and negative affect, as well as optimism and trait hypomania.

Trait positive affect predicts creative behavior at work as rated by supervisors (Gilmore et al., 2013). Moreover, trait positive affect is a personal resource that can compensate for the lack of a job resource of transformational leadership, which is a social/environmental facilitator of creative behavior at work (Koh et al., 2019). In a student sample, both positive and negative trait affect predicted creativity measured by a composite including creative activities and creativity attitudes (Ceci & Kumar, 2016). Similarly, optimism predicts employee creative behavior at work (rated by supervisors), both directly and through positive state affect and the positivity ratio (Rego et al., 2012). Furthermore, when optimism and pessimism are not treated as opposite ends on a single continuum, but as distinct dimensions of affective individual differences, the optimism-to-pessimism ratio shows a curvilinear inverted U-shape relationship with creative behavior at work, indicating that creativity is the highest when high optimism exists in combination with a certain moderate level of pessimism (Rego et al., 2018).

Trait hypomania is related to more creative leisure activities (Eckblad & Chapman, 1986) and is a descriptor of high creative achievers based on the latent class analysis of responses on the Biographical Inventory of Creative Behavior (von Stumm et al., 2011). Furthermore, patients during hypomanic episodes report engaging in creative activities, especially in the artistic domain (e.g., painting, writing; McCraw et al., 2013). However, it remains unclear whether this relationship is unique to trait hypomania. For instance, although Furnham and colleagues (2008) found that trait hypomania predicted creative behavior, this effect ceased to be significant when Big Five personality traits were controlled.

In addition to positive emotionality-related traits, achievement-related traits at the intersection of emotion and motivation are important predictors of creative behavior and achievement. Trait intrinsic motivation (Amabile et al., 1994) – operationally defined in terms of affective experiences of enjoyment and challenge in work – predicts frequency of engagement in creative activities (e.g., hours of work per week doing art, number of artworks produced), as well as ratings of creative achievement (e.g., instructor ratings of student commitment to art and potential as an artist). A meta-analysis showed the relationship between intrinsic motivation and product creativity to be reliable and moderate in size (de Jesus et al., 2013).

Passion can be defined as a relatively stable trait (Amiot et al., 2006; Cardon et al., 2009) that unites a strong desire and arousal evoked by anticipated, imagined, or physical engagement with activities that are important to one's identity and commitment and dedication to those activities (Fredricks et al., 2010; Moeller et al., 2017). Activities that adolescents identify being passionate about (in interview and experience sampling studies) are most often creative in nature (e.g., music, drama, art; Fredricks et al., 2010; Moeller et al., 2017) and passion for one's interests assessed by teacher-reports predicts peer-nominations of creativity of high school students (Grohman et al., 2017). Similarly, self-reported passion predicts observed creativity across samples and domains, from performing arts students (creative behavior/achievement assessed by instructors and program directors; Vallerand et al., 2007), professionals in the workplace (creativity measured by team leader ratings; Liu et al., 2011), and experienced entrepreneurs (CEOs of privately owned, independent, small to medium-sized firms self-reporting creative behavior, Cardon et al., 2013). In a study of design students, harmonious passion played a mediating role in the relationship between innovative cognitive style and self-reported creative achievement (Luh & Lu, 2012).

Some emotion-related traits predict creative activity and achievement in specific domains. Kaufman (2013) identified a dimension of affective engagement as a trait characterized by openness to a wide range of feelings, as well as preference for relying on gut feelings and empathy in decision making. This trait predicted creative achievement in the arts (including music, dance, humor, theatre, and film), but not intellectual domains such as science and technology. Other domain-specific effects concern the nature of emotion traits. Cardon et al. (2013) distinguished entrepreneurial passion for inventing, founding, and developing enterprises and found that passion for inventing and founding was related to self-reported creative behavior (Cardon et al., 2013). Furthermore, Kang et al. (2016) studied small and relatively young entrepreneurial firms and found that employee passion for inventing mediated the relationship between innovative work climate and employee innovative behavior (rated by firm CEOs).

As with the creativity decision, creative behavior and achievement are related to emotion-related traits that describe a sense of emotional efficacy. In a long-running longitudinal study of women, Helson et al. (1995) found that tolerance of ambiguity assessed at the end of college predicted occupational creativity at age 52. Trait emotional intelligence can facilitate engagement in specific cognitive and social creativity-relevant processes and is a reliable predictor of creative behavior (Xu et al., 2019). Trait emotional intelligence predicts knowledge sharing, which in turn is related to self-reported creative behavior (Goh & Lim, 2014). Carmeli and colleagues (2014) found that trait emotional intelligence is related to generosity toward colleagues and vigor, and that they in turn are associated with creative behavior at work. Furthermore, trait emotional intelligence interacts with proactive personality (personal resource) and organizational climate (job resource) in predicting higher self-reported creative behavior (Jafri et al., 2016).

Future Directions

Figure 12.1 offers an outline for a systematic program of research on the role of emotion-related traits on different aspects of creativity. The model suggests to jointly study Big Five traits and narrower functional traits. Similar to the study of affective states, emotion traits can be operationalized as typical experiences that capture both valence and arousal, thus including trait positive high activation affect, negative high activation affect, positive low activation affect, and negative low activation affect. This research will enable examining to what extent are state-level emotion processes similar to trait-level emotion processes in relation to creativity outcomes. Because prediction of outcomes is best when predictors and outcomes are similar in their breadth (Ackerman & Kanfer, 2004), it could be hypothesized that state-level emotion processes will be more closely related to short-term creative outcomes (e.g., performance on brief tasks of creative thinking and problem solving, such as typically employed in laboratory studies; Baas et al., 2008). On the other hand, emotion traits refer to typical behavior across time and situations and can be hypothesized to best predict outcomes that are accrued across time, such as creative achievement.

Beyond the study of overall trait affect, future research should examine specific emotion traits theoretically relevant to creativity and their mechanisms of influence. Although existing theory suggests that curiosity would affect different aspects of creativity, empirical research remains scarce. To what extent does curiosity affect creative attitudes and intentions? Existing research shows that curiosity predicts information seeking (Hardy et al., 2017). Does curiosity also increase the likelihood of other aspects of creative process engagement, including problem identification and idea generation? Does curiosity predict creative behavior differently across domains?

Although personality traits have been measured by self- and other-report, it can be argued that emotion-related traits specifically are best assessed by self-report because they are part of one's internal subjective experience. According to the self-other knowledge asymmetry model (Vazire, 2010), traits that describe internal attributes are relatively low on observability and thus the most accurate assessment is by oneself. On the other hand, assessment of different aspects of creativity can (and should be) diversified when possible. In the case of creativity decision, the options to go beyond self-reports might be limited because the relevant criteria describe internal evaluation and intentions. However, other aspects of creativity can be assessed by observations of the creative process (e.g., recording information seeking or sharing, generation of ideas) and by ratings from multiple knowledgeable others (e.g., different team members rating each other's creativity, employee ratings of supervisor creativity) or by evaluation of real-world products (ratings by experts or gatekeepers). It should be expected that trait measures are better predictors of creative behavior and performance on long-term tasks rather than on short-term tasks (such as those administered in the laboratory).

As depicted in Figure 12.1, future research will have to address potential moderating effects of emotion states, emotion abilities, and environmental factors on different aspects of creativity. Tamir (2005) proposed that trait-consistent negative affective states, such as worry, benefit performance on demanding tasks. Indeed, individuals higher in neuroticism chose to recall worrisome (as opposed to happy) memories before a creative thinking task, and they were also more creative on that task when worry was induced. It remains to be examined whether other emotion traits (e.g., trait positive affect) might similarly interact with state affect.

Although research on emotion abilities and creativity is only a nascent area of study, there is early support for the interaction between an emotion trait and ability. Parke et al. (2015) found that typical experience of positive activated affect at work (average ratings of enthusiasm and excitement across 25 workdays) did not predict supervisor-rated employee creativity at work; however, the interaction of typical positive affect and performance on an ability test of using emotions to facilitate thought predicted work creative behavior. Furthermore, emotion traits can interact with environmental factors to affect different aspects of creativity. Chamorro-Premuzic and Reichenbacher (2008) found that extraversion predicted higher divergent thinking test performance both in threat of evaluation and no evaluation conditions, but that neuroticism predicted lower performance only under threat of evaluation. The question for future research is how other theoretically relevant environmental factors (e.g., climate for creativity, Hunter et al., 2007; support for creativity, Amabile et al., 2004) interact with emotion traits to predict different aspects of creativity.

Finally, future research should expand the analytical techniques used in studying emotion traits and creativity beyond the traditional approach that examines inter-individual differences. People can be described in terms of their standing on different traits and examination of patterns of traits can provide new insights. Even attributes that are negatively correlated across individuals can co-occur in a subgroup of people. For instance, it is possible to identify a pattern of moderately high psychological vulnerabilities (anxiety, depression, stress) and psychological resources (psychological well-being, ego-resilience, hope) and this pattern is more common in artists than non-artists (Ivcevic et al., 2022). Patterns of other emotion-related traits can be relevant to different aspects of creativity (e.g., high trait emotional intelligence and high curiosity can be hypothesized as predicting greater creative process engagement in teams).

Conclusion

The model in Figure 12.1 summarizes and integrates existing research on emotion traits (situated among other functional divisions of traits and the broad Big Five trait dimensions) and their role in creative decision, domain-specific performance, creative process engagement, and creative behavior and achievement by directing and energizing attention and action. Moreover, the model points to likely groups of moderators pertaining to affective states, emotion abilities, and environmental factors relevant to creativity. Initial research illustrating such moderating effects exists, but more is called for to map the most theoretically relevant interactions. Our review concludes by making a full circle where scientific research begins, in a call for considering specification of emotion-related variables and creativity criteria under investigation, a call for diversity in assessment methods, and analytical techniques that include both inter-individual and intra-individual approaches.

References

Ackerman, P. L., & Kanfer, R. (2004). Cognitive, affective, and conative aspects of adult intellect within a typical and maximal performance framework. In D. Y. Dai & R. J. Sternberg (Eds.), *Motivation, Emotion, and Cognition: Integrative*

Perspectives on Intellectual Functioning and Development (pp. 119–141). Erlbaum.

Amabile, T. M., Hill, K. G., Hennessey, B. A., & Tighe, E. M. (1994). The work reference inventory: Assessing intrinsic and extrinsic motivational orientations. *Journal of Personality and Social Psychology, 66*(5), 950–967.

Amabile, T. M., Schatzel, E. A., Moneta, G. B., & Kramer, S. J. (2004). Leader behaviors and the work environment for creativity: Perceived leader support. *The Leadership Quarterly, 15*(1), 5–32. https://doi.org/10.1016/j.leaqua.2003.12.003

Amin, A., Basri, S., Rahman, M., et al. (2020). The impact of personality traits and knowledge collection behavior on programmer creativity, *Information and Software Technology, 128,* 106405. https://doi.org/10.1016/j.infsof.2020 .106405.

Amiot, C. E., Vallerand, R. J., & Blanchard, C. M. (2006). Passion and psychological adjustment: A test of the person-environment fit hypothesis. *Personality and Social Psychology Bulletin, 32*(2), 220–229. https://doi.org/10.1177/ 0146167205280250

Baas, M., De Dreu, C. K. W., & Nijstad, B. A. (2008). A meta-analysis of 25 years of mood-creativity research: Hedonic tone, activation, or regulatory focus? *Psychological Bulletin, 134*(6), 779–806. https://doi.org/10.1037/a0012815

Baer, J. (2010). Is creativity domain specific? In J. C. Kaufman & R. J. Sternberg (Eds.), *The Cambridge Handbook of Creativity* (pp. 321–341). Cambridge University Press. https://doi.org/10.1017/CBO9780511763205.021

Barbot, B., Besançon, M., & Lubart, T. (2016). The generality-specificity of creativity: Exploring the structure of creative potential with EPoC. *Learning and Individual Differences, 52,* 178–187. https://doi.org/10.1016/j.lindif.2016.06.005

Barrick, M. R., Mount, M. K., & Gupta, R. (2003). Meta-analysis of the relationship between the five-factor model of personality and Holland's occupational types. *Personnel Psychology, 56*(1), 45–74. https://doi.org/10.1111/j.1744-6570.2003 .tb00143.x

Barron, F., & Harrington, D. M. (1981). Creativity, intelligence, and personality. *Annual Review of Psychology, 32,* 439–476. https://doi.org/10.1146/annurev.ps .32.020181.002255

Beghetto, R. A., Karwowski, M., & Reiter-Palmon, R. (2021). Intellectual risk taking: A moderating link between creative confidence and creative behavior? *Psychology of Aesthetics, Creativity, and the Arts, 15*(4), 637–644. https://doi .org/10.1037/aca0000323

Biraglia, A., & Kadile, V. (2017). The role of entrepreneurial passion and creativity in developing entrepreneurial intentions: Insights from American homebrewers. *Journal of Small Business Management, 55*(1), 170–188. https://doi.org/10 .1111/jsbm.12242

Bonetto, E., Pichot, N., Pavani, J.-B., & Adam-Troian, J. (2020). Creative individuals are social risk-takers: Relationships between creativity, social risk-taking and fear of negative evaluations. *Creativity. Theories – Research – Applications, 7* (2), 309–320. https://doi.org/10.2478/ctra-2020-0016

Campos, H. M. (2017). Impact of entrepreneurial passion on entrepreneurial orientation with the mediating role of entrepreneurial alertness for technology-based firms in Mexico. *Journal of Small Business and Enterprise Development, 24*(2), 353–374. https://doi.org/10.1108/JSBED-10-2016-0166

Cardon, M. S., Gregoire D. A., Stevens, C. E., & Patel, P. C. (2013). Measuring entrepreneurial passion: Conceptual foundations and scale validation. *Journal of Business Venturing, 28*(3), 373–396. https://doi.org/10.1016/j .jbusvent.2012.03.003

Cardon, M. S., Wincent, J., Singh, J., & Drnovsek, M. (2009). The nature and experience of entrepreneurial passion. *The Academy of Management Review, 34*(3), 511–532. https://doi.org/10.5465/AMR.2009.40633190

Carmeli, A., McKay, A. S., & Kaufman, J. C. (2014). Emotional intelligence and creativity: The mediating role of generosity and vigor. *The Journal of Creative Behavior, 48*(4), 290–309. https://doi.org/10.1002/jocb.53

Carson, S. H., Peterson, J. B., & Higgins, D. M. (2005). Reliability, Validity, and Factor Structure of the Creative Achievement Questionnaire. *Creativity Research Journal, 17*(1), 37–50. https://doi.org/10.1207/s15326934crj1701_4

Ceci, M. W., & Kumar, V. K. (2016). A correlational study of creativity, happiness, motivation, and stress from creative pursuits. *Journal of Happiness Studies, 17* (2), 609–626. http://dx.doi.org/10.1007/s10902-015-9615-y

Chang, Y.-Y., & Shih, H.-Y. (2019). Work curiosity: A new lens for understanding employee creativity. *Human Resource Management Review, 29*(4), Article 100672. https://doi.org/10.1016/j.hrmr.2018.10.005

Chamorro-Premuzic, T., & Reichenbacher, L. (2008). Effects of personality and threat of evaluation on divergent and convergent thinking, *Journal of Research in Personality, 42*(4), 1095–1101. https://doi.org/10.1016/j.jrp.2007.12.007

Choi, J. N. (2004). Individual and contextual predictors of creative performance: The mediating role of psychological processes. *Creativity Research Journal, 16*(2–3), 187–199. https://doi.org/10.1207/s15326934crj1602&3_4

Choi, J. N. (2012). Context and creativity: The theory of planned behavior as an alternative mechanism. *Social Behavior and Personality, 40*(4), 681–692. http://dx.doi.org/10.2224/sbp.2012.40.4.681

Costa, P. T., & McCrae, R. R. (1995). Domains and facets: Hierarchical personality assessment using the Revised NEO Personality Inventory. *Journal of Personality Assessment, 64*(1), 21–50. https://doi.org/10.1207/ s15327752jpa6401_2

Csikszentmihalyi, M. (1988). Motivation and creativity: Toward a synthesis of structural and energistic approaches to cognition. *New Ideas in Psychology, 6*(2), 159–176. https://doi.org/10.1016/0732-118X(88)90001-3

de Jesus, S. N., Rus, C. L., Lens, W., & Imaginário, S. (2013). Intrinsic motivation and creativity related to product: A meta-analysis of the studies published between 1990–2010. *Creativity Research Journal, 25*(1), 80–84. https://doi.org/10.1080/ 10400419.2013.752235

DeYoung, C. G. (2015). Cybernetic Big Five Theory. *Journal of Research in Personality, 56*, 33–58. https://doi.org/10.1016/j.jrp.2014.07.004

DeYoung, C. G., Quilty, L. C., & Peterson, J. B. (2007). Between facets and domains: 10 aspects of the Big Five. *Journal of Personality and Social Psychology, 93*(5), 880–896. https://doi.org/10.1037/0022-3514.93.5.880

Diedrich, J., Jauk, E., Silvia, P. J., et al. (2018). Assessment of real-life creativity: The Inventory of Creative Activities and Achievements (ICAA). *Psychology of Aesthetics, Creativity, and the Arts, 12*(3), 304–316. https://doi.org/10.1037/ aca0000137

Eagly, A. H., & Chaiken, S. (2007). The advantages of an inclusive definition of attitude. *Social Cognition, 25*(5), 582–602. https://doi.org/10.1521/soco.2007.25.5.582

Eckblad, M., & Chapman, L. J. (1986). Development and validation of a scale for hypomanic personality. *Journal of Abnormal Psychology, 95*(3), 214–222. https://doi.org/10.1037/0021-843X.95.3.214

Farmer, S. M., & Tierney, P. (2017). Considering creative self-efficacy: Its current state and ideas for future inquiry. In M. Karwowski & J. C. Kaufman (Eds.), *The Creative Self: Effect of Beliefs, Self-Efficacy, Mindset, and Identity* (pp. 23–47). Elsevier Academic Press. https://doi.org/10.1016/B978-0-12-809790-8.00002-9

Feist, G. J. (1998). A meta-analysis of personality in scientific and artistic creativity. *Personality and Social Psychology Review, 2*(4), 290–309. https://doi.org/10.1207/s15327957pspr0204_5

Feist, G. J. (2019). The function of personality in creativity: Updates on the creative personality. In J. C. Kaufman & R. J. Sternberg (Eds.), *The Cambridge Handbook of Creativity* (pp. 353–373). Cambridge University Press. https://doi.org/10.1017/9781316979839.019

Feng, B., & Chen, M. (2020). The impact of entrepreneurial passion on psychology and behavior of entrepreneurs. *Frontiers in Psychology, 11*, 1733. https://doi.org/10.3389/fpsyg.2020.01733

Fredricks, J. A., Alfeld, C., & Eccles, J. (2010). Developing and fostering passion in academic and nonacademic domains. *Gifted Child Quarterly, 54*(1), 18–30. https://doi.org/10.1177/0016986209352683

Furnham, A., & Bachtiar, V. (2008). Personality and intelligence as predictors of creativity. *Personality and Individual Differences, 45*(7), 613–617. https://doi.org/10.1016/j.paid.2008.06.023

Furnham, A., Batey, M., Anand, K., & Manfield, J. (2008). Personality, hypomania, intelligence and creativity. *Personality and Individual Differences, 44*(5), 1060–1069. https://doi.org/10.1016/j.paid.2007.10.035

George, J. M., & Zhou, J. (2001). When openness to experience and conscientiousness are related to creative behavior: An interactional approach. *Journal of Applied Psychology, 86*(3), 513–524. https://doi.org/10.1037/0021-9010.86.3.513

Gilmore, P. L., Hu, X., Wei, F., Tetrick, L. E., & Zaccaro, S. J. (2013). Positive affectivity neutralizes transformational leadership's influence on creative performance and organizational citizenship behaviors. *Journal of Organizational Behavior, 34*(8), 1061–1075. https://doi.org/10.1002/job.1833

Goh, S.-K., & Lim, K.-Y. (2014). Perceived creativity: The role of emotional intelligence and knowledge sharing behaviour. *Journal of Information & Knowledge Management, 13*(4), 1450037. https://doi.org/10.1142/S0219649214500373

Goldberg, L. R. (1990). An alternative "description of personality": The Big-Five factor structure. *Journal of Personality and Social Psychology, 59*(6), 1216–1229. https://doi.org/10.1037/0022-3514.59.6.1216

Grohman, M. G., Ivcevic, Z., Silvia, P., & Kaufman, S. B. (2017). The role of passion and persistence in creativity. *Psychology of Aesthetics, Creativity, and the Arts, 11*(4), 376–385. https://doi.org/10.1037/aca0000121

Guastello, S. J., Guastello, D. D., & Hanson, C. A. (2004). Creativity, Mood Disorders, ond Emotional Intelligence. *The Journal of Creative Behavior, 38*(4), 260–281. https://doi.org/10.1002/j.2162-6057.2004.tb01244.x

Haller, C. S. & Courvoisier, D. S. (2010). Personality and thinking style in different creative domains. *Psychology of Aesthetics, Creativity and the Arts, 4*(3), 149–160. https://doi.org/10.1037/a0017084

Hardy, J. H. III, Ness, A. M., & Mecca, J. (2017). Outside the box: Epistemic curiosity as a predictor of creative problem solving and creative performance. *Personality and Individual Differences, 104*, 230–237. https://doi.org/10.1016/j.paid.2016.08.004

Harrison, S. H., & Dossinger, K. (2017). Pliable guidance: A multilevel model of curiosity, feedback seeking, and feedback giving in creative work. *Academy of Management Journal, 60*(6), 2051–2072. https://doi.org/10.5465/amj.2015.0247

Helson, R., Roberts, B., & Agronick, G. (1995). Enduringness and change in creative personality and the prediction of occupational creativity. *Journal of Personality and Social Psychology, 69*(6), 1173–1183. https://doi.org/10.1037/0022-3514.69.6.1173

Hoffmann, J. D., Ivcevic, Z., Zamora, G., Bazhydai, M., & Brackett, M. (2016). Intended persistence: Comparing academic and creative challenges in high school. *Social Psychology of Education: An International Journal, 19*(4), 793–814. https://doi.org/10.1007/s11218–016-9362-x

Hunter, S. T., Bedell, K. E., & Mumford, M. D. (2007). Climate for creativity: A quantitative review. *Creativity Research Journal, 19*(1), 69–90. https://doi.org/10.1080/10400410709336883

Huyghe, A., Knockaert, M., & Obschonka, M. (2016). Unraveling the "passion orchestra" in academia. *Journal of Business Venturing, 31*(3), 344–364. https://doi.org/10.1016/j.jbusvent.2016.03.002

Isaksen, S. G., Dorval, K. B., & Treffinger, D. J. (1994). *Creative Approaches to Problem Solving*. Kendall-Hunt.

Ivcevic, Z. (2007). Artistic and everyday creativity: An act-frequency approach. *The Journal of Creative Behavior, 41*(4), 271–290. https://doi.org/10.1002/j.2162-6057.2007.tb01074.x

Ivcevic, Z., & Brackett, M. A. (2015). Predicting creativity: Interactive effects of openness to experience and emotion regulation ability. *Psychology of Aesthetics, Creativity, and the Arts, 9*(4), 480–487. https://doi.org/10.1037/a0039826

Ivcevic, Z., Grossman, E., & Ranjan, A. (2022). Patterns of psychological vulnerabilities and resources in artists and nonartists. *Psychology of Aesthetics, Creativity, and the Arts, 16*(1), 3–15. https://doi.org/10.1037/aca0000309

Ivcevic, Z., & Hoffmann, J. D. (2019). Emotions and creativity: From process to person and product. In J. C. Kaufman & R. S. Sternberg (Eds.), *Cambridge Handbook of Creativity* (pp. 273–295). Cambridge University Press.

Ivcevic, Z., & Hoffmann, J. D. (2021). The creativity dare: Attitudes toward creativity and prediction of creative behavior in school. *The Journal of Creative Behavior*. Advance online publication. https://doi.org/10.1002/jocb.527

Ivcevic, Z., & Kaufman, J. C. (2013). The can and cannot do attitude: How self-estimates of ability vary across ethnic and socioeconomic groups. *Learning and Individual Differences, 27*, 144–148. https://doi.org/10.1016/j.lindif.2013.07.011

Ivcevic, Z., & Mayer, J. D. (2009). Mapping dimensions of creativity in the life-space. *Creativity Research Journal, 21*(2–3), 152–165. https://doi.org/10.1080/10400410902855259

Jafri, H., Dem, C., & Choden, S. (2016). Emotional intelligence and employee creativity: Moderating role of proactive personality and organizational climate. *Business Perspectives and Research, 4*(1), 54–66. https://doi.org/10.1177/2278533715605435

Kang, J. H., Matusik, J. G., Kim, T.-Y., & Phillips, J. M. (2016). Interactive effects of multiple organizational climates on employee innovative behavior in entrepreneurial firms: A cross-level investigation, *Journal of Business Venturing, 31*(6), 628–642. https://doi.org/10.1016/j.jbusvent.2016.08.002

Karwowski, M. (2012). Did curiosity kill the cat? Relationship between trait curiosity, creative self-efficacy and creative role identity. *Europe's Journal of Psychology, 8*, 547–558. http://dx.doi.org/10.5964/ejop.v8i4.513

Kaufman, S. B. (2013). Opening up openness to experience: A four-factor model and relations to creative achievement in the arts and sciences. *The Journal of Creative Behavior, 47*(4), 233–255. https://doi.org/10.1002/jocb.33

Kaufman, J. C., & Beghetto, R. A. (2009). Beyond big and little: The Four C model of creativity. *Review of General Psychology, 13*(1), 1–12. https://doi.org/10.1037/a0013688

Koh, D., Lee, K., & Joshi, K. (2019). Transformational leadership and creativity: A meta-analytic review and identification of an integrated model. *Journal of Organizational Behavior, 40*(6), 625–650. https://doi.org/10.1002/job.2355

Larson, L. M., Rottinghaus, P. J., & Borgen, F. H. (2002). Meta-analyses of Big Six interests and Big Five personality factors. *Journal of Vocational Behavior, 61*(2), 217–239. https://doi.org/10.1006/jvbe.2001.1854

Lee, D. Y., & Tsang, E. W. (2001). The effects of entrepreneurial personality, background and network activities on venture growth. *Journal of Management Studies, 38*(4), 583–602. https://doi.org/10.1111/1467-6486.00250

Li, C., Murad, M., Shahzad, F., Khan, M., Ashraf, S. F., & Dogbe, C. (2020). Entrepreneurial passion to entrepreneurial behavior: Role of entrepreneurial alertness, entrepreneurial self-efficacy and proactive personality. *Frontiers in Psychology, 11*, 1611. https://doi.org/10.3389/fpsyg.2020.01611

Liu, D., Chen, X.-P., & Yao, X. (2011). From autonomy to creativity: A multilevel investigation of the mediating role of harmonious passion. *Journal of Applied Psychology, 96*(2), 294–309. https://doi.org/10.1037/a0021294

Lloyd-Evans, R., Batey, M., & Furnham, A. (2006). Bipolar disorder and creativity: Investigating a possible link. In A. Columbus (Ed.), *Advances in Psychology Research* (pp. 111–141). Nova Science.

Loewenstein, G. F., Weber, E. U., Hsee, C. K., & Welch, N. (2001). Risk as feelings. *Psychological Bulletin, 127*(2), 267–286. https://doi.org/10.1037/0033-2909.127.2.267

Luh, D.-B., & Lu, C.-C. (2012). From cognitive style to creativity achievement: The mediating role of passion. *Psychology of Aesthetics, Creativity, and the Arts, 6*(3), 282–288. https://doi.org/10.1037/a0026868

Madjar, N., Greenberg, E., & Chen, Z. (2011). Factors for radical creativity, incremental creativity, and routine, noncreative performance. *Journal of Applied Psychology, 96*(4), 730–743. https://doi.org/10.1037/a0022416

Matthews, G., Deary, I. J., & Whiteman, M. C. (2003). *Personality Traits* (2nd ed.). Cambridge University Press.

Mayer, J. D. (2003). Structural divisions of personality and the classification of traits. *Review of General Psychology, 7*(4), 381–401. https://doi.org/10.1037/1089-2680.7.4.381

McCrae, R. R. (1996). Social consequences of experiential openness. *Psychological Bulletin, 120*(3), 323–337. https://doi.org/10.1037/0033-2909.120.3.323

McCraw, S., Parker, G., Fletcher, K., & Friend, P. (2013). Self-reported creativity in bipolar disorder: prevalence, types and associated outcomes in mania versus hypomania. *Journal of Affective Disorders, 151*(3), 831–836. https://doi.org/10.1016/j.jad.2013.07.016

McKay, A. S., Karwowski, M., & Kaufman, J. C. (2017). Measuring the muses: Validating the Kaufman Domains of Creativity Scale (K-DOCS). *Psychology of Aesthetics, Creativity, and the Arts, 11*(2), 216–230. https://doi.org/10.1037/aca0000074

Moeller, J., Dietrich, J., Eccles, J. S., & Schneider, B. (2017). Passionate experiences in adolescence: Situational variability and long-term stability. *Journal of Research on Adolescence, 27*(2), 344–361. https://doi.org/10.1111/jora.12297

Moriano, J.A., Gorgievski, M., Laguna, M., Stephan, U., & Zarafshani, K. (2012). A cross cultural approach to understanding entrepreneurial intention. *Journal of Career Development, 39*(2), 162–185. http://jcd.sagepub.com/content/39/2/162

Mumford, M. D., & Gustafson, S. B. (1988). Creativity syndrome: Integration, application, and innovation. *Psychological Bulletin, 103*(1), 27–43. https://doi.org/10.1037/0033-2909.103.1.27

Murnieks, C. Y., Mosakowski, E., & Cardon, M. S. (2014). Pathways of passion: Identity centrality, passion, and behavior among entrepreneurs. *Journal of Management, 40*(6), 1583–1606. https://doi.org/10.1177/0149206311433855

Parke, M. R., Seo, M. G., & Sherf, E. N. (2015). Regulating and facilitating: The role of emotional intelligence in maintaining and using positive affect for creativity. *Journal of Applied Psychology, 100*(3), 917–934. https://doi.org/10.1037/a0038452

Plucker, J. A., Beghetto, R. A., & Dow, G. T. (2004). Why isn't creativity more important to educational psychologists? Potentials, pitfalls, and future directions in creativity research. *Educational Psychologist, 39*(2), 83–96. https://doi.org/10.1207/s15326985ep3902_1

Puente-Díaz, R., & Cavazos-Arroyo, J. (2017). The influence of creative mindsets on achievement goals, enjoyment, creative self-efficacy and performance among business students. *Thinking Skills and Creativity, 24*, 1–11. https://doi.org/10.1016/j.tsc.2017.02.007

Puryear, J. S., Kettler, T., & Rinn, A. N. (2017). Relationships of personality to differential conceptions of creativity: A systematic review. *Psychology of Aesthetics, Creativity, and the Arts, 11*(1), 59–68. https://doi.org/10.1037/aca0000079

Rego, A., Cunha, M. P. e., Reis Júnior, D., Anastácio, C., & Savagnago, M. (2018). The optimism-pessimism ratio as predictor of employee creativity: The promise of duality, *European Journal of Innovation Management, 21*(3), 423–442. https://doi.org/10.1108/EJIM-07-2017-0087

Rego, A., Sousa, F., Marques, C., & Cunha, M. P. (2012). Optimism predicting employees' creativity: The mediating role of positive affect and the positivity ratio. *European Journal of Work and Organizational Psychology, 21*(2), 244–270. https://doi.org/10.1080/1359432X.2010.550679

Reiter-Palmon, R. (2017). The role of problem construction in creative production. *The Journal of Creative Behavior, 51*(4), 323–326. https://doi.org/10.1002/jocb.202

Roberts, B. W., Wood, D., & Caspi, A. (2008). The development of personality traits in adulthood. In O. P. John, R. W. Robins, & L. A. Pervin (Eds.), *Handbook of Personality: Theory and Research* (3rd ed., pp. 357–398). Guilford Press.

Schuldberg, D. (2001). Six subclinical spectrum traits in normal creativity. *Creativity Research Journal, 13*(1), 5–16. https://doi.org/10.1207/S15326934CRJ1301_2

Schutte, N. S., & Malouff, J. M. (2020). Connections between curiosity, flow and creativity, *Personality and Individual Differences, 152*, 109555, https://doi.org/10.1016/j.paid.2019.109555

Sheldon, K. M. (1995). Creativity and self-determination in personality. *Creativity Research Journal, 8*(1), 25–36. https://doi.org/10.1207/s15326934crj0801_3

Silvia, P. J. (2017). Curiosity. In P. A. O'Keefe & J. M. Harackiewicz (Eds.), *The Science of Interest* (pp. 97–107). Springer International. https://doi.org/10.1007/978-3-319-55509-6_5

Sordia, N., Jauk, E., & Martskvishvili, K. (2022). Beyond the big personality dimensions: Consistency and specificity of associations between the Dark Triad traits and creativity. *Psychology of Aesthetics, Creativity, and the Arts, 16*(1), 30–43. https://doi.org/10.1037/aca0000346

Soto, C. J., & John, O. P. (2017). The next Big Five Inventory (BFI-2): Developing and assessing a hierarchical model with 15 facets to enhance bandwidth, fidelity, and predictive power. *Journal of Personality and Social Psychology, 113*(1), 117–143. https://doi.org/10.1037/pspp0000096

Sternberg, R. J. (2002). "Creativity as a decision": Comment. *American Psychologist, 57* (5), 376. https://doi.org/10.1037/0003-066X.57.5.376a

Sung, S. Y., & Choi, J. N. (2009). Do Big Five personality factors affect individual creativity? The moderating role of extrinsic motivation. *Social Behavior and Personality: An International Journal, 37*(7), 941–956. https://doi.org/10.2224/sbp.2009.37.7.941

Syed, I., Butler, J. C., Smith, R. M., & Cao, X. (2020). From entrepreneurial passion to entrepreneurial intentions: The role of entrepreneurial passion, innovativeness, and curiosity in driving entrepreneurial intentions, *Personality and Individual Differences, 157*, 109758. https://doi.org/10.1016/j.paid.2019.109758

Tamir, M. (2005). Don't worry, be happy? Neuroticism, trait-consistent affect regulation, and performance. *Journal of Personality and Social Psychology, 89*(3), 449–461. https://doi.org/10.1037/0022-3514.89.3.449

Tang, C., Li, Q., & Kaufman, J. C. (2018). Problem clarity as a moderator between trait affect and self-perceived creativity. *The Journal of Creative Behavior, 52*(3), 267–279. https://doi.org/10.1002/jocb.152

Thomson, P., & Jaque, S. V. (2013). Exposing shame in dancers and athletes: Shame, trauma, and dissociation in a nonclinical population. *Journal of Trauma & Dissociation, 14*(4), 439–454. https://doi.org/10.1080/15299732.2012.757714

Tiwari, P., Bhat, A. K., & Tikoria, J. (2017). The role of emotional intelligence and self-efficacy on social entrepreneurial attitudes and social entrepreneurial intentions. *Journal of Social Entrepreneurship, 8*(2), 165–185. https://doi.org/10.1080/19420676.2017.1371628

To, M. L., Fisher, C. D., & Ashkanasy, N. M. (2015). Unleashing angst: Negative mood, learning goal orientation, psychological empowerment and creative behaviour. *Human Relations, 68*(10), 1601–1622. https://doi.org/10.1177/0018726714562235

To, M. L., Fisher, C. D., Ashkanasy, N. M., & Rowe, P. A. (2012). Within-person relationships between mood and creativity. *Journal of Applied Psychology, 97*(3), 599–612. https://doi.org/10.1037/a0026097

Turner, T., & Gianiodis, P. (2018). Entrepreneurship unleashed: Understanding entrepreneurial education outside of the business school, *Journal of Small Business Management, 56*(1), 131–149. https://doi.org/10.1111/jsbm.12365

Tyagi, V., Hanoch, Y., Hall, S. D., Runco, M., & Denham, S. L. (2017). The risky side of creativity: Domain specific risk taking in creative individuals. *Frontiers in Psychology, 8,* 1–9. https://doi.org/10.3389/fpsyg.2017.00145

Vallerand, R. J., Salvy, S.-J., Mageau, G. A., et al. (2007). On the role of passion in performance. *Journal of Personality, 75*(3), 505–534. https://doi.org/10.1111/j.1467-6494.2007.00447.x

von Stumm, S., Chung, A., & Furnham, A. (2011). Creative ability, creative ideation and latent classes of creative achievement: What is the role of personality? *Psychology of Aesthetics, Creativity, and the Arts, 5*(2), 107–114. https://doi.org/10.1037/a0020499

Vazire, S. (2010). Who knows what about a person? The self–other knowledge asymmetry (SOKA) model. *Journal of Personality and Social Psychology, 98*(2), 281–300. https://doi.org/10.1037/a0017908

Weber, E. U., Blais, A.-R., & Betz, N. E. (2002). A domain-specific risk-attitude scale: Measuring risk perceptions and risk behaviors. *Journal of Behavioral Decision Making, 15*(4), 263–290. https://doi.org/10.1002/bdm.414

Wong, C. S., & Law, K. S. (2002). The effects of leader and follower emotional intelligence on performance and attitude: An exploratory study. *Leadership Quarterly, 13*(3), 243–274. https://doi.org/10.1016/ S1048–9843(02)00099-1

Wille, B., & De Fruyt, F. (2014). Vocations as a source of identity: Reciprocal relations between Big Five personality traits and RIASEC characteristics over 15 years. *Journal of Applied Psychology, 99*(2), 262–281. https://doi.org/10.1037/a0034917

Wolfradt, U., & Pretz, J. E. (2001). Individual differences in creativity: Personality, story writing, and hobbies. *European Journal of Personality, 15*(4), 297–310. https://doi.org/10.1002/per.409

Xu, X., Liu, W., & Pang, W. (2019). Are emotionally intelligent people more creative? A meta-analysis of the emotional Intelligence–Creativity link. *Sustainability, 11*(21), 6123. http://dx.doi.org/10.3390/su11216123

Zhang, X., & Bartol, K. M. (2010). The influence of creative process engagement on employee creative performance and overall job performance: A curvilinear assessment. *Journal of Applied Psychology, 95*(5), 862–873. https://doi.org/10.1037/a0020173

Zhao, H., Seibert, S. E., & Lumpkin, G. T. (2010). The relationship of personality to entrepreneurial intentions and performance: A meta-analytic review. *Journal of Management, 36*(2), 381–404. https://doi.org/10.1177/0149206309335187

13 Gender Differences in Creativity and Emotions

Christa L. Taylor

Gender[1] differences in creativity and gender differences in emotions are both research topics for which existing literature is inconclusive. Although empirical evidence in both areas points to minimal gender differences overall, the results of individual studies are inconsistent and sometimes conflicting. Discrepant findings may be due, in part, to distinct characteristics of the studies, such as which indicators of creativity (e.g., ability vs. achievement) or emotions (e.g., feeling vs. expression) are assessed. Understanding in which contexts gender differences in creativity and emotions are more – or less – likely to be found is essential for identifying how these two lines of research may relate to one another. An exhaustive review of these vast literatures is not possible here. Rather, this chapter provides an overview of each body of literature, with a focus on the topics that may be most relevant to a connection between the two. Thus, this chapter discusses research examining gender differences in creativity and gender differences in emotions, and outlines how the two may be reciprocally linked by answering the question: What does research showing an emotions–creativity link mean for gender differences in creativity and emotions?[2]

Gender Differences in Creativity

Several key theoretical reviews of gender and creativity have concluded that there are minimal differences in the creative potential and ability of men/boys and women/girls overall (e.g., Abraham, 2016; Baer & Kaufman, 2008; Runco et al., 2010). Although most work in this area is based on mean differences on measures of divergent thinking, ratings of participants' creative productions and examinations of gender differences in the variability of creative

---

[1] This study discusses differences between men/boys and women/girls only (largely due to the lack of studies examining these issues in those with a nonbinary gender identification) and focuses on studies involving adults. Studies of childhood forms of creativity (e.g., play) are discussed elsewhere in this volume (Chapter 14).

[2] Although the distinction between mood and emotion (typically based on duration, intentionality, cause, consequences, and function) is important for our understanding of how these different forms of affect function (Beedie et al., 2005), studies from both literatures often use the terms interchangeably. Thus, this chapter discusses results from studies purporting to address either mood or emotion and uses the term emotion throughout for consistency.

ability are becoming increasingly more common. Relatively less empirical research has explicitly measured gender differences in creative behavior and achievement. However, real-world statistics paint a clear picture of women's underrepresentation as eminent creators (e.g., The Nobel Prize, 2021). Although many explanations have been proposed for why the gender gap in creative achievement persists, there are three types of theoretical perspectives that are most consistent with the general lack of gender differences in creative potential and ability.

Creative Potential and Ability

Differences in the mean creative ability of men/boys and women/girls have most frequently been examined using divergent thinking tasks, which assess a person's ability to generate many original responses to a stimulus (Guilford, 1956). Responses on divergent thinking tasks are most commonly scored based on the total number (i.e., fluency), statistical infrequency or uncommonness (i.e., originality), variability in the categories (i.e., flexibility), and/or amount of detail and depth (i.e., elaboration; Runco & Acar, 2012). Results for gender differences on divergent thinking performance are mixed, with some studies finding no difference (e.g., Richardson, 1985; Warren et al., 2018), some studies reporting a male advantage (e.g., Bender et al., 2013; Tara, 1981), and some studies reporting a female advantage (e.g., Lau & Cheung, 2010; Zhang & Zhang, 2017). It is common for results to differ based on the type of divergent thinking task (e.g., figural vs. verbal) or the type of indicator (e.g., fluency vs. originality; DeMoss et al., 1993; Kim & Michael, 1995; Szobiová, 2012), yet no consistent pattern of gender differences has been found (Abraham, 2016). Although meta-analyses of studies examining gender differences in divergent thinking report a female advantage in overall mean scores, effect sizes for the difference are trivial to small (Ma, 2009; Taylor et al., 2021; Thompson, 2016).

Mean gender differences in creative ability are also increasingly being examined using creative products generated by participants, such as stories or drawings. Products are typically rated for creativity using either rubrics, whereby products are rated based on specific researcher-defined criteria (Besemer & Treffinger, 1981), or the Consensual Assessment Technique (CAT; Amabile, 1982), whereby products are subjectively rated for creativity by a group of experts within a given creative domain. Results for studies examining mean gender differences in creative products are also mixed, even within the same domain and task type. For instance, one study asking participants to write musical compositions found that compositions created by males were more creative than those by females (Mawang et al., 2019), whereas other similar studies found no gender differences (Barbot & Lubart, 2012; Hassler et al., 1990). This type of inconsistency, wherein a gender effect is found in some studies and not others, is common on tasks across a range of creative domains, including creative writing (e.g., Kaufman et al., 2004, 2010), humor production (e.g., Kellner & Benedek, 2017; Sutu et al., 2021), and creative drawing (e.g., Chan & Zhao, 2010; Taylor & Barbot, 2021).

Recent work has also begun to examine gender differences in the *variability* of creative ability. The Greater Male Variability Hypothesis (GMVH) in creativity, which stems from early intelligence research (see Shields, 1982), suggests that although men do not outperform women on average, they *vary* more than women in creative ability (He & Wong, 2011). Given similar group means and a normal distribution in the population, greater male variability would translate to more men who score in the upper (and lower) extremes of creative ability. Several studies have found that males exhibit greater variability in scores on the Test for Creative Thinking-Drawing Production (TCT-DP; Urban & Jellen, 1996) across different populations (He & Wong, 2011; Karwowski, Jankowska, Gajda, et al., 2016; Karwowski, Jankowska, Gralewski, et al., 2016). However, other studies have reported mixed results, suggesting that the effect may differ based on various contextual factors, including the region in which the study was conducted (Ju et al., 2015), the age of participants (He, 2018; He et al., 2015), and the type of task or creative domain (Lau & Cheung, 2015; Taylor & Barbot, 2021). A recent meta-analysis (Taylor et al., 2021) found that gender differences in the variability of creativity scores were minimal overall and were smaller in countries that promoted greater gender equality.

Creative Behavior and Achievement

Although many studies have measured creative behavior and achievement, few report results by gender (Taylor et al., 2021). Creative behavior and achievement is typically measured with self-report checklists that ask participants to indicate how often they engage in a given creative behavior or activity and/or the level of recognition they have received in a given creative domain (e.g., Carson et al., 2005; Diedrich et al., 2018; Dollinger, 2003; Hocevar, 1979). Studies that have reported creative behavior and/or achievement by gender tend to find either trivial to small effects across all domains (Ahmetoglu et al., 2015; Elisondo, 2021; Runco, 1986) or moderate effects for a handful of domains in both directions (Diedrich et al., 2018; Jonason et al., 2015). Diedrich et al. (2018) found moderate to large gender effects (i.e., $r = |.30|$ to $|.61|$) for several subscales on the Inventory of Creative Activities and Achievement, which assesses both the frequency that participants engage in a set of creative activities and the level of achievement attained across eight domains (i.e., literature, music, arts and crafts, creative cooking, science and engineering, sports, visual arts, and performing arts). Whereas males reported engaging in more frequent creative behaviors in the science and engineering, sports, and music domains, females reported engaging more in the arts and crafts, creative cooking, and performing arts domains. However, considering only moderate effects, results for the achievement subscales differed: Males reported higher achievement in the performing arts and females reported higher achievement in music.

Real-world descriptive statistics for differences in men's and women's participation in, and recognition for, higher level creative pursuits paint a stark picture across domains. For instance, women received only 14% of Nobel Prizes awarded for literature and 3% of Nobel Prizes awarded for sciences (chemistry, economics, physics, and medicine) between 1901 and 2020 (The Nobel Prize, 2021). Within the visual arts, only 13.7% of living artists represented by galleries in Europe and North America in 2017 were women (Halperin, 2017) and artwork by women accounted for only 11% of acquisitions, across 26 prominent U.S. galleries, in the past decade (Halperin & Burns, 2019). Further, women are underrepresented among eminent creators, individuals recognized for enduring creative contributions, across domains (Piirto, 1991; Simonton, 1994). Indeed, Simonton (1994) suggested that only 3% of eminent individuals throughout the history of Western civilization have been women.

Theoretical Explanations

There are at least three main types of theoretical explanations for why the gender gap in creative achievement persists that are congruent with evidence of minimal gender differences observed at the potential/ability level. The first suggests that men and women pursue creative achievement at different rates or intensity. Central to this idea is differences in men's and women's socialization and relational roles (Helson, 1999; Piirto, 1991; Reis, 2002; Simonton, 1994), in which boys are socialized to be independent and agentic, whereas girls are socialized to be more relationship-focused and communal in many cultures (Leaper & Friedman, 2007). In addition to the time and effort that may be diverted away from creative pursuits in service of caregiving to others (Yavorsky et al., 2015), the commitment required for such pursuits may dissuade women from even attempting higher levels of creative achievement. Indeed, Piirto (1991) suggests that, especially after college, many talented women choose romantic relationships or family roles over advanced creative pursuits. Additionally, Reis (2002) suggests that whereas men may focus single-mindedly on a creative pursuit, women are more likely to engage in creative behavior across various, primarily domestic, areas (e.g., relationships, family and home, personal interests).

A second theoretical perspective points to differences in men's and women's abilities and characteristics that are independent of creative ability, but nonetheless critical for creative success. For example, girls have been found to be more likely to react negatively to evaluation and competition, wherein making external judgement salient diminishes the creative performance of girls, but not boys (Baer, 1997, 1998; Conti et al., 2001). Given that higher levels of creative achievement are dependent on public recognition (Csikszentmihalyi, 2014; Glăveanu, 2013), difficulty facing external evaluation presents a challenge to achieving creative success. Although gender differences in personality traits tend to be small and vary across cultures (Costa et al., 2001), males consistently report higher self-esteem than females across diverse cultures (see

Bleidorn et al., 2016). Although the relationship between general self-esteem and creative performance is not straightforward (Barbot, 2020), self-esteem is associated with initiative and the willingness to follow one's own path (Baumeister et al., 2003).

A third perspective suggests that external barriers prevent women from attaining high levels of creative achievement. This certainly seems to be the case throughout much of history, during which creative women faced overt discrimination (Simonton, 1994), such as female scientists in the early twentieth century seeing Nobel Prizes awarded solely to their male research partners (Bertsch McGrayne, 1993). Although women and girls in many modern societies have comparatively greater educational and vocational opportunities than those in the past, more covert forms of bias and discrimination continue to influence creative opportunities differently for men and women. For example, women receive less support and reward for creative behavior (Kwaśniewska & Nęcka, 2004; Luksyte et al., 2018; Taylor et al., 2020) and identical creative products are rated as more creative when accompanied by a stereotypically male, as opposed to female, name (Lebuda & Karwowski, 2013; Proudfoot et al., 2015).

Gender Differences in Emotions

Studies examining gender differences in emotions also report inconsistent and conflicting results (see Brody & Hall, 2008). One key to understanding these discrepancies may be the distinction between *felt* and *expressed* emotion (Rogers & Robinson, 2014). Felt emotion refers to the subjective experience of an emotional state, conceptualized as either a set of discrete, basic emotions (e.g., anger, sadness, joy; Ekman, 1992) or as a function of interacting dimensions (e.g., valence × intensity; Posner et al., 2005). On the other hand, expressed emotion refers to the display of a felt emotion (e.g., smiling when happy) or participants' tendency to either express or inhibit a set of given discrete emotions or emotions in general. Gender differences in emotional regulation strategies also play an important role in both the experience and expression of men's and women's emotions.

Felt Emotions

A sizable number of studies of the general population have found that women report more negative and less positive emotions in their daily lives than men, yet results for specific emotions vary (Ross & Willigen, 1996; Simon & Lively, 2010; Simon & Nath, 2004; Stevenson & Wolfers, 2009; Taylor et al., 2022). For example, Simon and Nath (2004) used data from a nationally representative survey of adults in the United States to examine men's and women's daily experience of emotions. Although men and women reported a similar frequency of experiencing emotions in general, gender differences emerged in the experience of positive and negative emotions: Men reported feeling excitement (i.e., excited and proud) more frequently than women, whereas women reported experiencing sadness (i.e., blue, sad, and lonely) more frequently than men, even after accounting for a range of sociodemographic and status characteristics. Taylor et al. (2022) used data from a nationwide sample of almost 15,000 workers across industries in the United States to examine gender differences in felt emotions at work. Women reported feeling more overwhelmed, frustrated, tense, discouraged, and stressed than men, whereas men reported feeling more respected and confident than women (though differences in feeling overwhelmed and respected were partially accounted for by women's greater tendency to work in occupations that require more emotional labor). Women, compared to men, have also reported a greater intensity of the emotions they experience (Diener et al., 1985; Fujita et al., 1991). However, because these results are based on retrospective accounts of how people believe they typically feel or have felt in the past, the validity of these gender difference effects have been questioned.

Although studies examining the emotions that people feel in their daily lives may necessarily rely on self-report methods, it is important to understand the limitations of this approach. Self-report measures of emotion used in studies examining gender differences are almost always global and retrospective (though see Feldman Barrett, 1997), requiring participants to rely on recollections that may be influenced by gender stereotypes (Plant et al., 2000). Indeed, participants' responses on self-report measures of emotion have been found to correspond with the extent to which they endorse gender stereotypes (Grossman & Wood, 1993; Hess et al., 2000; Robinson et al., 1998). For example, Grossman and Wood (1993) found that the more participants believed that the typical woman experiences more intense emotions than the typical man, the more they provided gender stereotypic ratings of their own emotional intensity. Accordingly, scores on self-report scales of affective intensity have been found to be unrelated to reports of intensity given at the time of an emotional event and studies using daily logs have found no gender effects across emotions (Feldman Barrett et al., 1998; Seidlitz & Diener, 1998). People also anticipate responding to negative situations in gender-stereotypic ways. For example, women's emotional profiles, created from ratings of the likelihood that they would feel each of seven basic emotions in response to a negative emotional situation, indicated more sadness, fear, and shame than that for men, which corresponded with participants reports from a prior study of how men and women in general would react to the same situations (Hess et al., 2000). Although it is important to keep these limitations in mind when considering the results of self-report studies of gender differences in emotion, it is unlikely that results are based only on stereotypes, as results based on self-report do not always align with cultural stereotypes (e.g., women have self-reported feeling angry more frequently than men in several studies; e.g., Ross & Willigen, 1996; Simon & Nath, 2004). Additionally, gender differences have also been found on other measures, such as those of emotional expression and regulation (Brody & Hall, 2008).

Emotional Expression and Regulation

Studies that measure gender differences in emotional expression tend to find that women both report themselves to be, and are observed to be, more emotionally expressive than men in general (Blier & Blier-Wilson, 1989; Kring & Gordon, 1998; Simon & Nath, 2004). Women report that they are more likely to express their feelings to a greater extent than men, and are less likely than men to endorse items such as "I keep my emotions to myself" (Simon & Nath, 2004). In two studies, Kring and Gordon (1998) found that after viewing a sad film, women displayed more facial expressions and more autonomic nervous system (ANS) activity (assessed via skin conductance) than men. In a meta-analysis of studies that used a variety of methods to measure emotional expression (e.g., facial, vocal, and/or behavioral cues) in boys and girls from infancy to 17 years old, Chaplin and Aldao (2013) found that girls expressed almost all emotions more than boys, with the exceptions of anger and pride (though most effects were small). However, some effects changed with age: Most notably, although boys expressed externalizing and negative emotions (such as anger) to a greater extent than girls in childhood, girls expressed more externalizing and negative emotions in adolescence. Although gender differences in the experience and frequency of expressing anger are mixed, there is some evidence that men and women express anger in different ways (see Fischer & Evers, 2010). For example, women have reported that they are more likely to cope with anger by talking about their feelings, whereas men are more likely to cope by using substances (e.g., alcohol or pills; Simon & Nath, 2004).

Differences in the way men and women express emotions are consistent with findings that men and women differ in the strategies they use to regulate their emotions. Men have been suggested to be more likely to use eternalizing strategies, such as blaming others and distracting themselves through activities, whereas women are more likely to use internalizing strategies, such as blaming themselves and ruminating on the emotion (see Brody & Hall, 2008). Indeed, women's greater tendency to ruminate in response to a negative emotional event is found consistently across many studies, including in two meta-analyses (see Nolen-Hoeksema & Aldao, 2011; Tamres et al., 2002). In light of evidence that people attribute women's emotions to their stable disposition and men's emotions to a given situation (Barrett & Bliss-Moreau, 2009), Nolen-Hoeksema (2012) suggests that this may make women less likely to take action to change distressing situations. However, evidence regarding other emotion regulation strategies (e.g., suppressing emotions or problem solving) is mixed. For example, although studies sometimes report that men suppress emotions to a greater extent than women (e.g., Gross & John, 2003), meta-analytic evidence suggests either no difference (Nolen-Hoeksema & Aldao, 2011) or that women engage in suppression more than men (Tamres et al., 2002).

Connecting Gender Differences in Creativity with Gender Differences in Emotions

The Link between Creativity and Emotions

The link between creativity and emotions is bidirectional, meaning emotions influence creativity and creativity influences emotions (Ivcevic & Hoffmann, 2019).

A large body of research has examined how emotions influence creative ideation (generating original ideas in response to open-ended problems; Barbot, 2018), providing us with a better understanding of how specific emotional states impact creative outcomes (see Baas et al., 2008). Early studies focused on the valence (i.e., pleasant vs. unpleasantness) of particular emotions, suggesting that emotions with a positive valence enhance creativity (Ashby et al., 1999; Isen et al., 1985, 1987). However, it has been well established in the previous decade or so that the level of activation (i.e., the engagement of motivational systems reflected in increased arousal; Baas et al., 2011) associated with an emotion may have a greater impact on creative outcomes (see Madrid et al., this volume). For example, although sadness and anger are both negatively valenced emotions, they are associated with different levels of activation (low and high, respectively) and predict creativity in different ways. Observational, experimental, and meta-analytic studies most frequently find that sadness is not associated, or is negatively associated, with creative ideation and behavior (e.g., Baas et al., 2008; Conner & Silvia, 2015; De Dreu et al., 2008). On the other hand, observational and experimental studies have found that anger enhances creativity (e.g., Gilet & Jallais, 2011; To et al., 2012; though see Silvia et al., 2014). However, happiness, a positive and activating emotion, has the most robust and strongest positive effect on creativity (Baas et al., 2008; Conner & Silvia, 2015; De Dreu et al., 2008; Gilet & Jallais, 2011; Silvia et al., 2014; To et al., 2012).

Although how creativity influences emotions has received less empirical attention historically, research demonstrating the emotional benefits of engaging in creative activity has grown in recent years (see Grossman & Drake, this volume). Professional artists, scientists, and writers (Glăveanu et al., 2013), as well as women engaging in everyday forms of creativity (cooking, handicrafts, solving everyday problems; Elisondo & Vargas, 2019), have described a sense of satisfaction and accomplishment following the completion of a creative project. In the lab, positive emotions have been shown to be enhanced after participants complete a creative activity (as opposed to a noncreative activity), such as completing a divergent versus convergent thinking task (Chermahini & Hommel, 2012) or inventing titles for a cartoon versus finding the difference between two cartoons (Bujacz et al., 2016). Daily diary studies, in which participants recorded their creative activity and emotions every day for a series of days, have shown that students (Conner et al., 2018; Conner & Silvia, 2015) experience greater positive emotions following engaging in creative activities. Supporting the directional role of creativity on positive emotions, Conner et al. (2018) showed that creative behavior one day predicted positive emotions and well-being the next. In contrast, positive emotions did not predict creative behavior on the subsequent day.

To connect research on the creativity–emotions link with gender differences in creativity or emotions, one must account for the conclusions of results from each of these literatures. Research on gender differences in creativity suggests that (1) men's and women's creative potential and ability are quite similar overall and (2) women are underrepresented across domains of creative achievement (though a small number of studies show that measured differences in everyday people are domain-specific). Research on gender differences in emotions suggests that (1) the most consistent finding for felt emotions is that women report feeling sadness (a negative, deactivating emotion) more frequently than men, whereas men report feeling happiness (a positive, activating emotions) more frequently than women and (2) women are more likely to engage in internalizing emotion regulation strategies and ruminate than men.

What Does the Creativity–Emotions Link Mean for Gender Differences in Creativity?

If women do indeed experience sadness in their daily lives to a greater extent than men, whereas men experience happiness to a greater extent than women, then gender differences in creativity should be expected. Further, if women have a greater tendency to ruminate and to view their emotional experiences as stemming from a dispositional tendency (see Nolen-Hoeksema, 2012), these detrimental effects may be relatively long lasting. Given limited gender differences in creative ability, any differences in creative achievement arising from emotions would likely be behavioral, particularly if emotions impact gender differences in creative achievement through their influence on motivation. The motivational consequences of such emotions, such as decreased frequency of creative ideation or activity, would be reflected on measures of creative behavior, for which results by gender are rarely reported (Taylor et al., 2021).

In any case, daily creative behavior may be best measured using more ecologically valid methods of assessment, such as experience sampling or daily diaries (as opposed to global, retrospective measures; see Cotter & Silvia, 2019). Indeed, in a daily diary study conducted over the course of 13 days, Conner and Silvia (2015) found that women reported engaging in significantly less creativity in general than men. However, this study asked people to report whether they engaged in creative activity in general. Future studies could assess more objective creative behavior by prompting responses for specific activities, as women may ascribe less creativity to their activities than do men (see Piirto, 1991).

What Does the Creativity–Emotions Link Mean for Gender Differences in Emotions?

How the creativity–emotions link may relate to gender differences in emotions depends on the exact causes of the gender gap in creative achievement. For example, women in general may not be engaging in creative behavior to the same extent as men (possibly due to differences in extra-creativity traits and abilities and/or roles and responsibilities). If this is the case, men may benefit from the boost to positive emotions gained from creative activity more than women, which may contribute to gender differences in emotions. Indeed, Taylor et al. (2020) found that women reported engaging in significantly less creative behavior at work than men, using the same sample in which women experienced more negative emotions (see Taylor et al., 2022). Although it is possible that women are simply engaging in creative behavior in more diverse areas, such as relationships or personal interests, creativity in these areas is undervalued (e.g., Reis, 2002). If the rate at which men and women engage in creative behavior does not differ overall, gender differences in emotions may still arise from the barriers to creative success that women are more likely to face, such as receiving less reward and acknowledgment for their creative output (Benedek et al., 2017; Kwaśniewska & Nęcka, 2004; Luksyte et al., 2017).

Future Directions

Given the bidirectional relationship between emotions and creativity, if there are gender-based differences in creativity and emotions, they also likely have a reciprocal relationship (Figure 13.1). Gender differences in creative pursuits, such as women either engaging in less creative behavior or experiencing less creative success than men, may contribute to women experiencing more negative, deactivating emotions. At the same time, women's greater experience of these emotions may lead to them engaging in less creative behavior, which further limits their opportunities for creative success. Given the absence of existing research connecting gender-based differences in creativity

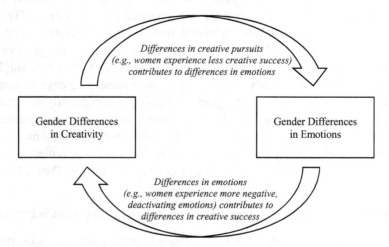

Figure 13.1 *How gender differences in creativity and emotions may influence one another reciprocally.*

with gender-based differences in emotions, this (albeit speculative) model presents diverse avenues for future research.

If girls and women do engage in less frequent creative behavior than boys and men, establishing whether emotions account for these differences can be accomplished in a number of ways. For example, one straightforward method of examining if gender differences in *felt* emotions account for gender differences in creative behavior would be to use a mediation model to examine if gender predicts creative behavior through reported emotions. However, this may be best accomplished using in-the-moment assessments (e.g., experience sampling), given that retrospective self-reports of emotions may be influenced by gender stereotypes, as well as longitudinally to establish directionality. One method of examining if gender differences in emotional *expression* and/or *regulation* account for gender differences in creative behavior would be to determine whether men (who may be more likely to distract themselves through activities; Brody & Hall, 2008) are more likely than women to turn to creative activities as a source of mood repair after experiencing a negative emotional event.

However, more complex models may be necessary to understand how gender differences in creative behavior and achievement influence differences in the emotional experiences of men and women. For example, even if women do engage in creative pursuits to the same extent (or more) as men, they face additional obstacles to creative success that may negatively influence their emotional experiences. Women may attribute gender-based disparities in the support, reward, and acknowledgement they receive for their creativity (Benedek et al., 2017; Kwaśniewska & Nęcka, 2004; Luksyte et al., 2017; Taylor et al., 2020) to internal causes, diminishing self-esteem, which is strongly associated with emotions (Weiner, 1985). If either directional component of the model proves true, this points to opportunities for interventions to improve individuals' creative achievement and/or emotional experiences.

Conclusion

Although conclusions regarding gender differences in creativity and gender differences in emotions are far from unanimous, an overview of the literature points to evidence of differences in specific areas. First, men and women may not differ in creative potential and ability, yet men reach higher levels of creative achievement than women. Second, men and women may not differ in how often they experience emotions, yet men report feeling more happiness and women report feeling more sadness. Based on these claims, as well as current knowledge regarding the link between creativity and emotions, I have presented a model of how gender differences in creativity and emotions may reciprocally influence one another. Although the model remains speculative pending further research, it may represent a fruitful starting point for research connecting these two literatures.

References

Abraham, A. (2016). Gender and creativity: An overview of psychological and neuroscientific literature. *Brain Imaging and Behavior*, *10*(2), 609–618. https://doi.org/10.1007/s11682-015-9410-8

Ahmetoglu, G., Harding, X., Akhtar, R., & Chamorro-Premuzic, T. (2015). Predictors of creative achievement: Assessing the impact of entrepreneurial potential, perfectionism, and employee engagement. *Creativity Research Journal*, *27*(2), 198–205. https://doi.org/10.1080/10400419.2015.1030293

Amabile, T. M. (1982). Social psychology of creativity: A consensual assessment technique. *Journal of Personality and Social Psychology*, *43*(5), 997–1013. https://doi.org/10.1037/0022-3514.43.5.997

Ashby, G. F., Isen, A. M., & Turken, A. U. (1999). A neuropsychological theory of positive affect and its influence on cognition. *Psychological Review*, *106*(3), 529–550. https://doi.org/10.1037/0033-295X.106.3.529

Baas, M., De Dreu, C. K. W., & Nijstad, B. A. (2008). A meta-analysis of 25 years of mood-creativity research: hedonic tone, activation, or regulatory focus? *Psychological Bulletin*, *134*(6), 779–806. https://doi.org/10.1037/a0012815

Baas, M., De Dreu, C. K. W., & Nijstad, B. A. (2011). When prevention promotes creativity: The role of mood, regulatory focus, and regulatory closure. *Journal of Personality and Social Psychology*, *100*(5), 794–809. https://doi.org/10.1037/a0022981

Baer, J. (1997). Gender differences in the effects of anticipated evaluation on creativity. *Creativity Research Journal*, *10*, 25–31. https://doi.org/10.1207/s15326934crj1001_3

Baer, J. (1998). Gender differences in the effects of extrinsic motivation on creativity. *The Journal of Creative Behavior*, *32*(1), 18–37. https://doi.org/https://doi.org/10.1002/j.2162-6057.1998.tb00804.x

Baer, J., & Kaufman, J. C. (2008). Gender differences in creativity. *Journal of Creative Behavior*, *42*(2), 75–105. https://doi.org/10.1002/j.2162-6057.2008.tb01289.x

Barbot, B. (2018). The dynamics of creative ideation: Introducing a new assessment paradigm. *Frontiers in Psychology*, *9*, 1–8. https://doi.org/10.3389/fpsyg.2018.02529

Barbot, B. (2020). Creativity and self-esteem in adolescence: A study of their domain-specific, multivariate relationships. *Journal of Creative Behavior*, *54*(2), 279–292. https://doi.org/10.1002/jocb.365

Barbot, B., & Lubart, T. (2012). Creative thinking in music: Its nature and assessment through musical exploratory behaviors. *Psychology of Aesthetics, Creativity, and the Arts*, *6*(3), 231–242. https://doi.org/10.1037/a0027307

Barrett, L. F., & Bliss-Moreau, E. (2009). She's emotional. He's having a bad day: Attributional explanations for emotion stereotypes. *Emotion*, *9*(5), 649–658. https://doi.org/10.1037/a0016821

Baumeister, R. F., Campbell, J. D., Krueger, J. I., & Vohs, K. D. (2003). Does high self-esteem cause better performance, interpersonal success, happiness, or healthier lifestyles? *Psychological Science in the Public Interest*, *4*(1), 1–44. https://doi.org/10.1111/1529-1006.01431

Beedie, C. J., Terry, P. C., & Lane, A. M. (2005). Distinctions between emotion and mood. *Cognition and Emotion*, *19*(6), 847–878. https://doi.org/10.1080/02699930541000057

Bender, S. W., Nibbelink, B., Towner-Thyrum, E., & Vredenburg, D. (2013). Defining characteristics of creative women. *Creativity Research Journal, 25*(1), 38–47. https://doi.org/10.1080/10400419.2013.752190

Benedek, M., Jauk, E., Kerschenbauer, K., Anderwald, R., & Grond, L. (2017). Creating art: An experience sampling study in the domain of moving image art. *Psychology of Aesthetics, Creativity, and the Arts, 11*(3), 325–334. https://doi.org/10.1037/aca0000102

Bertsch McGrayne, S. (1993). Nobel Prize women in science: Their lives, struggles, and momentous discoveries. *American Journal of Physics, 61*, 12. Joseph Henry Press. https://doi.org/10.1119/1.17318

Besemer, S. P., & Treffinger, D. J. (1981). Analysis of creative products: Review and synthesis. *The Journal of Creative Behavior, 15*(3), 158–178. https://doi.org/10.1002/j.2162-6057.1981.tb00287.x

Bleidorn, W., Arslan, R. C., Denissen, J. J. A., et al. (2016). Age and gender differences in self-esteem – A cross-cultural window. *Journal of Personality and Social Psychology, 111*(3), 396–410. https://doi.org/10.1037/pspp0000078

Blier, M. J., & Blier-Wilson, L. A. (1989). Gender differences in self-rated emotional expressiveness. *Sex Roles, 21*(3–4), 287–295. https://doi.org/10.1007/BF00289908

Brody, L. R., & Hall, J. A. (2008). Gender and emotion in context. In M. Lewis, J. M. Haviland-Jones, & L. Feldman Barrett (Eds.), *Handbook of Emotions* (3rd ed., pp. 395–408). Guilford Press.

Bujacz, A., Dunne, S., Fink, D., et al. (2016). Why do we enjoy creative tasks? Results from a multigroup randomized controlled study. *Thinking Skills and Creativity, 19*, 188–197. https://doi.org/10.1016/j.tsc.2015.11.002

Carson, S. H., Peterson, J. B., & Higgins, D. M. (2005). Reliability, validity, and factor structure of the Creative Achievement Questionnaire. *Creativity Research Journal, 14*(1), 37–50. https://doi.org/10.1207/s15326934crj1701

Chan, D. W., & Zhao, Y. (2010). The relationship between drawing skill and artistic creativity: Do age and artistic involvement make a difference? *Creativity Research Journal, 22*(1), 27–36. https://doi.org/10.1080/10400410903579528

Chaplin, T. M., & Aldao, A. (2013). Gender differences in emotion expression in children: A meta-analytic review. *Psychological Bulletin, 139*(4), 735–765. https://doi.org/10.1037/a0030737

Chermahini, S. A., & Hommel, B. (2012). Creative mood swings: Divergent and convergent thinking affect mood in opposite ways. *Psychological Research, 76*(5), 634–640. https://doi.org/10.1007/s00426-011-0358-z

Conner, T. S., DeYoung, C. G., & Silvia, P. J. (2018). Everyday creative activity as a path to flourishing. *Journal of Positive Psychology, 13*(2), 181–189. https://doi.org/10.1080/17439760.2016.1257049

Conner, T. S., & Silvia, P. J. (2015). Creative days: A daily diary study of emotion, personality, and everyday creativity. *Psychology of Aesthetics, Creativity, and the Arts, 9*(4), 463–470. https://doi.org/10.1037/aca0000022

Conti, R., Collins, M. A., & Picariello, M. L. (2001). The impact of competition on intrinsic motivation and creativity: Considering gender, gender segregation and gender role orientation. *Personality and Individual Differences, 31*(8), 1273–1289. https://doi.org/10.1016/S0191-8869(00)00217-8

Costa, P. T., Terracciano, A., & McCrae, R. R. (2001). Gender differences in personality traits across cultures: Robust and surprising findings. *Journal of Personality and Social Psychology*, *81*(2), 322–331. https://doi.org/10.1037/0022-3514.81.2.322

Cotter, K. N., & Silvia, P. J. (2019). Ecological assessment in research on aesthetics, creativity, and the arts: Basic concepts, common questions, and gentle warnings. *Psychology of Aesthetics, Creativity, and the Arts*, *13*(2), 211–217. https://doi.org/10.1037/aca0000218

Csikszentmihalyi, M. (2014). *The Systems Model of Creativity: The Collected Works of Mihaly Csikszentmihalyi*. Springer Science+Business Media. http://link.springer.com/10.1007/978-94-017-9085-7

De Dreu, C. K. W., Baas, M., & Nijstad, B. A. (2008). Hedonic tone and activation level in the mood-creativity link: Toward a dual pathway to creativity model. *Journal of Personality and Social Psychology*, *94*(5), 739–756. https://doi.org/10.1037/0022-3514.94.5.739

DeMoss, K., Milich, R., & DeMers, S. (1993). Gender, creativity, depression, and attributional style in adolescents with high academic ability. *Journal of Abnormal Child Psychology*, *21*(4), 455–467. https://doi.org/10.1007/BF01261604

Diedrich, J., Jauk, E., Silvia, P. J., et al. (2018). Assessment of real-life creativity: The Inventory of Creative Activities and Achievements (ICAA). *Psychology of Aesthetics, Creativity, and the Arts*, *12*(3), 304–316. https://doi.org/10.1037/aca0000137

Diener, E., Sandvik, E., & Larsen, R. J. (1985). Age and sex effects for emotional intensity. *Developmental Psychology*, *21*(3), 542–546. https://doi.org/10.1037/0012-1649.21.3.542

Dollinger, S. J. (2003). Need for uniqueness, need for cognition, and creativity. *Journal of Creative Behavior*, *37*(2), 99–116. https://doi.org/10.1002/j.2162-6057.2003.tb00828.x

Ekman, P. (1992). An argument for basic emotions. *Cognition and Emotion*, *6*(3–4), 169–200. https://doi.org/10.1080/02699939208411068

Elisondo, R. C. (2021). Creative Actions Scale: A Spanish scale of creativity in different domains. *Journal of Creative Behavior*, *55*(1), 215–227. https://doi.org/10.1002/jocb.447

Elisondo, R. C., & Vargas, A. (2019). Women's everyday creative activities: A qualitative study. *Creativity*, *6*(1), 91–111. https://doi.org/10.1515/ctra-2019-0006

Feldman Barrett, L. (1997). The relationships among momentary emotion experiences, personality descriptions, and retrospective ratings of emotion. *Personality and Social Psychology Bulletin*, *23*(10), 1100–1110. https://doi.org/10.1177/01461672972310010

Feldman Barrett, L., Robin, L., Pietromonaco, P. R., & Eyssell, K. M. (1998). Are women the "more emotional" sex? Evidence from emotional experiences in social context. *Cognition and Emotion*, *12*(4), 555–578. https://doi.org/10.1080/026999398379565

Fischer, A. H., & Evers, C. (2010). Anger in the context of gender. In M. Potegal, G. Stemmler, & C. Spielberger (Eds.), *International Handbook of Anger:*

Constituent and Concomitant Biological, Psychological, and Social Processes (pp. 349–360). Springer. https://doi.org/10.1007/978-0-387-89676-2

Fujita, F., Diener, E., & Sandvik, E. (1991). Personality processes and individual differences: Gender differences in negative affect and well-being: The case for emotional intensity. *Journal of Personality and Social Psychology, 61*(3), 427–434. https://doi.org/10.1037/0022-3514.61.3.427

Gilet, A. L., & Jallais, C. (2011). Valence, arousal and word associations. *Cognition and Emotion, 25*(4), 740–746. https://doi.org/10.1080/02699931.2010.500480

Glăveanu, V., Lubart, T., Bonnardel, N., et al. (2013). Creativity as action: Findings from five creative domains. *Frontiers in Psychology, 4*(April), 1–14. https://doi.org/10.3389/fpsyg.2013.00176

Glăveanu, V. P. (2013). Rewriting the language of creativity: The five A's framework. *Review of General Psychology, 17*(1), 69–81. https://doi.org/10.1037/a0029528

Gross, J. J., & John, O. P. (2003). Individual differences in two emotion regulation processes: Implications for affect, relationships, and well-being. *Journal of Personality and Social Psychology, 85*(2), 348–362. https://doi.org/10.1037/0022-3514.85.2.348

Grossman, M., & Wood, W. (1993). Sex differences in emotional intensity. *Journal of Personality and Social Psychology, 65*(5), 1010–1022.

Guilford, J. P. (1956). The structure of intellect. *Psychological Bulletin, 53*(4), 267–293. https://doi.org/10.1037/h0040755

Halperin, J. (2017). The 4 glass ceilings: How women artists get stiffed at every stage of their careers. *Artnet News,* 1–17. https://news.artnet.com/market/art-market-study-1179317?utm_content=from_&utm_source=Sailthru&utm_medium=email&utm_campaign=Europe December 18&utm_term=New Euro %2B Newsletter List

Halperin, J., & Burns, C. (2019). Museums claim they're paying more attention to female artists. That's an illusion. *Artnet News,* 1–13. https://news.artnet.com/womens-place-in-the-art-world/womens-place-art-world-museums-1654714?utm_content=from_&utm_source=Sailthru&utm_medium=email&utm_campaign=News Sunday 9/22/19&utm_term=artnet News Daily Newsletter USE

Hassler, M., Nieschlag, E., & De La Motte, D. (1990). Creative musical talent, cognitive functioning, and gender: Psychobiological Aspects. *Music Perception, 8*(1), 35–48. https://doi.org/10.2307/40285484

He, W. (2018). A 4-year longitudinal study of the sex-creativity relationship in childhood, adolescence, and emerging adulthood: Findings of mean and variability analyses. *Frontiers in Psychology, 9,* 1–14. https://doi.org/10.3389/fpsyg.2018.02331

He, W., & Wong, W. (2011). Gender differences in creative thinking revisited: Findings from analysis of variability. *Personality and Individual Differences, 51*(7), 807–811. https://doi.org/10.1016/j.paid.2011.06.027

He, W., Wong, W., & Hui, A. N. (2015). Gender differences in means and variability on creative thinking: Patterns in childhood, adolescence, and emerging adulthood. In A.-G. Tan & C. Perleth (Eds.), *Creativity, Culture, and Development* (pp. 85–98). Springer. https://doi.org/10.1007/978-981-287-636-2

Helson, R. (1999). A longitudinal study of creative personality in women. *Creativity Research Journal, 12*(2), 89–101. https://doi.org/10.1207/s15326934crj1202_2

Hess, U., Senécal, S., Kirouac, G., et al. (2000). Emotional expressivity in men and women: Stereotypes and self-perceptions. *Cognition & Emotion*, *14*(5), 609–642. https://doi.org/10.1080/02699930050117648

Hocevar, D. (1979, April 12–14). Measurement of creativity: Review and critique. [Conference presentation]. *Annual Meeting of the Rocky Mountain Psychological Association*, Denver, CO, United States.

Isen, A. M., Daubman, K. A., & Nowicki, G. P. (1987). Positive affect facilitates creative problem solving. *Journal of Personality and Social Psychology*, *52*(6), 1122–1131. https://doi.org/10.1037/0022-3514.52.6.1122

Isen, A. M., Johnson, M. M. S., Mertz, E., & Robinson, G. F. (1985). The influence of positive affect on the unusualness of word associations. *Journal of Personality and Social Psychology*, *48*(6), 1413–1426. https://doi.org/10.1037/0022-3514.48.6.1413

Ivcevic, Z., & Hoffmann, J. (2019). Emotions and creativity. In J. C. Kaufman & R. J. Sternberg (Eds.), *The Cambridge Handbook of Creativity* (2nd ed., pp. 273–295). Cambridge University Press.

Jonason, P. K., Richardson, E. N., & Potter, L. (2015). Self-reported creative ability and the Dark Triad traits: An exploratory study. *Psychology of Aesthetics, Creativity, and the Arts*, *9*(4), 488–494. https://doi.org/10.1037/aca0000037

Ju, C., Duan, Y., & You, X. (2015). Retesting the greater male variability hypothesis in mainland China: A cross-regional study. *Personality and Individual Differences*, *72*, 85–89. https://doi.org/10.1016/j.paid.2014.07.021

Karwowski, M., Jankowska, D. M., Gajda, A., et al. (2016). Greater male variability in creativity outside the WEIRD world. *Creativity Research Journal*, *28*(4), 467–470. https://doi.org/10.1080/10400419.2016.1229978

Karwowski, M., Jankowska, D. M., Gralewski, J., et al. (2016). Greater male variability in creativity: A latent variables approach. *Thinking Skills and Creativity*, *22*, 159–166. https://doi.org/10.1016/j.tsc.2016.10.005

Kaufman, J. C., Baer, J., & Gentile, C. A. (2004). Differences in gender and ethnicity as measured by ratings of three writing tasks. *Journal of Creative Behavior*, *38*(1), 56–69. https://doi.org/10.1002/j.2162-6057.2004.tb01231.x

Kaufman, J. C., Niu, W., Sexton, J. D., & Cole, J. C. (2010). In the eye of the beholder: Differences across ethnicity and gender in evaluating creative work. *Journal of Applied Social Psychology*, *40*(2), 496–511. https://doi.org/10.1111/j.1559-1816.2009.00584.x

Kellner, R., & Benedek, M. (2017). The role of creative potential and intelligence for humor production. *Psychology of Aesthetics, Creativity, and the Arts*, *11*(1), 52–58. https://doi.org/10.1037/aca0000065

Kim, J., & Michael, W. B. (1995). The relationship of creativity measures to school achievement and to preferred learning and thinking style in a sample of Korean high school students. *Educational and Psychological Measurement*, *55*(1), 60–74. https://doi.org/10.1177/0013164495055001006

Kring, A. M., & Gordon, A. H. (1998). Sex differences in emotion: Expression, experience, and physiology. *Journal of Personality and Social Psychology*, *74*(3), 686–703. https://doi.org/10.1037/0022-3514.74.3.686

Kwaśniewska, J., & Nęcka, E. (2004). Perception of the climate for creativity in the workplace: The role of the level in the organization and gender. *Creativity and Innovation Management*, *13*(3), 187–196. https://doi.org/10.1111/j.0963-1690.2004.00308.x

Lau, S., & Cheung, P. C. (2010). Developmental trends of creativity: What twists of turn do boys and girls take at different grades? *Creativity Research Journal, 22*(3), 329–336. https://doi.org/10.1080/10400419.2010.503543

Lau, S., & Cheung, P. C. (2015). A gender-fair look at variability in creativity: Growth in variability over a period versus gender comparison at a time point. *Creativity Research Journal, 27*(1), 87–95. https://doi.org/10.1080/10400419.2015.992685

Leaper, C., & Friedman, C. (2007). The socialization of gender. *Handbook of Socialisation: Theory and Research* (August), 561–587. http://psycnet.apa.org/psycinfo/2006-23344-022

Lebuda, I., & Karwowski, M. (2013). Tell me your name and I'll tell you how creative your work is: Author's name and gender as factors influencing assessment of products' creativity in four different domains. *Creativity Research Journal, 25*(1), 137–142. https://doi.org/10.1080/10400419.2013.752297

Luksyte, A., Unsworth, K. L., & Avery, D. R. (2018). Innovative work behavior and sex-based stereotypes: Examining sex differences in perceptions and evaluations of innovative work behavior. *Journal of Organizational Behavior, 39*(3), 292–305. https://doi.org/10.1002/job.2219

Ma, H.-H. (2009). The effect size of variables associated with creativity: A meta-analysis. *Creativity Research Journal, 21*(1), 30–42. https://doi.org/10.1080/10400410802633400

Mawang, L. L., Kigen, E. M., & Mutweleli, S. M. (2019). The relationship between musical self-concept and musical creativity among secondary school music students. *International Journal of Music Education, 37*(1), 78–90. https://doi.org/10.1177/0255761418798402

Nolen-Hoeksema, S. (2012). Emotion regulation and psychopathology: The role of gender. *Annual Review of Clinical Psychology, 8*, 161–187. https://doi.org/10.1146/annurev-clinpsy-032511-143109

The Nobel Prize. (2021, March). Nobel prize awarded women. www.nobelprize.org/prizes/lists/nobel-prize-awarded-women/

Nolen-Hoeksema, S., & Aldao, A. (2011). Gender and age differences in emotion regulation strategies and their relationship to depressive symptoms. *Personality and Individual Differences, 51*(6), 704–708. https://doi.org/10.1016/j.paid.2011.06.012

Piirto, J. (1991). Why are there so few? (Creative women: Visual artists, mathematicians, musicians). *Roeper Review, 13*(3), 142–147.

Plant, E. A., Hyde, J. S., Keltner, D., & Devin, P. G. (2000). The gender stereotyping of emotions. *Psychology of Women Quarterly, 24*(1), 81–92. https://doi.org/10.1111/j.1471-6402.2000.tb01024.x

Posner, J., Russell, J. A., & Peterson, B. S. (2005). The circumplex model of affect: An integrative approach to affective neuroscience, cognitive development, and psychopathology. *Development and Psychopathology, 17*(3), 715–734. https://doi.org/10.1017/S0954579405050340

Proudfoot, D., Kay, A. C., & Koval, C. Z. (2015). A gender bias in the attribution of creativity: Archival and experimental evidence for the perceived association between masculinity and creative thinking. *Psychological Science, 26*(11), 1751–1761. https://doi.org/10.1177/0956797615598739

Reis, S. M. (2002). Toward a theory of creativity in diverse creative women. *Creativity Research Journal, 14*(3–4), 305–316. https://doi.org/10.1207/S15326934CRJ1434_2

Richardson, A. G. (1985). Sex differences in creativity among a sample of Jamaican adolescents. *Perceptual and Motor Skills, 60,* 424–426.

Robinson, M. D., Johnson, J. T., & Shields, S. A. (1998). The gender heuristic and the database: Factors affecting the perception of gender-related differences in the experience and display of emotions. *Basic and Applied Social Psychology, 20*(3), 206–219. https://doi.org/10.1207/s15324834basp2003_3

Rogers, K. B., & Robinson, D. T. (2014). Measuring affect and emotions. In J. E. Stets & J. H. Turner (Eds.), *Handbook of Sociology of Emotions.* (vol. II, pp. 283–303). Springer Science+Business Media. https://doi.org/10.1007/978-94-017-9130-4_14

Ross, C. E., & Willigen, M. Van. (1996). Gender, parenthood, and anger. *Journal of Marriage and the Family, 58*(3), 572–584. https://doi.org/10.2307/353718

Runco, M. A. (1986). Predicting children's creative performance. *Psychological Reports, 59*(3), 1247–1254. https://doi.org/10.2466/pr0.1986.59.3.1247

Runco, M. A., & Acar, S. (2012). Divergent thinking as an indicator of creative potential. *Creativity Research Journal, 24*(1), 66–75. https://doi.org/10.1080/10400419.2012.652929

Runco, M. A., Cramond, B., & Pagnani, A. R. (2010). Gender and creativity. In J. C. Chrisler & D. R. McCreary (Eds.), *Handbook of Gender Research in Psychology* (pp. 343–357). Springer. https://doi.org/10.1007/978-1-4419-1467-5

Seidlitz, L., & Diener, E. (1998). Sex differences in the recall of affective experiences. *Journal of Personality and Social Psychology, 74*(1), 262–271. https://doi.org/10.1037/0022-3514.74.1.262

Shields, S. A. (1982). The variability hypothesis: The history of a biological model of sex differences in intelligence. *Signs: Journal of Women in Culture and Society, 7*(4), 769–797. https://doi.org/10.1086/493921

Silvia, P. J., Beaty, R. E., Nusbaum, E. C., et al. (2014). Everyday creativity in daily life: An experience-sampling study of "little c" creativity. *Psychology of Aesthetics, Creativity, and the Arts, 8*(2), 183–188. https://doi.org/10.1037/a0035722

Simon, R. W., & Lively, K. (2010). Sex, anger, and depression. *Social Forces, 88*(4), 1543–1568. https://doi.org/10.1353/sof.2010.0031

Simon, R. W., & Nath, L. E. (2004). Gender and emotion in the United States: Do men and women differ in self-reports of feelings and expressive behavior? *American Journal of Sociology, 109*(5), 1137–1176. https://doi.org/10.1086/382111

Simonton, D. K. (1994). *Greatness: Who Makes History and Why.* Guilford Press.

Stevenson, B., & Wolfers, J. (2009). The paradox of declining female happiness. *American Economic Journal: Economic Policy, 1*(2), 190–225. https://doi.org/10.1257/pol.1.2.190

Sutu, A., Phetmisy, C. N., & Damian, R. I. (2021). Open to laugh: The role of openness to experience in humor production ability. *Psychology of Aesthetics, Creativity, and the Arts, 15*(3), 401–411. https://doi.org/10.1037/aca0000298

Szobiová, E. (2012). Some psychological factors of creative development in family constellation: Intelligence and personality traits of artistically – technically gifted adolescents. *Creative and Knowledge Society, 2*(2), 70–89. https://doi.org/10.2478/v10212-011-0026-0

Tamres, L. K., Janicki, D., & Helgeson, V. S. (2002). Sex differences in coping behavior: A meta-analytic review and an examination of relative coping. *Personality and Social Psychology Review, 6*(1), 2–30. https://doi.org/10.1207/S15327957PSPR0601_1

Tara, S. N. (1981). Sex differences in creativity among early adolescents in India. *Perceptual and Motor Skills, 52,* 959–962.

Taylor, C. L., & Barbot, B. (2021). Gender differences in creativity: Examining the greater male variability hypothesis in different domains and tasks. *Personality and Individual Differences, 174,* 110661. https://doi.org/10.1016/j.paid.2021.110661

Taylor, C. L., Ivcevic, Z., Moeller, J., & Brackett, M. (2020). Gender and support for creativity at work. *Creativity and Innovation Management, 29,* 453–464. https://doi.org/10.1111/caim.12397

Taylor, C. L., Ivcevic, Z., Moeller, J., et al. (2022). Gender and emotions at work: Organizational rank has greater emotional benefits for men than women. *Sex Roles, 86,* 127–142. https://doi.org/10.1007/s11199-021-01256-z

Taylor, C. L., Said-Metwaly, S., Camarda A., & Barbot, B. (2021, August 27). Gender differences and variability in creative ability: A systematic review and meta-analysis of the greater male variability hypothesis in creativity. Manuscript submitted for publication.

Thompson, T. L. (2016). The mothers and fathers of invention: A meta-analysis of gender differences in creativity (unpublished dissertation). *In ProQuest Dissertations and Theses.* https://search.proquest.com/docview/1795577699?accountid=11440

To, M. L., Fisher, C. D., Ashkanasy, N. M., & Rowe, P. A. (2012). Within-person relationships between mood and creativity. *Journal of Applied Psychology, 97*(3), 599–612. https://doi.org/10.1037/a0026097

Urban, K. K., & Jellen, H. G. (1996). *Test for Creative Thinking-Drawing Production (TCT-DP).* Swets and Zeitlinger.

Warren, F., Mason-Apps, E., Hoskins, S., Azmi, Z., & Boyce, J. (2018). The role of implicit theories, age, and gender in the creative performance of children and adults. *Thinking Skills and Creativity, 28*(2010), 98–109. https://doi.org/10.1016/j.tsc.2018.03.010

Weiner, B. (1985). An attributional theory of achievement motivation and motion. *Psychological Review, 92*(4), 548–573. https://doi.org/10.1037/0033-295X.92.4.548

Yavorsky, J. E., Kamp Dush, C. M., & Schoppe-Sullivan, S. J. (2015). The production of inequality: The gender division of labor across the transition to parenthood. *Journal of Marriage and Family, 77*(3), 662–679. https://doi.org/10.1111/jomf.12189

Zhang, S., & Zhang, J. (2017). The association of TPH genes with creative potential. *Psychology of Aesthetics, Creativity, and the Arts, 11*(1), 2–9. https://doi.org/10.1037/aca0000073

14 Affect in Pretend Play and Creativity

Sandra W. Russ

Pretend play is a universal activity of childhood. Children in all cultures engage in play and in different forms of pretend play (Gaskins et al., 2007). We can wonder about the evolutionary advantage of pretend play, since it does occur in all cultures. Engaging in pretend play prepares children for problem solving in childhood and into adulthood. Pretend play also helps with accessing and processing emotions, which helps with developing creativity and emotion regulation (Russ, 2014). This chapter focuses on the emotional processes that occur during pretend play and how the expression of emotion contributes to creative problem solving, broadly defined.

What Is Pretend Play?

Pretend play is an observable behavior that occurs in children from about 3 through 9 or 10 years of age. Pretend play becomes more complex as children get older (Thompson & Goldstein, 2019). The fact that play is observable is important, because that means that we can measure and study pretend play in both correlational and experimental designs. When we watch children play, we can observe their imagination and affective expressions. How do they transform blocks into spaceships and houses? What kind of stories do they make up? What kinds of emotions do they express within the story?

The classic definitions of pretend play are, in my opinion, still the best. Fein defined pretend play as a symbolic behavior in which "one thing is playfully treated 'as if' it were something else" (1987, p. 282). The "as if" feature permits many kinds of activities to be classified as pretend play. When a block represents a fire truck, that is an example of a symbolic behavior.

The playful element speaks to the positive affect that usually accompanies play. Krasnor and Pepler (1980) add the features of nonlinearity, positive affect, intrinsic motivation, and flexibility of thought to the definition. Pretend play is not logical, includes positive emotions, is internally motivated, and requires flexibility in thinking. Flexibility of thought was also highlighted by Sherrod and Singer (1979) when they identified two cognitive abilities unique to fantasy and pretend play. One was the ability to recombine and integrate stored images as a source of internal stimulation and to divorce these images from reality. A second ability was reinforcement for skillful recombining of images. The ability to manipulate internal images and ideas is a kind of flexibility important in creativity.

Fein (1987) stressed the importance of affect in these mental images. The manipulation of affective ideation in play such as scary monsters, happy birthday parties, or a sick child in the hospital especially contributed to cognitive flexibility. She thought that affect in this form was an essential component of pretend play and was an important factor in developing creativity.

Russ (2016) stressed the self-generating component of pretend play as a precursor to the creative process of the adult. Children are making things up from scratch as they play. Even though they may be using fragments of TV shows, stories, daily experiences, and the like, they are choosing what they play out and are manipulating those ideas and memories. This self-generating process is a key component of creative production and the neurological processes that are active during creative activity (Beaty et al., 2016).

Pretend play is unique in that it is both a creative product and a venue for observing creative processes. Creative pretend play is a creative product in that it meets the criteria of being good/appropriate (a high-quality story) and novel (when compared to same-age peers). Of course, there is a continuum for originality and quality of the story. Play is also, however, an expression of the child's individuality and interpretation of the world. It is a form of self-expression. Runco (2004) proposed that all acts of interpreting the world are forms of creativity. This would certainly be true of the self-expression that occurs in children's play.

Because pretend play involves action and language, the process of creation can be studied and observed. We can see how often the block is transformed into other objects; how much fantasy is incorporated into the story; how much and what type of affect is expressed; how well the affect is integrated into the narrative. Many of the processes that occur in play are important components of creative production. Russ (1993, 2014) has proposed the following overlapping processes that occur in both pretend play and creativity: divergent thinking; broad remote associations; recombining images and ideas; narrative development; use of fantasy; joy and affective engagement in the task; expression of emotions; affect themes in cognition; and integration of affect into cognition. These last four abilities are affective processes important in both play and creativity. First, joy and engagement in the pretend play experience. Second, affect states, or perhaps more accurately, pretend affect states are expressed in the play narrative. Third, affective ideation in the form of affect themes occur throughout the play narrative. Fourth, the integration of the emotion into the story is an important characteristic.

Russ developed the Affect in Play Scale (APS; 1993, 2014) to measure these affective components, as well as cognitive components of play. This was an attempt to correct for what Rubin et al. (1983) called the "cognification of play." A measure of affect in play would enable investigation of the role of affect in the development of creativity in children. Russ theorized that children who are open to affective ideation and affect states and the joy of making things up would benefit in creative activities in three ways (1993, 2014). First, these children (and adults) could access affective cues that trigger and activate other ideation and memories in a search process. They would be comfortable thinking about emotion, both positive and negative emotions, and could easily access emotional content. Thus, they would have a broader associative network. Second, more emotionally salient content would be coded and stored from daily experience. There would be a richer network of emotional memories and associations to draw upon. Access to emotional memories is especially important in the arts. Third, affect could guide the selection process among associations. Perhaps this affective guidance is what is meant by intuition. In addition, experiencing joy in creation could plant the seeds for engaging in creative pursuits in later life.

Types of Affective Processes in Pretend Play and Creativity

Joy and Positive Emotion

Joy in creative discovery, on a small scale, can be seen in children's play. Play is one of the earliest experiences that children have with creative expression. Children are making things up from scratch. Yes, they are calling on memories of daily life, TV shows, dreams, stories, and so on, but the play narrative is their configuration and their choice.

I remember a 3-year-old running into my office and diving into the toys with great pleasure and beginning to play. His mother reported that he did this at home as well, especially when he returned from preschool. What was driving this child? What was so pleasurable? The freedom of self-expression? The love of creating story sequences at this young age? This love of play can be observed in many children who have the time and space to engage in play. Does this love of the play experience set the stage for the motivation to create in later childhood and adulthood? Torrance thought that "the essence of the creative person is being in love with what one is doing" (1988, p. 68). Pretend play, for many children, provides an early experience of joy and passion in an activity.

When children are deeply engaged in play, they experience the "flow state" that Csikszentmihalyi (1990) proposed was so important in creative production. The child is totally involved in the play task and loses a sense of time. Because play is self-paced, the child is in charge of the story and can find the right amount of challenge that they can handle – not too slow and not too fast. This balance is especially important when processing negative emotions such as sadness or anger.

Children engaged in play also demonstrate playfulness. Playfulness often accompanies pretend play and is accompanied by positive affect. Playfulness has been defined as the capacity to "frame or reframe a situation in such a way as to provide oneself (or possibly others) with amusement, humor, and/or entertainment" (Barnett, 2007, p. 977). Lieberman thought that manifest joy and humor were components of playfulness and an important part of pretend play. She found (1977) that playfulness in play was associated with divergent thinking in kindergarten children. She proposed that playfulness was the mediator between pretend play and creativity and that playfulness in play was the forerunner of the recombining of ideas important in the creative act. Other studies also found an association between playfulness and creativity (Christie & Johnson, 1983; Singer & Singer, 1990). Christian (2011), in a longitudinal study with a small sample of children, found that pretend play was related to teachers' ratings of playfulness in children 4 years later. Children with positive affect and imagination in organized narratives in play were considered more playful by their teachers after a 4-year period.

Pretend Affect States

What kinds of emotion do children experience in pretend play? When the dolls are fighting, is the child feeling anger? When the doll is expressing fear while being chased by a tiger, is the child truly in an affect state of fear? When the doll is caring for a hurt pretend dog, is the child experiencing empathy? These are key questions with complicated answers. During play, children are usually having fun and experiencing positive affect (Krasnor & Pepler, 1980). Playfulness is a major component of play. What does this mean for the nature of negative affect expressed in play?

We often observe children happily throttling an action figure in play – they are enjoying the experience and do not look angry. They might be experiencing some true negative affect, but it is in small doses that are not overwhelming.

Affect expressed in play are usually pretend affect states. Another way to conceptualize the states is that they are simulated affect states (Sutton-Smith, 2003). Affect in play may be similar to affect expressed by actors in a play. They are pretending to experience affect. Research in the area of acting can shed light on this area.

Goldstein and Winner (2010–2011) assessed elementary school children and adolescents who participated in a 10-month acting class and compared them to a class in visual arts or music. They found that the acting class children significantly increased in empathy and theory of mind (taking the perspective of the other). In a more recent study with 4-year-olds in Head Start, children who participated in dramatic pretend play games showed lower emotional distress and higher emotional control after engaging in dramatic pretend play games (Goldstein & Lerner, 2018). The authors thought that the physicalized expression of emotion was a major cause of the increased emotional control.

It is probable that there are many individual differences in the actual amount of the emotion experienced when pretending. As with actors, some children may experience intense emotions while others experience the idea of the emotion.

Affect in Ideation, Pretend Play, and Creativity: An Overlooked Connection

Affect in ideation is an important component of thought. We think about affect in a variety of forms. Different literatures use different labels to capture this construct:

- Affect in fantasy (scary snake)
- Affect in mental representations (loving mother)
- Emotion words (gun; monster; yummy)
- Emotion-laden cognition (Did I leave the water running?)
- Emotion-laden memories (happy, sad, scary memory images)
- Affect themes in stories (war themes; birthday party themes; losing a dog themes)

All of these versions of affective ideation occur and are expressed in children's pretend play. They also occur in stories, descriptions of memories, and drawings. An important point is that actual feeling states may or may not accompany this ideation. Affective ideation is a blend of cognition and affect. Theoretically, access to affective ideation should have advantages in creative production.

Theories of Role of Affect in Ideation in Creativity

There are a number of theories that propose an association between affective ideation and creativity. All of these theories focus on the facilitation of broad and remote associations. One key component of creativity is the ability to carry out a broad search for ideas and associations and to make remote associations (Mednick, 1962). This ability raises the probability of generating original ideas. The ability to access thoughts and images that contain affect should provide the individual with a rich repertoire of affective content to draw upon in creative work. In addition, individuals would be comfortable thinking about this affective content. Pretend play is a safe venue during which children can get comfortable with a range of affective content. This ability to access affective content should be especially important in the arts. Much of fiction, poetry, film, theater, and visual arts involves easy expression and use of affective memories and images. One quote I frequently turn to is that of the poet Stanley Kunitz (2005), who stated, "The poem has to be saturated with impulse, and that means getting down to the very tissue of experience" (p. 103). In other words, the poet must be able to deeply experience and think about emotion. This is true of many fiction authors and playwrights. Boyd (2009) has stressed the similarities between play and engaging in the arts. He saw the arts as training for a flexible mind and the same could be said for pretend play. Cognitive flexibility is also important in divergent thinking. Manipulating affective ideation in play should also contribute to cognitive flexibility in general, which has implications for all domains of creativity, not just that of the arts.

Fein's theory of affect and pretend play is especially relevant (1987). She proposed an affect symbol system that gets activated in pretend play and aids the development of creativity. Fein conceptualized this system as representing real or imagined affective experiences. This affect symbol system stores information about emotional events and is manipulated in pretend play. These symbolic units represent affective relationships such as fear of, love of, or anger at and can represent real or imagined events. These affective units are representational templates that store salient information about affect-laden events. These units are then manipulated and played with in pretend play. She thought that the manipulation of these affective representations was important in the development of creative thought.

Russ (1993) has pointed out the similarities between Fein's conceptualization of affective symbols and that of psychoanalytic theory. Freud's (1959) concept of repression theorized that when uncomfortable emotion-laden thoughts are walled off from conscious thought, there is a general constriction of thinking. Kris (1952) expanded Freud's concepts to the creativity area. Creative individuals would have access to affect-laden content, at times primitive and illogical (primary process thought), but in a controlled and organized fashion. The creative individual could switch between illogical, affect-laden thoughts and evaluative critical thinking in a controlled way. This kind of controlled switching is what often occurs in children's pretend play. Both theories of Fein and Kris propose that the manipulation of affect-laden cognition should foster flexibility in thinking and broad associations that are basic components of creativity.

Cognitive Integration of Affect

In typically developing children, affect is integrated into the story in an appropriate manner. The fight between the dolls has some context. They are fighting over a toy they both want, or they are in a boxing match. The scary monster is hiding under the bed and comes out to chase the dolls. At some level, there is an evaluation of the story sequence. This critical thinking or evaluative component is also important in creative production. The affective ideation is placed into an appropriate narrative. In the research on primary process thinking, it is the integration of the affective ideation into appropriate contexts that is related to creativity (Holt, 1967; Kris, 1952). Pretend play is an arena where the child can integrate affective content into an organized story and learn to regulate emotions (Singer & Singer, 1990). Because play is self-paced, the child can slowly experience uncomfortable emotions, especially negative affect, and play out worries and fears.

In summary, pretend play is a safe venue for the expression of various forms of affect that are important in creativity. Children can experience the joy of creating. They can express affect in fantasy in a way that involves physical involvement of the expression. In this way, pretend play is different from playing videogames. In pretend play, children are manipulating mental representations of affect. They are slowly gaining access to uncomfortable ideas and images. Throughout play, children are integrating the affect into a story narrative into an appropriate context.

Research Evidence

In conducting research on affective processes in play and creativity, the challenge is to separate affective components from cognitive components. This is a difficult task because pretend play involves cognitive–affective interactions much of the time. As Fein stated, affect is intertwined with fantasy in pretend play (1987). Russ (1993, 2004) developed the Affect in Play Scale (APS) to focus on affective processes, but imagination and story organization are also measured. However, the development of this measure was an attempt to isolate affective expression in play as much as possible and explore the association between affective processes and creativity.

The Affect in Play Scale is a comprehensive measure of the processes important in creativity in the domain of play. It is a standardized 5-minute play task developed to measure different processes in pretend play that are involved in creativity. Children receive two puppets and three blocks and are asked to play for 5 minutes. The instructions are unstructured in order to give as much room as possible for the child to express their typical play ability and to allow for individual differences. The child's play is scored from the videotape using a criterion-based rating scale. There are five main scores: (1) Organization, the quality of the plot and the complexity of the story, scored from 1 to 5; (2) Imagination, the novelty and uniqueness of the play and ability to pretend and transform the blocks, scored from 1 to 5; (3) Comfort, a global rating of the child's comfort engaging in play and their level of enjoyment, scored from 1 to 5; (4) Frequency of Affect, a total count of affect units expressed within the play narrative (e.g., A child might have the puppets say, "Yikes, a monster!" [fear] or "Whee! This slide is fun!" [happy]); and (5) Variety of Affect, a total count of the number of affect categories out of 11 possible categories, expressed during the play. The frequency of affect units counts both affect states and affect themes expressed in the narrative. There is also a sixth score, a rating of affect intensity, if relevant to a particular study. There are 11 categories of affect that can be subdived into positive (happy; nurturing) or negative (aggression; sadness). Thus, based on the theoretical model, the APS assesses simulated affect states; affective ideation themes; joy, pleasure, and engagement in the task; and cognitive integration of the affect into an organized and imaginative narrative. The APS was adapted for younger children by having more structured instructions with a variety of toys (APS-P; Kaugers & Russ, 2009). Scoring is similar to the APS.

Factor Analyses

In most studies with the APS, the imagination score and frequency of affect score are significantly related. However, in several factor analyses, the affect scores (frequency, variety, and intensity) form a separate factor from the cognitive scores (imagination, organization, and comfort). The factor analyses were conducted with different large samples in different research programs. Two were with samples of Italian children (Chessa et al., 2011; Delvecchio et al., 2016), and the other with U.S. children in a high-risk sample (Marcelo, 2016). Using the APS, Chessa found two factors with a large group (N = 519) of elementary school children. Delvecchio et al. (2016) carried out a large study of 300 Italian children from 4 to 9 years of age. They used the Affect in Play Scale–Preschool version (Kaugars & Russ, 2009), with minor adaptations for the older children. They found that older children had more organized play with a more sophisticated plot, a more complex story, more novelty and use of fantasy elements outside of daily experience. They also found more frequency of and more variety of affect expression in the narrative in older children. When looking at the factor structure of the play, they found a similar two-factor model with younger and older children. One factor was cognitive and one affective. These findings are important because even though pretend play becomes more complex with age, the factor structure of components of play remains the same.

Marcelo (2016) carried out a longitudinal study with 250 children in a racially diverse U.S. sample. She administered the APS-P to children at 4, 6, and 8 years of age. Her results were similar to the cross-sectional study with the APS-P of Delvecchio et al. (2016) with Italian children. Marcelo found a similar two-factor structure across childhood for both boys and girls and across race/ethnicity. There was a cognitive factor and an affective factor. Marcelo concluded that the same play constructs are captured by the APS-P over time across gender, race/ethnicity and poverty status. These findings are consistent with results from previous factor analyses with smaller samples (Russ, 2014) and support the theoretical conceptualization of the APS. The finding of two factors also suggests that affective processes can be studied separately from cognitive processes and might have different developmental trajectories and correlates.

Of note, Fehr and Russ (2014) with a U.S. sample of 4- and 5-year-olds found a separate factor for negative affect, while positive affect loaded with the cognitive factor. For younger children, cognitive and affective processes may be less differentiated and negative affect may be less integrated into cognition.

Cross-Situational Ability

Much of the research on affective processes in play and creativity has used the APS. The field in general continues to focus on cognitive processes in play, not affective. For example, level of complexity of the play or number of themes in the play is measured (Thompson & Goldstein, 2019). One important finding using the APS has been that expression of affect appears to be a cross-situational ability. Expression of affect in play, as measured by the APS, has been associated with expression of affect in memory narratives (Russ & Schafer,

2006). First and second grade children who expressed emotion in play were able to include emotion when talking about memories. A similar association occurred between affect in play and affect expressed in story narratives (Hoffmann & Russ, 2012). In this study with girls, only positive affect in play was associated with affect in stories. In the Russ and Schafer study (2006), both positive and negative affect in play related to affect in memories in a sample of boys and girls. In another study, for both boys and girls, affect in play related to primary process images on the Rorschach (Russ & Grossman-McKee, 1990). Finally, in preschool children, affect in play was associated with expression of daily emotion as rated by teachers (Kaugars & Russ, 2009). The associations among these cross-situational abilities are certainly bidirectional. However, theoretically it makes sense that if children can become more comfortable with expression of affect in the safe venue of play, they can develop this ability that can be expressed in a variety of situations.

Associations between Pretend Play and Creativity

A large number of carefully controlled studies have found an association between pretend play and creativity tasks (see Russ 2014, 2016 for reviews). However, the role of affect in the association is often unclear because affect has not been measured. In the Russ and colleagues research program, we have consistently found significant associations between affect in play and creativity measures. It should be noted that the frequency of affect score is composed of both pretend affect states and affect ideation and themes.

In an early study by Russ and Grossman-McKee (1990) with 60 first and second grade children, divergent thinking was significantly related to frequency of affect in the play narrative ($r = .42$, $p < .001$) and variety of affect categories ($r = .38$, $p < .001$). Both imagination ($r = .35$, $p < .001$) and quality of the organization of fantasy ($r = .30$, $p < .001$) also significantly related to the Alternate Uses Task. These correlations were independent of verbal intelligence. The finding that the relationship was independent of intelligence is important and is consistent with findings in the creativity literature. Russ and Schafer (2006) also found that affect in play related to divergent thinking in first and second grade children. In that study, negative affect was especially related to fluency and originality. Other studies with the APS and APS-P with different examiners, different child populations, and in different research labs have found similar results. Both affective process and imagination and organization of the story in play was associated with divergent thinking, independent of intelligence. For example, in a study by Kaugers and Russ (2009) with preschool children, frequency of affect expression was related to fluency and originality on a divergent thinking task. Affect in play also related to teachers' ratings of make-believe and enjoyment of play behavior. Fehr and Russ (2016) found a similar pattern of associations between affect in play and divergent thinking with a different sample of preschool children. However, in this sample, only positive affect was associated with divergent thinking, but not negative affect.

From these two samples, it appears that the relationship between positive affect in play and divergent thinking occurs as young as 4 years of age in typically developing children. Whereas in older children, both positive and negative affect are associated with creativity. Negative affect could have a different role in development in children younger than 6. Negative affect may not yet be integrated sufficiently to be used adaptively in other areas of functioning.

Hoffmann and Russ (2012) investigated the relationship between play and storytelling in 61 girls and found that play did relate to creativity in storytelling, independent of verbal ability. For the storytelling measure, using the consensus scoring system where stories were evaluated by several raters, imagination in pretend play positively related to creativity in storytelling, $r = .26$, $p < .05$. Children rated as more imaginative in pretend play were also rated as telling more creative stories. Positive affect in pretend play also significantly related to story likeability, $r = .30$, $p < .05$, creativity, $r = .31$, $p < .05$, and imagination, $r = .29$, $p < .05$. Children who expressed more positive affect during pretend play also tended to tell stories rated as more creative. Of note, divergent thinking was significantly related to creativity in storytelling. Those children who had higher divergent thinking scores also tended to have higher amounts of affect, larger varieties of affect, and greater amounts of fantasy in the stories they told. These children were also more likely to be rated as having stories that were more likeable, novel, creative, and imaginative. Originality during divergent thinking was also positively related to storytelling affect expression and fantasy, as well as ratings of creativity and novelty. These results suggest a common creative ability across creative tasks, which has implications for development of creative writing abilities. In the study by Fehr and Russ (2016) with preschool children using the APS-P, pretend play was related to divergent thinking and to creativity in storytelling. Divergent thinking and storytelling were also related. Thus, similar associations occurred between play, divergent thinking, and storytelling in preschool children and in school-age children.

Longitudinal Prediction

There have been several longitudinal studies with the APS that have found stability of the associations between pretend play ability and divergent thinking, independent of verbal intelligence. Russ and colleagues (1999) found that imagination in play of first and second grade children predicted divergent thinking four years later ($r = .42$). Interestingly, affect expression did not predict divergent thinking over time. We did not score for positive and negative affect and might have found different associations if we had done so.

In a second longitudinal study with a different population of girls, early imagination in play again predicted divergent thinking four years later ($r = .39$; Wallace & Russ, 2015). Positive affect predicted originality. Additional follow-up after seven years into high school found continued associations of medium effect size ($r = .39$) between imagination in play and divergent thinking, even after controlling for baseline divergent thinking (Lee & Russ, 2018). Affect was no longer predictive.

There were significant positive relations among cognitive and affective processes in play and, seven years later, corresponding domains on the Kaufman Domains of Creativity Scale (K-DOCS) as hypothesized (Lee & Russ, 2018). This measure is a self-perception measure of creative thoughts and behavior. Organization and imagination in play were positively associated with all five creative behavior domains with medium to large effect sizes. There were large associations between affective processes in play and Self/Everyday, Performance, and Artistic domains of creativity, whereas the associations between affective processes and Scholarly and Scientific domains were small. There were significant positive relations between positive affect and Self/Everyday creativity ($r = .75$, $p < .01$) and positive affect and Performance creativity ($r = .64$, $p < .05$). A non-significant positive relation was found between positive affect and Artistic creativity ($r = .42$). Additionally, there were significant positive relations between negative affect and Self/Everyday creativity ($r = .63$, $p < .05$) and negative affect and Performance creativity ($r = .67$, $p < .01$). A nonsignificant positive relation was found between negative affect and Artistic creativity ($r = .32$). Girls who expressed more affect in their play at baseline – both positive and negative affect – rated themselves as more creative relative to their peers on creative behavior domains that involve more emotional expression. The relationships between affective processes in play and Scholarly and Scientific domains of creativity ranged from $r = .10 - .25$. These results indicate that affect expression may not be as important in creative domains that involve nonfiction writing, debating, or building, for example. Finally, there were larger associations between comfort in play and Self/Everyday, Performance, and Artistic domains of creativity ($r = .45 - .69$) than between comfort in play and Scholarly and Scientific domains of creativity ($r = .15$ and $r = .26$), respectively. These associations remained similar after controlling for verbal ability. In addition, positive affect in play predicted affect expression in a happy memory, organization of a scared memory, and creativity in storytelling. Affect expression in both the happy and scared memories was associated with divergent thinking scores concurrently. These results are important because they suggest that girls who express more affect in play narratives as children perceive themselves to be more creative in the arts and in everyday life as adolescents.

Mullineaux and DiLalla (2009), in studying role-play, found that realistic role-play at age five predicted early adolescents' performance on a divergent thinking task at ages 10–15. They concluded that early play reflects creativity, an association that remains stable into adolescence. Although they did not specifically measure affect, it is probable that emotion was expressed in the role-playing.

The importance of the longitudinal results is two-fold. First, they suggest that the cognitive and affective processes involved in pretend play and in divergent thinking are trait-like, and relatively stable over time. This ability gives the individual an advantage in successfully engaging in creative activities as an adult. Second, they address the methodological issues raised by Lillard et al. (2013) about play and creativity research. One of their main criticisms of the research in the literature was that the same experimenters carried-out the play and creativity tasks. However, in these longitudinal studies, there were different researchers involved and scoring was blind. Even in many of the concurrent studies, there were different researchers and scoring was blind (see Russ & Wallace, 2013).

Facilitation Effects of Pretend Play on Creativity

An important question is whether we can utilize pretend play as a venue to increase creativity. Can we demonstrate cause and effect? Can we increase creativity through play interventions? Can we increase imagination and affect expression in play? Is it possible to harness what occurs in a natural developmental process and facilitate pretend play ability through an intervention protocol? The results of the studies examining play interventions are encouraging, as they provide evidence that even brief play interventions led by adults can be effective at improving pretend play abilities, and in some studies, creative abilities in other tasks. Dansky (1999) pointed out that brief play interventions can have long-term implications for a child's development and play skills as children enjoy playing and are likely to incorporate improvements into their own play, which provides further opportunities to enhance their skills. Russ and Wallace (2013) agreed with Dansky and concluded that there are a number of rigorous studies that have shown that different play interventions that scaffold the play have increased imagination and affect expression in play. Some of the studies also demonstrated increased creativity on other tasks. The research supports what child therapists have reported for years – that guided play in a safe environment can help children express emotions and become more comfortable with emotions.

In the original pilot study in the Russ research program, we developed a play intervention protocol that uses story stems and a variety of unstructured toys (Russ et al., 2004). Children are played with individually. First and second grade children in an inner-city school with a high degree of poverty received five individual 20-minute play sessions following a standard play intervention protocol. Different examiners blind to the group assignment assessed baseline play and outcome play on the APS. There were two play groups (imagination and affect) and one control group (puzzles and coloring). The play groups had a variety of toys available and played with the adult facilitator. They were asked to play out specific story themes that focused on imagination (have a boy go to the moon) or affect (have a girl be happy at a birthday party). The adult played with the child and followed the child's lead in the story, but also praised, modeled, and asked questions. We controlled for adult interaction in the control group as well.

The major result of this study was that the play interventions were effective in improving play skills on the APS. The affect play condition was most effective in that, after baseline play was controlled for, the affect play group had significantly higher play scores on all play processes. These children had more affect in their play (both positive affect and negative affect), a greater variety of affect content, and better imagination and organization of the story than did the control group. The imagination play group also had significantly more positive affect and variety of affect than the control group. Another major finding was that, on the outcome measure of divergent thinking, there were significant effects for group. Although the individual contrast comparisons did not reach significance, inspection of the profile plots indicated that the play groups (usually the affect play group) had higher scores on the divergent thinking test. However, one limitation of this study was that no baseline measure of divergent thinking was obtained. The finding that the group that played out affect in their stories had higher divergent thinking scores suggests that the combination of affect and imagination in play is most effective and, perhaps, more natural.

In a follow-up study of these children 4–8 months later by Moore and Russ (2008), the imagination group had improved play skills over time. The affect group did not maintain the play changes over this period. It may be that an increase in affect expression from a play intervention is temporary, whereas an increase in imagination and pretend in play could be longer lasting. In the follow-up study, there no longer was a significant group effect for divergent thinking. In fact, the control group now had significantly higher scores. Perhaps booster sessions would have been useful in maintaining the initial group effects.

Because the affect intervention was more effective in the short term, and the imagination intervention had longer term effects, in our current research we have combined the imagination and affect stories and prompts in each play intervention session. For example, after six small-group play sessions that were facilitated by adults, Hoffmann and Russ (2016) found that first and second grade girls had increased imagination and affect in play when compared to a control group who colored and did crafts. In addition, there was a transfer effect in that below-average players at baseline increased performance on a creativity task.

In a rigorous study by Thibodeau and colleagues (2016) with preschool children from 3 to 5 years of age, a total of 25 sessions over 5 weeks of pretend play group sessions did result in increased executive functioning. Children were randomly assigned to three groups: a pretend play group that used fantasy, a non-imagination play group that used action-oriented play such as action songs and coloring, and a control group. The measures of executive functioning were reflective of working memory and cognitive flexibility, important in creativity. The pretend play group showed significant improvement while the other two groups did not. Of note, children who were the most engaged and who had highly fantastical play had the most gains. One might assume that the fantastical play had accompanying affect. The authors theorized that the high fantastical players had more practice going back and forth between fantastical pretend and reality.

Children with Developmental Disabilities

In a study by Doernberg et al. (2021), a pretend play intervention was given to school-age children (ages 6–9 years) diagnosed with high-functioning Autism Spectrum Disorder (HF-ASD), to increase children's cognitive and affective play skills, and emotional understanding abilities. The intervention consisted of 5 weekly sessions, 15–20 minutes each. The play intervention was an adaptation of the play intervention used with typical children in the previous Russ intervention studies. The play facilitator played with the child, completing a series of play scenarios that were appropriate for children with ASD. At post-test, the intervention group significantly increased in imagination in play, which generalized to increased skills in emotional understanding. as measured by the Kusche Affective Inventory Revised. Interestingly, the group did not increase in affect expression. It may be that expression of affect content in fantasy play might be especially difficult to alter in these children with ASD, whereas it is possible to increase imagination and cognitive flexibility

Recently, we have been using video-based telehealth approaches where a play facilitator plays with a child. We have used this approach with a rare developmental disability – Prader–Willi Syndrome (PWS). PWS is a congenital genetic neurodevelopmental disorder that is characterized by intellectual impairments, intense food preoccupation, and cognitive and behavioral rigidity, among other symptoms. We found that if the play facilitator and child had the same toy set, and if there had been a face-to-face meeting originally to explain the process, it was feasible to scaffold the child's play over a remote platform. These children were 6–12 years of age and enjoyed the play interactions. The results of the feasibility study found good acceptability overall (Dimitropoulos et al., 2017). Preliminary results with a small sample found that the play intervention was effective in increasing imagination and affective processes in play. In addition, divergent thinking increased (Dimitropoulos et al., 2021). Play over a remote platform was also feasible with preschool children with PWS and their parents (Zyga et al., 2018). The results of these telehealth studies suggest that play intervention studies and interventions can be carried out over remote platforms and can be effective. In this time of COVID-19, play sessions with adults and with peers can be developmental aids to children.

In summary, one can conclude the following from the research:

- Affect expression and imagination in play are related, but separate constructs.
- Affect in play is associated with creativity measures.
- Expression of affect ideation is a cross-situational ability. Affect in play is associated with affect in memory descriptions, affect in stories, and affect in daily play.
- Play intervention modules can increase affect in play in typical children.
- Play intervention modules using a remote platform are feasible with children with developmental disabilities, such as PWS, and have been effective in increasing imagination and affect in play.

Future Research

A major recommendation for future research is to investigate the neurological correlates of pretend play. The role of affect in pretend play and creative thought can be illuminated by neuroscience. What is happening in the brain when a child expresses affect in pretend play? The expression of affect in pretend play includes many types of affect that engage a variety of neurological correlates. For example, one affective unit in play might include emotion words (Whee – this is fun!) which may or may not be accompanied by emotional expression (laughter) and motor movements (clapping). Each of these different expressions could involve different neurological processes and regions.

One recent study illustrates the utility of this approach. Hasmi et al. (2020) studied children from 4 to 8 years of age who played either with dolls or with a tablet. They measured brain activation by having the child wear a special cap while playing and using near-infrared spectroscopy. They found that areas of the brain were activated during doll play that are similar to areas activated during social play and empathy. Solitary doll play activated regions of the brain associated with empathy. This type of investigation of neurological correlates of pretend play should be the wave of the future. If we can learn what areas of the brain are activated during pretend play, then we can have a better understanding of how affect is involved in pretend play and implications for creativity.

It is also important that large samples be used when investigating the complexity of play (Lillard et al., 2013). Large samples are especially important in studies investigating correlates of cognitive and affective factors.

In the play intervention area, the field needs to develop standard guided play interventions for different ages and situations, and then disseminate those protocols to parents and teachers.

It is important that society value the importance of pretend play and expression of emotion in play, that contributes to the development of creativity in children. Pretend play is especially important in the preschool, kindergarten, and early elementary school years. Incorporating pretend play in various forms during the school day should help engage children in the learning enterprise and also develop their imagination and creative problem-solving abilities. Pretend play experiences should enable schools to focus on the whole child enabling optimal child development.

References

Barnett, L. A. (2007). The nature of playfulness in young adults. *Personality and Individual Differences, 43*, 948–958. https://doi.org/10.1016/j.paid.2007.02.018

Beaty, R., Benedek, M., Silvia. P., & Schacter, D. (2016). Creative cognition and brain network dynamics. *Trends in Cognitive Sciences, 20*, 87–95. https://doi.org/10.1016/j.tics.2015.10.004

Boyd, B. (2009). *On the Origin of Stories.* Harvard University Press.

Chessa, D., DiRiso, D., Delvecchio, E., Mazzeschi, C., Russ, S., & Lis, A. (2011). The Affect in Play Scale: Confirmatory factor analysis in elementary school children. *Psychological Reports, 109,* 759–774. https://doi.org/10.2466/09.10.21.PRO.109.6.759-774.

Christian, K. (2011). *The Construct of Playfulness: Relationships with Adaptive Behaviors, Humor, and Early Pretend Play.* Unpublished doctoral dissertation, Case Western Reserve University, Cleveland, Ohio.

Christie, J., & Johnson, E. (1983). The role of play in social-intellectual development. *Review of Educational Research, 53,* 93–115.

Csikszentmihalyi, M. (1990). *Flow: The Psychology of Optimal Experience.* Harper and Row.

Dansky, J. (1999). Play. In M. Runco & S. Pritzker (Eds.), *Encyclopedia of Creativity* (pp. 393–408). Academic Press.

Delvecchio, E., Li, J.-B., Pazzagli, C., Lis, A., & Mazzeschi, C. (2016). How do you play? A comparison among children aged 4–10. *Frontiers in Psychology, 7,* 1883. https://doi.org/10.3389/fpsyg.2016.01833

Dimitropoulos, A., Zyga, O., Doernberg, E., & Russ, S. (2021). Show me what happens next: Preliminary efficacy of a remote play-based intervention for children with Prader–Willi Syndrome. *Research in Developmental Disabilities,108.* https://doi.org/10.1016/j.ridd.2020.103820

Dimitropoulos, A., Zyga, O., & Russ, S. (2017). Evaluating the feasibility of a play-based telehealth intervention program for children with Prader–Willi Syndrome. *Journal of Autism and Developmental Disorders, 47(9),* 2814–2825. https://doi.org/10.1007/s10803–017-3196-z

Doernberg, E., Russ, S., & Dimitropoulos, A. (2021). Believing in make-believe: Efficacy of a pretend play intervention for school-aged children with high-functioning Autism Spectrum Disorder. *Journal of Autism and Developmental Disorders, 51,* 576–588. https://doi.org/10.1007/s10803-020-04547-8

Fehr, K., & Russ, S. (2014). Assessment of pretend play in preschool-aged children: Validation and factor analysis of the Affect in Play Scale – Preschool versions. *Journal of Personality Assessment, 96,* 350–357. https://doi.org/10.1080/00223891.2013.838171

Fehr, K., & Russ, S. (2016). Pretend play and creativity in preschool-aged children: Associations and brief intervention. *Psychology of Aesthetics, Creativity and the Arts, 10,* 296–308. https://doi.org/10.1037/aca0000054

Fein, G. (1987). Pretend play: Creativity and consciousness. In P. Gorlitz & J. Wohlwill (Eds.), *Curiosity, Imagination and Play* (pp. 281–304). Erlbaum.

Freud, S. (1959). Inhibitions, symptoms and anxiety. In. J. Stachey (Ed. & Trans.), *The Standard Edition of the Complete Psychological Works of Sigmund Freud* (vol. 20, pp. 87–172). Hogarth Press. (Original work published 1926.)

Gaskins, S., Haight, W., & Lancy, D. (2007). The cultural construction of play. In A. Goncu & S. Gaskins (Eds.), *Play and Development* (pp. 179–202). Taylor & Francis.

Goldstein, T., & Lerner, M. (2018). Dramatic pretend play games uniquely improve emotional control in young children. *Developmental Science, 21,* e12603. https://doi.org/10.1111/desc.12603.

Goldstein, T., & Winner, E. (2010–2011). Engagement in role play, pretense and acting classes predict advanced theory of mind skill in middle childhood. *Imagination, Cognition, and Personality, 30,* 249–258. https://doi.org/10.2190/IC.30.3.c

Hasmi, S., Vanderwert, R., Price, H., & Gerson, S. (2020). Exploring the benefits of doll play through neuroscience. *Frontiers in Human Neuroscience, 413.* https://doi .org/10.3389/fnhum.2020.560176

Hoffmann, J., & Russ, S. (2012). Pretend play, creativity, and emotion regulation in children. *Psychology of Aesthetics, Creativity, and the Arts, 6,* 175–184.

Hoffmann, J., & Russ, S. (2016). Fostering pretend play skills and creativity in elementary school girls: A group play intervention. *Psychology of Aesthetics, Creativity, and the Arts, 10,* 114–125.

Holt, R. (1967). The development of the primary process: A structural view. In R. Holt (Ed.), *Motivation and Thought* (pp. 344–384). International Universities Press.

Kaugars, A. S., & Russ, S. W. (2009). Assessing preschool children's pretend play: Preliminary validation of the affect in play scale – preschool version. *Early Education and Development, 20,* 733–755. https://doi.org/10.1080/ 10409280802545388

Krasnor, I., & Pepler, D. (1980). The study of children's play: Some suggested future directions. *New Directions for Child Development, 9,* 85–94.

Kris, E. (1952). *Psychoanalytic Explorations in Art.* International Universities Press.

Kunitz, S. (2005). *The Wild Braid.* Norton.

Lee, A., & Russ, S. (2018). Pretend play, divergent thinking, and self-perceptions of creativity: A longitudinal study. *International Journal of Creativity and Problem Solving, 28*(1), 73–88.

Lieberman, J. N. (1977). *Playfulness: Its Relationship to Imagination and Creativity.* Academic Press.

Lillard, A., Lerner, M., Hopkins, E., et al. (2013). The impact of pretend play on children. *Psychological Bulletin, 139,* 1–34. https://doi.org/10.1037/a0029321

Marcelo, A. K. (2016). The structure and development of pretend play across childhood. Doctoral dissertation, University of California Riverside.

Mednick, S. (1962). The associative bases of the creative process. *Psychological Review, 69,* 220–232. https://doi.org/10.1037/H0048850

Moore, M., & Russ, S. (2008). Follow-up of a pretend play intervention: Effects on play, creativity, and emotional processes in children. *Creativity Research Journal, 20,* 427–436. https://doi.org/10.1080/10400410802391892

Mullineaux, P. Y., & DiLalla, L. F. (2009). Preschool pretend play behaviors and early adolescent creativity. *Journal of Creative Behavior, 43,* 41–57. https://doi.org/10 .1002/j.2162-6057.2009.tb01305.x

Rubin, K., Fein, G., & Vandenberg, B, (1983). Play. In P. Mussen (Ed.), *Handbook of Child Psychology* (vol. 4, pp. 693–774). Wiley.

Runco, M. (2004). Everyone has creative potential. In R. J. Sternberg, E. L. Grigorenko, & J. L. Singer (Eds.), *Creativity: From Potential to Realization* (pp. 21–30). American Psychological Association.

Russ, S. W. (1993). *Affect and Creativity: The Role of Affect and Play in the Creative Process.* Erlbaum.

Russ, S. W. (2004). *Play in Child Development and Psychotherapy: Toward Empirically Supported Practice.* Erlbaum.

Russ, S. W. (2014). *Pretend Play in Childhood: Foundation of Adult Creativity.* American Psychological Association Books.

Russ, S. W. (2016). Pretend play: Antecedent of adult creativity. *New Directions in Child and Adolescent Development. Special Issue: Perspectives on Creativity Development,* 21–32.

Russ, S. W., & Grossman-McKee, A. (1990). Affective expression in children's fantasy play, primary process thinking on the Rorschach, and divergent thinking. *Journal of Personality Assessment, 54*(3–4), 756–771. https://doi.org/10.1080/00223891.1990.9674036

Russ, S. W., Moore, M., & Farber, B. (2004, July). Effects of play training on play, creativity, and emotional processes. Poster session presented at American Psychological Association, Honolulu, Hawaii.

Russ, S. W., Robins, A., & Christiano, B. (1999). Pretend play: Longitudinal prediction of creativity and affect in fantasy in children. *Creativity Research Journal, 12,* 129–139. https://doi.org/10.1207/s15326934crj1202_5

Russ, S. W., & Schafer, E. (2006). Affect in fantasy play, emotion in memories and divergent thinking. *Creativity Research Journal, 18,* 347–354. https://doi.org/10.1207/s15326934crj1803_9

Russ, S. W., & Wallace, C. (2013). Pretend play and creative processes. *American Journal of Play, 6,* 136–148.

Sherrod, L., & Singer, J. (1979). The development of make-believe play. In J. Goldstein (Ed.), *Sports, Games, and Play* (pp. 1–28). Erlbaum.

Singer, D. G., & Singer, J. L. (1990). *The House of Make-Believe: Children's Play and the Developing Imagination.* Harvard University Press.

Sutton-Smith, B. (2003). Play as a parody of emotional vulnerability. In D. Lytle (Ed.), *Play and Culture Studies* (vol. 5, pp. 3–17) Praeger.

Thibodeau, R., Gilpin, A., Brown, M., & Meyer, B. (2016). The effects of fantastical pretend play on the development of executive functions: An intervention study. *Journal of Experimental Child Psychology, 145,* 120–138. https://doi.org/10.1016/j.jecp.2016.01.001

Thompson, B., & Goldstein, T. (2019). Disentangling pretend play measurement: Defining the essential elements and developmental progression of pretense. *Developmental Review, 52,* 24–41. https://doi.org/10.1016/j.dr.2019.100867

Torrance, E. P. (1988). The nature of creativity as manifest in its testing. In R. Sternberg (Ed.), *The Nature of Creativity* (pp. 43–75). Cambridge University Press.

Wallace, C., & Russ, S. W. (2015). Pretend play, divergent thinking, and math achievement in girls: A longitudinal study. *Psychology of Aesthetics, Creativity, and the Arts. 9,* 296–305. https://doi.org/10.1037/a0039006

Zyga, O., Russ, S. W., & Dimitropoulos, A. (2018). The PRETEND Program: Evaluating the feasibility of a remote parent-training intervention for children with Prader-Willi Syndrome. *American Journal on Intellectual and Developmental Disabilities, 123,* 574–584. https://doi.org/10.1352/1944-7558-123.6.574

15 Creativity, Emotions, Emotion Regulation, and Aging

Older Adults Take on Life's Challenges with Creativity and Finesse

Polina Ermoshkina and Eva Kahana

The title of this chapter conjures up creative approaches to problem solving in late life and explores how older adults can use creativity to make the final phase of their life meaningful and to engage in successful aging. At the same time, we must acknowledge that older people face many challenging problems that require interpersonal and cognitive skills to ensure positive outcomes. As we traversed the recent literature related to emotion regulation in late life we had to be impressed by the focus on emotional intelligence as a primary resource for late-life interpersonal problem solving. This relative newcomer to theorizing coping and adaptation among older adults has enhanced our understanding of successful coping resources that promote problem solving in old age.

This chapter is written by two sociologists, and we are more familiar with the literature in gerontology and allied disciplines, such as nursing, than we are with psychological approaches that represent the mainstream of considering emotion regulation. Based on our background, we believe that we can broaden the scope of considering adaptive tasks faced by older adults and the adaptations they can employ to successfully deal with these tasks. As they age, people experience stressors associated with losses of friends and spouses, increased frailty, and the shrinking of life space that can affect their quality of life (Kahana & Kahana, 2003). Older adults encounter unpredictable and continually changing everyday problems that require them to draw on "accumulated experience in socioemotional realms" (Blanchard-Fields, 2007, p. 27).

As we discuss creativity and the various resources that older adults can draw upon, we refer to diverse theoretical approaches including the theory of resourcefulness that predominates in nursing (Zauszniewski, 1995, 1996). We want to recognize at the outset that emotion regulation and emotional intelligence are not explicitly included in some of these theoretical orientations. Nevertheless, they illuminate the options available to older adults for successfully addressing age-related challenges.

In the past, researchers were primarily focused on measuring older adults' cognitive functioning and mental abilities to understand the resources they can bring to solving age-related problems. Researchers found that cognitive abilities go through changes and generally decline with age (Hoyer & Verhaeghen, 2006; Schaie, 1989). However, there is immense variability in the individual paths of cognitive change. For instance, Colsher and Wallace (1991) found heterogeneity in rates of cognitive change; while Salthouse (2000) pointed out that "crystallized intelligence" (acquired through life experiences and education) does not decline with age, unlike "fluid intelligence" (ways of processing information). As the speed of processing information becomes less important in later life, researchers increasingly turned their gaze on everyday problem solving among older adults (Berg, 2008).

Everyday problem solving is defined as "the circumstances that we find ourselves in on a daily basis that involve using the skills, accumulated knowledge, and resources (e.g., time, money, and friends) that we have available to us to reach our goals and to sidestep obstacles to these goals" (Mienaltowski, 2011, pp. 75–76). Older adults must deal with everyday problems: trying to schedule an appointment with the doctor, learning to use telehealth, adapting to using a walker or a hearing aid, and navigating the Internet in order to find relevant information.

At the time of writing this chapter the world is still grappling with the COVID-19 pandemic that put the lives of older adults around the globe in danger. The pandemic presented older adults with additional everyday problems and stressors: social isolation (Smith et al., 2020), loneliness (Kotwal et al., 2021), misinformation regarding the severity and magnitude of COVID-19 (Radwan et al., 2020), limited access to healthcare providers, and a transition of routine health appointments to online (Schrack et al., 2020). Older adults also had trouble with household tasks, such as picking up, cleaning, and sanitizing groceries (Heid et al., 2021). All of the stressors associated with COVID-19 may have a long-term effect on older adults' well-being. For instance, one of the detrimental outcomes of social isolation on older adults is a greater risk of anxiety and depression (Santini et al., 2020). Fear of going to the grocery store during the pandemic may lead to poor nutritional choices (eating nonperishable food that tends to be high in sodium and sugar) and subsequent weight gain (Schrack et al., 2020). To deal with everyday problems and stressors, older adults have benefited from use of creativity, social resourcefulness, emotion regulation, and emotional intelligence.

Everyday Creativity during the COVID-19 Pandemic

During the COVID-19 pandemic many older adults were cut off from the rest of the world and had to adapt to a new life in isolation (at home or in institutional settings). It was reported (Lam & García-Román, 2020) that between 10% and 20% of older adults were spending all day alone. Everyday creativity (little-c creativity) can shape one's experience of loneliness and potentially mitigate it. Everyday creativity is defined as "original and meaningful acts that individuals perform in their ordinary lives, for example, as part of leisure or work" (Pauly et al., 2022, p. e31). Examples of everyday creativity include drawing, finding an innovative solution for a problem at home, quilting, inventing a new recipe, sculpting, and so on.

Everyday creativity can be a useful tool for older adults to generate ideas on how to structure their alone time (Thomas & Azmitia, 2019). Everyday creativity is different from Big-C Creativity (eminent creativity), where an individual's novel contribution has a profound societal impact (Simonton, 2013). Such work is often recognized as creative and innovative by peers, for example, the works of modern composers Leonard Bernstein and John Williams or artwork by Japanese artist Yayoi Kusama. It is important to note that there are examples of eminent creativity that had been shown in late life. In a recently published chapter (Kahana et al., 2021) we described evidence about continuing artistic and creative achievements in late life among artists and scientists who exhibited eminent creativity earlier in their lives. Accordingly, old age does not put an end to outstanding creative contributions among those who evidenced such achievements during their younger years.

When it comes to creativity in later life, ageism and deeply seated societal prejudice pose barriers for continuing creative pursuits. For example, prior research of NIH blogs and message boards revealed ageism in the scientific community toward funding elderly scientists with NIH grants (Kahana & Kahana, 2017). Creativity and innovativeness of the older scholars was openly doubted: "Innovative science is mostly an affair of younger men and women," "No more NIH grants for you, Elder. This is your sunset grant. Come on–make some room," "This is waste of NIH money. It only encourages more dead-woods to keep their labs open and keep their outdated ideas alive" (Kahana, Slone et al., 2018, p. 256).

While some scholars found support for a peak-decline hypothesis regarding age and divergent thinking (Reese et al., 2001), others found no differences between divergent thinking abilities of different age groups (Sharma & Babu, 2017). Hui and colleagues (2014) established a curvilinear relationship between age and self-assessed creative personality and creative activity participation. In comparison to other age groups, older adults in their study reported engagement in more creative activities, while younger age groups associated later life with a decline in creativity. Pauly and colleagues (2022) made a persuasive case that "creativity might not only have positive implications if it comprises a grandiose, novel accomplishment (eminent creativity) but that most individuals might be able to find small opportunities in daily life to express their creativity, in their own way" (p. e33). Scholars pointed out that many people were escaping reality during the COVID-19 pandemic by engaging in the act of creation. For instance, they benefited from learning to make bread from scratch (which led to a sudden shortage of yeast and flour around the country in 2020). The very act of creation can be therapeutic to cope with uncertainty caused by the pandemic (Kapoor & Kaufman, 2020).

Resourcefulness in Old Age

The Resourcefulness Theory anchored in the field of nursing (Zauszniewski, 1996) posits that older adults can deal with daily stressors and successfully solve everyday problems by using resourcefulness, which is "rooted in self-control and self-efficacy." Resourcefulness is defined as "a collection of cognitive and behavioral skills that are used to attain, maintain, or regain health" (Zauszniewski, 2012, p. 448). Resourcefulness is a skill and can be learned (Zauszniewski et al., 2002). Rosenbaum (1990) found that people who developed resourcefulness in the face of adversity could stay independent and productive.

Nursing scholars established two forms of resourcefulness: personal resourcefulness (based on self-help) and social resourcefulness (based on seeking help from others) (Bekhet & Zauszniewski, 2016). Personal and social resourcefulness were found to be associated with positive self-esteem (Zauszniewski, 1995), better self-reported physical health (Zauszniewski, 1996), enhanced performance of daily functions (Zauszniewski et al., 2006), and easier adjustment to relocation into a retirement community. Furthermore, resourcefulness training interventions (reframing a situation positively, relying on family and friends, seeking out professionals) improved older adults' adaptive functioning measured as personal care, socialization, leisure activities, and vocational skills (Bekhet & Zauszniewski, 2016).

If a creative person is defined as "one who is open to different paths to the same goal," older adults had years of experience in manipulating the resources at their disposal and more practice than younger people in "confronting limitations or barriers and push[ing] themselves to surmount these limits to find a different path to the same goal" (Fisher & Specht, 1999, p. 459). In the face of everyday challenges (such as lack of continuity of healthcare, driving cessation, need to schedule medical appointments, planning nutritious meals), older adults can rely on their social networks, cultural capital, and resourcefulness to solve their problems.

Although resourcefulness has been acknowledged as an important theoretical perspective within the nursing literature, this conceptualization has remained relatively isolated and is not discussed in mainstream gerontological or psychological orientations that address successful aging, effective coping, or emotion regulation. We propose further exploration of this concept in future research. Relating resourcefulness in late life to coping skills, such as Selective Optimization with Compensation (SOC), may prove to be a fruitful area of inquiry (Baltes & Freund, 2003).

Emotion Regulation in Later Life

Emotions and emotion regulation play a vital role in everyday problem solving. Emotion regulation has been defined as "a range of behavioral responses, including deliberate suppression of ongoing experience and/or expression, as well as anticipatory regulation and the active avoidance of emotionally provocative situations" (Magai, 2008, p. 386). Effective emotion regulation produces few negative emotional experiences (Blanchard-Fields et al., 2004). Emotion regulation (as a way of coping with normative stressors) is a contributing factor in successful aging (Gross & John, 2003). Older adults report better control over the display and experience of emotions than other age groups (Gross et al., 1997; Kessler & Staudinger, 2009). One possible explanation is that older adults experience emotions with lesser intensity (Sims et al., 2015). Another explanation is rooted in socioemotional selectivity theory, which postulates that with age individuals shift their goals in response to a foreshortened future and try to find meaning and satisfaction in their current relationships (Carstensen et al., 1999). Thus, as individuals get older, they become more adept at regulating their emotions. Older adults' networks become smaller (due to death, relocation to an assisted living facility, migration South), but their social integration into existing networks becomes greater (Carstensen et al., 1999). Since older adults tend to be invested in maintaining close interpersonal relationships, they are more likely than younger people to behave in a way that decreases negative emotions (Carstensen et al., 1999).

Age differences in emotion regulation can also be explained by Selective Optimization with Compensation (SOC) theory developed by Paul and Margaret Baltes (1990). SOC is a useful framework to understand successful development across the life course and is rooted in the idea that people's mental, physical, and environmental resources are limited and the losses and opportunities require allocation of those resources (Baltes & Rudolph, 2013). As older adults adapt to disability or late life physical limitations, they might use selection strategy (for example, limiting engagement in certain activities, such as driving at night). Older adults utilize compensation strategies such as assistive devices (walking aids, ergonomic utensils, shoes with Velcro) and home modifications (grip bed handles, shower chair, medical alert system) to preserve independence in the face of health limitations. Urry and Gross (2010), using SOC theory, made an argument that older adults achieve well-being even in the face of adversity by selecting and optimizing their emotion regulation process to compensate for the loss of resources (p. 355). Some older adults, who have good physical and mental health may be called "lucky agers." However for most older adults "facing aging-related stressors, such as health declines or losses in other domains, competent coping and adaptation to age-related changes and stressors is necessary in order to achieve or maintain positive quality of life outcomes" (Kahana et al., 2014, p. 3).

The life course literature suggests that as people grow older they become better at regulating reactions to problems and interpersonal tensions (Blanchard-Fields & Cooper, 2004). Self-report studies demonstrated that older adults were more likely to control their emotions than younger adults (Lawton et al., 1992) and less likely to report interpersonal tensions (Fingerman & Birditt, 2003) and anger in response to interpersonal problems (Birditt & Fingerman, 2003). Furthermore, memory is a "powerful regulation strategy" as it influences one's thoughts and behaviors (Charles & Carstensen, 2007, p. 317). Studies documented that with age there is a shift toward recalling positive information. Laboratory studies demonstrated that older adults remember events more positively than younger adults (Charles et al., 2003).

Magai (2008) problematized the overreliance of scholars on self-report studies as they are vulnerable to "presentational biases" (p. 387). The few experimental studies (Kunzmann et al., 2005; Magai et al., 2006) conducted on samples of older adults show that the ability to regulate emotions with age shows no decline.

In dealing with everyday problems, people use either problem-focused actions (direct action that aims to solve a problem) or emotion-passive strategies (such as not directly facing the problem). Blanchard-Fields and colleagues (1995) found that in low-emotion domains, all age groups tend to utilize problem-focused action. However, in dealing with interpersonal problems (conflicts with a family member), older adults are more likely than other age groups to use passive dependence or avoidance strategies. It is important to note that while the literature has called passive strategies less effective, some scholars point out that for older adults passive strategies can actually be adaptive as they "inhibit negative arousal before it occurs" (Blanchard-Fields et al., 2004, p. 262).

Emotional Intelligence in Later Life

Before introduction of emotional intelligence into the mainstream, scholars largely used a narrow definition of intelligence and relied on traditional academic abilities, such as IQ, as the indicators of intelligence (Ciarrochi et al., 2000). While cognitive intelligence is a strong predictor of professional success, it is not a good predictor of "successful functioning in everyday life" (Neubauer & Freudenthaler, 2005, p. 32). Conceptualization of intelligence has been expanded to include emotional intelligence. In their highly influential article, Peter Salovey and John Mayer (1990) defined emotional intelligence as "the subset of social intelligence that involves the ability to monitor one's own and others' feelings and emotions, to discriminate among them and to use this information to guide one's thinking and actions" (p. 189). The term *emotional intelligence* (EI) originally was used for "a type of intelligence that involved the ability to process emotional information" (Roberts et al., 2001, p. 197). There are two conceptualizations of emotional intelligence: ability EI and trait EI. Ability EI is measured with ability measures to establish "maximal performance," while trait EI is measured with self-reports and self-perceptions (Armstrong et al., 2011, p. 331). The former is conceptualized as cognitive ability, the latter as a personality trait (Petrides, 2011). Both approaches to EI have been critiqued for their measurement limitations. For example, Mayer and colleagues (2016) argued that the disadvantage of using a trait approach to EI is that people often estimate their abilities based on self-confidence and wishful thinking, while measuring EI with abilities tests is a good indicator of people's actual abilities. Other scholars (Austin, 2010) critiqued ability EI for disregarding the subjective nature of emotions.

An emotionally intelligent person accurately identifies emotions in oneself and others, effectively manages one's own emotions, uses emotions in decision making and understands how emotions are displayed (Mayer et al., 2016). Knowing how to regulate one's emotions in the face of everyday problems and stressors becomes especially important for older adults who have to deal with age-related limitations and disability and continue to engage in life and triumph over society's ageism.

Bringing the Concept of Emotional Intelligence into the Mainstream of Gerontology and Sociology

Emotional intelligence was popularized with the publication of Daniel Goleman's (1995) book *Emotional Intelligence: Why It Can Matter More than IQ*. The concept was introduced to the fields of business, leadership, and corporate employment with the publication of the book by the *New York Times* best-selling author Robert Cooper and entrepreneur Ayman Sawaf (1997), *Executive EQ: Emotion Intelligence in Leaderships and Organizations.* The emotional intelligence concept thus far received little attention in the gerontological and sociological communities. In this chapter, we attempt to bring this concept into the field of aging. There are conflicting findings regarding the relationship between emotional intelligence and age. One thing is clear: emotional intelligence is not stable over the life span (Conde-Pipó et al., 2021). Some studies found a positive relationship between emotional intelligence and age, with older adults having more emotional intelligence than younger people (Mayer et al., 1999). One explanation for increased emotional intelligence with age has to do with learning and accumulation of knowledge and experiences over time (Kaufman et al., 2008). Emotional intelligence, like other forms of intelligence, can increase with practice and older adults have more opportunities to practice than younger adults (Chen et al., 2016). Sliter and colleagues (2013) made a compelling argument that older adults improve their understanding of emotions and use better strategies than younger people. Other studies found that emotional intelligence decreases with age in some dimensions and increases in others (compensation) and reaches a positive balance (Dave et al., 2021).

Bringing the concept of emotional intelligence into the field of gerontology is essential. It is a concept that has proved to be associated with affective well-being (Liu et al., 2013) and resilience. In the face of adversity and major negative life events (serious illness, disability, job loss, widowhood), positive adaptation (resilience) is especially relevant for the daily experiences of older adults. Armstrong and colleagues (2011) found that trait emotional intelligence promotes resilience; those with higher emotional intelligence scores had less distress after major negative life events. Thus, emotional intelligence serves as a buffer to the effects of adversity (Armstrong et al., 2011). A positive correlation has been found between trait emotional intelligence and subjective well-being (Gallagher & Vella-Brodrick, 2008). There is only scarce research on the relationship between emotional intelligence and purpose in life. As older adults experience shrinking of their social circle due to interpersonal losses and health decline, finding purpose in life becomes especially important. The factors associated with purpose in life are happiness and subjective well-being. Ability emotional intelligence influences each of the aforementioned factors (Zysberg, 2012). Those with higher emotional intelligence and who are more aware of their emotions can regulate them more effectively, which in turn leads to enhanced subjective well-being (Salovey et al., 1999).

Emotional intelligence promises to be a useful resource to deal with adaptive tasks of aging. Adaptive tasks of old age have been described as efforts to (1) maintain a positive self-image, (2) maintain strong social ties, (3) plan for future care needs, and (4) find meaning in life in the face of losses (Sörensen et al., 2014). To deal with later life challenges and limitations, older adults benefit from drawing on past experiences in seeking novel and creative solutions. Such solutions are based on diverse skills. These include (1) seeing the situation from the perspective of the other (in order for people to help you, you need to understand their perspective); (2) engaging in proactive help-seeking and marshaling social support; (3) letting frustrations go, forgiving, and focusing on the positive; and (4) responding to social support with gratitude and appreciation. The constructive actions described are predicated on rejection of the stigma of ageism (Ayalon & Tesch-Römer, 2018).

Emotional Intelligence as a Component of Successful Aging and Creativity

Our chapter has focused on older adults who are encountering health challenges and may require social supports from family, friends, and formal institutions. However, it is important to note that large numbers of older adults maintain physical and mental health and good cognitive functioning well into late life (Van Hooren et al., 2007). These older adults may be referred to as successful agers.

Emotional intelligence might be a useful addition to the successful aging paradigm (sometimes called "vital aging" or "active aging" or "productive aging"). Successful aging captured the minds of gerontologists and sociologists in the past decades, and while there are several critiques of this paradigm (e.g. Liang & Luo, 2012), successful aging remains a powerful and important concept. John Rowe and Robert Kahn (1997) brought the concept of successful aging into mainstream gerontology. According to their definition, successful aging has three components: (1) low probability of disease and disease-related disability, (2) high cognitive and physical functional capacity, and (3) active engagement with life. The authors emphasize the importance of individual action ("attained through individual choice and effort") to achieve successful aging (Rowe & Kahn, 1998, p. 37).

After the publication of Rowe and Kahn's 1997 article, the concept of successful aging was further developed, expanded, and critiqued. For example, Glass (2003) pointed out that if the successful aging is taken seriously, it requires "substantial reorganization of healthcare systems, new and different outcome measures, and reconfigured funding strategies and priorities" (p. 382). Kahana and Kahana (2003) argued that older adults will face normative stressors (social losses, person-environment incongruence), but even in the face of these adversities, it is still possible to maintain a good quality of life.

Older adults can use social resources in order to adapt proactively (behavioral adaptations). Proactive adaptations have been defined as "temporally proximate behaviors that an older adult may engage in order to help enhance their quality of life. These behaviors are drawn from his/her existing resources such as active coping styles or family support resources" (Kahana et al., 2012, p. 4). Studies of older adults have moved from a focus on age-related deficits to considering positive adaptive skills. The greater the constraints posed by the environment, the more useful it becomes for older adults to come up with unique solutions reflecting cognitive creativity to deal with demands of their day-to-day situations. Thus, for example older adults who need assistance in driving, but are eager to participate in community activities, can express their creativity in choosing activities that would be of interest to family or friends who could drive them. Both emotional intelligence and creativity can compensate for deficits in other areas of intellectual and/or physical functioning and help older adults age successfully.

Those older adults who are fortunate to maintain physical, mental, and cognitive health encounter another important challenge related to ageism in our society (Ayalon & Gum, 2011). Ageism results in stereotypes that paint all older persons with a brush of infirmity and decline in abilities. Emotional intelligence as well as creativity provide important resources in counteracting and even fighting ageism. Older adults have a lot at stake in successfully counteracting ageist societal attitudes. They may need to fight off attempts to force them into early retirement or denying them well-deserved promotion (Malinen & Johnston, 2013).

Use of Emotional Intelligence and Creativity for Successful Care-Getting

With increased longevity in the Global North, older adults are more likely to experience chronic health limitations requiring a high level of care for a prolonged period of time. In the United States, older adults often rely on their family members for informal care, including instrumental activities (meal preparation, shopping, driving to appointments), personal care, and emotional support (Pope et al., 2012). A plethora of studies from diverse academic disciplines examined caregiving for aging parents, with particular attention to caregiving strain (Cohen et al., 2021; Silverstein et al., 2006; Willert & Minnotte, 2021). However little systematic attention has been given to care-getting.

Kahana and colleagues (2009) named successful care-getting "a critical goal of later life" (p. 72). Not only is caregiving associated with challenges but so is care-getting. How can older adults obtain high-quality care that allows them to exercise agency and independence, and to preserve dignity? How do older adults receive care that is not perfunctory or reluctant? There is an inherent power asymmetry in the caregiving relationship. Cushing (2003) made a compelling case that "caregiving relations are indeed a delicate site for negotiating and sharing power" (p. 90).

It is notable that providers of care are often burdened by their tasks. This leaves care receivers in the challenging position of minimizing the burden on their caregivers. Emotional intelligence is needed to accomplish this goal. In order to clarify the type of help needed by the care receiver, self-disclosure is required (Pennebaker, 1995). Effective help seeking (Nadler, 1991) also demands recognizing that caregiver availability and resources are limited. After receiving the requested assistance, the care receiver needs to offer appreciation and gratitude (Portocarrero et al., 2020) for the assistance provided. Such behaviors help demonstrate their emotional intelligence. If the caregiver is unable or unwilling to provide the type and amount of assistance needed the care receiver needs to be able to compromise (Gutmann & Thompson, 2014).

With early hospital discharges, older adults have to be creative to obtain responsive care (Kahana et al., 2009). There are a number of barriers to care-getting that may require emotional intelligence to solve. For example, personal barriers (e.g., lack of assertiveness in communicating needs), lack of social resources, and care-related resources can be obstacles (Zauszniewski et al., 2015). Furthermore, if older adults experience person–environment incongruence, it can lead to continuous stress and adverse physical and mental outcomes, which can lead to institutionalization (Kahana & Kahana, 2017).

In order to delay institutionalization, older adults can implement environmental modifications and strive to obtain high-quality home care. Lawton (1985) used the concept of proactivity in relation to the environment – a way for older adults to overcome environmental challenges that occur in late life. Kahana and Kahana (1996), building on Lawton's concept of environmental proactivity, developed a theory of Preventive and Corrective Proactivity. Proactive adaptations refer to "specific behavioral actions undertaken by older individuals to actively deal with impending or extant aging-related stressors" (Kahana et al., 2014, p. 3). In the face of stressors (both cumulative stressors and recent stressors) and in the presence of external resources (social support) and internal resources (e.g., altruism, locus of control, optimism, self-esteem), older adults are able to behaviorally adapt to the challenges. This can be achieved through preventive adaptations (planning ahead, advance care planning, drafting a will, moving closer to relatives in anticipation of declining health) and corrective adaptations, such as environmental modifications, marshaling support (Kahana et al., 2014). All of these adaptations can benefit from resources of emotional intelligence.

Using Emotional Intelligence and Creativity to Navigate the Broken Healthcare System

For older patients, especially those, who suffer from chronic illnesses, obtaining responsive and effective healthcare has become increasingly challenging (Kahana, Yu, et al., 2018). Scholars linked patient trust to continuity of care (Mechanic, 1996). Gone are the days of devoted family doctors who are familiar with the patient's history. Instead, patients now receive care from large bureaucratic organizations and providers who are seldom familiar with their backgrounds and unique needs. Calling patients consumers of care is not just a simple change in semantics, but a sign of a deeper change in the way we think about doctor–patient relationships and medical transactions (Mechanic, 1996).

Typically, the patient who is looking to see their regular doctor is directed first to a website or app, and even then only to see a physician's assistant or a nurse sharing the workload with the physician. The increased use of nonphysician professionals is partially explained by a shortage of physicians. Another reason is commodification, objectification, and standardization of healthcare (Timmermans & Almeling, 2009) brought on by the transition to a service-based economy.

The availability and demand for using telehealth can present both advantages and disadvantages for older patients (Seckin, 2010). Being involved in virtual medical visits eliminates transportation challenges. However, such long-distance communication further limits the personal dimensions of the inter-action. Older adults must exercise assertiveness to be sure that the long-distance interactions are not forced on them against their will.

Transportation Challenges

Transportation to the doctor can pose additional challenges to patients who are unable to drive. If the patient does not live in a neighborhood that provides transportation to medical appointments, they are left to their own devices. In the United States, the ability to drive is a central prerequisite of maintaining a good quality of life. Driving ability and car ownership are correlated with life satisfaction and independence among older adults (Choi et al., 2014; Fonda et al., 2001). Accordingly, limitations in driving present important challenges especially in settings and situations where transportation support is not avail-able and public transportation is limited.

Driving cessation and a perceived loss of control is strongly associated with a variety of adverse health outcomes, including depression (Choi et al., 2013). Furthermore, driving cessation can lead to a rapid health deterioration as ex-drivers have fewer out-of-home activities and tend to stay mostly indoors (Edwards et al., 2009). Creativity and emotional intelligence are dual resources for maintaining meaning in life in the face of adversity such as driving cessation. Emotional intelligence is needed whenever people are involved in negotiations. Creativity reflects an ability to think of novel and unique solutions and to think "outside the box." Accordingly, it greatly improves the success of older people to propose novel solutions to everyday problems. Thus, for example, the older person needing car rides for doctors' appointments can barter their services to babysit or oversee homework done by their own or their neighbor's grandchildren. In this situation, emotional intelligence may be reflected in the skillful way they ask for assistance with transportation, and propose to reciprocate while creativity may be reflected in their unique proposal to offer their own contribution for the favor asked. Furthermore, such bartering may best be accomplished as a long-term rather than an immediate exchange.

Emotional intelligence and creativity can benefit older patients as they involve their informal helping network in facilitating receiving formal healthcare. Therefore, there are many adaptive tasks involving both formal and informal care-getting that must be negotiated by older patients, and the use of creativity and emotional intelligence benefits the ultimate outcomes for older adults.

Conclusion

We were appreciative of the opportunity to bring sociological perspectives to consideration of emotional intelligence and creativity in late life. It is clear that older people must successfully negotiate diverse interpersonal situations as they aim to maintain good quality of life in old age. As more people live to older ages we can focus on the skills and talents they bring to navigating adaptive tasks of old age. Emotional intelligence can help these older adults maintain friendships and meaningful interpersonal exchanges even in the face of personal challenges. The resources and constructive behaviors of individuals can translate into more positive perceptions of late life in general.

An additional important contribution of emotional intelligence and creativity in late life relate to the broader success in changing perceptions and overcoming ageism (Ayalon & Tesch-Römer, 2018). To the extent that older adults can come up with creative solutions, they acquire respect from those helping them and counteract prevailing negative images of dependency and lack of competence in late life (Angus & Reeve, 2006). We conclude our chapter with the hopes to contribute to more macrophenomena of altering societal attitudes to further amplify the potential of older people for living their life the dignity and competence.

References

Angus, J., & Reeve, P. (2006). Ageism: A threat to "aging well" in the 21st century. *Journal of Applied Gerontology*, *25*(2), 137–152. https://doi.org/10.1177/0733464805285745

Armstrong, A. R., Galligan, R. F., & Critchley, C. R. (2011). Emotional intelligence and psychological resilience to negative life events. *Personality and Individual Differences*, *51*(3), 331–336. https://doi.org/10.1016/j.paid.2011.03.025

Austin, E. J. (2010). Measurement of ability emotional intelligence: Results for two new tests. *British Journal of Psychology, 101*(3), 563–578. https://doi.org/10.1348/000712609x474370

Ayalon, L., & Gum, A. M. (2011). The relationships between major lifetime discrimination, everyday discrimination, and mental health in three racial and ethnic groups of older adults. *Aging & Mental Health, 15*(5), 587–594. https://doi.org/10.1080/13607863.2010.543664

Ayalon, L., & Tesch-Römer, C. (2018). *Contemporary Perspectives on Ageism.* Springer Nature. https://doi.org/10.1007/978-3-319-73820-8

Baltes, B. B., & Rudolph, C. W. (2013). The theory of selection, optimization, and compensation. In M. Wang (Ed.), *The Oxford Handbook of Retirement* (pp. 88–101). Oxford University Press. https://doi.org/10.1093/oxfordhb/9780199746521.013.0044

Baltes, M. M., & Baltes, P. B. (1990). Psychological perspectives on successful aging: The model of selective optimization with compensation. In P. B. Baltes & M. M. Baltes (Eds.), *Successful Aging: Perspectives from the Behavioral Sciences* (pp. 1–34). Cambridge University Press. https://doi.org/10.1017/cbo9780511665684.003

Baltes, P. B., & Freund, A. M. (2003). Human strengths as the orchestration of wisdom and selective optimization with compensation. In L. G. Aspinwall & U. M. Staudinger (Eds.), *A Psychology of Human Strengths: Fundamental Questions and Future Directions for a Positive Psychology* (pp. 23–35). American Psychological Association. https://doi.org/10.1037/10566-002

Bekhet, A. K., & Zauszniewski, J. A. (2016). The effect of a resourcefulness training intervention on relocation adjustment and adaptive functioning among older adults in retirement communities. *Issues in Mental Health Nursing, 37*(3), 182–189. https://doi.org/10.3109/01612840.2015.1087606

Berg, C. (2008). Everyday problem solving in context. In S. Hofer, & D. F. Alwin (Eds.), *Handbook of Cognitive Aging: Interdisciplinary Perspectives* (pp. 207–223). Sage. https://doi.org/10.4135/9781412976589.n13

Birditt, K. S., & Fingerman, K. L. (2003). Age and gender differences in adults' descriptions of emotional reactions to interpersonal problems. *The Journals of Gerontology Series B: Psychological Sciences and Social Sciences, 58*(4), P237–P245. https://doi.org/10.1093/geronb/58.4.p237

Blanchard-Fields, F. (2007). Everyday problem solving and emotion: An adult developmental perspective. *Current Directions in Psychological Science, 16*(1), 26–31. https://doi.org/10.1111/j.1467-8721.2007.00469.x

Blanchard-Fields, F., & Cooper, C. (2004). Social cognition and social relationships. In F. R. Lang & K. L. Fingerman (Eds.), *Growing Together: Personal Relationships across the Lifespan* (pp. 268–289). Cambridge University Press. https://doi.org/10.1017/CBO9780511499852.011

Blanchard-Fields, F., Jahnke, H. C., & Camp, C. (1995). Age differences in problem-solving style: The role of emotional salience. *Psychology and Aging, 10*(2), 173–180. https://doi.org/10.1037/0882-7974.10.2.173

Blanchard-Fields, F., Stein, R., & Watson, T. (2004). Age differences in emotion-regulation strategies in handling everyday problems. *The Journals of Gerontology Series B: Psychological Sciences and Social Sciences, 59*(6), P261–P269. https://doi.org/10.1093/geronb/59.6.P261

Carstensen, L. L., Isaacowitz, D. M., Charles, S. T. (1999). Taking time seriously: A theory of socioemotional selectivity. *American Psychologist, 54*, 165–181. https://doi.org/10.1037/0003-066X.54.3.165

Charles, S. T., & Carstensen, L. L. (2007). Emotion regulation and aging. In J. Gross (Ed.), *Handbook of Emotion Regulation* (pp. 307–320). Guilford Press.

Charles, S. T., Mather, M., & Carstensen, L. L. (2003). Aging and emotional memory: The forgettable nature of negative images for older adults. *Journal of Experimental Psychology: General, 132*(2), 310–324. https://doi.org/10.1037/0096-3445.132.2.310

Chen, Y., Peng, Y., & Fang, P. (2016). Emotional intelligence mediates the relationship between age and subjective well-being. *The International Journal of Aging and Human Development, 83*(2), 91–107. https://doi.org/10.1177/0091415016648705

Choi, M., Adams, K. B., & Kahana, E. (2013). Self-regulatory driving behaviors: gender and transportation support effects. *Journal of Women & Aging, 25*(2), 104-118. https://doi.org/10.1080/08952841.2012.720212

Choi, M., Lohman, M. C., & Mezuk, B. (2014). Trajectories of cognitive decline by driving mobility: Evidence from the Health and Retirement Study. *International Journal of Geriatric Psychiatry, 29*(5), 447–453. https://doi.org/10.1002/gps.4024

Ciarrochi, J. V., Chan, A. Y., & Caputi, P. (2000). A critical evaluation of the emotional intelligence construct. *Personality and Individual Differences, 28*(3), 539–561. https://doi.org/10.1016/S0191–8869(99)00119-1

Cohen, S. A., Nash, C. C., & Greaney, M. L. (2021). Informal caregiving during the COVID-19 pandemic in the US: Background, challenges, and opportunities. *American Journal of Health Promotion 35*(7), 1032–1036. https://doi.org/10.1177/08901171211030142c

Colsher, P. L., & Wallace, R. B. (1991). Longitudinal application of cognitive function measures in a defined population of community-dwelling elders. *Annals of Epidemiology, 1*(3), 215–230. https://doi.org/10.1016/1047-2797(91)90001-S

Conde-Pipó, J., Melguizo-Ibáñez, E., Ramírez-Granizo, I., & González-Valero, G. (2021). Physical self-concept changes in adults and older adults: Influence of emotional intelligence, intrinsic motivation and sports habits. *International Journal of Environmental Research and Public Health, 18*(4), 1–14. https://doi.org/10.3390/ijerph18041711

Cooper, R., & Sawaf, A. (1997). *Executive EQ: Emotional intelligence in leadership and organizations.* Grosset/Putnam.

Cushing, P. (2003). Negotiating power inequities in caregiving relationships. *Journal on Developmental Disabilities, 10*(1), 83–91.

Dave, H. P., Keefer, K. V., Snetsinger, S. W., Holden, R. R., & Parker, J. D. (2021). Stability and change in trait emotional intelligence in emerging adulthood: A four-year population-based study. *Journal of Personality Assessment, 103* (1), 57–66. https://doi.org/10.1080/00223891.2019.1693386

Edwards, J. D., Lunsman, M., & Roth, D. L. (2009). Driving cessation and health trajectories in older adults. *Journals of Gerontology Series A, 64*(12), 1290–1295. https://doi.org/10.1093/gerona/glp114

Fingerman, K. L., & Birditt, K. S. (2003). Do age differences in close and problematic family ties reflect the pool of living relatives? *Journals of Gerontology, Series B, 58*(2), 80–87. https://doi.org/10.1093/geronb/58.2.p80

Fisher, B., & Specht, D. (1999). Successful aging and creativity in later life. *Journal of Aging Studies, 13*(4), 457–472. https://doi.org/10.1016/S0890–4065(99)00021-3

Fonda, S. J., Wallace, R., & Herzog, A. R. (2001). Changes in driving patterns and worsening depressive symptoms among older adults. *The Journals of Gerontology Series B, 56* (6), S343–S351. https://doi.org/10.1093/geronb/56.6.S343

Gallagher, E. N., & Vella-Brodrick, D. (2008). Social support and emotional intelligence as predictors of subjective well-being. *Personality and Individual Differences, 44* (7), 1551–1561. https://doi.org/10.1016/j.paid.2008.01.011

Glass, T. A. (2003). Assessing the success of successful aging. *Annals of Internal Medicine, 139*(5), 382–383. https://doi.org/10.7326/0003-4819-139-5_Part_1–200309020-00015

Goleman, D. (1995). *Emotional Intelligence: Why It Can Matter More Than IQ.* Bloomsbury.

Gross, J. J., Carstensen, L. L., Pasupathi, M., Tsai, J., & Hsu, A. Y. (1997). Emotion and aging: Experience, expression, and control. *Psychology & Aging, 12*(4), 590–599. https://doi.org/10.1037/0882-7974.12.4.590

Gross, J. J., & John, O. P. (2003). Individual differences in two emotion regulation processes: Implications for affect, relationships, and well-being. *Journal of Personality and Social Psychology, 85*(2), 348–362. https://doi.org/10.1037/0882-7974.12.4.590

Gutmann, A., & Thompson, D. F. (2014). *The Spirit of Compromise.* Princeton University Press. https://doi.org/10.1515/9781400851249

Heid, A. R., Cartwright, F., & Pruchno, R. (2021). Challenges experienced by older people during the initial months of the COVID-19 pandemic. *The Gerontologist, 61*(1), 48–58. https://doi.org/10.1093/geront/gnaa138

Hoyer, W. J., & Verhaeghen, P. (2006). Memory aging. In J. Birren & W. Schaie (Eds.), *Handbook of the Psychology of Aging* (pp. 209–232). Elsevier Academic Press. https://doi.org/10.1016/B9–78-012101-2/64950-0136

Hui, A. N., Yeung, D., & Cheng, S. T. (2014). Gains and losses in creative personality as perceived by adults across the life span. *Developmental Psychology, 50*(3), 709–713. https://doi.org/10.1037/a0034168

Kahana, E., & Kahana, B. (1996). Conceptual and empirical advances in understanding aging well through proactive adaptation. In V. L. Bengtson (Ed.), *Adulthood and Aging: Research on Continuities and Discontinuities* (pp. 18–40). Springer.

Kahana, E., & Kahana, B. (2003). Contextualizing successful aging: new directions in an age-old search. In R. Settersten (Ed.), *Invitation to the Life Course* (pp. 225–255). Baywood.

Kahana, J. S., & Kahana, E. (2017). *Disability and Aging: Learning from Both to Empower the Lives of Older Adults.* Lynne Rienner.

Kahana, E., Kahana, B., & Ermoshkina, P. (2021). The many faces of creativity in old age. In S. Russ, J. Hoffmann, & J. Kaufman (Eds.), *Cambridge Handbook of Lifespan Development of Creativity* (pp. 233–262). Cambridge University Press. https://doi.org/10.1017/9781108755726.014

Kahana, E., Kahana, B., & Lee, J. E. (2014). Proactive approaches to successful aging: One clear path through the forest. *Gerontology, 60*(5), 466–474. https://doi.org/10.1159/000360222

Kahana, E., Kahana, B., Wykle, M., & Kulle, D. (2009). Marshalling social support: A care-getting model for persons living with cancer. *Journal of Family Social Work, 12*(2), 168–193. https://doi.org/10.1080/10522150902874834

Kahana, E., Kelley-Moore, J., & Kahana, B. (2012). Proactive aging: A longitudinal study of stress, resources, agency, and well-being in late life. *Aging & Mental Health, 16*(4), 438–451. https://doi.org/10.1080/13607863.2011.644519

Kahana, E., Slone, M. R., & Reynolds, C. (2018). Beyond ageist attitudes: Researchers call for NIH action to limit funding for older academics. *The Gerontologist, 58* (2), 251–260. https://doi.org/10.1093/geront/gnw190

Kahana, B., Yu, J., Kahana, E., & Langendoerfer, K. (2018). Whose advocacy counts in shaping elderly patients' satisfaction with physicians' care and communication?. *Clinical Interventions in Aging, 13*, 1161–1168. https://doi.org/10.2147/CIA.S165086

Kapoor, H., & Kaufman, J. C. (2020). Meaning-making through creativity during COVID-19. *Frontiers in Psychology, 11*, 1–8. https://doi.org/10.3389/fpsyg.2020.595990

Kaufman, A. S., Johnson, C. K., & Liu, X. (2008). A CHC theory-based analysis of age differences on cognitive abilities and academic skills at ages 22 to 90 years. *Journal of Psychoeducational Assessment, 26*(4), 350–381. https://doi.org/10.1177/0734282908314108

Kessler, E. M., & Staudinger, U. M. (2009). Affective experience in adulthood and old age: The role of affective arousal and perceived affect regulation. *Psychology & Aging, 24*(2), 349–362. https://doi.org/10.1037/a0015352

Kotwal, A. A., Holt-Lunstad, J., Perissinotto, C. M. (2021). Social isolation and loneliness among San Francisco Bay Area older adults during the COVID-19 shelter-in-place orders. *Journal of the American Geriatrics Society, 69*(1), 20–29. https://doi.org/10.1111/jgs.16865

Kunzmann, U., Kupperbusch, C. S., & Levenson, R. W. (2005). Behavioral inhibition and amplification during emotional arousal: A comparison of two age groups. *Psychology & Aging, 20*(1), 144–158. https://doi.org/10.1037/0882-7974.20.1.144

Lam, J., & García-Román, J. (2020). Solitary day, solitary activities, and associations with well-being among older adults. *The Journals of Gerontology: Series B, 75* (7), 1585–1596. https://doi.org/10.1093/geronb/gbz036

Lawton, M. P. (1985). The elderly in context: Perspectives from environmental psychology and gerontology. *Environment and Behavior, 17*(4), 501–519. https://doi.org/10.1177/0013916585174005

Lawton, M. P., Kleban, M., Rajagopal, D., & Dean, J. (1992). Dimensions of affective experience in three age groups. *Psychology & Aging, 7*(2), 171–184. https://doi.org/10.1037/0882-7974.7.2.171

Liang, J., & Luo, B. (2012). Toward a discourse shift in social gerontology: From successful aging to harmonious aging. *Journal of Aging Studies, 26*(3), 327–334. https://doi.org/10.1016/j.jaging.2012.03.001

Liu, Y., Wang, Z., & Lü, W. (2013). Resilience and affect balance as mediators between trait emotional intelligence and life satisfaction. *Personality and Individual Differences, 54*(7), 850–855. https://doi.org/10.1016/j.paid.2012.12.010

Magai, C. (2008). Long-lived emotions: A lifecourse perspective on emotional development. In J. M. Haviland-Jones, & L. F. Barrett (Eds.), *Handbook of Emotions* (pp. 376–392). Guilford Press.

Magai, C., Consedine, N. S., & McPherson, R. (2006). Emotion experience and expression across the adult life span: Insights from a multimodal assessment study.

Psychology and Aging, 21(2), 303–317. http://dx.doi.org/10.1037/0882-7974.21
.2.303

Malinen, S., & Johnston, L. (2013). Workplace ageism: Discovering hidden bias. *Experimental Aging Research, 39*(4), 445–465. https://doi.org/10.1080/0361073X.2013.808111

Mayer, J. D., Caruso, D. R., & Salovey, P. (1999). Emotional intelligence meets traditional standards for an intelligence. *Intelligence, 27*(4), 267–298. https://doi.org/10.1016/S0160–2896(99)00016-1

Mayer, J. D., Caruso, D. R., & Salovey, P. (2016). The ability model of emotional intelligence: Principles and updates. *Emotion Review, 8*(4), 290–300. https://doi.org/10.1177/1754073916639667

Mechanic, D. (1996). Changing medical organization and the erosion of trust. *The Milbank Quarterly, 74*(2), 171–189. https://doi.org/3350245

Mienaltowski, A. (2011). Everyday problem solving across the adult life span: solution diversity and efficacy. *Annals of the New York Academy of Sciences, 1235,* 75–85. https://doi.org/10.1111/j.1749-6632.2011.06207.x

Nadler, A. (1991). Help-seeking behavior: Psychological costs and instrumental benefits. In M. S. Clark (Ed.), *Prosocial Behavior* (pp. 290–311). Sage.

Neubauer, A. C., & Freudenthaler, H. H. (2005). Models of emotional intelligence. In R. Schultz & R. D. Roberts (Eds.), *Emotional Intelligence: An International Handbook* (pp. 31–50). Hogrefe.

Pauly, T., Chu, L., & Hoppmann, C. A. (2022). COVID-19, time to oneself, and loneliness: Creativity as a resource. *The Journals of Gerontology: Series B, 77* (4), e30–e34. https://doi.org/10.1093/geronb/gbab070

Pennebaker, J. W. (ed.) (1995). *Emotion, Disclosure, and Health.* American Psychological Association. https://doi.org/10.1037/10182-000

Petrides, K. V. (2011). Ability and trait emotional intelligence. In T. Chamorro-Premuzic, A. Furnham & S. von Stumm (Eds.), *The Blackwell-Wiley Handbook of Individual Differences* (pp. 654–678). Wiley.

Pope, N. D., Kolomer, S., & Glass, A. P. (2012). How women in late midlife become caregiversfor their aging parents. *Journal of Women & Aging, 24*(3), 242–261. https://doi.org/10.1080/08952841.2012.639676

Portocarrero, F. F., Gonzalez, K., & Ekema-Agbaw, M. (2020). A meta-analytic review of the relationship between dispositional gratitude and well-being. *Personality and Individual Differences, 164,* 1–14. https://doi.org/10.1016/j.paid.2020.110101

Radwan, E., Radwan, A., & Radwan, W. (2020). Challenges facing older adults during the COVID-19 outbreak. *European Journal of Environment and Public Health, 5*(1), 1–6. https://doi.org/10.29333/ejeph/8457

Reese, H. W., Lee, L. J., Cohen, S. H., & Puckett, J. M. (2001). Effects intellectual variables, ages, and gender on divergent thinking in adulthood. *International Journal of Behavioral Development, 25,* 491–500. https://doi.org/10.1080/01650250042000483

Roberts, R. D., Zeidner, M., & Matthews, G. (2001). Does emotional intelligence meet traditional standards for an intelligence? Some new data and conclusions. *Emotion, 1*(3), 196–231. https://doi.org/10.1037/1528-3542.1.3.196

Rosenbaum, M. (1990). The role of learned resourcefulness in the self-control of health behavior. In M. Rosenbaum (Ed.), *Learned Resourcefulness: On Coping Skills, Self-Control, and Adaptive Behavior* (pp. 3–30). Springer.

Rowe, J. W., & Kahn, R. L. (1997). Successful aging. *The Gerontologist, 37*(4), 433–440. https://doi.org/10.1093/geront/37.4.433

Rowe, J. W., & Kahn, R. L. (1998). *Successful Aging*. Pantheon Books.

Salovey, P., Bedell, B. T., Detweiler, J. B., & Mayer, J. D. (1999). Coping intelligently: Emotional intelligence and the coping process. In C. Snyder (Ed.), *Coping: The Psychology of What Works* (pp. 141–164). Oxford University Press.

Salovey, P., & Mayer, J. D. (1990). Emotional intelligence. *Imagination, Cognition and Personality, 9*(3), 185–211. https://doi.org/10.2190/DUGG-P24E-52WK-6CDG

Salthouse, T. A. (2000). Aging and measures of processing speed. *Biological Psychology, 54*(1–3), 35–54. https://doi.org/10.1016/S0301–0511(00)00052-1

Santini, Z. I., Jose, P. E., & Koushede, V. (2020). Social disconnectedness, perceived isolation, and symptoms of depression and anxiety among older Americans: A longitudinal mediation analysis. *The Lancet Public Health, 5*(1), e62–e70. https://doi.org/10.1016/S2468–2667(19)30230-0

Schaie, K. W. (1989). The hazards of cognitive aging. *The Gerontologist, 29*(4), 484–493. https://doi.org/10.1093/geront/29.4.484

Schrack, J. A., Wanigatunga, A. A., & Juraschek, S. P. (2020). After the COVID-19 pandemic: The next wave of health challenges for older adults. *The Journals of Gerontology: Series A, 75*(9), e121–e122. https://doi.org/10.1093/gerona/glaa102

Seckin, G. (2010). Patients as information managers: The internet for successful self-health care & illness management. *Open Longevity Science, 4*(1), 36–42. https://doi.org/10.2174/1876326X01004010036

Sharma, S., & Babu, N. (2017). Interplay between creativity, executive function and working memory in middle-aged and older adults. *Creativity Research Journal, 29*, 71–77. https://doi.org/10.1080/10400419.2017.1263512

Silverstein, M., Gans, D., & Yang, F. M. (2006). Intergenerational support to aging parents: The role of norms and needs. *Journal of Family Issues, 27*(8), 1068–1084. https://doi.org/10.1177/0192513X06288120

Simonton, D. K. (2013). What is a creative idea? Little-c versus Big-C creativity. In J. Chan & K. Thomas (Eds.), *Handbook of Research on Creativity* (pp. 69–83). Edward Elgar. https://doi.org/10.4337/9780857939814.00015

Sims, T., Hogan, C. L., & Carstensen, L. L. (2015). Selectivity as an emotion regulation strategy: Lessons from older adults. *Current Opinion in Psychology, 3*, 80–84. https://doi.org/10.1016/j.copsyc.2015.02.012

Sliter, M., Chen, Y., Withrow, S., & Sliter, K. (2013). Older and (emotionally) smarter? Emotional intelligence as a mediator in the relationship between age and emotional labor strategies in service employees. *Experimental Aging Research, 39*(4), 466–479. https://doi.org/10.1080/0361073X.2013.808105

Smith, M. L., Steinman, L. E., & Casey, E. A. (2020). Combatting social isolation among older adults in a time of physical distancing: the COVID-19 social connectivity paradox. *Frontiers in Public Health, 8*, 1–9. https://doi.org/10.3389/fpubh.2020.00403

Sörensen, S., Hirsch, J. K., & Lyness, J. M. (2014). Optimism and planning for future care needs among older adults. *Journal of Gerontopsychology and Geriatric Psychiatry, 27*, 5–22. https://doi.org/10.1024/1662-9647/a000099

Thomas, V., & Azmitia, M. (2019). Motivation matters: Development and validation of the motivation for solitude scale–short form (MSS-SF). *Journal of Adolescence, 70*, 33–42. https://doi.org/10.1016/j.adolescence.2018.11.004

Timmermans, S., & Almeling, R. (2009). Objectification, standardization, and commodification in health care: A conceptual readjustment. *Social Science & Medicine, 69*(1), 21–27. https://doi.org/10.1016/j.socscimed.2009.04.020

Urry, H. L., & Gross, J. J. (2010). Emotion regulation in older age. *Current Directions in Psychological Science, 19*(6), 352–357. https://doi.org/10.1177/0963721410388395

Van Hooren, S. A. H., Valentijn, A. M., & Jolles, J. (2007). Cognitive functioning in healthy older adults aged 64–81: A cohort study into the effects of age, sex, and education. *Aging, Neuropsychology, and Cognition, 14*(1), 40–54. https://doi.org/10.1080/138255890969483

Willert, B., & Minnotte, K. L. (2021). Informal caregiving and strains: Exploring the impacts of gender, race, and income. *Applied Research in Quality of Life, 16*(3), 943–964. https://doi.org/10.1007/s11482–019-09786-1

Zauszniewski, J. A. (1995). Theoretical and empirical considerations of resourcefulness. *Image: the Journal of Nursing Scholarship, 27*(3), 177–180. https://doi.org/10.1111/j.1547-5069.1995.tb00855.x

Zauszniewski, J. A. (1996). Self-help and help-seeking behavior patterns in healthy elders. *Journal of Holistic Nursing, 14*(3), 223–236. https://doi.org/10.1177/089801019601400305

Zauszniewski, J. (2012). Resourcefulness. In J. J. Fitzpatrick & M. W. Kazer (Eds.), *Encyclopedia of Nursing Research* (3rd ed., pp. 448–449). Springer.

Zauszniewski, J. A., Au, T. Y., & Musil, C. M. (2012). Resourcefulness training for grandmothers raising grandchildren: Is there a need? *Issues in Mental Health Nursing, 33*(10), 680–686. https://doi.org/10.3109/01612840.2012.684424

Zauszniewski, J. A., Chung, C., & Krafcik, K. (2002). Predictors of resourcefulness in school-aged children. *Issues in Mental Health Nursing, 23*(4), 385–401. https://doi.org/10.1080/01612840290052587

Zauszniewski, J. A., Lai, C. Y., & Tithiphontumrong, S. (2006). Development and testing of the resourcefulness scale for older adults. *Journal of Nursing Measurement, 14*(1), 57–68. https://doi.org/10.1891/jnum.14.1.57

Zauszniewski, J. A., Lekhak, N., Yolpant, W., & Morris, D. L. (2015). Need for resourcefulness training for women caregivers of elders with dementia. *Issues in Mental Health Nursing, 36*(12), 1007–1012. https://doi.org/10.3109/01612840.2015.1075236

Zysberg, L. (2012). Loneliness and emotional intelligence. *The Journal of Psychology, 146*(1–2), 37–46. https://doi.org/10.1080/00223980.2011.574746

16 Interpersonal Relationships, Social Emotions, and Creativity

Izabela Lebuda, Aleksandra Zielińska, Dominik Gołąb, and Dorota M. Jankowska

> *To study creativity by focusing on the individual alone*
> *is like trying to understand how an apple tree produces fruit*
> *by looking only at the tree and ignoring*
> *an apple, the sun and the soil that support its life*
>
> Csikszentmihalyi, 1990, p. 202

Creativity as a sociocultural phenomenon is impossible to separate from interpersonal relationships (e.g., Amabile, 1982; Glăveanu et al., 2020; Lebuda & Glăveanu, 2019). Although the myth that creativity is a solitary activity is still present (Benedek et al., 2021), in fact, social interactions, directly or indirectly, influence the creative process and are crucial for creative development—through all stages of life and across all levels of creativity. In this chapter, we focus on the link between creativity and interpersonal relations from processual and developmental perspectives. As the importance of others in the creative process is largely related to the emotions of the creator, we will start with a brief description of the so-called *social emotions* and present their role in creative self-regulation. In the following section, we present the role of the most meaningful social relations in the life span development of creativity. We pay attention to facilitation of creative abilities development, especially in the early stages of life, and their reinforcement in creative activity by shaping creative self-beliefs.

Social Emotions in Self-Regulation of Creative Process

What or who is creative is based on social agreement (e.g., Kasof, 1995; Stein, 1953). Therefore, regardless of the stage of the process—looking for problems, working on ideas, or preparing for one's own or others' evaluation—authors keep in mind socially constructed criteria of creative works. One consequence of being concerned about social expectations and norms is activation of the so-called *social emotions* (Hareli & Parkinson, 2008). What distinguishes social emotions? Seeing that all affects are sensitive to social

The preparation of this chapter was partially supported by grant UMO-2017/27/B/HS6/00592 to Dorota Maria Jankowska from the National Science Center Poland.
Izabela Lebuda was supported by funding from the European Union's Horizon 2020 research and innovation programme under the Marie Sklodowska-Curie grant agreement No 896518.

context and serve as a signal to others, the discussion of borders between social and nonsocial emotions is ongoing (see e.g., Buck, 2014; Hareli & Parkinson, 2008; Sznycer et al., 2021). However, there is common agreement that not all emotions are social to the same extent; social ones are conceptualized as being solely based on social concerns and valuations, such as comparisons or responsibilities toward others (Buck, 2014; Hareli & Parkinson, 2008; Sznycer et al., 2021). They are aroused by an encounter with others, and these others could be real, recalled, anticipated, or even imagined (Leary, 2000, 2004). Admiration, embarrassment, gratitude, guilt, jealousy, shame, and pride are some examples of these kinds of emotions (de Hooge et al., 2018; Harris, 2006; Julle-Danière et al., 2020; Onu et al., 2016; Volling et al., 2002). They serve regulatory functions by signifying the meaning of interpersonal relationships, helping to maintain them, motivating behaviors that lead to socially appreciated outcomes, and helping to avoid social disapproval (Leary, 2004).

From the processual perspective, the role of emotions in creativity, including those evoked by various social circumstances, seems quite apparent. At the beginning of the creative process, both social and nonsocial emotions can be a source of inspiration and excitement; they may encourage people to act creatively from the initial moment or prevent them from doing so. Then, as the creative work unfolds, emotions play at least a twofold role: on the one hand, they drive people to search for new ideas and opportunities, thus spurring to maintain the creative pursuit; on the other, they may hinder the efforts, demotivate, and discourage from continuing the work. Finally, when a creative action ends and the results are ready to be shown, how people feel about what they have achieved may influence their decision to display work effects and motivation to engage in similar creative endeavors in the future. From this view, the creative process is regulated by social emotions.

Most research on the link between emotions and creativity has focused on exploring which emotional states are beneficial for creativity and which may rather suppress creative expression (e.g., Baas et al., 2008; Davis, 2009; De Dreu et al., 2008). Although positive, active, and promotion-related mood states are most likely to enhance creative performance (Baas et al., 2008), the way emotions influence creative work is neither straightforward nor always predictable. Looking for an example, the feelings of affection, compassion, caring, and tenderness for others, often referred to as companionate love, have been found diminishing for creativity as compared to anger that stimulated creative performance (Yang & Hung, 2015).

The complex mood–creativity relationship becomes even more pronounced when the creative process dynamics and social influences are considered. Indeed, different aspects of the same emotions sometimes play opposite roles. For example, while benign envy motivates to self-improvement through seeking and obtaining knowledge, and thus boosts team creativity, malicious envy is rather harmful for group creativity (Chu et al., 2021). Moreover, professionals working in different creative domains perceive various emotional components as both inhibitors and facilitators of the creative process (Botella, 2013).

Therefore, it is crucial to understand how people manage their affective states during a creative action and whether they use emotions to navigate through the complexities of the creative process. Such a perspective that highlights emotions' fluctuations and the resulting necessity to effectively control them is reflected in recent conceptions on self-regulation for creative action (see e.g., Ivcevic & Nusbaum, 2017; Rubenstein et al., 2018; Zielińska & Karwowski, 2022).

Self-regulation is an umbrella term that describes various psychological processes through which people control their thoughts, behaviors, and emotions to achieve a personally relevant goal (Hofmann et al., 2012; Malanchini et al., 2019). It was recently proposed that self-regulation of creative activity resembles self-directed learning and as such, it can be described as a cyclical process wherein various cognitive, metacognitive, motivational, and affective components are at play (Callan et al., 2021; Rubenstein et al., 2018). This self-regulatory repertoire varies across the three phases of guiding the creative process: forethought, performance, and self-reflection. Importantly, though, the ability to monitor and influence one's emotional states, often resulting from environmental and social contingencies (Bandura, 1986; Zimmerman, 2000), is crucial through the entire creative process.

Self-regulation of creative activity differs from managing such other goal-directed behaviors as saving money or running a marathon in two ways. The first is related to uncertainty embedded in the creative process (Beghetto, 2020, 2021). The second refers to the aforementioned social character of creative work (Glăveanu, 2015). Importantly, both characteristics are interrelated and almost directly point to the vital role of social emotions in effective self-regulation for creative action.

Indeed, the uncertain and unforeseeable nature of creative work partially stems from the social context in which creativity occurs. Without an audience (Glăveanu, 2013), a public (Sternberg & Karami, 2022), or simply other people interested in one's work, it is not possible to decide what is creative (i.e., original and meaningful). Participation of others and their informative and regulatory contribution to the creative process (Glăveanu & Lubart, 2014) constitutes the background for making social appraisals and experiencing such emotions as shame, pride, envy, and many others—often specific to a creative domain (Glăveanu et al., 2013). Importantly, though, how such affective states are incorporated in the creative endeavor, whether they hinder or stimulate an undertaken action, refers to the regulation of emotions triggered by social circumstances.

Emotion regulation encompasses monitoring and influencing how emotions are experienced and expressed (Gross, 2014). Going beyond a hedonistic pursuit toward pleasant mood states, people are able to recognize which emotions are most beneficial in a given situation and then change them accordingly (Tamir & Ford, 2012). For example, when facing a creative problem, people high in neuroticism may prefer to recall worrisome rather than happy social situations, which indeed allow them to achieve more creative results (Leung et al., 2014). Sometimes, however, socially relevant feelings may need to be suppressed rather than outwardly manifested in behavior to actually favor creativity. It was indeed demonstrated that shame experiences predict creativity in the organizational context but only when two factors are simultaneously in place: the first is the team environment that supports and cherishes creativity; the second refers to the regulation of shame by inhibiting its expression (González-Gómez & Richter, 2015).

Regulation of social emotions experienced during creative work seems especially important in the end of this process; namely, when presenting the outcomes to others, observing their reactions, and being evaluated. Although both positive and negative feedback may stimulate creativity (Kim & Kim, 2020), even when it is formulated in an angry way (Van Kleef et al., 2010), gaining social recognition is a source of satisfaction and pleasure (Glăveanu et al., 2013). Yet still, showing the results to others runs the risk of being criticized and unaccepted. Therefore, to sustain one's creative efforts despite discouragement, it is crucial to accept the uncertainty regarding the social evaluation of work (Bonetto et al., 2020) and to find ways to stay motivated even when being judged in an unfavorable way. While the role of social validation is the most profound in professional creativity (Lebuda, 2022), the mere willingness to share the effects of one's creative efforts is what characterizes effective self-regulators engaging in everyday creative activities (Zielińska et al., 2022).

In sum, the creative process is regulated *by* social emotions. Participation of other people—be it friends and family members, colleagues and opponents, domain representatives or wider public—in any creative endeavor is a source of social emotions, which in turn influence the course of creative actions. However, given that such influence may be beneficial but also detrimental to one's creative efforts, regulation *of* social emotions embedded in the creative process is the key self-regulatory ability allowing one to persist in an undertaken creative activity.

Significant Others and Creativity Development

Other people indirectly influence creativity by arousing *social emotions* and impact outright by providing support or setting challenges (Gute et al., 2008). Among the numerous social relationships, some are of particular importance for development. People crucial for one's goals and pursuits are called *significant others* (see Moretti & Higgins, 1999; Shah, 2003a). The presence or mental representation of *significant others* affects the standards used in self-evaluation and influences how the results are perceived (e.g., Baldwin, 1994; Shah, 2003b). It is also closely tied to self-concept and self-regulation, thus facilitating or hindering commitment and persistence in task realization. In creativity literature, the *significant others* are assigned to three main groups: predecessors (paragons, masters, and parents), contemporaries (siblings, peers, rivals, collaborators, and romantic partners/spouses), and successors (offspring, apprentices, and admirers) (Simonton, 1984a). But these interpersonal relationships can also be organized into groups linked to crucial areas of life, associated with the central developmental task in each stage of life. At an early age, it would be family in which someone was brought up and education, and later in life, family that someone created and professional domain. As the topics of emotions and social interaction at school are covered in different chapter of the Handbook (Karwowski, in this volume), we focus on family and professional relationships. In the work context, we limit the depiction to the role of significant others. For a discussion on creativity in organizations and team interactions—as these are separate and extensive areas of knowledge—please see Part V in this volume.

Family Interaction Patterns and Creativity Development through the Life Span

A child's interactions with the environment, especially with family members, are a crucial engine of developmental growth and early learning in childhood, contributing to the development of social, emotional, and cognitive competencies (Maccoby, 2000), including creativity (Miller & Gerard, 1979, for a review). Relevant to this development is the quality of interpersonal relationships within a family (Olson et al., 2019). Thus, in recent years, styles of family interactions that promote development of creativity in childhood have been extensively studied by many researchers (e.g., Gralewski & Jankowska, 2020; Guo et al., 2021; Karwowski et al., 2022; Liang & Yuan, 2020; Zhao & Yang, 2021). However, these works are replete with studies of dyadic subsystems within the family (mostly mother–child, less frequently father–child, and sibling interactions). Interestingly, despite the well-accepted dynamic family system framework, such family-level interaction constructs as cohesion, conflict, control, and organization, among others, are used relatively uncommonly (see Gardner & Moran, 1990; Lebuda et al., 2020).

Examining dyadic relationships, two main theoretical models are proposed to explain the family interaction patterns that contribute to the development of a child's creativity (Guo et al., 2021). The first is rooted in autonomy-supportive parenting theory (Rogers, 1954) and regards interactions based on emotional warmth that provide psychological safety and freedom (Harrington et al., 1987). Given that this sense of safety and freedom is established when parents are not only responsive and sensitive, but also skillfully combine parental stimulation and support (Rathunde, 1996), a number of studies have found that a constructive parenting style (most often authoritative parenting characterized by high levels of warmth and autonomy encouragements toward the child; see Baumrind, 1967) encourages development of children's creativity (e.g., Gralewski & Jankowska, 2020; Mehrinejad, et al., 2015; Si et al., 2018).

The second contrasting explanation derived from distance-conflicted family theory (Michel & Dudek, 1991) emphasizes the absence of harmony, tensions, and presence of conflicts in family interactions as an impetus for the development of (unintended) independence, autonomy, and creativity. The underlying logic to this argument is that some personality characteristics or coping strategies, such as rich fantasy life or development of creative problem-solving skills, that initially serve as defense mechanisms for the child in response to a conflicted family environment, may lead to creative achievement over time

(Olszewski-Kubilius, 2000). Consistent with these two explanation paths, both balanced family relationships and disharmony within the family system might be associated with the development of creativity in the early stage of life (Guo et al., 2021; Lebuda et al., 2020). Nevertheless, recent research provides suggestive evidence of a more complex relationship between parenting styles and a child's creativity. It turns out that a child's internal locus of control and self-esteem mediate the relationship between parenting styles and a child's creative thinking (Zhao & Yang, 2021); openness to experience plays a mediating role on the effect of parental warmth on a child's creativity; and Machiavellianism is the mediator between the effects of parental rejection on creative activities of the child (Guo et al., 2021).

At the level of the entire family interaction, one of the most frequently used creativity research frameworks is the Circumplex Model of Marital and Family Systems with three central dimensions of the family system (i.e., flexibility, cohesion, and communication) (Olson et al., 2019). In this regard, adaptability (a family's ability to flexibly change its power structure, role relationships, and rules) and control (monitoring of a child's behavior, discipline, and rule-setting) appear to be key family attributes for a child's creativity development. In families with flexible behavior control (Snowden & Christian, 1999) and high adaptability (flexible and even chaotic families), children can make their own mistakes, solve their problems, and learn to form their own ideas, and their creative potential likely develops as a result (Bomba et al., 1991; Gardner & Moran, 1990). Nevertheless, the role of family cohesion (emotional bonding that exists between family members) for a child's creativity continues to be something we do not fully understand. Evidence is mixed and could be a matter of cultural difference. Some findings have shown that high family cohesion is a positive predictor of a child's creativity (Chan, 2005), others do not (Gardner & Moran, 1990). One of the most recent studies on relationships between parents' creativity-related characteristics and family environment dimensions brought interesting results. Parents' creative self-beliefs (i.e., creative self-efficacy and creative personal identity) and their creative activity predicted support for creativity in the family and more generally balanced and satisfying family relationships (Lebuda et al., 2020). These findings underscore the importance of parents' characteristics as predictors of family lifestyle that stimulates the development of children's creative potential and suggest the need for deeper analysis of the social nuances of the family process (see Kwaśniewska et al., 2018).

Any discussion of the relation between family interactions and development of creativity would be incomplete without acknowledging siblings' relationships. In recent decades, research on the siblings' effect on creativity development has focused on structural variables, especially birth order, gender constellation, and age differences (Baer et al., 2005; Gaynor & Runco, 1992; Guo et al., 2018; Yang et al., 2017). Some of these studies compared only-child and non-only-child families (Yang et al., 2017), while other studies compared first-born and later-born children (Baer et al., 2005), and children in different ordinal positions, such as only versus first-, versus middle-, versus later-born (e.g., Gaynor & Runco, 1992), with the majority of them assessing divergent thinking (DT). And although these study results are inconclusive (see e.g., Baer et al., 2005; Gaynor & Runco, 1992), a new meta-analysis that examined the association of birth order and DT showed that first-borns had higher DT scores than later-born children, but non-significant differences were found between middle- and later-born ones (Abdulla Alabbasi et al., 2021).

The most common explanations for the link between birth order and child's creativity relate to (a) parental resources (money, time, parental investment in raising and cognition stimulation) and associated differential parental treatment and (b) sibling interactions. Theoretically, first-borns grow up in a more stimulating environment, receiving 100% of a parents' attention and better parental cognitive stimulation because they don't have to share parental resources at the start of their lives (Zajonc, 2001). On the other hand, if we assume that parental earnings, education level, and parental maturity tend to increase significantly over time, this is beneficial for later-born children. Moreover, later-born children may receive greater cognitive stimulation not only from more educated and aware parents but also from older siblings (Howe & Recchia, 2014).

Currently, a growing number of researchers are challenging findings regarding siblings' effect on creativity, regardless of the adopted interpretation framework of the results. They argue that the effects might have been overestimated due to a number of methodological and conceptual issues of this research, such as relatively small samples sizes or between-family analyses using cross-sectional data (see Baer et al., 2005; Damian & Spengler, 2020). Research examining the relation between birth order and intelligence suggests that results obtained from cross-sectional data might differ systematically from within-family data (Rodgers, 2001). Nonetheless, it should be pointed out that these problems are not only relevant to creativity research but are characteristic of sibling literature in general (Howe & Recchia, 2014). Yet, the literature on creativity still lacks longitudinal studies complemented for example by sibling and parent interviews, structured tasks, play sessions following siblings over time, and understanding of their social worlds. In light of the foregoing, it is concluded that we know relatively little about the role of siblings and their impact on creativity development.

As in the early stages of life, social interactions with parents and siblings are crucial for creativity development, relationships with the partner and one's offspring are undeniably decisive in adult life (see Karwowski & Wiśniewska, 2021). We start by looking at the link between romantic relationships and creativity. Evolutionary psychologists claim that creativity—as an indicator of fitness—plays a crucial role in attracting potential mates (see Varella et al., 2011) and develops as a result of sexual selection (Miller, 2001). It was indeed presented that creative abilities are desired in long- and short-term mating (e.g., Clegg et al., 2008; Griskevicius et al., 2006). Additionally, more creative males declare a greater number of sexual partners (Beaussart et al., 2012; Clegg et al.,

2011; Lange & Euler, 2014; Nettle, 2008); however, this does not translate to reproductive success (Lebuda et al., 2021a). Nevertheless, not only does creativity seem essential to attract or seduce a partner, but it also plays an indispensable role in fostering stability and lasting romantic relationships. Everyday creativity and self-assessed creativity (contrary to the artistic creativity) predict couples' passion, intimacy, and commitment (Campbell & Kaufman, 2017). Furthermore, a creative personality helps bolster romantic passion in established relations (Carswell et al., 2019).

But what do we know about the opposite direction of this relationship—how does romantic involvement influence creativity? Most information on this matter comes from research on professional and eminent creativity. Over the years, as in the case of parenthood, two opposing conclusions were reported. The first concerns the difficulties in combining family life with creativity and points out that achieving success in creative endeavors requires resigning or at least minimizing engagement in personal life. To illustrate this problem—based on the legend of Faust, who sold his soul to the devil for boundless knowledge—the term *Faustian bargain* was coined (Gardner, 1993). It was emphasized that this problem mainly affects women and has a tragic influence on their well-being (Gardner, 1993; Helson, 1999).

The opposite argumentation—that creators have satisfying family lives, and family relationships are vital for creative fulfilment—was also supported (Csikszentmihalyi, 1996; Mockros & Csikszentmihalyi, 2000). A recent analysis helps to untangle this inconsistency, but it also reveals a more complicated picture (Lebuda & Csikszentmihalyi, 2020). It was demonstrated that the relation between creators' professional success and their well-being is related to the perceived obligations of an occupation, as well as gender roles. Based on these beliefs, five types of links between family and creative work were formulated. The first one is called *supported creators* and describes creators who treat their work as social obligations and perceive a romantic partner as an assistant in their efforts. In their opinion, creative achievements are extremely demanding, so emotional support from the close one and help in organizing other life areas are necessary. The second type is *solitary creators* and characterizes people who are totally devoted to their work and temporarily resign from private life. In the other three types, creators see their profession as a choice, not superior to family life. *Professional creators* see the family–work mesosystems as complementary to each other and try to balance them. *After-hours creators* take care of their creative endeavors after fulfilling duties associated with different life roles. And the last type is *non-stop creators*—those who see creativity as a lifestyle, inseparable from family life and totally mixed with it. Even though all types of creators pointed to the tension between family relationships and professional tasks, each of them, except the *solidary creator*, presented romantic significant other as a source of unconditional acceptance, security, and belonging, and highly value their support, particularly during creative breakthroughs (Lebuda & Csikszentmihalyi, 2020).

Some of the challenges of balancing family life and creative development relate to parental obligations. Above, we have described a parent's role in their child's creative development, but obviously, parenthood influences the development of adults' creativity (see Dillon, 2002). It was presented that especially in the case of women, there are constant struggles to combine creative pursuit, especially at a professional level, with the role of child-caretaker (Ciciola-Izzo, 2014; Miller, 2010). And women creators, more often than their male peers, resign into having offspring (Gardner, 1993; Simonton 1999). On the other hand, in professional artistic creativity, offspring were presented as a source of inspiration and boost for the development of creative potential (Kirschenbaum & Reis, 1997).

Moreover, people often perceive parenthood as changing their style of thinking, enhancing their cognitive flexibility, and thus making them more creative and motivated to act creatively on a daily basis (Dillon, 2002). Interviews with mothers who value creativity clearly demonstrated that their striving to balance professional and personal life is manageable thanks to adopting creativity as a lifestyle (Kwaśniewska & Lebuda, 2017). They primarily fulfilled their creativity needs in family life, but in the professional context, they also expressed their creative potential by finding new ways of dealing with work challenges. It seems that the relationship between parenthood and creativity is reciprocal: providing nurturing presents challenges that may spur creativity, but a creative approach is also necessary to balance all duties from different areas of life (Dillon, 2002; Kwaśniewska & Lebuda, 2017).

However, based on the research conducted so far, little is known about the dynamics of partnership and parental relationships in the context of creative abilities development in adulthood. Therefore, longitudinal studies—which would allow for observing the dynamic changes over the course of the relationship while children grow up—seem to be particularly needed (see Helson & Pals, 2000). Finally, it also seems warranted to recommend looking beyond heteronormative, traditional marriages as well as employing a broader definition of family, for example by including grandparents, stepparents, and stepsiblings in research.

Professional Significant Others and Creative Self-Concept Development

Finally, we look at the role played by professional significant others in developing creativity in adult life. It was presented that being part of a professional network is essential for beginners, as well as career creators (Eubanks et al., 2016). Additionally, in the case of eminent creators, professional relations—particularly with paragons, rivals, associates, apprentices, and admirers—are even more impactful than the intimate one (Simonton, 1984a). Mentors play a crucial role in building the professional social network into a domain (Feist, 2006; Mumford et al., 2005; Torrance, 1983). Having a mentor is associated with a higher number of creative achievements (Torrance, 1983) and having eminent mentors often links to the mentee's higher achievements (Simonton, 1992; Zuckerman, 1996). The mentors' role is vital at the beginning of a creative career (Eubanks et al., 2014; Mumford et al., 2005). They support gaining new competencies, encourage taking the risk, and endure socialization into the domain. Irreplaceably, they ensure introduction to the field and convey tacit knowledge about unwritten rules of behavior and work (Csikszentmihalyi, 1996). The relation with a mentor—a person acclaimed by a domain—is essential in shaping the creative self-concept of young creators (Getzels & Csikszentmihalyi, 1976; Lebuda & Csikszentmihalyi, 2017). Acknowledgment of abilities and achievements by more experienced individuals enhances self-efficacy, provides a sense of belonging in the domain, and shapes, confirms, or enriches professional identity (Hung et al., 2008; Lebuda, 2022). To safeguard the positive influence of mentorship, the character of relations should be taken into consideration. In creative disciplines, the so-called *horizontal mentoring* (Keinänen & Gardner, 2004) is by far the most efficient. This kind of a relation is democratic in that the mentor lets the mentee explore and only assists and provides support mainly in the moments of necessity, ensuring a sense of security (see Eubanks et al., 2014).

Peers (collaborators as well as competitors) are the other work-related group of significant others. Colleagues provide intellectual stimulation and social support (Mumford et al., 2005). Acceptance from a reference group develops the sense of professional identity and helps establish career goals and set standards, but it also creates a context for the creator's own uniqueness (Haslam et al., 2013; Mockros & Csikszentmihalyi, 2000). Group belonging helps deal with challenging experiences and creative occupational uncertainty, such as constant assessment and unclear criteria of excellence (see Beghetto in this volume; Lebuda, 2022). The sense of being part of a creative group or organization could be strengthened by comparisons to main rivals and competitors (see Lebuda, 2016). Significant others, who are in a competitive relationship, help to reinforce assumptions about own creativity and have critical motivational functions (see Clydesdale, 2006). Moreover, competition and cooperation are often entwined. When creators co-work, in some aspects, they try to outperform one another, which could be a source of advancement and innovation at work (Abra, 1993; Gardner, 1993).

The role of younger generation apprentices and admirers increases in later career stages. Their attention confirms the lasting significance of the creators in the field and proves that expertise and experience of established creators are up-to-date and still desirable. The bond with successors provides a sense of continuity of the selected creative tradition, and at the same time, constitutes an inspiration to update and broaden horizons in a chosen area (Lebuda & Csikszentmihalyi, 2017). However, at this point, we do not know much more about the importance of experienced creators for the younger generation.

The role of significant others in the development of professional creativity contributes to intellectual exchange, social support, and shape of professional self-image. The last point is critical, because social validation, constant in creative work, could confirm but also shake the creative self-concept (Glăveanu & Tanggaard, 2014; Lebuda, 2022). Both attention and support from significant others as well as direct validation of the work play a crucial role in confirming creative self-beliefs.

Summary

Interpersonal relationships influence creative activity and development via various mechanisms, such as activating social emotions, creating the supporting environment, as well as, concurrently, independence and a sense of belonging and security. Social bonds are essential for facilitation of creativity skills, expression of creativity-related traits (e.g., openness to experiences, persistence, curiosity), and shaping creative self-beliefs: inviting to view creativity as necessary for fulfilling personal and professional roles and enhancing creative self-confidence (Kwaśniewska et al., 2018; Lebuda & Csikszentmihalyi, 2017). Creative self-concept is required to move from potential to creative behavior. To invest time and energy into creative challenges—in spite of an uncertain chance for success—one needs to value creativity but also believe in one's own skill to deal with the problem (Karwowski & Beghetto, 2019; Lebuda et al., 2021b). From early years through the entire life span, significant others, by direct information, by their own example, and by arranging context for creative success, strengthen the creator's creative self-beliefs.

However, we should not romanticize the link between social interactions and creativity and keep in mind that not all emotions and the social relations significant for creativity are pleasant. For example, jealousy and rivalry—even though they are usually undesirable—in specific circumstances can facilitate creative action and stimulate transgressive work (e.g., Baer et al., 2010; Chu et al., 2021). There are also many challenges and opposing forces to reconcile. To mention only a few, in the creative process, authors need to decide how to respond to social expectations, referral group norms, and mentors' teachings, and at the same time break the existing rules to be original, and create their own independence without being rejected (Rietzschel et al., 2010; Simonton, 1984b). What is more, matching personal creative needs with professional and family obligations could be equally satisfying and stressful. Even though looking for a way to balance many life roles may enhance creativity skills, for example, flexibility of thinking, it may also raise the risk of negligence of the actual, usually time-consuming creative activity.

To better comprehend the above struggles and stimulate creative growth more effectively, we need a closer look at the social interactions at each level and stage of creative development. More dynamic, longitudinal, and micro-longitudinal research is required to understand the role of social emotions in the creative process. In measuring emotions, it is worth to consider going beyond respondent declarations and analyzing indirect indications of emotional arousals, such as facial expression, pupil dilation, skin conductance, also with the employment of increasingly popular wearables (e.g., Dzedzickis et al., 2020; Schmidt et al., 2019). This type of data could give more objective and precise information about emotion fluctuation without interrupting the creative process.

We also see an urgent need for further research dedicated to significant others in creativity development. Notably, by using longitudinal research designs, adopting broader definitions of family (e.g., patchwork family), and observing how people reconcile work with family life, we could provide a more comprehensive picture of modern reality, thus extending our knowledge about social aspects of creative development meaningfully. In following this research direction, scholars may benefit from combining qualitative and quantitative data as well as using primary and secondary data sources. While data triangulation is relatively rare in creativity research (see Jankowska et al., 2018; Katz-Buonincontro et al., 2020 for some exceptions), we see great potential in using this approach to explore the complex and dynamic interactions between creativity, emotions, and interpersonal relationships.

References

Abdulla Alabbasi, A. M., Tadik, H., Acar, S., & Runco, M. A. (2021). Birth order and divergent thinking: A meta-analysis. *Creativity Research Journal*, 331–346. https://doi.org/10.1080/10400419.2021.1913559

Abra, J. (1993). Competition: Creativity's vilified motive. *Genetic, Social and General Psychology Monographs, 119*, 291–343.

Amabile, T. M. (1982). Social psychology of creativity: A consensual assessment technique. *Journal of Personality and Social Psychology, 43*, 997–1013.

Baas, M., De Dreu, C. K. W., & Nijstad, B. A. (2008). A meta-analysis of 25 years of mood-creativity research: Hedonic tone, activation, or regulatory focus? *Psychological Bulletin, 134*(6), 779–806. https://doi.org/10.1037/a0012815

Baer, M., Leenders, R. T. A. J., Oldham, G. R., & Vadera, A. K. (2010). Win or lose the battle for creativity: The power and perils of intergroup competition. *Academy of Management Journal, 53*(4), 827–845. https://doi.org/10.5465/AMJ.2010.52814611

Baer, M., Oldham, G. R., Hollingshead, A. B., & Jacobsohn, G. C. (2005). Revisiting the birth order-creativity connection: The role of sibling constellation. *Creativity Research Journal, 17*, 67–77. https://doi.org/10.1207/s15326934crj1701_6

Baldwin, M. W. (1994). Primed relational schemas as a source of self-evaluative reactions. *Journal of Social and Clinical Psychology, 13*, 380–403. https://doi.org/10.1521/jscp.1994.13.4.380

Bandura, A. (1986). *Social Foundations of Thought and Action: A Social Cognitive Theory*. Prentice-Hall.

Baumrind, D. (1967). Child care practices anteceding three patterns of preschool behavior. *Genetic Psychology Monographs, 75*, 43–88.

Beaussart, M., Kaufman, S., & Kaufman, J. (2012). Creative activity, personality, mental illness, and short-term mating success. *The Journal of Creative Behavior, 46*, 151–167. https://doi.org/10.1002/jocb.11

Beghetto, R. A. (2020). Uncertainty. In *The Palgrave Encyclopedia of the Possible* (pp. 1–7). Springer International. https://doi.org/10.1007/978-3-319-98390-5_122–1

Beghetto, R. A. (2021). There is no creativity without uncertainty: Dubito Ergo Creo. *Journal of Creativity, 31*, 100005.

Benedek, M., Karstendiek, M., Ceh, S., et al. (2021). Creativity myths: Prevalence and correlates of misconceptions on creativity. *Personality and Individual Differences, 182*, 111068. https://doi.org/10.1016/j.paid.2021.111068

Bonetto, E., Pichot, N., Pavani, J.-B., & Adam-Troïan, J. (2020). Creative individuals are social risk-takers: Relationships between creativity, social risk-taking and fear of negative evaluations. *Creativity. Theories – Research – Applications, 7*, 309–320. https://doi.org/10.2478/ctra-2020-0016

Botella, M. (2013). How artists create: Creative process and multivariate factors. *Learning and Individual Differences, 10*. https://doi.org/10.1016/j.lindif.2013.02.008

Bomba, A. K., Moran, J. D., & Goble, C. B. (1991). Relationship between familial style and creative potential of preschool children. *Psychological Reports, 68*, 1323–1326. https://doi.org/10.2466/PR0.68.4.1323-1326

Buck, R. (Ed.). (2014). Social emotions. In *Emotion: A Biosocial Synthesis* (pp. 246–295). Cambridge University Press. https://doi.org/10.1017/CBO9781139049825.011

Callan, G. L., Rubenstein, L. D., Ridgley, L. M., Neumeister, K. S., & Finch, M. E. H. (2021). Self-regulated learning as a cyclical process and predictor of creative problem-solving. *Educational Psychology, 41*(9), 1139–1159. https://doi.org/10.1080/01443410.2021.1913575

Campbell, K., & Kaufman, J. (2017). Do you pursue your heart or your art? Creativity, personality, and love. *Journal of Family Issues, 38*, 287–311. https://doi.org/10.1177/0192513X15570318

Carswell, K. L., Finkel, E. J., & Kumashiro, M. (2019). Creativity and romantic passion. *Journal of Personality and Social Psychology, 116*(6), 919–941. https://doi.org/10.1037/pspi0000162

Chan, D. W. (2005). Self-perceived creativity, family hardiness, and emotional intelligence of Chinese gifted students in Hong Kong. *Journal of Secondary Gifted Education, 16*, 47–56. https://doi.org/10.4219/jsge-2005-471

Chu, F., Zhang, W., Wu, S., & Liu, G. (2021). How does individual-level envy affect team creativity? Effects of knowledge seeking and moral reflection. *SAGE Open, 11*(4), 215824402110525. https://doi.org/10.1177/21582440211052554

Ciciola-Izzo, R. (2014). Mother/Art: A Journey into Selfhood, Motherhood and Art Education through Personal Works. MA thesis. Concordia University, Montreal.

Clegg, H., Nettle, D., & Miell, D. (2008). A test of Miller's aesthetic fitness hypothesis. *Journal of Evolutionary Psychology, 6*, 101–115. https://doi.org/10.1556/jep.2008.1009

Clegg, H., Nettle, D., & Miell, D. (2011). Status and mating success amongst visual artists. *Frontiers in Psychology, 2*, Article 310. https://doi.org/10.3389/fpsyg.2011.00310

Clydesdale, G. (2006). Creativity and competition: The Beatles. *Creativity Research Journal, 18*, 2, 129–139. https://doi.org/10.1207/s15326934crj1802_1

Csikszentmihalyi, M. (1990). *Flow: The Psychology of Optimal Experience*. Harper and Row.

Csikszentmihalyi, M. (1996). *Creativity: Flow and the psychology of discovery and invention*. HarperCollins.

Damian, R. I., & Spengler, M. (2020). Negligible effects of birth order on selection into scientific and artistic careers, creativity, and status attainment. *European Journal of Personality, 35*(6), 775–796. https://doi.org/10.1177/0890207020969010

Davis, M. A. (2009). Understanding the relationship between mood and creativity: A meta-analysis. *Organizational Behavior and Human Decision Processes, 108* (1), 25–38. https://doi.org/10.1016/j.obhdp.2008.04.001

De Dreu, C. K. W., Baas, M., & Nijstad, B. A. (2008). Hedonic tone and activation level in the mood-creativity link: Toward a dual pathway to creativity model. *Journal of Personality and Social Psychology, 94*, 739–756. https://doi.org/10.1037/0022-3514.94.5.739

de Hooge, I. E., Breugelmans, S. M., Wagemans, F. M. A., & Zeelenberg, M. (2018). The social side of shame: Approach versus withdrawal. *Cognition and Emotion, 32*(8), 1671–1677. https://doi.org/10.1080/02699931.2017.1422696

Dillon, J. J. (2002). The role of the child in adult development. *Journal of Adult Development, 9*, 267–275. https://doi.org/10.1023/A:1020286910678

Dzedzickis, A., Kaklauskas, A., & Bucinskas, V. (2020). Human emotion recognition: Review of sensors and methods. *Sensors, 20*(3), 592. https://doi.org/10.3390/s20030592

Eubanks, D. L., Palanski, M. E., Swart, J., Hammond, M. M., & Oguntebi, J. (2014). Creativity in early and established career: Insights into multi-level drivers from Nobel Prize winners. *The Journal of Creative Behavior, 50*, 229–251. https://doi.org/10.1002/jocb.70

Feist, G. J. (2006). *The Psychology of Science and the Origins of the Scientific Mind*. Yale University Press.

Gardner, H. (1993). *Creating Minds: An Anatomy of Creativity Seen through the Lives of Freud, Einstein, Picasso, Stravinsky, Eliot, Graham, and Gandhi*. Basic Books.

Gardner, K. G., & Moran, J. D. (1990). Family adaptability, cohesion, and creativity. *Creativity Research Journal, 3*, 281–286. https://doi.org/10.1080/10400419009534361

Gaynor, J., & Runco, M. (1992). Family size, birth-order, age-interval, and the creativity of children. *Journal of Creative Behavior, 26*, 108–118. https://doi.org/10.1002/j.2162-6057.1992.tb01166.x

Getzels, J. W., & Csikszentmihalyi, M. (1976). *The Creative Vision: A Longitudinal Study of Problem Finding in Art*. John Wiley & Sons.

Glăveanu, V. P. (2013). Rewriting the language of creativity: The five A's framework. *Review of General Psychology, 17*, 69–81. https://doi.org/10.1037/a0029528

Glăveanu, V. P. (2015). Creativity as a sociocultural act. *The Journal of Creative Behavior, 49*, 165–180. https://doi.org/10.1002/jocb.94

Glăveanu, V. P., Hanchett Hanson, M., Baer, J., et al. (2020). Advancing creativity theory and research: A Socio-cultural manifesto. *The Journal of Creative Behavior, 54*, 741–745. https://doi.org/10.1002/jocb.395

Glăveanu, V. P., & Lubart, T. (2014). Decentring the creative self: How others make creativity possible in creative professional fields: Decentring the creative self.

Creativity and Innovation Management, 23, 29–43. https://doi.org/10.1111/caim
.12049

Glăveanu, V., Lubart, T., Bonnardel, N., et al. (2013). Creativity as action: Findings
from five creative domains. *Frontiers in Psychology, 4*. https://doi.org/10.3389/
fpsyg.2013.00176

Glăveanu, V. P., & Tanggaard, L. (2014). Creativity, identity, and representation:
Towards a socio-cultural theory of creative identity. *New Ideas in
Psychology, 34*, 12–21. https://doi.org/10.1016/j.newideapsych.2014.02.002

González-Gómez, H. V., & Richter, A. W. (2015). Turning shame into creativity: The
importance of exposure to creative team environments. *Organizational
Behavior and Human Decision Processes, 126*, 142–161. https://doi.org/10
.1016/j.obhdp.2014.09.004

Gralewski, J., & Jankowska, D. M. (2020). Do parenting styles matter? Perceived
dimensions of parenting styles, creative abilities and creative self-beliefs in
adolescents. *Thinking Skills and Creativity, 38*, 100709. https://doi.org/10
.1016/j.tsc.2020.100709

Griskevicius, V., Cialdini, R., & Kenrick, D. (2006). Peacocks, Picasso, and parental
investment: The effects of romantic motives on creativity. *Journal of
Personality and Social Psychology, 91*, 63–76. https://doi.org/10.1037/0022-
3514.91.1.63

Gross, J. J. (2014). Emotion regulation: Conceptual and empirical foundations. In
Handbook of Emotion Regulation (2nd ed., pp. 3–20). Guilford Press.

Guo, J., Lin, S., & Guo, Y. (2018). Sex, birth order, and creativity in the context of
China's one-child policy and son preference. *Creativity Research Journal, 30*,
361–369.

Guo, J., Zhang, J., & Pang, W. (2021). Parental warmth, rejection, and creativity: The
mediating roles of openness and dark personality traits. *Personality and
Individual Differences, 168*, 110369. https://doi.org/10.1016/j.paid.2020.110369

Gute, G., Gute, D. S., Nakamura, J., & Csikszentmihalyi, M. (2008). The early lives of
highly creative persons: The influence of the complex family. *Creativity
Research Journal, 4*, 343–357. https://doi.org/10.1080/10400410802391207

Hareli, S., & Parkinson, B. (2008). What's social about social emotions? *Journal for the
Theory of Social Behaviour, 38*, 131–156. https://doi.org/10.1111/j.1468-5914
.2008.00363.x

Harrington, D. M., Block, J. H., & Block, J. (1987). Testing aspects of Carl Rogers's
theory of creative environments: Child-rearing antecedents of creative potential
in young adolescents. *Journal of Personality and Social Psychology, 52*,
851–856. https://doi.org/10.1037/0022-3514.52.4.851

Harris, C. R. (2006). Embarrassment: A form of social pain: This enigmatic emotion
likely evolved to smooth social interactions, but it can have less desirable
consequences in the modern world. *American Scientist, 94*, 524–533. www
.jstor.org/stable/27858867

Haslam, S. A., Adarves-Yorno, I., Postmes, T., & Jans, L. (2013). The collective origins
of valued originality: A social identity approach to creativity. *Personality and
Social Psychology Review, 17*(4), 384–401. https://doi.org/10.1177/
1088868313498001

Helson, R. (1999). A longitudinal study of creative personality in women. *Creativity
Research Journal, 12*, 89–101. https://doi.org/10.1207/s15326934crj1202_2

Helson, R., & Pals, J. L. (2000). Creative potential, creative achievement, and personal growth. *Journal of Personality, 68*(1), 1–27. https://doi.org/10.1111/1467-6494.00089

Hofmann, W., Schmeichel, B. J., & Baddeley, A. D. (2012). Executive functions and self-regulation. *Trends in Cognitive Sciences, 16*, 174–180. https://doi.org/10.1016/j.tics.2012.01.006

Howe, N., & Recchia, H. (2014). Sibling relationships as a context for learning and development. *Early Education and Development, 25*, 155–159. https://doi.org/10.1080/10409289.2014.857562

Hung, S., Huang, H., & Lin, S. S. J. (2008). Do significant others' feedback influence one's creative behavior? – Using structural equation modeling to examine creativity self-efficacy and creativity motivation mediation effect. *Bulletin of Educational Psychology, 2*, 321–338.

Ivcevic, Z., & Nusbaum, E. C. (2017). From having an idea to doing something with it: Self-regulation for creativity. In M. Karwowski & J. C. Kaufman (Eds.), *The Creative Self: Effects of Beliefs, Self-Efficacy, Mindset, and Identity* (pp. 343–365). Academic Press. https://doi.org/10.1016/B978-0-12-809790-8.00020-0

Jankowska, D. M., Czerwonka, M., Lebuda, I., & Karwowski, M. (2018). Exploring the creative process: Integrating psychometric and eye-tracking approaches. *Frontiers in Psychology, 9*, 1931. https://doi.org/10.3389/fpsyg.2018.01931

Julle-Danière, E., Whitehouse, J., Vrij, A., Gustafsson, E., & Waller, B. M. (2020). The social function of the feeling and expression of guilt. *Royal Society Open Science, 7*, 200617. https://doi.org/10.1098/rsos.200617

Karwowski, M., & Beghetto, R. A. (2019). Creative behavior as agentic action. *Psychology of Aesthetics, Creativity, and the Arts, 13*, 402–415. https://doi.org/10.1037/aca0000190

Karwowski, M., Jankowska, D. M., Lebuda, I., & Czerwonka, M. (2022). Do parents and children perceive creativity similarly? A dyadic study of creative mindsets. *Psychology of Aesthetics, Creativity, and the Arts, 16*(2), 233–241. https://doi.org/10.1037/aca0000358

Karwowski, M., & Wiśniewska, E. (2021). Creativity in adulthood. In J. D. Hoffman, S. W. Russ, and J. C. Kaufman (Eds.), *The Cambridge Handbook of Lifespan Development of Creativity* (pp. 206–232). Cambridge University Press. https://doi.org/10.1017/9781108755726.013

Kasof, J. (1995). Explaining creativity: The attributional perspective. *Creativity Research Journal, 8*, 311–366. https://doi.org/10.1207/s15326934crj0804_1

Katz-Buonincontro, J., Hass, R., & Perignat, E. (2020). Triangulating creativity: Examining discrepancies across self-rated, quasi-expert-rated and verbalized creativity in arts-based learning. *The Journal of Creative Behavior, 54*(4), 948–963. https://doi.org/10.1002/jocb.424

Keinänen, M., & Gardner, H. (2004). Vertical and horizontal mentoring for creativity. In R. J. Sternberg, E. L. Grigorenko, & J. L. Singer (Eds.), *Creativity from Potential to Realization* (pp. 169–193). American Psychological Association. https://doi.org/10.1037/10692-010

Kim, Y. J., & Kim, J. (2020). Does negative feedback benefit (or harm) recipient creativity? The role of the direction of feedback flow. *Academy of Management Journal, 63*, 584–612. https://doi.org/10.5465/amj.2016.1196

Kirschenbaum, R. J., & Reis, S. M. (1997). Conflicts in creativity: Talented female artists. *Creativity Research Journal, 10,* 251–263. https://doi.org/10.1080/10400419.1997.9651224

Kwaśniewska, J. M., Gralewski, J., Witkowska, E. M., Kostrzewska, M., & Lebuda, I. (2018). Mothers' personality traits and the climate for creativity they build in the relationship with their children. *Thinking Skills and Creativity, 27,* 13–24. https://doi.org/10.1016/j.tsc.2017.11.002

Kwaśniewska, J. M., & Lebuda, I. (2017). Balancing between the roles and duties – creativity of mothers. *Creativity. Theories – Research – Applications, 4,* 137–158. https://doi.org/10.1515/ctra-2017-0007

Lange, B., & Euler, H. (2014). Writers have groupies, too: High quality literature production and mating success. *Evolutionary Behavioral Sciences, 8,* 20–30. https://doi.org/10.1037/h0097246

Leary, M. R. (2000). Affect, cognition, and the social emotions. In J. P. Forgas (Ed.), *Feeling and Thinking: The Role of Affect in Social Cognition* (pp. 331–356). Cambridge University Press.

Leary, M. R. (2004). Digging deeper: The fundamental nature of "self-conscious" emotions. *Psychological Inquiry, 15,* 129–131. www.jstor.org/stable/20447215

Lebuda, I. (2016). Political pathologies and Big-C creativity – eminent polish creators' experience of restrictions under the communist regime. In V. P. Glăveanu (Ed.), *The Palgrave Handbook of Creativity and Culture Research* (pp. 329–354). Palgrave MacMillan. https://doi.org/10.1057/978-1-137-46344-9_16

Lebuda, I. (2022). (Un)certain relation between social validation and creators' self-concept. In R. A. Beghetto & G. J. Jaeger (Eds.), *Uncertainty: A Catalyst for Creativity, Learning and Development* (pp. 269–291). Springer.

Lebuda, I., & Csikszentmihalyi, M. (2017). Me, myself, I, and creativity: Self-concepts of eminent creators. In M. Karwowski & J. C. Kaufman (Eds.), *The Creative Self: Effect of Beliefs, Self-Efficacy, Mindset, and Identity* (pp. 137–152). Elsevier Academic Press. https://doi.org/10.1016/B978-0-12-809790-8.00008-X

Lebuda, I., & Csikszentmihalyi, M. (2020). All you need is love: The importance of partner and family relations to highly creative individuals' well-being and success. *The Journal of Creative Behavior, 54,* 100–114. https://doi.org/10.1002/jocb.348

Lebuda, I., & Glăveanu, V. P. (2019). Re/searching the social in creativity, past, present and future: An introduction to the Palgrave Handbook of Social Creativity Research. In I. Lebuda & V. P. Glăveanu (Eds.), *The Palgrave Handbook of Social Creativity Research* (pp. 1–10). Palgrave Macmillan. https://doi.org/10.1007/978-3-319-95498-1_1

Lebuda, I., Jankowska, D. M., & Karwowski, M. (2020). Parents' creative self-concept and creative activity as predictors of family lifestyle. *International Journal of Environmental Research and Public Health, 17,* 9558. https://doi.org/10.3390/ijerph172495

Lebuda, I., Sorokowski, P., Groyecka, A., et al. (2021a). Creation and procreation: Creative ability and reproductive success outside the WEIRD world. *Creativity Research Journal, 33*(3), 255–263. https://doi.org/10.1080/10400419.2020.1870816

Lebuda, I., Zielińska, A., & Karwowski, M. (2021b). On surface and core predictors of real-life creativity. *Thinking Skills and Creativity, 42.* https://doi.org/10.1016/j.tsc.2021.1009

Leung, A. K. y., Liou, S., Qiu, L., et al. (2014). The role of instrumental emotion regulation in the emotions–creativity link: How worries render individuals with high neuroticism more creative. *Emotion, 14*, 846–856. https://doi.org/10.1037/a0036965

Liang, C.-C., & Yuan, Y.-H. (2020). Exploring children's creative self-efficacy affected by after-school program and parent–child relationships. *Frontiers in Psychology, 11,* 2237. https://doi.org/10.3389/fpsyg.2020.02237

Maccoby, E. E. (2000). Parenting and its effects on children: On reading and misreading behavior genetics. *Annual Review of Psychology, 51*, 1–27. https://doi.org/10.1146/annurev.psych.51.1.1

Mockros, C.A., & Csikszentmihalyi, M. (2000). The social construction of creative lives. In A. Montuori & R. E. Purser (Eds.), *Social Creativity* (vol. 1, pp. 175–219). Hampton Press. https://doi.org/10.1007/978-94-017-9085-7_9

Malanchini, M., Engelhardt, L. E., Grotzinger, A. D., Harden, K. P., & Tucker-Drob, E. M. (2019). "Same but different": Associations between multiple aspects of self-regulation, cognition, and academic abilities. *Journal of Personality and Social Psychology, 117*, 1164–1188. https://doi.org/10.1037/pspp0000224

Mehrinejad, S. A., Rajabimoghadam, S., & Tarsafi, M. (2015). The relationship between parenting styles and creativity and the predictability of creativity by parenting styles. *Procedia – Social and Behavioral Sciences, 205*, 56–60. https://doi.org/10.1016/j.sbspro.2015.09.014

Michel, M., & Dudek, S. Z. (1991). Mother-child relationships and creativity. *Creativity Research Journal, 4*(3), 281–286. https://doi.org/10.1080/10400419109534400

Miller, B. C., & Gerard, D. (1979). Family influences on the development of creativity in children: An integrative review. *The Family Coordinator, 28*, 295. https://doi.org/10.2307/581942

Miller, G. (2001). Aesthetic fitness: How sexual selection shaped artistic virtuosity as a fitness indicator and aesthetic preferences as mate choice criteria. *Bulletin of Psychology and the Arts, 2*, 20–25.

Miller, G. W. (2010). Mothering and creativity. In A. O'Reilly (Ed.), *Encyclopedia of Motherhood* (pp. 832–834). Sage. https://dx.doi.org/10.4135/9781412979276.n442

Moretti, M. M., & Higgins, E. T. (1999). Internal representations of others in self-regulation: A new look at a classic issue. *Social Cognition, 17*, 186–208. https://doi.org/10.1521/soco.1999.17.2.186

Mumford, M. D., Connelly, M. S., Scott, G., et al. (2005). Career experiences and scientific performance: A study of social, physical, life, and health sciences. *Creativity Research Journal, 17*, 105–129. https://doi.org/10.1207/s15326934crj1702&3_1

Nettle, D. (2008). Why is creativity attractive in a potential mate? *Behavioral and Brain Sciences, 31*, 275–276. https://doi.org/10.1017/S0140525X08004366

Olson, D. H., Waldvogel, L., & Schlieff, M. (2019). Circumplex model of marital and family systems: An update. *Journal of Family Theory & Review, 11*, 199–211. https://doi.org/10.1111/jftr.12331

Olszewski-Kubilius, P. (2000). The transition from childhood giftedness to adult creative productiveness: Psychological characteristics and social supports. *Roeper Review, 23*, 65–71. https://doi.org/10.1080/02783190009554068

Onu, D., Kessler, T., & Smith, J. R. (2016). Admiration: A conceptual review. *Emotion Review, 8*(3), 218–230. https://doi.org/10.1177/1754073915610438

Rathunde, K. (1996). Family context and talented adolescents' optimal experience in school-related activities. *Journal of Research on Adolescence, 6*, 605–628.

Rietzschel, E., Nijstad, B., & Stroebe, W. (2010). The selection of creative ideas after individual idea generation: Choosing between creativity and impact. *British Journal of Psychology, 101*, 47–68. https://doi.org/10.1348/000712609X414204

Rodgers, J. L. (2001). What causes birth order–intelligence patterns? The admixture hypothesis, revived. *American Psychologist, 56*, 505–510. https://doi.org/10.1037/0003-066X.56.6-7.505

Rubenstein, L. D., Callan, G. L., & Ridgley, L. M. (2018). Anchoring the creative process within a self-regulated learning framework: Inspiring assessment methods and future research. *Educational Psychology Review, 30*, 921–945. https://doi.org/10.1007/s10648–017-9431-5

Schmidt, P., Reiss, A., Dürichen, R., & Laerhoven, K. V. (2019). Wearable-based affect recognition – A review. *Sensors, 19*(19), 4079. https://doi.org/10.3390/s19194079

Shah, J. (2003a). Automatic for the people: How representations of significant others implicitly affect goal pursuit. *Journal of Personality and Social Psychology, 84*, 661–681. https://doi.org/10.1037/0022-3514.84.4.661

Shah, J. (2003b). The motivational looking glass: How significant others implicitly affect goal appraisals. *Journal of Personality and Social Psychology, 85*, 424–439. https://doi.org/10.1037/0022-3514.85.3.424

Si, S., Zhang, S., Yu, Q., & Zhang, J. (2018). The interaction of DRD2 and parenting style in predicting creativity. *Thinking Skills and Creativity, 27*, 64–77. https://doi.org/10.1016/j.tsc.2017.11.001

Simonton, D. K. (1984a). Artistic creativity and interpersonal relationships across and within generations. *Journal of Personality and Social Psychology, 6*, 1273–1286.

Simonton, D. K. (1984b). *Genius, Creativity, and Leadership: Histriometric Inquiries.* Harvard University Press.

Simonton, D. K. (1992). Leaders of American psychology, 1879–1967: Career development, creative output, and professional achievement. *Journal of Personality and Social Psychology, 62*, 5–17. https://doi.org/10.1037/0022-3514.62.1.5

Simonton, D. K. (1999). *Origins of Genius: Darwinian Perspectives on Creativity.* Oxford University Press.

Snowden, P. L., & Christian, L. G. (1999). Parenting the young gifted child: Supportive behaviors. *Roeper Review, 21*, 215–222. https://doi.org/10.1080/02783199909553964

Stein, M. I. (1953). Creativity and culture. *Journal of Psychology, 36*, 311–322. https://doi.org/10.1080/00223980.1953.9712897

Sternberg, R. J., & Karami, S. (2022). An 8P theoretical framework for understanding creativity and theories of creativity. *The Journal of Creative Behavior, 56*(1), 55–78. https://doi.org/10.1002/jocb.516

Sznycer, D., Sell, A., & Lieberman, D. (2021). Forms and functions of the social emotions. *Current Directions in Psychological Science, 30*(4), 292–299. https://doi.org/10.1177/09637214211007451

Tamir, M., & Ford, B. Q. (2012). When feeling bad is expected to be good: Emotion regulation and outcome expectancies in social conflicts. *Emotion, 12*, 807–816. https://doi.org/10.1037/a0024443

Torrance, E. P. (1983). Role of mentors in creative achievement. *The Creative Child and Adult Quarterly, 8*, 8–16.

Van Kleef, G. A., Anastasopoulou, C., & Nijstad, B. A. (2010). Can expressions of anger enhance creativity? A test of the emotions as social information (EASI) model. *Journal of Experimental Social Psychology, 46,* 1042–1048. https://doi .org/10.1016/j.jesp.2010.05.015

Varella, M., de Souza, A., & Ferreira, J. (2011). Evolutionary aesthetics and sexual selection in the evolution of rock art aesthetics. *Rock Art Research, 28,* 153–163.

Volling, B. L., McElwain, N. L., & Miller, A. L. (2002). Emotion regulation in context: The jealousy complex between young siblings and its relations with child and family characteristics. *Child Development, 73,* 581–600. https://doi.org/10.1111/ 1467-8624.00425

Yang, J., Hou, X., Wei, D., et al. (2017). Only-child and non-only-child exhibit differences in creativity and agreeableness: Evidence from behavioral and anatomical structural studies. *Brain Imaging and Behavior, 11,* 493–502. https://doi .org/10.1007/s11682-016-9530-9

Yang, J.-S., & Hung, H. V. (2015). Emotions as constraining and facilitating factors for creativity: Companionate love and anger: Emotions as constraining and facilitating factors for creativity. *Creativity and Innovation Management, 24,* 217–230. https://doi.org/10.1111/caim.12089

Zajonc, R. B. (2001). Birth order debate resolved? *American Psychologist, 56*(6–7), 522–523. https://doi.org/10.1037/0003-066X.56.6-7.522

Zhao, H., & Yang, J. (2021). Fostering creative thinking in the family: The importance of parenting styles. *Thinking Skills and Creativity, 41,* 100920. https://doi.org/ 10.1016/j.tsc.2021.100920

Zielińska, A., & Karwowski, M. (2022). Living with uncertainty in creative process: A self-regulatory perspective. In R. A. Beghetto & G. J. Jaeger (Eds.), *Uncertainty: A Catalyst for Creativity, Learning and Development.* Springer.

Zielińska, A., Lebuda, I., Ivcevic, Z., & Karwowski, M. (2022). How adolescents develop and implement their ideas? On self-regulation of creative action. *Thinking Skills and Creativity, 43,* 100920. https://doi.org/10.1016/j.tsc.2022 .100998

Zimmerman, B. J. (2000). Attaining self-regulation: A social cognitive perspective. In M. Boekaerts, P. R. Pintrich, & M. Zeidner (Eds.), *Handbook of Self-Regulation* (pp. 13–39). Academic Press. https://doi.org/10.1016/B978–012109890-2/ 50031-7

Zuckerman, H. (1996). *Scientific Elite: Nobel Laureates in the United States.* The Free Press. https://doi.org/10.1177/027046769701700446

PART IV

Emotions and Creative Products

17 Emotional Creativity

Emotional Experience as Creative Product

Radek Trnka

Emotional creativity (EC) is an interesting psychological construct that combines creative abilities on one hand and emotional processing on the other. It is a set of cognitive abilities and personality traits related to originality and appropriateness in emotional experience (Averill, 1999; Ivcevic et al., 2007). When considering the four basic stages of the creative process – preparation, incubation, illumination and verification   emotional creativity abilities play an important role at the preparation stage as well as at the verification stage of the creative process (Averill, 1999; Soroa et al., 2015). It supports making connections with the reasons for and consequences of emotional responses at the preparation stage of the creative process and is related to the experience of and expression of novel and original emotions at the verification stage (for more detail, see Averill, 1999).

In the original theoretical conceptualization of EC, three components of EC were distinguished: novelty, preparedness, and effectiveness/authenticity (Averill, 1999). Emotional novelty denotes how a person perceives his or her own emotions as being original, unique, uncommon, and improbable. This ability describes the personal disposition of how a person understands the originality of their own emotional experience. In contrast, emotional preparedness includes thinking about one's own emotional reactions and emotional experiences, searching for the reasons for one's own feelings, as well as paying attention to other people's emotions in an effort to better understand one's own feelings. This dispositional ability is closely related to the processing of emotional life events and memory retrieval of details from emotional life events. Finally, emotional effectiveness/authenticity includes responding effectively in situations requiring new or unusual emotional responses and the tendency to believe that emotions may help to achieve one's life goals. This component is more heterogeneous in comparison to emotional novelty and preparedness and covers the aspects of emotional responding in real life situations as well as deeper personal beliefs about the role of emotions in one's life.

Figure 17.1 provides a more complex view of EC. In the upper cone of this theoretical model, personal dispositions related to EC can be found, namely,

Many thanks to all collaborators who worked, for more than ten years, on our projects focused on emotional creativity and also to the editors for inspiring comments on earlier versions of this chapter.

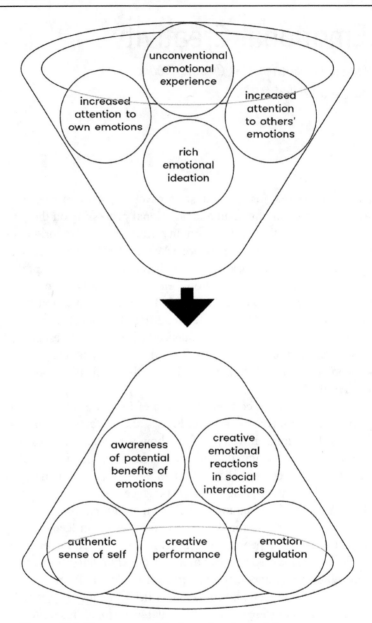

Figure 17.1 *Two-cone model of emotional creativity.*

unconventional emotional experience, rich emotional ideation, increased atten-tion to one's own emotional life, and increased attention to the emotions of others. These personal dispositions are suggested to be underlying "prerequis-ites" of EC. For example, unconventional emotional experience is a disposition to experience highly original emotions in comparison to other people. In other words, this aspect of EC is related to how different an emotional experience is in comparison to the norm (Ivcevic et al., 2017). In contrast, rich emotional ideation is an imaginative disposition and denotes the ability to imagine various instances of hypothetical emotional situations, reactions, episodes, or experiences. Increased attention to one's own emotional life and increased attention to the emotions of others are dispositional aspects of EC closely related to the cognitive style of an individual. These aspects consider the degree to which an individual is accustomed to focusing his or her attention on his or her own emotional life or to the emotions of others. Consistent with the definition of emotional preparedness (Averill, 1999), people who pay increased attention to their own emotions are also suggested to think more about their own emotional reactions and emotional experiences and to search for the reasons for their feelings. This means that focusing attention on emotions is closely linked to more effort to cognitively process one's own emotional experience.

Among the personal dispositions related to EC in the upper cone of the model (Figure 17.1), unconventional emotional experience seems to play a primary role and may also influence other personal dispositions related to EC. For example, it can be expected that a disposition to experience highly original emotions may also attract more attention and thinking about a person's own emotions in the long-term perspective. At the same time, a disposition to experience highly original emotions may also stimulate imaginative ideation related to emotional aspects of life. Together, personal dispositions related to EC in the upper cone are expected to be highly interconnected and to work as a complex in a coherent manner.

In the lower cone of the model (Figure 17.1), there are aspects of EC that represent rather the consequences of personal dispositions related to the EC depicted in the upper cone. The awareness of potential benefits of emotions is a part of the subjective knowledge of how emotions may help one to achieve his or her life goals or improve well-being. This awareness is an outcome of the dispositional aspects of EC, namely, increased attention to one's own emotions, increased attention to others' emotions, and rich emotional ideation. People who pay increased attention to their own emotional life and to the emotions of others and have rich emotional ideation are expected to also have deeper and more diverse awareness of the potential benefits of emotions. This EC-related knowledge, as well as the perceptual information gained from observing others' emotions, may be utilized in social interactions, for example, by the performance of creative emotional reactions that respond suitably to the actual development of a social interaction.

Furthermore, personal dispositions related to EC depicted in the upper cone are also suggested to influence creative performance. An unconventional emotional life and rich emotional imagination may in particular stimulate creativity during creative performance. These dispositions for being emotionally creative are considered to be resources for the creative process. People who have an unconventional emotional life and a rich emotional imagination may utilize these resources in creative production (e.g., artistic creative production or development of problem-focused creative solutions).

Unconventional emotional experience may also support an authentic sense of self. EC is generally suggested to involve the dispositions to be genuine and sincere (Ivcevic et al., 2017). This indicates that one's reaction accurately reflects one's inner feelings, meaning they are therefore authentic. However, it is necessary to point out that accuracy in reflecting one's own inner feelings cannot alone predict high EC, because even though the reactions of an individual may accurately reflect his/her inner feelings, the individual may indeed have an ordinary emotional life in comparison to others.

Increased attention to one's own emotions can also be expected to influence emotion regulation. For example, people who pay increased attention to their own emotions may detect emotional feelings earlier and start to regulate these feelings more effectively, if necessary. However, sometimes increased attention to one's own emotions may also be maladaptive. For example, people who ruminate too much about their past failures may experience more stress and unpleasant feelings.

From the perspective of cognitive psychology, EC is linked to both exploratory and generative cognitive processes (Trnka et al., 2020). The experience of an unusual combination of discrete emotions, a variety of different emotions at the same time, or responding to emotional situations with original emotional reactions all are abilities that require cognitive flexibility in generative processes. In contrast, creative thinking about past emotional reactions and experiences is closely linked to exploratory cognitive processes. During cognitive processing of a new emotional event, a subject tries to ascribe sense to this emotional event by categorizing it. The conceptual knowledge of the subject involves prototypical categories of emotional events built on the basis of events that the subject experienced in the past. By seeking the common attributes of a new emotional event with the prototypical categories of emotional events, the subject constructs the subjective meaning of the new emotional event. Highly emotionally creative people have a rich past emotional life, and they are even suggested to have a more differentiated spectrum of prototypical categories of emotional events in their conceptual knowledge about emotions. High EC thus enables more flexibility in the conceptual interpretation of past emotional events due to the presence of more differentiated prototypical categories in the conceptual knowledge about emotions, which provide a broader and more fine-grained basis for exploratory cognitive processing of emotional events.

The construct of EC is relatively young (Averill, 1999) and its investigation is in dynamic progress. The Emotional Creativity Inventory (ECI, Averill, 1999) is the only available trait measure of EC at present. The ECI consists of 30 items rated on a 5-point scale divided into three subscales: Preparedness, Novelty, and Effectiveness/Authenticity. A recent meta-analysis examined the reliability of use of the ECI across past empirical studies (total n = 5,479) and revealed excellent generalized reliability for the ECI total score and very good, generalized reliabilities for all three of its subscales: Preparedness, Novelty, and Effectiveness/Authenticity (Kuška et al., 2020).

Aside from the ECI, there are also two ability measures of EC, the Emotional Consequences test and the Emotional Triads test (Averill & Thomas-Knowles, 1991). In the Emotional Consequences test, participants are presented with emotionally salient hypothetical situations and are asked to produce various possible consequences. In the Emotional Triads test, participants are given four sets of three dissimilar emotions and are asked to imagine a situation in which all three feelings would occur simultaneously. Responses from the tasks are then scored by external evaluators using the Consensual Assessment Technique.

This chapter aims to provide an overview of research conducted on EC. At the beginning, EC is introduced in the context of its relationships to basic personality traits and everyday behavior. The chapter then shows how EC and other cognitive creative abilities are mutually related. The next subsection explains how EC varies with age and how EC is related to age-related cognitive changes in older adulthood. The subsequent subsections then describe the gender differences found in EC and introduce research on EC within the applied and clinical contexts. Finally, current promising avenues for future research on EC are outlined.

Emotional Creativity, Personality, and Everyday Behavior

Past research explored how EC relates to basic personality traits. The ECI has been positively correlated with openness to experience (Averill, 1999, Study 3; Ivcevic et al., 2007; Luke & Zychowicz, 2014), with agreeableness (Averill, 1999, Study 3), and with hope and positive affectivity (Sharma & Mathur, 2016). The correlation found between EC and openness to experience in particular was quite strong (Averill, 1999), and this finding was also replicated in the study of Ivcevic et al. (Study 3, 2007). It is not clear whether openness to experience is a key ingredient in EC or whether EC independently predicts behavioral creativity in cases when the creative product involves the direct expression of emotion (e.g., during artistic creative activities (Ivcevic et al., 2007)). However, for persons high in openness to experience, involvement in creative activities is suggested to be internally satisfying, because engagement in creative activities is in accordance with their openness to new experience trait.

Research investigating real-life involvement in creative leisure-time activities revealed that higher EC was related to five of the seven proposed types of creative hobbies (Trnka et al., 2016). Specifically, real-life engagement in creative writing (poems, prose, or blogs), painting, composing music or music improvisation, performing drama (i.e., dance improvisation or theatrical improvisation), and do-it-yourself activities (i.e., handmade production of material creative products for daily use) was found to be significantly related to higher EC in participants (Trnka et al., 2016). In contrast, making creative sculptures or ceramics and any kind of inventing were found to be unrelated to EC. Ivcevic et al. (2007) suggested that emotional abilities play a significant role in creativity only when the products express emotional content. This may explain why inventing was found to be unrelated to EC. Even though inventing definitely requires creative cognition and possibly also divergent thinking, its products are often practically oriented and do not involve emotional content.

Emotional Creativity and Other Cognitive Creative Abilities

Research on the relationship of EC and cognitive creative abilities involving divergent thinking has thus far brought inconsistent results. Past studies used either a trait measure of EC (i.e., the ECI (Alzoubi et al., 2021; Martsksvishvili et al., 2017; Zenasni & Lubart, 2008), or both the ECI and ability measures of EC (Study 1, Ivcevic et al., 2007).

Starting with a study that utilized only a trait measure of EC, Alzoubi et al. (2021) found a positive relationship between EC and the ability to generate novel unfamiliar associations to stimuli words. In this study, the participants were required to find another word that can be associated with the stimuli words in a meaningful way. All three components of EC were found to predict creative performance in this experiment. In contrast, EC was not found to be related to the ability to produce original and useful ideas about the potential uses of common objects in a study by Martsksvishvili et al. (2017). Nor was any direct link between EC and divergent thinking creative performances found when participants were asked to generate unusual uses for a cardboard box and generate unusual ideas when imagining what would happen if there were no traffic in their city (Zenasni & Lubart, 2008).

Let us turn our attention to the results of a study that used both the trait measure as well as the ability measures of EC (Study 1, Ivcevic et al., 2007). This study explored how EC relates to the ability to generate possible consequences of hypothetical situations and the ability to make connections between distant ideas when associating with similar semantic meaning to stimuli words. The trait emotional novelty was found to be positively correlated with both creative event consequences and remote associations, whereas the trait emotional preparedness and the trait effectiveness/authenticity were not. This study also involved two ability measures of EC, Emotional Consequences and Emotional Triads (Averill & Thomas-Knowles, 1991). The cognitive ability measured by the Emotional Triads task (i.e., the ability to imagine a situation in which a combination of three dissimilar emotions would be experienced simultaneously) was found to be unrelated to the above-mentioned cognitive creativity measures. The cognitive ability measured by the Emotional Consequences task (i.e., the ability to produce various possible consequences to hypothetical emotional situations) was found to be related to the ability to generate the possible consequences of hypothetical situations measured by the Torrance Tests of Creative Thinking (Torrance, 1974) but was unrelated to the ability to make connections between distant ideas when associating with similar semantic meaning to stimuli words (Study 1, Ivcevic et al., 2007).

Furthermore, the study of Gutbezahl and Averill (1996) examined the relations between EC and artistic creativity. In this case, the participants drew pictures of discrete emotions. Participants with higher EC used a more expressionistic style: that is, they used color and space more creatively and represented emotions in a symbolic, nonfigurative way. In contrast, less emotionally creative participants used a more pictographic style: that is, they used figurative forms and articulated the story through pictures.

A further question is: how is EC related to emotional intelligence (EI), the set of abilities related to emotional processing that appears to be quite similar to EC? EI is defined as the ability to perceive emotions accurately, use emotions to enhance thinking, understand and label emotions, and regulate emotions in the self and others (Mayer & Salovey, 1997). Empirical evidence shows that EI and EC are distinct but related abilities (Ivcevic et al., 2007). The main difference lies in the engagement of convergent and divergent thinking in EI and EC. EI requires convergent thinking and the solving of emotional problems. This includes accurate recognition, reflection, and regulation of the subject's emotions in order to cope more successfully with negative feelings or maintain or increase positive feelings. In contrast to EI, EC requires divergent thinking and the generation of an appropriate, but also original, response. EC often involves manipulation and transformation of the subject's emotional experience to deal with an emotional problem or challenge.

Age-Related Changes in Emotional Creativity

The levels of EC have been found to differ with age. A cross-sectional study involving younger, midlife, and older adults revealed that age was negatively associated with the ECI total score and two of the three ECI components, emotional novelty and emotional preparedness (Trnka et al., 2020). In contrast, age was not associated with emotional effectiveness/authenticity. This ECI component was found to be constant across adulthood (Figure 17.2).

When taking a closer look at these age-related differences, the lower emotional preparedness in older age implies a decreased tendency to think about one's emotional reactions and emotional experiences and to search for reasons for one's own feelings in older adulthood. These results are in accordance with the more flexible and emotionally mature functioning of older adults (Blanchard-Fields, 2007, 2009). This advantage is suggested to be reached due to the accumulation of experience with various emotions during the life course. Investing less effort into thinking about one's own and other's emotions may be an adaptive strategy enabling cognitive resources to be saved in older adulthood (Trnka et al., 2020).

The accumulation of experience with varied emotional events with aging may also explain the other finding, that is, why older adults perceive their emotions as less unique, novel, and uncommon than younger adults (Figure 17.2). In other words, the older the participants were, the weaker was their tendency to evaluate their emotions as novel and unique (Trnka et al., 2020). Older people are expected to have met with more emotional episodes during their lives, and this experience may also cause lower emotional novelty in older age compared to younger age. Repeated experience of similar emotional events may lead to future utilization of patterns and scripts from previously experienced emotional

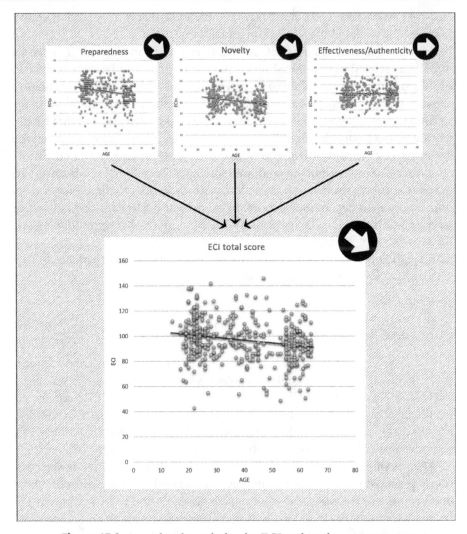

Figure 17.2 *Age-related trends for the ECI and its three components: Preparedness, Novelty, and Effectiveness/Authenticity. (Source: Trnka et al., 2020)*

episodes stored in memory, which may explain the decreased emotional novelty in older adulthood.

The weakened tendency to evaluate emotions as novel and unique in older adulthood is also in accordance with the decrease of the trait openness to experience in older adulthood (Lucas & Donnellan, 2009; Roberts et al., 2006). As mentioned above in this chapter, openness to experience is a trait highly correlated with trait EC. A meta-analysis of longitudinal studies (Roberts et al., 2006) revealed that the trait openness to experience started to decrease after the age of 55 years but interestingly increases from adolescence to middle adulthood. In contrast to these findings, the trait emotional novelty was found to be highest in adolescents and lowest in older adults (Figure 17.2).

In contrast to decreased emotional novelty and emotional preparedness in older age, emotional effectiveness/authenticity was found to be constant across adulthood. This component of EC includes effective responding in situations requiring new or unusual emotional responses and the tendency to believe that emotions may help a person achieve his or her life goals. Because longitudinal research on EC has been lacking, these insights may inspire future longitudinal studies of EC.

Interestingly, the levels of EC were found to be sensitive to the degree of age-related cognitive decline. For example, older adults with more apathy were less emotionally creative than older adults with less apathy (Trnka et al., 2019). Increased apathy is an indicator of cognitive decline caused by worsened functioning of the frontal-subcortical brain circuits in older adulthood (Grace & Malloy, 2001). As apathy is linked with symptoms such as unconcern, loss of interest, or lack of energy, the lower levels of EC in more apathic older adults is not surprising.

However, some findings in this area are very interesting. Older adults with more cognitive deficits in inhibitory control were found to have higher EC compared to older adults without cognitive deficits in inhibitory control (Trnka et al., 2019). In this study, the deficits in inhibitory control were measured in line with the conception of Grace and Malloy (2001), that is as a decreased cognitive control of emotions given by worsened functioning of the frontal-subcortical brain circuits in older adulthood. Cognitive deficits in inhibitory control are expressed by behavioral hallmarks, such as irritability, emotional lability, sudden emotional outbursts, disinhibited emotional expressions, or increased swearing. It is possible that the experience of disinhibited emotional reactions may represent a source of novelty for older adults (Trnka et al., 2019). As disinhibited emotional expressions involve irritability, emotional lability, and frequent sudden emotional outbursts (Grace & Malloy, 2001; Prado-Jean et al., 2010; Zuidema et al., 2009), the experience of such emotional reactions may be perceived as a divergence from common experience and may stimulate the cognitive processing of emotional events. For this reason, deficits in inhibitory control may surprisingly also lead to increased EC compared to older adults without such inhibitory deficits (Trnka et al., 2019).

It is important to note that older adults are otherwise considered to show some improvements in controlling their emotions in late age (see Scheibe & Carstensen, 2010; Urry & Gross, 2010). However, when age-related changes in the brain start, they perform lesser levels of cognitive control of emotions (Opitz et al., 2012), which may explain the findings mentioned above.

Interestingly, higher EC related to deficits in inhibitory control in older adults (Trnka et al., 2019) is also in line with research in other domains of creativity. For example, diminished inhibitory control in cognitive functioning was found to cause more creative performance in creative tasks in older adults compared to younger adults (Carpenter et al., 2020; Kim et al., 2007). These experiments involved distractions, and older adults were found to generate more creative solutions when exposed to distracting information. In the context of EC, disinhibited emotional expressions, such as sudden emotional outbursts or increased swearing, may be considered to play the role of an emotional distractor for a person. Such emotional distractions may focus the subject's attention on their emotional reactions more and also stimulate more thinking about emotional events.

Gender Differences in Emotional Creativity

A meta-analysis covering the available nine empirical studies presenting gender differences revealed that women tend to be more emotionally creative than men (Kuška et al., 2020). The total sample size was 3,555 participants and involved samples from studies that varied in sample sizes as well as the countries where the research was conducted (Figure 17.3). All of these studies measured EC as a trait using the ECI (Averill, 1999).

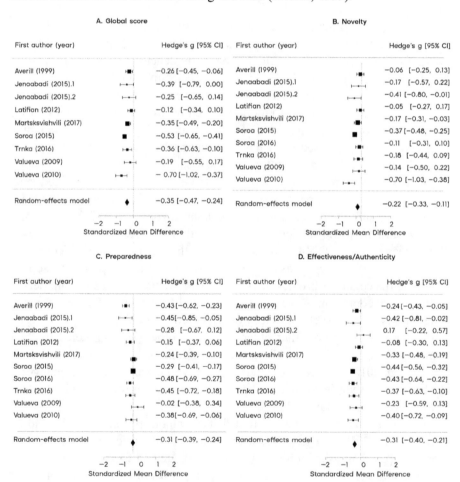

Figure 17.3 *Summarization of gender differences in EC from past studies. Negative values mean higher scores in women than in men. (Source: Kuška et al., 2020)*

This meta-analysis identified higher ECI total scores in women than in men and also showed that women scored higher in all three subscales – Novelty, Preparedness, and Effectiveness/Authenticity (Figure 17.3). Let us take a closer look at these gender differences found from the perspective of the three main trait components of EC. From the perspective of emotional novelty, women were found to perceive their own emotions as more original, unique, uncommon, and improbable when compared to men. From the perspective of emotional preparedness, women also reported thinking more about their own emotional reactions and emotional experiences and searching for the reasons for their own feelings. They also pay more attention to other people's emotions than men in an effort to better understand their own feelings. The higher scores of women in the authenticity/effectiveness component indicate that women respond more effectively in situations requiring new or unusual emotional responses and have a stronger belief that emotions may help in achieving one's own life goals.

Emotional Creativity in Applied Settings

There are few studies exploring the role of EC in applied contexts. Wang et al. (2015) explored EC in both employees and their supervisors in 18 commercial enterprises in China. The organizations were engaged in the management of electronic information and technologies focused on resources, environmental, and new materials. The participants were employed in production, marketing, research and development, and management activities. The results showed that high EC had significant positive effects on the innovative performance of employees. This relationship was moderated by the employees' intrinsic motivation and supervisors' support for creativity. The authors interpreted the results such that EC enhances the employees' self-efficacy and motivation for engagement in future innovative performance, because it stimulates innovative activities and solutions that are in accordance with the needs of organizations. High EC is suggested to be a very desirable personality trait, especially in positions with high uncertainty, such as research and development, front service reception, service, and sales. Thus, assessing EC is generally recommended during the selection of applicants for these positions.

Song (2016) explored EC, professional identity, teaching efficacy, and their relationships to the leadership style of teachers' supervisors in college English teachers. The leadership style of supervisors was measured as the degree of "paternalistic leadership." Paternalistic leadership is a fatherlike leadership style in which strong authority is combined with concern and considerateness. Taken together, a stronger paternalistic leadership style among supervisors and the teachers' EC were found to have a moderating effect on the teaching efficacy of teachers. At the same time, this moderating effect was found to be mediated via the teachers' professional identity (covering professional competence, behavior, and emotions). Based on these results, the following recommendations for organizational and university leaders were formulated: (a) strengthen the ability of staff members at the management level to handle their emotions; (b) encourage staff members to improve their EC, such as making time for regular emotional management; (c) suggest that staff members take part in psychological counseling training; (d) improve staff members' ability to deal with their emotions; and (e) strengthen staff members' ability to express themselves in innovative ways.

The role of EC in applied settings has evidently been studied only rarely thus far. The above-mentioned studies have brought first very interesting findings, but this field is still waiting for further exploration in the future.

Emotional Creativity in Clinical Practice

Interestingly, the construct of EC seems to have quite big potential to be utilized in clinical psychological assessment. Already in 2007 (Fuchs et al., 2007), EC was found to be negatively related to alexithymia (the inability to identify, describe, and express one's own emotions). This study was conducted on a general sample of students, not on a clinical population sample. Less emotionally creative participants also reported higher dispositional alexithymia.

Furthermore, EC was investigated in the context of psychodiagnostics of neurodegenerative diseases. Early diagnosis of neurodegenerative diseases via neuropsychological assessment is highly desirable because psychic changes often occur before the apparent motor symptoms are detectable. Early diagnosis of neurodegenerative diseases supports the efficacy of further treatment and the possibility of decelerating the development of degenerative changes in patients. Because EC was found to be related to cognitive decline in a sample of healthy older adults (Trnka et al., 2019), it was plausible to ask if changes in EC could be detected in early stages of some neurodegenerative diseases that are also accompanied by cognitive decline. This idea was explored on patients suffering from Parkinson's disease (PD), a progressive neurodegenerative disease affecting the nerve cells in the brain that produce dopamine (Nikolai et al., 2022). PD is characterized by cardinal motor symptoms, such as tremor, bradykinesia, and muscular rigidity, as well as a wide range of non-motor symptoms (e.g., cognitive deficit, apathy, or anhedonia: a reduced ability to experience pleasure). Both PD patients and healthy controls underwent a complex neuropsychological assessment and were administered the ECI. PD patients showed lower scores in the cognitive tests and a lower score in emotional preparedness compared to healthy adults (Table 17.1). The decreased emotional preparedness in PD patients indicates that PD influences processes such as thinking about one's emotional reactions and emotional experiences and paying attention to other people's emotions (Nikolai et al., 2022). Interestingly, the trait measure of EC was found to be uncorrelated to most neuropsychological tests for monitoring cognitive functions. It seems that the

Table 17.1 *Differences in the ECI components between patients suffering from Parkinson's disease and healthy controls (Source: Nikolai et al., 2022)*

	HC (*n* = 40)		**PD** (*n* = 22)				
	M±SD	*(min-max)*	*M±SD*	*(min-max)*	*Z*	*p*	r_b
Preparedness	25.5±5.1	(14–35)	20.6±4.6	(11–29)	−3.41	**0.001**	**−0.525**
Novelty	39.4±8.7	(20–57)	37.5±7.4	(26–55)	−1.00	0.317	−0.155
Effectiveness/ Authenticity	29.6±4.6	(19–38)	27.3±4.9	(18–38)	−1.92	0.055	−0.295

Note. HC – healthy controls; PD – Parkinson's disease; *M* – arithmetic mean; *SD* – standard deviation; *Z* – test statistic of the Mann-Whitney test. The *p* is for the *p*-value of the Mann-Whitney test. The *p*-values for significant differences are marked in bold. r_b is the rank-biserial correlation representing the effect size (absolute values close to zero represent no effect, 0.3 is considered as a threshold for the medium effect and 0.5 as a threshold for a strong effect).

levels of trait EC could be a distinctive diagnostic marker of patients' emotional functioning, independent of other measures of cognitive functions (Nikolai et al., 2022). This study opens up an area for future psychodiagnostic use of the construct of EC in clinical practice.

EC was also examined in relation to the degree of schizotypy of participants (Holt et al., 2008). Schizotypal traits include being warily apprehensive, watchful, and suspicious, being alienated from the self and others, having a sense of strangeness and nonbeing, and feeling to be bland, barren, indifferent, and insensitive. Schizotypal traits indicate a greater trait disposition toward schizophrenia and are suggested to increase the risk of future development of psychopathology, such as Schizotypal Personality Disorder (Claridge, 1997). The study of Holt et al. (2008) distinguished between several types of schizotypal personality: high schizotypes (scoring highly on cognitive disorganization and introvertive anhedonia, i.e., a reduced ability to experience pleasure), negative schizotypes (reporting only introvertive anhedonia), positive schizotypes (reporting only unusual experiences, such as hallucinations, paranormal ideation, or psychopathological delusion), and low schizotypes. High schizotypes and positive schizotypes were also found to show higher trait EC. These results indicate that high trait EC could be related to a schizotypal personality involving the use of nonlinear cognition, cognitive disorganization, and impulsive nonconformity (disinhibited and impulse-ridden characteristics). At the same time, high trait EC was also found to be related to "positive schizotypal" personality with a disposition to hallucinations, paranormal ideation, and psychopathological delusion. This study was conducted on a healthy, non-clinical sample of undergraduate and graduate students; thus, research on samples of patients suffering from schizophrenia or other schizotypal disorders is needed in the future.

Emotional Creativity: Future Directions

Currently, the ECI (Averill, 1999) is the most frequently used method for measuring EC. It is a measure based on self-reporting of the subject's inner traits and abilities and provides information about the subject's self-perception of his or her own EC. In other words, it provides insights about how subjects perceive their own emotionally creative behaviors, mental processes, and personality traits. For future possible use of the construct of EC in clinical practice, the development of new performance tests that could measure EC as an ability is needed. Currently, there are two ability measures of EC available, the Emotional Consequences test and the Emotional Triads test (Averill & Thomas-Knowles, 1991). However, the scoring of these tests is based on the Consensual Assessment Technique, which involves evaluations of creative performance by several independent evaluators. This scoring technique can be utilized in experimental research; however, it cannot be used in clinical practice because it is too lengthy and time-demanding. For clinical use of EC, for example, in the context of early psychodiagnosis of neurodegenerative diseases, the validation of EC ability tests in different clinical populations and the establishing of norms for such performance tests for healthy populations are needed. This is an important task for future applied research on EC and methodological development in the field.

In the context of basic research on EC, a further question is whether EC varies from moment to moment. Thus far, EC has been approached and defined as a sum of relatively stable dispositional traits and abilities. However, one may ask if and how EC varies in different creative experimental tasks or different real-life situations. Furthermore, how a subject's actual mood (see Ying et al., 2021) or emotional state may influence the actual levels of EC and how strongly they may influence creative production or performance is not known. When looking back at Figure 17.1 depicting the theoretical model of EC, some possible hypotheses for future research can be developed. First, more creative production can be expected from a subject who has a sufficient actual cognitive capacity available to utilize their dispositional trait EC in creative activity. For example, in the case when a subject's cognitive capacity is loaded by another parallel task or tasks (e.g., work duties or real-life demands unrelated to creative performance), it is less likely to expect a subject to invest as much cognitive effort into emotional ideation, which could possibly influence the degree of subsequent creative performance, despite their trait disposition to rich emotional ideation. Second, it can also be hypothesized that there are more dispositional types in terms of dispositions to unconventional experience. For example, some types of personalities may tend to experience more positive emotions simultaneously, because they are high in trait positive emotionality and generally tend to experience pleasant emotions more frequently than negative ones. In contrast, some other types of personalities may show high trait negative emotionality and tend to experience unpleasant emotions more frequently across various real-life situations. It can be hypothesized that trait positive emotionality may positively interact with EC and together support more creative performance compared to trait negative emotionality. The experience of positive emotions was found to broaden people's momentary thought action repertoires, which support building both intellectual and physical personal resources (see Fredrickson, 2001). Merely the broadened momentary thought action space related to the experience of positive emotions may support the utilization of personal trait EC-dispositions in creative performance. The outlined hypotheses may be incentives for further detailed exploration.

Past research has also shown inconsistent results in the field of the relationship between EC and cognitive creative abilities (for a detailed description, see the subsection Emotional Creativity and Other Cognitive Creative Abilities). This inconsistency may indicate that the influence of EC on creative performance could be dependent on the nature of the creative experimental task. When comparing the results of studies that measured EC as a trait, EC was found to be positively related to the ability to generate novel, unfamiliar associations to stimuli words (Alzoubi et al., 2021). On the other hand, EC was found to be unrelated to the ability to produce original ideas about the potential uses of common objects (Martsksvishvili et al., 2017) and to the ability to generate unusual uses for a cardboard box (Zenasni & Lubart, 2008). These opposite findings may be possibly interpreted by the assumption that EC influences performance in relatively simple associative cognitive tasks but does not influence performance in tasks requiring more complicated cognitive activity, such as mental manipulation with objects. Indeed, the studies of Martsksvishvili et al. (2017) and Zenasni and Lubart (2008) both measured cognitive creative abilities requiring mental manipulation with objects (i.e., the ability to produce original ideas about the potential uses of common objects and the ability to generate unusual uses for a cardboard box). These mental processes can be expected to require more complex cognitive activity than the creation of novel unfamiliar associations to stimuli words, as measured in the study of Alzoubi et al. (2021). More research is needed in this field to verify this assumption.

Furthermore, another study found that the trait emotional novelty positively influenced the ability to generate possible consequences of hypothetical situations, but the trait emotional preparedness and the trait effectiveness/authenticity did not (Study 1, Ivcevic et al., 2007). The ability to generate possible consequences of hypothetical situations can also be expected to require more complex cognitive activity in comparison to the ability to generate novel associations to stimuli words (measured in the study of Alzoubi et al., 2021). Taking all these insights together, it can be hypothesized that the influence of EC on cognitive creative performance may be dependent on the complexity of the cognitive creative task. For future research, it can be proposed that EC influences cognitive creative performance in tasks requiring relatively simple associative cognitive processes, but its influence weakens with increasing complexity of the cognitive creative task. More experimental studies are needed in this field to show further insights on the variations of the impact of trait EC on creative performance in different types of creative tasks.

A recent study by Zhai et al. (2021) has opened a new, topical avenue for future research. This study explored the role of EC in a population of college students and employed people during the COVID-19 pandemic in China. Under the control of COVID-19-related life events and age, EC was found to support post-traumatic growth as well as protect participants against mental health problems, including somatization, depression, and anxiety. These results showed that trait EC played an important role in coping with stressful life events during the COVID-19 pandemic. Thus, EC can be expected to be an important predictor of a subject's resiliency against stress. At the same time, another study indicated that a negative mood during the COVID-19 pandemic could promote an individual's creative ideation and EC (Ying et al., 2021). Nevertheless, it is necessary to point out that causal effects are difficult to determine in this study, as it is a purely correlational one.

This chapter defined EC, reviewed past research on EC, and showed some avenues for future research at the end. As mentioned at the beginning, research on EC is relatively young and is still undergoing dynamic development. Many questions about EC still remain unanswered, as was also shown in this concluding section. A big part of past research measured EC as a trait. For the future, more studies approaching EC as an ability are needed to contribute to a more complex understanding of EC. Some preliminary studies also indicate that the construct of EC could be utilized practically in clinical settings as well as in commercial and educational sectors. Future applied research should pay increased attention to the potential of EC to be used in these areas.

References

Alzoubi, A. M. A., Qudah, M. F. A., Albursan, I. S., Bakhiet, S. F. A., & Alfnan, A. A. (2021). The predictive ability of emotional creativity in creative performance among university students. *SAGE Open*, *11*(2). https://doi.org/10.1177/21582440211008876

Averill, J. R. (1999). Individual differences in emotional creativity: Structure and correlates. *Journal of Personality, 67*, 331–371. https://doi.org/10.1111/1467-6494.00058

Averill, J. R., & Thomas-Knowles, C. (1991). Emotional creativity. In K. T. Strongman (Ed.), *International Review of Studies on Emotion* (pp. 269–299). Wiley.

Blanchard-Fields, F. (2007). Everyday problem solving and emotion: An adult developmental perspective. *Current Directions in Psychological Science*, *16*(1), 26–31. https://doi.org/10.1111/j.1467-8721.2007.00469.x

Blanchard-Fields, F. (2009). Flexible and adaptive socio-emotional problem solving in adult development and aging. *Restorative Neurology and Neuroscience*, *27*(5), 539–550. https://doi.org/10.3233/RNN-2009-0516

Carpenter, S. M., Chae, R. L., & Yoon, C. (2020). Creativity and aging: Positive consequences of distraction. *Psychology and Aging, 35*(5), 654–662. https://doi.org/10.1037/pag0000470

Claridge, G. (Ed.). (1997). *Schizotypy: Implications for Illness and Health*. Oxford University Press.

Fredrickson, B. L. (2001). The role of positive emotions in positive psychology: the broaden-and-build theory of positive emotions. *American Psychologist, 56*(3), 218–226. https://doi.org/10.1037/0003-066X.56.3.218

Fuchs, G. L., Kumar, V. K., & Porter, J. (2007). Emotional creativity, alexithymia, and styles of creativity. *Creativity Research Journal, 19*, 233–245. https://doi.org/10.1080/10400410701397313

Grace, J., & Malloy, P. F. (2001). *Frontal Systems Behavior Scale: Professional Manual.* Psychological Assessment Resources.

Gutbezahl, J., & Averill, J. (1996). Individual differences in emotional creativity as manifested in words and pictures. *Creativity Research Journal, 9*(4), 327–337. https://doi.org/10.1207/s15326934crj0904_4

Holt, N. J., Simmonds-Moore, C., & Moore, S. (2008). Benign schizotypy: Investigating differences between clusters of schizotype on paranormal belief, creativity, intelligence and mental health. In *Proceedings of Presented Papers: The Parapsychological Association 51st Annual Convention* (pp. 82–96). Parapsychological Association.

Ivcevic, Z., Brackett, M. A., & Mayer, J. D. (2007). Emotional intelligence and emotional creativity. *Journal of Personality, 75*, 199–236. https://doi.org/10.1111/j.1467-6494.2007.00437.x

Ivcevic, Z., Ebert, M., Hoffmann, J. D., & Brackett, M. A. (2017). Creativity in the domain of emotions. In J. C. Kaufman, J. Baer, & V. Glăveanu (Eds.), *Cambridge Handbook of Creativity across Different Domains* (pp. 525–548). Cambridge University Press. https://doi.org/10.1017/9781316274385.029

Jenaabadi, H., Marziyeh, A., & Dadkan, A. M. (2015). Comparing emotional creativity and social adjustment of gifted and normal students. *Advances in Applied Sociology, 5*(3), 111–118. https://doi.org/10.4236/aasoci.2015.53010

Lattifian, M., & Delavarpour, M. A. (2012). An investigation into the relationship between attachment style and mental health by the mediating role of emotional creativity. *Advances in Cognitive Science, 2*(14), 45–62.

Kim, S., Hasher, L., & Zacks, R. T. (2007). Aging and benefit of distractibility. *Psychonomic Bulletin & Review, 14*(2), 301–305. https://doi.org/10.3758/BF03194068

Kuška, M., Trnka, R., Mana, J., & Nikolai, T. (2020). Emotional creativity: A meta-analysis and integrative review. *Creativity Research Journal, 32*(2), 151–160. https://doi.org/10.1080/10400419.2020.1751541

Lucas, R. E., & Donnellan, M. B. (2009). Age differences in personality: Evidence from a nationally representative Australian sample. *Developmental Psychology, 45*(5), 1353–1363. https://doi.org/10.1037/a0013914

Luke, D., & Zychowicz, K. (2014). Comparison of outcomes with nonintentional and intentional precognition tasks. *The Journal of Parapsychology, 78*, 223–234.

Martsksvishvili, K., Abuladze, N., Sordia, N., & Neubauer, A. (2017). Emotional creativity inventory: Factor structure, reliability and validity in a Georgian-speaking population. *Problems of Psychology in the 21st Century, 11*(1), 31–41. https://doi.org/10.33225/ppc/17.11.31

Mayer, J. D., & Salovey, P. (1997). What is emotional intelligence? In P. Salovey & D. Sluyter (Eds.), *Emotional Development and Emotional Intelligence: Educational Implications* (pp. 3–34). Basic Books.

Nikolai, T., Sulc, Z., Balcar, K., et al. (2022). Decreased emotional creativity and its relationship with cognitive functions in Parkinson's disease: A preliminary study. *Applied Neuropsychology: Adult, 29*(6), 1484–1491. https://doi.org/10.1080/23279095.2021.1891901

Opitz, P. C., Rauch, L. C., Terry, D. P., & Urry, H. L. (2012). Prefrontal mediation of age differences in cognitive reappraisal. *Neurobiology of Aging, 33*(4), 645–655. https://doi.org/10.1016/j.neurobiolaging.2010.06.004

Prado-Jean, A., Couratier, P., Druet-Cabanac, M., et al. (2010). Specific psychological and behavioral symptoms of depression in patients with dementia. *International Journal of Geriatric Psychiatry, 25*(10), 1065–1072. https://doi.org/10.1002/gps.2468

Roberts, B. W., Walton, K. E., & Viechtbauer, W. (2006). Patterns of mean-level change in personality traits across the life course: A meta-analysis of longitudinal studies. *Psychological Bulletin, 132*(1), 1–25. https://doi.org/10.1037/0033-2909.132.1.1

Scheibe, S., & Carstensen, L. L. (2010). Emotional aging: Recent findings and future trends. *The Journals of Gerontology: Series B, 65*(2), 135–144. https://doi.org/10.1093/geronb/gbp132

Sharma, D., & Mathur, R. (2016). Linking hope and emotional creativity: Mediating role of positive affect. *The International Journal of Indian Psychology, 58*, 50–61. https://doi.org/10.25215/0304.044

Song, C. (2016). Supervisors' paternalistic leadership influences college English teachers' teaching efficacy in China. *Social Behavior and Personality, 44*, 1315–1328. https://doi.org/10.2224/sbp.2016.44.8.1315

Soroa, G., Aritzeta, A., Balluerka, N., & Gorostiaga, A. (2016). Adaptation and validation of the Basque version of the Emotional Creativity Inventory in higher education. *The Spanish Journal of Psychology, 19*, 1–13. https://doi.org/10.1017/sjp.2016.26

Soroa, G., Gorostiaga, A., Aritzeta, A., & Balluerka, N. (2015). A shortened Spanish version of the Emotional Creativity Inventory (the ECI-S). *Creativity Research Journal, 27*, 232–239. https://doi.org/10.1080/10400419.2015.1030313

Torrance, E. P. (1974). *Torrance Tests of Creative Thinking*. Ginn.

Trnka, R., Cabelkova, I., Kuška, M., & Nikolai, T. (2019). Cognitive decline influences emotional creativity in the elderly. *Creativity Research Journal, 31*(1), 93–101. https://doi.org/10.1080/10400419.2019.1577205

Trnka, R., Kuška, M., & Cabelkova, I. (2020). Emotional creativity across adulthood: Age is negatively associated with emotional creativity. *Studia Psychologica, 62*(2), 164–177. https://doi.org/10.31577/sp.2020.02.798

Trnka, R., Zahradnik, M., & Kuška, M. (2016). Emotional creativity and real-life involvement in different types of creative leisure activities. *Creativity Research Journal, 28*(3), 348–356. https://doi.org/10.1080/10400419.2016.1195653

Urry, H. L., & Gross, J. J. (2010). Emotion regulation in older age. *Current Directions in Psychological Science, 19*(6), 352–357. https://doi.org/10.1177/0963721410388395

Valueva, E. A. (2009). Diagnostics of emotional creativity: Adaptation of the questionnaire of J. Averill [Engl. transl.]. In D. V. Lusin & D. V. Ushakov (Eds.), *Social and Economic Intelligence: From Processes to Measurement* [Engl. transl.]. (pp. 216–227). Institute of Psychology of the Russian Academy of Sciences.

Valueva, E. A., & Ushakov, D. V. (2010). Empirical verification of the model of the correlation of subject and emotional abilities [Engl. transl.]. *Psychology: Journal of the Higher School of Economics, 7*, 103–114.

Wang, G., Huang, H., & Zheng, Q. (2015). Effect of Chinese employees' emotional creativity on their innovative performance. *Social Behavior and Personality, 43*, 1147–1160. https://doi.org/10.2224/sbp.2015.43.7.1147

Ying, D., Yang, Y., Xie, C., et al. (2021). A positive role of negative mood on creativity: The opportunity in the crisis of the COVID-19 epidemic. *Frontiers in Psychology, 11*, 3853. https://doi.org/10.3389/fpsyg.2020.600837

Zenasni, F., & Lubart, T. I. (2008). Emotion-related traits moderate the impact of emotional state on creative performances. *Journal of Individual Differences, 29*(3), 157–167. https://doi.org/10.1027/1614-0001.29.3.157

Zhai, H. K., Li, Q., Hu, Y. X., et al. (2021). Emotional creativity improves posttraumatic growth and mental health during the COVID-19 Pandemic. *Frontiers in Psychology, 12*. https://doi.org/10.3389/fpsyg.2021.600798

Zuidema, S. U., de Jonghe, J. F., Verhey, F. R., & Koopmans, R. T. (2009). Predictors of neuropsychiatric symptoms in nursing home patients: Influence of gender and dementia severity. *International Journal of Geriatric Psychiatry, 24*(10), 1079–1086. https://doi.org/10.1002/gps.222

18 Affective Factors in Dark Creativity

Hansika Kapoor and Urvi Mange

Thief pretends to puke on bus passenger; aides steal Rs 50k.
–Times News Network, 2021

This headline from an Indian newspaper draws an image of a clever yet devious individual who leveraged a basic emotion, disgust, to their advantage. Another headline from the same edition went on to describe how a couple was arrested for stealing gold from COVID-19 corpses and patients (Buddi, 2021). Both stories describe acts that are contrary to social norms surrounding purity (Wagemans et al., 2018), where actors have ignored dominant expectations in order to attain a self-serving goal. Not only that, the individuals have tried to achieve this in an original way, so that they may be more likely to get away with the theft. If these headlines elicited an emotional response in you, the reader, then an understanding of affective factors at play in dark creativity is already underway.

Ivcevic and Hoffmann (2019) argued that human emotions aid in laying the foundation of creative processes. They compared emotions to fuel and stated that human emotions ignite creativity. Although extensive reviews on this interplay exist (e.g., Baas et al., 2008), current creativity scholarship is limited in its overall understanding when it comes to affect and creativity. For decades, researchers have studied the processes (i.e., cognitive styles, personality correlates, emotions, and contexts) surrounding positive, benevolent, or at least neutral creativity. That is, real-world creativity is generally understood to be original, task-oriented, and valuable, generating out-of-the-box solutions for prevailing problems and applying these for the common good (e.g., James & Taylor, 2010). Although creativity has been often conceptualized as a positive force, it is not exempt from being used negatively, that is, for self-benefit or for the deliberate destruction of others. This chapter discusses the broad affective factors driving dark creativity, which can be negative (James et al., 1999) and malevolent (Cropley et al., 2008), presenting suggestions for future research in this new domain of creativity scholarship.

Negative and malevolent creativity are characterized by task-oriented behaviors with the end result being harmful. The former leads to harming others

The authors declare that there are no potential conflicts of interest with respect to the research, authorship, and/or publication of this chapter. We are thankful to Anirudh Tagat for useful comments on an earlier version of this chapter.

without deliberation, more like a by-product of their actions, whereas the latter involves a calculated and conscious decision or intent to hurt others. An instance of negative creativity would be to use an original lie to cover up for incomplete homework, whereas malevolent creativity consists of deploying a disguised explosive to double the number of fatalities. Cropley et al. (2008) argued that malevolent creativity is primarily focused on self-benefit using creative solutions, although the extent of harm done by the counterproductive strategies is contingent upon the intentions of the individual.

Such intentions are included in the Person facet of the four Ps model of creativity (Rhodes, 1961), along with motivational states, emotions, and other individual differences. The other Ps include the process (cognitive processes underlying the creative product), press (environmental factors that facilitate/ constrain creativity), and product (the creative output itself). Cropley and Cropley's (2013) 6Ps model differentiated the Person P into three subcomponents: personal properties, personal motivation, and personal feelings/mood. The granular distinction between these Ps, particularly the individual's motivational and emotional aspects, can expand our understanding of the dark side.

Traditional definitions of creativity view the construct as epitomizing novelty and task-appropriateness with some degree of social consensus (Plucker et al., 2004). However, the concept of effectiveness is a moral quandary, as the effectiveness or use of a solution depends on the need of the individual. For instance, a thief who devises a new method to break into houses may find this solution useful, but the victim of the theft is unlikely to concur. Further, a one-to-one correspondence between a person's motive and the resultant outcome can be lacking; consider that the thief is caught and offered to join law enforcement to prevent further robberies in the area. They may eventually use their malevolent creative methods for social good. As compared to positive/ bright/benevolent creativity, dark creativity is more difficult to conceptualize by solely gauging its novelty and usefulness; rather it can be formulated better by considering underlying processes and intent (motivation, desire, emotions) held by creators. For instance, a thief pretending to be a police officer to surpass security personnel in a museum and being able to steal a diamond shows that the process (a disguise in this case) and press (the presence of security) acted in concert with the intent of the thief (desire for money). Therefore, the influence of the press and process on the creative outcome and how it interacts with the intent of the actor is also necessary to be considered.

The remainder of the chapter is organized as follows: first, a discussion about the association between dark personality characteristics and creativity is presented, owing to scant research directly associating dark creativity and affect. Using dark personality traits as a springboard, with their associated affective features and emotional profiles, an extension is made to dark creative intent and actions. Associated constructs like empathy, perspective-taking, and the desire for self-benefit are also explored. The next section dives deeper into affective factors associated with dark creativity, highlighting past research in this domain and connecting theoretical models to propose future work. Owing to the intertwined nature of morality (including moral preferences and behaviors) with dark creativity, the role of deception and emotions (moral, basic, and aesthetic) is also presented. Last, suggestions for future research in affect and dark creativity are proposed, focusing on novel measurements and interdisciplinary methods.

Bridges from Personality to Affect to Dark Creativity

Affective factors as they directly relate to dark creativity have been studied sparingly. The closest research in this domain has been done in the context of dark personality traits, such as psychopathy, narcissism, Machiavellianism, sadism, and how these relate to dark creativity (e.g., Kapoor, 2015). Although research has examined the bright circumplex of the Big Five traits in this context as well (e.g., Gutworth et al., 2016), the Dark Triad/Tetrad and their associations with morally dubious behaviors (see also Furnham et al., 2013; Paulhus, 2014) may be more relevant to dark creativity. These subclinical personality traits are often found in everyday contexts, illustrated by common features such as lack of empathy, self-centeredness, cynicism, callous social attitudes, and manipulation, emotional or otherwise.

Of relevance to the current chapter is the relationship of this socially aversive circumplex of traits with empathy. The Dark Triad has been associated with deficits in emotional empathy (*I feel what you feel*), but with little impairment in cognitive empathy (*I understand what you feel*); however, research is yet to reach a consensus (Jonason & Krause, 2013; Pajevic et al., 2018; Wai & Tiliopoulos, 2012). A lack of empathy relates to a lack of regard for others' wellbeing, lack of guilt, and little concern when engaging in moral wrongdoing (Decety & Cowell, 2014). Further, empathy and morality are intertwined and share a complex relationship. For instance, empathizing with a family member who is a criminal might lead a police officer to protect their relative, even though the family member has engaged in immoral behavior. Therefore, empathy can also become a basis of engaging in moral wrongdoing, depending on group membership. Taking the same example, if the police officer identifies with being a law enforcement official more strongly than a member of their own family, then they may empathize with the victim of the crime more than their family member.

In addition, emotional recognition is also impaired in those high on psychopathy (Puthillam et al., 2019) and sadism (Pajevic et al., 2018). And although a meta-analysis found that emotional intelligence was negatively related to Machiavellianism and to psychopathy (Miao et al., 2019), research has also suggested that socioemotional skills can be used by dark personalities to emotionally manipulate others (Nagler et al., 2014). Examining these affective factors – empathetic concern toward others, general empathy levels, emotional intelligence, emotional recognition – can forge links from personality dispositions to emotional correlates with dark creative behaviors. For instance, research has identified how empathy deficits in psychopathy are associated with indirect relational aggressive behaviors, like engaging in malicious humor (Heym et al., 2019). Formulating malicious humor in turn is a dark creative behavior worthy of investigation (see also Kapoor & Karandikar, 2019).

Perspective-taking is another social skill that helps individuals consider and appreciate the viewpoints of others by figuratively stepping into their shoes. Research has found that individuals high on dark traits are more likely to be morally disengaged (Erzi, 2020), possibly via lower considerations for empathic concern and perspective-taking (Wu et al., 2020). Relatedly, moral perspective-taking or assessing the moral impacts of one's decisions on others is also worthy of investigation in this context (see also Walker, 1980). Combined with tendencies to seek original solutions to problems, such individuals are theoretically more likely to engage in dark creativity. In all, there seems to be substantial overlap between the conceptualization of dark traits and dark creativity, via socio-moral and affective factors, which needs to be investigated in future research.

Affective Features of Dark Creativity

Before delving into preliminary investigations in the area of affective factors and dark creativity, it is important to define some affect-related terminology. Affect is defined as the general term inclusive of both dispositional traits and affective states, that is, they are more transient states dependent on the current context a person is in (Barsade & Gibson, 2007). Emotions, on the other hand, can be defined as a response to an immediate event or stimulus that warrants attention and for which necessary action needs to be taken (Davis, 2009; Fredrickson, 2001). Mood is a generalized state of human emotion and is not contingent on another stimulus (Davis, 2009). Thus, emotion is a more specialized reaction as opposed to mood and is short lived as it is context dependent (Kumar, 1997).

Scholarship associating emotions with dark creativity is scarce, but this lack of research does not imply an absence of the phenomenon. Interestingly, most of the work on dark innovation is in the context of organizational behaviors, relating it to dark personality clusters. A famous prototype of the selfish boss was Apple founder Steve Jobs who, for his own creative ambitions, did not hesitate to manipulate other people (Fouché et al., 2017). Further, the inaugural study of negative creativity was in an organizational context, manipulated a justice treatment, and aimed to induce feelings of perceived fairness or unfairness in participants (Clark & James, 1999). Specifically, although all participants were led to believe that they would receive an incentive for performing a mundane task, only half were eligible for such an incentive. Subsequent creative behavior was recorded, with preliminary evidence that perceived injustice contributed to the generation of negative creative ideas.

Similarly, imagine a situation where you've been overlooked for a long-due promotion at your workplace. Such a situation would make most people angry and hamper efficiency at work, and maybe even encourage some workplace deviance like cyberloafing (De Lara, 2007). However, in a study where anger of moderate levels was induced in participants, this did more good than harm by stimulating the creation of novel ideas (Yang & Hung, 2015). Further, many studies exploring associations between creativity and emotions show that activating emotions, such as anger, produce higher levels of creativity in comparison to deactivating (e.g., sadness) or neutral ones (Baas et al., 2011; De Dreu et al., 2008; Van Kleef et al., 2010). Research has also found that moderate levels of stress and anxiety aid creativity (Du et al., 2021); however, the valence of creativity depends on the context the individual is in. For instance, some individuals used COVID-19 to engage in creativity and make meaning of ongoing events (Kapoor & Kaufman, 2020), whereas others used the crisis to spread propaganda, and in turn, citizens suffered the ills of not only a pandemic but also an infodemic.

Literature has largely focused on emotional valence (positive and negative) when examining the antecedents of creative behavior. For instance, motivational compatibility purports that a positive mood leads to higher creative output in tasks involving leisure and fun, whereas negative moods do the same for more serious tasks (Friedman et al., 2007). However, Baas et al. (2008) and De Dreu et al. (2008) argued that looking at valence alone would not provide a comprehensive investigation of creativity, making it imperative to consider not only mood variability but also intentions of the individual. For instance, if an employee feels that organizational goals are not beneficial for them, the employee's subsequent workplace behaviors could simply be based on the valence of their (negative) mood. However, such a link is not straightforward, and hence De Dreu et al. (2008) suggested that it may be better to use a dual pathway model of creativity that considers both arousal and valence while predicting creative output:

1. The first pathway helps individuals reach creative outcomes as a result of the cognitive flexibility that stems from positive emotions.
2. The second pathway helps individuals reach creative outcomes as a result of perseverance and effort stemming from negative emotions. Most often this pathway is employed to generate innovative solutions to a problematic situation.

Another important attribute is the activation level of emotions (i.e., whether the emotion encourages an action); it is more likely that higher (compared to lower) activation provides one with energy and resources to come up with creative solutions (Baas et al., 2008). Therefore, it is likely that creative outcomes emerge from a combination of valence, activation, intentions, and other motivational processes, all of which need to be acknowledged when affect is studied in creativity. For instance, an employee who is wrongly accused of social loafing (negative affect), can be motivated to come up with a novel product strategy to gain recognition (bright creativity), whereas an employee who is charismatic and popular (positive affect) can manipulate other employees to get them to do the employee's work (dark creativity). Hence, relying on valence alone may not provide a comprehensive understanding of the interplay between affect and creativity; it is recommended to include other aspects like arousal and intent. For instance, feeling threatened by coworkers of foreign origin (arousing negative emotion) can lead to implementing unfriendly or discriminatory organizational policies and is most often a means to restore equilibrium as well as destroy the threat of having members of diasporic communities in the organization.

Research on dark creativity has included affective factors such as emotional intelligence (Harris et al., 2013), implicit aggression (Harris & Reiter-Palmon, 2015), and anger (Cheng et al., 2021; Perchtold-Stefan et al., 2020a). Further, research has also found how cognitive reappraisal strategies can reduce malevolent ideation (Cheng et al., 2021) and how thinking about revenge in stressful situations impairs such reappraisal (Perchtold-Stefan et al., 2021). Emotional intelligence (EI), the ability to perceive, process, and manage one's and others' emotions (Mayer et al., 1999), is essential to study with dark creativity. EI aids in emotional control, which in turn influences how people perceive and respond to problems. In fact, Harris et al. (2013) found that those with lower EI were more likely to come up with malevolently creative solutions.

Thus, dark creativity can arise from a combination of the intent of the creator, their socioemotional skills, and the requirements of the situation. For instance, Perchtold-Stefan et al. (2020b) examined the social function of malevolent creativity by studying humor styles. They found that participants who used humor for shaming, hurting others, or proving their superiority were more malevolently creative when using humor than others who had more prosocial intentions. Attributes such as prosociality at first seem unrelated to creativity; however, possessing certain traits or lack thereof (such as empathy and perspective-taking) can contribute to differences in the valence of creative output produced. Hui et al. (2021) found that students with poor perspective-taking ability adopted a more flexible moral reasoning, only if they were creative. In line with this finding, a chapter on dark creativity would be nearly incomplete without addressing morality, moral flexibility, and morally dubious behaviors, such as deception (see also Kapoor & Kaufman, 2021; Kapoor & Khan, 2017).

Lying Can Be Creative, Too

Despite varied studies in the area, the relationship between morality and creativity seems muddy. Two review papers, only a year apart, found contradictory results: one concluding that creativity and *morality* are positively related (Shen et al., 2019) and the other identifying a weak positive relationship between creativity and *unethicality* (Storme et al., 2021). However, the latter paper made a distinction between studies that used objective (behavioral, other reports) or subjective self-reports of dishonesty; as social desirability can contaminate results in the morality–creativity space, the overall positive relationship was driven by studies using objective measures of unethicality, such as observations of dishonest behavior.

Broadly in this domain, studies have suggested that (a) creative individuals tend to be able to justify their wrongdoings more easily (e.g., Mai et al., 2015), (b) creative and morally flexible behaviors like deception can be bi-directional and share a common link of not being restricted by rules (Gino & Wiltermuth, 2014), and (c) lying can be creative, in both prosocial and antisocial ways (Walczyk et al., 2008). Specifically, the role of deception in dark creativity has been outlined by Kapoor and Khan (2017), identifying deception as a fundamental cognitive process in the generation of creative ideation meant to meet negative goals. This is not to say that creative prosocial lying does not include deception (e.g., original lies that spare someone's feelings), but that it may be less common.

Consider a coworker who always leaves the microwave dirty after using it. Also suppose that this coworker is actively looking to enter a romantic relationship. If one has the proclivity to be original and deceptive, and is annoyed by this behavior, they could start an office rumor that the coworker is in a relationship with whoever keeps the microwave dirty, targeting their reputation. Consider now that the relationship-seeking coworker is someone who frequently mocks one's outfits at work; they could get back at the coworker by setting them up on a fake blind date and getting them stood up. Let's increase this a notch and now consider that the coworker had an extramarital relationship with one's spouse, due to which a legal separation ensued. If one wants to be deviously creative, they could pretend to be someone else on a dating app that the coworker uses (catfishing them) and lead them down a winding path paved with emotional manipulation.

Each of the antecedent situations is coupled with differing intensities of negative emotions (anger, disgust, to name a few) toward the coworker with several caveats. One, the individual planning and executing the rumor, blind date, or catfish expedition needs to be able to morally justify these deceptive actions. Second, this individual also needs to be cognitively flexible enough to come up with these ideas to cause reputational or long-term emotional damage to their coworker. And last, the person would need to prefer inflicting the harm surreptitiously, to avoid identification and backlash.

Thus, deception can be the route to express dark creativity across several contexts. Research has also identified how individuals with higher Dark Tetrad traits have a higher propensity to lie (Forsyth et al., 2021). There can also be degrees of deceptiveness, varying based on the quantity, quality, manner, and relevance of information communicated (see also Information Manipulation Theory; McCornack, 1992). Further, the complex cognitive decision to deceive has been associated with the influence of emotions, both as an antecedent and consequence. Much of this research comes from organizational psychology literature on the use of deception in negotiation contexts, which feature informational and power asymmetries. In such scenarios, negative emotions increase the likelihood of using deception as a negotiation tactic, and vice versa for positive emotions (e.g., Olekalns & Smith, 2009). To explain this interplay further, Gaspar and Schweitzer (2013) proposed the emotion deception model, where a priori, context-specific, and anticipated emotions determined whether and how to engage in deception. Extending this to dark creativity, negative emotional states can encourage original deception for self-serving purposes (like in a negotiation setting, see also Baas et al., 2019) or to inflict harm on others (like in the catfishing example).

Research has also identified positive emotions as antecedents of prosocial lying, including compassion (Fang et al., 2020) and empathy toward another's sadness (Xu et al., 2020). Another study also suggested that induced and trait compassion promote benevolent lying when mediated by the desire to prevent emotional harm (Lupoli et al., 2017). Therefore, it can be theorized that individuals who want to willfully cause harm may use emotional awareness differently, and may choose to engage in antisocial deception. Consider a situation where one only experiences cognitive, but not affective, empathy toward another's distress (e.g., Cuff et al., 2016). An individual predisposed to being darkly creative may choose to leverage the knowledge of another's emotions to their own benefit and lie or manipulate them in turn. Of course, this has to be empirically validated; however, it is important to build off literature on emotional factors in deception more broadly and postulate hypotheses in dark creativity.

Moral, Basic, and Aesthetic Emotions

Whereas deception is a behavioral manifestation of unethicality, we propose that dark creativity can be more directly linked to certain affective factors. Moral emotions, as conceptualized by Haidt (2003), are associated with larger societal welfare and concerns beyond the individual themselves. These emotions influence whether one upholds moral standards, tolerates moral transgressions, and engages in moral behavior (see also Tangney et al., 2007). Moral emotions can be largely classified in a 2 (target) × 2 (valence) matrix: self-condemning (e.g., shame, guilt, embarrassment), other-condemning (e.g., contempt, anger, disgust), self-praising (e.g., pride), and other-praising emotions (e.g., gratitude, awe, compassion).[1] Apart from briefly exploring anger (e.g., Perchtold-Stefan et al., 2020a), scholarship in dark creativity has yet to examine relationships with these moral emotions.

Returning to the examples at the start of the chapter, dark creative actors may exploit others' moral emotions by violating social expectations. Throwing up in public transportation is objectively disgusting, transgresses the purity foundation (Graham et al., 2013), and is likely to lead to some chaos and misdirection in this case. The thief, however, was undeterred from pretending to vomit, implying lesser moral concern for the same, as their goal was to steal

---

[1] For a detailed review of these emotions, the reader is directed to Haidt (2003) and Tangney et al. (2007).

money in a novel way. Similarly, the couple who stole jewelry from COVID-19 corpses and patients were less likely to have experienced disgust, which may have otherwise served as a moral speed bump. Therefore, the manner in which dark creative actors experience moral emotions in social contexts can help us understand whether and how they will transgress social norms (see also Wang & Wei, 2021) and act creatively.

Take the example of guilt, an emotion that is often confused with shame. Whereas the former is associated with lapses in moral judgement/behavior in interpersonal contexts, the latter is more likely experienced in hierarchical settings, particularly when norm violation becomes known to others. Therefore, guilt-proneness is an adaptive characteristic that can influence moral decisions, often preventing unethical behaviors (e.g., Cohen et al., 2012). Further, the experience of guilt can help preserve and strengthen relationships (e.g., Baumeister et al., 1994), owing to better perspective-taking by guilt-prone individuals (Leith & Baumeister, 1998). Further, there is evidence that guilt-proneness is associated with disapproving the use of false promises, misrepresentation, and lying as negotiation tactics (Cohen, 2010; see also Gino & Shea, 2012).

However, consider an individual who is less prone to experiencing guilt and thereby less likely to take on another's perspective; such an individual is unlikely to be keen on safeguarding relationships too. It can be argued that this individual may be more likely to approve the use of deception in interpersonal settings, which when used in novel ways can constitute dark creativity (Figure 18.1). Therefore, we propose that the use of deception may mediate the relationship between guilt-proneness and dark creativity, wherein less guilt-prone persons would be more likely to think of dark creative outcomes that deploy deception. In this model, the main relationship to be tested is the negative association between guilt proneness and dark creativity. The negative link between guilt proneness and deception (Cohen, 2010) and the positive association between deception and dark creativity (Kapoor & Khan, 2017) have already been established. Similarly, extensions can be proposed using existing literature on moral emotions and behavioral/cognitive processes associated with dark creativity.

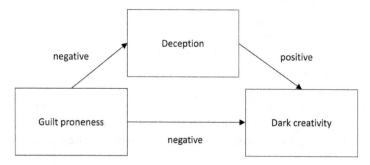

Figure 18.1 *A hypothesized model depicting guilt proneness and dark creativity mediated by deception.*

Basic emotions, such as fear, also have a role to play in the production of dark creative actions. Conspiracy theories are often creative narratives that give meaning to random events for a certain section of the population who believe these explanations (Bonetto & Arciszewski, 2021). Conspiracies can become a dangerous, albeit creative way of instilling and maintaining fear among populations susceptible to such beliefs. For instance, conspiratorial beliefs about COVID-19 vaccinations can endanger lives by preventing widespread immunization (e.g., Scrima et al., 2022). Similarly, other forms of information exchange, such as gossip and rumors, can be weaponized to prey on basic emotions in a novel manner. Conversely, negative emotions can also be antecedents and motivate the generation of a retaliatory and original rumor; however, this is yet to be investigated. It can be proposed that unpleasant, active, and highly arousing emotions, like anger (Reisenzein, 1994), can promote malevolent problem solving across contexts. Similarly, the underlying reason for an angry response, such as a failure to reappraise a situation or to act in a vengeful way (Perchtold-Stefan et al., 2021), can also moderate the extent of dark creativity. In fact, James and colleagues' (1999) study on perceived unfairness provided preliminary evidence for the same.

There is considerable overlap between moral, basic, and aesthetic emotions, the last of these being subjective feelings elicited during an aesthetic encounter, such as being moved when listening to classical music (Menninghaus et al., 2019). In addition to positive appraisals (e.g., awe and surprise) of aesthetic objects or experiences, there can also be negative appraisals and associated emotions, like anger and confusion (Schindler et al., 2017; Silvia, 2009). Cooper and Silvia (2009) illustrated how anger and disgust toward offensive artwork can lead to behavioral consequences like rejection and opposition (see also Silvia & Brown, 2007). Extending this, hostile aesthetic emotions may function in two ways in the context of dark creativity: (a) emotions like boredom, confusion, anger, disgust, and the like toward aesthetic artifacts (art, music, literature, and so on) may encourage novel ways to oppose or destroy the same, including vandalism and (b) aesthetic emotions that overlap with moral emotions, like disgust, may have to be overcome by creators themselves to generate provocative works of art. These artworks in turn may be misperceived by audiences as malevolently creative and intending to harm sentiments, instead of as artists expressing their creative freedom. For instance, when M. F. Hussain painted Mother India and Indian goddesses in the nude, he received death threats from Hindu nationalists (Buncombe, 2011), who attributed malice to the artist's intent.

Shining a Light on Dark Creativity in the Future

Although scholarship on dark creativity is accumulating slowly and steadily, research on the intersection of affective factors and the dark side has a long way to go. This chapter reviewed how dark personality traits and their associated emotional features can be used as a springboard to connect to dark creative behaviors. The use of deception, both as a cognitive process and behaviorally, can be included in affect-driven paradigms to assess dark creativity. Similarly, moral perspective-taking and (lack of) empathy are relevant variables in future studies on dark creativity and affective antecedents or consequences. Last, the investigation of moral, basic, and aesthetic emotions can be merged with any of the above areas for a comprehensive overview of how emotions operate in dark creativity.

That said, the element of intent is important to be considered in arguments of dark creativity. First, because there may not always be a one-to-one correspondence between the valence of an actor's intent and eventual outcome (see also Cropley, 2010), and second, because motivations can be manipulated in experimental contexts. Therefore, what drives a darkly creative act in the presence of emotional antecedents can help explain the extent of damage that a subsequent idea can cause. For instance, although Forgeard and Mecklenburg's (2013) model illustrates intended beneficiaries and prosocial goals as motivations that guide creative behavior, in a dark creativity context, these can conversely represent antisocial or self-interested goals.

In the affective domain, mood-induction procedures are often used to place participants in a specific mood state prior to performing an experimental task. For instance, the use of self-referent statements (e.g., I feel disappointed in myself now), multimedia (e.g., pictures/videos of laughing babies), or providing positive or negative feedback on task performance can induce specific moods (e.g., Westermann et al., 1996). Mood induction paradigms have also been implemented and validated in online settings (Göritz & Moser, 2006; Marcusson-Clavertz et al., 2019), expanding their scope. In the context of dark creativity, frustration or another active, high-arousal negative emotion can be contextually induced to determine its effects on the generation of dark creative ideas, perhaps through a real-world divergent thinking task (see also Perchtold-Stefan et al., 2020a). Similarly, attempts can be made to induce moral (like guilt) and aesthetic emotions (like disgust) to study their effects on the generation of dark creative ideas, with appropriate ethics approval.

Future research can also develop real-world divergent thinking tasks to explore the role of empathy and perspective-taking among participants. For instance, a gossip generation task can be used to examine whether and how individuals generate content about a third-party entity, which can be fueled by this entity's moral or immoral behaviors (e.g., a business protecting/damaging the environment or an individual's tax evasion behaviors). Other work can also use creativity tasks to explore whether and how individuals emotionally manipulate others in novel ways to meet their goals (see also Ivcevic et al., 2007). An example would be trying to convince someone not to break up with you, via emotional blackmail.

Affect in dark creativity can also be explored across disciplines. Joy of destruction games (Abbink & Sadrieh, 2009) can be used to explore creative justifications for burning others' money in an economic game setup. In political science, the use of novel propaganda to induce fear and thereby effect compliant behaviors can become the basis of a case study in dark creativity. Original laws that prevent certain social groups from equal participation in expressing their rights can be darkly creative, as can benevolent -isms (e.g., sexism, racism). Group membership can be permitted or threatened in creative ways to maintain social order within the in-group; for instance, disparaging initiation rituals or deliberate exclusions from exclusive societies. Moreover, as culture and affect are intertwined especially in the moral domain (e.g., Haidt et al., 1993), it is imperative to consider cultural variations in future research with diverse participant samples.

In sum, there are several avenues by which affective factors in dark creativity can be investigated. It is important to remember that understanding the emergence of dark creative ideas and behaviors is not with the intent to promote them, but rather to examine the circumstances and individual properties that foster their emergence.

References

Abbink, K., & Sadrieh, A. (2009). The pleasure of being nasty. *Economics Letters, 105* (3), 306–308. https://doi.org/10.1016/j.econlet.2009.08.024

Baas, M., De Dreu, C. K. W., & Nijstad, B. A. (2008). A meta-analysis of 25 years of mood-creativity research: Hedonic tone, activation, or regulatory focus? *Psychological Bulletin, 134*(6), 779–806. https://doi.org/10.1037/a0012815

Baas, M., De Dreu, C. K. W., & Nijstad, B. A. (2011). Creative production by angry people peaks early on, decreases over time, and is relatively unstructured. *Journal of Experimental Social Psychology, 47*(6), 1107–1115. https://doi.org/10.1016/j.jesp.2011.05.009

Baas, M., Roskes, M., Koch, S., Cheng, Y., & De Dreu, C. K. W. (2019). Why social threat motivates malevolent creativity. *Personality and Social Psychology Bulletin, 45*(11), 1590–1602. https://doi.org/10.1177/0146167219838551

Barsade, S. G., & Gibson, D. E. (2007). Why does affect matter in organizations? *Academy of Management Perspectives, 21*(1), 36–59. https://doi.org/10.5465/AMP.2007.24286163

Baumeister, R. F., Stillwell, A. M., & Heatherton, T. F. (1994). Guilt: An interpersonal approach. *Psychological Bulletin, 115*(2), 243–267. https://doi.org/10.1037/0033-2909.115.2.243

Bonetto, E., & Arciszewski, T. (2021). The creativity of conspiracy theories. *The Journal of Creative Behavior, 54*(4), 916–924. jocb.497. https://doi.org/10.1002/jocb.497

Buddi, M. (2021, July 9). Hyderabad: Couple arrested for stealing jewelry from Covid patients at hospital. *The Times of India.*

Buncombe, A. (2011, October 23). MF Husain: Indian artist who spent his last five years in self-imposed exile after death threats from Hindu nationalists. *Independent.*

Cheng, R., LU, K., & HAO, N. (2021). The effect of anger on malevolent creativity and strategies for its emotion regulation. *Acta Psychologica Sinica, 53*(8), 847. https://doi.org/10.3724/sp.j.1041.2021.00847

Clark, K., & James, K. (1999). Justice and positive and negative creativity. *Creativity Research Journal*, *12*(4), 311–320. https://doi.org/10.1207/s15326934crj1204_9

Cohen, T. R. (2010). Moral emotions and unethical bargaining: The differential effects of empathy and perspective taking in deterring deceitful negotiation. *Journal of Business Ethics*, *94*(4), 569–579. https://doi.org/10.1007/s10551-009-0338-z

Cohen, T. R., Panter, A. T., & Turan, N. (2012). Guilt proneness and moral character. *Current Directions in Psychological Science*, *21*(5), 355–359. https://doi.org/10.1177/0963721412454874

Cooper, J. M., & Silvia, P. J. (2009). Opposing art: Rejection as an action tendency of hostile aesthetic emotions. *Empirical Studies of the Arts*, *27*(1), 109–126. https://doi.org/10.2190/em.27.1.f

Cropley, D. H. (2010). Summary – The dark side of creativity: A differentiated model. In D. H. Cropley, A. J. Cropley, J. C. Kaufman, & M. A. Runco (Eds.), *The Dark Side of Creativity* (pp. 360–373). Cambridge University Press.

Cropley, D. H., & Cropley, A. J. (2013). *Creativity and Crime: A Psychological Analysis.* Cambridge University Press.

Cropley, D. H., Kaufman, J. C., & Cropley, A. J. (2008). Malevolent creativity: A functional model of creativity in terrorism and crime. *Creativity Research Journal*, *20*(2), 105–115. https://doi.org/10.1080/10400410802059424

Cuff, B. M. P., Brown, S. J., Taylor, L., & Howat, D. J. (2016). Empathy: A review of the concept. *Emotion Review*, *8*(2), 144–153. https://doi.org/10.1177/1754073914558466

Davis, M. A. (2009). Understanding the relationship between mood and creativity: A meta-analysis. *Organizational Behavior and Human Decision Processes*, *108*(1), 25–38. https://doi.org/10.1016/j.obhdp.2008.04.001

De Dreu, C. K. W., Baas, M., & Nijstad, B. A. (2008). Hedonic tone and activation level in the mood-creativity link: Toward a dual pathway to creativity model. *Journal of Personality and Social Psychology*, *94*(5), 739–756. https://doi.org/10.1037/0022-3514.94.5.739

De Lara, P. Z. M. (2007). Relationship between organizational justice and cyberloafing in the workplace: Has "anomia" a say in the matter? *Cyberpsychology and Behavior*, *10*(3), 464–470. https://doi.org/10.1089/cpb.2006.9931

Decety, J., & Cowell, J. M. (2014). Friends or foes: Is empathy necessary for moral behavior? *Perspectives on Psychological Science*, *9*(5), 525–537. https://doi.org/10.1177/1745691614545130

Du, Y., Yang, Y., Wang, X., et al. (2021). A positive role of negative mood on creativity: The opportunity in the crisis of the COVID-19 epidemic. *Frontiers in Psychology*, *11*(January), 1–14. https://doi.org/10.3389/fpsyg.2020.600837

Erzi, S. (2020). Dark Triad and schadenfreude: Mediating role of moral disengagement and relational aggression. *Personality and Individual Differences*, *157*(January), 109827. https://doi.org/10.1016/j.paid.2020.109827

Fang, X., Chen, L., Wang, J., Zhang, Q., & Mo, L. (2020). Do all types of compassion increase prosocial lying? *Psychology Research and Behavior Management*, *13*, 437–451. https://doi.org/10.2147/PRBM.S238246

Forgeard, M. J. C., & Mecklenburg, A. C. (2013). The two dimensions of motivation and a reciprocal model of the creative process. *Review of General Psychology*, *17*(3), 255–266. https://doi.org/10.1037/a0032104

Forsyth, L., Anglim, J., March, E., & Bilobrk, B. (2021). Dark Tetrad personality traits and the propensity to lie across multiple contexts. *Personality and Individual Differences, 177*(110792). https://doi.org/10.1016/j.paid.2021.11079

Fouché, P., du Plessis, R., & van Niekerk, R. (2017). Levinsonian seasons in the life of Steve Jobs: A psychobiographical case study. *Indo-Pacific Journal of Phenomenology, 17*(1), 1–18. https://doi.org/10.1080/20797222.2017.1331970

Fredrickson, B. L. (2001). The role of positive emotions in positive psychology: The broaden-and-build theory of positive emotions. *American Psychologist, 56*(3), 218–226. https://doi.org/10.1037//0003-066x.56.3.218

Friedman, R. S., Förster, J., & Denzler, M. (2007). Interactive effects of mood and task framing on creative generation. *Creativity Research Journal, 19*(2–3), 141–162. https://doi.org/10.1080/10400410701397206

Furnham, A., Richards, S. C., & Paulhus, D. L. (2013). The Dark Triad of personality: A 10 year review. *Social and Personality Psychology Compass, 7*(3), 199–216. https://doi.org/10.1111/spc3.12018

Gaspar, J. P., & Schweitzer, M. E. (2013). The emotion deception model: A review of deception in negotiation and the role of emotion in deception. *Negotiation and Conflict Management Research, 6*(3), 160–179. https://doi.org/10.1111/ncmr.12010

Gino, F., & Shea, C. (2012). Deception in negotiations: The role of emotions. In G. E. Bolton & R. T. A. Croson (Eds.), *The Oxford Handbook of Economic Conflict Resolution* (pp. 47–60). Oxford University Press.

Gino, F., & Wiltermuth, S. S. (2014). Evil genius? How dishonesty can lead to greater creativity. *Psychological Science, 25*(4), 973–981. https://doi.org/10.1177/0956797614520714

Göritz, A. S., & Moser, K. (2006). Web-based mood induction. *Cognition and Emotion, 20*(6), 887–896. https://doi.org/10.1080/02699930500405386

Graham, J., Haidt, J., Koleva, S., et al. (2013). Moral foundations theory: The pragmatic validity of moral pluralism. *Advances in Experimental Social Psychology, 47*, 55–130. https://doi.org/10.1016/B978-0-12-407236-7.00002-4

Gutworth, M. B., Cushenbery, L., & Hunter, S. T. (2018). Creativity for deliberate harm: Malevolent creativity and social information processing theory. *The Journal of Creative Behavior, 52*(4), 305–322. https://doi.org/10.1002/jocb.155

Haidt, J. (2003). The moral emotions. In R. J. Davidson, K. R. Scherer, & H. H. Goldsmith (Eds.), *Handbook of Affective Sciences* (pp. 852–870). Oxford University Press. https://doi.org/10.1093/mnras/stx1358

Haidt, J., Koller, S. H., & Dias, M. G. (1993). Affect, culture, and morality, or is it wrong to eat your dog? *Journal of Personality and Social Psychology, 65*(4), 613–628. https://doi.org/10.1037/0022-3514.65.4.613

Harris, D. J., & Reiter-Palmon, R. (2015). Fast and furious: The influence of implicit aggression, premeditation, and provoking situations on malevolent creativity. *Psychology of Aesthetics, Creativity, and the Arts, 9*(1), 54–64. https://doi.org/10.1037/a0038499

Harris, D. J., Reiter-Palmon, R., & Kaufman, J. C. (2013). The effect of emotional intelligence and task type on malevolent creativity. *Psychology of Aesthetics, Creativity, and the Arts, 7*(3), 237–244. https://doi.org/10.1037/a0032139

Heym, N., Firth, J., Kibowski, F., et al. (2019). Empathy at the heart of darkness: Empathy deficits that bind the dark triad and those that mediate indirect relational aggression. *Frontiers in Psychiatry*, *10*, 1–10. https://doi.org/10.3389/fpsyt.2019.00095

Hui, P. P., Chiu, W. C. K., Pang, E., Coombes, J., & Tse, D. Y. P. (2021). Seeing through and breaking through: The role of perspective taking in the relationship between creativity and moral reasoning. *Journal of Business Ethics*, 0123456789. https://doi.org/10.1007/s10551-021-04876-3

Ivcevic, Z., Brackett, M. A., & Mayer, J. D. (2007). Emotional intelligence and emotional creativity. *Journal of Personality*, *75*(2), 199–236. https://doi.org/10.1111/j.1467-6494.2007.00437.x

Ivcevic, Z., & Hoffmann, J. (2019). Emotions and creativity: From process to person and product. In J. C. Kaufman & R. J. Sternberg (Eds.), *The Cambridge Handbook of Creativity* (pp. 273–295). Cambridge University Press.

James, K., Clark, K., & Cropanzano, R. (1999). Positive and negative creativity in groups, institutions, and organizations: A model and theoretical extension. *Creativity Research Journal*, *12*(3), 211–226. https://doi.org/10.1207/s15326934crj1203

James, K., & Taylor, A. (2010). Positive creativity and negative creativity (and unintended consequences). In D. H. Cropley, A. J. Cropley, J. C. Kaufman, & M. A. Runco (Eds.), *The Dark Side of Creativity* (pp. 33–56). Cambridge University Press.

Jonason, P. K., & Krause, L. (2013). The emotional deficits associated with the Dark Triad traits: Cognitive empathy, affective empathy, and alexithymia. *Personality and Individual Differences*, *55*(5), 532–537. https://doi.org/10.1016/j.paid.2013.04.027

Kapoor, H. (2015). The creative side of the Dark Triad. *Creativity Research Journal*, *27*(1), 58–67. https://doi.org/10.1080/10400419.2014.961775

Kapoor, H., & Karandikar, S. (2019). Darkness all around: Humor, personality, and creativity. *In-Mind Magazine*. www.in-mind.org/blog/post/darkness-all-around-humor-personality-and-creativity

Kapoor, H., & Kaufman, J. C. (2020). Meaning-making through creativity during COVID-19. *Frontiers in Psychology*, *11*, 595990. https://doi.org/10.3389/fpsyg.2020.595990

Kapoor, H., & Kaufman, J. C. (2021). Unbound: The relationship between creativity, moral foundations, and dark personality. *The Journal of Creative Behavior*. https://doi.org/10.1002/jocb.523

Kapoor, H., & Khan, A. (2017). Deceptively yours: Valence-based creativity and deception. *Thinking Skills and Creativity*, *23*, 199–206. https://doi.org/10.1016/j.tsc.2016.12.006

Kumar, R. (1997). The role of affect in negotiations. *The Journal of Applied Behavioral Science*, *33*(1), 84–100. https://doi.org/10.1177/0021886397331007

Leith, K. P., & Baumeister, R. F. (1998). Empathy, shame, guilt, and narratives of interpersonal conflicts: Guilt-prone people are better at perspective taking. *Journal of Personality*, *66*(1), 1–37. https://doi.org/10.1111/1467-6494.00001

Lupoli, M. J., Jampol, L., & Oveis, C. (2017). Lying because we care: Compassion increases Prosocial lying. *Journal of Experimental Psychology: General*, *146*(7), 1026–1042. https://doi.org/10.1037/xge0000315

Mai, K. M., Ellis, A. P. J., & Welsh, D. T. (2015). The gray side of creativity: Exploring the role of activation in the link between creative personality and unethical behavior. *Journal of Experimental Social Psychology*, *60*, 76–85. https://doi.org/10.1016/j.jesp.2015.05.004

Marcusson-Clavertz, D., Kjell, O. N. E., Persson, S. D., & Cardeña, E. (2019). Online validation of combined mood induction procedures. *PLoS ONE, 14*(6), 1–16. https://doi.org/10.1371/journal.pone.0217848

Mayer, J. D., Caruso, D. R., & Salovey, P. (1999). Emotional intelligence meets traditional standards for an intelligence. *Intelligence, 27*(4), 267–298. https://doi.org/10.1016/S0160-2896(99)00016-1

McCornack, S. A. (1992). Information manipulation theory. *Communication Monographs, 59*(1), 1–16. https://doi.org/10.1080/03637759209376245

Menninghaus, W., Wagner, V., Wassiliwizky, E., et al. (2019). What are aesthetic emotions? *Psychological Review, 126*(2), 171–195. https://doi.org/10.1037/rev0000135

Miao, C., Humphrey, R. H., Qian, S., & Pollack, J. M. (2019). The relationship between emotional intelligence and the dark triad personality traits: A meta-analytic review. *Journal of Research in Personality, 78*, 189–197. https://doi.org/10.1016/j.jrp.2018.12.004

Nagler, U. K. J., Reiter, K. J., Furtner, M. R., & Rauthmann, J. F. (2014). Is there a "dark intelligence"? Emotional intelligence is used by dark personalities to emotionally manipulate others. *Personality and Individual Differences, 65*, 47–52. https://doi.org/10.1016/j.paid.2014.01.025

Olekalns, M., & Smith, P. L. (2009). Mutually dependent: Power, trust, affect and the use of deception in negotiation. *Journal of Business Ethics, 85*(3), 347–365. https://doi.org/10.1007/s10551-008-9774-4

Pajevic, M., Vukosavljevic-Gvozden, T., Stevanovic, N., & Neumann, C. S. (2018). The relationship between the Dark Tetrad and a two-dimensional view of empathy. *Personality and Individual Differences, 123*, 125–130. https://doi.org/10.1016/j.paid.2017.11.009

Paulhus, D. L. (2014). Toward a taxonomy of dark personalities. *Current Directions in Psychological Science, 23*(6), 421–426. https://doi.org/10.1177/0963721414547737

Perchtold-Stefan, C. M., Fink, A., Rominger, C., & Papousek, I. (2020a). Creative, antagonistic, and angry? Exploring the roots of malevolent creativity with a real-world idea generation task. *Journal of Creative Behavior.* https://doi.org/10.1002/jocb.484

Perchtold-Stefan, C. M., Fink, A., Rominger, C., & Papousek, I. (2020b). Motivational factors in the typical display of humor and creative potential: The case of malevolent creativity. *Frontiers in Psychology, 11.* https://doi.org/10.3389/fpsyg.2020.01213

Perchtold-Stefan, C. M., Fink, A., Rominger, C., & Papousek, I. (2021). Failure to reappraise: Malevolent creativity is linked to revenge ideation and impaired reappraisal inventiveness in the face of stressful, anger-eliciting events. *Anxiety, Stress, & Coping, 34*(4), 437–439. https://doi.org/10.1080/10615806.2021.1918682

Plucker, J. A., Beghetto, R. A., & Dow, G. T. (2004). Why isn't creativity more important to educational psychologists? Potentials, pitfalls, and future directions in creativity research. *Educational Psychologist, 39*(2), 83–96. https://doi.org/10.1207/s15326985ep3902_1

Puthillam, A., Karandikar, S., & Kapoor, H. (2019). I see how you feel: How the Dark Triad recognizes emotions. *Current Psychology*, 1–8. https://doi.org/10.1007/s12144-019-00359-x

Reisenzein, R. (1994). Pleasure-arousal theory and the intensity of emotions. *Journal of Personality and Social Psychology*, *67*(3), 525–539. https://doi.org/10.1037/0022-3514.67.3.525

Rhodes, M. (1961). An analysis of creativity. *The Phi Delta Kappan*, *42*(7), 305–310. www.jstor.org/stable/20342603

Schindler, I., Hosoya, G., Menninghaus, W., et al. (2017). Measuring aesthetic emotions: A review of the literature and a new assessment tool. *PLoS ONE*, *12*(6), e0178899. https://doi.org/10.1371/journal.pone.0178899

Scrima, F., Miceli, S., Caci, B., & Cardaci, M. (2022). The relationship between fear of COVID-19 and intention to get vaccinated. The serial mediation roles of existential anxiety and conspiracy beliefs. *Personality and Individual Differences*, *184*(January), 111188. https://doi.org/10.1016/j.paid.2021.111188

Shen, W., Yuan, Y., Yi, B., Liu, C., & Zhan, H. (2019). A theoretical and critical examination on the relationship between creativity and morality. *Current Psychology*, *38*, 469–485. https://doi.org/10.1007/s12144-017-9613-9

Silvia, P. J. (2009). Looking past pleasure: Anger, confusion, disgust, pride, surprise, and other unusual aesthetic emotions. *Psychology of Aesthetics, Creativity, and the Arts*, *3*(1), 48–51. https://doi.org/10.1037/a0014632

Silvia, P. J., & Brown, E. M. (2007). Anger, disgust, and the negative aesthetic emotions: Expanding an appraisal model of aesthetic experience. *Psychology of Aesthetics, Creativity, and the Arts*, *1*(2), 100–106. https://doi.org/10.1037/1931-3896.1.2.100

Storme, M., Celik, P., & Myszkowski, N. (2021). Creativity and unethicality: A systematic review and meta-analysis. *Psychology of Aesthetics, Creativity, and the Arts*, *15*(4), 664–672. https://doi.org/10.1037/aca0000332

Tangney, J. P., Stuewig, J., & Mashek, D. J. (2007). Moral emotions and moral behavior. *Annual Review of Psychology*, *58*(1), 345–372. https://doi.org/10.1146/annurev.psych.56.091103.070145

Times News Network. (2021, July 10). Thief pretends to puke on BMTC bus passenger, aides steal Rs 50k. *The Times of India*.

Van Kleef, G. A., Anastasopoulou, C., & Nijstad, B. A. (2010). Can expressions of anger enhance creativity? A test of the emotions as social information (EASI) model. *Journal of Experimental Social Psychology*, *46*(6), 1042–1048. https://doi.org/10.1016/j.jesp.2010.05.015

Wagemans, F. M. A., Brandt, M. J., & Zeelenberg, M. (2018). Disgust sensitivity is primarily associated with purity-based moral judgments. *Emotion*, *18*(2), 277–289. https://doi.org/10.1037/emo0000359

Wai, M., & Tiliopoulos, N. (2012). The affective and cognitive empathic nature of the dark triad of personality. *Personality and Individual Differences*, *52*(7), 794–799. https://doi.org/10.1016/j.paid.2012.01.008

Walczyk, J. J., Runco, M. A., Tripp, S. M., & Smith, C. E. (2008). The creativity of lying: Divergent thinking and ideational correlates of the resolution of social dilemmas. *Creativity Research Journal*, *20*(3), 328–342. https://doi.org/10.1080/10400410802355152

Walker, L. J. (1980). Cognitive and perspective-taking prerequisites for moral development. *Child Development*, *51*(1), 131–139.

Wang, B., & Wei, P. (2021). Moral emotion: A new perspective on the relationship between morality and creativity. *Advances in Psychological Science*, *29*(2), 268–275.

Westermann, R., Spies, K., Stahl, G., & Hesse, F. W. (1996). Relative effectiveness and validity of mood induction procedures: A meta-analysis. *European Journal of Social Psychology*, *26*, 557–580.

Wu, W., Su, Y., Huang, X., Liu, W., & Jiang, X. (2020). The dark triad, moral disengagement, and social entrepreneurial intention: Moderating roles of empathic concern and perspective taking. *Frontiers in Psychology*, *11*. https://doi.org/10.3389/fpsyg.2020.01520

Xu, L., Chen, G., & Li, B. (2020). Sadness empathy facilitates prosocial lying. *Social Behavior and Personality*, *47*(9), 1–11. https://doi.org/10.2224/SBP.8371

Yang, J.-S., & Hung, H. V. (2015). Emotions as constraining and facilitating factors for creativity: Companionate love and anger. *Creativity and Innovation Management*, *24*(2), 217–230. https://doi.org/10.1111/caim.12089

19 For Emotion's Sake . . . The Centrality of Emotions in the Art Experience

Pablo P. L. Tinio and Eva Specker

Art is a fundamentally human phenomenon. It accompanies us throughout the life span, from the early, seemingly random scribbles of a young child, the realistic sketches of an adolescent, and the complex multimedia creations of a high-schooler to the highly conceptual and abstract creations of an adult artist. Art is a deeply ingrained expressive and aesthetic activity within our cultures and it almost always surrounds us. It is in our computer screen savers and in phone background images. It is on book covers and in magazine and television advertisements. Even everyday activities, such as driving a car, expose us to a consistent flow of art in the architectural designs of buildings we pass, the music that we listen to, and the street signs and billboards that we see along the way. And beyond the informal presence of art in everyday life, we continue to encounter art in more dedicated contexts such as school auditoriums and grand concert halls, small galleries and big museums, and outdoor public art spaces and professional art studios.

Scholars have long debated, and will likely continue to debate, whether art is utilitarian and has a function (Dissanayake, 2007). What we do know – both anecdotally and through empirical research on the aesthetic experience of art – is that interaction with works of art provokes emotional reactions in the viewer and can evoke memories and even powerful physiological responses. While these reactions are not specific to art encounters, we know that emotional reactions to art, even those that seem on the surface to be minor, might just be the surface manifestation of complex, deeply personal, and even personally transformative aesthetic experiences (Smith & Carr, 2001).

Emotions evoked by art are not only central to the experiences of perceivers, but also commonly discussed by artists in relation to their works and creative processes (Tinio & Gartus, 2018). It is also regularly mentioned in museum exhibition catalogs and artwork labels and widely written about by art historians and critics. According to the English critic Clive Bell (1914), "The starting-point for all systems of aesthetics must be the personal experience of a peculiar emotion. The objects that provoke this emotion we call works of art" (p. 3). The centrality of emotion in art is reflected in Kandinsky's (1914, as cited in Harrison & Wood, 2003) famous statement that "Every work of art is the child of its time, often it is the mother of our emotions" (p. 83). Referring to the artist, Kandinsky also wrote, "He himself leads a relatively refined and complex existence, and the work he produces will necessarily awaken finer emotions in the spectator who is capable of them, emotions that we cannot put into words" (p. 84).

In this chapter, we focus on the emotions involved in the art experience: the most commonly described emotions, how they are expressed by the artist and experienced by the audience, the factors involved in influencing emotional expression, how emotions are considered and integrated into models of the aesthetic experience of art, and what issues surrounding emotions and art we must keep in mind in future research. The best way to research and theorize about emotions in art will continue to be debated (e.g., Menninghaus et al., 2017, 2019; Nadal et al., 2017), and we discuss here why there might never be a resolution to the question of whether emotions felt through the context of art are entirely different from those felt during everyday situations (e.g., Frijda, 1988; Frijda & Schram, 1995; Juslin, 2013; Levinson, 1997; Scherer, 2005; Scherer & Zentner, 2008). It is not our intention to provide a definitive answer to these questions, but rather to provide an overview of the scientific discourse associated with them. Despite disagreement on specific issues, what can be agreed upon is that emotions are central to the experience of art. As Kreitler and Kreiter (1972) asserted, "Regardless of the various qualitative and restrictive epithets often attached to the description of emotions evoked through art, it can hardly be disputed that emotions are frequently a dominant element in the experience of art" (p. 264). Emphasis here is placed on visual art, although many of the topics covered in this chapter are relevant to other forms of art, such as music (Koelsch & Siebel, 2005), design (Locher, 2003), and architecture (Vartanian et al., 2013, 2019). Furthermore, this chapter considers a wide range of emotions, both positive, like pleasure, and negative, like anger, and those that might not fit neatly in the positive–negative dimension, such as nostalgia and surprise (Silvia, 2009; Tinio & Gartus, 2018).

Aesthetic and Everyday Emotions

One of the most intensely debated topics in the psychology of art and aesthetics is whether emotions experienced during encounters with art are different from emotions experienced in daily life. The debate surrounding the addition of the word *aesthetic* to the word *emotion* is succinctly captured by Skov and Nadal (2020):

> The very concept of aesthetic emotions entails that they can be distinguished from nonaesthetic emotions. To accept the concept of aesthetic emotions is to accept that the adjective *aesthetic* denotes a meaningful class of emotions that are defined by distinct properties. But what exactly does aesthetic mean? In what way does the adjective *aesthetic* modify the noun *emotion*? What quality does aesthetic confer to emotion? (p. 640)

According to Scherer (2005), aesthetic emotions are fundamentally different from what he calls utilitarian emotions, which help us adapt to the demands of everyday situations and which might call for specific, intense, and immediate actions. Utilitarian emotions are often related to survival, goal attainment, and the need to cope with a particular life event. For example, the emotions of fear and anger might lead to a fight-or-flight response. Shame and guilt help to constrain one's behaviors to those that are socially acceptable. Happiness and joy promote approach behaviors toward people, ideas, and things that might promote positive social relationships, health, and well-being.

In contrast, aesthetic emotions are not immediately adaptive and are much less intense than utilitarian emotions – they do not dictate whether one lives, one dies, or one is shunned from their social group. For example, awe and wonder might be felt when beholding a beautiful and imposing landscape such as the Grand Canyon. Harmony and solemnity might result from viewing an abstract painting by Mondrian or Kandinsky. The emotions of awe, wonder, harmony, and solemnity may be quite intense and be accompanied by physiological arousal, such as chills. However, they will not be as intense as utilitarian emotions (Scherer, 2005). The idea that aesthetic emotions are distinct from everyday emotions was also shared by Frijda (1988), Kubovy (1999), and Bell (1914).

More recently, Menninghaus et al. (2019; see also Menninghaus et al., 2017) also argued for the idea that aesthetic emotions are their own class of emotions that are different from ordinary emotions, and they provided a systematic and nuanced account of why this is so. Unlike ordinary emotions, aesthetic emotions are sensitive to aesthetic virtues, such as the experience of beauty, fascination, and being moved. Aesthetic emotions also predict pleasure or displeasure and liking and disliking and contribute to the formation of aesthetic preferences. Menninghaus et al. (2019) used the feeling of being moved as an example of the distinctiveness of aesthetic emotions: "Like all aesthetic emotions that are linguistically derived from ordinary emotion terms (further examples being suspense, surprise, interest, boredom), being moved can be an 'everyday' emotion, an art-elicited emotion in the broader sense, and, to the extent that it directly predicts aesthetic appreciation, an aesthetic emotion in the narrower sense" (p. 177). Stated another way, being moved may be considered not an ordinary emotion, but an aesthetic one because it could lead to aesthetic appreciation. Therefore, according to Menninghaus et al. (2019), aesthetic emotions are directly associated with the aesthetic appreciation of aspects of our world. In other words, aesthetic emotions predict aesthetic appreciation, such as when one likes a painting.

Both Scherer's (2005) and Menninghaus and colleagues' (2019) characterizations of aesthetic emotions draw on appraisal theories of emotions (Lazarus, 2001; Scherer, 2001, 2005). These theories state that events (e.g., interactions with artworks in a museum) themselves do not cause emotions; rather, people's subjective evaluations of events cause emotions. Evaluations could involve determining whether an event is relevant to one's particular goal, whether one has the cognitive resources to cope with the event, or whether the event is compatible with one's social and moral beliefs. These evaluations make up the appraisal structure of an event, which in turn leads to emotions. If events themselves cause emotions, then everyone experiencing the same event should have the same emotional reaction to the event. However, the same event might be emotionally experienced differently by different people. Two people can attend the same dance performance, listen to the same piece of music, read the same book, and look at the same painting and come out of these experiences with wholly different emotional reactions because their appraisal structures, not the events, were different (see Silvia, 2005 and Silvia & Brown, 2007 for an overview of appraisal theories of emotion in relation to art).

Appraisals themselves could be influenced by top-down, higher-order cognitive processes that could, in turn, affect emotional responses to art. One such cognitive process is psychological distancing, which involves art perceivers experiencing aesthetic artifacts (e.g., a piece of music, a fictional story, or an art object) as safe, harmless, or nonconsequential (Scherer, 2005). This is the case even for an artifact that is negative in content or in emotional valence. Examples of these might include a scene in a film showing a man alone in the wilderness being stalked and devoured by wild animals; a realistic painting that depicts a scene of a massacre, with dead and mutilated bodies scattered on the ground; a photograph showing captured soldiers in a warzone being beaten by their captors. A perceiver beholding any of these works might feel sadness, fear, or anger. However, they are not likely to run out of the theatre, gallery, or museum in sheer terror because they are psychologically distanced from what they are seeing (Frijda, 1988). They do not feel directly threatened by the experience and know that they are not in harm's way.

Gerger et al. (2014) provided empirical support for the psychological distancing phenomenon. Participants in their study viewed positively and negatively valenced artworks (artistic photographs of objects and scenes) and positively and negatively valenced photographs belonging to the International Affective Picture System (IAPS; Lang et al., 1999). The IAPS is a commonly used set of photographic images varying in content and emotional valence. The stimuli were presented in two conditions: as artworks or as realistic press photographs. The authors collected subjective emotion and liking ratings, as well as data using facial electromyography (EMG). The latter measures facial muscle activity and has been shown to be an effective and objective indicator of people's emotional reactions to stimuli such as artworks. Greater activation of the zygomaticus major muscle (smiling muscle) indicates a positive emotional reaction and greater activation of the corrugator supercilii muscle (frowning muscle) indicates a negative emotional reaction (Dimberg, 1990; Gerger et al., 2011; Lang et al., 1993). Gerger et al.'s results showed that positive emotional reactions as indicated by EMG data were lower and liking ratings for stimuli with negative emotional valence were higher, when the stimuli were presented as artworks versus as press photographs. This finding is consistent with the psychological distancing effect in which negative stimuli could be evaluated positively in an art context, which poses no immediate threat to the perceiver.

Aesthetic emotions being a special class of emotions, as proposed by Scherer (2005), Menninghaus et al. (2019), and others, is but one side of the coin. The other side states that aesthetic emotions are no different from everyday emotions. For example, Skov and Nadal (2020) have argued that empirical evidence does not support the idea that aesthetic emotions are a distinct class of emotions. Concerning appraisal theories of emotions, Skov and Nadal state that aesthetic appreciation could be understood in terms of appraisal structures that are common in everyday, nonaesthetic appreciation. Put simply, emotions are emotions regardless of whether one is experiencing a famous sculpture in a museum or beholding a well-plated and appetizing plate of food. In fact, Skov and Nadal (2020) state that "available evidence suggests that the opposite view is more likely: that the ability of humans to attend to almost every aspect of the physical world, including the parts of it constructed by humans, and assess them for their pleasing qualities, relies on an engagement of affective processes that are shared with other forms of appraisal" (p. 646). The same reward systems and processes that are active in the brain when dealing with everyday objects and situations are also active when dealing with what we typically consider "aesthetic" objects and situations, such as music, poetry, and artworks.

Finally, Fingerhut and Prinz (2020) recently provided an additional perspective that helps to add nuance to the above debate. They proposed that instead of differentiating between "normal" and "aesthetic" emotions, one should differentiate between art-elicited and aesthetic emotions. Art-elicited emotions are experienced as a consequence of engaging with art (e.g., experiencing fear when watching a horror film) while aesthetic emotions are emotions that are relevant for our aesthetic evaluation of objects. For instance, the experience of wonder when looking at an artwork is an aesthetic emotion because it influences our aesthetic evaluation of the work (i.e., we consider the artwork good because it elicits wonder).

Factors That Impact Emotions and other Aesthetic Outcomes: Artwork, Context, and Viewer

The Genuine Artifact in a Curated Space

Although this chapter focuses on emotions, it is important to set emotions within the context of the full suite of responses to art. For example, a museum visitor's attention might be seized by a particular painting in a gallery full of other objects and people. This visitor approaches the painting and reads the accompanying label describing the creator of the work, its provenance, and the materials of which it is made. They may not only learn something new from this experience, but they may also judge whether they like the work or not. It could also be the case that the work elicits emotions in the visitor, such as nostalgia and longing, because it brought back fond memories from childhood. The visitor might even feel goosebumps as a result of the experience. This example will not be the same for different people, artworks, and contexts. However, it illustrates the power of art to evoke complex and varied outcomes related to attention, approach-avoid behaviors, learning, liking-disliking, and physiological and emotional responses.

Emotions and all other possible outcomes of the aesthetic experience result from an interaction among what Tinio (2020) referred to as the *aesthetics triumvirate* that includes the art viewer, the artwork itself, and the nature of the context in which the artwork is presented. There are certain aspects of artworks that have been shown to influence how they are experienced and that have bearings on the types of emotions that they evoke in the art viewer. For example, because aesthetic experiences involve a search for meaning (Millis, 2001; Russell, 2003), representational works allow the viewer to more easily feel emotions from identifying and thinking about the objects and subjects that might be depicted in the artworks. In contrast, abstract works – especially those that are purely abstract, such as the paintings of Kazimir Malevich or Piet Mondrian or Jackson Pollock – are more difficult for viewers to make meaning of and grasp. To engage deeply with abstract works, viewers often need to be scaffolded with additional information about the artist, the historical context in which the artwork was created, and the concepts and ideas behind the works.

The nature of the context in which artworks are presented is also incredibly important as it sets the tone for how one might interact with the artworks on view (e.g., Bourdieu, 1984; Carr, 1991, 1992, 2003; Pelowski, Forster et al., 2017). Certain contextual elements may even be a requirement for deep emotional engagement with art to be possible. As Van de Cruys and Wagemans (2011) stated, "An experience of deep aesthetic appreciation is not so easily reproduced in the lab" (p. 1042), and more recently, Carbon (2020) noted that "the deeper effects of aesthetic experience are quite rare in standard laboratory contexts, and therefore their existence might even be questionable if we always carry out our aesthetic research in laboratory settings that are mostly far from reality" (p. 3). In contrast, museums elevate the perceived quality of art (Carr, 2003). They have the reputation as authoritative cultural institutions that select artifacts deemed worthy of being included in their collections and presented formally to the public. In doing so, museums have the power to declare an artwork (and by default its creator; and vice versa) as having a special quality that distinguishes it from other similar objects (Smith & Wolf, 1996; Tröndle, 2014). As we mentioned above, just telling the viewer that a photograph is an artwork (instead of a news photograph) leads to a more positive emotional experience, even for images with negative content (Gerger et al., 2014). Similarly, telling people that the artwork they are viewing came from a gallery results in increased activations in pleasure and emotion areas of the brain (Kirk et al., 2009).

Museums and galleries also positively impact the way artworks are perceived because these spaces are known to exhibit original works of art, the very artifacts that artists themselves have made. To art viewers, authenticity matters (Benjamin, 1969; Specker et al., 2021). Authentic works are perceived as being imbued with the maker's touch and other special qualities (Newman & Bloom, 2012). One of the more robust findings in psychology of art research is that people respond more positively to authentic artworks than their corresponding reproductions (e.g., Huang et al., 2011; Kruger et al., 2004; Wolz & Carbon, 2014). Not only are authentic artworks liked more, they are also deemed as more valuable (Newman & Bloom, 2012).

Perhaps the most impactful contextual factor that directly impacts emotional and aesthetic responses is that artworks displayed in museums and galleries are carefully curated to be displayed in a purposeful, systematic, and contextualized manner. Museums do not just display monetarily, culturally, and historically valuable artworks; instead, they present these works within the context of art history, the personal lives of the artists including their social circles and influences, and the provenance of the works such as how they came to become a part of museum collections (Illes & Tinio, in press). These contextual elements are presented along with the artworks (such as labels and wall texts about the works), and the sequencing and physical placements of the works help to create themes and narratives (e.g., Mullennix et al., 2020; Reitstätter et al., 2020; Specker et al., 2020).

Thus, by having the reputation of authority and by presenting genuine artifacts in a systematic and curated manner, museums are able to elevate the perception of artworks and impact people's experiences of art. For example, one of the most renowned modern art museums in the world is the Solomon R. Guggenheim Museum, which was designed by the celebrated architect Frank Lloyd Wright. The museum is located in New York City in a highly affluent neighborhood adjacent to Central Park. The impressive building itself is considered a work of modern art with its organic, spiraling form that provides a unique approach to displaying art. The main feature of the building's interior is a ramp that spirals from the ground floor to the top of the structure. This physical feature leads visitors to experience the displayed works sequentially – bottom-up or top-down. Visitors to the Guggenheim experience genuine artworks in a grand museum presented in a highly structured and curated manner. Altogether, these contextual factors have a tremendous influence on visitors' aesthetic experiences.

Art Expertise

In addition to the features of artworks and the nature of the context in which they are presented, certain characteristics of art perceivers themselves also impact their aesthetic experiences in general, and their emotional responses to art in particular. The characteristic that has been of particular interest to researchers is art expertise, which usually refers to the level of art knowledge that a person has, but is also often operationally defined to include formal training and interest in art (Specker et al., 2018; Specker, 2021). This area of research has a long history in the psychology of art and aesthetics and has led to important insights into how people experience and emotionally respond to art.

Although people tend to prefer representational to abstract works, art expertise could moderate such preference, as described below. Aesthetic experiences are the result of an interplay between cognitive and emotional processes (e.g., Leder et al., 2004; Leder & Nadal, 2014). However, the correlation between cognitive and emotional processes decreases as level of art expertise increases (Leder et al., 2012). Art perceivers with little to no knowledge of the artworks they are viewing are more likely to focus on what is being depicted and the emotional elements being evoked by the works. In contrast, those with more art knowledge pay attention to other aspects of an artwork, such as the personal history of the artist and the provenance of the work as well as its materials, compositional structure, conceptual foundation, and similarity to other works by the same artist and artistic style to which it belongs (e.g., Augustin & Leder, 2006; Leder et al., 2014; Locher, 1996; Tinio et al., 2014). Those with high level of art expertise also pay attention to the manner in which the artwork is presented by the museum (Illes & Tinio, in press).

Although the impact of art expertise might seem to relate mainly to cognitive aspects of the art experience (e.g., knowledge about a specific art style), art expertise can directly impact emotional responses to art. Leder et al. (2014) used facial EMG to examine whether art expertise modulates the emotions that people experience when looking at negatively and positively valenced artworks. They found that art experts had weaker EMG muscle activations (in the corrugator supercilii) toward negatively valenced artworks as compared to non-art experts. Furthermore, art experts showed stronger EMG muscle activations toward positively valenced artworks than non-experts. As discussed above, high activation of the corrugator supercilii is an indicator of a negative (frowning) response. The results therefore show that art experts find negatively valenced artworks less negative, and positively valenced artworks more positive, than non-art experts. Expertise in this case seems to serve as an insulator against extreme negative reactions.

It is important to note that Leder et al.'s (2014) results also show that the effects of expertise on the aesthetic experience of art are immediate and automatic, as facial EMG – like many other physiological measures such as skin conductance, heart rate variability, and, to an extent, eye-movement tracking – has great temporal sensitivity and is able to detect facial muscle activations of which people are often unaware and which serve as indicators of emotional reactions (Gerger et al., 2011). Another method, event-related potential (ERP) measures, with millisecond precision, neural processes (in the form of electrical activity measured by electrodes placed on specific areas of the scalp) in response to viewing visual stimuli. Analyses of ERP data focus on determining the presence of electrical activities in specific sites on the scalp – referred to as *components* – that are established indicators of emotional and cognitive processes. Relevant to this chapter, the ERP method can indicate not only attention to art being viewed, but also whether the viewer is sensitive to the emotional content of the artworks they are viewing and the time course associated with emotional responses to the artworks.

Else et al. (2015) used the ERP method to examine the impact of art expertise on emotional responses to art. Visual artists (formally trained artists, art historians, and curators) and non-artists viewed a large set of representational, abstract, and semi-abstract artworks while ERP data were recorded. The participants also rated the extent to which the artworks affected them emotionally (positively or negatively). The results showed that the strength of neural activity was highly related to expertise. Specifically, for artists, neural activity was highest in response to abstract art relative to the other two types of art. In contrast, for non-artists, neural activity was lowest in response to abstract art relative to the other two types of art. Moreover, artists also showed more emotional arousal in response to all three types of artworks than non-artists. Finally, Else et al. (2015) found that the N1 component – which is associated with the very early processing of the emotional aspects of visual stimuli – was found only in the artists. The authors concluded that these differences between the two groups indicate that compared to non-artists, artists were able to direct attention much earlier and allocate more attentional resources to abstract art. Furthermore, while viewing the artworks, the artists' attention to the art persisted when those of the non-artists began to fade. Thus, compared to non-artists, experts were more aroused by, and attentive toward, art but especially abstract art.

Art expertise influences not only the intensity of emotions that one experiences during encounters with art, but also the ability to distinguish emotions that one is experiencing. This ability is referred to as emotion differentiation, or emotional granularity, and it has been linked to positive outcomes such as better emotion regulation, the ability to cope with stressful situations, and psychological well-being (Barrett et al., 2001; Kashdan et al., 2015). Because art experiences often involve a wide variety and different intensities of emotions, it follows that emotion differentiation could play a key role in aesthetic experiences. Recently, Fayn et al. (2018) tackled this issue by examining whether levels of emotion differentiation during aesthetic experiences of art might be related to levels of knowledge about art. Specifically, they examined if those with more art knowledge would have deeper and more nuanced engagement with art and, in turn, greater emotion differentiation abilities. They also measured participants' level of curiosity (as an indicator of their motivation to engage deeply with art) and their perceived comprehension of the artworks that they viewed (Silvia, 2006). They found that participants who had more art knowledge showed more emotion differentiation of negative emotions. This effect was driven by the extent to which the participants reported comprehending the artworks and, to a lesser extent, participants' level of curiosity. Fayn et al.'s (2018) findings are consistent with previous studies that have shown that art experts are more likely to prefer and gravitate toward the less pleasant (Silvia, 2013) and the more complex artworks (Parsons, 1987).

Research on the effects of art expertise on aesthetic experience has been a part of the field of psychology of aesthetics and the arts during most of its history. Studies that have focused specifically on the impact of art expertise on art-related emotions have been sporadic but have steadily increased in the past decade. This increase is partly owed to new methods that have made it possible to more rigorously and objectively measure emotions beyond simply asking people what they felt after looking at a work of art (e.g., Tinio & Gartus, 2018). We hope that this methodological development will continue in the coming years and be accompanied by similar developments in how expertise is conceptually and operationally defined (see also Specker et al., 2018; Specker, 2021).

Emotions and Models of the Aesthetic Experience of Art

As discussed above, the aesthetic triumvirate consists of the artwork, perceiver, and context in which the artwork is presented. The nature of the interaction among these three components determines the nature of the aesthetic experience as well as resulting cognitive and emotional outcomes, such as preferences for, and understanding of, the artwork and emotions felt as a result of the experience. This constellation of processes and outcomes during interactions with art has been characterized by a number of models of the aesthetic experience. In this section, we explore how emotions are situated within these models.

Perhaps the most dominant and cited of these models is Leder et al.'s (2004; see also Leder & Nadal, 2014; Pelowski, Markey et al., 2017) *model of aesthetic appreciation and aesthetic judgments*, which consists of five processing stages: (1) perception – analysis of a work's basic visual characteristics such as symmetry, complexity, contour, clarity, and contrast; (2) implicit memory integration – largely nonconscious processing of a work's familiarity, prototypicality, and peak-shift characteristics (i.e., exaggeration of salient features of an object, such as in caricatures where specific facial features or body parts are enlarged to bring emphasis to those features); (3) explicit classification – deliberate processing of an artwork's content (what is depicted and how it is depicted) and style (whether a work belongs to a specific art historical style, such as Abstract Expressionism) that is heavily influenced by art-related knowledge; (4) cognitive mastery – developing an understanding of various aspects of an artwork including ideas, technical and material characteristics, and concepts associated with the work; and (5) evaluation – an assessment of the success of the cognitive mastery stage such as in terms of a reduction in ambiguity (e.g., comprehending the idea behind a purely abstract artwork). There is a continuous feedback loop between the cognitive mastery and evaluation stages. On the one hand, successful cognitive mastery leads to a pleasurable and emotionally positive experience. On the other hand, failure to reach cognitive mastery could lead to a cycling back to earlier stages of the model. The two outcomes identified by the model are aesthetic judgments and aesthetic emotions. One of the defining features of the Leder et al. (2004) model is that emotional processing occurs in parallel to the five stages. In other words, emotional processing occurs from the moment the perceiver first glances at an artwork to the moment when an aesthetic judgment is made. Emotions in this sense are pervasive and critical aspects of the art experience.

Another comprehensive model of the aesthetic experience of art is Chatterjee's (2003) *neuroscientific model of visual aesthetics*, which shares similar features with Leder et al.'s (2004) model. The former refers to the aesthetic experience of visual objects more generally, while the latter focuses on the aesthetic experience of visual art more specifically (see Vartanian & Nadal, 2007 for a detailed discussion and comparison of the two models). However, both models characterize the aesthetic experience as progressing from three broad stages: the early, automatic processing of low-level visual features (e.g., symmetry and complexity; Leder et al.'s stage 1), to intermediate memory-based processing (identifying objects and scenes; Leder et al.'s stages 2 and 3), and to higher-level cognitive processing involving meaning-making, aesthetic judgments, and aesthetic emotions (Leder et al.'s stages 4 and 5).

A third model that includes the above three broad stages is Chatterjee and Vartanian's (2014) *aesthetic triad model*, which describes the interaction among sensory-motor, meaning-knowledge, and emotion-valuation neural systems. According to this model, the nature of the interaction among these three systems defines the resulting aesthetic experience, and unlike the two previous models, Chatterjee and Vartanian's model does not characterize aesthetic experience as resulting from a sequence of processing stages. Instead, the contribution of each neural system varies (relative to the other two systems) depending on what is being aesthetically experienced. Thus, while there are differences, the models by Leder et al. (2004), Chatterjee (2003), and Chatterjee and Vartanian (2014) have a number of key similarities in their accounts of the experience of art. Especially relevant to the present chapter is the centrality of emotion in all three models.

The above models are focused solely on the experience of the perceiver as they interact with art. Tinio (2013), in the *mirror model of art*, developed on the Leder et al. (2004) and Chatterjee (2003) models to include the creative art-making process. According to the mirror model, the aesthetic experience of art mirrors, in reverse order, the art-making process. In addition, the emotional experience of the perceiver of an artwork mirrors the emotional profile of that artwork. Tinio and Gartus (2018) referred to the emotional profile inherent in an artwork as the *emotion affordance,* which they examined in studies conducted in a museum and that involved both museum visitors' experiences of entire exhibitions and individual works of art. Tinio and Gartus focused on determining correspondences between an exhibition's or an artwork's emotional affordance and the primary emotions that visitors reported after having seen the exhibition or the work. For example, a painting might have primarily nostalgic or mainly lighthearted and playful elements as determined by historical records and writings about the work. Entire exhibitions can similarly have specific emotion affordances. According to their hypotheses, these emotion affordances should correspond to the emotions that visitors report experiencing after viewing the exhibition or the work. Results showed visitors' emotions corresponded strongly with the affordances of the art that they experienced (see also Specker et al., 2017 for a similar test of the mirror model). This was the case for individual artworks and entire exhibitions (see Smith, 2014 for a discussion of the cumulative effects of viewing multiple artworks).

Tinio and Gartus (2018) showed that art perceivers are sensitive to specific emotions inherent in artworks, which is consistent with one of the central tenets of the mirror model: "The mirror model suggests that during an encounter with an artwork, perceivers recapture some of the thoughts, concepts, and emotions of the artist, and that the perceivers reinterpret these within the context of their current motivational states, emotions, thought processes, and viewing environments" (p. 274). Additional support for the mirror model were obtained by Pelowski et al. (2020), who examined artists and the perceivers of their artworks. They found that the viewers were able to guess which emotions the artists intended to evoke in their works and were able to feel the same emotions that the artists felt during the art-making process. Recently, Pelowski et al. (2021) replicated these findings with art by professional artists at the Venice Biennale, the oldest and one of the most prestigious exhibitions in the world.

Conclusion

Common to the models discussed in this chapter is the fact that emotions are fundamental to the experience of art, and along with aesthetic judgments (e.g., preference and liking), emotions constitute one of the main set of outcomes of aesthetic experiences. As Tinio and Gartus (2018) and Pelowski et al. (2020) showed, perceivers are able to pick up the emotional characteristics inherent in works they are beholding. Art conveys and evokes emotions. It is therefore not surprising that emotions are so pervasive when people speak and write about art.

As much as we have learned about the role of emotions in the experience of art, there is much left to discover as important open questions remain, questions that will fuel future research on emotions in art. For example, how does cultural background impact one's emotional responses to art? Factors related to the individual and those related to broader influences stemming from society and culture have rarely been examined and will prove to be promising areas for future work. Mikuni et al. (2021), for instance, recently examined the well-known museum fatigue effect and whether it manifests differently for art perceivers from different cultures. Although they discovered evidence for the universality of the museum fatigue effect, their findings suggest other fruitful areas for examination. Another question that needs to be addressed more systematically is what types of art media (e.g., sculpture, painting, installation art) are more likely to elicit certain emotions? The early stages of visual perception are common across different types of objects. However, there may be specific components of late cognitive processing that are specific for certain art media (Chatterjee, 2003), which in turn could influence the types of emotions experienced by the viewer. Finally, how do existing mood and affective state interact with the emotion affordance of an artwork and what are the resulting cognitive and affective outcomes of this interaction? Research on emotions experienced through art have typically used a one-shot strategy in which data are only collected during or immediately following an interaction with an artwork. Future studies should consider viewers' baseline emotions, such as those that they are experiencing as they enter a gallery and how these change during the course of viewing multiple works. As has been evident in the past two decades, continuous innovations in research design and instrumentation will certainly allow us to tackle such challenging questions in the future.

References

Augustin, D., & Leder, H. (2006). Art expertise: A study of concepts and conceptual spaces. *Psychology Science, 48*(2), 135–156.

Barrett, L. F., Gross, J., Christensen, T. C., & Benvenuto, M. (2001). Knowing what you're feeling and knowing what to do about it: Mapping the relation between emotion differentiation and emotion regulation. *Cognition & Emotion, 15*(6), 713–724. https://doi.org/10.1080/02699930143000239

Bell, C. (1914). *Art*. Frederick A. Stokes Company.

Benjamin, W. (1969). *Illuminations*. Schocken Books.

Bourdieu, P. (1984). *Distinction: A Social Critique of the Judgement of Taste*. Harvard University Press.

Carbon, C. C. (2020). Ecological art experience: How we can gain experimental control while preserving ecologically valid settings and contexts. *Frontiers in Psychology, 11*, 800. https://doi.org/10.3389/fpsyg.2020.00800

Carr, D. (1991). Minds in museums and libraries: The cognitive management of cultural institutions. *Teachers College Record, 93*, 6–27.

Carr, D. (1992). Cultural institutions as structures for cognitive change. *New Directions for Adult and Continuing Education, 53*, 21–35. https://doi.org/10.1002/ace.36719925305

Carr, D. W. (2003). *The Promise of Cultural Institutions*. AltaMira Press.

Chatterjee, A. (2003). Prospects for a cognitive neuroscience of visual aesthetics. *Bulletin of Psychology and the Arts, 4*, 55–60. https://doi.org/10.1037/e514602010–003

Chatterjee, A., & Vartanian, O. (2014). Neuroaesthetics. *Trends in Cognitive Sciences, 18*(7), 370–375. https://doi.org/10.1016/j.tics.2014.03.003

Dimberg, U. (1990). Facial electromyography and emotional reactions. *Psychophysiology, 27*, 481–494. http://dx.doi.org/10.1111/j.1469-8986.1990.tb01962.x

Dissanayake, E. (2007). What art is and what art does: An overview of contemporary evolutionary hypotheses. In C. Martindale, P. Locher, & V. M. Petrov (Eds.), *Evolutionary and Neurocognitive Approaches to Aesthetics, Creativity and the Arts* (pp. 1–14). Baywood.

Else, J. E., Ellis, J., & Orme, E. (2015). Art expertise modulates the emotional response to modern art, especially abstract: An ERP investigation. *Frontiers in Human Neuroscience, 9*, 525. https://doi.org/10.3389/fnhum.2015.00525

Fayn, K., Silvia, P. J., Erbas, Y., Tiliopoulos, N., & Kuppens, P. (2018). Nuanced aesthetic emotions: Emotion differentiation is related to knowledge of the arts and curiosity. *Cognition and Emotion*, *32*(3), 593–599. https://doi.org/10.1080/02699931.2017.1322554

Fingerhut, J., & Prinz, J. J. (2020). Aesthetic emotions reconsidered. *The Monist*, *103*(2), 223–239. https://doi.org/10.1093/monist/onz037

Frijda, N. H. (1988). The laws of emotion. *American Psychologist*, *43*, 349–358. http://dx.doi.org/10.1037//0003-066x.43.5.349.

Frijda, N., & Schram, D. (1995). Emotions and cultural products: Psychological reaction to the arts and literature. *Poetics*, *23*, 1–6. http://dx.doi.org/10.1016/0304-422X(95)90009-W.

Gerger, G., Leder, H., & Kremer, A. (2014). Context effects on emotional and aesthetic evaluations of artworks and IAPS pictures. *Acta Psychologica*, *151*, 174–183. https://doi.org/10.1016/j.actpsy.2014.06.008

Gerger, G., Leder, H., Tinio, P. P. L., & Schacht, A. (2011). Faces versus patterns: Exploring aesthetic reactions using facial EMG. *Psychology of Aesthetics Creativity and the Arts*, *5*, 241–250. http://dx.doi.org/10.1037/a0024154

Harrison, C., & Wood, P. (2003). *Art in Theory 1900–2000: An Anthology of Changing Ideas*. Blackwell.

Huang, M., Bridge, H., Kemp, M. J., & Parker, A. J. (2011). Human cortical activity evoked by the assignment of authenticity when viewing works of art. *Frontiers in Human Neuroscience*, *5*, 134. http://dx.doi.org/10.3389/fnhum.2011.00134

Illes, A., & Tinio, P. P. L. (in press). Experiencing art in museums: Empirical aesthetics, neuroaesthetics, and museum studies. In M. Nadal & M. Skov (Eds.), *The Routledge International Handbook of Neuroaesthetics*.

Juslin, P. N. (2013). From everyday emotions to aesthetic emotions: Towards a unified theory of musical emotions. *Physics of Life Reviews*, *10*, 235–266. http://dx.doi.org/ 10.1016/j.plrev.2013.05.008

Kashdan, T. B., Barrett, L. F., & McKnight, P. E. (2015). Unpacking emotion differentiation: Transforming unpleasant experience by perceiving distinctions in negativity. *Current Directions in Psychological Science*, *24*(1), 10–16. https://doi.org/10.1177/0963721414550708

Kirk, U., Skov, M., Hulme, O., Christensen, M. S., & Zeki, S. (2009). Modulation of aesthetic value by semantic context: An fMRI study. *NeuroImage*, *44*, 1125–1132. http://dx.doi.org/10.1016/j.neuroimage .2008.10.009

Koelsch, S., & Siebel, W. A. (2005). Towards a neural basis of music perception. *Trends in Cognitive Sciences*, *9*, 578–584. https://doi.org/10.1016/j.tics.2005.10.001

Kreitler, H., & Kreitler, S. (1972). *Psychology of the Arts*. Duke University Press.

Kruger, J., Wirtz, D., Van Boven, L., & Altermatt, T. W. (2004). The effort heuristic. *Journal of Experimental Social Psychology*, *40*(1), 91–98. https://doi.org/10.1016/S0022-1031(03)00065-9

Kubovy, M. (1999). *On the Pleasures of the Mind*. Russell Sage Foundation.

Lang, P. J., Bradley, M. M., & Cuthbert, B. N. (1999). *International Affective Picture System: Technical Manual and Affective Ratings*. The Center for Research in Psychophysiology, University of Florida.

Lang, P. J., Greenwald, M. K., Bradley, M. M., & Hamm, A. O. (1993). Looking at pictures: Affective, facial, visceral, and behavioral reactions. *Psychophysiology*, *30*(3), 261–273. https://doi.org/10.1111/j.1469-8986.1993.tb03352.x

Lazarus, R. S. (2001). Relational meaning and discrete emotions. In K. R. Scherer, A. Schorr, & T. Johnstone (Eds.), *Appraisal Processes in Emotion: Theory, Methods, Research* (pp. 37–67). Oxford University Press.

Leder, H., Belke, B., Oeberst, A., & Augustin, D. (2004). A model of aesthetic appreciation and aesthetic judgments. *British Journal of Psychology, 95*, 489–508. https://doi.org/10.1348/0007126042369811

Leder, H., Gerger, G., Brieber, D., & Schwarz, N. (2014). What makes an art expert? Emotion and evaluation in art appreciation. *Cognition and Emotion, 28*(6), 1137–1147. https://doi.org/10.1080/02699931.2013.870132

Leder, H., Gerger, G., Dressler, S., & Schabmann, A. (2012). How art is appreciated. *Psychology of Aesthetics, Creativity, and the Arts, 6*, 2–10. https://doi.org/10.1037/a0026396

Leder, H., & Nadal, M. (2014). Ten years of a model of aesthetic appreciation and aesthetic judgments: The aesthetic episode – developments and challenges in empirical aesthetics. *British Journal of Psychology, 105*, 443–464. https://doi.org/10.1111/bjop.12084

Levinson, J. (1997). Emotion in response to art. In M. Hjort & S. Laver (Eds.), *Emotion and the Arts* (pp. 20–34). Oxford University Press.

Locher, P. J. (1996). The contribution of eye-movement research to an understanding of the nature of pictorial balance perception: A review of the literature. *Empirical Studies of the Arts, 14*, 143–163. https://doi.org/10.2190/D77M-3NU4-DQ88-H1QG

Locher, P. J. (2003). An empirical investigation of the visual rightness theory of picture perception. *Acta Psychologica, 114*, 147–164. https://doi.org/10.1016/j.actpsy.2003.07.001

Menninghaus, W., Wagner, V., Hanich, J., et al. (2017). The distancing-embracing model of the enjoyment of negative emotions in art reception. *Behavioral and Brain Sciences, 40*, 1–63. https://doi.org/10.1017/S0140525X17000309

Menninghaus, W., Wagner, V., Wassiliwizky, E., et al. (2019). What are aesthetic emotions? *Psychological Review, 126*(2), 171–195. https://doi.org/10.1037/rev0000135

Mikuni, J., Specker, E., Pelowski, M., Leder, H., & Kawabata, H. (2021). Is there a general "art fatigue" effect? A cross-paradigm, cross-cultural study of repeated art viewing in the laboratory. *Psychology of Aesthetics, Creativity, and the Arts, 16*(2). https://doi.org/10.1037/aca0000396

Millis, K. (2001). Making meaning brings pleasure: The influence of titles on aesthetic experiences. *Emotion, 1*, 320–329. https://doi.org/10.1037/1528-3542.1.3.320

Mullennix, J. W., Kristo, G. M., & Robinet, J. (2020). Effects of preceding context on aesthetic preference. *Empirical Studies of the Arts, 38*(2), 149–171. https://doi.org/10.1177/0276237418805687

Nadal, M., Vartanian, O., & Skov, M. (2017). Psychological models of art reception must be empirically grounded. *Behavioral and Brain Sciences, 40*, 36–37. https://doi.org/10.1017/S0140525X17001790

Newman, G. E., & Bloom, P. (2012). Art and authenticity: The importance of originals in judgments of value. *Journal of Experimental Psychology General, 141*, 558–569. https://doi.org/10.1037/a0026035

Parsons, M. J. (1987). *How We Understand Art: A Cognitive Developmental Account of Aesthetic Experience.* Cambridge University Press.

Pelowski, M., Forster, M., Tinio, P. P. L., Scholl, M., & Leder, H. (2017). Beyond the lab: Framework for examining interactions with art in museums. *Psychology of Aesthetics, Creativity, and the Arts, 11*, 245–264. https://doi.org/10.1037/aca0000141

Pelowski, M., Markey, P. S., Forster, M., Gerger, G., & Leder, H. (2017). Move me, astonish me … delight my eyes and brain: The Vienna integrated model of top-down and bottom-up processes in art perception (VIMAP) and corresponding affective, evaluative, and neurophysiological correlates. *Physics of Life Reviews, 21*, 80–125. https://doi.org/10.1016/j.plrev.2017.02.003

Pelowski, M., Specker, E., Boddy, J., et al. (2021). Together in the dark? Investigating the understanding and feeling of intended emotions between viewers and professional artists at the Venice Biennale. *Psychology of Aesthetics Creativity and the Arts.* https://doi.org/10.1037/aca0000436.

Pelowski, M., Specker, E., Gerger, G., Leder, H., & Weingarden, L. S. (2020). Do you feel like I do? A study of spontaneous and deliberate emotion sharing and understanding between artists and perceivers of installation art. *Psychology of Aesthetics, Creativity, and the Arts, 14*(3), 276–293. https://doi.org/10.1037/aca0000201

Reitstätter, L., Brinkmann, H., Santini, T., et al. (2020). The display makes a difference: A mobile eye tracking study on the perception of art before and after a museum's rearrangement. *Journal of Eye Movement Research, 13*(2). https://doi.org/10.16910/jemr.13.2.6

Russell, P. A. (2003). Effort after meaning and the hedonic value of paintings. *British Journal of Psychology, 94*, 99–110. https://doi.org/10.1348/000712603762842138

Scherer, K. R. (2001). Appraisal considered as a process of multilevel sequential checking. In K. R. Scherer, A. Schorr, & T. Johnstone (Eds.), *Appraisal Processes in Emotion: Theory, Methods, Research* (pp. 92–120). Oxford University Press.

Scherer, K. R. (2005). What are emotions? And how can they be measured? *Social Science Information, 44*, 695–729. http://dx.doi.org/10.1177/0539018405058216

Scherer, K. R., & Zentner, M. (2008). Music evoked emotions are different – More often aesthetic than utilitarian. *Behavioral and Brain Sciences, 31*, 595–596. http://dx.doi.org/10.1017/s0140525x08005505

Silvia, P. J. (2005). Cognitive appraisals and interest in visual art: Exploring an appraisal theory of aesthetic emotions. *Empirical studies of the arts, 23*(2), 119–133. https://doi.org/10.2190/12AV-AH2P-MCEH-289E

Silvia, P. J. (2006). Artistic training and interest in visual art: Applying the appraisal model of aesthetic emotions. *Empirical studies of the arts, 24*(2), 139–161. https://doi.org/10.2190/DX8K-6WEA-6WPA-FM84

Silvia, P. J. (2009). Looking past pleasure: anger, confusion, disgust, pride, surprise, and other unusual aesthetic emotions. *Psychology of Aesthetics, Creativity, and the Arts, 3*(1), 48. https://doi.org/10.1037/a0014632

Silvia, P. J. (2013). Interested experts, confused novices: Art expertise and the knowledge emotions. *Empirical Studies of the Arts, 31*(1), 107–115. https://doi.org/10.2190/EM.31.1.f

Silvia, P. J., & Brown, E. M. (2007). Anger, disgust, and the negative aesthetic emotions: Expanding an appraisal model of aesthetic experience. *Psychology of*

Aesthetics, Creativity, and the Arts, 1(2), 100. https://doi.org/10.1037/1931-3896 .1.2.100

Skov, M., & Nadal, M. (2020). There are no aesthetic emotions. *Psychological Review, 126*(2), 640–649. https://doi.org/10.1037/rev0000187

Smith, J. K. (2014). *The Museum Effect: How Museums, Libraries, and Cultural Institutions Educate and Civilize Society*. Rowman & Littlefield.

Smith, J. K., & Carr, D. W. (2001). In Byzantium. *Curator, 44*, 335–354. https://doi.org/ 10.1111/j.2151-6952.2001.tb01174.x

Smith, J. K., & Wolf, L. F. (1996). Museum visitor preferences and intentions in constructing aesthetic experience. *Poetics, 24*, 219–238. https://doi.org/10 .1016/0304-422X(95)00006-6

Specker, E. (2021). Further validating the VAIAK: Defining a psychometric model, configural measurement invariance, reliability, and practical guidelines. *Psychology of Aesthetics, Creativity, and the Arts*. Advance online publication. https://doi.org/10.1037/aca0000427

Specker, E., Fekete, A., Trupp, M. D., & Leder, H. (2021). Is a "real" artwork better than a reproduction? A meta-analysis of the genuineness effect. *Psychology of Aesthetics, Creativity, and the Arts*. Advance online publication. https://doi .org/10.1037/aca0000399

Specker, E., Forster, M., Brinkmann, H., et al. (2018). The Vienna Art Interest and Art Knowledge Questionnaire (VAIAK): A unified and validated measure of art interest and art knowledge. *Psychology of Aesthetics, Creativity, and the Arts, 14*(2), 172. https://doi.org/10.1037/aca0000205

Specker, E., Stamkou, E., Pelowski, M., & Leder, H. (2020). Radically revolutionary or pretty flowers? The impact of curatorial narrative of artistic deviance on perceived artist influence. *Psychology of Aesthetics, Creativity, and the Arts*. Advance online publication. https://doi.org/10.1037/aca0000320

Specker, E., Tinio, P. P. L., & van Elk, M. (2017). Do you see what I see? An investigation of the aesthetic experience in the laboratory and museum. *Psychology of Aesthetics, Creativity, and the Arts, 11*, 265–275. https://doi.org/10.1037/ aca0000107

Tinio, P. P. L. (2013). From artistic creation to aesthetic reception: The mirror model of art. *Psychology of Aesthetics, Creativity, and the Arts, 7*, 265–275. https://doi .org/10.1037/a0030872

Tinio, P. P. L. (2020). Aesthetics. In R. Runco & S. Pritzker (Eds.), *Encyclopedia of Creativity* (3rd ed., pp. 18–22). Elsevier. https://doi.org/10.1016/B978–0-12- 809324-5.23690-0

Tinio, P. P. L., & Gartus, A. (2018). Characterizing the emotional response to art beyond pleasure: Correspondence between the emotional characteristics of artworks and viewers' emotional responses. *Progress in Brain Research, 237*, 319–342. https://doi.org/10.1016/bs.pbr.2018.03.005

Tinio, P. P. L., Smith, J. K., & Smith, L. F. (2014). The walls do speak: Psychological aesthetics and the museum experience. In P. P. L. Tinio & J. K. Smith (Eds.), *Cambridge Handbook of the Psychology of Aesthetics and the Arts* (pp. 195–218). Cambridge University Press. https://doi.org/10.1017/CBO9781139207058.011

Tröndle, M. (2014). Space, movement and attention: Affordances of the museum environment. *International Journal of Arts Management, 17*(1), 4–17. www.jstor.org/ stable/24587224

Van de Cruys, S., & Wagemans, J. (2011). Putting reward in art: A tentative prediction error account of visual art. *i-Perception*, *2*(9), 1035–1062. https://doi.org/10.1068/i0466aap

Vartanian, O., & Nadal, M. (2007). A biological approach to a model of aesthetic experience. In L. Dorfman, C. Martindale, & V. Petrov (Eds.), *Aesthetics and Innovation* (pp. 429–444). Cambridge Scholars.

Vartanian, O., Navarrete, G., Chatterjee, A., et al. (2013). Impact of contour on aesthetic judgments and approach-avoidance decisions in architecture. *Proceedings of the National Academy of Sciences*, *110*, 10446–10453. https://doi.org/10.1073/pnas.1301227110

Vartanian, O., Navarrete, G., Chatterjee, A., et al. (2019). Preference for curvilinear contour in interior architectural spaces: Evidence from experts and nonexperts. *Psychology of Aesthetics, Creativity, and the Arts*, *13*(1), 110–116. https://doi.org/10.1037/aca0000150

Wolz, S. H., & Carbon, C. C. (2014). What's wrong with an art fake? Cognitive and emotional variables influenced by authenticity status of artworks. *Leonardo*, *47*, 467–473. http://dx.doi.org/10.1162/LEON_a_00869

20 The Affective Benefits of Creative Activities

Eliana Grossman and Jennifer E. Drake

Grief over loss, exuberance at receiving a promotion, or anxiety facing a work deadline are just three examples of the emotionally arousing situations we all face and manage with emotion regulation strategies. According to Thompson (1994), "emotion regulation consists of extrinsic and intrinsic processes responsible for monitoring, evaluating, and modifying emotional reactions, especially their intensive and temporal features, to accomplish one's goals" (pp. 27–28). This includes the management of positive and negative emotions and the ability to respond to the environment in an "adaptive and flexible manner" (Morris et al., 2007, p. 363). An important aspect of emotion regulation is learning not only which strategies to use, but which *activities* to pursue when confronted with an emotionally arousing situation.

Engaging in creative activities has been shown to improve affect. Artists and writers have often talked about the powerful emotional benefits of engaging in the arts. For the author Graham Greene (1980), writing was a "form of therapy" and he wondered how it was that "all those who do not write, compose, or paint can manage to escape the madness, the melancholia, the panic fear which is inherent in the human situation" (p. 285). For the painter Paul Cézanne, in "paint, there lies salvation" (Paul Cézanne Quotes, 2021). While creativity is fundamental to the arts, many non-artistic activities also call for creativity – from scholarly activities such as scientific or historical research to more commonplace activities such as cooking, gardening, sewing, or rearranging furniture. The cardiologist Richard Bing spoke about the emotional benefits of research: "It helps me emotionally to feel more about science. You see, I am a romanticist. I perceive science as an emotional exercise of searching the unknown" (quoted in Root-Bernstein, 2002, p. 64). Therefore, the emotional benefits of engaging in creative activities are likely not exclusive to the arts.

The terms *emotion, mood, arousal,* and *affect* are sometimes used interchangeably. Emotions are discrete and subtle states that can be observed through facial expressions, body posture, physiological arousal, and tone of voice (Niedenthal et al., 2006). A person can experience a wide range of positive

Jennifer E. Drake https://orcid.org/0000-0001-7494-3624
Address correspondence to: Jennifer E. Drake, Department of Psychology, Brooklyn College, CUNY, 2900 Bedford Avenue, Brooklyn, NY 11210. Phone: 718-951-5000, extension 3585. Fax: 718-951-4814. E-mail: jdrake@brooklyn.cuny.edu.

or negative emotions such as happiness, surprise, fear, or despair. Whereas emotions are short in duration, mood is considered a long-lasting state. Both emotions and moods vary in valence from positive (e.g., content) to negative (e.g., sad) and in arousal from deactivated (e.g., lethargic) to activated (e.g., exuberant). Arousal is a psychological and physiological state of alertness that is a feature of both emotions and moods. Affect can be understood to encompass emotion, mood, and arousal (Juslin & Sloboda, 2010). Since the use of these terms varies from study to study, we use the term *affect* to refer to emotions, mood, and arousal.

Creativity scholars have made a distinction between four types of creativity: "Big-C," "Pro-C," "little-c," and "mini-c" (Kaufman & Beghetto, 2009). "Big-C" refers to the kind of creativity seen in eminent artists and scholars who transform a field (e.g., scientist Marie Curie for her research on radioactivity; Charles Darwin for the theory of evolution; Pablo Picasso and Georges Braque for cubism; George Balanchine for his revolutionary choreography). "Pro-C" is creativity at a professional level (e.g., a researcher designing a new study), "little-c" is everyday creativity (e.g., decorating cupcakes), and "mini-c" is personal creativity (e.g., creating a secret handshake with friends). "Big-C" creativity is positively skewed (meaning very few people reach creative eminence), whereas "little-c" creativity is normally distributed in the general population (meaning many of us engage in such creative acts daily; Jauk et al., 2014).

In this chapter, we review the research on the affective benefits of artistic and non-artistic creative activities, and we explore whether these activities reduce negative affect, increase positive affect, or both. We examine the ways in which these activities elicit different emotion regulation strategies, including whether these strategies are effective in reducing negative affect and/or increasing positive affect. Finally, we consider the mechanisms underlying their affective benefits allowing us to ascertain whether there is something unique about engaging in creative activities that leads to improved affect.

Literature Review

We conducted an extensive literature search of peer-reviewed journal articles using *APA PsycInfo* and *Google Scholar*. First, we used the broad search terms "creativity" or "creative activities" AND "emotion regulation" or "mood improvement" or "emotional benefits." Then, we narrowed our search by looking at specific creative activities (described below) and paired these activities with the search terms "emotion regulation" OR "mood improvement" OR "emotional benefits." We included the following artistic activities, identified in the work by Davies et al. (2012): (1) music (singing, playing a musical instrument, composing music); (2) dance and theatre (dancing, acting); (3) visual arts (drawing, painting, printmaking, sculpture, pottery, jewelry making, digital artmaking, animating, photography, sewing, knitting, crocheting, embroidery, woodwork, coloring); and (4) narrative arts (creative writing, journaling, making films or videos). We excluded those activities that might be considered artistic but were passive (e.g., going to a museum, listening to music) and therefore did not generate a creative product. When searching for non-artistic creativities, we searched for activities that had been included in the work by Fancourt et al. (2020) and included gardening, cooking, magic and circus tricks,[1] and science.

In our review, we excluded studies with clinical populations (e.g., individuals suffering from depression) or those investigating the benefits of various kinds of art therapy. While engaging in creative activities can benefit clinical populations, our focus was on how creative activities can improve affect as opposed to reducing symptoms. We also focused on how the creative activity itself, uncoupled from therapy, impacts affect improvement and emotion regulation in everyday life. Our review included experimental studies where an affective state was induced, longitudinal studies assessing the emotion regulation strategies elicited by creative activities, as well as observational and case studies.

The Use of Creative Activities to Improve Affect

When examining the benefits of creative activities, it is important not only to focus on *which* activities improve affect, but also *when* we pursue these activities, *how* they improve our affect, and *why* these benefits occur. To answer these questions, we applied van Goethem and Sloboda's (2011) model of emotion regulation to study affect improvement of creative activities at four different levels: goals (the when), tactics (the which), strategies (the how), and mechanisms (the why). This model has been previously used when examining the affective benefits of listening to music (Baltazar & Saarikallio, 2016) and artistic activities more generally (Fancourt et al., 2020). The goal is the desired state or outcome that we hope to achieve from engaging in an activity (e.g., feeling less anxious). The tactic is the activity that we engage in to improve our affect (e.g., drawing, cooking). The strategy is the emotion regulation strategy used to manage affect (e.g., drawing something unrelated to the source of the anxiety). Finally, the mechanism is the aspect of the activity that leads to improved affect (e.g., the activity of drawing something unrelated to one's anxiety is effective because it shifts attention away from the feeling of anxiety).

Goals

The goal of emotion regulation is to achieve a desired state or outcome (e.g., reduce feelings of anxiety). Often the goal is to decrease negative affect while simultaneously increasing positive affect. In what follows, we describe a clear and somewhat surprising distinction in the affective benefits of engaging in artistic versus non-artistic creative activities.

When experiencing negative affect (e.g., sadness, anger, anxiety), one goal of engaging in artistic activities is to reduce that negative affect. This has been

---

[1] A search for magic and circus tricks did not yield a single peer-reviewed article and therefore these activities are not included in this chapter.

shown experimentally by inducing a negative affective state by having partici-pants watch a sad film clip (Drake et al., 2011), recall a personally distressing event (e.g., Drake & Winner, 2012), write about a traumatic experience (e.g., Pennebaker & Chung, 2011), or watch someone else experience pain (Goldstein & Lerner, 2018). When participants engaged in an artistic activity after the negative affect induction, their negative feelings were reduced and positive feelings were enhanced.

Few studies have examined how engaging in an artistic activity improves affect without an affect induction. Some researchers have compared activities that vary in valence (e.g., writing or drawing about a negative or positive life event) without any affect induction (e.g., Curl & Folks, 2008; Pennebaker, 1997). However, it could be argued that an activity that requires someone to write or draw about a negative personal event is an affect induction itself – a person is in a neutral affective state and must recall a personally upsetting event that inevitably will lower positive affect and increase negative affect. To the best of our knowledge, no studies have examined how the arts can be used to maintain or enhance positive affect decoupled from reducing negative affect. However, there are studies examining how the arts result in better emotion regulation skills without any affect induction (e.g., Brown & Saxe, 2013; Hoffmann & Russ, 2012).

Non-artistic activities such as cooking and gardening have been shown to maintain or enhance a current positive affective state like optimism (Koay & Dillon, 2020) or enjoyment (Güler & Haseki, 2021; Mosko & Delach, 2021). Cooking has also been used to enhance a mixed affective state (both positive and negative affect) like nostalgia (Baker et al., 2005). These kinds of activities create a sense of purpose and accomplishment (Sunga & Advincula, 2021) and are sources of inspiration (Russo, 2000). Fewer studies of non-artistic activities have examined the reduction of negative affect or have involved some type of negative affect induction. Thus, the findings on non-artistic activities may more accurately represent what occurs in our everyday lives when we pursue creative activities from a neutral state.

Activities

We use the term *activities* (instead of *tactics*) to refer to both artistic and non-artistic creative behaviors.

Artistic Activities

Music. Many studies on the affective benefits of creative activities have focused on music. Perhaps this is not surprising given the pervasiveness of music in our everyday lives: music is played at social gatherings, in stores, and at places of worship and can be listened to at home, in our cars, and on the go. Despite the volume of studies on the affective benefits of music, we found only one study on the benefits of singing and not a single study on composing music or playing a musical instrument. The one study on singing examined the emotion regulation strategies used when singing and therefore will be reviewed in the strategies section below (Fancourt & Steptoe, 2019).

Dance. Many dancers describe dance and creative movement as a way to express their affect (van Vugt, 2014). Modern dancer Isadora Duncan once said: "If I could tell you what it meant, there would be no point in dancing it" (Goodreads, 2021). A bidirectional link has been demonstrated between our emotions, facial expressions, and posture (Friedman, 2010). Our bodies not only reflect our affect but can be used to improve it. After a stress induction, being in an upright posture improved affect (increased positive affect and decreased negative affect) more for adults than being in a slumped over posture with shoulders rolled forward (Nair et al., 2015).

Very few studies have examined the benefits of dance outside of a dance therapy setting, except for one study that compared the benefits of a single session of a movement activity to an art activity for college students (Zimmerman & Mangelsdorf, 2020). After recalling and writing about a perceived stressor, participants were randomly assigned to engage in a movement activity or a visual art activity for 20 minutes and then write about the perceived stressor again for 5 minutes. The movement and art activities covered similar content: warm-up (breathing activity), imagery activity (embody or draw animals, objects, places), prompted actions (move or draw fast, slow, etc.), and circle activity (participants mirrored each other's movements or drawings). Both groups showed self-reported improvements in affect (increases in positive affect and decreases in negative affect) and reductions in stress from before to after the activity. While this study does demonstrate the affective benefits of movement and arts-based activities, it is unclear whether the benefits were due to the activities themselves or the passage of time, as there was no control group given the stress induction and then asked to sit quietly. It is also possible that the improvements were due to participants engaging in the 5-minute expressive writing activity prior to and after their assigned movement or art activity.

Theatre. Like dance, theatre is an art form where the experience of affect is encouraged. In Method Acting, actors are taught to feel the emotions of their character on stage in real time (Goldstein, 2009). As argued by Goldstein (2009), actors must have the ability to recall and experience an affective state when the scene calls for it, as well as simultaneously managing their own affect with that of their character. Since one of the main components of acting is self-expression, it may not be surprising that acting students may express their affect more effectively than non-acting students. Gentzler et al. (2020) found that undergraduate acting students (as compared to non-acting students) self-reported greater perception of their ability to amplify emotions (e.g., intensify their emotions, use their emotions to their advantage, or prolong their experience of emotion).

The affective benefits of acting also extend to drama and pretend play for young children. Preschoolers who engaged in 8 weeks of dramatic pretend play showed more emotional control than preschoolers who engaged in block building or reading as evidenced by less personal distress (e.g., feeling of sadness or fear, or physically freezing) when the researcher experienced pain (Goldstein & Lerner, 2018). Another study found that children who engaged in more complex pretend play (e.g., organized plot, use of imagination, affective expressions that are frequent and varied) had better parent-reported emotion regulation skills (Hoffmann & Russ, 2012).

Visual Arts. Artmaking (e.g., drawing, painting, coloring) has been shown to improve affect in children and adults after a single session lasting no more than 10 minutes. De Petrillo and Winner (2005) found that drawing improved affect for adults more than non-drawing activities such as copying shapes or a word puzzle. A similar finding was reported with children: Drake and Winner (2013) showed that drawing improved affect more than copying line drawings. Subsequent work on this topic conducted by Drake et al. (2011) with adults comparing two different art forms found that drawing improved affect more than writing. In a study of adults, Drake and Winner (2012) showed that drawing improves affect more than sitting quietly, demonstrating that it is not the mere passage of time that improves affect but the act of creating something.

Similar affective benefits for adults may be achieved from coloring (which arguably is less creative than drawing, but might be more accessible regardless of level of expertise or years of training). However, the results are mixed. One study found that coloring a mandala was as beneficial as drawing to distract (participants were asked to draw a design) for improving affect (Forkosh & Drake, 2017). However, other researchers have found that coloring a mandala is more beneficial for improving affect than free drawing with no instructions given or drawing to distract (Curry & Kasser, 2005; van der Vennet & Serice, 2012). Perhaps there is something inherently calming about the mandala's circular design; surprisingly, coloring a blank circle improves affect more after a negative induction than coloring a blank square (Babouchkina & Robins, 2015).

Narrative Arts. Multiple sessions of expressive writing (writing about an upsetting event) compared to writing about everyday events is associated with many positive outcomes in adults and children (Pennebaker & Chung, 2011). Pennebaker (1997) found that initially writing about a stressful event is painful, but ultimately beneficial for adults over several writing sessions. It may be that the immediate affective benefits of writing are found in the body's psycho-physiological response such as respiratory sinus arrhythmia (RSA), a physiological indicator of emotion regulation (Bazhenova et al., 2001). Differences in resting RSA (before engaging in an activity) may reflect individual differences in emotional reactivity with a higher resting RSA associated with better emotion regulation abilities (Beauchaine, 2001). In fact, expressive writing was found to be particularly beneficial for those adults with the highest resting RSA, compared to writing about everyday events (Sloan & Epstein, 2005). Finally, expressive writing has been shown to decrease negative affect (Soliday et al., 2004) and reduce anxiety symptoms (Reynolds et al., 2000) in children and adults weeks to months beyond the intervention.

Non-artistic Activities

Cooking. Creativity in cooking is not reserved for master chefs on *Iron Chef* and can simply be seen when someone comes up with a novel way to poach an egg (Beghetto et al., 2015). Cooking a favorite recipe can elicit feelings of nostalgia (a mixed positive and negative affective state) as adults recall the ritual of cooking as well as its connection to family (Baker et al., 2005). Cooking has also been shown to improve affect over longer periods of time. In one study, adults were asked to identify personal moments of meaning and value during their cooking process (Mosko & Delach, 2021). Not only did cooking improve participants' affect, but they consistently reported enjoying the creative and independent aspects of cooking as "it's something you come up with yourself" (p. 354). In this same study, six months later, participants reported that cooking continued to have a positive impact on their well-being. More recently, adults have turned to cooking to cope with the COVID-19 pandemic. At the beginning of the pandemic, individuals in Turkey cooked to relax and increase happiness (Güler & Haseki, 2021). In addition to improvements in affect, cooking resulted in gains in skills and knowledge as well as increased self-actualization and self-enhancement.

Gardening. Like cooking, gardening is an activity marked by creativity and innovation. Actively planting flowers was shown to improve affect more than passively walking through a garden (Hayashi et al., 2008). Gardening has also been shown to reduce stress levels. After a stress induction, middle aged participants were randomly assigned to an outdoor gardening activity (e.g., pruning branches, planting bulbs) or an indoor reading activity (Van Den Berg & Custers, 2011). Although both activities resulted in reductions in cortisol levels following the activity, gardening was associated with a significantly greater reduction. Additionally, positive affect increased from before to after the activity for those who gardened but decreased for those who read. While these findings do suggest the potential benefits of gardening, these two activities involved different settings – outdoor for gardening and indoor for reading. Thus, we cannot tease apart whether the benefits were due to the activity themselves or the setting, or the combination of the two.

Similar to cooking, gardening has been a respite of pleasure and distraction for individuals during the COVID-19 pandemic. A qualitative study of Filipinos in September 2020 examined their experience of gardening during the pandemic, including their motivations for engaging in the activity as well as the perceived mental health benefits (Sunga & Advincula, 2021). Adults reported a relief from stress, anxiety, and boredom as well as a boost in sense of purpose and accomplishment from home gardening.

Science. There exists no experimental work on the affective benefits of scientific research. All that we have at present are personal reports from scientists. The path to scientific discovery is inherently creative and scientists report experiencing positive affect during periods of creative problem solving and idea generation, a concept called "aesthetic cognition" (Root-Bernstein,

2002). Scientists often report experiencing joy in their pursuit of scientific discovery. Biologist and Nobel Prize winner Gerald Edelman recounted "the splendid feeling, almost a lustful feeling, of excitement when a secret of nature is revealed" (Wolpert & Richards, 1997, p. 137). In fact, this experience has been so widely shared among scientists that it has been termed "shuddering at the beautiful," a phrase coined by Subrahmanyan Chandrasekhar, astrophysicist and Nobel Prize winner (1987). Scientists also experience feelings of inspiration and captivation. Chemist Dudley Herschbach describes a common characteristic of Nobel laureates: ". . . you really have to become completely captivated by something, like falling in love . . . You can't imagine why everyone else isn't chasing after this wonderful person" (Russo, 2000).

Strategies

Engagement with the arts helps to regulate our affect in three different ways: approach, avoidance, and self-development. It is important to note that, as discussed by Fancourt et al. (2019), these three sets of strategies are all related to positive health outcomes and therefore one strategy is not considered better than the other. We will examine how creative activities improve affect using these three sets of strategies.

Approach

The approach strategy involves addressing negative emotions through reappraisal, acceptance, or problem solving (Fancourt et al., 2019). Reappraisal refers to changing or altering our mental state to a particular situation (Wu et al., 2017). In one study, researchers developed a Reappraisal Intervention where college students were presented with four anger-inducing vignettes and were asked to list as many ways as possible to reappraise the situation (Weber et al., 2014). To assess creativity, college students were asked to complete a divergent thinking task. Responses to the reappraisal intervention and divergent thinking task were coded for fluency (total number of responses) and flexibility (number of different responses). A positive correlation was found between the two tasks on both fluency and flexibility, suggesting that the act of reappraising affect is in and of itself a creative activity since it involves finding new solutions or new perspectives. Indeed, a neuroscientific study found that reappraising affect (as assessed by the Reappraisal Intervention; Weber et al., 2014) and creative ideation (as assessed by an Alternative Uses Task, Fink et al., 2012) involved similar brain activation with reappraising affect associated with increased activation in the prefrontal sites and creative ideation associated with increased activation in the posterior cortical sites (Fink et al., 2017).

Whereas both of these studies demonstrate a positive association between reappraisal and creative thinking, they did not assess the effectiveness of this strategy in regulating affect. Wu and colleagues (2017) asked adults to view pictures from the International Affective Picture System (IAPS) and describe their reappraisal of the pictures aloud. Another group of adults rated the responses on creativity, effectiveness, and appropriateness. Creativity of responses and effectiveness of the reappraisal strategy were positively correlated, suggesting that creativity plays an important role in emotion regulation.

In some cases, however, reappraisal may not be helpful. Hemenover et al. (2008) found that those who were asked to write about the positive consequences of an emotionally charged film clip (about a child serial killer) did not reap the same affective benefits as those who were asked to write about a personally positive experience. Based on our review of the literature, we did not find any studies that focused on the use of the acceptance or problem-solving strategies when engaging in creative activities.

Avoidance

The avoidance strategy involves ignoring negative emotions through distraction, suppression, or detachment (Fancourt et al., 2019). Distraction is shifting our attention away from a situation or feeling (Fancourt et al., 2020). Using drawing to distract has been found to improve affect more than drawing to express. These benefits are found across a range of negative affective states (e.g., sadness, anger, anxiety) for children (Drake, 2021; Drake & Winner, 2013) and adults (e.g., Drake & Winner, 2012), and after a single session of drawing as well as multiple sessions of drawing over several days (Drake et al., 2016) and one month (Drake, 2019).

Research has also shown that children spontaneously use drawing to distract after a negative affect induction (Brechet et al., 2022; Drake, 2021). One study asked children to draw freely for 5 minutes after recalling a disappointing event (Drake, 2021). Drawings were coded as "distract" if they were unrelated to the remembered disappointing event, and as "express" if they were related to the disappointing event. The majority of children spontaneously used drawing as a form of distraction rather than expression. A similar finding was reported by Brechet et al. (2022), who found that in a free drawing condition, only 5 out of 47 children drew the event that had made them sad, and those 5 children reframed the event that had saddened them. Thus, children do not need to be given specific instructions on the content of what to draw to reap the affective benefits of drawing. They will naturally use drawing as a form of distraction.

Distraction is not limited to drawing. Poetry and narrative writing improved affect in adults more when used to distract rather than express (Fink & Drake, 2016). When assessing which set of strategies (approach, avoidance, or self-development) we are most likely to use when engaging in music, Fancourt and Steptoe (2019) found that singers were more likely to use avoidance (which includes distraction) than the other two strategies. Other work, while not assessing emotion regulations per se, has shown that individuals seek out creative activities like gardening because they serve as a form of distraction (Sunga & Advincula, 2021).

Research on suppression – inhibiting an emotional response – has compared the use of this strategy between actors and non-actors. Because actors actively express their affect on stage, they may be less likely to suppress their affect in their daily lives (Goldstein et al., 2013). In a study comparing adolescent actors and non-actors, no difference was found in affect expression or intensity between the two groups, but actors reported less use of suppression than non-actors. In a second study, Goldstein and colleagues (2013) assessed whether acting training impacts the use of suppression by comparing children engaging in a 10-month acting and visual arts training. Whereas the acting group endorsed more suppression at the beginning of the training, they significantly decreased their use of suppression from before to after training with no differences found in the visual arts group. However, this finding has not been replicated with college students studying acting: Gentzler et al. (2020) found no differences in the use of suppression (or other emotion regulation strategies) between actors and non-actors.

Self-Development

The self-development strategy involves refocusing oneself through enhanced self-identity, improved self-esteem, or increased agency. When cooking and gardening, individuals have reported a sense of accomplishment and purpose (Mosko & Delach, 2021; Sunga & Advincula, 2021) and increased levels of self-acceptance (Mosko & Delach, 2021). In one of the only studies to examine the benefits of singing, Fancourt and Steptoe (2019) examined the emotion regulation strategies used when singing in a live versus virtual choir (where participants record their piece individually). While virtual choir participants reported using less emotion regulation strategies than live choir participants overall, they did report using more self-development strategies. The authors suggest this may be because the virtual choir singers could re-record their sessions, hear their contribution as a single voice, and that their desire to engage in a virtual choir may be due to improving their self-confidence.

Mechanisms

It is important to examine the underlying factors that contribute to *how* creative activities improve affect. Why does cooking reduce stress levels? How does expressive writing improve our affect? Why is drawing to distract more effective in reducing sadness than drawing to express?

There may be aspects of the activity that lend themselves to certain emotion regulation strategies and affective benefits. Expressive writing may improve affect because it involves reframing and reworking the experience, thereby allowing us to come to terms with and understand upsetting experiences over time (Pennebaker & Chung, 2011). On the other hand, drawing invites us to focus on the aesthetic properties of color, line, and composition. Therefore, drawing may allow us to engage with the medium and shift our attention away from negative thoughts and feelings. Acting invites us to express the feelings of our character and may train children and adults to express (rather than suppress) their affect. Finally, gardening has a restorative and relaxing quality as individuals engage with nature and the outdoors (Hayashi et al., 2008; Sunga & Advincula, 2021), which may allow for reflection and use of the self-development strategy. Thus, the underlying mechanisms of how these activities improve affect may be due to which emotion regulation strategies these activities elicit.

The valence of an activity may also be related to affect improvement, though the results are mixed. For example, Diliberto-Macaluso and Stubblefield (2015), found that drawing something neutral in valence improved affect just as much as drawing something positive in valence. However, Monnier et al. (2016) found that valence did play a role in affect improvement for children: children who drew or described a positive memory had greater affect improvement than children who drew or described a neutral memory.

Other researchers have examined our subjective experience when pursuing creative activities. First, these activities may improve affect because of the pleasure we experience from creating something (White, 1959). Indeed, work has shown that enjoyment is related to affect improvement when cooking (Güler & Haseki, 2021; Mosko & Delach, 2021), drawing (Drake, 2021; Drake & Winner, 2013), and gardening (Sunga & Advincula, 2021). Second, these activities are associated with perceived competency (Drake, 2021; Drake & Winner, 2013; Güler & Haseki, 2021) as individuals report increasing their skills and knowledge of the activity. Third, affect improvement may be related to the sense of accomplishment, self-acceptance, and mastery that we experience from creating something (Mosko & Delach, 2021; Sunga & Advincula, 2021). Fourth, these activities may lead to states of flow where individuals are fully immersed and absorbed in the activity (Drake, 2021; Forkosh & Drake, 2017). Finally, activities like cooking and gardening may promote social bonds and community building as groups of individuals work together toward a common goal (Baker et al., 2005; Koay & Dillon, 2020; Mosko & Delach, 2021).

Limitations and Future Directions

Most of the studies reviewed here involved a negative affect induction and then examined the effects of various kinds of activities on that affect. Far less is known about how these activities improve our affect when we freely choose a creative activity with no negative affect induction. Perhaps more importantly, there is much we do not know on the underlying mechanisms of how creative activities achieve this improvement.

Even though learning how to regulate affect is a key component of children's development (Denham et al., 2003; Eisenberg et al., 2002; Saarni, 1999), the majority of the studies have focused on how engaging in creative activities improves affect in adults. Yet children are natural artists: they love to pretend, dance, sing, and create images on paper. It seems very plausible that engaging in creatives activities would help children cope with emotionally arousing and distressing situations and lead to improvements in their affect.

It is important to note that while creative activities do improve our affect, many of the studies presented here did not compare the benefits of creative and non-creative activities. There are likely many non-creative activities that have the potential to improve affect (e.g., exercising, walking the dog, cleaning the house) that have not been investigated. We therefore cannot draw any conclusions on how non-creative activities may be used to improve affect. The extent to which the affective benefits that we derive from creative activities are specific to the activities themselves rather than a result of involvement in any kind of engaging task is an important area of future study.

Studies have also tended to focus on the affective benefits of a particular emotion regulation strategy (e.g., drawing to distract, expressive writing). As a result, the studies are limited in scope and cannot speak to how pervasive various strategies are used within and across activities. An important avenue for future research is to continue to examine how different activities may elicit different emotion regulation strategies. For example, when might it be more effective to engage in drawing versus acting versus cooking and do these activities improve our affect using different emotion regulation strategies?

In our review of the literature, it was clear that not all art forms and not all creative activities have been given equal attention. Far more research has been conducted on the passive activity of listening to music than the active activity of singing. More work has been conducted on drawing and writing than dance and theatre. Whether these differences are due to the activities themselves or the accessibility of the activities (e.g., we engage in writing daily) is unclear. It would also be important for future research to examine the extent to which the activities we engage in are truly creative – in the sense of an individual doing something novel and inventive. For example, singing a familiar song or making a favorite recipe might not be creative but instead habitual. Future research should examine the level of novelty involved when engaging in what are considered creative activities.

Future research should also examine whether there are creative activities that are better suited for certain populations. Previous research with adults (Pennebaker, 1997) has shown that writing is effective in improving affect, but it is likely that writing as a form of affect improvement may be ineffective for young children who are still mastering this skill or those with autism who may struggle to express themselves through this medium (Zajic et al., 2018). The non-verbal activity of drawing may be a far more effective way for children to process and cope with their affect. It is also possible that different populations may reap different affective benefits from the same creative activity. For example, older adults may experience feelings of nostalgia while cooking as they remember family, but children may experience the joy of cooking as they create something new. Future work should investigate whether there are developmental differences in the affective benefits of creative activities.

Finally, this work has implications for non-artistic creative activities that are not typically recognized as creative such as teaching, learning, and problem solving. Teaching is full of creativity as teachers design lessons, classroom exercises, and assignments all well as keeping their students engaged. Teachers report experiencing positive affect such as joy while teaching (Hagenauer & Volet, 2014). This positive affect has not only been related to their own efficacy while teaching but also their students' affect (Chen, 2019; Frenzel, 2014). This work has the potential to illuminate the affective benefits of different kinds of pursuits that are not traditionally viewed as creative.

Conclusions

Using the model of emotion regulation (van Goethem & Sloboda, 2011), we draw four conclusions from the studies reported here. First, from the research thus far, we can conclude that there is a difference in our affective goals for artistic versus non-artistic creative activities. Artistic activities are used to reduce negative affect, whereas non-artistic activities are used to enhance or maintain positive affect. However, it is possible that this difference is due to the experimental designs of the studies: the studies on artistic activities often involved a negative affect induction and the non-artistic activities examined affect improvement from a neutral state. Future research is needed to examine whether this is due to a genuine difference or an artifact of study design.

Second, creative activities are effective and engaging ways to improve affect, and these benefits are found across a range of activities. It was evident from our review of the literature that far more research has examined the affective benefits of artistic than non-artistic activities. It is possible that we more readily see the connection between art and improved affect or that we associate creativity more with artistic than non-artistic activities. Even though more work has examined the affective benefits of artistic activities, the art forms have not received equal attention and conclusions cannot be drawn of whether one art form might be better suited for a particular situation or group of individuals.

Third, we found that the use and effectiveness of the three sets of emotion regulation strategies identified by Fancourt and colleagues (2019) differed by activity. Drawing improved affect more when used as a form of avoidance (distraction); non-artistic activities as a form of self-development; and writing and creative problem solving as a form of approach. There were also activities that improved affect using all three strategies including singing, gardening, and cooking. Thus, there is a broad range of strategies that can be used to improve affect, and it is possible that the use of these strategies may be related more to individual differences than to the effectiveness of the strategies per se.

Finally, researchers have only begun to examine *how* creative activities regulate our affect. There might be aspects of the activity that lend themselves to specific emotion regulation strategies. For example, writing may afford expression due to the referential nature of the symbol system of language, while drawing may afford distraction due to the immediately engaging aesthetic properties of the medium. This work also suggests that these activities may improve affect due to the pleasure we experience from creating. Taken together, however, the existing work clearly demonstrates that engaging in creative activities is one effective way to improve and regulate our affect.

References

Babouchkina A., & Robbins, S. J. (2015). Reducing negative mood through mandala creation: A randomized control trial. *Art Therapy: Journal of the American Art Therapy Association, 32*(1), 34–39. https://doi.org/10.1080/07421656.2015.994428

Baker, S. M., Karrer, H. C., & Veeck, A. (2005). My favourite recipes: Recreating emotions and memories through cooking. *Advances in Consumer Research, 32*(1), 304–305.

Baltazar M., & Saarikallio, S. (2016). Toward a better understanding and conceptualization of affect self-regulation through music: A critical, integrative literature review. *Psychology of Music, 44*(6), 1500–1521. https://doi.org/10.1177/0305735616663313

Bazhenova, O. V., Plonskaia, O., & Porges, S. W. (2001). Vagal reactivity and affective adjustment in infants during interaction challenges. *Child Development, 72*(5), 1314–1326. https://doi.org/10.1111/1467-8624.00350

Beauchaine, T. (2001). Vagal tone, development, and Gray's motivational theory: Toward an integrated model of autonomic nervous system functioning in psychopathology. *Development and Psychopathology, 13*(2), 183–214. https://doi.org/10.1017/s0954579401002012

Beghetto, R. A., Kaufman, J. C., & Hatcher, R. (2015). Applying creativity research to cooking. *The Journal of Creative Behavior, 50*(3), 171–177. https://doi.org/10.1002/jocb.124

Brechet, C., D'Audigier, L., & Audras-Torrent, D. (2022). The use of drawing as an emotion regulation technique with children. *Psychology of Aesthetics, Creativity, and the Arts, 16*(2), 221–232. https://doi.org/10.1037/aca0000314

Brown, E. D., & Sax, K. L. (2013). Arts enrichment and preschool emotions for low-income children at risk. *Early Childhood Research Quarterly, 28*(4), 337–346. https://doi.org/10.1016/j.ecresq.2012.08.002

Chandrasekhar, S. (1987). *Truth and Beauty.* University of Chicago Press.

Chen, J. (2019). Exploring the impact of teacher emotions on their approaches to teaching: A structural equation modelling approach. *British Journal of Educational Psychology, 89*(1), 57–74. https://doi.org/10.1111/bjep.12220

Curl, K., & Forks, G. (2008). Assessing stress regulation as a function of artistic creation and cognitive focus. *Art Therapy: Journal of the American Art Therapy Association, 25*(4), 164–169. https://doi.org/10.1080/07421656.2008.1012955

Curry, N. A., & Kasser, T. (2005). Can coloring mandalas reduce anxiety? *Art Therapy: Journal of the American Art Therapy Association, 22*(2), 81–85. https://doi.org/10.1080/07421656.2005.10129441

Davies, C. R., Rosenberg, M., Knuiman, M., et al. (2012). Defining arts engagement for population-based health research: Art forms, activities and level of engagement, *Arts & Health: An International Journal for Research, Policy and Practice, 4*(3), 203–216. https://doi.org/10.1080/17533015.2012.656201

Denham, S. A., Blair, K. A., DeMulder, E., et al. (2003). Preschool emotional competence: Pathway to social competence. *Child Development, 74*(1), 238–256. https://doi.org/10.1111/1467–8624.00533

De Petrillo, L., & Winner, E. (2005). Does art improve mood? A test of a key assumption underlying art therapy. *Art Therapy, 22*(4), 205–212. https://doi.org/10.1080/07421656.2005.10129521

Diliberto-Macaluso, K. A., & Stubblefield, B. L. (2015). The use of painting for short-term mood and arousal improvement. *Psychology of Aesthetics, Creativity, and the Arts, 9*(3), 228–234. http://dx.doi.org/10.1037/a0039237

Drake, J. E. (2019). Examining the psychological and psychophysiological benefits of drawing over one month. *Psychology of Aesthetics, Creativity, and the Arts, 13*(3), 338–347. https://doi.org/10.1037/aca0000179

Drake, J. E. (2021). How drawing to distract improves mood in children. *Frontiers in Psychology, 12*, 622927. https://doi.org/10.3389/fpsyg.2021.622927

Drake, J. E., Coleman, K., & Winner, E. (2011). Short-term mood repair through art: Effects of medium and strategy. *Art Therapy: Journal of the American Art Therapy Association, 28*(1), 26–30. https://doi.org/10.1080/07421656.2011.557032

Drake, J. E., Hastedt, I., & James, C. (2016). Drawing to distract: Examining the psychological benefits of drawing over time. *Psychology of Aesthetics, Creativity, and the Arts, 10*(3), 325–331. https://doi.org/10.1037/aca0000064

Drake, J. E., & Winner, E. (2012). Confronting sadness through art-making: Distraction is more beneficial than venting. *Psychology of Aesthetics, Creativity, and the Arts, 6*(3), 251–266.https://doi.org/10.1037/a0026909

Drake, J. E., & Winner, E. (2013). How children use drawing to regulate their emotions. *Cognition and Emotion, 27*(3), 512–520. https://doi.org/10.1080/02699931.2012.720567

Eisenberg, N., Spinard, T. L., & Morris, A. S. (2002). Regulation, resiliency, and quality of social functioning. *Self and Identity, 1*(2), 121–128. https://doi.org/10.1080/152988602317319294

Fancourt, D., Garnett, C., & Müllensiefen, D. (2020). The relationship between demographics, behavioral and experiential engagement factors, and the use of artistic creative activities to regulate emotions. *Psychology of Aesthetics, Creativity, and the Arts.* Advance online publication. http://dx.doi.org/10.1037/aca0000296

Fancourt, D., Garnett, C., Spiro, N., West, R., & Müllensiefen, D. (2019). How do artistic creative activities regulate our emotions? Validation of the Emotion Regulation Strategies for Artistic Creative Activities Scale (ERS-ACA). *PLoS ONE,14*(2), e0211362. https://doi.org/10.1371/journal.pone.0211362

Fancourt, D., & Steptoe, A. (2019). Present in body or just in mind: Differences in social presence and emotion regulation in live vs. virtual singing experiences. *Frontiers in Psychology, 10*, 778. https://doi.org/10.3389/fpsyg.2019.00778

Fink, L., & Drake, J. E. (2016). Writing and flow: Comparing the benefits of narrative versus poetry writing. *Empirical Studies of the Arts, 34*(2), 177–192. https://doi.org/10.1177/0276237416636368

Fink, A., Koschutnig, K., Benedek, M., et al. (2012). Stimulating creativity via the exposure to the other people's ideas. *Human Brain Mapping, 33*, 2603–2610. https://doi.org/10.1002/hbm.21387

Fink, A., Weiss, E. M., Schwarzl, U., et al. (2017). Creative ways to well-being: Reappraisal inventiveness in the context of anger-evoking situations. *Cognitive, Affective & Behavioral Neuroscience, 17*(1), 94–105. https://doi.org/10.3758/s13415–016-0465-9

Forkosh, J., & Drake, J. E. (2017). Coloring versus drawing: Effects of cognitive demand on mood repair, flow, and enjoyment. *Art Therapy: Journal of the American Art Therapy Association, 34*(2), 75–82. https://doi.org/10.1080/07421656.2017.1327272

Frenzel, A. C. (2014). Teacher emotions. In R. Pekrun & L. Linnenbrink-Garcia (Eds.), *International Handbook of Emotions in Education* (pp. 494–519). Routledge. https://doi.org/10.4324/9780203148211

Friedman, B. H. (2010). Feelings and the body: The Jamesian perspective on automatic specific of emotion. *Biological Psychology, 84*(3), 383–393. https://doi.org/10.1016/j.biopsycho.2009.10.006

Gentzler, A. L., DeLong, K. L., & Smart, R. (2020). Theater majors compared with nonmajors: Investigating temperament and emotion beliefs, awareness, regulation, and perception. *Psychology of Aesthetics, Creativity, and the Arts, 14*(3), 301–312. https://doi.org/10.1037/aca0000219

Goldstein, T. R. (2009). Psychological perspectives on acting. *Psychology of Aesthetics, Creativity, and the Arts, 3*(1), 6–9. https://doi.org/10.1037/a0014644

Goldstein, T. R. & Lerner, M. (2018). Dramatic pretend play games uniquely improve emotional control in young children. *Developmental Science, 21*(4), e12603. https://doi.org/10.1111/desc.12603

Goldstein, T. R., Tamir, M., & Winner, E. (2013). Expressive suppression and acting. *Psychology of Aesthetics, Creativity, and the Arts, 7*(2), 191–196. https://doi.org/10.1037/a0030209

Goodreads. *Isadora Duncan.* (2021). www.goodreads.com/author/show/160918.Isadora_Duncan

Greene, G. (1980). *Ways of Escape.* Simon & Schuster.

Güler, O., & Haseki, M. İ. (2021). Positive psychological impacts of cooking during the COVID-19 lockdown period: A qualitative study. *Frontiers in Psychology, 12* (635957), 829. https://doi.org/10.3389/fpsyg.2021.635957

Hagenauer, G., & Volet, S. E. (2014). "I don't think I could, you know, just teach without any emotion": Exploring the nature and origin of university teachers' emotions. *Research Papers in Education, 29*(2), 240–262. https://doi.org/10.1080/02671522.2012.754929

Hayashi, N., Wada, T., Hirai, H., et al. (2008). The effects of horticultural activity in a community garden on mood change. *Environmental Control in Biology, 46*(4), 233–240. https://doi.org/10.2525/ecb.46.233

Hemenover, S. H., Augustine, A. A., Shulman, T. E., Tran, T. Q., & Barlett, C. (2008). Individual differences in the ability to repair negative affect. *Emotion, 8*(4), 468–478. https://doi.org/10.1037/1528-3542.8.4.468

Hoffmann, J., & Russ, S. (2012). Pretend play, creativity, and emotion regulation in children. *Psychology of Aesthetics, Creativity, and the Arts, 6*(2), 175–184. https://doi.org/10.1037/a0026299

Jauk, E., Benedek, M., & Neubauer, A. C. (2014). The road to creative achievement: A latent variable model of ability and personality predictors. *European Journal of Personality, 28*(1), 95–105. https://doi.org/10.1002/per.1941

Juslin, P. N., & Sloboda, J. A. (2010). Introduction: Aims, organization, and terminology. In P. N. Juslin & J. A. Sloboda (Eds.), *Handbook of Music and Emotion: Theory, Research, Applications* (pp. 3–12). Oxford University Press.

Kaufman, J. C., & Beghetto, R. A. (2009). Beyond big and little: The Four C model of creativity. *Review of General Psychology, 13*(1), 1–12. https://doi.org/10.1037/a0013688

Koay, W. I., & Dillon, D. (2020). Community gardening: Stress, well-being, and resilience potentials. *International Journal of Environmental Research and Public Health, 17*(18), 6740. https://doi.org/10.3390/ijerph17186740

Monnier, C., Syssau, A., Blanc, N., & Brechet, C. (2016). Assessing the effectiveness of drawing an autobiographical memory as a mood induction procedure in children. *The Journal of Positive Psychology, 13*(2), 174–180. https://doi.org/10.1080/17439760.2016.1257048

Morris, A. S., Silk, J. S., Steinberg, L., Myers, S. M., & Robinson, L. R. (2007). The role of the family context in the development of emotion regulation. *Social Development, 16*(2), 361–388. https://doi.org/10.1111/j.1467-9507.2007.00389.x

Mosko, J. E., & Delach, M. J. (2021). Cooking, creativity, and well-being: An integration of quantitative and qualitative methods. *The Journal of Creative Behavior, 55*(2), 348–361. https://doi.org/10.1002/jocb.459

Nair, S., Sagar, M., Sollers, J., III, Consedine, N., & Broadbent, E. (2015). Do slumped and upright postures affect stress responses? A randomized trial. *Health Psychology, 34*(6), 632–641. https://doi.org/10.1037/hea0000146

Niedenthal, P., Krauth-Gruber, S., & Ric, F. (2006). *Psychology of Emotions: Interpersonal, Experiential, and Cognitive Approaches*. Psychology Press.

Paul Cezanne Quotes. (2021). www.brainyquote.com/quotes/paul_cezanne_370522

Pennebaker, J. W. (1997). Writing about emotional experiences as a therapeutic process. *Psychological Science, 8*(3), 162–166. https://doi.org/10.1111/j.1467-9280.1997.tb00403.x

Pennebaker, J. W., & Chung, C. K. (2011). Expressive writing and its links to mental and physical health. In H. S. Friedman (Ed.), *Oxford Handbook of Health Psychology* (pp. 417–430). Oxford University Press. https://doi.org/10.1093/oxfordhb/9780195342819.013.0018

Reynolds, M., Brewin, C. R., & Saxton, M. (2000). Emotional disclosure in school children. *Journal of Child Psychology and Psychiatry and Allied Disciplines, 41*(2), 151–159. https://doi.org/10.1017/S0021963099005223

Root-Bernstein, R. S. (2002). Aesthetic cognition. *International Studies in the Philosophy of Science, 16*(1), 61–77. https://doi.org/10.1080/02698590120118837

Russo, E. (2000). Nobel impact. *The Scientist, 14*(24),10.

Saarni, C. S. (1999). *The Development of Emotional Competence*. Guilford Press.

Sloan, D. M., & Epstein, E. M. (2005). Respiratory sinus arrhythmia predicts written disclosure outcome. *Psychophysiology, 42*(5), 611–615. https://doi.org/10.1111/j.0048-5772.2005.347.x

Soliday, E., Garofalo, J. P., & Rogers, D. (2004). Expressive-writing intervention for adolescents' somatic symptoms and mood. *Journal of Clinical Child and Adolescent Psychology, 33*(4), 792–801. https://doi.org/10.1207/s15374424jccp3304_14

Sunga, A. B., & Advincula, J. L. (2021). The "plantito/plantita" home gardening during the pandemic. *Community Psychology in Global Perspective, 7*(1), 88–105. https://doi.org/10.1285/i24212113v7i1p88

Thompson, R. A. (1994). Emotion regulation: A theme in search of definition. *Monographs of the Society for Research in Child Development, 59*(2/3), 250–283. https://doi.org/10.2307/1166137

Van Den Berg, A. E., & Custers, M. H. (2011). Gardening promotes neuroendocrine and affective restoration from stress. *Journal of Health Psychology, 16*(1), 3–11. https://doi.org/10.1177/1359105310365577

van der Vennet, R., & Serice, S. (2012). Can coloring mandalas reduce anxiety? A replication study. *Art Therapy: Journal of the American Art Therapy Association, 29*(2), 87–92. https://doi.org/10.1080/07421656.2012.680047

van Goethem, A., & Sloboda, J. (2011). The functions of music for affect regulation. *Musicae Scientiae, 15*(2), 208–228. http://doi.org/10.1177/1029864911401174

van Vugt, M. K. (2014). Ballet as a movement-based contemplative practice? Implications for neuroscientific studies. *Frontiers in Human Neuroscience, 8* (513). https://doi.org/10.3389/fnhum.2014.00513

Weber, H., de Assunção, V. L., Martin, C., Westmeyer, H., & Geisler, F. C. (2014). Reappraisal inventiveness: The ability to create different reappraisals of critical situations. *Cognition and Emotion, 28*(2), 345–360. https://doi.org/10.1080/02699931.2013.832152

White, R. W. (1959). Motivation reconsidered: The concept of competence. *Psychological Review, 66*(5), 297–333. https://doi.org/10.1037/h0040934

Wolpert, L., & Richards, A. (1997). *Passionate Minds: The Inner World of Scientists.* Oxford University Press.

Wu, X., Guo, T., Tang, T., Shi, B., & Luo, J. (2017). Role of creativity in the effectiveness of cognitive reappraisal. *Frontiers in Psychology, 8,* 1598. https://doi.org/10.3389/fpsyg.2017.01598

Zajic, M. C., McIntyre, N., Swain-Lerro, L., et al. (2018). Attention and written expression in school-age, high-functioning children with autism spectrum disorders. *Autism, 22*(3), 245–258. https://doi.org/10.1177/1362361316675121

Zimmerman, N., & Mangelsdorf, H. H. (2020). Emotional benefits of brief creative movement and art interventions. *The Arts in Psychotherapy, 70.* https://doi.org/10.1016/j.aip.2020.101686

21 Everyday Creativity as a Pathway to Meaning and Well-Being

Molly Holinger and James C. Kaufman

The day-to-day stress of life makes it easy, with its increasing demands for time and attention, to put one's well-being on the back burner. Even easier is to ignore bigger picture concerns such as one's meaning in life. Sometimes it can take major world events that have a traumatic personal impact, such the recent pandemic and subsequent lockdown, to take a step back and consider such larger issues (Kapoor & Kaufman, 2020). In these cases, everyday creativity can provide one such pathway toward pursuing well-being.

Indeed, a work that had strong implications for Humanism, *Man's Search for Meaning* (Frankl, 2006/1946), emerged from the insight reached from the author surviving the Holocaust. Frankl discussed three ways of finding meaning in life, one of which encompassed creating something. Other leading scholars in the Humanism tradition also embraced the power of everyday creativity. For example, both Rogers' (1961) seven traits of a fully functioning person and Maslow's (1943) self-actualization level of his hierarchy of needs include creativity as a core component.

This connection of everyday creativity to such essential human desires as well-being and meaning continues to this day. For example, design thinkers have applied creativity to planning and enriching one's personal and professional life (Burnett & Evans, 2016). Scholars across fields such as positive psychology (e.g., Kaufman, 2020), and of course creativity (e.g., Acar et al., 2020), have used sophisticated analyses and methodological designs to the study of *everyday creativity* (e.g., McKay et al., 2022). Scholarly work on *the creativity and well-being connection* has advanced (e.g., Acar et al., 2020) past its theoretical foundations (Richards, 2007), partly boosted by the positive psychology movement. Informed by such new developments, this chapter offers an updated perspective on the positive outcomes of creativity (as advocated by Forgeard & Kaufman, 2016).

We want to first note that the phrase "positive *outcomes* of everyday creativity" implies causality, and we focused on synthesizing and compiling intervention studies. We also see merit in correlational studies that have told us most of what we know on creativity, well-being, and meaning to this point and incorporate daily diary and ecological momentary assessment studies that have made significant contributions in recent years, but most still do not establish causality. Readers should also consider that, by nature, the therapeutic intervention studies begin with a lower baseline of mental health than the average population. Thus, the benefits uncovered in the literature may not generalize given that the participants begin at a "deficit" in terms of mental health. Finally, several creativity and well-being studies focus on another group of at-risk individuals: aging adults. Therefore, we devote a section of this chapter to this specific demographic.

Everyday Creativity

Everyday creative activities may range from cooking to gardening to entertaining a small child to trying to fix a broken household item. They may include artistic endeavors, such as painting or music or writing, but they may extend to other domains. They may be done at home as part of one's personal life, as a specific hobby, or at work or school (Reiter-Palmon et al., 2012). They may occur as much as four times more frequently at work than outside of work (Karwowski et al., 2017).

Everyday creativity can be seen as part of a larger trajectory of creative development, as proposed by the Four C Model. This model begins with mini-c, or personal creativity (Beghetto & Kaufman, 2007). Mini-c represents moments of insight that carry personal meaning for the creator. Such creativity may not be recognized by others; it may not even be articulated. With enough feedback (Holinger & Kaufman, 2018) and metacognition (Kaufman & Beghetto, 2013), mini-c may evolve into everyday creativity, or little-c. Little-c creativity can be enjoyed and appreciated by others, from a poem read at a coffee shop, to an interesting meal served to friends, to a painting sold at a craft fair. With enough deliberate practice (Ericsson et al., 2007) and upon having some type of impact on a field (e.g., Sternberg et al., 2003), little-c can become Pro-c, or expert-level creativity (Kaufman & Beghetto, 2009). If such creativity continues to have an impact over many generations (typically past the creator's death), then it can be considered creative genius, or Big-C (Simonton, 2009). Many of the core benefits of creativity that we will discuss may apply to all Four Cs, but our emphasis will be on little-c, or everyday creativity.

Well-Being

The positive outcomes we discuss in these studies are grounded in well-established theoretical models, including subjective well-being (SWB; Diener, 1984), psychological well-being (Ryff, 1995), flourishing (Seligman, 2011), and self-determination theory (Ryan & Deci, 2017). First, Diener's (1984) model of subjective well-being includes three components: positive affect, negative affect, and life satisfaction. SWB researchers stress that objective measures such as socioeconomic status, physical health, or geographic location do not fully explain how good one's life is because, "people react differently to the same circumstances, and they evaluate conditions based on their unique expectations, values, and previous experiences" (Diener et al., 1999, p. 277). To put it plainly, the distinguishing characteristic of subjective well-being is subjectivity (Diener, 1984) – based on an individual's inner perspective.

Another theory of well-being is Ryff's (1995) model of psychological well-being (PWB). In contrast to SWB, for which individuals determine their own judgments of the good life (Ryan & Deci, 2001), with PWB people are given predetermined criteria of well-being including: self-acceptance, environmental mastery, positive relations with others, autonomy, purpose in life, and personal growth. The emphasis on self-actualization, personal growth, and accepting the whole self, both positive and negative, resonate with the humanists, including Maslow, Rogers, and Jung. Some researchers (e.g. Ryff, 1995) argue that psychological well-being theory captures well-being more fully than subjective well-being because it includes a broad range of wellness markers whereas subjective well-being largely focuses on happiness and life satisfaction.

Next, the PERMA model (Seligman, 2011) encompasses the five components of Positive Emotions, Engagement, Relationships, Meaning, and Accomplishment. PERMA includes short-term factors of well-being such as positive emotions (similar to the "positive affect" marker of subjective well-being) and long-term factors (such as meaning).

Finally, Self-Determination Theory (SDT; Ryan & Deci, 2017) is a theory of motivation and human development that features autonomy, competence, and relatedness. The degree to which these three types of motivation, or "satisfactions" (p. 5) are supported or inhibited, influenced by social-contextual factors, influences well-being. "SDT research documents that in social contexts in which there is psychological support for these satisfactions, people's curiosity, creativity, productivity, and compassion are most robustly expressed" (p. 5).

Drawing from these various models (see Table 21.1), we will explore five positive outcomes associated with creativity: socialization/connectedness, personal growth, meaning/legacy, positive emotion, and mastery/engagement/flow.

Table 21.1 *Well-being model and specific component*

	Subjective well-being	Psychological well-being	PERMA	Self-determination theory
Socialization/ connectedness		Positive relations with others	Relationships	Relatedness
Personal growth		Personal growth		
Meaning		Purpose in life	Meaning	
Positive emotion	Positive affect		Positive emotion	
Flow			Engagement	Competence

PERMA: Positive emotions, Engagement, Relationships, Meaning, Accomplishment

We will then spotlight the ways that creativity can specifically benefit older adults, and finally offer directions for the future.

Personal Growth

Personal growth has meaningful implications for both professional and personal well-being. According to Spreitzer and colleagues (2005), vitality (feeling invigorated and alive) and learning (obtaining new knowledge and developing new skills) chiefly characterize thriving at work. This definition aligns with the findings of Kleine and colleagues (2019) who, in a meta-analysis of the factors that contribute to thriving at work, reported a relationship between positive attitudes toward personal growth and thriving. Moreover, Cho and colleagues (2009) found that employees who described their workplace as supportive of self-improvement and goal-identification had greater desire to stay in their current workplace environment. Ivcevic (2007) found a small association between personal growth (Ryff, 1989) and everyday creativity. There was no significant association with artistic creativity, suggesting that artistic and everyday creativity have defining attributes discrete from one another. There were also differences in frequency of engagement (people engaged in everyday creative activities more frequently than artistic creative activities); personality traits (extraversion and conscientiousness significantly related to everyday creativity but not artistic creativity); and psychological health (artistic creativity showed a small positive correlation with psychopathology).

Negative events can lead to diversifying experiences that promote creative growth by inciting individuals to think in new ways, encounter new stimuli, think flexibly, and reappraise existing relationships. For example, Tang et al. (2021) explored the relationship between creativity, personal growth, and social connection in response to crisis, namely, the COVID-19 pandemic. In large samples of employees from China, Germany, and the United States, individuals' self-reported impact of COVID-19 was linked to creative behavior which, in turn, related to participants' perceived creative growth, and ultimately increased their sense of well-being. Survivors of Hurricane Katrina who lost their homes perceived flexibility and originality as enablers of resilience (Metzl, 2009).

Calhoun and Tedeschi (2001) compare these momentous life events to an earthquake because they call into question our views of the world and cause us to restructure our assumptions and beliefs. This type of growth, known as posttraumatic growth, is defined as the positive changes that individuals may make in response to a serious adverse experience in their lives. These changes tend to occur in five areas: improving relationships, seeing new opportunities in life, making use of personal strengths, appreciating life more, and increasing spirituality (Tedeschi & Calhoun, 1996). Connecting this concept back to creativity, growth in the areas of improving relationships and identifying new opportunities for one's life has been shown to lead to self-reported creative growth, or increased drive/demonstration of creativity (Forgeard, 2013). That both positive *and* negative changes in relationships led to greater creativity reinforces that creative work can emerge from both positive and negative social experiences.

Engaging purposefully in creative activities, such as expressive writing, can help people process these negative (or simply emotional) events (Pennebaker, 1997; Pennebaker & Beall, 1986). It becomes possible to find meaning in the form of coherence, which is when one can look back at one's life and feel as though it makes sense. In addition to coherence, two other conceptions of meaning are associated with creativity: significance, or believing that one has a life that is worth living (Heintzelman & King, 2014; King et al., 2016; Martela & Steger, 2016), and legacy, or feeling as though one will leave part of themselves behind even after their physical life has ended. In the next section, we focus on this third key component of meaning.

Meaning/Legacy

When people are faced with the concept of eventual death, they are apt to seek out symbolic immortality, or some way that they can live on (metaphorically) after death. There is a body of theory and research that suggests people primed to think about death may respond by seeking out other people as opposed to participating in creative acts (e.g., Arndt et al., 1999). However, most conceptions of symbolic immortality (e.g., Lifton, 1979, 2011) are quite tied to creative actions; indeed, one specific pathway is to leave a legacy of one's creative work. In younger people, a need to find purpose and seek out a legacy may lead to a desire to engage in prosocial creativity. Those high on this need also showed higher levels of positive emotions (Shoshani & Russo-Netzer, 2017).

As one grows to adulthood, Erikson's (1982) core psychosocial stage reflects generativity, which can encompass having children, being productive (such as at work), and being creative. Generativity was found to connect to positive well-being with symbolic immortality as a mediating variable (Huta & Zuroff, 2007). Perach and Wisman (2019) reviewed several studies and found a link between creative achievement and the ability to cope with death anxiety. Cui et al. (2020) looked at benevolent versus malevolent creativity's relationship with death-related anxiety during the COVID-19 pandemic. Only benevolent creativity helped ease anxiety, particularly in those who sought meaning.

Positive Emotion

Laypeople often conflate well-being solely with positive emotions, and yet most models of well-being consider feeling happy or joyful as only one among several other essential components. This being said, positive emotion is indeed an important aspect of well-being and one that creativity researchers have explored in depth. An exciting line of new research has emerged in recent years on the topic of creativity and emotion using ecological momentary assessment (EMA). Partially due to the increased ease of use enabled by technology and statistical advancements, EMA has grown in popularity (Silvia & Cotter, 2021) across fields and within creativity research, specifically. In this approach, a variety of tools such as texts, surveys, or phone calls are used to ask participants about the frequency and the nature of creative activity in their daily lives. Across studies (Conner & Silvia, 2015; Conner et al., 2018; Karwowski et al., 2017; Silvia et al., 2014), positive high-activation emotions, such as being elated or exhilarated, were reported on days or at times when individuals were involved in creative activities, which is consistent with past research on creative thinking and mood (Baas et al., 2008). As Conner and Silvia put it, "creative days are characterized by greater emotional zest and engagement" (p. 463). Negative emotions, such as feeling angry, stressed, or self-conscious, had either no relationship or were negatively related to creativity.

Importantly, EMA research enables researchers to explore causality by analyzing trends across days. Using this approach, Conner et al. (2018) found that people felt more "energetic, enthusiastic, and excited" (p. 184) the day after doing something creative the previous day. These carryover effects also extended to flourishing, or feeling a sense of purpose, human connection, and interest in life. Neither positive affect nor flourishing led to increased creativity the following day, suggesting that creativity may lead to increased positive affect and flourishing but not vice versa.

Does everyday creativity have the same benefits at work? Amabile was prescient in her use of daily diary methods (one type of EMA design) to examine everyday creativity at work almost a decade before the current wave of EMA research. Creative days were characterized by positive emotions (Amabile et al., 2005). Eighty-six percent of reactions to creative events involved experiences of "joy, pride, satisfaction, relief, or other positive feelings" (p. 387) and only 14 percent involved negative responses such as "anger, sadness, or fear" (p. 387). Time-lagged analyses, however, found no evidence for creativity as an antecedent for positive affect. Creativity did not predict positive affect on days following the initial event, suggesting that the positive affect experienced as a consequence of a creative event does not extend beyond the day it occurs. Exploring this relationship further is especially important given (a) the central role that work plays in our lives and (b) as mentioned earlier, creative activity occurs much more frequently at work as compared to outside of work (Karwowski et al., 2017).

In another workplace study by Sherman and Shavit (2018), individuals were asked, "How much creative effort do you invest in order to make your work more enjoyable?" (p. 2055). Self-reported creative effort, or striving to incorporate imagination, and creative skills and knowledge into one's work, was associated with positive emotions as well as meaning and purpose in life. Seeking out enjoyment through creative work was itself a source of enjoyment and increased quality of life.

Mastery/Engagement/Flow

The next positive outcome associated with creativity that we discuss in this chapter is flow, which occurs when the level of challenge matches or slightly exceeds an individual's abilities (Csikszentmihalyi, 1990). Getting into flow requires a delicate balance, as the activity requires a certain level of struggle but not to the point where the individual feels overwhelmed. Tasks that exceed the creator's skill level often end in frustration, anxiety, or giving up; tasks that are well below a creator's skill level often result in boredom or disinterest. Most flow activities provide inherent feedback through which the individual can learn, adjust, and develop mastery, one of the components of the self-determination theory (Ryan & Deci, 2017). People typically find flow activities highly enjoyable and intrinsically rewarding. In fact, Csikszentmihalyi describes flow as an "optimal state." In his view, "Contrary to what we usually believe, moments like these, the best moments in our lives, are not the passive, receptive, relaxing times – although such experiences can also be enjoyable, if we have worked hard to attain them. The best moments usually occur when a person's body or mind is stretched to its limits in a voluntary effort to accomplish something difficult and worthwhile" (Csikszentmihalyi, 1990, p. 3). Flow is less a direct outcome of creativity, but more accurately a state often involved in creative activity that is associated with such outcomes as positive affect, well-being (Asakawa, 2004), self-esteem (Wells, 1988), and life satisfaction (Han, 1988). Flow is relatively common as only about one-third of people report never or infrequently experiencing flow (Gallup Poll, 1988).

Flow occurs both in and outside of work to varying degrees and a few studies have explored how leisure and work experiences relate. For example, in a sample of adult employees, the vast majority of flow experiences occurred at work as opposed to outside of work. Such moments were characterized by happiness, strength, focus, and creativity (Csikszentmihalyi & LeFevre, 1989). Even though employees had more optimal experiences at work than during leisure time, they nevertheless reported that they preferred to be at leisure than at work. This suggests that the requisite nature of work undermines intrinsic motivation and subverts the positive outcomes it begets. Eschleman et al. (2014) explored how the activities that employees engage in to recover from work (i.e., "recovery experiences") related to creative performance at work. One type, mastery experiences, through which individuals challenge themselves and build new skills (qualities inherent in flow), mediated the effect of creative activity outside of work and creative performance. Creative activities were positively related to mastery, which was in turn positively related to behaviors at work that related to the organization, such as defending one's company from criticisms from other workers.

Socialization or Connectedness

> A generation ago, when *Annie Hall* won the Oscar for Best Picture, talk therapy occupied a prominent place in our collective imagination, whether or not you partook. If you wanted to spend several hours a week baring your soul to a stranger who was professionally obligated to listen and react, you went to therapy. Today you join a writing workshop. – Steve Almond (2012)

As Almond observed, group creative activities have been shown to produce feelings of social connection through common interest, providing an environment and context for sharing personal experiences, and working together (e.g., Johnson & Sullivan-Marx, 2006; Packer & Ballantyne, 2011). Developing social connections is an established therapeutic practice (Martin et al., 2000) and is often an element in successful creativity-focused interventions.

One can feel connected with others while experiencing other people's creativity. Consider Smith's (2014) Museum Effect. Smith assessed art museum–goers' feelings about the degree to which they were focused on their connection with friends, social issues, and the general well-being of the planet. He surveyed them at the beginning, middle, and end of their visit, finding a peak of connectedness in the middle of their visit. Although there was a slight decline by the end, these levels were still notably higher than when the museum-goers first entered the museum. Smith interprets these findings with the lens of Leder et al. (2004) and other theoretical perspectives, which proposes that interacting with art can cause one to self-reflect and even potentially enter a flow-like state.

Why else might everyday creativity be associated with feeling socially connected? Another reason may be creativity's connection to perspective-taking (Glăveanu, 2015). This ability to understand and empathize with other people is associated with creativity both in the workplace (Hoever et al., 2012) and schools (Doron, 2017). People with higher levels of perspective-taking were more likely to be able to successfully manage their emotions and, hence, be more likely to forgive others (Rizkalla et al., 2008). Interventions designed for tolerance that build off of cognitive flexibility (Gocłowska et al., 2013) or openness (Gocłowska et al., 2017) have been shown to increase creativity. More recently, creativity interventions have been shown to reduce prejudice (Groyecka-Bernard et al., 2021).

Many everyday creative activities are social in nature (Ivcevic & Mayer, 2009) and thus facilitate well-being. Much of the research on creativity and socialization focuses on older adults. Thus we continue our discussion of this line of research in the next section.

Creativity and Well-Being Among Older Adults

Several aspects of cognitive functioning associated with creativity decline with age (Seligman et al., 2016), including, short-term memory, fluid reasoning, originality, and mind-wandering. Furthermore, openness to experience, which has been consistently linked to creativity in past research, also has been shown to decline in later life (Donnellan & Lucas, 2008; Graham et al., 2020; Specht et al., 2011). On the other hand, factors such as the accumulation of domain-specific and domain-general knowledge, pattern recognition, self-efficacy, and effective collaboration may increase or at least remain constant with age. As previously discussed, the desire to leave a legacy can also motivate creativity later in life. For example, Simonton (1989) found a pattern that many eminent creators produced significant works, or a "swan song," toward the end of their lives. Overall, weighing the factors that develop or regress with age, creativity likely decreases later in life. Historiometric studies of creative productivity have produced similar findings (e.g., Simonton, 2012; Zuckerman, 1977).

If creativity declines with age, then why do we concentrate on older adults to end this chapter? First, a practical justification: a substantial proportion of the research on well-being and creativity targets this specific population. Second, we are more concerned about the positive outcomes of creativity (What good things can creativity do for us as people?) rather than what we can do to increase or enhance creativity (What are the factors or contexts that drive creative performance/achievement?). As people age, they often shift their perspective on life's priorities, perhaps becoming less concerned with outward markers of success and more concerned with the topics discussed in this chapter such as family, relationships, and meaning. While creativity may decline in later years, the benefits reaped from engaging in creative activity do not. In fact, the literature points to several positive outcomes of arts-related and everyday creative engagement for older adults.

Gerontologic research has particular relevance to Ryan and Deci's (2017) self-determination theory, as two major lines of research on older adults focus on sense of control and social connection (Cohen, 2006). For example, in one study, socially isolated older people engaged in weekly group creative activities, such as painting, print-making, creative writing, computing, and cookery. In addition, a mentor was assigned to each participant, with support gradually lessening over time, to facilitate opportunities for social connection and help tailor the activity to participants' personal interests. Participants reported increased quality of social interactions, and this effect remained one year post-intervention (Greaves & Farbus, 2006). Providing activities that were personally meaningful and engaging, appeared to be a key component in developing self-efficacy from trying and succeeding at new creative endeavors.

Other studies have also linked purposeful activity to well-being later in life (e.g., Herzog & House, 1991). Collins et al. (2008) explored the relationship between flow experiences and happiness later in life through experience sampling over a seven day period. Most participants experienced flow at least once during the study window. Flow activity on a certain day was not related to emotion (positive or negative), nor life satisfaction, however, "higher quality flow, defined by intense concentration, loss of self-awareness, and rewarding outcomes," (p. 715) was related to high activation positive emotions (such as elation). As mentioned earlier, these types of emotions (positive, high-activation) are also associated with creative thinking (Baas et al., 2008). Looking at the data on the intra-individual level, patterns among variables shifted: participants with a greater number of flow experiences had lower average levels of positive affect and life satisfaction. One explanation for these results is that these individuals sought out flow as a coping mechanism to manage or distract from negative emotions. Following this logic, people who engaged flow more frequently would also have higher levels of negative affect. One study found that older individuals described flow using similar terms as other age groups (Massimini et al., 1988), though more research is needed to understand if flow also functions the same way in later years.

Arts-related everyday creative activities appear to benefit older adults in a variety of ways (Malchiodi, 2012). For example, when Fisher and Specht (1999) asked 36 aging adults about their perceptions of how their artistic creativity contributed to their successful aging, six common themes emerged: a sense of purpose, interactions with others, personal growth, self-acceptance, autonomy, and health. Their findings summarized, "The older individuals in this study are not only active, but have a sense of purpose, accomplishment, and something to look forward to ... . Their artwork draws them onward, does not permit disengagement, and demands active involvement in both the cognitive realm of their inner being and the physical world manipulating resources into unique expressions of self" (p. 469).

Another study placed 150 older adults in a control and 150 matched older adults in a treatment condition. Participants in the treatment condition participated weekly in a community-based art programs run by professional artists that ranged from painting, pottery, oral histories in a creative framework, poetry, and dance. They spent additional time attending concerts and other cultural events, as well as producing original artistic work. The control group engaged in community activities unrelated to the arts. One year after baseline measures, findings showed lower levels of loneliness and depression, and higher morale in the treatment group as compared to the control group (Cohen, 2006).

In summary, some common positive outcomes of arts-related and general everyday creativity across studies have included building self-efficacy and self-esteem, increased social interactions, reduced depression, and heightened motivation/morale (Flood & Phillips, 2007; Gladding & Martin, 2010). There are several obvious benefits inherent in arts-related activities. For example, they are often enjoyable, motivational, cognitively stimulating, and involve social interaction (Noice et al., 2014). Finally, although unclear whether flow causes higher or lower positive affect or life satisfaction, we do know that "people who reported a higher number of days with flow had lower average levels of positive affect and life satisfaction, yet participants were happier on the days that they had higher quality of flow" (Collins et al., 2008, p. 715).

Conclusion and Future Directions

In this chapter, we focused on five outcomes of creativity that enrich quality of life: socialization, personal growth, meaning, positive emotion, and flow. Future research might explore how other dimensions of well-being relate to creativity, such as awe or hope. Other opportunities to push this area of research forward include:

- Using experimental research methods that not only determine a relationship between well-being and creativity but also elucidate causality.
- Examining multiple measures/conceptualizations of creativity to better determine how, for example, rated creative work may differ from divergent thinking performance or self-beliefs.
- Moving beyond the largely arts-based focus of existing work to look at more domains, from everyday to STEM and beyond.
- Considering different levels of creative achievement, from professional-level work (beyond organizational creativity; see Boldt & Kaufman, in press) to exploring the scope of mini-c and little-c.
- Finally, conducting additional meta-analyses now that a large body of research exists.

References

Acar, S., Tadik, H., Myers, D., Van der Sman, C., & Uysal, R. (2020). Creativity and wellbeing: A meta-analysis. *Journal of Creative Behavior, 55,* 738–751. https://doi.org/10.1002/jocb.485

Almond, S. (2012, March 23). Why talk therapy is on the wane and writing workshops are on the rise. *The New York Times.* www.nytimes.com/2012/03/25/magazine/why-talk-therapy-is-on-the-wane-and-writing-workshops-are-on-the-rise.html

Amabile, T. M., Barsade, S. G., Meuller, J. S., & Staw, B. M. (2005). Affect and creativity at work. *Administrative Science Quarterly, 50,* 367–403. https://doi.org/10.2189/asqu.2005.50.3.367

Arndt, J., Greenberg, J., Solomon, S., Pyszczynski, T., & Schimel, J. (1999). Creativity and terror management: The effects of creative activity on guilt and social projection following mortality salience. *Journal of Personality and Social Psychology, 77,* 19–32. https://doi.org/10.1037/0022-3514.77.1.19

Asakawa, K. (2004). Flow experience and autotelic personality in Japanese college students: How do they experience challenges in daily life? *Journal of Happiness Studies, 5,* 123–154. https://doi.org/10.1023/B:JOHS.0000035915.97836.89

Baas, M., De Dreu, C. K., & Nijstad, B. A. (2008). A meta-analysis of 25 years of mood-creativity research: Hedonic tone, activation, or regulatory focus? *Psychological Bulletin, 134,* 779–806. https://doi.org/10.1037/a0012815

Beghetto, R. A., & Kaufman, J. C. (2007). Toward a broader conception of creativity: A case for "mini-c" creativity. *Psychology of Aesthetics, Creativity, and the Arts, 1,* 73–79. https://doi.org/10.1037/1931-3896.1.2.73

Boldt, G., & Kaufman, J. C. (in press). Creativity and meaning at work. In R. Reiter-Palmon & S. T. Hunter (Eds.), *Handbook of Organizational Creativity* (2nd ed.). Academic Press.

Burnett, W., & Evans, D. J. (2016). *Designing Your Life: How to Build a Well-Lived, Joyful Life.* Alfred A. Knopf.

Calhoun, L. G., & Tedeschi, R. G. (2001). Posttraumatic growth: The positive lesson of loss. In R. A. Neigmeyer (Ed.), *Meaning Reconstruction and the Experience of Loss* (pp. 157–172). American Psychological Association.

Cho, S., Johanson, M. M., & Guchait, P. (2009). Employees intent to leave: A comparison of determinants of intent to leave versus intent to stay. *International Journal of Hospitality Management, 28,* 374–381. https://doi.org/10.1016/j.ijhm.2008.10.007

Cohen, G. D. (2006). Research on creativity and aging: The positive impact of the arts on health and illness. *Generations: Journal of the American Society on Aging, 30,* 7–15. www.jstor.org/stable/26555432

Collins, A. L., Sarkisian, N., & Winner, E. (2008). Flow and happiness in later life: An investigation into the role of daily and weekly flow experiences *Journal of Happiness Studies, 10,* 703–719. https://doi.org/10.1007/s10902-008-9116-3.

Conner, T. S. DeYoung, C. G., & Silvia, P. J. (2018) Everyday creative activity as a path to flourishing, *The Journal of Positive Psychology, 13,* 181–189. https://doi.org/10.1080/17439760.2016.1257049

Conner, T. S., & Silvia, P. J. (2015). Creative days: A daily diary study of emotions, personality, and everyday creativity. *Psychology of Aesthetics, Creativity, and the Arts, 10,* 287–295. https://doi.org/10.1037/aca0000022

Csikszentmihalyi, M. (1990). *Flow: The Psychology of Optimal Experience.* Harper & Row.

Csikszentmihalyi, M., & LeFevre J. (1989). Optimal experience in work and leisure. *Journal of Personality and Social Psychology, 56,* 815–822. https://doi.org/10.1037/0022-3514.56.5.815

Cui, Y. X., Zhou, X., Zu, C., et al. (2020). Benevolent creativity buffers anxiety aroused by mortality salience: Terror management in COVID-19 Pandemic. *Frontiers in Psychology, 11,* 3705. https://doi.org/10.3389/fpsyg.2020.601027

Diener, E. (1984). Subjective well-being. *Psychological Bulletin, 95,* 542–575. https://doi.org/10.1037/0033-2909.95.3.542

Diener, E., Suh, E. M., Lucas, R. E., & Smith, H. L. (1999). Subjective well-being: Three decades of progress. *Psychological Bulletin, 125,* 276–302. https://doi.org/10.1037/0033-2909.125.2.276

Donnellan, M. B., & Lucas, R. E. (2008). Age differences in the Big Five across the life span: evidence from two national samples. *Psychology and Aging, 23,* 558–566. https://doi.org/10.1037/a0012897

Doron, E. (2017). Fostering creativity in school aged children through perspective taking and visual media based short term intervention program. *Thinking Skills and Creativity, 23,* 150–160. https://doi.org/10.1016/j.tsc.2016.12.003

Ericsson, K. A. Roring, R. W., & Nandagopal, K. (2007). Giftedness and evidence for reproducibly superior performance: An account based on the expert-performance framework. *High Ability Studies, 18,* 3–56. https://doi.org/10.1080/13598130701350593

Erikson, E. H. (1982). *The Life Cycle Completed.* W. W. Norton.

Eschleman, K. J., Madsen, J., Alarcon, G., & Barelka, A. (2014). Benefiting from creative activity: The positive relationships between creative activity, recovery experiences, and performance-related outcomes. *Journal of Occupational and Organizational Psychology*, *87*, 579–598. https://doi.org/10.1111/joop.12064

Fisher, B. J., & Specht, D. K. (1999). Successful aging and creativity in later life. *Journal of Aging Studies, 13*, 457–472. https://doi.org/10.1016/S0890-4065(99)00021-3

Flood, M., & Phillips, K. D. (2007). Creativity in older adults: A plethora of possibilities. *Issues in Mental Health Nursing, 28*, 389–411. https://doi.org/10.1080/01612840701252956

Forgeard, M. J. (2013). Perceiving benefits after adversity: The relationship between self-reported posttraumatic growth and creativity. *Psychology of Aesthetics, Creativity, and the Arts*, *7*, 245–264. https://doi.org/10.1037/a0031223

Forgeard, M. J. C., & Kaufman, J. C. (2016). Who cares about imagination, creativity, and innovation, and why? A review. *Psychology of Aesthetics, Creativity, and the Arts, 10*(3), 250–269. https://doi.org/10.1037/aca0000042

Frankl, V. E. (2006). *Man's Search for Meaning*. Beacon Press. (Original work published 1946)

Gallup Poll. (1988). Omnibus, III

Gladding, S. T., & Martin, B. (2010). Creativity and self-esteem in later life. In M. H. Guindon (Ed.), *Self-Esteem across the Lifespan: Issues and Interventions* (pp. 311–323). Routledge/Taylor & Francis Group. https://doi.org/10.1080/08952841.2011.561147

Glăveanu, V. P. (2015). Creativity as a sociocultural act. *The Journal of Creative Behavior*, *49*, 165–180. https://doi.org/10.1002/jocb.94

Gocłowska, M. A., Baas, M., Elliot, A. J., & De Dreu, C. K. W. (2017). Why schema-violations are sometimes preferable to schema-consistencies: The role of interest and openness to experience. *Journal of Research in Personality*, *66*, 54–69. https://doi.org/10.1016/j.jrp.2016.12.005

Gocłowska, M. A., Crisp, R. J., & Labuschagne, K. (2013). Can counter-stereotypes boost flexible thinking? *Group Processes & Intergroup Relations, 16*, 217–231. https://doi.org/10.1177/1368430212445076

Graham, E. K., Weston, S. J., Gerstorf, D., et al. (2020). Trajectories of big five personality traits: A coordinated analysis of 16 longitudinal samples. *European Journal of Personality, 34*, 301–321. https://doi.org/10.1002/per.2259

Greaves, C. J., & Farbus, L. (2006). Effects of creative and social activity on the health and well-being of socially isolated older people: Outcomes from a multi-method observational study. *The Journal of the Royal Society for the Promotion of Health*, *126*, 134–142. https://doi.org/10.1177/1466424006064303

Groyecka-Bernard, A., Karwowski, M., & Sorokowski, P. (2021). Creative thinking components as tools for reducing prejudice: Evidence from experimental studies on adolescents. *Thinking Skills and Creativity*, *39*, 100779. https://doi.org/10.1016/j.tsc.2020.100779

Han, S. (1988). The relationship between life satisfaction and flow in elderly Korean immigrants. In M. Csikszentmihalyi & I. S. Csikszentmihalyi (Eds.), *Optimal Experience: Psychological Students of Flow in Consciousness* (pp. 138–149). Cambridge University Press.

Heintzelman, S. J., & King, L. A. (2014). Life is pretty meaningful. *American Psychologist, 69*, 561–574. https://doi.org/10.1037/a0035049

Herzog, A. R., & House, J. S. (1991). Productive activities and aging well. *Generations: Journal of the American Society on Aging, 15,* 49–54. www.jstor.org/stable/44876955

Hoever, I. J., Van Knippenberg, D., Van Ginkel, W. P., & Barkema, H. G. (2012). Fostering team creativity: perspective taking as key to unlocking diversity's potential. *Journal of Applied Psychology, 97,* 982–996. https://doi.org/10.1037/a0029159

Holinger, M., & Kaufman, J. C. (2018). The relationship between creativity and feedback. In A. Lipnevich & J. Smith (Eds), *Cambridge Handbook of Instructional Feedback* (pp. 575–588). Cambridge University Press.

Huta, V., & Zuroff, D. C. (2007). Examining mediators of the link between generativity and well-being. *Journal of Adult Development, 14,* 47–61. https://doi.org/10.1007/s10804-007-9030-7

Ivcevic, Z. (2007). Artistic and everyday creativity: An act-frequency approach. *The Journal of Creative Behavior, 41,* 271–290. https://doi.org/10.1002/j.2162-6057.2007.tb01074.x

Ivcevic, Z., & Mayer, J. D. (2009). Mapping dimensions of creativity in the life-space. *Creativity Research Journal, 21,* 152–165. https://doi.org/10.1080/10400410902855259

Johnson, C. M., & Sullivan-Marx, E. M. (2006). Art therapy: Using the creative process for healing and hope among African American older adults. *Geriatric Nursing, 27,* 307–316.

Kapoor, H., & Kaufman, J. C. (2020). Meaning-making through creativity during COVID-19. *Frontiers in Psychology, 11,* 595990. https://doi.org/10.3389/fpsyg.2020.595990

Karwowski, M., Lebuda, I., Szumski, G., & Firkowska-Mankiewicz, A. (2017). From moment-to-moment to day-to-day: Experience sampling and diary investigations in adults' everyday creativity. *Psychology of Aesthetics, Creativity, and the Arts, 11*(3), 309–324. https://doi.org/10.1037/aca0000127

Kaufman, J. C., & Beghetto, R. A. (2009). Beyond big and little: The Four C Model of Creativity. *Review of General Psychology, 13,* 1–12. https://doi.org/10.1037/a0013688

Kaufman, J. C., & Beghetto, R. A. (2013). In praise of Clark Kent: Creative metacognition and the importance of teaching kids when (not) to be creative. *Roeper Review, 35,* 155–165. https://doi.org/10.1080/02783193.2013.799413

Kaufman, S. B. (2020). *Transcend: The New Science of Self-Actualization.* TarcherPerigee.

King, L. A., Heintzelman, S. J., & Ward, S. J. (2016). Beyond the search for meaning: A contemporary science of the experience of meaning in life. *Current Directions in Psychological Science, 25,* 211–216. https://doi.org/10.1177/0963721416656354

Kleine, A.-K., Rudolph, C. W., & Zacher, H. (2019). Thriving at work: A meta-analysis. *Journal of Organizational Behavior, 40,* 973–999. https://doi.org/10.1002/job.2375

Leder, H., Belke, B., Oeberst, A., & Augustin, D. (2004). A model of aesthetic appreciation and aesthetic judgments. *British Journal of Psychology, 95*(4), 489–508. https://doi.org/10.1348/0007126042369811

Lifton, R. J. (1979). *The Broken Connection.* Simon & Schuster.

Lifton, R. J. (2011). *Witness to an Extreme Century: A Memoir*. Free Press.

Malchiodi, C. A. (2012). Creativity and aging: An art therapy perspective. In C. A. Malchiodi (Ed.), *Handbook of Art Therapy* (2nd ed., pp. 275–287). Guilford Press.

Martela, F., & Steger, M. F. (2016). The three meanings of meaning in life: Distinguishing coherence, purpose, and significance. *The Journal of Positive Psychology*, *11*(5), 531–545. https://doi.org/10.080/17439760.2015.1137623

Martin, D. J., Garske, J. P., & Davis, M. K. (2000). Relation of the therapeutic alliance with outcome and other variables: A meta-analytic review. *Journal of Consulting and Clinical Psychology*, *68*, 438–450. https://doi.org/10.1037/0022-006X.68.3.438

Maslow, A. H. (1943). A theory of human motivation. *Psychological Review, 50*, 370–396.

Massimini, F., Csikszentmihalyi, M., & Delle Fave, A. (1988). Flow and biocultural evolution. In M. Csikszentmihalyi & I. Csikszentmihalyi (Eds.), *Optimal Experience: Psychological Studies of Flow in Consciousness* (pp. 60–81). Cambridge University Press.

McKay, A. S., Mohan, M., & Reina, C. S. (2022). Another day, another chance: Daily workplace experiences and their impact on creativity. *Journal of Product Innovation Management*, *39*(3), 292–311. https://doi.org/10.1111/jpim.12573

Metzl, E. S. (2009). The role of creative thinking in resilience after hurricane Katrina. *Psychology of Aesthetics, Creativity, and the Arts, 3*, 112–123. https://doi.org/10.1037/a0013479

Noice T., Noice H., & Kramer A. F. (2014). Participatory arts for older adults: A review of benefits and challenges. *Gerontologist, 54*, 741–753. https://doi.org/10.1093/geront/gnt138

Packer, J., & Ballantyne, J. (2011). The impact of music festival attendance on young people's psychological and social well-being. *Psychology of Music, 39*, 164–181. https://doi.org/10.1177/0305735610372611

Pennebaker, J. W. (1997). Writing about emotional experiences as a therapeutic process. *Psychological Science, 8*, 162–166. https://doi.org/10.1111/j.1467-9280.1997.tb00403.x

Pennebaker, J. W., & Beall, S. (1986). Confronting a traumatic event: Toward an understanding of inhibition and disease. *Journal of Abnormal Psychology, 95*, 274–281. https://doi.org/10.1037//0021-843x.95.3.274

Perach, R., & Wisman, A. (2019). Can creativity beat death? A review and evidence on the existential anxiety buffering functions of creative achievement. *The Journal of Creative Behavior, 53*, 193–210. https://doi.org/10.1002/jocb.171

Reiter-Palmon, R., Robinson-Morral, E. J., Kaufman, J. C., & Santo, J. B. (2012). Evaluation of self-perceptions of creativity: Is it a useful criterion? *Creativity Research Journal, 24*, https://doi.org/107-114. 10.1080/10400419.2012.676980

Richards, R. L. (2007). Everyday creativity: Our hidden potential. In R. Richards (Ed.), *Everyday Creativity and New Views of Human Nature* (pp. 25–54). American Psychological Association.

Rizkalla, L., Wertheim, E. H., & Hodgson, L. K. (2008). The roles of emotion management and perspective taking in individuals' conflict management styles and disposition to forgive. *Journal of Research in Personality, 42*, 1594–1601. https://doi.org/10.1016/j.jrp.2008.07.014

Rogers, C. (1961). *On Becoming a Person*. Houghton Mifflin.

Ryan, R. M., & Deci, E. L. (2001). On happiness and human potentials: A review of research on hedonic and eudaimonic well-being. *Annual Review of Psychology, 52*, 141–166. https://doi.org/10.1146/annurev.psych.52.1.141

Ryan, R. M., & Deci, E. L. (2017). *Self-Determination Theory: Basic Psychological Needs in Motivation, Development, and Wellness*. Guilford Press. https://doi .org/10.1521/978.14625/28806

Ryff, C. D. (1989). Happiness is everything, or is it? Explorations on the meaning of psychological well-being. *Journal of Personality and Social Psychology, 57*, 1069–1081. https://doi.org/10.1037/0022-3514.57.6.1069

Ryff, C. D. (1995). Psychological well-being in adult life. *Current Directions in Psychological Science, 4*, 99–104. https://doi.org/10.1111/1467-8721.ep10772395

Seligman, M. E. P. (2011). *Flourish*. Simon & Schuster.

Seligman, M. E. P., Forgeard, M., & Kaufman, S. B. (2016). Creativity and aging: What we can make with what we have left. In M. E. P. Seligman, P., Railton, R. F. Baumeister, & C. Sripada (Eds,), *Homo Prospectus* (pp. 305–350). Oxford University Press.

Sherman, A., & Shavit, T. (2018). The thrill of creative effort at work: An empirical study on work, creative effort and well-being. *Journal of Happiness Studies, 19*, 2049–2069. https://doi.org/10.1007/s10902-017-9910-x

Shoshani, A., & Russo-Netzer, P. (2017). Exploring and assessing meaning in life in elementary school children: Development and validation of the meaning in life in children questionnaire (MIL-CQ). *Personality and Individual Differences, 104*, 460–465. https://doi.org/10.1016/j.paid.2016.09.014

Silvia, P. J., Beaty, R. E., Nusbaum, E. C., et al. (2014). Everyday creativity in daily life: An experience-sampling study of "little c" creativity. *Psychology of Aesthetics, Creativity, and the Arts, 8*, 183–188. https://doi.org/10.1037/a0035722

Silvia, P. J., & Cotter, K. N. (2021). *Researching Daily Life: A Guide to Experience Sampling and Daily Diary Methods*. American Psychological Association.

Simonton, D. K. (1989). The swan-song phenomenon: Last-works effects for 172 classical composers. *Psychology and Aging, 4*, 42–47. https://doi.org/10.1037//0882-7974.4.1.42

Simonton, D. K. (2009). *Genius 101*. Springer.

Simonton, D. K. (2012). Creative productivity and aging: An age decrement – or not? In S. K. Whitbourne & M. J. Sliwinski (Eds.), *The Wiley-Blackwell Handbook of Adulthood and Aging* (pp. 477–496). Wiley-Blackwell.

Smith, J. K. (2014). *The Museum Effect: How Museums, Libraries, and Cultural Institutions Educate and Civilize Society*. Rowman & Littlefield.

Specht, J., Egloff, B., & Schmukle, S. C. (2011). Stability and change of personality across the life course: The impact of age and major life events on mean-level and rank-order stability of the Big Five. *Journal of Personality and Social Psychology, 101*, 862–882. https://doi.org/10.1037/a0024950

Spreitzer, G., Sutcliffe, K., Dutton, J., Sonenshein, S., & Grant, A. M. (2005). A socially embedded model of thriving at work. *Organization Science, 16*, 537–549. https://doi.org/10.1287/orsc.1050.0153

Sternberg, R. J., Pretz, J. E., & Kaufman, J. C. (2003). Types of innovations. In L. Shavinina (Ed.), *The International Handbook of Innovation* (pp. 158–169). Erlbaum.

Tang, M., Hofreiter, S., Reiter-Palmon, R., Bai, X., & Murugavel, V. (2021). Creativity as a means to well-being in times of COVID-19 pandemic: Results of a cross-cultural study. *Frontiers in Psychology*, *12*, 601389. https://doi.org/10.3389/fpsyg.2021.601389

Tedeschi, R. G., & Calhoun, L. G. (1996). The posttraumatic growth inventory: Measuring the positive legacy of trauma. *Journal of Traumatic Stress*, *9*, 455–471. https://doi.org/10.1007/BF02103658

Wells, A. J. (1988). Self-esteem and optimal experience. In M. Csikszentmihalyi & I. Csikszentmihalyi (Eds.), *Optimal Experience: Psychological Studies of Flow in Consciousness* (pp. 327–341). Cambridge University Press.

Zuckerman, H. (1977). *Scientific Elite: Nobel Laureates in the United States*. Free Press.

22 Creative Arts Therapies

Processes and Outcomes for Emotional Well-Being

Hod Orkibi and Shoshi Keisari

While the associations between creativity and mental illness have been widely explored (Carson, 2019), creativity has also been recognized as an important human quality in the humanistic (Maslow, 1962; Rogers, 1961) and positive psychology literature (Peterson & Seligman, 2004). Within this wider context, the *creative arts therapies* (CAT) is an umbrella term for mental health professions that apply the creative processes and their outcomes to optimize health and well-being within a therapeutic relationship. The CAT consist of several specialized disciplines: art therapy, dance movement therapy, drama therapy, psychodrama, music therapy, and poetry/bibliotherapy. The definition of each CAT discipline is presented in Table 22.1.

Training in the CAT takes place at the MA level in the United States (www.nccata.org/) and many European countries, as well as in Israel (www.ecarte.info/). The prerequisites for enrollment usually include having a bachelor's degree in the related art form (e.g., a theatre degree for drama therapy) or in a related social science (e.g., psychology, social work, counseling). Candidates are typically required to provide proof of a specified number of hours or a documented experience in the art form as well as completion of specific courses in psychology. Programs normally take 2–3 years, and are comprised of theoretical, experiential, assessment and research courses as well as extensive hands-on supervised clinical field training with actual clients (Orkibi, 2018). Creative arts therapists work with clients of all ages, including individuals, dyads, families, and groups across a variety of mental healthcare, medical, rehabilitation, educational, and community settings (Orkibi, 2020). Whereas in some countries the CAT have yet to be legislated, in others they are protected titles by law with a distinct licensure (e.g., South Africa, the United Kingdom, and some states in the United States) or licensed through related professions (e.g., counseling, marriage and family therapy, social work). The next section provides a brief overview of the history of the CAT as a modern profession.

Brief History of the CAT as a Profession

The origins of the CAT can be traced back to indigenous healers and shamans who used the arts in healing and illness-prevention rituals that included dancing, singing, drumming, storytelling, and purposeful use of

Table 22.1 *Creative arts therapies (CAT) disciplines*

CAT discipline	Description
Art therapy (AT)	Uses a spectrum of 2- and 3-dimensional structured and unstructured visual arts media (e.g., pencils, paints, chalk, crayons, found objects, clay, fabrics) within a therapeutic relationship with an art therapist. The art therapist facilitates nonverbal and verbal self-expression and reflection through the process of artmaking and the resulting artwork.
Dance movement therapy (DMT)	Uses dance and movement as a way into and a means of therapy, within a therapeutic relationship, with the goal of promoting physical, emotional, cognitive, social, and spiritual integration. DMT is based on the premise of the interconnection between body and mind.
Drama therapy (DT) and Psychodrama (PD)	DT involves the intentional use of drama and theatre processes such as embodiment, dramatic projection, improvisation, role-play, and performance to facilitate physiological, psychological, and social change. PD uses guided role-play and specific techniques to explore clients' personal and interpersonal problems and possible solutions. While both operate in a dramatic reality, in DT the story and characters move along a continuum between reality-based and a fantasy-based, whereas in PD they are mostly reality-based.
Music therapy (MT)	Uses music and its properties (e.g., melody, rhythm, tempo, dynamics, pitch), as well as song writing, improvisation, and singing within a therapeutic relationship to optimize clients' quality of life and improve their physical, social, communicative, emotional, intellectual, and spiritual health and well-being. MT can involve active music making and/or receptive music listening, according to the client's needs.
Biblio/Poetry therapy (BPT)	Uses written language, poetry writing and reading, expressive writing, journal writing, as well as story writing and reading within a therapeutic relationship.

Note. Based on Orkibi, 2020.

costumes, masks, and various instruments and props (McNiff, 1979, 1981, 2009). In ancient Greece, dramatic enactments with dance, music, and story-telling aimed to stimulate a cathartic emotional release in the audience (*Aristotle's Poetics*, 1961). There is also evidence that the arts were used in medical and therapeutic settings in the Middle Ages, and later during the Enlightenment in the late seventeenth century, which led to more rational scientific accounts about the place of the arts in medicine, followed by the rise of psychiatry in the nineteenth century when new ways of integrating the arts within healthcare emerged (Fancourt, 2017). However, a professional group should have a specialized body of knowledge and set of skills, specified training requirements, standards of conduct and ethics, licensing systems and protected titles, a professional association with a credentialing system, and a service recognized by the society and the administration (Orkibi, 2012). What follows is a brief overview of the emergence of each CAT discipline as a modern profession in the United States and United Kingdom.

Psychodrama and Drama Therapy

Among the CAT, **psychodrama** is probably the oldest discipline that emerged as a profession. It originated in the early 1920s with the work of psychiatrist and theatre director Jacob Levy Moreno from his creative experiments with children involving storytelling and role-playing in the parks of Vienna (Moreno, 1964). Moreno also worked with groups of female prostitutes whose discussions on various health issues turned into therapeutic interactions where one prostitute became the others' therapeutic agent to alleviate their suffering (Moreno, 1964, pp. 155–157). Moreno also founded a Therapeutic Theater in Vienna, where he focused on impromptu enactments, but it was only after he immigrated to the United States in 1925 that he gradually developed psychodrama into a structured therapeutic method (Blatner, 2000). In 1942, Moreno founded the American Society of Group Psychotherapy and Psychodrama (https://asgpp.org/). Given Moreno's background in psychiatry, psychodrama "began to stray from the aesthetics of its theatrical roots" (Johnson & Emunah, 2009, p. 5).

This difference between psychodrama's theatrical roots and its actual practice may have contributed to the emergence of **drama therapy** in the United States (Johnson & Emunah, 2009). The first drama therapy article in the United States was published in the 1970s by Eleanor Irwin who worked with children using a psychoanalytic approach to drama therapy (Irwin et al., 1972). This was followed by the emergence of various approaches in drama therapy, including Robert Landy's Distancing Theory (Landy, 1986) and Role Method (Landy, 1993), Renée Emunah's Integrative Five Phase approach (Emunah, 1994), and David Johnson's Developmental Transformations (Johnson et al., 1996). What was later called the North American Drama Therapy Association was founded in 1979 (www.nadta.org/).

In the United Kingdom, dramatherapy[1] evolved in the 1960s from drama-in-education (Jennings, 1994) and the earlier work of Peter Slade, a pioneer in using educational drama and children's theatre for expression and development (Slade, 1954); he was familiar with Moreno's work and coined the term *dramatherapy* as early as 1939 (Jones, 2007, p. 51). Dramatherapy was further developed in the United Kingdom by Sue Jennings who implemented Remedial Drama in schools and hospitals (Jennings, 1973; Jones, 2007) and by Marian (Billy) Lindkvist who founded the Sesame course in drama and movement therapy (Karkou & Sanderson, 2006). The British Association for Dramatherapists was founded in 1977, and the British Psychodrama Association was founded in 1984 (www.psychodrama.org.uk/).

---

[1] Note the UK spelling of *dramatherapy* as one word (as in psychotherapy or psychodrama) versus the U.S. spelling *drama therapy*.

Art Therapy

The birth of art therapy (AT) as a profession in the United States is credited to Margaret Naumburg, a psychologist who is often called "the mother of art therapy" (Gussak & Rosal, 2016). In the 1940s, Naumburg worked in psychiatric settings and began to publish clinical case studies influenced by the psychoanalytic principle of making the unconscious conscious through the analysis of clients' artworks (Naumburg, 1966). Another pioneer in the United States was Edith Kramer, an artist who also relied on psychoanalytic theory in her therapy work but viewed AT differently from Naumburg, since she focused on the inherent therapeutic potential of the artmaking process rather than on the product (Kramer, 1972). The American Art Therapy Association was founded in 1969 (https://arttherapy.org/). In the United Kingdom, AT emerged when British artist Adrian Hill used the term *art therapy* in 1942, after he observed the therapeutic benefits of drawing while he was recovering from tuberculosis in the hospital (Waller, 1991). The British Association of Art Therapists was founded in 1964 (www.baat.org/).

Music Therapy

Although music was used in hospitals in different ways such as playing pre-recorded music to patients, music therapy (MT) in the United States originated in post–World War II veterans' hospitals where musicians and hospital workers used music to treat wounded veterans (Bradt, 2006). E. Thayer Gaston is considered "the father of music therapy". He worked with adults in a psychiatric clinic. The American Music Therapy Association was founded in 1998 as a merger between two separate MT associations that were created in 1950 and 1971 (www.musictherapy.org/). Similarly, after World War II, musicians in the United Kingdom were invited to play *to* and *with* veterans in hospitals (Karkou & Sanderson, 2006). The development of MT as a profession in the United Kingdom is credited to Juliette Alvin, a professional musician who used musical improvisation in her work with children with learning difficulties and/or autism, and who founded the British Society for Music Therapy and Remedial Music in 1958 (Ansdell, 2002). Two other prominent pioneers are pianist Paul Nordoff and special education teacher Clive Robbins who also worked with children in the early 1960s (Wheeler, 2015). The current British Association for Music Therapy was founded in 2011 as a merger of two separate MT associations that were established in 1958 and 1976 (www.bamt.org/).

Dance Movement Therapy

Marian Chace, originally a dancer and dance teacher who viewed modern dance as a means of emotional expression, is considered to be the founder of dance therapy in the United States where she applied dance in psychiatric hospitals as early as 1942 (Nemetz, 2006). Chace was the first president of the

American Dance Therapy Association that was founded in 1966 (www.adta .org/). In the United Kingdom dance movement psychotherapy evolved out of dance and physical education in the 1970s (Karkou & Sanderson, 2006; Payne, 1992). Some of the pioneers were trained in Rudolf Laban's movement analysis method and were influenced by his early writings on the educational and therapeutic value of dance (Laban, 1970), while others implemented the Sesame approach for drama and movement in therapy. The UK Association for Dance Movement Psychotherapy was founded in 1982 (https://admp.org.uk/).

Biblio/Poetry Therapy

The term *bibliotherapy* was coined in 1916 by the American Unitarian minister and essayist Samuel McCord Crothers and was soon adopted by hospital librarians, both in the United States and the United Kingdom, who recommended self-help books to psychiatric patients for specific health problems (McCulliss, 2012; McNicol & Brewster, 2018). Later in the United States, poet and pharmacist Eli Griefer, who is credited with giving poetry therapy its name, conducted *poemtherapy* groups as a volunteer in hospitals in the early 1950s (Mazza, 2017). In 1959, Griefer facilitated a poetry therapy group with psychiatrist Jack L. Leedy who later published the first collective volume on poetry therapy (Leedy, 1969). In 1969, Leedy founded what in 1981 was renamed the National Association for Poetry Therapy (https://poetrytherapy.org/). No similar association exists in the United Kingdom, but there is an International Federation for Biblio/Poetry Therapy (https://ifbpt.org/). Compared to other CAT, biblio/poetry therapy is an under-researched discipline, probably because it is not yet offered at the graduate level in university-based programs (except at the University of Haifa in Israel).

Change Factors Shared by the CAT

Unlike talk therapy, the therapeutic process in the CAT relies heavily on arts-based factors of change, some of which are shared by all disciplines.

Aesthetic distance: The art form and the creative process establish "distance from everyday reality and it is this fluidity which makes exploration of self through the art form safe" (Cattanach, 1999, p. 192). Landy's (1983, 1996) concept of distancing in drama therapy refers to clients' ability to express and withhold emotions. It relates to the balance between identifications and separations in the creative process, which enables the participants to simultaneously be *close* enough to the experience to be able to affectively enact it, and *distant* enough to cognitively reflect upon it. There are three forms of distancing: underdistance (i.e., being overflooded with emotions), overdistance (i.e., being disconnected from emotions, cognitively reflecting, rationalizing, and analyzing), and aesthetic distance (i.e., a balanced state of both being and observing, feeling and thinking). The therapist's task is to modulate the distance according to the client's emotional needs in the here-and-now to move between everyday and dramatic content and between the client's roles as active participant and observer (Landy, 1983, p. 184). Aesthetic distance is similar to the concept of psychological self-distancing that has been associated with adaptive self-regulation of emotions (White et al., 2015) as well as thoughts and behaviors (White & Carlson, 2016). Johnson (1985) suggested that an aesthetic theory of the CAT should "be described in terms of increasing beauty, balance, or harmony in the person" (p. 236). However, such aesthetic properties are secondary in the CAT, where beauty does not necessarily refer to an aesthetically pleasing artistic expression. Rather, if an artistic expression reflects the client's emotional experience authentically and coherently, it is beautiful. This notion is somewhat consistent with expression theories of art where the creator's personal emotions are central to the aesthetic experience (Wilkinson, 1992).

Playfulness and spontaneity: A safe therapeutic space encourages playfulness, which refers to an intrinsically motivating state of being flexible and open to an arts-based experience, self-exploration and expression that facilitates creativity and change (Bateson & Martin, 2013). In the context of the CAT, playfulness does not imply frivolity, being humorous or amused (cf. Barnett, 1990; Proyer, 2013); rather that clients spontaneously "play" with difficult emotional experiences. Specifically, for Moreno, spontaneity is a procreative state of readiness that propels "the individual towards an adequate response to a new situation or a new response to an old situation" (Moreno, 1953/1993, p. 42). Thus, spontaneity is different from mindless instinctive or uninhibited impulsivity because it moves in a prescribed direction and hence contains an element of self-regulation (Kipper, 1986). Fredrickson (2001) argued that play and playfulness in adults can facilitate the emergence of positive emotions and creativity. Correlational data indicate that playfulness is positively related to positive emotions and negatively to negative emotions (Chang et al., 2013). In children, experimental studies have shown that expression of more positive emotions during pretend play is associated with telling stories that are more creative and imaginative, and that children with higher scores on emotional pretend play variables also have higher emotion regulation (Hoffmann & Russ, 2012; Russ, 2014). Recent evidence suggests that being in a state of openness to experiences and tolerance of ambiguity is associated with creativity, and that emotion regulation plays a role in the process of generating a creative outcome (Ivcevic & Hoffmann, 2019). In a COVID-19-related study, fathers' playfulness was related to less stress reactions and improved emotion regulation in their children, which may hint at the potential impact of therapists' playfulness on clients' emotional experience (Shorer & Leibovich, 2020; Shorer et al., 2021).

Creativity and imagination: Moreno believed that creativity is essential for adapting to life changes (Moreno & Moreno, 1944) and that "people must be creative in order to survive" (Moreno, 1964, p. 158). In contrast to traditional definitions of creativity (Runco & Jaeger, 2012), the creative process and outcome in the CAT do not necessarily require an external frame of reference to be considered creative; namely, original (new) and useful (effective). Rather, the client's own personal frame of reference is often the primary criterion for the novelty and effectiveness of the creative process and outcome. This notion echoes Runco's (1996, 2011) theory of personal creativity, where creativity does not necessarily require an external frame of reference, as well as Beghetto and Kaufman's (2007, 2015) "mini-c" concept that refers to a more subjective experience of creativity that is personally meaningful, in contrast to little-c (everyday) or Big-C (eminent) creativity. Relatedly, a recent construct termed *creative adaptability* refers to individuals' cognitive-behavioral-emotional ability to respond creatively and adaptively to stressful situations (Orkibi, 2021; Orkibi et al., 2021). The emotional aspect of creative adaptability refers to one's ability to generate personally new and potentially effective emotional reactions to a stressful situation, which can be explored and rehearsed, for example, through role-play in psychodrama. Because in the CAT the creative arts are used for therapeutic aims, the aesthetics of the work are not primordial (McNiff, 2009). Rather "imagination is the central concept which informs the understanding of the use of arts and play in therapy … [because] imagination gives us access to that which is hidden from us" (Levine, 1999, p. 259). The artistic process not only involves intentional interactions with creative imagination, but the CAT envision the clients as artmakers who use their imagination to create their own self and life (Johnson, 1985).

Symbols, metaphors, and imagery: The arts endow symbolic form to a broad range of human feelings (Langer, 1953). In the CAT, symbols, metaphors, and images are manifested and explored through the creative artmaking process and the resulting artwork (Malchiodi, 2005; Samaritter, 2009). They deliver succinct implicit messages about the clients' inner experiences and sensations by conveying the maximum meaning of rich inner experiences through a minimum of words or nonverbally, thus often bypassing communication barriers (Azoulay & Orkibi, 2015; Ronen, 2011). Symbolic and metaphoric expressions often help bring the subconscious to conscious awareness (Imus, 2021). The creative process and the artwork can deepen communication and understanding of the self and others, beyond rationality. They convey meaning in symbolic forms and are external metaphorical depictions of the inner emotional world of those who create them (Moon, 2007), thus facilitating a process of meaning making (Jones, 2021). The aim of the CAT can be expressed as creating "a meaningful symbol of oneself that captures the beauty in one's soul" (Johnson, 1985, p. 236).

Concretization: The arts in the CAT facilitate concretization, that is, the changing of abstract and formless internal psychological content into an externalized tangible artistic presentation (Kushnir & Orkibi, 2021). Blatner (1992) suggested that in AT, concretization occurs through the use of color, shape, or composition. In drama, this is achieved through physical enactment of roles in situations, and in dance through movement, posture, and gesture. Music provides auditory concretization through melody, rhythm, tempo, pitch, and so on, and writing concretizes through words. Overall, concretization enables clients to project or embody intangible inner emotional experiences, observe them from new perspectives, and ultimately gain new insights and therapeutic transformation. For instance, in psychodrama, the therapist first aims to capture an emotionally loaded (i.e., charged) content from clients' words, and then invite them to use role-play to transform this content into an externalized, tangible, and embodied representation of their emotional experiences that can be observed, explored creatively (i.e., to generate new and more effective emotional responses), and then positively altered (Kushnir & Orkibi, 2021).

Active involvement: Client involvement in psychotherapy consists of actively participating in the therapeutic process in terms of *experiential* depth; namely, "the degree of a client's involvement in the exploration of new feelings and meanings in relation to the self" (Pascual-Leone & Yeryomenko, 2017, p. 653). This notion is crucial to the CAT because they are action-oriented interventions, which have been associated with entering a *flow*-like state of mind (Baker & MacDonald, 2013; de Felice et al., 2019) characterized by deep involvement that is associated with well-being (Csikszentmihalyi, 1991). The participatory and sensory nature of any artistic engagement relates to a sense of *vitality* and *aliveness*, thus acknowledging the *embodied body–mind* connection (Malchiodi, 2005). In studies of psychodrama, in-session dramatic engagement predicted adolescents' emotional exploration (Orkibi, Azoulay, Regev, et al., 2017), which was positively associated with gains in their academic self-concept (Orkibi, Azoulay, Snir, et al., 2017). In an AT study, improvement in elementary school children's involvement in therapy was positively correlated with improvement in their emotional internalizing problems such as anxiety and depression (Regev, 2021). These meaningful association warrant further investigation on the role of the CAT in helping clients to name, explore, process, regulate, and express their emotions adaptively.

The Evidence Base for the CAT

There are several systematic reviews and meta analyses on the effects of the CAT interventions on a range of outcomes (e.g., de Witte, Pinho, et al., 2020; Dunphy et al., 2019; Feniger-Schaal & Orkibi, 2020; Glavin & Montgomery, 2017; Gold et al., 2009; Karkou & Meekums, 2017; Koch et al., 2019; Masika et al., 2020; Orkibi & Feniger-Schaal, 2019; Van Lith, 2016). This section provides an overview of studies on the mounting evidence for the contribution of the CAT to various facets of *emotional well-being*, used here in a broad sense of encompassing a range of emotion-related outcomes. Change factors that reflect the in-session processes that lead to therapeutic change are also discussed.

Regulating and Processing Emotions

Emotion regulation refers to "attempts to influence which emotions one has, when one has them, and how one experiences or expresses these emotions"

(Gross, 2015, pp. 4–5). Emotion regulation goals include decreasing or increasing negative emotions or positive emotions, changing the intensity and duration of emotions, or changing the quality of emotional responses. Evidence indicates the effectiveness of the CAT in improving emotional regulation and processing.

For instance, psychodrama with university freshmen increased the emotion regulation strategy of cognitive reappraisal and decreased the emotion regulation strategy of suppression, compared to a control group (Soysal, 2021)[2]. The qualitive data in this mixed methods study revealed that the most common emotions that participants asked to process in the psychodrama group were anxiety, shame, anger, and sadness. In the interviews, the participants identified specific psychodrama techniques that improved their emotion regulation skills. *Role-playing* and particularly *role-reversal* (in which participants take on the role of "the other" in their psychodrama) enabled them to reenact their experiences, recognize their own emotions, and see various perspectives, which may have facilitated the improvement in cognitive reappraisal. Similarly, the emotion regulation strategy of cognitive reappraisal was also fostered by the *double technique* (in which the therapist or a group member expresses emotions or/and thoughts the participant is unable to express), which helps to reframe the situation. The *mirroring* technique (in which participants watch someone else replaying what they previously did) also helped them observe the situation from the outside, and hence promotes cognitive reappraisal. Finally, the *concertation* technique (in which the participants are asked to translate their abstract emotions into concrete and externalized expressions; Kushnir & Orkibi, 2021), enhanced self-expression and reduced suppression. Psychodrama also helped the group members who were in the audience (watching the psychodrama), to identify their own feelings and at times experience emotional release (i.e., catharsis).

Studies on visual AT indicate it can foster emotion regulation in two main ways. One is by increasing the participants' ability to modulate emotions through the creative artmaking process itself, which involves a pleasurable sensory experience with the arts materials as well as relief. The second is by increasing participants' ability to reflect on their emotions, express and communicate them to others, and discover new meaning and insights related to emotional states (Czamanski-Cohen & Weihs, 2016; Haeyen et al., 2015).

Increased *emotional processing* is thought to be the main way AT leads to psychological and physical symptom reduction in patients with breast cancer (Czamanski-Cohen et al., 2019, 2020). In their line of studies, *emotion processing* consisted of three aspects: (1) *emotional awareness*, when bodily sensations or unconscious knowledge experienced somatically is transferred to explicit

---

[2] The literature distinguishes between two main emotional regulation strategies. One strategy is *cognitive reappraisal*, a form of cognitive change that involves construing a potentially emotion-eliciting situation in a way that changes its emotional impact. The second is the *expressive suppression* strategy, a form of response modulation that involves inhibiting ongoing emotion-expressive behavior (Gross, 2015).

thoughts; (2) *expression*, the way in which emotions are communicated with others, intentionally or nonintentionally, verbally and nonverbally; and (3) acceptance of *emotion*, where individuals are accepting and nurturing of their feelings (Czamanski-Cohen et al., 2020). The first in this series of studies examined the effect of an AT group on emotion processing among women with breast cancer (Czamanski-Cohen et al., 2019). The AT group was compared to a group activity of coloring shapes of mandalas followed by a short lecture on self-care. The AT group yielded greater improvement in enhancing emotional awareness and acceptance, which are indicators of emotion processing, as well as a decrease in depressive symptoms with a large effect size, indicating a meaningful difference between groups. In addition, the qualitative data showed that only the women in the AT group reported connecting with difficult emotions and that therapy helped them to process their breast cancer experience.

The AT in this study was based on the body–mind model (Czamanski-Cohen & Weihs, 2016) that consists of four core therapeutic change processes: (1) *the triangular relationship* between the art therapist, the patient, and the art process and product; (2) *self-engagement* in the sensory experience of artmaking that activates the amygdala through the engagement with art materials and concrete visual imagery, which allows for easier access to emotional material than verbal communication alone. This sensory experience also involves a sense of pleasure, which make difficult content explored through the artmaking tolerable, and can provide a sense of relief; (3) *embodied self-expression,* as the core of emotion processing, provides an opportunity to express (implicit) somatic knowledge that is not easily translatable into (explicit) words. Externalization of implicit knowledge via the artmaking process and through reflection on the art product facilitate the use of language to express this somatic-emotional knowledge and make it explicit; (4) *meta-cognitive processes*, engagement in a reflective process that provides the opportunity for both perspective taking and meaning-making. Overall, the evidence indicates that artistic engagement in the CAT is a facilitator of emotion regulation and processing across various populations.

Stress Relief

Stress is the physiological or psychological response to internal or external stressors and involves changes affecting nearly every system of the body, thus influencing how people feel and behave. Stress is a well-known risk factor for the onset and progression of a range of emotional and physical problems (American Psychological Association, 2021). A MT systematic review and meta-analysis showed an overall medium to large effect on physiological and psychological stress-related outcomes in both mental healthcare and medical settings (de Witte, Pinho, et al., 2020). The authors suggested several reasons for the stress-reducing effect of MT. One is the delivery of musical activities that fostered interpersonal synchrony among the client and therapist and group members, which was associated with an increase in positive feelings of togetherness and bonding (Linnemann et al., 2016; Tarr et al., 2014). Interpersonal synchrony is also associated with the release of the neurotransmitters endorphin and oxytocin that play an important role in reducing stress (Elheja et al., 2021; Papasteri et al., 2020). The authors noted that synchronization in the therapeutic encounter may also be considered as a mirror reaction, since the musical activity of the therapist and the client become simultaneous through similar musical expression. Then, by changing the intensity of the music, playing slower and less loudly, emotion regulation can be achieved (de Witte, Pinho, et al., 2020). Another factor relates to the ability of musical experiences to provide distraction from stressful feelings or thoughts (Chanda & Levitin, 2013) and increase the intensity of pleasant emotional valence, which has a stress-reducing effect (Jiang et al., 2016). MT also includes receptive interventions, where the clients listen to music and verbally process their own emotions and/or experiences. During both active and receptive interventions, music therapists use the specific qualities of music, such as rhythm, tempo, dynamics, melody, and harmony, to facilitate and promote emotion expression and regulation (de Witte, Pinho, et al., 2020). Overall, this meta-analysis of MT interventions indicated there was a greater effect on stress-related outcomes than a meta-analysis of general music interventions that only found small to medium effects (de Witte, Spruit, et al., 2020), possibly because of the qualifications of the facilitators, since qualified music therapists are specifically trained to tailor the musical activities to both the participants' musical preferences and their clinical needs.

In a series of dance movement therapy (DMT) studies, a randomized control trial reported a positive effect of a short-term DMT intervention for breast cancer patients on perceived stress, pain severity, and pain interference (Ho et al., 2016). The second study indicated that DMT positively affected a stress-sensitive hormone (diurnal cortisol slopes) in breast cancer patients with high levels of perceived distress (Ho et al., 2018). The researchers attributed the results of both studies (Ho et al., 2016, 2018) to the spontaneous rhythmic movement in DMT, which allows participants to relax and freely express their feelings and release their psychological tension.

In AT, drawing and coloring mandalas are common interventions for stress reduction. A study on undergraduate students reported that coloring mandalas and plaid coloring groups reduced the level of anxiety more than in an unstructured coloring group, possibly because the coloring of geometric patterns induces a meditative state (Curry & Kasser, 2005). In another study on the stress-reducing effect of drawing mandalas in individuals with intellectual disabilities (Schrade et al., 2011), the findings suggested that mandala making could be considered an effective stress reducer, though it was not more effective at reducing stress than the free drawing or the control conditions. In a different study, after drawing within a mandala shape, participants reported improved mood compared to patients who colored within a square (Babouchkina & Robbins, 2015). Based on Jungian theory (Jung, 1972), the authors suggested that the mandala is a representative archetype of one's self, and that the process of mandala making promotes a reorganization of the self through the creation of a new center, leading to a positive experience with relaxing qualities.

A systematic review of the stress-reducing and managing effects of the CAT reported a significant reduction in participants' stress (Martin et al., 2018). Interestingly, this review did not report findings from drama therapy or psychodrama interventions, possibly due to the specific characteristics of dramatic action, which are often based on the intensification of emotional experience. Some studies have, however, reported the contribution of drama therapy and psychodrama to treating symptoms of posttraumatic stress disorder (Giacomucci & Marquit, 2020; Hamidi & Sobhani Tabar, 2021; Sajnani et al., 2019). Here, the core premise is that the dramatic reality provides a safe place with aesthetic-dramatic distancing (Landy, 1996), which enables the therapists and the clients to control the degree to which traumatic events are directly addressed.

Depressive Symptoms and Grief Processing

Depression is a widely researched negative emotional experience characterized by persistent sadness and a lack of interest or pleasure, that has profound implications for all areas of life, including physical health, daily functioning, and relationships with others (World Health Organization, 2021). There is vast literature on the effectiveness of the CAT in treating depressive symptoms (Jasemi et al., 2016; Koch et al., 2014; Meekums et al., 2015). The change factors include not only emotion regulation and processing, but also the process and resolution of inner conflicts to build a more coherent and integrative view of the self, which ultimately reduces depressive symptoms (Keisari, 2021).

An increase in positive emotions and a reduction of depressive symptoms were reported in several studies on the effectiveness of drama therapy groups integrated with a life review in older adults (Keisari, Gesser-Edelsburg, et al., 2020; Keisari, Palgi, et al., 2020). Participants and staff members reported that spontaneous dramatic improvisation was enjoyable and enhanced the positive experience in the groups. The process of dramatically acting the life stories of other group members generated a sense of having a valuable role in life and being able to contribute to one's community. The program provided opportunities for creative expression and enhanced the experience of social connectedness in the group and more generally in the adult day center community. The findings indicated that the drama therapy intervention helped the participants to process their life-stories in a more integrative manner and to resolve unfinished business from the past, an essential developmental task in old age. These transformative aspects contributed to the reduction in depressive symptoms and the increase in positive affect and other well-being indicators.

A MT study examined how songwriting affects negative emotions and depressive symptoms in people with spinal cord injury or acquired brain injury (Baker et al., 2015). This MT intervention was based on previous findings that songwriting about personal experiences generates strong experiences of flow and that participants derive meaning from both the songwriting process and the resulting song product (Baker & MacDonald, 2013). However, the results indicated that participants who reported meaningful songwriting also reported less emotional suppression and more negative affect and anxiety. The authors suggested that in a meaningful songwriting process, these individuals who had experienced loss, were more likely to accept all their emotions and as a result also experience an increase in anxiety and depression. The results also suggested that the songwriting process could help process grief and facilitate the building of a healthy post-injured self-concept (Baker et al., 2015). Similarly, studies have shown how the CAT make it possible to process the experience of loss by retelling and reconstructing the loss story, creating opportunities to explore the new identity, maintain continuous bonds with their loved ones who passed away, and resolve unfinished business (Dominguez, 2018; Hill & Lineweaver, 2016; Keisari, 2021; O'Callaghan & Michael, 2015).

Psychodrama, for instance, provides a specific approach to working with the mental, emotional, and behavioral aspects of complicated grief, in response to losses caused by death or other circumstances such as divorce (Dayton, 2005; Testoni et al., 2019). Psychodrama concretizes a lost object or person (Kushnir & Orkibi, 2021), allowing the participant to interact with the loss with the support and witnessing of others. According to a group of 25 psychodramatists, the techniques that facilitate the processing of complicated grief include the empty chair and role reversal techniques that enable the participant to conduct a dialogue in the here-and-now with the deceased, and speak the unspoken (Testoni et al., 2019). The double technique enables participants to express their inner voice and overcome emotional blocks. The future projection technique dramatizes what is thought to happen after imminent death or separation. Yet another study found that a psychodrama and movie-making intervention was effective in helping 268 high school students process the suicide of a peer (Testoni et al., 2018). Specifically, the students in the experimental group reported decreased death anxiety and an increase in spirituality and life-meaning compared to the control group.

Overall, the literature points to the effectiveness of the CAT to enhance emotion regulation, emotion processing, and stress relief, while reducing depressive symptoms. The studies also highlight specific aspects of the CAT in processing loss experiences and grief. Several in-session change factors through which the creative process leads to these outcomes were identified.

Future Directions for CAT Research

Whereas psychotherapy outcome research inquires whether or not treatment leads to change, change process research inquires *how* or *why* psychotherapy leads to change (Kazdin, 2009). Given the growing interest in psychotherapy research beyond outcome studies, it is important to identify CAT factors that lead to therapeutic change. *Change process research* is crucial to the advancement of the CAT because it can help (a) identify specific change factors that can account for the ways in which therapeutic change occurs, (b) improve the effectiveness of CAT interventions, (c) refine a theory of change that provides a rationale and structure for CAT interventions, and (e) develop more effective training and supervision on effective change factors that are supported by evidence (Hardy & Llewelyn, 2015). Therapeutic change can stem from the client, therapist, or relational factors that tap the interaction between them (Elliott, 2012). Data can be collected from one or, preferably, several sources including the client, therapists, and observers. The type of change can be emotional, cognitive, behavioral, and/or physiological.

Elliott (2010) identified four main types of change process research. The first type is *qualitative helpful factors* research that examines which factors lead to client-reported change as assessed post-session or post-treatment. The second is *quantitative micro-analytic sequential process* research that examines the associations between process factors themselves by coding clients' and therapists' recorded responses and interactions (e.g., how specific responses or techniques provided by the therapist are associated with client involvement or insight). This design is best suited to quantitatively testing theory of change hypotheses. The third is *significant events* research that examines what happens in client-identified important (helpful or hindering) moments in therapy and may involve both qualitative and quantitative data collection and analyses. The fourth type is quantitative *process-outcome* research, which involves measuring process variables and testing whether they relate to or influence therapeutic outcomes.

In a recent scoping review of therapeutic change factors in the CAT the authors called for greater specificity in conceptualizing and operationalizing change factors in the CAT (de Witte et al., 2021). They appealed to researchers to adopt a shared terminology and use it more accurately, systematically, and consistently to minimize redundancy, confusion, and contraindications across CAT studies. Another crucial step would be to formulate a parsimonious *theory of change* and use it as a guide to explain how a change factor (e.g., playfulness, aesthetic distance, concretization) operates across the CAT and/or in each discipline, to improve health and well-being.

A truly operational theory of change should be logical, parsimonious, consistent with data, elegant (i.e., straightforward), and explain a range of outcomes (Runco, 2007, p. 400). A generic theory of change for the CAT is suggested below, which builds largely on the above-mentioned change factors that are shared by all CAT. As can be seen in Figure 22.1, the upper left square consists of common change factors, which are nonspecific factors that are "common to all psychotherapeutic approaches" (de Felice et al., 2019, p. 50). Thus, they are prerequisites to any form of therapy, including the CAT. In turn, these prerequisites lay the groundwork for the intentional induction of change factors that are unique to the CAT, depicted in the upper right square, which facilitate client's readiness (i.e., warm-up) to engage with the arts within a therapeutic *creative space*. Next, as indicated in the bottom left square, arts-based work within this creative space may facilitate a range of arts-based

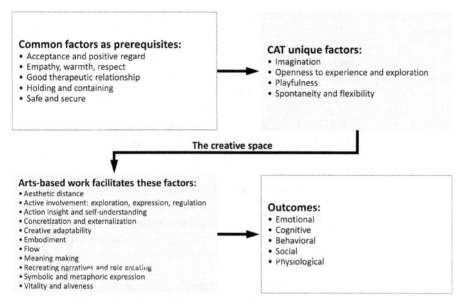

Common factors as prerequisites:
• Acceptance and positive regard
• Empathy, warmth, respect
• Good therapeutic relationship
• Holding and containing
• Safe and secure

CAT unique factors:
• Imagination
• Openness to experience and exploration
• Playfulness
• Spontaneity and flexibility

The creative space

Arts-based work facilitates these factors:
• Aesthetic distance
• Active involvement: exploration, expression, regulation
• Action insight and self-understanding
• Concretization and externalization
• Creative adaptability
• Embodiment
• Flow
• Meaning making
• Recreating narratives and role creating
• Symbolic and metaphoric expression
• Vitality and aliveness

Outcomes:
• Emotional
• Cognitive
• Behavioral
• Social
• Physiological

Figure 22.1 *Generic theory of change in the CAT.*

change factors (see de Witte et al., 2021). The notion of the creative space echoes the psychoanalyst D. W. Winnicott's concept of the *potential space*, which first emerges between the primary caregiver and the infant, and is a space between fantasy and reality that nurtures play, imagination, and creativity (Winnicott, 2016). In the creative space, a triangular relationship emerges, which involves the therapist, client, and the creative process and/or product (Jones, 2005, p. 215) that reflect a personally new and more effective way of psychological responding to the problem. For instance, the aesthetic–dramatic realm where psychodrama takes place is called the "surplus reality" in which clients are invited to actively explore any past, present, or future experiences (Moreno, 1965) and may *recreate* their *narratives*, *create* new and more adaptive *roles*, and gain *action insights* that cannot be achieved through conversation alone but rather arise from the experiential drama-based work. Such in-session experiences are reasoned to lead to the desired outcomes as indicated in the bottom right square. To sum, the change factors in our model are by no means exhaustive. Rather, this model aims to inspire further development of change theory to operationalize how the CAT promote clients' emotional and general well-being.

References

American Psychological Association. (2021). *Stress*. https://dictionary.apa.org/stress
Ansdell, G. (2002). Music therapy in the United Kingdom. Voices Resources. https://voices.no/community/index.html?q=country-of-the-month%252F2002-music-therapy-united-kingdom

Aristotle's Poetics. (1961). S. H. Butcher (Trans.). Hill and Wang.

Azoulay, B., & Orkibi, H. (2015). The four-phase CBN Psychodrama model: A manualized approach for practice and research. *The Arts in Psychotherapy, 42*, 10–18. https://doi.org/10.1016/j.aip.2014.12.012

Babouchkina, A., & Robbins, S. J. (2015). Reducing negative mood through mandala creation: A randomized controlled trial. *Art Therapy, 32*(1), 34–39. https://doi.org/10.1080/07421656.2015.994428

Baker, F. A., & MacDonald, R. A. R. (2013). Flow, identity, achievement, satisfaction and ownership during therapeutic songwriting experiences with university students and retirees. *Musicae Scientiae, 17*(2), 131–146. https://doi.org/10.1177/1029864913476287

Baker, F. A., Rickard, N., Tamplin, J., & Roddy, C. (2015). Flow and meaningfulness as mechanisms of change in self-concept and well-being following a songwriting intervention for people in the early phase of neurorehabilitation. *Frontiers in Human Neuroscience, 9*(299). https://doi.org/10.3389/fnhum.2015.00299

Barnett, L. A. (1990). Playfulness: Definition, design, and measurement. *Play & Culture, 3*(4), 319–336.

Bateson, P., & Martin, P. (2013). *Play, Playfulness, Creativity and Innovation.* Cambridge University Press. https://doi.org/10.1017/CBO9781139057691

Beghetto, R. A., & Kaufman, J. C. (2007). Toward a broader conception of creativity: A case for "mini-c" creativity. *Psychology of Aesthetics, Creativity, and the Arts, 1*(2), 73–79. https://doi.org/10.1037/1931-3896.1.2.73

Beghetto, R. A., & Kaufman, J. C. (2015). Promise and pitfalls in differentiating amongst the cs of creativity. *Creativity Research Journal, 27*(2), 240–241. https://doi.org/10.1080/10400419.2015.1030300

Blatner, A. (1992). Theoretical principles underlying creative arts therapies. *The Arts in Psychotherapy, 18*(5), 405–409. https://doi.org/10.1016/0197-4556(91)90052-c

Blatner, A. (2000). *Foundations of Psychodrama: History, Theory, and Practice* (4th ed.). Springer.

Bradt, J. (2006). The history of music therapy. In S. L. B. (Ed.), *Creative Arts Therapies Manual: A Guide to the History, Theoretical Approaches, Assessment, and Work with Special Populations of Art, Play, Dance, Music, Drama, and Poetry Therapies* (pp. 168–174). Charles C. Thomas.

Carson, S. H. (2019). Creativity and mental illness. In J. C. Kaufman & R. J. Sternberg (Eds.), *The Cambridge Handbook of Creativity* (2nd ed., pp. 296–318). Cambridge University Press. https://doi.org/10.1017/9781316979839.016

Cattanach, A. (1999). Links between the arts therapies. In A. Cattanach (Ed.), *Process in the Arts Therapies* (pp. 191–197). Kingsley.

Chanda, M. L., & Levitin, D. J. (2013). The neurochemistry of music. *Trends in Cognitive Sciences, 17*(4), 179–193. https://doi.org/10.1016/j.tics.2013.02.007

Chang, P.-J., Qian, X., & Yarnal, C. (2013). Using playfulness to cope with psychological stress: Taking into account both positive and negative emotions. *International Journal of Play, 2*(3), 273–296. https://doi.org/10.1080/21594937.2013.855414

Csikszentmihalyi, M. (1991). *Flow: The Psychology of Optimal Experience.* HarperPerennial.

Curry, N. A., & Kasser, T. (2005). Can coloring mandalas reduce anxiety? *Art Therapy, 22*(2), 81–85. https://doi.org/10.1080/07421656.2005.10129441

Czamanski-Cohen, J., & Weihs, K. L. (2016). The bodymind model: A platform for studying the mechanisms of change induced by art therapy. *The Arts in Psychotherapy, 51*, 63–71. https://doi.org/10.1016/j.aip.2016.08.006

Czamanski-Cohen, J., Wiley, J. F., Sela, N., Caspi, O., & Weihs, K. (2019). The role of emotional processing in art therapy (REPAT) for breast cancer patients. *Journal of Psychosocial Oncology, 37*(5), 586–598. https://doi.org/10.1080/07347332.2019.1590491

Czamanski-Cohen, J., Wiley, J., & Weihs, K. (2020). Protocol for the REPAT study: role of emotional processing in art therapy for breast cancer palliative care patients. *BMJ Open, 10*(11), e037521. https://doi.org/10.1136/bmjopen-2020-037521

Dayton, T. (2005). The use of psychodrama in dealing with grief and addiction-related loss and trauma. *Journal of Group Psychotherapy Psychodrama and Sociometry, 58*(1), 15–35.

de Felice, G., Giuliani, A., Halfon, S., et al. (2019). The misleading dodo bird verdict. How much of the outcome variance is explained by common and specific factors? *New Ideas in Psychology, 54*, 50 55. https://doi.org/10.1016/j.newideapsych.2019.01.006

de Witte, M., Orkibi, H., Zarate, R., et al. (2021). From therapeutic factors to mechanisms of change in the creative arts therapies: A scoping review. *Frontiers in Psychology, 12*(2525). https://doi.org/10.3389/fpsyg.2021.678397

de Witte, M., Pinho, A. D. S., Stams, G.-J., et al. (2020). Music therapy for stress reduction: A systematic review and meta-analysis. *Health Psychology Review*, 1–26. https://doi.org/10.1080/17437199.2020.1846580

de Witte, M., Spruit, A., van Hooren, S., Moonen, X., & Stams, G.-J. (2020). Effects of music interventions on stress-related outcomes: A systematic review and two meta-analyses. *Health Psychology Review, 14*(2), 294–324. https://doi.org/10.1080/17437199.2019.1627897

Dominguez, K. M. (2018). Encountering disenfranchised grief: An investigation of the clinical lived experiences in dance/movement therapy. *American Journal of Dance Therapy, 40*(2), 254–276. https://doi.org/10.1007/s10465–018-9281-9

Dunphy, K., Baker, F. A., Dumaresq, E., et al. (2019). Creative arts interventions to address depression in older adults: A systematic review of outcomes, processes, and mechanisms. *Frontiers in Psychology, 9*(2655). https://doi.org/10.3389/fpsyg.2018.02655

Elheja, R. A., Palgi, Y., Feldman, R., et al. (2021). The role of oxytocin in regulating loneliness in old age. *Psychoneuroendocrinology, 133*, 105413.

Elliott, G. R. (2012). Qualitative methods for studying psychotherapy change processes. In D. Harper & A. R. Thompson (Eds.), *Qualitative Research Methods in Mental Health and Psychotherapy* (pp. 69–81). Wiley https://doi.org/10.1002/9781119973249.ch6

Elliott, R. (2010). Psychotherapy change process research: Realizing the promise. *Psychotherapy Research, 20*(2), 123–135. https://doi.org/10.1080/10503300903470743

Emunah, R. (1994). *Acting for Real: Drama Therapy Process, Technique, and Performance*. Brunner/Mazel.

Fancourt, D. (2017). A history of the use of arts in health. In *Arts in Health: Designing and Researching Interventions* (pp. 3–22) Oxford University Press. https://doi.org/10.1093/oso/9780198792079.003.0001

Feniger-Schaal, R., & Orkibi, H. (2020). Integrative systematic review of drama therapy intervention research. *Psychology of Aesthetics, Creativity, and the Arts, 14*(1), 68–80. https://doi.org/10.1037/aca0000257

Fredrickson, B. L. (2001). The role of positive emotions in positive psychology: The broaden-and-build theory of positive emotions. *American Psychologist, 56*(3), 218–226. https://doi.org/10.1037/0003-066x.56.3.218

Giacomucci, S., & Marquit, J. (2020). The effectiveness of trauma-focused psychodrama in the treatment of PTSD in inpatient substance abuse treatment [Original Research]. *Frontiers in Psychology, 11*(896). https://doi.org/10.3389/fpsyg.2020.00896

Glavin, C. E. Y., & Montgomery, P. (2017). Creative bibliotherapy for post-traumatic stress disorder (PTSD): A systematic review. *Journal of Poetry Therapy, 30*(2), 95–107. https://doi.org/10.1080/08893675.2017.1266190

Gold, C., Solli, H. P., Krüger, V., & Lie, S. A. (2009). Dose–response relationship in music therapy for people with serious mental disorders: Systematic review and meta-analysis. *Clinical Psychology Review, 29*(3), 193–207. https://doi.org/https://doi.org/10.1016/j.cpr.2009.01.001

Gross, J. J. (2015). Emotion regulation: Current status and future prospects. *Psychological Inquiry, 26*(1), 1–26. https://doi.org/10.1080/1047840X.2014.940781

Gussak, D., & Rosal, M. (Eds.). (2016). *The Wiley-Blackwell Handbook of Art Therapy.* Wiley-Blackwell.

Haeyen, S., van Hooren, S., & Hutschemaekers, G. (2015). Perceived effects of art therapy in the treatment of personality disorders, cluster B/C: A qualitative study. *The Arts in Psychotherapy, 45*, 1–10. https://doi.org/10.1016/j.aip.2015.04.005

Hamidi, F., & Sobhani Tabar, S. (2021). Effect of psychodrama on post-traumatic stress disorder symptoms in primary school students living in earthquake-stricken areas [Original Research]. *Iranian Journal of Psychiatry and Clinical Psychology, 26*(4), 400–417. https://doi.org/10.32598/ijpcp.26.3.3190.2

Hardy, G. E., & Llewelyn, S. (2015). Introduction to psychotherapy process research. In O. C. G. Gelo, A. Pritz, & B. Rieken (Eds.), *Psychotherapy Research: Foundations, Process, and Outcome* (pp. 183–194). Springer Vienna. https://doi.org/10.1007/978-3-7091-1382-0_9

Hill, K. E., & Lineweaver, T. T. (2016). Improving the short-term affect of grieving children through art. *Art Therapy, 33*(2), 91–98. https://doi.org/10.1080/07421656.2016.1166414

Ho, R. T. H., Fong, T. C. T., Cheung, I. K. M., Yip, P. S. F., & Luk, M.-y. (2016). Effects of a short-term dance movement therapy program on symptoms and stress in patients with breast cancer undergoing radiotherapy: A randomized, controlled, single-blind trial. *Journal of Pain and Symptom Management, 51*(5), 824–831. https://doi.org/10.1016/j.jpainsymman.2015.12.332

Ho, R. T. H., Fong, T. C. T., & Yip, P. S. F. (2018). Perceived stress moderates the effects of a randomized trial of dance movement therapy on diurnal cortisol slopes in breast cancer patients. *Psychoneuroendocrinology, 87*, 119–126. https://doi.org/10.1016/j.psyneuen.2017.10.012

Hoffmann, J., & Russ, S. W. (2012). Pretend play, creativity, and emotion regulation in children. *Psychology of Aesthetics, Creativity, and the Arts, 6*(2), 175–184. https://doi.org/10.1037/a0026299

Imus, S. D. (2021). Creating breeds creating. In H. Wengrower & S. Chaiklin (Eds.), *Dance and Creativity within Dance Movement Therapy: International Perspectives* (pp. 124–140). Routledge. https://doi.org/10.4324/9780429442308

Irwin, E., Levy, P., & Shapiro, M. (1972). Assessment of drama therapy in a child guidance setting. *Group Psychotherapy & Psychodrama, 25*(3), 105–116.

Ivcevic, Z., & Hoffmann, J. (2019). Emotions and creativity. In J. C. Kaufman & R. J. Sternberg (Eds.), *The Cambridge Handbook of Creativity* (2nd ed., pp. 273–295). Cambridge University Press.

Jasemi, M., Aazami, S., & Zabihi, R. E. (2016). The effects of music therapy on anxiety and depression of cancer patients. *Indian Journal of Palliative Care, 22*(4), 455–458. https://doi.org/10.4103/0973-1075.191823

Jennings, S. (1973). *Remedial Drama: A Handbook for Teachers and Therapists.* Pitman.

Jennings, S. (1994). *The Handbook of Dramatherapy.* Routledge.

Jiang, J., Rickson, D., & Jiang, C. (2016). The mechanism of music for reducing psychological stress: Music preference as a mediator. *The Arts in Psychotherapy, 48*, 62–68. https://doi.org/10.1016/j.aip.2016.02.002

Johnson, D. R. (1985). Envisioning the link among the creative arts therapies. *The Arts in Psychotherapy, 12*(4), 233–238. https://doi.org/10.1016/0197-4556(85)90036-X

Johnson, D. R., & Emunah, R. (2009). *Current Approaches in Drama Therapy* (2nd ed.). Charles C. Thomas.

Johnson, D. R., Forrester, A., Dintino, C., James, M., & Schnee, G. (1996). Towards a poor drama therapy. *The Arts in Psychotherapy, 23*(4), 293–306. www .sciencedirect.com/science/article/B6V9J-3VV41S4-1/2/ cd26a5151af0987e0399552ab140e574

Jones, P. (2005). *The Arts Therapies: A Revolution in Healthcare.* Brunner-Routledge.

Jones, P. (2007). *Drama as Therapy: Theory, Practice, and Research* (2nd ed.). Routledge. www.loc.gov/catdir/toc/ecip0711/2007007576.html

Jones, P. (2021). *The Arts Therapies: A Revolution in Healthcare* (2nd ed.). Routledge.

Jung, C. G. (1972). *Mandala Symbolism.* Princeton University Press.

Karkou, V., & Meekums, B. (2017). Dance movement therapy for dementia. *Cochrane Database of Systematic Reviews.* https://doi.org/10.1002/14651858.CD011022 .pub2

Karkou, V., & Sanderson, P. (2006). *Arts Therapies: A Research-Based Map of the Field.* Elsevier-Churchill Livingstone.

Kazdin, A. E. (2009). Understanding how and why psychotherapy leads to change. *Psychotherapy Research, 19*(4–5), 418–428. https://doi.org/10.1080/ 10503300802448899

Keisari, S. (2021). Expanding the role repertoire while aging: A drama therapy model. *Frontiers in Psychology, 12*, 635975–635975. https://doi.org/10.3389/fpsyg.2021 .635975

Keisari, S., Gesser-Edelsburg, A., Yaniv, D., & Palgi, Y. (2020). Playback theatre in adult day centers: A creative group intervention for community-dwelling older adults. *PLoS ONE, 15*(10), e0239812. https://doi.org/10.1371/journal.pone .0239812

Keisari, S., Palgi, Y., Yaniv, D., & Gesser-Edelsburg, A. (2020). Participation in life-review playback theater enhances mental health of community-dwelling older adults: A randomized controlled trial. *Psychology of Aesthetics, Creativity, and the Arts.* Advance online publication. https://doi.org/10.1037/aca0000354

Kipper, D. A. (1986). *Psychotherapy through Clinical Role Playing*. Brunner/Mazel.

Koch, S., Kunz, T., Lykou, S., & Cruz, R. (2014). Effects of dance movement therapy and dance on health-related psychological outcomes: A meta-analysis. *The Arts in Psychotherapy, 41*(1), 46–64. https://doi.org/10.1016/j.aip.2013.10.004

Koch, S. C., Riege, R. F. F., Tisborn, K., et al. (2019). Effects of dance movement therapy and dance on health-related psychological outcomes: A meta-analysis update. *Frontiers in Psychology, 10*(1806). https://doi.org/10.3389/fpsyg.2019.01806

Kramer, E. (1972). *Art as Therapy with Children*. Schocken Books.

Kushnir, A., & Orkibi, H. (2021). Concretization as a mechanism of change in psychodrama: Procedures and benefits. *Frontiers in Psychology, 12*(176). https://doi.org/10.3389/fpsyg.2021.633069

Laban, R. V. (1970). *Principles of Dance and Movement Notation*. Dance Horizons.

Landy, R. J. (1983). The use of distancing in drama therapy. *The Arts in Psychotherapy, 10*(3), 175–185. https://doi.org/10.1016/0197-4556(83)90006-0

Landy, R. J. (1986). *Drama Therapy: Concepts and Practices*. Charles C. Thomas.

Landy, R. J. (1993). *Persona and Performance: The Meaning of Role in Drama, Therapy, and Everyday Life*. Guilford Press.

Landy, R. J. (1996). Drama therapy and distancing: Reflections on theory and clinical application. *The Arts in Psychotherapy, 23*(5), 367–373. https://doi.org/10.1016/S0197-4556(96)00052-4

Langer, S. K. (1953). *Feeling and Form: A Theory of Art*. Charles Scribner's Sons.

Leedy, J. J. (1969). *Poetry Therapy: The Use of Poetry in the Treatment of Emotional Disorders*. Lippincott.

Levine, E. (1999). On the play ground: Child psychotherapy and expressive arts therapy. In S. K. Levine & E. G. Levine (Eds.), *Foundations of Expressive Arts Therapy: Theoretical and Clinical Perspectives* (pp. 257–273). Jessica Kingsley.

Linnemann, A., Strahler, J., & Nater, U. M. (2016). The stress-reducing effect of music listening varies depending on the social context. *Psychoneuroendocrinology, 72*, 97–105. https://doi.org/10.1016/j.psyneuen.2016.06.003

Malchiodi, C. A. (2005). *Expressive Therapies*. Guilford Press.

Martin, L., Oepen, R., Bauer, K., et al. (2018). Creative arts interventions for stress management and prevention – a systematic review. *Behavioral Sciences, 8*(2), 28. www.mdpi.com/2076-328X/8/2/28

Masika, G. M., Yu, D. S. F., & Li, P. W. C. (2020). Visual art therapy as a treatment option for cognitive decline among older adults: A systematic review and meta-analysis. *Journal of Advanced Nursing, 76*(8), 1892–1910. https://doi.org/10.1111/jan.14362

Maslow, A. H. (1962). Creativity in self-actualizing people. In *Toward a Psychology of Being*. (pp. 127–137). D. Van Nostrand. https://doi.org/10.1037/10793-010

Mazza, N. (2017). *Poetry Therapy: Theory and Practice* (2nd ed.). Routledge, Taylor & Francis Group.

McCulliss, D. (2012). Bibliotherapy: Historical and research perspectives. *Journal of Poetry Therapy, 25*(1), 23–38. https://doi.org/10.1080/08893675.2012.654944

McNicol, S., & Brewster, L. (2018). *Bibliotherapy*. Facet.

McNiff, S. (1979). From shamanism to art therapy. *Art Psychotherapy, 6*(3), 155–161. https://doi.org/10.1016/0090-9092(79)90039-5

McNiff, S. (1981). *The Arts and Psychotherapy*. Charles C. Thomas.

McNiff, S. (2009). *Integrating the Arts in Therapy: History, Theory, and Practice.* Charles C. Thomas.

Meekums, B., Karkou, V., & Nelson, E. A. (2015). Dance movement therapy for depression. *Cochrane Database of Systematic Reviews.* https://doi.org/10.1002/14651858.CD009895.pub2

Moon, B. L. (2007). *The Role of Metaphor in Art Therapy: Theory, Method, and Experience.* Charles C. Thomas.

Moreno, J. L. (1953/1993). *Who Shall Survive? Foundations of Sociometry, Group Psychotherapy, and Sociodrama – Student Edition.* American Society of Group Psychotherapy and Psychodrama.

Moreno, J. L. (1964). The third psychiatric revolution and the scope of psychodrama. *Group Psychotherapy, 17*(2–3), 149–171.

Moreno, J. L. (1965). Therapeutic vehicles and the concept of surplus reality. *Group Psychotherapy, 18*(4), 211–216.

Moreno, J. L., & Moreno, F. B. (1944). Spontaneity theory of child development. *Sociometry, 7*(2), 89–128. https://doi.org/10.2307/2785405

Naumburg, M. (1966). *Dynamically Oriented Art Therapy: Its Principles and Practices* Grune & Stratton.

Nemetz, L. D. (2006). Moving with meaning: The historical progression of dance/movement therapy. In S. L. Brooke (Ed.), *Creative Arts Therapies Manual: A Guide to the History, Theoretical Approaches, Assessment, and Work with Special Populations of Art, Play, Dance, Music, Drama, and Poetry Therapies* (pp. 95–108). Charles C. Thomas.

O'Callaghan, C., & Michael, N. (2015). Music therapy in grief and mourning. In J. Edwards (Ed.), *The Oxford Handbook of Music Therapy* (pp. 405–414). Oxford University Press.

Orkibi, H. (2012). Arts therapies students' scores in profession-related variables: Quantitative results of a longitudinal study. *Body, Movement and Dance in Psychotherapy, 7*(2), 129–144. https://doi.org/10.1080/17432979.2012.659678

Orkibi, H. (2018). The user-friendliness of drama: Implications for drama therapy and psychodrama admission and training. *The Arts in Psychotherapy, 59*, 101–108. https://doi.org/10.1016/j.aip.2018.04.004

Orkibi, H. (2020). Creative arts therapies. Society for the Psychology of Aesthetics, Creativity, & the Arts. www.div10.org/creative-arts-therapies/

Orkibi, H. (2021). Creative adaptability: Conceptual framework, measurement, and outcomes in times of crisis. *Frontiers in Psychology, 11*(3695). https://doi.org/10.3389/fpsyg.2020.588172

Orkibi, H., Azoulay, B., Regev, D., & Snir, S. (2017). Adolescents' dramatic engagement predicts their in-session productive behaviors: A psychodrama change process study. *The Arts in Psychotherapy, 55*, 46–53. https://doi.org/10.1016/j.aip.2017.04.001

Orkibi, H., Azoulay, B., Snir, S., & Regev, D. (2017). In-session behaviours and adolescents' self-concept and loneliness: A psychodrama process–outcome study. *Clinical Psychology and Psychotherapy, 24*, O1455–O1463. https://doi.org/10.1002/cpp.2103

Orkibi, H., Ben-Eliyahu, A., Reiter-Palmon, R., et al. (2021). Creative adaptability and emotional well-being during the COVID-19 pandemic: An international study.

Psychology of Aesthetics, Creativity, and the Arts. Advance online publication. https://doi.org/10.1037/aca0000445

Orkibi, H., & Feniger-Schaal, R. (2019). Integrative systematic review of psychodrama psychotherapy research: Trends and methodological implications. *PLoS ONE, 14*(2), e0212575. https://doi.org/10.1371/journal.pone.0212575

Papasteri, C. C., Sofonea, A., Boldasu, R., et al. (2020). Social feedback during sensorimotor synchronization changes salivary oxytocin and behavioral states [Original Research]. *Frontiers in Psychology, 11*(2495). https://doi.org/10.3389/fpsyg.2020.531046

Pascual-Leone, A., & Yeryomenko, N. (2017). The client "experiencing" scale as a predictor of treatment outcomes: A meta-analysis on psychotherapy process. *Psychotherapy Research, 27*(6), 653–665. https://doi.org/10.1080/10503307.2016.1152409

Payne, H. (1992). *Dance Movement Therapy: Theory and Practice.* Tavistock/Routledge.

Peterson, C., & Seligman, M. E. P. (2004). *Character Strengths and Virtues: A Handbook and Classification.* American Psychological Association.

Proyer, R. T. (2013). Playfulness over the lifespan and its relation to happiness. *Zeitschrift für Gerontologie und Geriatrie,* 1–5. https://doi.org/10.1007/s00391-013-0539-z

Regev, D. (2021). A process-outcome study of school-based art therapy. *International Journal of Art Therapy,* 17–25. https://doi.org/10.1080/17454832.2021.1957960

Rogers, C. R. (1961). Toward a theory of creativity. In *On Becoming a Person: A Therapist's View of Psychotherapy* (pp. 347–359). Houghton Mifflin.

Ronen, T. (2011). *The Positive Power of Imagery: Harnessing Client Imagination in CBT and Related Therapies.* Wiley-Blackwell.

Runco, M. A. (1996). Personal creativity: Definition and developmental issues. *New Directions for Child and Adolescent Development, 1996*(72), 3–30. https://doi.org/10.1002/cd.23219967203

Runco, M. A. (2007). *Creativity –Theories and Themes: Research, Development, and Practice.* Elsevier Academic Press. http://books.google.com/books?id=nJlfKEmeqEC&hl=iw&source=gbs_navlinks_s

Runco, M. A. (2011). Personal creativity. In M. A. Runco & S. R. Pritzker (Eds.), *Encyclopedia of Creativity* (2nd ed., vol. 2, pp. 220–223). Academic Press.

Runco, M. A., & Jaeger, G. J. (2012). The standard definition of creativity. *Creativity Research Journal, 24*(1), 92–96. https://doi.org/10.1080/10400419.2012.650092

Russ, S. W. (2014). *Pretend Play in Childhood: Foundation of Adult Creativity.* American Psychological Association.

Sajnani, N., Mayor, C., Burch, D., et al. (2019). Collaborative discourse analysis on the use of drama therapy to treat trauma in schools. *Drama Therapy Review, 5*(1), 27–47. https://doi.org/10.1386/dtr.5.1.27_1

Samaritter, R. (2009). The use of metaphors in dance movement therapy. *Body, Movement and Dance in Psychotherapy, 4*(1), 33–43. www.informaworld.com/10.1080/17432970802682274

Schrade, C., Tronsky, L., & Kaiser, D. H. (2011). Physiological effects of mandala making in adults with intellectual disability. *The Arts in Psychotherapy, 38*(2), 109–113. https://doi.org/10.1016/j.aip.2011.01.002

Shorer, M., & Leibovich, L. (2020). Young children's emotional stress reactions during the COVID-19 outbreak and their associations with parental emotion regulation and parental playfulness. *Early Child Development and Care*, 1–11. https://doi.org/10.1080/03004430.2020.1806830

Shorer, M., Swissa, O., Levavi, P., & Swissa, A. (2021). Parental playfulness and children's emotional regulation: The mediating role of parents' emotional regulation and the parent–child relationship. *Early Child Development and Care, 191*(2), 210–220. https://doi.org/10.1080/03004430.2019.1612385

Slade, P. (1954). *Child Drama*. University of London Press.

Soysal, F. S. Ö. (2021). The effects of psychodrama on emotion regulation skills in emerging adults. *Current Psychology*. https://doi.org/10.1007/S12144-021-01800-W

Tarr, B., Launay, J., & Dunbar, R. I. M. (2014). Music and social bonding: "self-other" merging and neurohormonal mechanisms [Hypothesis and Theory]. *Frontiers in Psychology, 5*(1096). https://doi.org/10.3389/fpsyg.2014.01096

Testoni, I., Cichellero, S., Kirk, K., Cappelletti, V., & Cecchini, C. (2019). When death enters the theater of psychodrama: Perspectives and strategies of psychodramatists. *Journal of Loss and Trauma, 24*(5–6), 516–532. https://doi.org/10.1080/15325024.2018.1548996

Testoni, I., Ronconi, L., Palazzo, L., et al. (2018). Psychodrama and moviemaking in a death education course to work through a case of suicide among high school students in Italy. *Frontiers in Psychology, 9*(441). https://doi.org/10.3389/fpsyg.2018.00441

Van Lith, T. (2016). Art therapy in mental health: A systematic review of approaches and practices. *The Arts in Psychotherapy, 47*, 9–22. https://doi.org/https://doi.org/10.1016/j.aip.2015.09.003

Waller, D. (1991). *Becoming a Profession: The History of Art Therapy in Britain, 1940–82*. Tavistock/Routledge.

Wheeler, B. L. (2015). *Music Therapy Handbook*. Guilford Press.

White, R. E., & Carlson, S. M. (2016). What would Batman do? Self-distancing improves executive function in young children. *Developmental Science, 19*(3), 419–426. https://doi.org/10.1111/desc.12314

White, R. E., Kross, E., & Duckworth, A. L. (2015). Spontaneous self-distancing and adaptive self-reflection across adolescence. *Child Development, 86*(4), 1272–1281. https://doi.org/10.1111/cdev.12370

Wilkinson, R. (1992). Art, emotion and expression. In O. Hanfling (Ed.), *Philosophical Aesthetics: An Introduction* (pp. 179–238). Wiley-Blackwell.

Winnicott, D. W. (2016). Living creatively. In *The Collected Works of D. W. Winnicott*, vol. 9, 1969–1971 (pp. 213–224). Oxford University Press. https://doi.org/10.1093/med:psych/9780190271411.003.0043

World Health Organization. (2021). *Depression*. www.who.int/health-topics/depression#tab=tab_1

23 Developing Emotion Abilities through Engagement with the Arts

Megan G. Stutesman and Thalia R. Goldstein

The arts (visual arts, theatre, dance, music) have been connected to emotion by philosophers and psychologists for centuries, and have been proposed to represent, express, and engage emotions through both creation and perception (Barwell, 1986; Hjort & Laver, 1997). All art forms have been theorized as able to foster emotional skills in the practice of expressing emotion through art creation and through interpretation of emotion in art observation. Simultaneously, each art form has shown differential effects in empirical testing. For example, adult actors and dancers have shown higher empathy and emotion recognition abilities than the general population (Schmidt et al., 2021) and visual arts training and viewing have been used as interventions to better the empathy and emotional intelligence of business and medical professionals (Bentwich & Gilbey, 2017; Ebert et al., 2015a; Morris et al., 2005; Wikström, 2003). Educational psychologists have promoted using arts education as an avenue for social and emotional development because emotional skill-building strategies are theorized as already employed in arts classrooms (Holochwost et al., 2021; Hutzel et al., 2010; Quaglia et al., 2015). However, the connection between engagement in the arts and emotion ability development is more nuanced than a simple "any and all art engagement leads to any and all emotion abilities" causal pathway.

Recognizing, interpreting, and acting on emotions in art often involve more than one type of sensory and perception cue (visual, auditory, physical, etc.; Haq & Jackson, 2011). Creating art may also engage emotions multimodally, as different art forms tap more heavily into different channels for emotion cues (Melcher & Bacci, 2013; Schellenberg & von Scheve, 2012). For example, visual arts emphasize emotion expressed and perceived visually, while music places more emphasis on auditory cueing, and dance places more emphasis on physical cueing. Therefore, repeated engagement in a particular art form may, theoretically, alter emotional development uniquely. Each art form's effects on emotional development should therefore be considered individually (Holochwost et al., 2021).

In this chapter, we present an overview of evidence for various emotion abilities' development through the arts; we focus on the past 10 years of

The writing of this chapter was supported in part by a National Endowment for the Arts grant to the second author.

published research and delineate among art disciplines. We also focus on emotion ability development in early and middle childhood. This age, from 5 to 12 years old, is a sensitive period for development when many of the largest changes in emotion abilities occur (Pons et al., 2004; Sommerville & Decety, 2017), and thus, may be the most malleable period for emotion ability development through arts engagement (Huston & Ripke, 2006).

Generally, emotion abilities begin in infancy as babies begin to recognize facial expressions as containing meaning (emotional and otherwise), and the cultural implications of those meanings. Infants and toddlers continue to develop emotion abilities as they move from depending on others' soothing to their own emotional control and soothing when distressed. Emotion abilities then develop quickly during early and middle childhood years, as children become more adept at recognizing emotions in others and controlling emotions in themselves. In adolescence, development continues, but less rapidly (LoBue et al., 2019; Saarni et al., 2006). Importantly, emotional development does not occur maturationally, along a set pathway without environmental influences. Nor does emotional development exist separately from cognitive development; children's cognitive abilities such as appraisals, executive functions (e.g. Simonds et al., 2007), and intelligence affect their emotional development. Developmental trajectories are also highly affected by the child's cultural and contextual environment, parental and peer influences (Dishion & Tipsord, 2011; Stack et al., 2010), and other temporal factors.

Emotion Ability Development and the Arts

Multiple factors hinder the creation and development of a unified, thorough, and experimentally testable theory of emotional development and the arts. The first is the wide variety of experiences that a child can have in the arts. Children's experiences in the arts can range from afterschool programs, recreational programs, professional training programs, within-school arts classes, arts as integrated into other academic coursework, and at-home art-making. Children can view the arts in theatres, concert halls, museums, schools, field trips, and at home, formally or informally. Experiences can be creative (such as drawing whatever they feel like) or not (such as analyzing the structure of a musical piece). The type (visual, music, theatre, dance), time, depth, purpose, teacher characteristics, and intensity of arts engagement also vary widely for children (as it does for adults) (Holochwost et al., 2021). There is not yet strong evidence or theory as to how these various factors affect children's engagement with or learning from the arts.

The second factor preventing a unified theory is the various definitional issues with the term *emotion abilities*. *Emotion abilities* encompasses a variety of skills as broad as emotional intelligence, empathy, affective theory of mind, emotion perception, emotion recognition, emotion contagion, compassion, sympathy, social understanding, emotional control, and emotion regulation (Jones et al.,

2016). Problematically, researchers working in these constructs often use the same term for different abilities, or measure the same concept across studies using different definitions (Bridges et al., 2004; Decety & Moriguchi, 2007). Other times, researchers use umbrella terms (e.g., *Social-Emotional Learning*) but actually measure a small and specific ability (e.g., emotion matching to a partner). Investigations of the arts and emotion abilities are not immune to these issues.

Primarily, "emotion abilities" fall into two categories: other-oriented, and self-oriented. Other-oriented abilities include emotion recognition, emotion perception, and theory of mind. *Emotion recognition* is the ability to perceptually or cognitively see that someone else is experiencing an emotion, while *emotion perception* is the ability to understand the content or label of that emotion. Emotion recognition and perception are tied to each other in functioning, but an individual must first recognize that an emotional state exists (emotion recognition) before perceiving what that emotion is (emotion perception) (Sweeny et al., 2013). A related ability, *theory of mind* (ToM), is the ability to attribute mental states, including emotion, to oneself and others (Altschuler et al., 2018; Dvash & Shamay-Tsoory, 2014; Gallant et al., 2020). *Affective theory of mind* (AToM), is a subcomponent of ToM defined as the attribution of emotional states specifically (Altschuler et al., 2018; Duval et al., 2011; Shamay-Tsoory & Aharon-Peretz, 2007). Related to ToM are empathic abilities, often defined in two ways: cognitive empathy and affective empathy. *Cognitive empathy* is closely related to ToM, in that it requires knowing what others are feeling and thinking, whereas *affective empathy* refers to feeling the same emotions as others (Cox et al., 2012; Laird, 2015). In fact, cognitive empathy might be better conceptualized as equivalent to AToM because they both can employ the same underlying cognitive mechanisms to arrive at an understanding of what another is feeling (Maibom, 2017). For example, both AToM and cognitive empathy could employ the cognitive mechanism of "Theory Theory," which proposes that one assumes a causal theory of another's emotional states and how they interact to predict behavior, or "Simulation Theory," which explains the process of understanding another's emotional state by simulating it in your own mind (Apperly, 2008).

Developing concurrently with other-oriented emotion abilities, self-oriented emotion abilities are typically characterized as regulatory capacities, including the ability to recognize that you yourself are experiencing an emotion, and then successfully regulate that emotion in accordance to your goals and needs of the immediate situations (LoBue et al., 2019). This regulation includes magnitude and duration of emotions (Gross, 2013). *Emotion regulation* can also be described as the ability to influence when and how we experience and express emotions (Fischer et al., 2016). A large variety of emotion regulation strategies develop over time, with different consequences (Gross, 2013).

As mentioned above, instead of focusing on individual abilities as unique constructs in emotional development (whether self- or other-oriented), researchers often group emotion abilities under umbrella terms such as *social-emotional learning*, which includes a broad range of skills from self-awareness, social-awareness, responsible decision making, self-management, and relationship skills (Durlak, 2015; Payton et al., 2000). *Emotional intelligence* (EI), often used as a more general term, encompasses four major subcategories of skills including emotion perception, emotion understanding, reasoning with emotion, and emotion management (Mayer et al., 2016; Schellenberg, 2011). EI is not a unique emotion construct of its own, but rather a conceptualization of the suite of emotion abilities that work together as a set of unified abilities (Petrides et al., 2006). Critics have argued that EI is often poorly defined, and does not necessarily refer to a distinct ability (Humphrey et al., 2007; Pool & Qualter, 2018; Zeidner et al., 2003). Proponents of EI have instead suggested that EI is a set of cascading abilities where emotion perception precedes emotion understanding, which then leads to emotion reasoning and management (Joseph & Newman, 2010), or that the integration of its subcomponents form a cohesive, global ability (Mayer et al., 2008). These varying conceptualizations affect how researchers chose to operationalize and measure the outcomes of arts-based activities.

In addition to the above factors constraining our knowledge, the arts may affect emotion development differently across the life span. Engagement in the arts can also differentially affect the development of neurodiverse trajectories such as those with autism or disabilities (Alter-Muri, 2017; Lee et al., 2017; Wexler, 2014), and children who have experienced early life hardships (i.e., ACES; Shakoor et al., 2021) or are who are resource lacking (Wexler, 2014).

Considering the effects of art are multifaceted and may look different across age groups and populations, in what follows, we outline evidence for arts engagement interactions with emotional development in typical development, specifically during the critical emotional development period of early and middle childhood. We discuss child engagement in the creation and consumption of arts for art's sake (Winner et al., 2013), which includes active participation in art creation and the perception and appreciation of art. We do not include the use of arts for alternative purposes (i.e., therapeutic benefits or improved learning in academic subjects). We present supporting evidence for and against the development of emotion abilities in childhood through individual art forms including visual, theatre, dance, and music with an emphasis on research conducted within the past 10 years (for earlier reviews, see Winner & Hetland, 2000; Winner et al., 2013). In Table 23.1, we present an overview of each study reviewed for ease of reference. There are also numerous databases and other reviews that have covered these studies, including a searchable reviewed database: ArtsEdSearch.org.

Evidence for Emotion Ability Development through Art

As it has been for many years (see Winner & Hetland, 2000), recent evidence for the development of emotion abilities through engagement in

Table 23.1 *Early and middle childhood emotion development in the arts*

Citation	Art form	Emotion ability	Age group	Type of study	Findings
Zakaria et al. (2021)	Visual	ER	Preschool	Qualitative	+
Drake & Winner (2013)	Visual	ER	6–12 years	Experimental	+
Drake (2021)	Visual	ER	6–12 years	Experimental	+
Morizio et al. (2021)	Visual	Empathy	Elementary school	Case study, intervention	+
Bradshaw (2016)	Visual	Empathy	Middle school	Qualitative	+
Watson et al. (2019)	Visual	Empathy	4th and 5th grades	Randomized controlled trial	x
Ebert et al. (2015b)	Visual	Emotion knowledge (AToM)	6–12 years	Intervention	+
Hoffmann et al. (2021)	Visual	EI	9 years	Quasi-experimental intervention	+/x (increased ability not shown at follow-up)
Maierna & Camodeca (2021)	Theatre	ER	Elementary school	Randomized controlled trial	+
Goldstein et al. (2013)	Theatre	ER	7–10 years	Quasi-experimental	+
Goldstein & Lerner (2018)	Theatre	ER, ToM, Empathy	Pre-Kindergarten	Randomized controlled trial	+/x (emotional distress lowered but no ToM or empathy effects)
Goldstein & Winner (2011)	Theatre	ToM	7–10 years	Quasi-experimental	x
Goldstein & Winner (2011)	Theatre	ToM	7–10 years	Correlational	+

Study	Art form	Outcome	Age	Design	Result
Goldstein & Winner (2011)	Theatre	ToM	4–5 years	Quasi-experimental	x
Mages (2018)	Theatre	ToM	Middle school	Randomized controlled trial	+
Greene et al. (2015)	Theatre	Empathy	Elementary school	Quasi-experimental	+/x (difference between groups found at pre-test, no differences at post-test)
Goldstein & Winner (2011)	Theatre	Empathy	6 years	Randomized controlled trial; Qualitative analysis	+
Gil et al. (2014)	Theatre	Empathy			
Pereira & Marques-Pinto (2017)	Dance	ER	9–13 years	Quasi-experimental	+/x (one measure found increases, one found no effect)
Williams & Berthelsen (2019)	Music	ER	4–5 years	Quasi-experimental intervention	+
Boucher et al. (2021)	Music	Emotion comprehension	4–5 years	Intervention	+/− (5-year-olds increased ability, 4-year-olds did not)
Ilari et al. (2018)	Music	ToM	6–7 years	Quasi-experimental	x
Schellenberg & Mankarious (2012)	Music	Emotion comprehension: Emotion matching and ER	7–8 years	Quasi-experimental	+
Mualem & Lavidor (2015)	Music	ER	Adults (Retrospective, longitudinal childhood participation in music)	Quasi-experimental	x
Rabinowitch et al. (2013)	Music	ToM and Empathy	Elementary school	Randomized controlled trial	+/x (increased empathy, no difference for ToM)

Table 23.1 (cont.)

Citation	Art form	Emotion ability	Age group	Type of study	Findings
Kim & Kim (2018)	Music	EI	7–12 years	Quasi-experimental intervention	+/x (subsection of EI increased, but no holistic EI group differences)
Schellenberg (2011)	Music	EI	Adults (retrospective, longitudinal childhood participation in music)	Quasi-experimental	x
Tsortanidou (2020)	Multimodal	General emotion ability	9–10 years	Qualitative	+
Andersen et al. (2019)	Multimodal	ER	6–9 years	Quasi-experimental Intervention	+
Brown & Sax (2013)	Multimodal	ER	Preschool	Quasi-experimental intervention	+

Note: + = positive relationship between art engagement and ability; - = negative relationship; x = no effect. AToM = Affective Theory of Mind; ER = Emotion Regulation; EI = Emotional Intelligence, ToM = Theory of Mind. Only original research published in English between 2011 and 2021 included.

various art forms continues to be siloed, domain specific, varying in strength, and underdefined. There are assorted studies across visual arts, dance, theatre, and music, and there are studied outcomes across emotion regulation, theory of mind, emotional intelligence, and so on. Some studies are correlational, some are quasi-experimental, some are qualitative, and a very few (although more than previously) are randomized controlled trials. Ages of participants in this literature vary from preschool to adult professionals, and arts engagement varies from school classes in which everyone is forced to participate to highly selective audition-only programs to museums with field trips. This makes broad conclusions outside of "arts engagement is related to emotional development" hard to make – firm understanding of causal direction, mediating abilities, or moderating factors is basically unknown. This is not to say that the field has not made progress since philosophical musings of Plato or calls to move away from high-stakes, far transfer empirical work into research that is more based on art forms themselves (Winner et al., 2013). However, as seen below, while small steps are continuing to be made, large leaps have yet to be taken.

Evidence in Visual Arts

Visual arts have been connected to emotion abilities including emotion regulation, empathy, emotion understanding, and emotional intelligence, and has shown some positive effects across these emotion domains for children during early and middle childhood. However, to our knowledge, visual arts have not yet been empirically tied to more cognitive emotion abilities, such as emotion perception and ToM in early and middle childhood.

Recent findings show how creating visual art could be implicated in teaching children emotion regulation. Qualitative work has shown that the visual arts affect preschoolers' emotion control through the process of engaging with and communicating different emotions in a creative way during drawing activities (Zakaria et al., 2021). More experimental work has shown how art can be used to bolster emotion regulation skills. Drake and Winner (2013) demonstrated that 5 minutes of drawing increases 6- to 12-year-old children's mood after negative mood induction, and Drake (2021) replicated these findings. This study also revealed that regardless of whether the content of the drawing was real or imaginary, children's mood still improved through drawing. Furthermore, Drake (2021) showed that children spontaneously use drawing to distract from sad mood and that mood improvement via drawing is greater for younger children than older children. Therefore, while these studies do not directly investigate whether and how arts engagement affects emotion abilities, they hint at visual arts as a way to spontaneously regulate or distract from sad emotion, implying a baseline ability of emotion understanding (understanding one's sad emotional state) is needed before employing the use of art to act on the sad mood.

Beyond regulation, the effects of visual arts on children's empathy abilities have been assessed in several ways. One case study demonstrated increases in empathy by following elementary school children through an afterschool visual arts intervention where children engaged in art projects and then discussed and observed their artwork (Morizio et al., 2021). Another took a qualitative approach to examine a 4-month-long visual arts intervention in middle schoolers and concluded that employment of the collaborative discourse required to complete visual arts projects increased empathy in the students (Bradshaw, 2016).

Empathy development through art has also been assessed, but did not show positive effects, using a randomized controlled trial: Watson et al. (2019) randomly assigned 4th- and 5th-graders to a control group or to art intervention groups that took field trips to view a theatrical production, symphony, or visual arts museum. Children took either three or six field trips, and their 4th- and 5th-grade classroom instructors also met with artists in a professional development session. Teachers were encouraged to incorporate artistic learning activities into the everyday classroom; however, this was not controlled for or measured. No effects of empathy or perspective taking for either the control or experimental arts groups were found in comparison of pre- and post-test scores on Likert scale self-report surveys (Watson et al., 2019).

Other work has found more positive effects. In a 6-week intervention, children aged 6- to 12-years-old attended visual arts workshops in an exhibition space. At post-test, children demonstrated improved emotion knowledge assessed with story vignettes that required naming the most appropriate emotion (Ebert et al., 2015b). In a similar intervention study by Hoffmann et al. (2021), 9- to 11-year-olds (i.e., 4th- to 6th-graders) participated in a visual arts intervention consisting of artmaking and art appreciation, and were compared to a no-intervention control group on EI. A subsection of an EI measure was used, requiring children to match social events to emotions. The visual arts group outperformed the control group on EI at the immediate post-test, but this difference did not remain at a 2-month follow-up (Hoffmann et al., 2021).

While the above work has showed researchers' focus on emotion responding and regulation, there have been no studies to date, to our knowledge, that examine how visual arts engagement may affect children's emotion recognition, perception, or ToM, a gap in the literature. There is some evidence that visual arts could foster these skills in other age groups (see Kastner et al., 2021), but particular considerations of early and middle childhood have yet to be investigated.

Evidence in Theatre

Children's theatre engagement has been examined across different activities including dramatic pretend play and drama-based pedagogy, acting training, and live theatre attendance. Taken together, research suggests positive outcomes including increased emotion regulation, cognitive and affective ToM, empathy, and EI. However, findings are mixed and there is a lack of longitudinal studies and randomized controlled trials. We suggest theatre positively impacts some children's emotion development within certain contexts; however, researchers should not claim effects are widespread or generalizable.

Theatre experience has been connected to emotion regulation capacity in a few studies. In a study of elementary school–age children, girls were randomly assigned to a theatre group or a no treatment control group. The theatre group participated in 4 months of theatre workshops. Between the start and end of the program, the theatre group increased emotion regulation skills, measured by the Emotion Regulation Checklist, and the control group decreased emotion regulation skills (Maierna & Camodeca, 2021). Looking at emotion regulation strategy, Goldstein et al. (2013) tested 7- to 10-year-olds enrolled in extracurricular acting or visual arts classes. Using the Coping Strategies Interview, the acting group showed decreased use of emotion suppression (a maladaptive emotion regulation strategy) over time, whereas the visual arts group did not show decreased use of the maladaptive emotion suppression (Goldstein et al., 2013). This study suggests that children who participate in acting may decrease the use of maladaptive emotion regulation strategies such as emotion suppression. In a randomized controlled trial of drama games with 5-year-old children, Goldstein and Lerner (2018) found that an 8-week, three times per week, intervention led to better distress regulation, measured through a distress response task and child interview self-report, but did not increase ToM, altruism, or empathy compared to children in the two control groups, block play and story time.

As the basis of character performance in theatre is understanding emotions, thoughts, and beliefs of a character, increased emotion recognition and ToM have been theorized as related to theatre practice. In two studies, Goldstein and Winner (2011) looked at effects of theatre training (compared to music or visual arts training) on the ToM of children aged 7–11. There were no group differences at pre- or post-test on ToM, indicating children's ToM was not affected by the acting intervention. With these same data, acting class involvement was correlated with superior ToM (composite cognitive and affective scores) than was involvement in dance or non-art activities (Goldstein & Winner, 2011). This demonstrates a self-selection effect, where those who elect to partake in acting classes have superior ToM to those who elect to partake in dance and non-art activities. Theatre has not been shown to affect ToM in preschool age children either. Mages (2018) tested 4- and 5-year-olds who received either a supplementary theatre program with 14 days of theatre activities integrated into their regular preschool curricula or no theatre program activities (control group). No differences in ToM were found between groups at pre- or post-test, and theatre group children did not increase their ToM ability more than control children (Mages, 2018).

Different from theatre participation as an actor, as in the above reviewed studies, engagement in theatre can also take the form of watching live performance. The effects of watching live performance on ToM were examined in middle and high school students who were selected via lottery to attend a live theatre performance on a field trip. Students in this group performed better on the Reading the Mind in the Eyes Test, an affective ToM measure, after attending the performance than matched control students who did not attend the performance (Greene et al., 2015).

Taken together, then, the findings from studies on children's theatre participation and ToM are mixed; 7- to 11-year-old children who elect to take acting have superior ToM than those who do not elect to partake in acting classes, but an acting intervention did not impact 7- to 11-year-olds' ToM. Furthermore, theatre is not related to younger (aged 4–5 years) children's ToM ability. These null findings for children aged 4–5 years old could, at least in part, be due to the developmental trajectory of ToM. Typically, full ToM, as defined by false belief reasoning, emerges from 4 to 5 years old (Dunn et al., 1991; Wellman et al., 2001); therefore, a theatre intervention may not advance ToM in this age group because these children have not yet developed baseline ToM ability. Watching live theatre has also been connected to increased ToM, but this has only been shown in middle and high school children thus far.

Like the connection between children's theatre participation and ToM, the findings from children's theatre participation and empathy are also mixed. In Goldstein and Winner (2011), mentioned above, empathy was also tested after 10 months of acting intervention. Elementary school children in the acting group made more gains, measured by Index of Empathy scores, than the non-acting group. Acting group children also scored higher on the Fiction Emotion-Matching empathy measure, but this difference was found at pretest and was not affected by the intervention.

Children's empathy and theatre participation have also been examined using augmented reality to induce role-play. In an augmented reality dramatic story-book intervention, children role-played stories and their empathy was qualitatively measured with behavior observation of empathetic responses in video recordings; the 6-year-olds demonstrated enhanced empathy compared to a control group who read the same stories but did not enact them (Gil et al., 2014).

Collectively, the studies of children's theatre participation suggest that theatre may positively impact emotion development. However, there are gaps in this literature. Namely, theatre participation in some childhood age groups has not been examined for some emotion development abilities yet, and the ties from preschool-age theatre engagement through middle childhood into adolescence are not well developed. Is theatre experience the same in the age groups? How can theatre intervene on maturational development across time?

Evidence in Dance

Experience in dance has been connected to emotion regulation, emotion perception, and emotional intelligence. Though scant, evidence suggests some positive developmental effects across these abilities for individuals in early and middle childhood. However, to our knowledge, dance has not yet been empirically associated with childhood empathy abilities. Dance has received less attention than other arts and, thus, much of the literature has not been published within the past 10 years. For example, Van Meel et al. (1993) showed dance experience positively impacts emotion perception abilities of 5- and 8-year-olds, and von Rossberg-Gempton et al. (1999) showed social-emotional growth in the areas of cooperation, communication, and awareness of others in 8-year-olds from a dance intervention.

One recent study has examined the effect of children's dance on social-emotional skills, including self-management, akin to emotion regulation as operationalized in the study (Pereira & Marques-Pinto, 2017). Children in 5th to 7th grades (aged 9–12) who participated in an afterschool dance program were compared to a control group in a non-arts afterschool program. The dance group improved their teacher-rated social-emotional skills above and beyond the control group, specifically for self-management. However, no differences were found between groups on the child-reported measure (Pereira & Marques-Pinto, 2017).

In a systematic review of dance and EI, San-Juan-Ferrer and Hípola (2020) analyzed work on EI and its related abilities, including self-control, emotion recognition, prosocial skills, emotional competence, and empathy. The authors discussed articles that used multiple foundational definitions of EI including the following: the ability model by Mayer et al. (2001, 2016), which conceptualizes EI as perception, emotion understanding and regulation, and facilitating thought through emotion; the mixed model by O'Neil (1996), which conceptualizes EI as knowledge of one's own emotions, emotion management, emotion recognition, motivation, and ability to establish relationships; and Petrides and Furnham's (2000, 2001) model, which identifies the dichotomy between emotional self-efficacy (trait EI) and emotional cognitive ability (ability EI). Most articles were from the sports literature, robotics engineering, and non–English speaking conference reports. Across a wide range of ages, the authors proposed that dance participation in primary school–age children positively benefits the multiple facets and models of EI and may positively serve childhood development (San-Juan-Ferrer & Hípola, 2020). However, there were no additional empirical studies other than those reviewed above.

Evidence in Music

The literature on music and emotion abilities is more robust than other art forms, yet results are still mixed. From the evidence to date, it is unclear what parameters facilitate connections between childhood music training and emotion ability advancement and the direction of the connection. Studies examining EI suggest that relations between music engagement and emotion abilities may be better characterized as a relationship between music engagement and general intelligence. This suggests instead of music being the catalyst of change in ability, children with superior cognitive capacity are drawn to music participation, leading to superior emotion abilities. Thus, observed associations between music participation and emotion abilities might be mediated by preexisting general intelligence differences, although evidence for preexisting differences is mixed (Habibi et al., 2014; Winsler et al., 2020).

There is enough research in music that several systematic reviews have been published. One examined effects of music on emotional, educational, and prosocial skills in 3- to 12-year-olds and concluded that music participation positively impacts emotion perception, assessment, expression, and regulation (Blasco-Magraner et al., 2021). Other studies have found that 4- and 5-year-olds who received rhythm and movement classes demonstrated superior emotion regulation than control group children (Williams & Berthelsen, 2019). However, this study may be better characterized as a dance intervention because it consisted of coordinated rhythmic movement activities. Another intervention study examined emotion comprehension abilities of 4- and 5-year-olds after participating in 40 minutes of music once a week for 12 weeks. Both age groups increased their comprehension of emotions on the Test of Emotion Comprehension (TEC) (Boucher et al., 2021).

For theory of mind, 6- and 7-year-olds who self-enrolled into afterschool swimming, soccer, music, or control programs showed no group differences on ToM (Reading the Mind in the Eyes task) at baseline or after 3 years of programming (Ilari et al., 2018). In another study, 7- and 8-year-olds with at least 8 months of music training performed better on the TEC and demonstrated higher Wechsler Abbreviated Scale of Intelligence scores than non-musically trained children, even after controlling for demographic variables such as family income (Schellenberg & Mankarious, 2012). Interestingly, differences in TEC scores did not remain when intelligence scores were held constant, suggesting cognitively advanced children are drawn to music rather than music affecting emotion abilities (Schellenberg & Mankarious, 2012). Alternatively, this could suggest that parents of cognitively advanced children choose to enroll them in music, or that music is part of a general "enrichment" strategy that parents use for their children.

Studies with adults have compared emotion abilities of individuals with longitudinal childhood music participation to those without music participation to retrospectively reveal effects of childhood music engagement. No differences were found between college-age adults with at least 6 years of music education (most beginning in childhood) and those without music training on auditory emotion recognition tasks with voice or music stimuli (Mualem & Lavidor, 2015). Another study showed higher Kaufman Brief Intelligence Test (IQ) scores for musically trained individuals than untrained individuals, but these differences did not extend to the Mayer-Salovey-Caruso Emotional Intelligence Test (EI) (Schellenberg, 2011). These studies do not support longitudinal childhood music participation necessarily impacting emotion perception or EI.

One randomized controlled trial studied children's music participation and found no connection to emotion abilities. Rabinowitch et al. (2013) showed elementary schoolers assigned to a music group had greater gains between pre- and post-test on empathy, using the Index of Empathy and a novel task, than a games group or no intervention group. However, no group differences were found for cognitive empathy (AToM) using the Matched Faces measure (Rabinowitch et al., 2013).

Conversely, some brain-imaging studies indicate associations between childhood music and increased empathy. Building on behavioral research, Wu and Lu (2021) emphasized neuroscience research connecting childhood music training and empathy in a systematic review. Prior to music training, children's brain structures showed no differences between music and non-music groups. After music training, compared to non-music children, musically trained children's brains show structural differences in brain regions connected to empathy (Habibi et al., 2018; Wu & Lu, 2021). Taken together, it is hard to see an emergent picture with simple causal associations. More likely, unmeasured latent mediating and moderating factors affect the association between music engagement and empathy.

Turning to more global indices of emotion abilities, the EI of 7- to 12-year-olds was compared in an intervention group enrolled in two music classes (one general music and one music performance class) and a control group enrolled in only the general music class. EI was measured by the Emotional Intelligence Scale, a self-report scale validated for use with children. The music group had greater increases in EI than the control group for the scale's emotion perception subsection. But with all subsections included, there were no differences between groups (Kim & Kim, 2018).

Evidence in Multimodal Art

While art forms individually are hypothesized as connected to emotion abilities, researchers also study combinations, or multimodal art, where art forms are grouped or experienced simultaneously. These can include immersive art such as a dance piece that includes visual arts, or theatre and music together. Though limited, studies on multimodal art participation present promising results for positively impacting childhood emotion ability development. For example, qualitative teacher interviews and quantitatively coded classroom observations revealed that social-emotional skills were cultivated though a combination of storytelling, visual arts, and drama for 9- and 10-year-olds (Tsortanidou et al., 2020). In another study, 6- to 9-year-olds participated an arts program where artists worked with academic teachers to conduct sessions on dance, music, theatre, visual arts, and literary and digital arts (Andersen et al., 2019) across multiple days. Immediately after and 6 months after intervention, art group children had greater improvement in emotion and behavior regulation, measured with the Behavior Rating Inventory of Executive Function, than control group children who did not receive the multiple days of intervention (Andersen et al., 2019). Another integrated arts program compared preschoolers' Emotion Regulation Checklist scores before and after music, dance, and visual arts components, compared to a control group. The arts group demonstrated emotion regulation improvements from pre- to post- test, compared to control group preschoolers (Brown & Sax, 2013).

Remaining Questions and Limitations

The state of the evidence for developing emotion abilities in and through the arts should be considered with its limitations in mind to provide context for much of the extant research and implications for practice and developing theory. First, many studies are quasi-experimental or correlational by design, meaning individuals self-select into arts participation. Improved emotion abilities observed in these studies may be present because individuals who are better at emotional skills are attracted to the arts, and that art engagement itself is not responsible for augmented emotion abilities. The arts would then be theorized as a conduit to expression and practice of heightened emotion abilities already present.

Second, increased emotion ability development could be mediated by a third variable. For example, Blasco-Magraner et al. (2021) call attention to a meta-analysis that found effects of music on children's emotion ability were mediated by IQ; others have posited that emotion ability gains are rooted in executive function (EF) gains and should not be considered separate (Riggs et al., 2006). Additional variables that could mediate emotion ability gains include vocabulary, language knowledge (Bosacki & Moore, 2004; Nook et al., 2017), general intelligence (Izmaylova et al., 2021), motivation, teacher encouragement, mindset, self-concept, creativity, transportation, flow, topic of the art, physical engagement, and materials used. Findings could also be mediated by another variable yet to be identified in this research area. When studies show emotion abilities fostered through the arts, the abilities examined may be but one small snippet of developmental cascades that involve or follow from other non-emotion-related abilities. Researchers have also noted associations between arts and social-emotional abilities may occur because arts training often takes place within social-emotional contexts (Schellenberg & Mankarious, 2012). With the state of the research to date, we must caution against drawing causal conclusions about relationships between childhood arts participation and emotion development.

There is also little research on underlying processes in arts participation that are driving forces of observed emotion ability change. The arts are multifaceted and can involve dynamic and variable components (e.g., collaboration, individual self-reflection, responding to criticism, interdisciplinary settings; Winner et al., 2007). Additionally, arts interventions are multifaceted, and vary widely. It could be that some arts interventions are more focused on connecting the art form to emotion abilities (e.g., perceiving emotions and portraying emotions with art), and others are more focused on specific technical training components of the art form (e.g., reading music or paintbrush-stroke technique). Which components of the artistic process or of the art intervention push emotion ability development forward? This is a large opening for future research in this area, and one that will depend on engaging with artists and arts educators themselves.

In addition to unknown underlying causal artistic mechanisms for emotion development, emotion development discussions even outside of arts contexts are riddled with inconsistencies and ongoing debates. There is not a clear consensus in the emotion literature itself about developmental cascades of distinct emotion abilities and definitions of operationalized emotion abilities, or if they should be considered distinct processes (Hoemann et al., 2020; Sarmento-Henrique et al., 2020). On its own, the emotion development field has limitations due to measurement inconsistencies, definition overlaps, lab-setting versus real-world application differences, and so forth, adding to the complexity of examining emotion development in and through the arts.

There are also measurement and study design limitations. We considered each art form separately, which allowed for delineation between emotion ability measures used within empirical research on each art form. While there are some emotion ability measures consistently used in the research across different art forms, such as the Reading the Mind in the Eyes test (e.g., Illari et al., 2018 for music; Greene et al., 2015 for theatre), measurement type is often siloed within the art form. For example, studies of music on emotion perception use auditory/vocal emotion perception measures (i.e., speech prosody), while studies of acting use visual facial emotion perception measures (i.e., facial expression). Measures used typically approximate skills within the art form at hand, making it difficult to generalize ties between art form and emotion abilities. This relates to the issue of abilities gained through the arts potentially not transferring to domains outside of the arts (Goldstein et al., 2017).

Another generalizability issue centers on the lack of longitudinal research. Few studies have examined correlations longitudinally between emotion development and childhood arts participation, and in intervention studies, few have conducted follow-up tests after initial post-test. This limits generalizing emotion ability outcomes past immediate changes – we cannot suggest lasting impacts without more longitudinal studies and intervention studies with follow-up tests.

While we focused on childhood, a time of emotion ability growth, it is unclear which age(s) may reap the most benefit from arts engagement. Children in early and middle childhood are particularly plastic in their emotion ability development (Sommerville & Decety, 2017), but empirical arts research has not been able to suggest whether or not one age group may experience more emotion ability gain from the arts over another. This leaves open fruitful future research directions: to narrow which developmental group(s) may be most susceptible to developing emotion abilities through the arts. Additionally, future research could parse which ages are best suited to benefit from which art forms and which emotion abilities. For example, does theatre participation better encourage empathy abilities in elementary school over high school children? Is emotion perception better fostered through arts engagement in early childhood or adolescence?

Lastly, when interpreting the empirical evidence, we must bear in mind that the research is most robust for visual arts and music; theatre and dance are underrepresented in comparison. Therefore, we caution against holistic claims of "the arts" bettering development of emotion abilities until all art forms are adequately represented in scholarly work.

Future Directions: How Can We Move Forward?

The past 10 years of research in this field have extended the long history of connections between the arts and emotion abilities, yet the field is hindered because scholars across art domains and emotion ability domains are still siloed from one another. The same questions are continuing to be asked across art forms, but they are examined in disparate ways with different methodologies. This means we cannot, as a field of art and emotion development scholars, make broad claims about how "art positively affects emotion development" unless the ways in which we study these phenomena are cohesive and integrated. It is time to stop going in circles – studying the same set of questions with no common denominator – rendering us unable to claim much of anything general. We must unify and name the field in order to move forward. For anyone who studies the arts and emotion development, we encourage the forging of interdisciplinary teams across the arts and academic topics.

Conclusion

In this chapter, we highlighted evidence that connects participation in various art forms with development of various emotion abilities in childhood. While the literature covered is not exhaustive, it suggests visual arts, music, theatre, and dance may provide unique platforms for emotional skill development. Importantly, these conclusions must be taken with the limitation that they are provisional for typical development; when atypical developmental trajectories are considered, conclusions may look different. Future research is needed both to identify which specific processes within art forms allow for emotional development and to compare efficacy between art forms. Finally, a renewed focus on interdisciplinary work that unifies research agendas across art and emotion ability domains will allow researchers in psychology and in the arts to explore new connections in these topics, discover new truths, and develop new ways to understand opportunities for intervention.

References

Alter-Muri, S. B. (2017). Art education and art therapy strategies for Autism Spectrum disorder students. *Art Education, 70*(5), 20–25. https://doi.org/10.1080/00043125.2017.1335536

Altschuler, M., Sideridis, G., Kala, S., et al. (2018). Measuring individual differences in cognitive, affective, and spontaneous theory of mind among school-aged children with Autism Spectrum disorder. *Journal of Autism and Developmental Disorders, 48*(11), 3945–3957. https://doi.org/10.1007/s10803-018-3663-1

Andersen, P. N., Klausen, M. E., & Skogli, E. W. (2019). Art of learning – an art-based intervention aimed at improving children's executive functions. *Frontiers in Psychology, 10*, 1769. https://doi.org/10.3389/fpsyg.2019.01769

Apperly, I. A. (2008). Beyond Simulation–Theory and Theory–Theory: Why social cognitive neuroscience should use its own concepts to study "theory of mind." *Cognition, 107*(1), 266–283. https://doi.org/10.1016/j.cognition.2007.07.019

Barwell, I. (1986). How does art express emotion? *The Journal of Aesthetics and Art Criticism, 45*(2), 175–181. https://doi.org/10.2307/430558

Bentwich, M. E., & Gilbey, P. (2017). More than visual literacy: Art and the enhancement of tolerance for ambiguity and empathy. *BMC Medical Education, 17*(1), 200. https://doi.org/10.1186/s12909-017-1028-7

Blasco-Magraner, J. S., Bernabe-Valero, G., Marín-Liébana, P., & Moret-Tatay, C. (2021). Effects of the educational use of music on 3- to 12-year-old children's emotional development: A systematic review. *International Journal of Environmental Research and Public Health, 18*(7), 3668. https://doi.org/10.3390/ijerph18073668

Bosacki, S. L., & Moore, C. (2004). Preschoolers' understanding of simple and complex emotions: Links with gender and language. *Sex Roles, 50*(9), 659–675. https://doi.org/10.1023/B:SERS.0000027568.26966.27

Boucher, H., Gaudette-Leblanc, A., Raymond, J., & Peters, V. (2021). Musical learning as a contributing factor in the development of socio-emotional competence in children aged 4 and 5: An exploratory study in a naturalistic context. *Early Child Development and Care, 191*(12), 1922–1938. https://doi.org/10.1080/03004430.2020.1862819

Bradshaw, R. D. (2016). Art integration fosters empathy in the middle school classroom. *The Clearing House: A Journal of Educational Strategies, Issues and Ideas, 89*(4–5), 109–117. https://doi.org/10.1080/00098655.2016.1170441

Bridges, L. J., Denham, S. A., & Ganiban, J. M. (2004). Definitional issues in emotion regulation research. *Child Development, 75*(2), 340–345. https://doi.org/10.1111/j.1467-8624.2004.00675.x

Brown, E. D., & Sax, K. L. (2013). Arts enrichment and preschool emotions for low-income children at risk. *Early Childhood Research Quarterly, 28*(2), 337–346. https://doi.org/10.1016/j.ecresq.2012.08.002

Cox, C. L., Uddin, L. Q., Di Martino, A., et al. (2012). The balance between feeling and knowing: Affective and cognitive empathy are reflected in the brain's intrinsic functional dynamics. *Social Cognitive and Affective Neuroscience, 7*(6), 727–737. https://doi.org/10.1093/scan/nsr051

Decety, J., & Moriguchi, Y. (2007). The empathic brain and its dysfunction in psychiatric populations: Implications for intervention across different clinical conditions. *BioPsychoSocial Medicine, 1*(1), 22. https://doi.org/10.1186/1751-0759-1-22

Dishion, T. J., & Tipsord, J. M. (2011). Peer contagion in child and adolescent social and emotional development. *Annual Review of Psychology, 62*(1), 189–214. https://doi.org/10.1146/annurev.psych.093008.100412

Drake, J. E. (2021). How drawing to distract improves mood in children. *Frontiers in Psychology, 12*, 78. https://doi.org/10.3389/fpsyg.2021.622927

Drake, J. E., & Winner, E. (2013). How children use drawing to regulate their emotions. *Cognition & Emotion, 27*(3), 512–520. https://doi.org/10.1080/02699931.2012.720567

Dunn, J., Brown, J., Slomkowski, C., Tesla, C., & Youngblade, L. (1991). Young children's understanding of other people's feelings and beliefs: Individual differences and their antecedents. *Child Development, 62*(6), 1352–1366.

Durlak, J. A. (2015). *Handbook of Social and Emotional Learning: Research and Practice*. Guilford Press.

Duval, C., Piolino, P., Bejanin, A., Eustache, F., & Desgranges, B. (2011). Age effects on different components of theory of mind. *Consciousness and Cognition, 20*(3), 627–642. https://doi.org/10.1016/j.concog.2010.10.025

Dvash, J., & Shamay-Tsoory, S. G. (2014). Theory of mind and empathy as multidimensional constructs: Neurological foundations. *Topics in Language Disorders, 34*(4), 282–295. https://doi.org/10.1097/TLD.0000000000000040

Ebert, M., Hoffmann, J. D., Ivcevic, Z., Phan, C., & Brackett, M. A. (2015a). Creativity, emotion, and art: development and initial evaluation of a workshop for professional adults. *International Journal of Creativity and Problem Solving, 25*(2), 47–59.

Ebert, M., Hoffmann, J. D., Ivcevic, Z., Phan, C., & Brackett, M. A. (2015b). Teaching emotion and creativity skills through art: A workshop for children. *International Journal of Creativity and Problem Solving, 25*(2), 25–35.

Fischer, A. H., & Manstead, A. S. R. (2016). Social functions of emotion and emotion regulation. In L. Feldman Barrett, M. Lewis, & J. M. Haviland-Jones (Eds.), *Handbook of Emotions* (4th ed., pp. 424–438). Guilford Press.

Gallant, C. M. M., Lavis, L., & Mahy, C. E. V. (2020). Developing an understanding of others' emotional states: Relations among affective theory of mind and empathy measures in early childhood. *British Journal of Developmental Psychology, 38*(2), 151–166. https://doi.org/10.1111/bjdp.12322

Gil, K., Rhim, J., Ha, T., Doh, Y. Y., & Woo, W. (2014). AR Petite Theater: Augmented reality storybook for supporting children's empathy behavior. *2014 IEEE International Symposium on Mixed and Augmented Reality – Media, Art, Social Science, Humanities and Design (ISMAR-MASH'D)*, 13–20. https://doi.org/10.1109/ISMAR-AMH.2014.6935433

Goldstein, T. R., & Lerner, M. D. (2018). Dramatic pretend play games uniquely improve emotional control in young children. *Developmental Science, 21*(4), e12603. https://doi.org/10.1111/desc.12603

Goldstein, T. R., Lerner, M. D., & Winner, E. (2017). The arts as a venue for developmental science: Realizing a latent opportunity. *Child Development, 88*(5), 1505–1512. https://doi.org/10.1111/cdev.12884

Goldstein, T. R., Tamir, M., & Winner, E. (2013). Expressive suppression and acting classes. *Psychology of Aesthetics, Creativity, and the Arts, 7*(2), 191–196. https://doi.org/10.1037/a0030209

Goldstein, T. R., & Winner, E. (2011). Engagement in role play, pretense, and acting classes predict advanced theory of mind skill in middle childhood. *Imagination, Cognition and Personality, 30*(3), 249–258. https://doi.org/10.2190/IC.30.3.c

Greene, J. P., Hitt, C., Kraybill, A., & Bogulski, C. A. (2015). Learning from live theater. *Education Next, 15*(1), 54–61.

Gross, J. J. (2013). Emotion regulation: Taking stock and moving forward. *Emotion, 13*(3), 359–365. https://doi.org/10.1037/a0032135

Habibi, A., Damasio, A., Ilari, B., et al. (2018). Childhood music training induces change in micro and macroscopic brain structure: Results from a longitudinal study. *Cerebral Cortex, 28*(12), 4336–4347. https://doi.org/10.1093/cercor/bhx286

Habibi, A., Ilari, B., Crimi, K., et al. (2014). An equal start: Absence of group differences in cognitive, social, and neural measures prior to music or sports training in children. *Frontiers in Human Neuroscience*, *8*, 690. https://doi.org/10.3389/fnhum.2014.00690

Haq, S., & Jackson, P. J. B. (2011). Multimodal emotion recognition. In W. Wang (Ed.), *Machine Audition: Principles, Algorithms and Systems* (pp. 398–423). IGI Global. https://doi.org/10.4018/978-1-61520-919-4.ch017

Hjort, M., & Laver, S. (1997). *Emotion and the Arts*. Oxford University Press.

Hoemann, K., Wu, R., LoBue, V., Oakes, L. M., Xu, F., & Barrett, L. F. (2020). Developing an understanding of emotion categories: Lessons from objects. *Trends in Cognitive Sciences*, *24*(1), 39–51. https://doi.org/10.1016/j.tics.2019.10.010

Hoffmann, J. D., Ivcevic, Z., & Maliakkal, N. (2021). Emotions, creativity, and the arts: Evaluating a course for children. *Empirical Studies of the Arts*, *39*(2), 123–148. https://doi.org/10.1177/0276237420907864

Holochwost, S. J., Goldstein, T. R., & Wolf, D. P. (2021). Delineating the benefits of arts education for children's socioemotional development. *Frontiers in Psychology*, *12*, 1435. https://doi.org/10.3389/fpsyg.2021.624712

Humphrey, N., Curran, A., Morris, E., Farrell, P., & Woods, K. (2007). Emotional intelligence and education: A critical review. *Educational Psychology*, *27*(2), 235–254. https://doi.org/10.1080/01443410601066735

Huston, A. C., & Ripke, M. N. (2006). Experiences in middle childhood and children's development: A summary and integration of research. In *Developmental Contexts in Middle Childhood: Bridges to Adolescence and Adulthood* (pp. 409–434). Cambridge University Press. https://doi.org/10.1017/CBO9780511499760.021

Hutzel, K., Russell, R., & Gross, J. (2010). Eighth-graders as role models: A service-learning art collaboration for social and emotional learning. *Art Education*, *63*(4), 12–18. https://doi.org/10.1080/00043125.2010.11519074

Ilari, B., Fesjian, C., & Habibi, A. (2018). Entrainment, theory of mind, and prosociality in child musicians. *Music & Science*, *1*, 2059204317753153. https://doi.org/10.1177/2059204317753153

Izmaylova, E. I., Kuzmishina, T. L., Gorelkina, M. A., Korneva, E. N., & Lukinova, A. V. (2021). The relationship between general and emotional intelligence in pre-school children. *SHS Web of Conferences*, *117*, 02001. https://doi.org/10.1051/shsconf/202111702001

Jones, S. M., Zaslow, M., Darling-Churchill, K. E., & Halle, T. G. (2016). Assessing early childhood social and emotional development: Key conceptual and measurement issues. *Journal of Applied Developmental Psychology*, *45*, 42–48. https://doi.org/10.1016/j.appdev.2016.02.008

Joseph, D. L., & Newman, D. A. (2010). Emotional intelligence: An integrative meta-analysis and cascading model. *Journal of Applied Psychology*, *95*(1), 54–78. https://doi.org/10.1037/a0017286

Kastner, L., Umbach, N., Jusyte, A., et al. (2021). Designing visual-arts education programs for transfer effects: Development and experimental evaluation of (digital) drawing courses in the art museum designed to promote adolescents' socio-emotional skills. *Frontiers in Psychology*, *11*, 603984. https://doi.org/10.3389/fpsyg.2020.603984

Kim, H.-S., & Kim, H.-S. (2018). Effect of a musical instrument performance program on emotional intelligence, anxiety, and aggression in Korean elementary school children. *Psychology of Music*, *46*(3), 440–453. https://doi.org/10.1177/0305735617729028

Laird, L. (2015). Empathy in the classroom: Can music bring us more in tune with one another? *Music Educators Journal*, *101*(4), 56–61. https://doi.org/10.1177/0027432115572230

Lee, G. T., Chou, W.-C., & Feng, H. (2017). Social engagements through art activities for two children with Autism Spectrum disorders. *International Journal of Education Through Art*, *13*(2), 217–233. https://doi.org/10.1386/eta.13.2.217_1

LoBue, V., Pérez-Edgar, K., & Buss, K. A. (Eds.). (2019). *Handbook of Emotional Development*. Springer International. https://doi.org/10.1007/978-3-030-17332-6

Mages, W. K. (2018). Does theatre-in-education promote early childhood development? The effect of drama on language, perspective-taking, and imagination. *Early Childhood Research Quarterly*, *45*, 224–237. https://doi.org/10.1016/j.ecresq.2017.12.006

Maibom, H. L. (2017). Affective empathy. In H. Maibom (Ed.), *The Routledge Handbook of Philosophy of Empathy* (pp. 22–31). Routledge. https://doi.org/10.4324/9781315282015

Maierna, M. S., & Camodeca, M. (2021). Theatrical activities in primary school: Effects on children's emotion regulation and bullying. *International Journal of Bullying Prevention*, *3*(1), 13–23. https://doi.org/10.1007/s42380-019-00057-z

Mayer, J. D., Caruso, D. R., & Salovey, P. (2016). The Ability Model of Emotional Intelligence: Principles and updates. *Emotion Review*, *8*(4), 290–300. https://doi.org/10.1177/1754073916639667

Mayer, J. D., Perkins, D. M., Caruso, D. R., & Salovey, P. (2001). Emotional intelligence and giftedness. *Roeper Review*, *23*(3), 131–137. https://doi.org/10.1080/02783190109554084

Mayer, J. D., Roberts, R. D., & Barsade, S. G. (2008). Human abilities: Emotional intelligence. *Annual Review of Psychology*, *59*(1), 507–536. https://doi.org/10.1146/annurev.psych.59.103006.093646

Melcher, D., & Bacci, F. (2013). Perception of emotion in abstract artworks: A multidisciplinary approach. In S. Finger, D. W. Zaidel, F. Boller, & J. Bogousslavsky (Eds.), *Progress in Brain Research* (vol. 204, pp. 191–216). Elsevier. https://doi.org/10.1016/B978-0-444-63287-6.00010-5

Morizio, L. J., Cook, A. L., Troeger, R., & Whitehouse, A. (2021). Creating compassion: Using art for empathy learning with urban youth. *Contemporary School Psychology*. Advance online publication https://doi.org/10.1007/s40688-020-00346-1

Morris, J. A., Urbanski, J., & Fuller, J. (2005). Using poetry and the visual arts to develop emotional intelligence. *Journal of Management Education*, *29*(6), 888–904. https://doi.org/10.1177/1052562905277313

Mualem, O., & Lavidor, M. (2015). Music education intervention improves vocal emotion recognition. *International Journal of Music Education*, *33*(4), 413–425. https://doi.org/10.1177/0255761415584292

Nook, E. C., Sasse, S. F., Lambert, H. K., McLaughlin, K. A., & Somerville, L. H. (2017). Increasing verbal knowledge mediates development of multidimensional emotion representations. *Nature Human Behaviour*, *1*(12), 881–889. https://doi.org/10.1038/s41562-017-0238-7

O'Neil, J. (1996). On emotional intelligence: A conversation with Daniel Goleman. *Educational Leadership*, *54*(1), 6–11.

Payton, J. W., Wardlaw, D. M., Graczyk, P. A., et al. (2000). Social and emotional learning: A framework for promoting mental health and reducing risk behavior in children and youth. *Journal of School Health*, *70*(5), 179–185. https://doi.org/10.1111/j.1746-1561.2000.tb06468.x

Pereira, N. S., & Marques-Pinto, A. (2017). Including educational dance in an after-school socio-emotional learning program significantly improves pupils' self-management and relationship skills? A quasi experimental study. *The Arts in Psychotherapy*, *53*, 36–43. https://doi.org/10.1016/j.aip.2017.01.004

Petrides, K. V., & Furnham, A. (2000). On the dimensional structure of emotional intelligence. *Personality and Individual Differences*, *29*(2), 313–320. https://doi.org/10.1016/S0191-8869(99)00195-6

Petrides, K. V., & Furnham, A. (2001). Trait emotional intelligence: Psychometric investigation with reference to established trait taxonomies. *European Journal of Personality*, *15*(6), 425–448. https://doi.org/10.1002/per.416

Petrides, K. V., Niven, L., & Mouskounti, T. (2006). The trait emotional intelligence of ballet dancers and musicians. *Psicothema*, *18*, Suppl, 101–107.

Pons, F., Harris, P. L., & de Rosnay, M. (2004). Emotion comprehension between 3 and 11 years: Developmental periods and hierarchical organization. *European Journal of Developmental Psychology*, *1*(2), 127–152. https://doi.org/10.1080/17405620344000022

Pool, L. D., & Qualter, P. (2018). *An Introduction to Emotional Intelligence*. John Wiley & Sons.

Quaglia, R., Longobardi, C., Iotti, N. O., & Prino, L. E. (2015). A new theory on children's drawings: Analyzing the role of emotion and movement in graphical development. *Infant Behavior and Development*, *39*, 81–91. https://doi.org/10.1016/j.infbeh.2015.02.009

Rabinowitch, T.-C., Cross, I., & Burnard, P. (2013). Long-term musical group interaction has a positive influence on empathy in children. *Psychology of Music*, *41*(4), 484–498. https://doi.org/10.1177/0305735612440609

Riggs, N. R., Jahromi, L. B., Razza, R. P., Dillworth-Bart, J. E., & Mueller, U. (2006). Executive function and the promotion of social–emotional competence. *Journal of Applied Developmental Psychology*, *27*(4), 300–309. https://doi.org/10.1016/j.appdev.2006.04.002

Saarni, C., Campos, J. J., Camras, L. A., & Witherington, D. (2006). Emotional development: Action, communication, and understanding. In N. Eisenberg (Ed.), *Handbook of Child Psychology*, vol. 3, *Social, Emotional, and Personality Development* (6th ed., pp. 226–299). John Wiley & Sons.

San-Juan-Ferrer, B., & Hípola, P. (2020). Emotional intelligence and dance: A systematic review. *Research in Dance Education*, *21*(1), 57–81. https://doi.org/10.1080/14647893.2019.1708890

Sarmento-Henrique, R., Quintanilla, L., Lucas-Molina, B., Recio, P., & Giménez-Dasí, M. (2020). The longitudinal interplay of emotion understanding, theory of mind, and language in the preschool years. *International Journal of Behavioral Development*, *44*(3), 236–245. https://doi.org/10.1177/0165025419866907

Schellenberg, E. (2011). Music lessons, emotional intelligence, and IQ. *Music Perception*, *29*(2), 185–194. https://doi.org/10.1525/mp.2011.29.2.185

Schellenberg, E. G., & Mankarious, M. (2012). Music training and emotion comprehension in childhood. *Emotion*, *12*(5), 887–891. https://doi.org/10.1037/a0027971

Schellenberg, E. G., & von Scheve, C. (2012). Emotional cues in American popular music: Five decades of the Top 40. *Psychology of Aesthetics, Creativity, and the Arts*, *6*(3), 196–203. https://doi.org/10.1037/a0028024

Schmidt, I., Rutanen, T., Luciani, R. S., & Jola, C. (2021). Feeling for the other with ease: prospective actors show high levels of emotion recognition and report above average empathic concern, but do not experience strong distress. *Frontiers in Psychology*, *12*, 1979. https://doi.org/10.3389/fpsyg.2021.543846

Shakoor, S., Mankee-Williams, A., Otis, M., & Bhui, K. (2021). Creative arts and digital interventions: A discussion for prevention and recovery from mental health consequences of Adverse Childhood Experiences (ACEs). PsyArXiv. https://doi.org/10.31234/osf.io/gz3q9

Shamay-Tsoory, S. G., & Aharon-Peretz, J. (2007). Dissociable prefrontal networks for cognitive and affective theory of mind: A lesion study. *Neuropsychologia*, *45*(13), 3054–3067. https://doi.org/10.1016/j.neuropsychologia.2007.05.021

Simonds, J., Kieras, J. E., Rueda, M. R., & Rothbart, M. K. (2007). Effortful control, executive attention, and emotional regulation in 7–10-year-old children. *Cognitive Development*, *22*(4), 474–488. https://doi.org/10.1016/j.cogdev.2007.08.009

Sommerville, J. A., & Decety, J. (Eds.). (2017). *Social Cognition: Development across the Life Span*. Routledge, Taylor & Francis Group.

Stack, D. M., Serbin, L. A., Enns, L. N., Ruttle, P. L., & Barrieau, L. (2010). Parental effects on children's emotional development over time and across generations. *Infants & Young Children*, *23*(1), 52–69. https://doi.org/10.1097/IYC.0b013e3181c97606

Sweeny, T. D., Suzuki, S., Grabowecky, M., & Paller, K. A. (2013). Detecting and categorizing fleeting emotions in faces. *Emotion (Washington, D.C.)*, *13*(1), 76–91. https://doi.org/10.1037/a0029193

Tsortanidou, X., Daradoumis, T., & Barberá, E. (2020). Developing social-emotional skills through imaginative teaching methods in elementary education. *Early Child Development and Care*. Advance online publication. https://doi.org/10.1080/03004430.2020.1854241

Van Meel, J., Verburgh, H., & De Meijer, M. (1993). Children's interpretations of dance expressions. *Empirical Studies of the Arts*, *11*(2), 117–133. https://doi.org/10.2190/V69N-VB0T-A9Q3-TJ04

von Rossberg-Gempton, I. E., Dickinson, J., & Poole, G. (1999). Creative dance: Potentiality for enhancing social functioning in frail seniors and young children. *The Arts in Psychotherapy*, *26*(5), 313–327. https://doi.org/10.1016/S0197-4556(99)00036-2

Watson, A., Greene, J., Holmes Erickson, H., & Beck, M. I. (2019). Altered attitudes and actions: Social-emotional effects of multiple arts field trips (SSRN Scholarly Paper ID 3340163). Social Science Research Network. https://doi.org/10.2139/ssrn.3340163

Wellman, H. M., Cross, D., & Watson, J. (2001). Meta-analysis of theory-of-mind development: The truth about false belief. *Child Development*, *72*(3), 655–684. https://doi.org/10.1111/1467-8624.00304

Wexler, A. (2014). Reaching higher? The impact of the common core state standards on the visual arts, poverty, and disabilities. *Arts Education Policy Review, 115*(2), 52–61. https://doi.org/10.1080/10632913.2014.883897

Wikström, B.-M. (2003). A picture of a work of art as an empathy teaching strategy in nurse education complementary to theoretical knowledge. *Journal of Professional Nursing, 19*(1), 49–54. https://doi.org/10.1053/jpnu.2003.5

Williams, K. E., & Berthelsen, D. (2019). Implementation of a rhythm and movement intervention to support self-regulation skills of preschool-aged children in disadvantaged communities. *Psychology of Music, 47*(6), 800–820. https://doi.org/10.1177/0305735619861433

Winner, E., Goldstein, T. R., & Vincent-Lancrin, S. (2013). *Art for Art's Sake? The Impact of Arts Education*. OECD. https://doi.org/10.1787/9789264180789-en

Winner, E., & Hetland, L. (2000). The arts in education: Evaluating the evidence for a causal link. *Journal of Aesthetic Education, 34*(3/4), 3–10.

Winner, E., Hetland, L., Veenema, S., & Sheridan, K. (2007). *Studio Thinking: The Real Benefits of Visual Arts Education*. Teachers College Press.

Winsler, A., Gara, T. V., Alegrado, A., Castro, S., & Tavassolie, T. (2020). Selection into, and academic benefits from, arts-related courses in middle school among low-income, ethnically diverse youth. *Psychology of Aesthetics, Creativity, and the Arts, 14*(4), 415–432. https://doi.org/10.1037/aca0000222

Wu, X., & Lu, X. (2021). Musical training in the development of empathy and prosocial behaviors. *Frontiers in Psychology, 12*, 661769. https://doi.org/10.3389/fpsyg.2021.661769

Zakaria, M. Z., Yunus, F., & Mohamed, S. (2021). Drawing activities enhance pre-schoolers socio emotional development. *Southeast Asia Early Childhood Journal, 10*(1), 18–27. https://doi.org/10.37134/saecj.vol10.1.2.2021

Zeidner, M., Matthews, G., Roberts, R. D., & MacCann, C. (2003). Development of emotional intelligence: Towards a multi-level investment model. *Human Development, 46*(2–3), 69–96. https://doi.org/10.1159/000068580

PART V

Emotions and Creativity at School and Work

24 Anxiety, Fear of Failure, and Creativity

Ross C. Anderson

> The fear of failure kills creativity and intelligence. The only thing it produces is conformity.
>
> –Anup Kochhar, from *The Failure Project*

Anup Kochhar asserts in his book, *The Failure Project*, that "the fear of failure is not just the greatest fear of man, it is *the* fear of man. All other fears are avatars of the fear of failure" (Kochhar, 2016, p. 10). So, where does fear of failure, and the anxiety it may produce, fit into the creative process? Are fear and anxiety barriers we should try to remove to become more creative? Are they catalysts for creative risk-taking and the enhanced alertness that help us recognize an opportunity for innovation, invention, and growth? Research provides some new understanding about how fear of failure and anxiety fit into the creative process, and ways to help us manage, and even leverage, these subjective experiences to benefit ourselves and others.

Creativity has been defined with a focus on the originality and effectiveness of an idea, solution, or product (Runco & Jaeger, 2012) as a way to enhance clarity in research and measurement. Creativity has also been defined as the "interaction among aptitude, process, and environment" that results in an individual or group's production of something novel and useful (Plucker et al., 2004, p. 90). A plethora of theories exists to try to understand, study, and enhance the creative potential of individuals or groups (see Kozbelt et al., 2010). These definitions and theories, often cited in the literature, largely exclude attention to the underlying affective aspect of creative experience. At the heart of this affective experience resides fundamental relationships between uncertainty, anxiety, fear of failure, and the associated risk-taking necessary to produce something creative. Even if only mild in intensity, anxiety may arise at different stages of the creative process, especially when there will be an audience responding to the creative output or when someone is reaching their limits of knowledge and skill.

Ross Anderson, PhD, is Co-Founder of Creative Engagement Lab, LLC. Correspondence concerning this chapter should be addressed to Ross Anderson, 275 W 27th Ave, Eugene, OR 97405. E-mail: ross@creativeengagementlab.com. This research was supported by a grant from the U.S. Department of Education (U351D140063).

Though largely considered a negative emotion within many contexts, such as education (see math anxiety as an example in Lyons & Beilock, 2012), anxiety plays an inescapable role in creative experience where uncertainty exists. At the heart of creativity is the unknown and the new, the breaking from conventions and conformity, and the challenging of existing norms and ideas. Those essential parts of creativity come with the threat of failure, rejection, embarrassment, exclusion, and nonconformity. However, the experience and intensity of this threat and the resulting anxiety and fear are likely different for each of us. This chapter explores features of creativity and the creative process that relate to the affective states of anxiety and fear of failure with the goal to illustrate the research on how these states can be managed, and even leveraged, to enhance creativity.

Uncertainty Is Essential

To begin understanding how anxiety and fear of failure fit into creativity specifically, it is important to accept that uncertainty is a necessary condition for creativity to occur. Uncertainty describes a state of doubt, of not knowing, and a lack of predictability and control over what to expect (Beghetto, 2019). Uncertainty can be thought of on a spectrum of intensity from the mundane faced in everyday life (e.g., *Do I have enough groceries to make dinner later?*) to profound uncertainties, which feel entirely unknowable (e.g., *Will I still have my job and good health in a year?*). According to Beghetto (2019), between those extremes resides actionable uncertainty where creative opportunities become possible. For instance, when evening arrives and you open your fridge to find miscellaneous random ingredients remaining, that uncertainty opens the door to a creative combination of materials for a unique and, hopefully, delicious meal. External factors, such as needing to prepare a meal for a new significant other, could make the level of threat feel less manageable, blocking the cognitive effort needed to be inventive in the kitchen.

As the antecedent of creative thought and action, sources of uncertainty can be thought of as social, internal, material, and societal-situational ruptures (Beghetto, 2019). To understand those sources, we can place uncertainty in the context of the educational setting in a middle school science classroom (Anderson, Irvin, et al., 2022). Daily, students actively make sense of complex science concepts together with scaffolded instruction, experiencing a state of doubt that should feel like actionable uncertainty on several levels. At the internal level, each student holds some confusion and, potentially, frustration and anxiety, about the meaning of specific concepts they are expected to learn. (*What is the difference between evaporation and condensation?*) At the social level, each student feels some doubt about whether others will put effort toward understanding their creative and potentially discrepant ideas and contributions and whether they may be judged negatively and potentially ridiculed. (*Do you all think evaporation is a shrivelling grape, clouds over the ocean, or the cracked earth in the desert, or all three?*) At the material level, if students are asked to construct a 3D model to illustrate the water cycle, they will feel actionable uncertainty when sitting around a ball of clay, a shoebox, and popsicle sticks. (*Am I creative and skilled enough to make something that looks good? How will I start?*)

These students will need to use their own creative ideas to reshape the materials into a meaningful story. These students may experience uncertainty as societal-situational ruptures when class discussion relates the water cycle to increased drought due to climate change. (*Will there be enough clean water to grow food for everyone in 50 years?*) That level of uncertainty may feel too great to be actionable unless the teacher frames the discussion through the innovative solutions being developed to avert or manage those consequences. Each type of uncertainty fosters creative opportunities, but each can also result in powerful negative emotions, such as fear of failure and anxiety if they do not feel actionable. This range and threshold will likely be determined by both individual and contextual factors. For instance, one student may feel much stronger social pressure to conform than others, potentially due to past trauma, such as bullying by peers or being harshly criticized publicly by a teacher. Or the teacher may not have provided enough low-stakes practice with the materials to make the creative model-building process feel like a manageable risk.

Negative Emotions and Creativity

Generally, on a negative-to-positive spectrum, anxiety and fear of failure can be thought of as negative aspects of any subjective experience. In Brackett's (2019) book, *Permission to Feel*, a classroom tool called the *mood meter* places emotions in four quadrants with low- to high-energy sorting emotions on the Y-axis and low- to high-pleasantness sorting emotions along the X-axis. The mood meter tool places anxiety and fear side by side in the high-energy and low-pleasantness quadrant, meaning they are highly arousing but do not feel very good. That approach to emotions follows the circumplex model (Posner et al., 2005; Russell, 1980), which suggests that the two dimensions of energy and pleasantness account for the core properties of human emotion and can provide important insight on moment-to-moment emotional experience.

In creative experience, those emotions may be accompanied by frustration at dead ends or negative self-beliefs reinforced by critical feedback from others, demotivating a person to take creative risks (Beghetto & Dilley, 2017). There is evidence that positive emotions, such as excitement and enthusiasm, can enhance motivation and engagement in the creative process across different domains, from work to education (Hennessey & Amabile, 1987, 2010). Conversely, there is also evidence that negative emotions, depending on the valence and activation of the emotion, can be an important part of the creative process to enhance alertness (De Dreu et al., 2008). The role of some emotional states, such as anxiety and fear, have a complex relationship with the creative process. On the one hand, they may inhibit creative action by working in opposition to the creative beliefs, mindsets, values, and attitudes that underlie an individual's agency to take creative action. On the other hand, they may stimulate creative thinking and action, enhance alertness and attention, and increase the critical thinking necessary to move novelty into reality.

Agentic Beliefs

If an individual or group does not feel confident in a specific creative task, such as developing a metaphor to represent a scientific process, fear of failure and anxiety could become major barriers to action. New research and theory highlight how adaptive and growth-oriented beliefs and mindsets are key factors that translate creative potential into creative production (e.g., Anderson & Haney, 2021; Karwowski & Beghetto, 2018). Those beliefs and mindsets will depend on a variety of factors, such as personal experiences, and interact with the risks an individual is willing to take. In fact, in a study of more than 800 adults, researchers found that a person's willingness to take intellectual risks (e.g., doing new things or sharing ideas even when unsure) moderated the link between their creative confidence and creative behavior (Beghetto et al., 2021). That finding suggests that the contribution creative confidence makes to actual creative action may depend, in part, on an individual's willingness to take risks.

Though not included in that research, it is easy to imagine that this capacity to take risks could be stymied by anxiety and fear, based on a variety of possible factors. A recent study with high school students found three relevant attitudes toward creativity: anticipating negative social consequences, anxious risk aversion, and valuing creativity. An attitude of anxious risk aversion correlated with avoidance goals in academic performance, and more positive attitudes toward creativity predicted students' motivation to engage in creative behavior and creative challenges at school (Ivcevic & Hoffman, 2021). That research illustrates the important role attitudes can play, especially during adolescence when the need for social acceptance is monumental (Dahl et al., 2018).

Putting the role of risk-taking in context, we can imagine a design student might be confident in their capacity for creative furniture designs based on receiving past recognition and developing several designs into actual furniture. However, the student may be wary of taking a big design risk in their current class because of a harsh critique they received publicly at the last design charrette from visiting faculty. The context of perceived or real social consequences (e.g., public ridicule or being judged harshly by peers) of those risks will likely matter, as well. The dread of repeating this public embarrassment might suppress their typical willingness to try out new ideas, create an anxious risk aversion, and lead to a less creative final product. In this way, anxiety and fear can overpower the confidence necessary for creative risk-taking if a person lacks skills to manage and regulate those emotions or if the social consequences feel too high stakes. These disruptive emotions may also compromise a person's concentration and focus, interrupting their *flow*.

On the flip side, anxiety and fear can also overlap with external motivators to push a group or individual to apply more effort and resourcefulness and take bigger risks (Karwowski & Anderson, 2021). For instance, when inventing something new, students reported that failure was seen by some groups as an opportunity to learn – high and low points in the process – rather than through the lens of finality as a goal unmet or as an unsuccessful outcome (Estabrooks & Couch, 2018). The difference between leaning into that fear and anxiety versus becoming avoidant may come down to using strategies such as self-coaching statements (e.g., *You can do this!*), and stress reduction techniques, such as breath control (Fried & Chapman, 2012). At a mild level, anxiety might be one of the best physiological indicators to detect the uncertainty necessary for a creative risk. In this way, following an *affect-as-information* approach (Clore et al., 2001), anxiety is a signal of uncertainty and hence a creative opportunity. The emotional feeling of anxiety serves as affective feedback guiding judgment, decision making, and information processing. When this attribution is made explicit through cognitive effort, the anxiety may be turned into an opportunity rather than deterrent.

Flow State and Anxiety

Reaching the optimal level of anxiety and fear in creative experience can be viewed through our understanding of *flow state* engagement provided by the late Mihaly Csikszentmihalyi (1997). Csikszentmihalyi proposed that an optimal level of challenge and risk in work should be balanced by the level of skill and competence. This optimal zone allows a person to feel that growth and success are possible to avoid the distracting negative emotions that can accompany risk-taking. When the challenge level is too low in reference to current skill level, a person may become bored and unmotivated. Conversely, when a challenge level is too high, the resulting anxiety and fear of failure may overwhelm their motivation to continue making an effort. Theory and research on flow state have covered a wide array of industries and aspects of motivation and engagement in education to optimize conditions for creative development (Csikszentmihalyi & Rathunde, 1993; Kowal & Fortier, 1999; Shernoff et al., 2003). Researchers found that when high school students in the United States and Finland felt challenged and skilled in science learning (e.g., the main ingredients for a flow state), they also felt more confident, successful, and happy (Schneider et al., 2016).

In one longitudinal study across the middle school grades, latent class groups were identified to represent different trajectories of divergent thinking development across time. Frequency of flow state in learning was included as a predictor of students' assignments to a latent class. Flow predicted students' assignment to classes that remained stable or experienced growth in divergent thinking originality across 6th through 8th grades compared to the largest class showing a steady decline in originality. Conversely, students' academic anxiety was not a statistically significant predictor of assignment to any groups

(Anderson, 2019), which suggested that some anxiety in school did not necessarily detract from creative development in early adolescence. In fact, the correlation between anxiety and flow at the 6th grade ($r = .08$) was small but positive and statistically significant at $p < .05$. When thinking about how anxiety fits into the creative process, flow provides one way to understand how challenge and uncertainty, and the anxiety that results, are inherent in the creative process within a certain range. That range, or *tolerance*, will likely be different for individuals and groups. A related approach to understanding anxiety and fear of failure in the creative process is through the concept of tolerance for ambiguity.

Tolerance for Ambiguity

Tolerance for ambiguity is considered an attitudinal or dispositional trait-like factor determining a person's "tendency to support and perhaps even be attracted to ambiguous situations" (Lubart et al., 2013, p. 45), where information for a problem, task, or situation may be missing or confusing. Research has illustrated how the natural tendency to find closure as quickly as possible to resolve uncertainty may result in inadequate processing and a lack of quality and novel thinking (Zenasni et al., 2008). Lay Epistemic Theory (Kruglanski, 2013) proposes that this need for closure is a trait-like motivational tendency reflecting a desire for fast and firm answers to a question. That theory proposes that both the stable beliefs held by a group, such as political conservatism, and contextual factors, such as time pressure, mental fatigue, group makeup, and boredom, can catalyze the need for closure. Three experimental studies found that the need for closure, manipulated by contextual factors, led to less creative output by groups, and that this negative relationship was mediated by conformity pressure (Chirumbolo et al., 2004). The need for closure and the associated lower tolerance for ambiguity can negatively impact the creative process.

Tolerance for ambiguity might also be thought of as acceptance of multiple meanings. For instance, in the context of visual and performing arts, works are often purposefully ambiguous to create room for personal interpretation and different perspectives. There is some evidence that tolerance for ambiguity is a characteristic that can be developed with practice, and that making sense of artworks and other types of ambiguous subject matter, through a technique such as visual thinking strategies (Yenawine, 2013), may support this development, even in adulthood (Bentwich & Gilbey, 2017). Visual thinking strategies practice the ability to see multiple perspectives and possibilities within a piece of art, potentially tapping into a malleable aspect of tolerating ambiguity that is trainable. Abstract and complex music, choreography, theatre, and other types of contemporary art can be valuable subject matter to cultivate greater tolerance for ambiguity across age groups. Research with elementary school–age students found using visual thinking strategies fostered aspects of critical thinking, important to having a tolerance for ambiguity, such as being open to multiple interpretations (Housen, 2001).

Research has described tolerance for ambiguity from multiple related angles, such as the spectrum from *uncertainty avoidance* to *risk-taking propensity*. Those ideas have been studied from a sociological and cultural perspective to identify how some groups establish institutions and beliefs to avoid the threat of ambiguous situations (Furnham & Marks, 2013). At the individual level, intolerance for uncertainty has been linked to higher levels of anxiety, a higher appraisal and sensitivity to threat, and more negative affect. Greater intolerance is associated with more negative health outcomes. In contrast, higher tolerance for uncertainty has been linked with a greater acceptance of challenge, more positive affect, and greater level of openness (Bardi et al., 2009). Intolerance of uncertainty has even been used as a diagnostic tool for generalized anxiety disorder, highlighting the link between worry and the desire for predictability and paralysis of cognition facing uncertainty (Birrell et al., 2011). Based on this past research, individuals or groups characterized by a tolerance for ambiguity and uncertainty reflect a combination of beliefs, affect, and cognition. It may be helpful to think of tolerance for ambiguity in any given situation as a facet of a larger umbrella phenomenon that has recently been added to the lexicon of creativity research – *creative anxiety*.

Creative Anxiety

Recently, researchers bridged that past work on tolerance for uncertainty to the specific anxiety experienced when facing creative demands (Daker et al., 2020). This initial work on creative anxiety began with the objective of understanding this phenomenon further to develop interventions for educational and professional settings. Those aims follow in the footsteps of new practices to address other educationally relevant anxieties, such as math anxiety[1] (see Park et al., 2014). Anxiety that emerges when facing creative challenges can be thought of as the subjective experience of uncertainty to a degree that can immobilize effective cognition (Hirsh et al., 2012). Within the sphere of creativity, this anxiety may also be related to social or personal expectations for originality and threat of risk-taking and unconventionality that may be required to achieve this novelty, as demonstrated in recent research with high school students (Ivcevic & Hoffman, 2021). Those expectations can result in a fear of failure or being judged negatively (Daker et al., 2020). Depending on the task, that anxiety will likely be related to anxieties about the noncreative aspects of the task, such as not having adequate technical skill and prior knowledge – differentiating between those two sources of anxiety in creative demands is important.

---

[1] High math anxiety is linked to feelings of tension, apprehension, and fear of math and results in underperformance in math, avoidance of math, and actual physiological sensations of fear, pain, and threat. Math anxiety research has demonstrated the potential of interventions, such as expressive writing.

When controlling for noncreative sources of anxiety, Daker et al. (2020) found that creativity-specific anxiety predicted creative attitudes and achievement over and above anxiety for the noncreative aspects of a presented situation. Across ten different content domains, from visual arts to science to humor, individuals expressed higher anxiety for creatively demanding situations than for similar situations not requiring creativity, which was especially salient for women. That result supports the idea that the creative process – and its inherent uncertainty – involves the experience of some degree of anxiety. Moreover, individuals reporting higher creativity-specific anxiety felt less capable of creativity and reflected that creativity was a less significant part of their identity compared to individuals with less anxiety. The authors found that negative effects of domain-specific creative anxiety were generalized across a range of potential fields and pursuits, even those that may be considered inherently creative, such as music. Those results indicate creative anxiety may present a very real and prolific barrier to creative pursuits and development in creative professional pathways.

This kind of anxiety may limit the development of an individual's identity as a creative person or professional, which could have a broad influence on their self-regulation, choices, and behavior based on the postulates of identity-based motivation (Oyserman & Destin, 2010). From that perspective, if one's creative identity is weak, that person is more likely to see challenges and failure as diagnostic of their own shortcomings, rather than as normative for everyone. They will make choices and take action that align with that noncreative identity. To see how this anxiety relates to other underlying factors of creative identity development for individuals, recent research in the teaching context offers a helpful example.

Creative Anxiety in the Teaching Context

Recent work with teachers built from Daker et al.'s (2020) framework to understand how the need for closure in tolerating ambiguity and creative anxiety may function together in the context of teacher development during the uncertainty experienced in the early months of the COVID-19 pandemic. Anderson et al. (2021) studied a small sample of U.S. teachers engaging in an innovative online professional development program and found a large correlation ($r = .50$) between teachers' higher need for closure facing ambiguity and their creative anxiety. Teachers' secondary traumatic stress correlated with both constructs; however, when included together as predictors of this stress on teachers, only creative anxiety remained statistically significant. That finding supports the idea that the tendency to tolerate or even seek out ambiguity and uncertainty may be a facet of the subjective experience of creative anxiety that people experience and manage differently.

Additionally, higher levels of creative anxiety were negatively correlated with teachers' self-efficacy for creative teaching and predicted feeling greater negative affect (e.g., distressed, guilty, nervous, and irritable) while teaching. In the context of teaching, these results taken together illustrate how creative anxiety works against teachers' confidence to respond creatively to the demands of teaching. Creative anxiety may also work against their ability to support the creativity of students and their capacity to manage stress in their work. One of those stressors is the secondary trauma taken on by caring for students who are dealing with trauma, from violence in their neighborhood to school closure from a global pandemic (Anderson, Katz-Buonincontro, Livie, et al., 2022). To be able to understand and support the trauma of students, especially during a universally traumatic experience such as the COVID-19 pandemic, requires balancing the fatigue of holding that empathy with the ability to be proactive to take realistic action. This adaptability and resilience sheds light on the connection between the creative capacities of individuals and the anxiety, stress, and uncertainty that result from open-ended challenges in life. To effectively manage the intrusive, arousing, and avoidant aspects of this particular kind of stress represents a considerable creative challenge teachers may face on a regular basis (Bride et al., 2004).

Fear of Failure

Fear of failure may sit alongside intolerance of uncertainty and creative anxiety in the dualistic role of potential barrier and necessary – perhaps even beneficial – catalyst within the creative process. Creativity research has found the experience of failure and impasse to often be a prerequisite for reaching insight (Sawyer, 2012). Though fixation on failure can block the progression to insights and solutions in the creative process, multiple moments of impasses and insights can play out in a cyclical process, ultimately landing on a breakthrough solution (see Finke et al., 1992; Lubart, 2001). In this way, impasse and failure may seem impossible on the one hand, but those moments may signify the threshold for a breakthrough. The meaning that failure and impasse hold will likely determine whether they result in negative fixation or productive insight.

How meaning of failure takes shape may depend on the sociocultural context. Is failure penalized or inspected? Is failure seen as a weakness or opportunity? From a constructionist approach to creativity and development, failure is just a natural and expected step in the inventive process of creating something new (Martinez & Stager, 2013). From that constructionist perspective, a culture of invention expects failure, hailing it as progress filled with useful information. Constructionist theory builds on sociocultural and constructivist ideas to understand how learning and human development occur in the process of making and tinkering in an iterative, experimental process where new knowledge and understanding are informed by mistakes. Mistakes are waypoints on the unique constructed journey of an individual or group toward inventing something new. A classic example from industry is Spencer Silver and Art Fry's repeated trial and error across years seeking out a use for an accidental weak adhesive developed in labs at 3M Company, until arriving at the final solution of the ubiquitous Post-it note (Anderson, 2015).

When asking adolescent students to portray the meaning of failure in the creative and inventive process some use terms such as *high point* and *low point* as descriptors rather than mentioning the term itself. This mental model highlights failure as a part of the process rather than as an outcome or end point (Estabrooks & Couch, 2018). Those students shared a variety of ways to think about creative failure: (a) feelings of not succeeding personally, (b) quitting or giving up, (c) not achieving a goal or intended result, (d) a course correction or setback, (e) a learning opportunity, and (f) part of getting closer to success. Importantly, those definitions contrast a fixed versus growth creative mindset about creative capacity (Karwowski, 2021) – another connective tissue between anxiety and fear of failure and resilience in the creative process.

Fear of failure in a creative pursuit can feel like *creative impossibility*, as Karwowski (2021) describes. That feeling contrasts with a creative growth mindset seeing mistakes and failure as an inevitable side effect to effort and persistence toward growth. A fixed creative mindset emerges from the *entity* belief that we are each born with a certain amount of creative ability, which cannot be changed, no matter how hard we try. Entity beliefs about creativity demotivate creative behavior by seeing failure as a reinforcement of lack of ability and too high a threat to risk. As with other domains (Burnette et al., 2013), a growth creative mindset emerges from incremental beliefs that creative development progresses with effort, mistakes, failure, and incremental improvement. People holding stronger incremental theories about ability manage failure better by seeing it as a learning opportunity. Reframing individuals' creative mindsets may be a key mechanism and point of intervention to helping individuals and groups manage – and, perhaps, even leverage – creative anxiety and fear of failure in creative pursuits.

Extensive research in education (see Jacovidis et al., 2020) indicates that messaging and modeling from both parents and teachers can have a powerful influence on the motivation and resilience of students. For instance, messaging, such as "it's okay, not everyone can be good at mathematics" may seem comforting but can have the contradictory effect of demotivating a learner. Alternatively, when a teacher focuses on effort rather than ability and offers clear feedback on what a student did correctly and where they can put more effort, they are more likely to reinforce a growth mindset about math for students. Undoubtedly, messaging and modeling will shape the meaning that failure can take on for someone engaging in a creative challenge. Similarly, when students are asked about what works to cultivate a growth mindset in their creative learning, they suggested more playful, process-focused creative work that frames mistakes as "a portal to a new discovery" (Anderson et al., 2020). Similarly, teachers shared that feeling permission to be playful in low-stakes creative activities and letting go of the idea of perfection helped them cultivate a creative growth mindset (Anderson, Katz-Buonincontro, Bousselot, et al. 2022).

Strategies to Address Creative Anxiety and Fear of Failure

As the research on creative anxiety reinforces, any approach to helping individuals and groups manage anxiety and fear in creative challenges and pursuits may need to be both general and domain specific. The creative demands of theatre and the expectations to perform are different from those experienced in facing an engineering or mechanical challenge. However, developing a range of emotional awareness and regulation strategies may be essential no matter the domain. Fostering a creative growth mindset, generally, and within a domain will require a mix of development in knowledge, skill, experience, and the resulting shifts in beliefs. Creative skill development has a history of research and practice, but programs addressing creative mindset and anxiety have only recently been underway. In fact, in the education sphere, scholars recently suggested that it was unclear if teachers' beliefs and attitudes about creativity could be changed (Bereczki & Kárpáti, 2018; Kettler et al., 2018).

One Strategy in Education

One teacher professional development program, called makeSPACE,[2] specifically targets teachers' creative mindsets, self-beliefs, and affect in a scaffolded approach (Anderson et al., 2021). The program introduces theory and research on creativity to illustrate the malleability and development of different creative resources (Lubart et al., 2013), beyond aspects most often associated with creativity, such as original thinking or skill in visual arts. Teachers reflect on their own creative resources, consider those they want to develop, and then experience a range of creative and reflective exercises with the goal of integrating them gradually into their classroom teaching for the benefit of students. Each stage of that experiential and reflective learning process frames creative potential through a multidimensional and malleable lens. Figure 24.1 illustrates the hypothetical change in teacher beliefs, affect, and practices (Anderson, Katz-Buonincontro, Livie, et al., 2022). In a mixed methods study, researchers found the first stage of the program contributed to a large reduction in teachers' fixed creative mindsets and creative anxiety and increased their creative self-efficacy and perceived value of creativity for students (Anderson, Katz-Buonincontro, Bousselot, et al., 2022). A second study replicated these results and also found increased resilience and joy and decreased stress across teachers' experience in the program during the 2020–2021 school year when COVID-19 shut down most schools (Anderson, Katz-Buonincontro, Livie, et al., 2022).

In focus groups, teachers provided in-depth explanations about how these shifts took place. Their preexisting creative anxiety resulted from pressure they felt to perform creatively as a teacher and the negative expectations they had.

---

[2] Find out more information about the makeSPACE approach and research at www .makespaceproject.org.

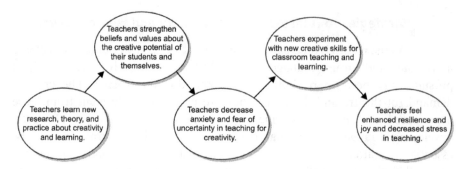

Figure 24.1 *The pathway to shift teacher beliefs, affect, perceptions, practices for creative teaching and learning, and overall resilience and well-being in the makeSPACE project.*

They carried ideas about perfection that made creative risks and potential failure feel paralyzing. Teachers were worried about being judged as not creative while they shared their work and ideas in the online course. The professional development experience helped them learn to take manageable risks in preparation for taking bigger creative leaps in the classroom. Teachers felt they needed to be "perfect," which fed their creative anxiety. By practicing quick creative exercises and learning why and how mistakes are essential for new insights, teachers realized the limitations of adhering to ideas of perfection. Teachers' perceptions of creative potential as a natural gift changed to seeing the creative process as something universally accessible. By embracing this new understanding in their own creative practice, teachers appeared to shift their creative mindset and reduce their creative anxiety. Learning to face and manage this anxiety and fear across different domains also enhanced teachers' understanding and awareness of their students' experience taking risks, trying something new, and sharing ideas with others.

A second study with a new sample replicated some of those same effects during the 2020–2021 school year of COVID-related distance learning, though teachers in that sample began with a substantially lower mean level of creative anxiety, which did not appear to change across the professional development. However, that study also found a statistically significant medium-to-large effect in reduced secondary traumatic stress, increased joy and resilience in teaching, and increased cognitive empathy for students' risk-taking (Anderson, Katz-Buonincontro, Livie, et al., 2022). Those results within the world of teaching and education may generalize to a broader population and different domains. Learning about the complex but accessible nature of the creative process in an experiential, reflective, and contextually relevant approach may shift the creative mindset, anxiety, and fear of failure to help individuals or groups face ambiguous challenges more adaptively. Those shifts can result in greater awareness and empathy for others who may have less tolerance for ambiguity and greater creative anxiety in a certain domain. One key aspect of research from the makeSPACE program is the focus on reflection toward the development of creative metacognition – each person's unique approach to observe and regulate their thinking, emotions, and action in the creative process.

Creative Metacognition

Creative metacognition can serve as a mechanism for self-awareness, creative strategy, contextual understanding, and self-regulation of emotions and thoughts as emotional states change through the creative process (Beghetto & Karwowski, 2017). In early adolescence, this creative metacognition was the strongest mediating factor translating different aspects of students' creative potential, such as divergent thinking, into creative production (Anderson & Haney, 2021). Strengthening creative metacognition requires focusing attention on the creative process and explicit development of emotional awareness and techniques for expressing and regulating those emotions, effectively. Emotion abilities contribute to school success (Ivcevic & Brackett, 2014), and these skills can be developed by social and emotional learning programs. Creative metacognition can likely establish a greater understanding for the unique conditions that benefit the creative engagement of each of us, individually, across the different professional, recreational, and personal settings we inhabit.

Toward a Model of Creative Agency

The beliefs, metacognition, and affect related to anxiety and fear of failure in the creative process appear to be some of the underlying factors of developing creative agency (Anderson, Katz-Buonincontro, Bousselot, et al., 2022). The model of creative behavior as agentic action (Karwowski & Beghetto, 2018) builds on the decades of work from the late Albert Bandura to shine a spotlight on how feelings, values, and beliefs shape how we navigate the social-cognitive reality of our world. Work on creative anxiety (Daker et al., 2020) and the role of emotional intelligence in creativity (Parke et al., 2015) suggests creative agency must go beyond the social-cognitive to incorporate how we regulate and facilitate our emotions to enhance the creative process. In learning and life, habits and routines that nurture and reinforce adaptive feelings and beliefs in our creative potential may go far in buttressing ourselves and those around us to resist the power that anxiety and fear of failure holds to stymie effort and risk-taking. The way that individuals leverage those emotion states for greater creativity may reflect an emotional intelligence and adaptability (Ivcevic & Hoffman, 2021) that can benefit others through modeling. Greater understanding of how these emotions fit into the creative process and the creative development of individuals and groups could have a huge impact on well-being and adaptability. When we take meaningful creative risks, we not only grow our own confidence and understanding we also model this strength for others.

Conclusion

Uncertainty is a necessary ingredient for creative experience, but it will stimulate anxiety and fear of failure under many circumstances. These are powerful but often unpleasant emotions to experience and can be demotivating if people do not develop strategies to manage or even leverage them to enhance creativity. As such, these affective components of creativity can be considered as important sources of information rather than as potent detractors. The field of creativity can further our understanding if we learn how people leverage these emotions throughout the creative process. For people to grow creative agency, they will likely need to become metacognitive about their creative process not only to take advantage of the full spectrum of emotions but also to reinforce a growth mindset, a value for creative risk taking, and a self-efficacy to be successful in the specific creative endeavor. The field is learning about this agentic process from adolescence into adulthood and more research is needed, especially about earlier developmental stages. Creative metacognition may help people set the conditions and scaffolding to achieve flow in the creative process for optimal performance. What those conditions look like in different sociocultural settings will be a rich area for future research. Achieving and maintaining a balance of challenge and skill can help transform anxiety and fear of failure from emotions to avoid into building blocks for richer creative engagement, empowered creative agency, and sustained creative success across a variety of domains in life.

References

Anderson, R. C. (2015). The makers: Creativity and entrepreneurial spirit. In Y. Zhao (Ed.), *Counting What Counts: Reframing Education Outcomes* (pp. 93–112). Solution Tree Press.

Anderson, R. C. (2019). Becoming *Creative Agents*: Trajectories of *Creative Development* during the *Turbulence* of *Early Adolescence*. Doctoral dissertation. University of Oregon. University of Oregon Scholar's Bank. https://scholarsbank.uoregon.edu/xmlui/handle/1794/24881

Anderson, R. C., Bousselot, T., Katz-Buoincontro, J., & Todd, J. (2021). Generating buoyancy in a sea of uncertainty: Teachers creativity and well-being during the COVID-19 pandemic. *Frontiers in Psychology, 11*. https://doi.org/10.3389/fpsyg.2020.614774

Anderson, R. C., & Haney, M. (2021). Reflection in the creative process of early adolescents: The mediating roles of creative metacognition, self-efficacy, and self-concept. *Psychology of Aesthetics, Creativity, and the Arts, 15*(4), 612–626. https://doi.org/10.1037/aca0000324

Anderson, R. C., Haney, M., Pitts, C., Porter, L., & Bousselot, T. (2020). "Mistakes can be beautiful": Creative engagement in arts integration for early adolescent learners. *Journal of Creative Behavior, 54*(3), 662–675.

Anderson, R. C., Irvin, S., Bousselot, T., Beard, N., & Beach, P. (2022). Grasping the uncertainty of scientific phenomena: A creative, agentic, and multimodal model of sensemaking. In R. Beghetto and G. Jaeger (Eds.), *Uncertainty: A Catalyst for Creativity, Learning, and Development*. Springer.

Anderson R. C., Katz-Buonincontro, J., Bousselot, T., et al. (2022). How am I a creative teacher? Foundational beliefs, values, and affect for integrating creativity in the classroom. *Teaching and Teacher Education, 110*, 103583. https://doi.org/10.1016/j.tate.2021.103583

Anderson, R. C., Katz-Buonincontro, J., Livie, M., et al. (2022). Reinvigorating the desire to teach: Teacher professional development for creativity, agency, stress, and well-being. *Frontiers in Education*. https://www.frontiersin.org/articles/10.3389/feduc.2022.848005/full

Bardi, A., Guerra, V. M., & Ramdeny, G. S. D. (2009). Openness and ambiguity intolerance: Their differential relations to well-being in the context of an academic life transition. *Personality and Individual Differences, 47*(3), 219–223. https://doi.org/10.1016/j.paid.2009.03.003

Beghetto, R. A. (2019). Structured uncertainty: How creativity thrives under constraints and uncertainty. In C. A. Mullen (Ed.), *Creativity under Duress in Education?* (pp. 27–40). Springer.

Beghetto, R. A., & Dilley, A. E. (2017). Creative aspirations or pipe dreams? Toward understanding creative mortification in children and adolescents. *New Directions for Child and Adolescent Development* (151), 79–89. https://doi.org/10.1002/cad

Beghetto, R. A., & Karwowski, M. (2017). Toward untangling creative self-beliefs. In M. Karwowski & J. C. Kaufman (Eds.), *The Creative Self: Effect of Beliefs, Self-Efficacy, Mindset, and Identity* (pp. 3–22). Academic Press. https://doi.org/10.1016/B978-0-12-809790-8.00001-7

Beghetto, R. A., Karwowski, M., & Reiter-Palmon, R. (2021). Intellectual risk taking: A moderating link between creative confidence and creative behavior? *Psychology of Aesthetics, Creativity, and the Arts, 15*(4), 637–644. https://doi.org/10.1037/aca0000323

Bentwich, M. E., & Gilbey, P. (2017). More than visual literacy: Art and the enhancement of tolerance for ambiguity and empathy. *BMC Medical Education, 17*(1), 1–9. https://doi.org/10.1186/s12909-017-1028-7

Bereczki, E. O., & Kárpáti, A. (2018). Teachers' beliefs about creativity and its nurture: A systematic review of the recent research literature. *Educational Research Review, 23*, 25–56. https://doi.org/10.1016/j.edurev.2017.10.003

Birrell, J., Meares, K., Wilkinson, A., & Freeston, M. (2011). Toward a definition of intolerance of uncertainty: A review of factor analytical studies of the Intolerance of Uncertainty Scale. *Clinical Psychology Review, 31*(7), 1198–1208. https://doi.org/10.1016/j.cpr.2011.07.009

Bracket, M. (2019). *Permission to Feel: Unlocking the Power of Emotions to Help Our Kids, Ourselves, and Our Society Thrive*. Celadon Books.

Bride, B. E., Robinson, M. R., Yegidis, B., & Figley, C. R. (2004). Development and validation of the Secondary Traumatic Stress Scale. *Research on Social Work Practice, 14*(7), 27–35.

Burnette, J. L., O'Boyle, E. H., VanEpps, E. M., Pollack, J. M., & Finkel, E. J. (2013). Mind-sets matter: A meta- analytic review of implicit theories and self-regulation. *Psychological Bulletin, 139*, 655–701.

Chirumbolo, A., Livi, S., Mannetti, L., Pierro, A., & Kruglanski, A. W. (2004). Effects of need for closure on creativity in small group interactions. *European Journal of Personality*, *18*(4), 265–278. https://doi.org/10.1002/per.51

Clore, G., Gasper, K., & Garvin, E. (2001). Affect as information. In J. P. Forgas, (Ed.), *Handbook of Affect and Social Cognition* (pp. 121–144). Erlbaum.

Csikszentmihalyi, M. (1997). *Finding Flow: The Psychology of Engagement with Everyday Life*. Basic Books.

Csikszentmihalyi, M., & Rathunde, K. (1993). The measurement of flow in everyday life: Toward a theory of emergent motivation. In J. Jacobs (Ed.), *Current Theory and Research in Motivation: Nebraska Symposium on Motivation 1992: Developmental Perspectives on Motivation* (vol. 40, pp. 57–97). University of Nebraska Press.

Dahl, R. E., Allen, N. B., Wilbrecht, L., & Suleiman, A. B. (2018). Importance of investing in adolescence from a developmental science perspective. *Nature*, *554* (7693), 441–450.

Daker, R. J., Cortes, R. A., Lyons, I. M., & Green, A. E. (2020). Creativity anxiety: Evidence for anxiety that is specific to creative thinking, from STEM to the arts. *Journal of Experimental Psychology: General*, *149*(1), 42–57. https://doi .org/10.1037/xge0000630

De Dreu, C. K. W., Baas, M., & Nijstad, B. A. (2008). Hedonic tone and activation level in the mood-creativity link: Toward a dual pathway to creativity model. *Journal of Personality and Social Psychology*, *94*(5), 739–756. https://doi.org/ 10.1037/0022-3514.94.5.739

Estabrooks, L. B., & Couch, S. R. (2018). Failure as an active agent in the development of creative and inventive mindsets. *Thinking Skills and Creativity*, *30*, 103–115. https://doi.org/10.1016/j.tsc.2018.02.015

Finke, R. A., Ward, T. B., & Smith, S. M. (1992). *Creative Cognition: Theory, Research, and Applications*. MIT Press.

Fried, L., & Chapman, E. (2012). An investigation into the capacity of student motivation and emotion regulation strategies to predict engagement and resilience in the middle school classroom. *Australian Educational Researcher*, *39*(3), 295–311. https://doi.org/http://dx.doi.org/10.1007/s13384-011-0049-1

Furnham, A., & Marks, J. (2013). Tolerance for ambiguity: A review of the literature. *Psychology*, *4*(9), 717–728. https://doi.org/10.1080/10848770.2018.1437991

Hennessey, B. A., & Amabile, T. M. (1987). *Creativity and Learning: What Research Says to the Teacher*. National Education Association.

Hennessey, B. A., & Amabile, T. M. (2010). Creativity. *Annual Review of Psychology*, *61* (1), 569–598. https://doi.org/10.1146/annurev.psych.093008.100416

Hirsh, J. B., Mar, R. A., & Peterson, J. B. (2012). Psychological entropy: A framework for understanding uncertainty-related anxiety. *Psychological Review*, *119*(2), 304–320. https://doi.org/10.1037/a0026767

Housen, A. C. (2001). Aesthetic thought, critical thinking and transfer. *Arts and Learning Research Journal*, *18*(1), 99–132.

Ivcevic, Z., & Brackett, M. (2014). Predicting school success: Comparing conscientiousness, grit, and emotion regulation ability. *Journal of Research in Personality*, *52*, 29–36. https://doi.org/10.1016/j.jrp.2014.06.005

Ivcevic, Z., & Hoffman, J. (2021). The creativity dare: Attitudes toward creativity and prediction of creative behavior in school. *Journal of Creative Behavior* (early view). https://doi.org/10.1002/jocb.527

Jacovidis, J. Anderson, R., Beach, P., & Chadwick, K. (2020). *Growth Mindset Thinking and Beliefs in Teaching and Learning*. International Baccalaureate.

Karwowski, M. (2021). Creative mindsets. In V. P. Glăveanu (Ed.), *The Palgrave Encyclopedia of the Possible* (pp. 1–6). Palgrave Macmillan. https://doi.org/10.1007/978-3-319-98390-5_58-1

Karwowski, M., & Anderson, R. C. (2021). Goal orientations. In V. P. Glăveanu (Ed.), *The Palgrave Encyclopedia of the Possible* (pp. 1–6). Palgrave Macmillan. https://doi.org/10.1177/0013164405282473

Karwowski, M., & Beghetto, R. A. (2018). Creative behavior as agentic action. *Psychology of Aesthetics, Creativity, and the Arts*, *13*(4), 402–415. https://doi.org/10.1037/aca0000190

Kettler, T., Lamb, K. N., Willerson, A., & Mullet, D. R. (2018). Teachers' perceptions of creativity in the classroom. *Creativity Research Journal*, *30*(2), 164–171. https://doi.org/10.1080/10400419.2018.1446503

Kochhar, A. (2016). *The Failure Project*. Body & Soul Books.

Kowal, J., & Fortier, M. S. (1999). Motivational determinants of flow: Contributions from self-determination theory. *Journal of Social Psychology*, *139*(3), 355–368. https://doi.org/10.1080/00224549909598391

Kozbelt, A., Beghetto, R. A., & Runco, M. A. (2010). Theories of creativity. In J. C. Kaufman & R. J. Sternberg (Eds.), *The Cambridge Handbook of Creativity* (pp. 20–47). Cambridge University Press.

Kruglanski, A. W. (2013). *Lay Epistemics and Human Knowledge: Cognitive and Motivational Bases*. Springer Science & Business Media.

Lubart, T. I. (2001). Models of the creative process: Past, present and future. *Creativity Research Journal*, *13*(3-4), 295–308.

Lubart, T. I., Zenasni, F., & Barbot, B. (2013). Creative potential and its measurement. *International Journal for Talent Development and Creativity*, *1*(2), 41–50.

Lyons, I. M., & Beilock, S. L. (2012). When math hurts: Math anxiety predicts pain network activation in anticipation of doing math. *PLoS ONE*, *7*(10). https://doi.org/10.1371/journal.pone.0048076

Martinez, S. L., & Stager, G. (2013). *Invent to Learn: Making, Tinkering, and Engineering in the Classroom*. Constructing Modern Knowledge Press.

Oyserman, D., & Destin, M. (2010). Identity-based motivation: Implications for intervention. *The Counseling Psychologist*, *38*(7), 1001–1043.

Park, D., Ramirez, G., & Beilock, S. L. (2014). The role of expressive writing in math anxiety. *Journal of Experimental Psychology: Applied*, *20*(2), 103–111. https://doi.org/10.1037/xap0000013

Parke, M. R., Seo, M.-G., & Sherf, E. N. (2015). Regulating and facilitating: The role of emotional intelligence in maintaining and using positive affect for creativity. *Journal of Applied Psychology*, *100*(3), 917–934. https://doi.org/10.1037/a0038452

Plucker, J. A., Beghetto, R. A., & Dow, G. T. (2004). Why isn't creativity more important to educational psychologists? Potentials, pitfalls, and future directions in creativity research. *Educational Psychologist*, *39*(2), 83–96.

Posner, J., Russell, J., & Peterson, B. (2005). The circumplex model of affect: An integrative approach to affective neuroscience, cognitive development, and psychopathology. *Developmental Psychopathology*, *17*(3), 715–734.

Runco, M. A., & Jaeger, G. J. (2012). The Standard Definition of Creativity. *Creativity Research Journal, 24*(1), 92–96. https://doi.org/10.1080/10400419.2012.650092

Russell, J. (1980). A circumplex model of affect. *Journal of Personality and Social Psychology, 39*(6), 1161–1178.

Sawyer, R. K. (2012). *Explaining Creativity: The Science of Human Innovation* (2nd ed.). Oxford University Press.

Schneider, B., Krajcik, J., Lavonen, J., et al. (2016). Investigating optimal learning moments in U.S. and Finnish science classes. *Journal of Research in Science Teaching, 53*(3), 400–421. https://doi.org/10.1002/tea.21306

Shernoff, D. J., Csikszentmihalyi, M., Shneider, B., & Shernoff, E. S. (2003). Student engagement in high school classrooms from the perspective of flow theory. *School Psychology Quarterly, 18*(2), 158–176. https://doi.org/10.1521/scpq.18.2.158.21860

Yenawine, P. (2013). *Visual Thinking Strategies: Using Art to Deepen Learning across School Disciplines.* Harvard University Press.

Zenasni, F., Besançon, M., & Lubart. T. (2008). Creativity and tolerance of ambiguity: An empirical study. *Journal of Creative Behavior, 42*(1), 61–72.

25 Peers, Affect, and Creativity at School

Maciej Karwowski

Imagine your first reaction when someone uses the phrase *creativity in school*. For some people, it might sound like an oxymoron; for others, it could bring back memories of those class activities when their creativity flourished. So, are your school memories regarding creativity nightmares, seeing your classes as hampering originality, or perhaps they are more positive, with teachers and peers remembered as allowing for your curiosity and imagination to bloom? These questions are not only rhetorical; they illustrate people's attitudes and opinions when they think and talk about creativity (Ivcevic & Hoffmann, 2021). It goes without saying that often (Robinson, 2006), yet not necessarily fairly (Karwowski, 2022), schools are being criticized as anti-creative. The situation, however, is more complex than unnuanced claims frequently propose. Consider, for example, the broadly advertised "creativity crisis" (Kim, 2011). According to a new analysis, support for its existence is weak at best (Barbot & Said-Metwaly, 2021).

This chapter discusses the role of creativity in the classroom, focusing on two categories mentioned in the title: peers and affect. I discuss how both are related to creativity, particularly regarding classroom and school functioning. I briefly explore some definitional issues and debunk some shared myths about creativity and school. Next, I focus on three main points. First, I discuss research results showing how peers perceive creative students: whether they are liked or perhaps instead they are being rejected and ridiculed. Second, I discuss how creative abilities and behaviors in the classroom might – directly or not – influence students' creative self-perception. Thus, I explore whether being surrounded by creative peers is helpful, harmful, or neutral for their classmates' creative confidence. Third and finally, I discuss the role of creative climate in the classroom and teachers' behaviors as factors that shape students' affective reactions – both positive and negative.

Defining Creativity in the Classroom and School Contexts

Saying that creativity is complex and multifaced is a cliché, yet *creativity indeed is complex*. Notably, though, despite this complexity and contrary to many

Maciej Karwowski, Institute of Psychology, University of Wroclaw, Poland. Address: Dawida 1, St., 50-527 Wroclaw, e-mail: maciej.karwowski@uwr.edu.pl. This chapter was supported by a grant from National Science Centre Poland (2016/22/E/HS6/00118).

critiques, creativity scholars mostly share the definition of their central research construct of interest, perceiving it as an activity that leads to original (novel) and relevant (appropriate, useful) effects (Runco & Jaeger, 2012). While other criteria are sometimes proposed – such as aesthetical appeal (Kharkhurin, 2014) or surprisingness of the outcomes (Simonton, 2012) – originality and relevance are critical aspects of thinking, action, or product to be called creative (see Weisberg et al., 2021 for an opposing stance). A recent extension (Glăveanu & Beghetto, 2021) of these classic approaches focuses on creative experiences, caring less about outcomes and focusing more on the process that leads to original and effective solutions. More specifically, as Glăveanu and Beghetto (2021) propose, creative experience requires "a principled engagement with the unfamiliar and a willingness to approach the familiar in unfamiliar ways" (p. 76).

Focus on experiences instead of outcomes resolves some well-known issues with the so-called standard definition of creativity. Indeed, originality and relevance, or effectiveness, for that matter, are not void of problems. Something new for one person could be evident for another. Usefulness or relevance is also relative; it largely depends on time, place, the creator's experience, or the audience. The situation becomes even more complicated when we situate creativity in the educational context. Students scarcely create something novel and relevant in the strict sense, yet they constantly use imagery or remote associations or they develop new ideas while playing, learning, or engaging in hobbyist activities (Ivcevic & Mayer, 2009; Zielińska, 2020; Zielińska et al., 2022a). The same applies to teachers; only a few create brand-new curricula or develop teaching strategies that revolutionize school life, but so many use their creativity to make the learning process more engaging and effective by introducing small-scale innovations (Gajda, Beghetto, et al., 2017). Moreover, teachers have multiple ways to create opportunities to develop or hamper creativity in their classrooms.

Thus, one way to better understand creativity in the classroom is to analyze it in terms of students' and teachers' experiences. A related way is to situate it within the conceptual space proposed by the Four C model of creativity (Kaufman & Beghetto, 2009). This widely accepted model proposes hierarchically organized levels of creativity, from mini-c to little-c, to Pro-c, and Big-C creativity. Mini-c denotes mental processes, such as combining and restructuring pieces of information or applying creative operations in learning or problem-solving. Little-c applies to the activity that often, albeit not always, results in products that are of personal rather than social importance. Various *do-it-yourself* gadgets and solutions (i.e., creating a new gift for a friend, decorating someone's room, or solving the problem of broken furniture) might serve as examples of this level of creativity (Ivcevic, 2007; Zielińska, 2020). Such activity often forms a precondition for professionalized creativity, but perhaps even more importantly, it brings joy and positive emotions (Chi et al., 2021; Conner & Silvia, 2015). Pro-c and Big-C levels describe more professionalized creativity, either in work settings (Pro-c), or those that apply to the most outstanding achievements of famous creators (Big-C).

When children and adolescents are considered (although this applies to adults as well, see Karwowski & Wiśniewska, 2021), mini-c and little-c creativity are central to educational scholars' interests. Solving open-ended and ill-defined problems during math classes, experiencing flashes of insight during science experiments, developing alternative explanations for historical events – all this happens in school every day. While too often teaching and learning are rote, surface, and shallow, there is much space for mini-c in learning processes in virtually any school subject (Beghetto, 2016). In the same vein, little-c is quite prevalent among adolescents and young adults (Ivcevic, 2007; Karwowski et al., 2021). Although such hobbyist-like creativity tends to be fulfilled outside rather than inside of the classroom (Liang et al., 2021; Runco et al., 2017), many longer term projects that students conduct provide opportunities for little-c creativity in school settings. That might involve generating and testing hypotheses during a biology class, finding new ways to solve math problems, or providing alternative explanations of the consequences of well-known historical facts.

This chapter focuses primarily on the two lower levels of creativity: mini-c and little-c. When creative students are mentioned, it is done keeping in mind those students who effectively solve problems or engage their thinking and imagination in learning. Additionally, considering creativity as a form of experience is particularly fruitful when emotions and peer interactions come into play. Experiencing situations in different ways is reciprocally associated with perceiving themselves as more, rather than less creative, hence addressing different levels of agency and confidence. This chapter also discusses how classroom composition and interactions might shape students' self-perception and why it matters.

Peer Relationships of Creative Students

Highly creative people, especially geniuses, are often described as isolated and poorly adapted. Indeed, implicit or lay theories that people hold emphasize that creators are lone wolves or "mad geniuses" (Kaufman et al., 2007; Simonton, 2014). Although it sometimes happens to be so, such perception is among the most prevalent creativity myths (Sawyer, 2012). Consider, for example, Jane Austen or Bill Gates – to provide just two random examples – not only extraordinarily creative individuals, but also well connected to others and effectively cooperating with them (Sawyer, 2012).

Does this stereotypical perception apply to "lower levels" of creativity; namely, are creative students perceived as lone wolves? Studies on implicit theories of creativity often corroborate such a conclusion, even if this perception is at odds with empirical evidence. In short, research about peer relationships and creativity contradicts these opinions and leads to perceiving creativity as socially attractive. As a recent study demonstrated (Bonetto et al., 2021), creative individuals are perceived not only as competent, but also as warm.

Social connections for creativity have been highlighted many times in theoretical models (Boekhorst et al., 2021), yet there is a scarcity of research that empirically explores it, particularly when it refers to children and adolescents. Creativity literature has a long and fruitful history of studying individual conditions of creativity, including personality (Feist, 1998; Feist & Barron, 2003), intelligence (Gerwig et al., 2021), creative self-beliefs (Beghetto & Karwowski, 2017; Karwowski & Lebuda, 2016), and emotions (Ivcevic & Hoffmann, 2019). Many fewer studies explored the role of social connections (Kéri, 2011; Lau & Li, 1996; Simonton, 1984). The relationships creative students have with their peers were almost completely overlooked. This is surprising and unfortunate, given that social connections and relations are often essential drivers of individual creativity in schools (Gajda, Beghetto, et al., 2017).

An interesting way to approach and study social relations of creative people is based on social network methods (Cattani & Ferriani, 2008; Perry-Smith, 2006; Perry-Smith & Shalley, 2003). Such studies established that information-sharing ties allow for more creative solutions in companies and teams in organizational settings. While it might also apply to classrooms, what seems particularly important from the educational perspective is how informal ties, such as friendships, relate to creativity.

According to homophily and similarity-attraction hypotheses (McPherson et al., 2001), individuals form friendship ties with similar others. This similarity refers to such external, sociodemographic attributes as gender, race, or social status, and to psychological traits such as personality, for instance (Byrne et al., 1967; Izard, 1960; Kao & Jouyner, 2004; McPherson et al., 2001). The question is whether it also applies to creativity; is there a *creativity similarity effect*? Do creative people more often form friendship relations with one another? A related question is whether more creative students are perceived as interpersonally attractive (someone people want to be around) by their peers, so whether *creativity attractiveness* exists.

Homophily has been demonstrated across various settings, but only very few studies explored its role with reference to creativity. These investigations were driven by the assumption that creativity influences friendship formation, because people share the same values and preferences, and, consequently, their interpersonal experiences are more rewarding (Izard, 1960). Let's take an example of openness to experience: a personality engine of creativity. Given that openness shapes hobbies (Wolfradt & Pretz, 2001), it might make creative people drawn to others who are similarly creative, because they share a preference for engaging in similar activities and engaging in new experiences. Moreover, people with a similar level of creativity might feel more comfortable sharing their ideas (Mueller et al., 2012). Dissimilarity might make people feel uncomfortable with sharing new ideas for fear of criticism. Thus, there is a reason to expect that students with a similar level of creative abilities, activities, and hobbies will be more likely to form reciprocal friendship ties.

At the same time, however, it seems vital to consider the potentially different role of creative activities and achievements when discussing the role of creativity in friendship formation. While creative activity – doing something together for the sake of intrinsic motives – does indeed seem to be beneficial for creating networks, it is not that clear in the case of creative achievement. Creative accomplishments are rare among adolescents and young adults (Karwowski & Wiśniewska, 2021), even if they often engage in everyday creative activities (Ilha Villanova & Pina e Cunha, 2021; Ivcevic & Mayer, 2009; Zielińska et al., 2022a). This is, however, not to say that such achievements are entirely nonexistent. After all, it still happens that students who are talented in a specific domain (be it music, dance, or sport) demonstrate creative achievement despite their young age. Thus, based on the homophily and similarity hypothesis, we might expect that having similar creative achievements would indeed increase their chances for positive mutual relationships, friendship included. There are, however, some caveats. As classic social psychology theorizing posits (Tesser, 1988), when a trait (in this case, creativity) is vital for self-perception and self-esteem, social comparisons with highly creative people might be problematic and eventually detrimental for self-esteem. Imagine that your friend's achievement is greater than yours. Such a situation might negatively influence your self-worth, particularly if being creative is important to you. That might lead to either weakening the ties with similarly (and highly) creative individuals or depreciating the value of your own creativity and of creativity as a worthwhile trait in general.

Friendship ties among people who have high creative achievements in different domains is a case of particular interest. In this hypothetical case, people can stay close to each other without the risk of being negatively influenced by comparisons. Focus on various creative fields makes it less likely to affect self-perception negatively. Quite the opposite, they could bask in the reflected glory (Cialdini et al., 1976). However, when it comes to students' creative achievements and relationships, including friendship, there is a lack of studies that might resolve this controversy.

Another question is whether students are likely drawn to creative others in general (*creativity attractiveness* hypothesis). Previous studies demonstrated that creativity is perceived as a valuable trait of a potential partner (Li & Kenrick, 2006) and that creative people are considered both interpersonally and sexually attractive (Clegg et al., 2008; Nettle, 2008). Thus, students and adults alike are expected to report friendship ties with (or nominate as friends) creative others, whether this friendship is reciprocated or not. In one study (Lau & Li, 1996), "popular" students were more often perceived as creative by their peers and teachers, compared to students who were "average." In an investigation on adults (Kéri, 2011), the size of one's primary network (i.e., close friends and family) positively predicted creative achievements. Given that Keri's (2011) study was correlational, it is unclear whether creativity makes someone interpersonally attractive or richer social relations help people become more creative. While both these possibilities seem quite likely, experimental studies are lacking to date.

Previous studies focused on perceived rather than actual creativity. A more recent investigation (McKay, Grygiel, et al., 2017) approached this problem by testing whether students who perform better in creativity tests are more liked in the classroom and whether students similar in their creativity tend to form close ties with one another. An essential strength of McKay and colleagues' (2017) studies was associated with using more objective measures of creativity – both studies used figural creative imagery tasks (Jankowska & Karwowski, 2015). The results confirmed that mutual friendship nominations were more likely to occur when scores on a creativity task were similar. Additionally, children's popularity was positively related to their original thinking and creativity in general. Therefore, McKay et al.'s (2017) findings tend to confirm both the *creativity similarity hypothesis* (students indicated as friends those peers who were similar to them in the level of creative potential) and the *creativity attractiveness hypothesis* (there was a positive relationship between popularity and creativity in general).

Moreover, a recent study (Hopp et al., 2019) longitudinally demonstrated that gifted students select friends based on their perceived level of creativity in a summer program. An open question for future research should explore the mechanisms behind these effects. Most importantly, two questions seem critical to answer. The first is about the specificity of creativity and the second is why exactly creativity is attractive among classmates.

Regarding the specificity of creativity as a factor that is perceived as attractive, unfortunately the studies mentioned did not control for relevant covariates and potential confounds. Consider, for example, intelligence or school achievement. Creativity is positively related to intelligence (Gerwig et al., 2021; Karwowski et al., 2016; Silvia, 2015) and school successes (Gajda, Karwowski, et al., 2017). At the same time, more intelligent people are more interpersonally attractive (Sprecher & Regan, 2002; but see Driebe et al., 2021), similarly to students who do well in school (van der Wilt et al., 2018). Therefore, it seems vital to replicate previous findings and test whether the effect of creative attractiveness holds when relevant covariates are controlled for.

Second, assuming that more creative students are often sociometric stars – people who are liked and admired by others (Torrance, 2004) – there is a natural question of why that is the case. What exactly makes them interpersonally attractive? So far, we can only propose some speculations as the evidence is indirect at best. Thus, some well-established correlates or consequences of creative thinking, such as a sense of humor (Murdock & Ganim, 1993), energy in play (Proyer et al., 2019), solving everyday problems (Zielińska, 2020), or optimism (Michael et al., 2011), could make such students perceived more positively. At the same time, however, creative students are – or at least are sometimes perceived by their teachers as – impulsive, arrogant, or nonconformist (Gralewski & Karwowski, 2013; Kettler et al., 2018). Such traits are obviously less likely to build interpersonal attractiveness. Therefore, there is a gap in our understanding of why creative students are liked in the classroom. One particularly fruitful route for future investigation is to analyze peers' affective responses caused by interactions with more creative students. Given a highly developed sense of humor, one might assume that such contacts will result in positive affect and increased engagement. At the same time, however, the high energy such students often demonstrate, and their uncommon ideas, in the long run might also create exhaustion among peers and result in communication difficulties (Chen & Agrawal, 2017). Therefore, there is still much to be done to better understand why creative students are liked by their peers. However, the important take-home message is that they are liked, which seems to be at odds with what is usually observed when teachers' attitudes toward creative students are analyzed (Dawson, 1997; Kettler et al., 2018; Westby & Dawson, 1995).

Do Classmates Influence Students' Self-Perception?

A growing interest in the creative self-beliefs that people hold is a recent trend in creativity literature. The category of self-beliefs covers a broad range of interrelated yet distinct phenomena that describe what people think about creativity (e.g., their implicit theories of creativity) and how they perceive themselves in terms of creative potential (Karwowski, Lebuda, et al., 2019). Among the most often analyzed aspects of creative self-beliefs studied to date, four seem exceptionally well researched: creative self-concept, creative self-efficacy, creative identity, and creative mindsets.

Creative self-concept describes a relatively stable self-perceived potential to behave creatively and solve problems that require creativity. Its stability means that creative self-concept is conceptualized similarly to traits. However, there are some arguments that self-concept is more plastic and malleable than personality traits or abilities (Lebuda et al., 2021; Zandi et al., 2022). Although previous research (Beghetto, 2006) focused mainly on domain-general creative self-concept, thus presenting participants with items like "I think I am a creative person," individuals quite naturally have different self-perceptions of their potential across different domains (Snyder et al., 2021). This perception is shaped by their experiences, previous successes in these domains, feedback from other people (e.g., teachers, parents, or peers, see Karwowski et al., 2015), or social comparisons.

Creative self-efficacy, a construct inspired by Bandura's influential theorizing (Bandura, 1982, 1997), is understood as a self-perceived prospective potential to behave creatively (Beghetto & Karwowski, 2017). Therefore, while self-concept is rather oriented toward thinking in terms of "I am a creative person," self-efficacy more often deals with such statements as "I am able to deal with problems that require me to think outside the box." A recent reconceptualizations (Beghetto & Karwowski, 2017; Karwowski, Lebuda, et al., 2019) call for vivacious understanding of creative self-efficacy, considering it highly dynamic, domain- or even task-specific and changeable in time. According to this perspective, creative self-efficacy is closer to a state than trait (Marsh et al., 2019).

Creative confidence factor plays an important self-regulatory role in initiating activity and sustaining it. A creative behavior as agentic action (CBAA) model (Karwowski & Beghetto, 2019) postulates that creative confidence is driven by people's creative potential (as thanks to higher skills and abilities, they learn that they can be effective and their confidence grows), but subsequently, confidence translates into creative activity and achievement. Therefore, although the links between creative potential and creative confidence are rarely strong (meta-analytical correlation between them was estimated at $r = .23$, Haase et al., 2018), which also speaks to people's restricted metacognitive skills, it serves as one of the important mechanisms that allows people to use their abilities in the service of creative activity.

Notably, the decision to engage in creativity is also driven by whether people perceive it as a vital part of their identity or not. As demonstrated elsewhere (Karwowski & Beghetto, 2019), the centralness that creativity occupies in one's personal identity moderates the relationship between creative potential and behavior. More precisely, there is a robust correlation between people's creative potential and their activities and accomplishments, but only among those who consider creativity essential for themselves. Even effective divergent thinkers and problem solvers are unlikely to achieve a lot if they do not care about creativity or do not perceive it as valuable. Such people usually take a different route in their careers and lives without engaging in risky creative activities.

Creative mindsets cover an important part of people's implicit theories of creativity, particularly the extent to which people believe that creativity is fixed, unchangeable, or possible to be developed (growth). This perspective, inspired by Dweck's (Dweck & Yeager, 2019) model, was not only successfully applied to the context of creativity (Karwowski, 2014), but mindsets were demonstrated to play a regulatory role in initiating people's creative behavior. Indeed, believing that creativity is fixed and nothing can really change it was found to be detrimental for creative activity and associated with a set of less adaptive beliefs and strategies. People perceiving creativity as unchangeable, often called "entity theorists," were found to avoid risk and new challenges, be less engaged in everyday creative activities (Hass et al., 2019), and have fewer creative accomplishments. On the other hand, incremental theorists (people who perceive creativity as possible to be developed) were found to be more engaged in risky creative endeavors and were more effective problem solvers. One interesting finding that previous studies demonstrated is that about a quarter of the population tends to hold both mindsets simultaneously, quite paradoxically believing that creativity is both changeable and stable (Karwowski, Royston, et al., 2019). Such a pattern looks contrary to logic that assumes that fixed and growth mindsets are two ends of one continuum. However, given how complex creativity is, this paradox is not that surprising. Several people are fully convinced that we might strengthen our creative abilities during dedicated sessions of creativity training (Alves-Oliveira et al., 2021; Scott et al., 2004), yet at the same time, some levels of creativity, like Big-C, for instance, are impossible to be achieved without talent.

How are creative self-beliefs related to or influenced by peer relationships in the classroom? This is an important yet relatively overlooked question when it comes to creativity literature. However, a related problem has been intensively studied in educational psychology, thus providing some indirect yet helpful inspirations. Several theoretical models propose useful explanations of how students' self-perception (primarily their academic self-concept or self-efficacy) is shaped and developed. One widely accepted set of conditions of self-efficacy was proposed by Bandura (1997). He described four primary sources of people's self-efficacy. The first is mastery experiences – previous successes people reinterpret as indicating that they can solve similar or more complex problems in the future. The second condition is vicarious experiences – mainly modeling and observing how other people (critical ones for the individual) deal with the problem at hand. Such observation-based learning allows the individual to build the conviction that they are able to use the same strategies or ways of dealing with the problem. The third source of self-efficacy is social persuasion: usually verbal or nonverbal feedback people receive from parents, teachers, bosses, or peers. Indeed, comparisons with others and encouraging words received from someone we care about can serve as a self-efficacy builder. The fourth and final source, according to Bandura (1997), relates to people's physiological experiences – signals their body sends, early signs of stress or relaxation in the face of the task, are reinterpreted as indicating that we can or cannot deal with a task at hand. Sudden anxiety felt when the problem is presented might be interpreted as indicating that something is wrong, and they can't solve the task.

Another useful perspective that explains how our self-perception is shaped refers to three critical mechanisms people tend to use (Wolff et al., 2018). The first is of a temporal character. Indeed, people in general and students in particular conclude about their potential based on how their effectiveness changed over time. Perceived progress (i.e., better current than the previous achievement) builds self-concept by proving that "I'm able to achieve this."

The second mechanism refers to dimensional comparisons. As illustrated by educational psychology research (Marsh et al., 2018), students' academic self-concept is domain-specific, that is, self-perceived competencies in language, math, or science are usually quite loosely related. What is even more interesting is that students tend to compare their abilities across domains, for instance by asking themselves how good are they in math compared to biology. Such intraindividual comparisons lead to interesting effects. For example, "students with identical verbal (or math) ability differ in their verbal (math) self-concept when they differ in their math (verbal) achievement: students performing better in math than in the verbal domain tend to have lower self-perceptions of their verbal ability than do students with identical verbal ability but lower math ability" (Moller & Marsh, 2013, p. 544). "Translating" this effect to creativity, one might expect that higher creative skills in one domain could lead to underestimation of creative potential in the other, even if – objectively – performance in this second domain is high as well. This hypothesis, however, is yet to be tested.

However, the effect that seems to be most relevant for the topic of this chapter is the third mechanism that stands behind our self-perception. This mechanism involves external comparisons, usually conducted within a specific group: primarily the classroom. Students conclude about their abilities by comparing themselves to their classmates. As the so-called Big-Fish-Little-Pond Effect (BFLPE, see Marsh, 1987; Marsh & Hau, 2003) posits, students' academic self-concept is positively associated with their school achievement but, at the same time, negatively influenced by their peers' achievement. In other words, the higher the individual achievements are, the higher the self-concept will be. But, the higher the overall class achievement is – so the more demanding comparison group – the lower the individual's academic self-concept will be.

The natural question is whether BFLPE applies to creative self-concept. Is being surrounded by more creative peers making us doubt our creative poten-tial, or perhaps making creativity salient, valued, and consequently more often attributed to ourselves? BFLPE is robust and cross-culturally universal (Marsh & Hau, 2003), yet its generalizability beyond academic self-concept is unknown. Contrary to school achievement, creativity is less evident in the classroom; students have fewer opportunities to observe it directly from their peers. Academic achievement is highly valued and desired in the classroom; the value ascribed to creativity is often much lower (Westby & Dawson, 1995). Therefore, whether being surrounded by more-versus-fewer creative peers strengthens or weakens creative self-perception is not that clear.

So far, only one study addressed this research question directly (Karwowski, 2015). An extensive investigation (more than 3,600 students placed in 179 classes at 89 schools) tested students' creative self-concept (measured with the Short Scale of Creative Self, Karwowski, et al., 2018; Zielińska et al., 2022b), and their creative potential (divergent thinking) as well as creative activity (a scale from the Inventory of Creative Activities and Achievements, Diedrich et al., 2018). Three-level hierarchical linear models regressed students' creative self-concept and creative personal identity on their abilities and activities as well as their classmates' average level of creative activity and divergent thinking. It was expected that, at the students' level, there would be positive links between creative potential and activity, and creative self-concept. At the same time, following the BFLPE, it was assumed that the average classroom level of potential and activity would be negatively linked to creative self-perception.

The individual-level predictors were found significant and consistent with expectations and previous theorizing. Indeed, the better the students' divergent thinking and previous creative activity were, the stronger their creative self-concept and creative personal identity were. However, there were no main effects of peers' divergent thinking or creative activity on creative self-perception. Thus, what adolescents thought about their creativity was inde-pendent of the reference group formed by their classmates. The open question is whether this pattern would replicate in more creativity-oriented school settings. Finally, an intriguing interaction effect at the classroom level occurred.

Contrary to the BFLPE, students' creative self-concept and creative personal identity were stronger in those classes that *simultaneously* held higher average divergent thinking and creative activity. Therefore, although none of the main effects of divergent thinking or activity was significant, their interaction indeed was. It might be interpreted as showing a synergetic result of peers' ability and activity or the role of the specific creative climate in the classroom (Karwowski, 2019). It was not sufficient for peers to have high creative potential (divergent thinking) but to use the opportunities to apply this potential to observable creative activities in their classrooms. If such opportunities to *think and act creatively* were indeed used, peers' creative self-concept benefited.

My secondary and previously unpublished analyses on this extensive data set examined whether students' creative self-concept and the extent to which they valued creativity were associated with the climate in their classroom (particularly, emotional and social relationships with peers and the support their creativity received in the classroom). Using the Creative Climate Questionnaire (Karwowski, 2019), peers' relationship was measured using such items as: "our class is well-knit," "I like most of the students in my class," or "my classmates are cool." Student-perceived support for the creativity that teachers provide was measured using items like: "our teachers encourage us to propose our own solutions to the problems we solve," "teachers support our original ideas," or "teachers spur our creativity."

A series of multilevel models demonstrated that not only students' domain-general self-perception of creativity (creative self-concept) and valuing it (creative personal identity), but also domain-specific perceptions measured by the Kaufman Domain of Creativity Scale (Kaufman, 2012; McKay, Karwowski, et al., 2017) were positively associated with the climate in the classroom. The more positive the relationship with classmates was, the higher the perceived creative self-concept, valuing creativity, everyday, and scholarly creativity was. Perceived support provided by teachers at the class level was positively associated with self-perceived creativity in the performance and artistic domains.

Thus, this study not only suggests a skepticism regarding whether the BFLPE effect applies to creative self-perception but also confirms that peer relations in the classroom might shape, or at least be positively associated with, the self-perception of creativity. More specifically, this investigation indicates the existence of an effect opposite to what BFLPE would suggest: in classrooms composed of more creative peers, other students felt more rather than less creative. This, however, happens only if these creative students have some space and opportunity to experience their creativity in the classroom. Moreover, this opportunity to behave creatively was higher in the classes where peers' relationships were more positive and creativity was supported.

Concluding Thoughts

Creativity is an underappreciated driver of successful learning, a factor that allows students to take the perspective of others and a source of positive emotions. As this chapter argued, creativity in school settings is often mythologized, with several biases and myths being too often and too easily applied to creative students. That might include perceiving school as an anti-creative environment in general or seeing creative students as rejected individuals.

Based on network studies and extensive classroom investigations, the conclusions this chapter brings are much less radical and spectacular than school critics proclaim. These conclusions apply to two broad spheres of students' functioning: their relations with classmates, including interpersonal attractiveness in the classroom, and the potential influences peers might have on how students perceive their creativity in the classroom. Based on the research discussed in this chapter, both these aspects require a more nuanced perspective.

First, creativity makes students attractive to their peers. It makes sense, as students able to generate new and original ideas could make class activities exciting and the effects of projects they work on unique. Even if being original sometimes means being ridiculed (Beghetto & Dilley, 2016), there is more to admire and like in creative students. That might include their sense of humor, engagement in play, and the quality of ideas they propose. So, contrary to what is sometimes observed among famous creators, creative students are often sociometric stars rather than solitaries.

Second, the well-known homophily effect applies to the classroom as well. Students who share their interests are naturally more likely to become friends. This effect seems to apply to creativity as well – students characterized by a similar level of creative activity are quite often clustered together and occupy central places in their networks. It does not preclude the situation that highly creative students are individualistic and rejected, yet the dominant pattern is their high cohesiveness and attractiveness.

Third, as discussed above, what students think about their creative abilities shapes the likelihood of solving open-ended, ill-defined tasks. Disbelief in one's creative possibilities or considering creativity as something irrelevant for oneself makes these chances close to zero. This is precisely why creativity literature analyzes what people think about their creative potential and whether their confidence is accurate. Social conditions, including peer relationships and comparisons, were theorized as vital elements that influence people's self-belief. As the Big-Fish-Little-Pond Effect illustrates, while academically successful students are usually convinced about their potential (academic self-concept), this effect weakens or even disappears when they are surrounded by high achieving peers. Does this effect translate to creative self-concept? More research is needed to offer a definitive answer to this question, yet the results discussed so far put generalizability of the BFLPE to creativity into doubt. As illustrated, adolescent students tended to appreciate creativity and believe in their potential more when surrounded by more effective divergent thinkers engaged in creative activities. Importantly, these two aspects (i.e., peers' creative abilities *and* activities) had to occur together to affect students' creative self-concept positively. Thus, it is not enough to be among potentially creative students to think about ourselves as creative; what is needed is that this creative potential has chances to be presented in the social context of the classroom. To be so, a creative climate is necessary.

The fourth and final conclusion this chapter brings is that certain aspects of school and classroom climate, particularly positive relationships with peers based on high interpersonal integration and cohesiveness, predict students' creative self-concept across various domains and the intensity of their creative activity. Given that this relationship is correlational, a firm conclusion about causality is premature. It is possible that peer relationships based on trust and positive emotions make creativity in the classroom more likely thanks to broader accessibility of different ideas and solutions, and to feeling safe. Similarly, however, it is quite possible that in the classes where creativity is exercised and appreciated, cohesiveness among students increases due to their exchange of ideas, the possibility of working together, and opportunities to present their "new faces" during creative tasks. And while future longitudinal studies should provide a more robust answer to the question about causality, peer relationships in the classroom matter for creativity.

To conclude, there are plenty of reasons why creativity should occupy a more prominent place in the everyday lives of our classrooms. One of them is its role in peer relationships and – reciprocally – the extent to which it benefits from a positive climate and relationships. Humans are indeed social animals; this sociality is inevitably associated with creative thought and action.

References

Alves-Oliveira, P., Arriaga, P., Xavier, C., Hoffman, G., & Paiva, A. (2021). Creativity landscapes: Systematic review spanning 70 years of creativity interventions for children. *The Journal of Creative Behavior*. Advance online publication. https://doi.org/10.1002/jocb.514

Bandura, A. (1982). Self-efficacy mechanism in human agency. *American Psychologist*, *37*(2), 122.

Bandura, A. (1997). *Self-Efficacy: The Exercise of Control*. W. H. Freeman.

Barbot, B., & Said-Metwaly, S. (2021). Is there really a creativity crisis? A critical review and meta-analytic re-appraisal. *The Journal of Creative Behavior*, *55*(3), 696–709. https://doi.org/10.1002/jocb.483

Beghetto, R. A. (2006). Creative self-efficacy: Correlates in middle and secondary students. *Creativity Research Journal*, *18*(4), 447–457. https://doi.org/10.1207/s15326934crj1804_4

Beghetto, R. A. (2016). Creative learning: A fresh look. *Journal of Cognitive Education and Psychology*, *15*(1), 6–23. https://doi.org/10.1891/1945-8959.15.1.6

Beghetto, R. A., & Dilley, A. E. (2016). Creative aspirations or pipe dreams? Toward understanding creative mortification in children and adolescents? *New Directions for Child and Adolescent Development*, *2016*(151), 85–95. https://doi.org/10.1002/cad.20150

Beghetto, R. A., & Karwowski, M. (2017). Toward untangling creative self-beliefs. In M. Karwowski & J. C. Kaufman (Eds.), *The Creative Self: Effect of Beliefs,*

Self-Efficacy, Mindset, and Identity (pp. 3–22). Elsevier Academic Press. https://doi.org/10.1016/B978-0-12-809790-8.00001-7

Boekhorst, J. A., Halinski, M., & Good, J. R. L. (2021). Fun, friends, and creativity: A social capital perspective. *The Journal of Creative Behavior*, *55*(4), 970–983. https://doi.org/10.1002/jocb.502

Bonetto, E., Pichot, N., Girandola, F., & Bonnardel, N. (2021). The normative features of creativity: Creative individuals are judged to be warmer and more competent. *The Journal of Creative Behavior*, *55*(3), 649–660. https://doi.org/10.1002/jocb.477

Byrne, D., Griffitt, W., & Stefaniak, D. (1967). Attraction and similarity of personality characteristics. *Journal of Personality and Social Psychology*, *5*, 82–90. https://doi.org/10.1037/h0021198

Cattani, G., & Ferriani, S. (2008). A core/periphery perspective on individual creative performance: Social networks and cinematic achievements in the Hollywood film industry. *Organization Science*, *19*, 824–844. https://doi.org/10.1287/orsc.1070.0350

Chen, M.-H., & Agrawal, S. (2017). Do communication barriers in student teams impede creative behavior in the long run? – A time-lagged perspective. *Thinking Skills and Creativity*, *26*, 154–167. https://doi.org/10.1016/j.tsc.2017.10.008

Chi, N., Liao, H., & Chien, W. (2021). Having a creative day: A daily diary study of the interplay between daily activating moods and physical work environment on daily creativity. *The Journal of Creative Behavior*, *55*(3), 752–768. https://doi.org/10.1002/jocb.488

Cialdini, R., B., Borden, R. J., Avril, T., et al. (1976). Basking in reflected glory: Three (football) field studies. *Journal of Personality and Social Psychology*, *34*(3), 366–375. https://doi.org/10.1037/0022-3514.34.3.366

Clegg, H., Nettle, D., & Miell, D. (2008). A test of Miller's aesthetic fitness hypothesis. *Journal of Evolutionary Psychology*, *6*(2), 101–115. https://doi.org/10.1556/JEP.2008.1009

Conner, T. S., & Silvia, P. J. (2015). Creative days: A daily diary study of emotion, personality, and everyday creativity. *Psychology of Aesthetics, Creativity, and the Arts*, *9*(4), 463.

Dawson, V. L. (1997). In search of the wild bohemian: Challenges in the identification of the creatively gifted. *Roeper Review*, *19*(3), 148–152.

Diedrich, J., Jauk, E., Silvia, P. J., et al. (2018). Assessment of real-life creativity: The Inventory of Creative Activities and Achievements (ICAA). *Psychology of Aesthetics, Creativity, and the Arts*, *12*(3), 304–316. https://doi.org/10.1037/aca0000137

Driebe, J. C., Sidari, M. J., Dufner, M., et al. (2021). Intelligence can be detected but is not found attractive in videos and live interactions. *Evolution and Human Behavior*, *42*(6), 507–516. https://doi.org/10.1016/j.evolhumbehav.2021.05.002

Dweck, C. S., & Yeager, D. S. (2019). Mindsets: A view from two eras. *Perspectives on Psychological Science*, *14*(3), 481–496. https://doi.org/10.1177/1745691618804166

Feist, G. J. (1998). A meta-analysis of personality in scientific and artistic creativity. *Personality and Social Psychology Review*, *2*(4), 290–309. https://doi.org/10.1207/s15327957pspr0204_5

Feist, G. J., & Barron, F. X. (2003). Predicting creativity from early to late adulthood: Intellect, potential, and personality. *Journal of Research in Personality, 37*(2), 62–88. https://doi.org/10.1016/S0092-6566(02)00536-6

Gajda, A., Beghetto, R. A., & Karwowski, M. (2017). Exploring creative learning in the classroom: A multi-method approach. *Thinking Skills and Creativity, 24,* 250–267, https://doi.org/10.1016/j.tsc.2017.04.002

Gajda, A., Karwowski, M., & Beghetto, R. A. (2017). Creativity and academic achievement: A meta-analysis. *Journal of Educational Psychology, 109*(2), 269–299. https://doi.org/10.1037/edu0000133

Gerwig, A., Miroshnik, K., Forthmann, B., et al. (2021). The relationship between intelligence and divergent thinking: a meta-analytic update. *Journal of Intelligence, 9,* 23. https://doi.org/10.3390/jintelligence9020023

Glăveanu, V. P., & Beghetto, R. A. (2021). Creative experience: A non-standard definition of creativity. *Creativity Research Journal, 33*(2), 75–80. https://doi.org/10.1080/10400419.2020.1827606

Gralewski, J., & Karwowski, M. (2013). Polite girls and creative boys? Students' gender moderates accuracy of teachers' ratings of creativity. *The Journal of Creative Behavior, 47*(4), 290–304. https://doi.org/10.1002/jocb.36

Haase, J., Hoff, E. V., Hanel, P. H. P., & Innes-Ker, Å. (2018). A meta-analysis of the relation between creative self-efficacy and different creativity measurements. *Creativity Research Journal, 30*(1), 1–16. https://doi.org/10.1080/10400419.2018.1411436

Hass, R. W., Katz-Buonincontro, J., & Reiter-Palmon, R. (2019). The creative self and creative thinking: An exploration of predictive effects using Bayes factor analyses. *Psychology of Aesthetics, Creativity, and the Arts, 13*(4), 375–387. https://doi.org/10.1037/aca0000169

Hopp, M. D. S., Zhang, Z. S., Hinch, L., O'Reilly, C., & Ziegler, A. (2019). Creative, thus connected: The power of sociometric creativity on friendship formation in gifted adolescents – a longitudinal network analysis of gifted students. *New Directions for Child and Adolescent Development, 2019*(168), 47–73. https://doi.org/10.1002/cad.20324

Ilha Villanova, A. L., & Pina e Cunha, M. (2021). Everyday creativity: A systematic literature review. *The Journal of Creative Behavior, 55*(3), 673–695. https://doi.org/10.1002/jocb.481

Ivcevic, Z. (2007), Artistic and everyday creativity: An act-frequency approach. *The Journal of Creative Behavior, 41,* 271-290. https://doi.org/10.1002/j.2162-6057.2007.tb01074.x

Ivcevic, Z., & Hoffmann, J. (2019). Emotions and creativity: From process to person and product. In J. C. Kaufman & R. J. Sternberg (Eds.), *The Cambridge Handbook of Creativity* (2nd ed., pp. 273–295). Cambridge University Press. https://doi.org/10.1017/9781316979839.015

Ivcevic, Z., & Hoffmann, J. D. (2021). The creativity dare: Attitudes toward creativity and prediction of creative behavior in school. *The Journal of Creative Behavior.* https://doi.org/10.1002/jocb.527

Ivcevic, Z., & Mayer, J. D. (2009). Mapping dimensions of creativity in the life-space. *Creativity Research Journal, 21*(2–3), 152–165. https://doi.org/10.1080/10400410902855259

Izard, C. E. (1960). Personality similarity and friendship. *Journal of Abnormal and Social Psychology, 61,* 47–51. https://doi.org/10.1037/h0042147

Jankowska, D. M., & Karwowski, M. (2015). Measuring creative imagery abilities. *Frontiers in Psychology, 6.* https://doi.org/10.3389/fpsyg.2015.01591

Kao, G., & Jouyner, K. (2004). Do race and ethnicity matter among friends? Activities among interracial, interethnic, and intraethnic adolescent friends. *The Sociological Quarterly, 45,* 557–573. https://doi.org/10.1111/j.1533-8525.2004.tb02303.x

Karwowski, M. (2014). Creative mindsets: Measurement, correlates, consequences. *Psychology of Aesthetics, Creativity, and the Arts, 8*(1), 62–70. https://doi.org/10.1037/a0034898

Karwowski, M. (2015). Peer effect on students' creative self-concept. *The Journal of Creative Behavior, 49*(3), 211–225, https://doi.org/10.1002/jocb.102

Karwowski, M. (2019). Classroom creative climate: From a static to a dynamic perspective. In I. Lebuda & V. P. Glăveanu (Eds.), *The Palgrave Handbook of Social Creativity Research* (pp. 487–499). Springer International. https://doi.org/10.1007/978-3-319-95498-1_30

Karwowski, M. (2022). School does not kill creativity. *European Psychologist, 27*(3), 263–275. https://doi.org/10.1027/1016-9040/a000449

Karwowski, M., & Beghetto, R. A. (2019). Creative behavior as agentic action. *Psychology of Aesthetics, Creativity, and the Arts, 13*(4), 402–415. https://doi.org/10.1037/aca0000190

Karwowski, M., Dul, J., Gralewski, J., et al. (2016). Is creativity without intelligence possible? A necessary condition analysis. *Intelligence, 57,* 105–117. https://doi.org/10.1016/j.intell.2016.04.006

Karwowski, M., Gralewski, J., & Szumski, G. (2015). Teachers' effect on students' creative self-beliefs is moderated by students' gender. *Learning and Individual Differences, 44,* 1–8. https://doi.org/10.1016/j.lindif.2015.10.001

Karwowski, M., & Lebuda, I. (2016). The big five, the huge two, and creative self-beliefs: A meta-analysis. *Psychology of Aesthetics, Creativity, and the Arts, 10*(2), 214–232. https://doi.org/10.1037/aca0000035

Karwowski, M., Lebuda, I., & Beghetto, R. A. (2019). Creative self-beliefs. In J. C. Kaufman & R. J. Sternberg (Eds.), *The Cambridge Handbook of Creativity* (pp. 396–417). Cambridge University Press. https://doi.org/10.1017/9781316979839.021

Karwowski, M., Lebuda, I., & Wiśniewska, E. (2018). Measuring creative self-efficacy and creative personal identity. *The International Journal of Creativity & Problem Solving, 28,* 45–57.

Karwowski, M., Royston, R. P., & Reiter-Palmon, R. (2019). Exploring creative mindsets: Variable and person-centered approaches. *Psychology of Aesthetics, Creativity, and the Arts, 13*(1), 36–48. https://doi.org/10.1037/aca0000170

Karwowski, M., & Wiśniewska, E. (2021). Creativity in adulthood. In S. W. Russ, J. D. Hoffmann, & J. C. Kaufman (Eds.), *The Cambridge Handbook of Lifespan Development of Creativity* (pp. 206–232). Cambridge University Press. https://doi.org/10.1017/9781108755726.013

Karwowski, M., Zielińska, A., Jankowska, D. M., et al. (2021). Creative lockdown? A daily diary study of creative activity during pandemics. *Frontiers in Psychology, 12,* 23, https://doi.org/10.3389/fpsyg.2021.600076

Kaufman, J. C. (2012). Counting the muses: Development of the Kaufman Domains of Creativity Scale (K-DOCS). *Psychology of Aesthetics, Creativity, and the Arts, 6*(4), 298–308. https://doi.org/10.1037/a0029751

Kaufman, J. C., & Beghetto, R. A. (2009). Beyond big and little: The Four C model of creativity. *Review of General Psychology*, *13*(1), 1–12. https://doi.org/10.1037/a0013688

Kaufman, J. C., Bromley, M. L., & Cole, J. C. (2007). Insane, poetic, lovable: Creativity and endorsement of the "mad genius" stereotype. *Imagination, Cognition and Personality*, *26*, 149–161. https://doi.org/10.2190/J207-3U30-R401-446J

Kéri, S. (2011). Solitary minds and social capital: Latent inhibition, general intellectual functions and social network size predict creative achievements. *Psychology of Aesthetics, Creativity, and the Arts*, *5*, 215–221. https://doi.org/10.1037/a0022000

Kettler, T., Lamb, K. N., Willerson, A., & Mullet, D. R. (2018). Teachers' perceptions of creativity in the classroom. *Creativity Research Journal*, *30*(2), 164–171. https://doi.org/10.1080/10400419.2018.1446503

Kharkhurin, A. V. (2014). Creativity.4in1: Four-criterion construct of creativity. *Creativity Research Journal, 26*(3), 338–352. https://doi.org/10.1080/10400419.2014.929424

Kim, K. H. (2011). The creativity crisis: The decrease in creative thinking scores on the Torrance Tests of Creative Thinking. *Creativity Research Journal*, *23*(4), 285–295. https://doi.org/10.1080/10400419.2011.627805

Lau, S., & Li, W.-L. (1996). Peer status and perceived creativity: Are popular children viewed by peer and teachers as creative? *Creativity Research Journal*, *9*, 295–306. https://doi.org/10.1207/s15326934crj0904

Lebuda, I., Zielińska, A., & Karwowski, M. (2021). On surface and core predictors of real-life creativity. *Thinking Skills and Creativity*, *42*, 100973. https://doi.org/10.1016/j.tsc.2021.100973

Li, N. P., & Kenrick, D. T. (2006). Sex similarities and differences in preferences for short-term mates: What, whether, and why. *Journal of Personality and Social Psychology*, *90*(3), 468–489. https://doi.org/10.1037/0022-3514.90.3.468

Liang, Q., Niu, W., Cheng, L., & Qin, K. (2021). Creativity outside school: The influence of family background, perceived parenting, and after-school activity on creativity. *The Journal of Creative Behavior*. https://doi.org/10.1002/jocb.521

Marsh, H. W. (1987). The Big-Fish-Little-Pond Effect on academic self-concept. *Journal of Educational Psychology*, *79*(3), 280–295. https://doi.org/10.1037/0022-0663.79.3.280

Marsh, H. W., & Hau, K.-T. (2003). Big-Fish-Little-Pond Effect on academic self-concept: A cross-cultural (26-country) test of the negative effects of academically selective schools. *American Psychologist*, *58*(5), 364–376. https://doi.org/10.1037/0003-066X.58.5.364

Marsh, H. W., Pekrun, R., Murayama, K., et al. (2018). An integrated model of academic self-concept development: Academic self-concept, grades, test scores, and tracking over 6 years. *Developmental Psychology*, *54*(2), 263–280., https://doi.org/10.1037/dev0000393

Marsh, H. W., Pekrun, R., Parker, P. D., et al. (2019). The murky distinction between self-concept and self-efficacy: Beware of lurking jingle-jangle fallacies. *Journal of Educational Psychology*, *111*(2), 331–353. https://doi.org/10.1037/edu0000281

McKay, A. S., Grygiel, P., & Karwowski, M. (2017). Connected to create: A social network analysis of friendship ties and creativity. *Psychology of Aesthetics, Creativity, and the Arts*, *11*(3), 284–294. https://doi.org/10.1037/aca0000117

McKay, A. S., Karwowski, M., & Kaufman, J. C. (2017). Measuring the muses: Validating the Kaufman Domains of Creativity Scale (K-DOCS). *Psychology of Aesthetics, Creativity, and the Arts, 11*(2), 216–230. https://doi.org/10.1037/aca0000074

McPherson, M., Smith-Lovin, L., & Cook, J. M. (2001). Birds of a feather: Homophily in social networks. *Annual Review of Sociology, 27*, 415–444. https://doi.org/10.1146/annurev.soc.27.1.415

Michael, L. A. H., Hou, S.-T., & Fan, H.-L. (2011). Creative self-efficacy and innovative behavior in a service setting: Optimism as a moderator. *The Journal of Creative Behavior, 45*(4), 258–272. https://doi.org/10.1002/j.2162-6057.2011.tb01430.x

Möller, J., & Marsh, H. W. (2013). Dimensional comparison theory. *Psychological Review, 120*(3), 544–560. https://doi.org/10.1037/a0032459

Mueller, J. S., Melwani, S., & Goncalo, J. A. (2012). The bias against creativity: Why people desire but reject creative ideas. *Psychological Science, 23*, 13–17. https://doi.org/10.1177/0956797611421018

Murdock, M. C., & Ganim, R. M. (1993). Creativity and humor: Integration and incongruity. *The Journal of Creative Behavior, 27*(1), 57–70. https://doi.org/10.1002/j.2162-6057.1993.tb01387.x

Nettle, D. (2008). Why is creativity attractive in a potential mate? *Behavioral and Brain Sciences, 31*(3), 275–276. https://doi.org/10.1017/S0140525X08004366

Perry-Smith, J. E. (2006). Social yet creative: The role of social relationships in facilitating individual creativity. *Academy of Management Journal, 49*, 85–101. https://doi.org/10.5465/AMJ.2006.20785503

Perry-Smith, J. E., & Shalley, C. E. (2003). The social side of creativity: A static and dynamic social network perspective. *Academy of Management Review, 28*, 89–106. https://doi.org/10.2307/30040691

Proyer, R. T., Tandler, N., & Brauer, K. (2019). Playfulness and creativity: A selective review. In S. R. Luria, J. Baer, & J. C. Kaufman (Eds.), *Creativity and Humor* (pp. 43–60). Elsevier Academic Press. https://doi.org/10.1016/B978-0-12-813802-1.00002-8

Robinson, Ken. (2006). Do schools kill creativity? [Video]. TED Conferences. https://www.ted.com/talks/sir_ken_robinson_do_schools_kill_creativity?utm_campaign=tedspread&utm_medium=referral&utm_source=tedcomshare

Runco, M. A., Acar, S., & Cayirdag, N. (2017). A closer look at the creativity gap and why students are less creative at school than outside of school. *Thinking Skills and Creativity, 24*, 242–249. https://doi.org/10.1016/j.tsc.2017.04.003

Runco, M. A., & Jaeger, G. J. (2012). The standard definition of creativity. *Creativity Research Journal, 24*(1), 92–96. https://doi.org/10.1080/10400419.2012.650092

Sawyer, R. K. (2012). *Explaining Creativity: The Science of Human Innovation*. Oxford University Press.

Scott, G., Leritz, L. E., & Mumford, M. D. (2004). The effectiveness of creativity training: A quantitative review. *Creativity Research Journal, 16*(4), 361–388. https://doi.org/10.1080/10400410409534549

Silvia, P. J. (2015). Intelligence and creativity are pretty similar after all. *Educational Psychology Review, 27*(4), 599–606. https://doi.org/10.1007/s10648-015-9299-1

Simonton, D. K. (1984). Artistic creativity and interpersonal relationships across and within generations. *Journal of Personality and Social Psychology, 46*, 1273–1286. https://doi.org/10.1037//0022-3514.46.6.1273

Simonton, D. K. (2012). Taking the U.S. Patent Office criteria seriously: A quantitative three-criterion creativity definition and its implications. *Creativity Research Journal, 24*(2-3), 97–106. https://doi.org/10.1080/10400419.2012.676974

Simonton, D. K. (2014). The mad-genius paradox: Can creative people be more mentally healthy but highly creative people more mentally ill? *Perspectives on Psychological Science, 9*, 470–480. https://doi.org/10.1177/1745691614543973

Snyder, H. T., Sowden, P. T., Silvia, P. J., & Kaufman, J. C. (2021). The creative self: Do people distinguish creative self-perceptions, efficacy, and personal identity? *Psychology of Aesthetics, Creativity, and the Arts, 15*(4), 627–636. https://doi.org/10.1037/aca0000317

Sprecher, S., & Regan, P. C. (2002). Liking some things (in some people) more than others: Partner preferences in romantic relationships and friendships. *Journal of Social and Personal Relationships, 19*(4), 463–481. https://doi.org/10.1177/0265407502019004048

Tesser, A. (1988). Toward a self-evaluation maintenance model of social behavior. In L. Berkowitz (Ed.), *Advances in Experimental Social Psychology* (vol. 21, pp. 181–227). Elsevier. https://doi.org/10.1016/S0065-2601(08)60227-0

Torrance, E. P. (2004). Great expectations: Creative achievements of the sociometric stars in a 30-year study. *Journal of Secondary Gifted Education, 16*(1), 5–13. https://doi.org/10.4219/jsge-2004-465

van der Wilt, F., van der Veen, C., van Kruistum, C., & van Oers, B. (2018). Popular, rejected, neglected, controversial, or average: Do young children of different sociometric groups differ in their level of oral communicative competence? *Social Development, 27*(4), 793–807. https://doi.org/10.1111/sode.12316

Weisberg, R., Pichot, N., Bonetto, E., et al. N. (2021). From explicit to implicit theories of creativity and back: The relevance of naive criteria in defining creativity. *The Journal of Creative Behavior, 55*(3), 839–856. https://doi.org/10.1002/jocb.492

Westby, E. L., & Dawson, V. L. (1995). Creativity: Asset or burden in the classroom? *Creativity Research Journal, 8*(1), 1–10. https://doi.org/10.1207/s15326934crj0801_1

Wolff, F., Helm, F., Zimmermann, F., Nagy, G., & Möller, J. (2018). On the effects of social, temporal, and dimensional comparisons on academic self-concept. *Journal of Educational Psychology, 110*(7), 1005–1025. https://doi.org/10.1037/edu0000248

Wolfradt, U., & Pretz, J. E. (2001). Individual differences in creativity: Personality, story writing, and hobbies. *European Journal of Personality, 15*, 297–310. https://doi.org/10.1002/per.409

Zandi, N., Karwowski, M., Forthmann, B., & Holling, H. (2022). How stable is the creative self-concept? A latent state-trait analysis. *Psychology of Creativity, Aesthetics, and the Arts*, Advance online publication. https://doi.org/10.1037/aca0000521.

Zielińska, A. (2020). Mapping adolescents' everyday creativity. *Creativity. Theories – Research – Applications, 7*(1), 208–229. https://doi.org/10.2478/ctra-2020-0012

Zielińska, A., Lebuda, I., Ivcevic, Z., & Karwowski, M. (2022a). How adolescents develop and implement their ideas? On self-regulation of creative action. *Thinking Skills and Creativity, 43*. https://doi.org/10.1016/j.tsc.2022.100998

Zielińska, A., Lebuda, I., & Karwowski, M. (2022b). Scaling creative self: An Item Response Theory analysis of the Short Scale of Creative Self. *Creativity Research Journal*, Advance online publication. https://doi.org/10.1080/10400419.2022.2123139.

26 Creative Curricular Experiences

Navigating Uncertainties and Emotions toward Creative Expression

Ronald A. Beghetto and Annette C. Schmidt

Creative endeavors are inherently uncertain activities, because one is never certain how a given creative effort will turn out. Consequently, it is not surprising that when engaging in such efforts one will encounter obstacles, setbacks, and failures along the way. Encounters with uncertainties and setbacks are emotionally laden (Berns, 2010; von Thienen et al., 2017) and can, in some cases, be experienced as profoundly negative and demoralizing. When this occurs, it can result in what has been called *creative mortification*. Creative mortification refers to the abandonment or indefinite suspension of future creative efforts and aspirations (Beghetto, 2014; Beghetto & Dilley, 2016). An aspiring poet who is ridiculed by peers may, for instance, stop sharing and writing poetry. Fortunately, this need not be the case.

Uncertainty and setbacks, even profoundly painful and disappointing ones, can lead to creative learning and growth. One way of thinking about encountered uncertainties and setbacks is that they open up at least two potential pathways, one leading to creative expression and the other leading to avoidance or suspension of one's creative expression. A key question for educators, researchers, and anyone interested in supporting creative development is: *How might young people be supported in pursuing the pathway of learning and growth when experiencing emotionally laden encounters with uncertainty and setbacks?*

The aim of this chapter is to address this question. Specifically, this chapter outlines how creative curricular experiences can serve as a vehicle for students to learn how to navigate uncertainty and setbacks toward creative expression and development. In particular, we introduce a process model that can help researchers and educators conceptualize the roles creative self-beliefs and emotions play in shaping different pathways that students can take when they encounter uncertainties and setbacks. Practical implications and future directions for research are also discussed.

Diverging Pathways in Creative Expression and Development

Our primary assertion in this chapter is that creative expression and development can occur in most any educational context if students have opportunities to engage in creative curricular experiences that provide necessary structures and supports to help them anticipate and productively navigate the

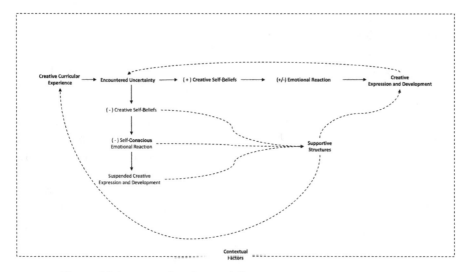

Figure 26.1 *Potential pathways following creative impasse.*

uncertainties encountered along the way. This includes developing the confidence and capacity to regulate the kinds of beliefs and emotions associated with transforming encounters with uncertainty and setbacks into creative action. Alternatively, when young people engage in creative curricular experiences without supportive structures in place, then we would assert that it will be more likely that students' creative expression and development will be curtailed.

To better understand the rationale for these assertions, it may be helpful to introduce a general process model that depicts differential pathways that students can take when engaging with the uncertainties inherent in creative curricular experiences. Figure 26.1 depicts these pathways. We acknowledge, at the outset, that our representation of this process is somewhat underspecified as there are likely a host of factors not accounted for that can also play a role. Still, we feel that the factors we highlight can go a long way in helping educators and researchers conceptualize and further refine efforts aimed at supporting young people's creative expression and development.

As depicted in Figure 26.1, the process starts with young people engaging in a creative experience, encountering uncertainty, and working through creative self-beliefs, and emotional reactions, with the assistance of supportive structures and contexts, toward creative expression and development. Each of these features of the process is discussed in the sections that follow.

Creative Curricular Experience

Given that our focus is on creative endeavors situated in educational contexts, our process model starts with students having the opportunity to engage in a creative curricular experience. Creative curricula refer to "curricular technologies, techniques, or experiences that have the potential to provide students with opportunities to meet preestablished criteria by sharing their own unique perspectives, developing their own approach to doing something, or coming up with their own creative outcomes" (Beghetto, 2019, p. 92). Students in a science class who are required to develop and conduct a novel research project about the wetlands outside of their school is an example of a creative curricular experience.

A key feature of creative curricular experiences, as with any creative experience, is that they provide students with structured and supported encounters with uncertainty. These experiences represent a blend of predetermined and to-be-determined elements. The predetermined elements represent the goals and criteria for success, which are specified in advance, and the to-be-determined elements represent the myriad ways students can meet those goals and criteria. In this way, uncertainty is designed into the process. Importantly, the uncertainty designed into the experience represents a state of genuine uncertainty in that teachers do not know how students will ultimately meet the learning goals and criteria. Consequently, creative curricular experiences represent structured opportunities for both teachers and students to engage with uncertainty and have creative learning experiences in an otherwise supportive and structured learning environment.

Creative curricular experiences include the following eight design elements (adapted from Beghetto, 2019, p. 97):

1. **Creative openings.** This first feature is what makes creative curricular experiences different from other curricular experiences because students have opportunities to meet learning goals and criteria in their own creative ways. Without the opportunity for students to be invited, encouraged, and even expected to meet criteria in different ways, then creative learning outcomes are unlikely to occur.

2. **Connections to academic content.** Supporting students' academic learning is the primary objective in most K–12 and higher education settings; consequently, students engaging in creative curricular experiences in such settings are expected to use and demonstrate key academic content and skills while engaging in the experience.

3. **Clear criteria for success.** Clear criteria for success represent a foundational instructional support, which becomes particularly pronounced in creative curricular experiences because students need a clear understanding of the parameters and guidelines necessary for success when developing their own approach to meeting criteria. Without clear criteria for success, students can become overwhelmed by the uncertainty of creative curricular experiences.

4. **Multiple opportunities for student feedback.** Multiple opportunities for student feedback represent another foundational instructional structure and source of support when engaging students in creative curricular experiences. Frequent feedback, from multiple sources (e.g., teachers, peers, outside experts), can help ensure that students are on track and making progress toward meeting the criteria necessary for success (Lipnevich & Smith, 2018).

Given that students will be trying out different ways of meeting criteria, feedback will help ensure that their efforts move beyond simple novelty and toward a blend of novelty and meeting required task constraints (Beghetto & Kaufman, 2007).

5. **Opportunities for multiple iterations.** Creative curricular experiences, like other creative experiences, often include aspects of nonlinearity (Glăveanu & Beghetto, 2020) involving some level of "messiness" (Tanggaard & Juelsbo, 2016) and unpredictable twists and turns. Consequently, creative curricular experiences are designed to provide students with flexibility and encouragement to try out different ideas and actions in an effort to meet their goals and the specified criteria, which includes the option to make necessary changes (based on feedback) and to take different directions in their work.

6. **Work can be exhibited.** Creative curricular experiences have the potential to make creative contributions to others (e.g., peers, teachers, and people beyond the immediate educational environment). As such, creative curricular experiences are often designed to be exhibited to others so that they can inspire and contribute to peers, teachers, and outside audiences.

7. **Focus on the process.** Although creative curricular experiences do have outcomes (including tangible products), the focus is on what is learned through the process of engaging in these experiences (Glăveanu & Beghetto, 2020). Creative curricular experiences therefore should include opportunities for students to reflect on and share their experiences with the process, including the challenges, setbacks, and mistakes they have made and what they have learned from the process of encountering and attempting to work through those setbacks.

8. **Informs instruction.** Creative curricular experiences should also be designed to ensure that teachers can gather timely information that can inform instructional decisions and the selection of supports teachers can provide to current and future students. This information includes identifying the challenges, successes, and emotional reactions that students experience while engaged in these kinds of curricular activities.

Encountering Uncertainty

The next step in the pathway, as illustrated in Figure 26.1, is an encounter with uncertainty. The uncertainty young people (and even teachers) experience when engaged in creative curricular experiences is designed to propel them into a state of creative inquiry – providing them with an opportunity to think and act in new and meaningful ways. Throughout the process students (and teachers) may encounter multiple states of uncertainty, because there will likely be surprising twists and turns in how creative endeavors proceed as well as surprising outcomes of creative efforts. Indeed, creative endeavors typically entail some level of emergence (Sawyer, 2012), surprise (Simonton, 2016), and inconclusiveness (Corazza, 2016).

Consequently, not all encounters with uncertainty will motivate creative action. As mentioned, uncertainty can be experienced as so emotionally intense or overwhelming that people feel stifled by it. Indeed, uncertainty and creativity have a somewhat nuanced and interdependent relationship. On one hand, uncertainty can serve as a driver of creative thought and action, because experiences with uncertainty cause a state of unknowing or doubt (Beghetto, 2021) that require creative (i.e., new and meaningful) action in order to resolve the uncertainty. In the context of creative curricular experiences, the uncertainty is represented by the to-be-determined elements of the activity as well as surprises and setbacks encountered throughout the process. If students have the creative-self beliefs (Karwowski & Kaufman, 2017), regulatory strategies (Hoffmann et al., in press; Ivcevic & Nusbaum, 2017; Zielinska & Karwowski, in press), and instructional and contextual supports necessary to navigate these uncertainties (Beghetto, 2019), then students will be more likely to respond creatively. On the other hand, encounters with uncertainty can be so overwhelming that people may feel unable to resolve it. In such cases, students may believe they are not capable of resolving the uncertainty they face, experience a range of negative emotions (e.g., frustration, embarrassment, anger, shame), and ultimately give up on subsequent creative efforts (Beghetto, 2014).

In this way, uncertainty can serve as a catalyst or impediment for creative endeavors and actions. As mentioned, young people (and teachers) can experience potentially stifling uncertainty at any point of the process – from the moment the creative curricular experience is introduced, throughout the process, and even at the end of the process. In some cases, this uncertainty can be quickly resolved by teachers intervening and providing clarifying feedback, instructional supports, and other supportive structures (e.g., learning materials, connections with outside experts). However, even when students have supportive structures and clear criteria in place, it is still possible that they will find themselves at an impasse because they are engaging with nonroutine problems and tasks (Pólya, 1966) or because their efforts are thwarted (e.g., what they thought would work, does not work; their efforts are belittled or ridiculed).

Consequently, if people feel overwhelmed by the uncertainty they are experiencing, then they likely will avoid taking action or defer their actions to trusted others in the hopes that someone else will provide a way for resolving the uncertainty they encounter. In sum, uncertainty has the *potential* to motivate creative action if people view the uncertainty they experience as *actionable*; otherwise, they likely will attempt to avoid taking action or defer action to others (Beghetto, 2021). Moreover, regardless of when the encounters with uncertainty occur, we assert that these encounters activate sociocognitive (i.e., creative self-beliefs) and emotional reactions that play an important role in whether young people will act on the uncertainty they encounter and persist in their creative endeavors.

Finally, even seemingly resolved creative endeavors maintain a level of inconclusiveness (Corrazza, 2016). A finished artwork can, for instance, later be reinterpreted by future audiences in different contexts. A seemingly established creative contribution in science can later be revised or even refuted. The consequences of creative efforts can also have unexpected and unintended aspects to them, which can reintroduce uncertainty in how they are judged, experienced and engaged with by current and future audiences and stakeholders (Baert, 1991; Beghetto, 2021). In some cases, these secondary unintended consequences can be beneficial (e.g., discovering a new creative contribution to student learning). In other cases, secondary unintended consequences can be harmful (e.g., a solution to one ill-defined problem leading to a new set of ill-defined problems). Consequently, uncertainty serves as a catalyst and condition of creative endeavors, which can move through cycles of temporary resolution, only to later prompt new creative responses and engagements.

Finally, the punctuated disequilibrium caused by experiences with uncertainty can evoke a range of self-beliefs and emotions in and across any creative endeavor. This can occur across broad time spans or shorter duration creative tasks and experiences. Karwowski et al. (2019), for instance, demonstrate that positive and negative emotions can dynamically move across tasks and potentially influence creative confidence and creative outcomes. Given that creative work is punctuated by experiences of uncertainty and sometimes negative emotions, it is important that educators anticipate and support such experiences in the design and enactment of learning activities. Suggestions for how educators might anticipate and incorporate supports and structures in young people's learning experiences are discussed in the sections that follow.

Creative Self-Beliefs

We assert, along with similar social cognitive perspectives (e.g., Bandura, 1997; Karwowski & Kaufman, 2017), that people's self-beliefs play an important role in determining whether they will take creative action when encountering uncertainty. Indeed, there is evidence that even people who have the potential to act creatively, may only do so if they feel confident in their ability to take creative action, see value doing so, and are willing to take the creative risks necessary to take action (see Beghetto et al. 2021; Karwowski & Beghetto, 2019; Karwowski et al. 2019).

In this way, creative self-beliefs make up people's broader creative identity (Beghetto & Karwowski, 2017; Karwowski & Kaufman, 2017). A person's creative identity is made up of a dynamic set of more specific self-beliefs about themselves and their creative abilities. When people encounter particular opportunities to take creative action, they will make more specific appraisals of their confidence and willingness to take creative action based on the task at hand and situational factors (e.g., physiological state, other people in the setting, the sociomaterial and environmental features of the setting). Uncertain and ambiguous tasks can, for instance, influence people's self-judgments of their ability to successfully take creative action (Bandura, 2006; Beghetto & Karwowski, 2017). As a result, even people who otherwise consider themselves creative may lack confidence to successfully engage with and creatively work through the uncertainty encountered in a particular task. We further assert that this ambiguity can be compounded if there are not clear criteria for success or clear pathways for seeking assistance and support as needed.

We can therefore say that although people hold general beliefs about their creative self, creative self-beliefs are not static (Karwowski et al. 2019). Creative self-beliefs become activated once students encounter the uncertainty of a creative curricular task. Students likely will experience additional uncertainties throughout the process of engaging with a task and even following completion of the task. With respect to the initial encounter of uncertainty when presented with a creative curricular task, we would thereby assert whether students actually take creative action is, in part, determined by at least three, interrelated creative self-beliefs, which include: their creative *confidence beliefs* (i.e., their confidence in their ability to be successful in resolving the uncertainty encountered in a particular creative curricular experience); their *creative value* beliefs (i.e., whether they value taking creative action); and their *creative risk-taking* beliefs (i.e., whether they view the benefits of taking creative action outweigh the potential hazards).

In cases where young people face uncertainty with this trio of positive creative self-beliefs, we would assert that they would move toward creative learning (as illustrated by the horizontal path in Figure 26.1). Conversely, in cases where young people hold this trio of negative creative self-beliefs, they would move away from or avoid engaging with the task and thereby would be more likely to be on the path toward suspension of creative expression and development (as illustrated by the downward, vertical path in Figure 26.1). These assertions align with the more general approach-avoidance motivational orientation described by motivation researchers (Elliot, 2008). This is not to say that students who lack the confidence and willingness to engage with the uncertainty they encounter are destined to move toward the suspension of creative expression and development, but rather that they likely need additional structured supports to redirect their movement toward creative action (see also our discussion in the section on supportive structures).

With respect to additional encountered uncertainties that occur after engaging with a creative curricular task, we would assert that in addition to the trio of self-beliefs we've already mentioned, at least two additional and related creative self-beliefs become activated and play a role in determining whether students will move toward creative expression and development. Specifically, creative metacognitive beliefs and creative mindset would seem to play an increasingly important role when students are engaged in creative tasks and encounter new uncertainties.

Creative metacognition refers to one's creative self and contextual knowledge that helps regulate behavior when engaged in creative tasks (Kaufman & Beghetto, 2013). When students encounter the uncertainties that come from unexpected setbacks or challenges, creative metacognitive beliefs become activated and help determine how young people will respond (e.g., seek additional assistance or give up on a task) to the setbacks, challenges, and impasses they face in the midst of creative endeavors. If students accurately assess their strengths and the situational challenges they face and regulate their behavior accordingly (e.g., seek assistance and support), then we would expect them to be more likely to continue their movement toward creative expression and development (illustrated in the horizontal pathway of Figure 26.1). Conversely, if students have misjudged their strengths or the complexity of the task when they encounter uncertainty, their efforts and willingness to persist may wane and eventually become suspended (illustrated in the vertical pathway of Figure 26.1).

In addition, students' creative mindsets (Karwowski, 2014) also play an important role in whether students will ultimately decide to persist or (at least temporarily) abandon their creative efforts. Creative mindset refers to people's beliefs as to whether their creative ability is fixed and limited or incremental and malleable (i.e., able to grow). In the context of a creative curricular task, we maintain that students' creative mindsets become activated and inform decisions on whether to persist or abandon creative efforts whenever they encounter unexpected setbacks and challenges. If they believe they have exhausted their creative ability (fixed mindset), then we would expect them to suspend or abandon their efforts. Conversely, if they believe they can be successful (be it from additional effort or socioenvironmental supports), then we would expect them to persist toward creative expression and development. Again, we would assert that creative effort that has been suspended can be reactivated if students receive timely structural supports from teachers, peers, and trusted others.

Finally, creative self-beliefs also play a role once students have completed a creative curricular experience. Students' appraisals of their various creative self-beliefs and more broadly their creative identity can undergo recalibration based on their performance, experience, self-appraisals, and feedback they received once a creative curricular experience has ended. The accuracy of this recalibration process plays an important role in determining subsequent creative engagement. Given that there is evidence (see Beghetto et al. 2011; Kaufman et al. 2015) that young people sometimes underestimate their creative performance in relation to the ratings of teachers (or other external judges), it is important that educators support young people in developing healthy, accurate, and positive creative self-beliefs following their performance on creative curricular tasks. In some cases, students will overestimate their creative self-beliefs and in other cases they may underestimate their creative self-beliefs. Both over- and under-estimating one's creative self-beliefs can lead to problematic outcomes (e.g., becoming demoralized when encountering new creative challenges); therefore, it is important that students have multiple opportunities to continue to test out and develop healthy self-beliefs through structured and supportive engagement with the uncertainties inherent in creative endeavors.

Emotional Reactions

Creative learning endeavors, as with all challenging learning endeavors, are shot through with emotion (Rosiek & Beghetto, 2009). It can be difficult to predict how a particular young person might respond to the uncertainties encountered in creative curricular experiences. It is therefore important to recognize that experiencing uncertainty can elicit a range of emotions. Given the uncomfortable nature of such emotions, people tend to avoid or at least quickly resolve the uncertainty. The unpleasantness of the emotions experienced can be compounded when young people engage with uncertainty and their efforts are thwarted through setbacks and failures (Beghetto & McBain, 2022).

There are many slogans, in and beyond education, that are related to transforming failure into learning opportunities, including "you haven't succeeded, yet ..." "learn from your mistakes," "fail forward," and so on. The problem with such slogans, no matter how well-intended or seemingly motivational, is that when we find ourselves in the throes of failure, these slogans fall flat. One reason is because they are focused more on the cold cognition of our experiences and do not adequately speak to the sometimes intense and emotionally painful nature of failure and setbacks.

The emotions people experience following failure and setbacks can be thought of as falling under two broad categories of negative emotions (Tracy & Robbins, 2004). The first type, often referred to as "basic" negative emotions, include anger, sadness, frustration. Although this first type is unpleasant, these emotions tend to be more transitory, and their source is externalized to a situation or event (Russell & McAuley, 1986; Tracy & Robbins, 2004). The second type of reaction is called negative self-conscious emotions, which include shame, guilt, and embarrassment (Lewis & Sullivan, 2005; Tracy & Robbins, 2004). The experience of shame seems to be a particularly stifling emotional response, because it can impede or indefinitely suspend creative expression and development (Beghetto, 2014). Indeed, shame represents an indictment of the self and, when coupled with negative self-beliefs, can result in young people believing in the emotional painful futility of subsequent efforts (Beghetto & Dilley, 2016).

Consequently, young people who experience negative self-conscious emotions, coupled with negative creative self-beliefs, may be more likely to abandon their creative efforts and move toward the indefinite suspension of creative expression and development (moving down the vertical pathway of Figure 26.1). Experiencing negative emotions, of course, does not necessarily stifle creative expression and development. Negative emotional states, much like creative self-beliefs, are quite dynamic and situated. Indeed, recent conceptualizations and research on emotions (Barrett, 2017; Boiger et al. 2018) have highlighted a far more dynamic and situated conception of emotions between and across people and cultures. Moreover, there is evidence that throughout the course of a creative curricular experience, people can experience a range of positive and negative emotions (Hoffmann et al. in press), which tend to be associated with their creative self-beliefs (Karwowski et al., 2019). Timely instructional supports that help young people experience small wins

(Amabile & Kramer, 2011) can not only bolster their creative confidence but also seem to enhance their emotional reactions (Karwowski et al., 2019). It is not only possible but likely that young people who experience negative emotions while engaging with the uncertainties and potential setbacks inherent in creative endeavors can still, with support, move toward creative expression and development. This emotionally dynamic movement toward creative learning is illustrated in the horizontal pathway of Figure 26.1.

Moreover, much like the work highlighting the importance of helping young people develop their creative metacognition to help them regulate their creative efforts, there is also compelling and growing work highlighting the importance of supporting young people's emotional regulation (Hoffmann et al., in press; Ivcevic & Brackett, 2015; Ivcevic & Nusbaum, 2017). Hoffmann and colleagues (Hoffmann et al., in press), for instance, discuss how a full spectrum of emotions (from negative to positive) can be converted into creative outcomes. One way this occurs is that emotions are viewed as information that can be monitored and directed in order to reach a creative goal or outcome (Hoffmann et al., in press; Ivcevic & Brackett, 2015). Although young people can learn how to regulate emotions, much like they can learn how to regulate their creative beliefs and actions (Zielinska & Karwowski, in press), they do need supportive instructional structures to help them develop these skills, particularly when experiencing the sometimes intense and unpleasant emotional reactions that can come from encounters with uncertainty and setbacks.

Finally, providing students with opportunities for creative learning can also provide them with authentic moments where their work is valued and seen as meaningful, thus improving their sense of well-being. In this way, students engaging in creative curricular experiences can also serve to support the development of their own sense of emotional and creative resilience and well-being. This, of course, does not mean that students will not need support to help them get through the challenges of facing uncertainty and negative creative outcomes, but rather highlights that successfully working through uncertainty can help students improve their confidence, competence, and sense of well-being (Seligman, 2011; Seligman et al., 2007). Indeed, Seligman et al. (2007) have described the conversations people have within themselves between the moment something happens and the moment they react to that event. When experiencing negative creative outcomes students may catastrophize the moment by blaming themselves (global-self) or they can blame others (external other) or they can acknowledge their negative performance and build on their strengths (Beghetto, 2021; Seligman et al., 2007). Catastrophizing, or blaming oneself for failures and believing that there is no hope for improvement, can lead to depression (Seligman et al., 2007) and creative mortification (Beghetto, 2014). A key takeaway for educators is to anticipate and incorporate supportive structure into creative curricular experiences to help ensure that students can move toward (rather than away from) creative expression and development.

Supportive Structures

What can educators do to help support young people through encounters with uncertainty so that they can move toward creative expression and development? The first step is for educators to anticipate the sociocognitive and emotional challenges inherent in creative endeavors and recognize that for many young people they may not yet know how to productively work through such challenges (Kapur, 2016). When educators recognize and anticipate the challenges and setbacks that young people likely will face when engaging in creative curricular experiences, they can be in a better position to provide "just-in-time" sociocognitive and emotional scaffolds.

Although the concept of skilled others providing "scaffolding" or targeted support to students to promote learning and development has a somewhat long and well-known history in education (Vygotsky, 1978; Wood et al., 1976), the concept of emotional scaffolding (Rosiek, 2003; Rosiek & Beghetto, 2009) is a more recent and less widely understood or applied concept. Emotional scaffolding refers to "teachers' pedagogical use of analogies, metaphors, and narratives to influence students' emotional response to specific aspects of the subject matter in a way that promotes student learning" (Rosiek, 2003, p. 402). Emotional scaffolding works in conjunction with the creative imagination to help animate and promote learning and development (Rosiek & Beghetto, 2009). Recent work (Han, 2019) on the concept of emotional scaffolding has been extended to explore how students can also serve as important sources of emotional support to one another, including helping them not only engage with content but also work through and navigate difficult and unpleasant emotions and uncertainties inherent in learning and schooling.

In the context of the process model presented in Figure 26.1, we assert that creative self-beliefs and emotions play an important role and have a potentially profound influence on whether students will persist in the face of uncertainties and setbacks or, alternatively, disengage and suspend their creative efforts. Although low levels of creative confidence and negative emotions can serve as deterrents to sustained creative efforts, students can be supported in learning how to regulate and transform their encounters with uncertainty in ways that promote creative expression and development.

Educators can support students in developing a key facet of their creative metacognition (Kaufman & Beghetto, 2013), referred to as *creative self-regulation,* which is a set of processes and strategies that people use to make their creative efforts more effective (Ivcevic & Nusbaum, 2017; Zielinska & Karwowski, in press). Students can learn how to engage in creative self-regulation, which enables them to monitor and calibrate their efforts and emotions when attempting to attain their creative goals. Importantly, creative self-regulation strategies focus on developing a combination of sociocognitive (i.e., creative self-beliefs) and emotional self-regulation strategies that can help ensure that students move toward creative expression and development. More specifically, Zielinksa and Karwowski (in press) describe three core strategies that educators can help young people to learn and develop, which include: creative *forethought* strategies (prior to engaging in a creative task); creative *performance* strategies (during a creative task); and creative *self-reflection* strategies (following engagement with a creative task).

Creative forethought strategies include efforts aimed at helping young people anticipate and accept uncertainties and obstacles that they likely will encounter during their engagement with creative curricular experiences (Zielinksa & Karwowski, in press). Accepting uncertainties and obstacles does not imply that students should persist in unproductive thoughts and behaviors, but rather can help orient them to engage in possibility thinking when encountering uncertainties and setbacks, which includes being prepared to seek help when needed and even dropping a particular approach or perspective to explore, identify, and try out more promising possibilities.

Once students engage in creative curricular experiences, educators can also support young people in developing creative performance strategies by helping them anticipate and recognize when it might be beneficial to adjust their approach or even their goals in the face of ambiguities and setbacks. Learning how to pivot or explore new options is a key strategy in productively working through uncertainties and setbacks encountered in creative endeavors (Ivcevic & Nusbaum, 2017). Adaptive performance strategies also include learning how to regulate emotions throughout the process, particularly when encountering difficulties and obstacles (Hoffman et al. in press; Zielinksa & Karwowski, in press). It is both unrealistic and likely ineffective to try to eliminate or quickly resolve the negative emotions that students experience when working through the uncertainties and setbacks inherent in creative curricular experiences. Indeed, teachers' well-intended efforts to quickly resolve or eliminate negative emotions (e.g., "Don't get upset," "You shouldn't be angry or frustrated") can actually be experienced as controlling rather than supportive (Reeve, 2009). As previously noted, working through positive and negative emotions plays an important role in movement toward creative expression and development.

Consequently, instead of trying to control and eliminate negative reactions, it is important for educators to allow students to experience negative emotions when working through uncertainties and setbacks, within reasonable parameters (e.g., It's okay to be upset, but it's not okay to destroy property, yell at others). It can also be helpful to anticipate and normalize negative emotions and experiences by having a place where students can step away from the tasks and briefly take a break in a different context. Indeed, there is evidence (Amicone, et al., 2018; Kaplan, 1995) that taking breaks, particularly by moving to more calming and restorative settings (e.g., a space in the school or classroom that includes elements or features of the natural environment) or going outdoors into the natural environment (e.g., taking breaks to walk in the schoolyard), can have restorative effects on attention and cognitive functions. Allowing students to step away to green spaces and to reflect on their creative work can relieve stress, regulate emotions, both positive and negative that may emerge from the creative experience, and come back to the task more focused and possibly more open to creative risks.

In addition to providing a nature-inspired space for restoration, students can be supported in their creative endeavors by learning when it might be useful to seek assistance as needed, draw on negative emotional states as a means to increase creative focus and engagement (Hoffman et al. in press), as well as remind students that they do have the capacity to manage setbacks effectively, which can also boost their creative confidence beliefs (Zielinksa & Karwowski, in press).

Finally, creative self-regulation also involves incorporating self-reflection during and following engagement with creative curricular experiences. Students can be supported in developing their creative self-regulation by being encouraged to engage in self-reflection on their performance (including the emotional features of their performance) and self-evaluate their performance in light of feedback received from their teachers, peers, and anyone else involved in the creative curricular experience. The focus of this reflection should be on sharing one's work with others with the emphasis being placed on learning (Beghetto, 2019; Zielinksa & Karawoski, in press).

Two promising instructional activities that can support young people in developing the core features of creative self-regulation (i.e., forethought, performance, and reflection) include the sharing of *my favorite failure* narratives (Beghetto & McBain, 2022) and *exhibitions of creative learning* (Beghetto, 2019). My favorite failure narratives use a simple five-element design, which invites people to: (1) identify and describe a failure or setback they've previously experienced; (2) describe what emotions they experienced during that setback or failure; (3) describe what they learned about the situation; (4) describe what they learned about themselves as result of that setback; and (5) explain why it is their favorite failure (or setback).

Prior to engaging in a creative curricular experience, educators can share their own and other people's narratives of favorite failures with students (see Beghetto & McBain, 2022) *and* invite students to share their own narratives. Sharing narratives of favorite failures represents an important sociocognitive and emotional support, because these narratives can promote vicarious and direct models of creative expression and development from failures. In this way, young people can be better equipped to anticipate and work through potential setbacks they may encounter in a new creative curricular experience based on models for how others (and themselves) have worked through previous setbacks. Such narratives also model the core features of creative self-regulation (Zielinska & Karwowski, in press), because they stimulate *forethought*, include self-regulated *performance* illustrating how others and students themselves have made necessary adjustments, reframing and emotional regulation during encounters with uncertainty and setbacks, and serve as examples of *self-reflection* and creative learning.

Similarly, exhibitions of creative expression and development at the end of the curricular experience can help develop *self-reflection* strategies by having students and educators share their experiences, perceptions, learning, and possible future directions for students *and* teachers. One simple set of reflective questions (based on Beghetto, 2019, pp. 100–102) that educators can use (or modify for their purposes) involves establishing a specific date and time at the end of a creative curricular experience whereby individual students or student teams share their responses, in the form of a presentation, to the following questions:

- What worked well and what was surprising or didn't work well?
- What did you learn from the process?
- What did you learn about creativity?
- What did you learn about yourself?
- What suggestions would you have for next year's students who engage in this creative curricular experience?
- What do you wish you knew at the beginning that you know now?
- What would have helped improve or make this a better experience?
- What is your biggest takeaway from this experience?

Taken together, we would assert that these kinds of instructional supports can help young people develop the confidence and strategies to productively work through uncertainties encountered in creative curricular experiences.

Contextual Factors

Creative curricular experiences do not occur in a vacuum. Indeed, the sociopsychological and material context plays a key role when it comes to how students experience creative curricular experiences. Researchers (Amabile, 1996; Bandura, 1997; Beghetto & Kaufman, 2014; Davies et al., 2013) have long recognized that the context can play an instrumental role in shaping creativity, learning, and development. Moreover, researchers have also demonstrated how the natural environment and even incorporating features of the natural environment into curricular experiences can promote a sense of well-being and serve as a context for learning and creative expression (Guerra, et al. 2020; Kuo, et al., 2019). A creative rooftop garden project that students design without ever leaving their 9th grade science classroom likely would be quite different from a project that involves going out into the community and accessing and working in the context of an actual rooftop to develop and design the project.

How then might educators think about context in the design of creative curricular experiences? There are at least two major considerations. One pertains to the understanding and actively monitoring the sociopsychological environment. The other is to understand how the physical environment influences creative efforts and consider these features in our creative curricular designs. We briefly discuss each of these major factors in the sections that follow.

The Sociopsychological Environment

Teresa Amabile and colleagues have extensively documented how the socio-psychological messages of the learning environment, even well-intended messages, can curtail and suppress creative expression (Amabile, 1996; Amabile & Pillemer, 2012; Hennessey & Amabile, 2010; Hennessey, 2010). More specifically, when students feel monitored, experience time pressures, and become focused on evaluation, competition, social comparison, and attaining rewards, then they may avoid creative risk-taking because they are focused on extrinsic motives for their actions rather than being willing to take the risks necessary for creative engagement and expression.

This is not to say that extrinsic motives cannot motivate creativity (see Eisenberger & Cameron, 1998; Eisenberger & Shanock, 2003), but rather that when the primary reason for engaging in a task is extrinsically motivated it may inadvertently curtail creative expression. As creativity scholars have long noted (Guilford, 1950), a student who feels compelled to meet expectations in expected ways, even when invited to "be original," may in fact focus more on conforming to expectations to receive a high grade rather than try something new and risk receiving a lower grade. Similarly, when social comparison is salient in the learning environments, students' creative confidence may be diminished and they may even feel demoralized, because they believe they fall short in comparison to others (e.g., "I'm not as creative as the other students in this class"). Creatively curtailing motivational messages can even be unintentionally communicated by the material features of a learning environment (Beghetto, 2019), such as homogeneous displays of student work around the classroom (i.e., reinforcing sameness instead of creative difference) and "best work walls" (i.e., highlighting it is best to meet expected outcomes in expected ways).

A key take-away for educators when it comes to the sociopsychological environment is to monitor the kinds of intentional (and unintentional) motivational messages being sent to and among students in the interactions, expectations, and displays in the classroom. This kind of monitoring includes self-monitoring and reflection on the part of educators and students, including actively checking in with each other. The following reflective prompts and active reminders for teachers and students can be helpful in this regard (adapted from Beghetto, 2019, pp. 66, 73–74):

- *Do we communicate in a creativity supportive tone?*
- *Do the routines, procedures, and classroom displays send creativity supportive messages to students?*
- *Do we allow for the messiness, frustration, and other potentially negative emotions that come with creative efforts?*
- *How are we reinforcing the idea that more effort and asking for help are signs of strength in creative efforts (rather than signs of weakness)?*
- *Do we support each other through productive creative struggles?*
- *Are we okay with making mistakes, starting over, trying something completely different, and focusing on what we have learned from setbacks?*

The Physical and Natural Environment

Another way educators can help promote creative expression and development is to consider how the physical and natural features of the environment influence students' behaviors and emotional states. With respect to the influence of context on creativity, Davies and colleagues (2013) summarize findings from studies that highlight how flexible use of learning materials and the use of inside and outside environments can support creativity. More specifically, Davies et al. (2013) report on research that highlights how flexible use of material features of the environment that promote a sense of openness, movement, and different uses of spaces and objects in spaces can promote the growth of creative ideas and creative expression (Gandini et al. 2005). This includes taking into consideration how the different sensory features of an environment (e.g., light, color, sound, opportunities to display creative works) might be used to support creative expression and students' perceptions of their own creativity (Addison et al. 2010, Vecchi, 2010). Even simple material objects, like math counting sticks and blocks, can be used flexibly to help students communicate their creative ideas and insights (see Ball, 1993; Beghetto & Vasquez, in press).

Creative expression can also be supported when learning is moved beyond the walls of the immediate school and classroom environment and into different non-school settings (e.g., museums, art galleries, community settings) and natural environments (Davies et al. 2013). These different contexts and environments can support young people in encountering and developing new perspectives in themselves and in collaboration with others beyond the walls of the classroom. Natural environments seem to have the doubly mutual benefit of providing opportunities to creatively engage with uncertainty, while offering both the potential to develop adaptive creative self-beliefs and the potential to experience emotionally supportive and restorative states (e.g., calmness, restorative focus, and well-being) in natural settings (Kaplan, 1995). Creative curricular experiences in natural environments can provide students with greater autonomy and "loose parts" with which to build and create (Kuo, et al., 2019). Non-school environments can provide students with a new space to learn and explore the world around them. Novel, non-school environments offer a wide range of unique learning experiences and stimuli, which can include everything from rocks, flowers, ponds, insects, trees, leaves, and blades of grass to inspiring encounters with accomplished creators and creative works.

The features and experiences of non-school environments can be used to fuel the creative imagination of students. Natural outdoor spaces provide students with a calm, relaxing environment (Kaplan, 1995) that is simultaneously dynamic, unpredictable, and ever changing, culminating in a space conducive to creativity (Guerra et al. 2020). In addition to moving learning out of the classroom into novel and natural environments, it may also be beneficial to bring in features of novel and natural environments into classroom settings. Creative curricular activities that use natural elements, such as plants, animals, climate, all contain an element of natural uncertainty that may be generative to creative ideation and expression.

Educators and students may benefit from reflecting and acting on the following prompts and reminders when it comes to the physical environment:

- *What environments beyond the classroom and school might serve as potentially generative sites for creative curricular activities?*
- *How might we partner with community organizations to develop creative curricular experiences?*
- *How might we incorporate the natural environment in creative curricular experiences by moving learning outdoors and bringing features of the natural environment to our in-class learning?*
- *How might we use experiences in the natural environment to help restore focus and a sense of well-being when experiencing frustrations with creative curricular efforts?*

Concluding Thoughts and Directions for Research

The aim of this chapter was to introduce a process model that can help educators and creativity researchers conceptualize, design, and examine how creative curricular experiences might serve as a vehicle for supporting young people's creative expression and development. As we have discussed, creative curricular experiences provide structured and supportive learning activities that can help them develop adaptive, creative self-beliefs and self-regulatory strategies necessary for working through emotionally laden encounters with uncertainty and setbacks. We also discussed the central role that supportive structures and context play in the process.

We conclude by highlighting a few directions for research. With respect to research, it is important to note that although the process model depicted in Figure 26.1 and described throughout is based on prior theoretical and empirical work, the assertions are still somewhat speculative and thereby require additional study, testing, and development. There are at least three broad areas that can serve as the basis for further inquiry and development.

The first pertains to exploring the domain-general and domain-specific features of this model. Creativity researchers have demonstrated important domain differences in how creativity is expressed and developed within and across domains (see Baer, 2015; Kaufman, 2016 for an extended discussion). In the context of educational settings, it is highly likely that students' creative expression and development will vary depending on the subject area (e.g., mathematics vs. science vs. language arts). It is also likely that there will be important differences within micro-domains (Baer & Kaufman, 2005; Kaufman & Baer, 2005), such as writing poetry versus writing a literary critique in the domain of language arts. It is also possible that there may be some broad similarities across domains and micro-domains (Baer & Kaufman, 2005; Kaufman & Baer, 2005; Plucker & Beghetto, 2004), such as the general role that creative self-beliefs, emotions, supportive structures play in creative expression. The same can be said for the role of context (Beghetto & Kaufman, 2014; Davies et al. 2013). Studies aimed at testing the consistency and variances of the experiences of young people within and across domains and sociocultural and physical contexts (e.g., natural vs. artificial and even digital environments; similarities and differences within and across different sociocultural contexts) is an important and needed direction for future research.

There is also a need for subsequent research to explore potentially important dynamics in the role that creative self-beliefs and emotions play in the process. Although we have asserted that these two factors are central to whether young people will move toward creative expression and development, how specifically these beliefs and emotions play a role, including the role of taught and learned metacognitive and self-regulative strategies, remains as an area in need of further specification and clarity. Similar to domain generality versus domain specificity of creative expression and development, we anticipate that there likely are important general (or trait-like) and specific (or state-like) features of creative self-beliefs (see Karwowski & Kaufman, 2017), emotional reactions (see chapters in this volume), and the creative metacognitive skills (Kaufman & Beghetto, 2015) and emotional self-regulative (Hoffmann et al. in press; Zielinksa & Karawoski, in press) strategies employed by young people.

Finally, given that a key aim of education is to prepare young people for successfully transferring learning experiences outside of school and into the future (Cheng, 2016; Mayer, 1989), it is important for researchers to examine whether and how young people transfer the metacognitive skills and self-regulatory strategies developed through creative curricular experiences to future opportunities to respond creatively to uncertainty in learning and life (Ivcevic & Eggers, 2021). Taking a broader, life span approach can help ensure that we understand how educators might extend their efforts to support the development of adaptive creative and emotional strategies well into adulthood (see Hoffmann et al. 2020). Such research efforts are a bit more ambitious given that they require longitudinal (or at least micro-longitudinal) designs. Fortunately, creativity researchers have and continue to develop more dynamic methods and measures (e.g., diary-based studies) that can be used to examine this important area of future research (see Zielinksa & Karawoski, in press).

These areas of future directions for research represent a much broader program of research, which will require collaborations among teams of researchers, educators, and young people. In the meantime, we hope that the ideas presented in this chapter will inspire researchers and educators to conceptualize, design, and study various kinds of creative curricular experiences that can help young people develop the creative self-beliefs and emotional regulatory strategies necessary for navigating challenging uncertainties in learning and life.

References

Addison, N., Burgess, L., Steers, J., & Trowell, J. (2010). *Understanding Art Education: Engaging Reflexively with Practice*. Routledge.

Amabile, T. M. (1996). *Creativity in Context: Update to the Social Psychology of Creativity*. Westview.

Amabile, T. M., & Kramer, S. J. (2011). The power of small wins. *Harvard Business Review, 89*(5), 70–80.

Amabile, T. M., & Pillemer, J. (2012). Perspectives on the social psychology of creativity. *The Journal of Creative Behavior, 46*, 3–15.

Amicone, G., Petruccelli, I., De Dominicis, S., et al. (2018). Green breaks: The restorative effect of the school environment's green areas on children's cognitive performance. *Frontiers in Psychology, 9*, 1579. https://doi.org/10.3389/fpsyg.2018.01579

Ball, D. L. (1993). With an eye on the mathematical horizon: Dilemmas of teaching elementary school mathematics. *The Elementary School Journal, 93*(4), 373–397. https://doi.org/10.1086/461730

Baer, J. (2015). *Domain Specificity of Creativity*. Academic Press.

Baer, J., & Kaufman, J. C. (2005). Bridging generality and specificity: The Amusement Park Theoretical (APT) model of creativity. *Roeper Review, 27*, 158–163.

Baert, P. (1991). Unintended consequences: A typology and examples. *International Sociology, 6*, 201–210. https://doi.org/10.1177/026858091006002006

Bandura, A. (1997). *Self-Efficacy: The Exercise of Control*. W. H. Freeman.

Bandura, A. (2006). Guide for constructing self-efficacy scales. In F. Pajares, & T. Urdan (Eds.), *Self-Efficacy Beliefs of Adolescents* (pp. 307–337). Information Age.

Barrett, L. F. (2017). *How Emotions Are Made: The Secret Life of the Brain*. Houghton Mifflin Harcourt.

Beghetto, R. A. (2014). Creative mortification: An initial exploration. *Psychology of Aesthetics, Creativity, and the Arts, 8*, 266–276. https://psycnet.apa.org/doi/10.1037/a0036618

Beghetto, R. A. (2019). *Beautiful Risks: Having the Courage to Teach and Learn Creatively*. Rowman & Littlefield. https://doi.org/10.1007/978-3-319-98390-5_122-1

Beghetto, R. A. (2021). There is no creativity without uncertainty: Dubito Ergo Creo. *Journal of Creativity, 31*. https://doi.org/10.1016/j.yjoc.2021.100005

Beghetto, R. A., & Dilley, A. E. (2016). Creative aspirations or pipe dreams? Toward understanding creative mortification in children and adolescents. *New Directions for Child and Adolescent Development, 151*, 85–95. https://10.1002/cad.20150

Beghetto, R. A., & Karwowski, M. (2017). Toward untangling creative self-beliefs. In M. Karwowski & J. C. Kaufman (Eds.), *The Creative Self* (pp. 3–22). Academic Press. http://dx.doi.org/10.1016/ B978–0-12-809790-8.00001-7

Beghetto, R. A., Karwowski, M., & Reiter-Palmon, R. (2021). Intellectual risk taking: A moderating link between creative confidence and creative behavior? *Psychology of Aesthetics, Creativity, and the Arts, 15*(4), 637–634. https://doi.org/10.1037/aca0000323

Beghetto, R. A., & Kaufman, J. C. (2007). Toward a broader conception of creativity: A case for mini-c creativity. *Psychology of Aesthetics, Creativity, and the Arts, 1*, 73–79. https://psycnet.apa.org/doi/10.1037/1931-3896.1.2.73

Beghetto, R. A., & Kaufman, J. C. (2014). Classroom contexts for creativity. *High Ability Studies, 25*(1), 53–69. https://doi.org/10.1080/13598139.2014.905247

Beghetto, R. A., Kaufman, J. C., & Baxter, J. (2011). Answering the unexpected questions: Exploring the relationship between students' creative self-efficacy and teacher ratings of creativity. *Psychology of Aesthetics, Creativity, and the Arts, 5*, 342–349. https://doi.org/10.1037/a0022834

Beghetto, R. A., & McBain, L. (2022). *My Favorite Failure*. Rowman & Littlefield.

Beghetto, R. A., & Vasquez, A. M. (in press). Creative learning: A pedagogical perspective. In L. J. Ball & F. Vallee-Tourangeau (Eds.), *Routledge International Handbook of Creative Cognition*. Routledge.

Berns, G. (2010). *Iconoclast: A Neuroscientist Reveals How to Think Differently*. Harvard Business Press.

Boiger, M., Ceulemans, E., De Leersnyder, J., et al. (2018). Beyond essentialism: Cultural differences in emotions revisited. *Emotion.18*(8), 1142–1162. https://doi.org/10.1037/emo0000390

Cheng, V. M. Y. (2016). Understanding and enhancing personal transfer of creative learning. *Thinking Skills and Creativity, 22*, 58–73. https://doi.org/10.1016/j.tsc.2016.09.001

Corazza, G. E. (2016). Potential originality and effective-ness: The dynamic definition of creativity. *Creativity Research Journal, 28*(3), 258–267. https://doi.org/10.1080/10400419.2016.1195627

Davies, D., Jindal-Snape, D., Collier, C., et al. (2013). Creative learning environments in education: A systematic literature review. *Thinking Skills and Creativity, 8*, 80–91. https://doi.org/10.1016/j.tsc.2012.07.004

Eisenberger, R., & Cameron, J. (1998). Reward, intrinsic interest, and creativity: New findings. *American Psychologist, 53*, 676–679. https://doi.org/10.1037/0003-066X.53.6.676

Eisenberger, R., & Shanock, L. (2003). Rewards, intrinsic motivation, and creativity: A case study of conceptual and methodological isolation. *Creativity Research Journal, 15*, 121–130. https://doi.org/10.1080/10400419.2003.9651404

Elliot, A. J. (Ed.). (2008). *Handbook of Approach and Avoidance Motivation*. Psychology Press. https://doi.org/10.4324/9780203888148

Gandini, L., Hill, L., Cadwell, L., & Schwall, C. (Eds.). (2005). *In the Spirit of the Studio: Learning from the Atelier of Reggio Emilia*. Teachers' College Press.

Glăveanu, V. P., & Beghetto, R. A. (2020). Creative experience: A non-standard definition of creativity. *Creativity Research Journal*. https://doi.org/10.1080/10400419.2020.1827606

Guerra, M., Villa, F. V., & Glăveanu, V. (2020). The teacher's role in the relationship between creativity and outdoor education: A review of the literature. *RELADeI, 9*(2), 131–149.

Guilford, J. P. (1950). Creativity. *American Psychologist, 5*, 444–454. https://doi.org/10.1037/h0063487

Han, M. (2019). *Exploring the Nexus between Bilingual Learning, Emotions and Creativity: A Case Study of a Former Korean Bilingual Student's Creative*

Artifact (Book). Doctoral dissertation. University of Connecticut. Doctoral Dissertations, 2352. https://opencommons.uconn.edu/dissertations/2352

Hennessey, B. A. (2010). Intrinsic motivation and creativity in the classroom: Have we come full circle? In R. A. Beghetto & J. C. Kaufman (Eds.), *Nurturing Creativity in the Classroom* (pp. 329–361). Cambridge University Press.

Hennessey, B. A., & Amabile, T. (2010). Creativity. *Annual Review of Psychology, 61*, 569–598.

Hoffmann, J. D., Ivcevic, Z., & Maliakkal, N. (2020). Creative thinking strategies for life: A course for professional adults using art. *The Journal of Creative Behavior, 54*(2), 293–310. https://doi.org/10.1002/jocb.366

Hoffmann, J. D., McGarry, J., & Seibyl, J. (in press). Beyond tolerating ambiguity: How emotionally intelligent people can channel uncertainty into creativity. In R. A. Beghetto & G. Jaeger (Eds.), *Uncertainty: A Catalyst for Creativity, Learning and Development*. Springer.

Ivcevic, Z., & Brackett, M. A. (2015). Predicting creativity: Interactive effects of openness to experience and emotion regulation ability. *Psychology of Aesthetics, Creativity, and the Arts, 9*(4), 480. https://doi.org/10.1037/a0039826

Ivcevic, Z., & Eggers, C. (2021). Emotion regulation ability: Test performance and observer reports in predicting relationship, achievement and well-being outcomes in adolescents. *International Journal of Environmental Research and Public Health, 18*. https://doi.org/10.3390/ijerph18063204

Ivcevic, Z., & Nusbaum, E. C. (2017). From having an idea to doing something with it: Self-regulation for creativity. In M. Karwowski & J. C. Kaufman (Eds.), *The Creative Self: Effect of Beliefs, Self-Efficacy, Mindset, and Identity* (pp. 343–365). Elsevier Academic Press. https://doi.org/10.1016/B978-0-12-809790-8.00020-0

Kaplan, S. (1995). The restorative benefits of nature: Toward an integrative framework. *Journal of Environmental Psychology, 15*(3), 169–182. https://doi.org/10.1016/0272-4944(95)90001-2

Kapur, M. (2016). Examining productive failure, productive success, unproductive failure, and unproductive success in learning. *Educational Psychologist, 51*(2), 289–299. https://doi.org/10.1080/00461520.2016.115545

Karwowski, M. (2014). Creative mindsets: Measurement, correlates, consequences. *Psychology of Aesthetics, Creativity, and the Arts, 8*, 62–70. http://dx.doi.org/10.1037/a0034898

Karwowski, M., & Beghetto, R. A. (2019). Creative behavior as agentic action. *Psychology of Aesthetics, Creativity, and the Arts, 13*(4), 402–415. https://doi.org/10.1037/aca0000190

Karwowski, M., Han, M. H., & Beghetto, R. A. (2019). Toward dynamizing the measurement of creative confidence beliefs. *Psychology of Aesthetics, Creativity, and the Arts, 13*(2), 193–202. https://doi.org/10.1037/aca0000229

Karwowski, M., & Kaufman, J. C. (Eds.). (2017). *The Creative Self*. Academic Press.

Kaufman, J. C. (2016). *Creativity 101*. Springer.

Kaufman, J. C., & Baer, J. (Eds.). (2005). *Creativity across Domains: Faces of the Muse*. Erlbaum.

Kaufman, J. C., & Beghetto, R. A. (2013). In praise of Clark Kent: Creative metacognition and the importance of teaching kids when (not) to be creative. *Roeper Review, 35*, 155 – 165. https://doi.org/10.1080/02783193.2013.799413

Kaufman, J. C., Beghetto, R. A, & C. Watson. (2015). Creative metacognition and self-ratings of creative performance: A 4-C perspective. *Learning and Individual Difference, 51,* 394–399. https://doi.org/10.1016/j.lindif.2015.05.004

Kuo, M., Barnes, M., & Jordan, C. (2019). Do experiences with nature promote learning? Converging evidence of a cause-and-effect relationship. *Frontiers in Psychology, 10,* 305. https://doi.org/10.3389/fpsyg.2019.00305

Lewis, M., & Sullivan, M. W. (2005). The development of self-conscious emotion. In A. J. Elliot & C. S. Dweck (Eds.), *Handbook of Competence and Motivation* (pp. 185-201). Guilford Press.

Lipnevich, A. A., & Smith, J. K. (Eds.). (2018). *The Cambridge Handbook of Instructional Feedback.* Cambridge University Press. https://doi.org/10.1017/9781316832134

Mayer, R. E. (1989). Cognitive views of creativity: Creative teaching for creative learning. *Contemporary Educational Psychology, 14*(3), 203–211. https://doi.org/10.1016/0361-476X(89)90010-6

Pólya, G, (1966) On teaching problem solving. In *Conference Board of the Mathematical Sciences, The Role of Axiomatics and Problem Solving in Mathematics* (pp. 123–129). Ginn.

Plucker, J. A., & Beghetto, R. A. (2004). Why creativity is domain general, why it looks domain specific, and why the distinction doesn't matter. In R. J. Sternberg, E. L. Grigorenko, & J. L. Singer (Eds.), *Creativity: From Potential to Realization* (pp. 153–168). American Psychological Association.

Reeve, J. (2009). Why teachers adopt a controlling motivating style toward students and how they can become more autonomy supportive. *Educational Psychologist, 44,* 159–175. https://doi.org/10.1080/00461520903028990

Rosiek J. (2003) Emotional scaffolding: An exploration of teacher knowledge at the intersection of student emotion and subject matter content. *Journal of Teacher Education, 54,* 399–412 https://doi.org/10.1177/0022487103257089

Rosiek, J., & Beghetto, R. A. (2009). Emotional scaffolding: The emotional and imaginative dimensions of teaching and learning. In P. A. Schutz & M. Zembylas (Eds.), *Advances in Teacher Emotion Research* (pp. 175–194). Springer. https://doi.org/10.1007/978-1-4419-0564-2_9

Russell, D., & McAuley, E. (1986). Causal attributions, causal dimensions, and affective reactions to success and failure. *Journal of Personality and Social Psychology, 50*(6), 1174–1185. https://doi.org/10.1037/0022-3514.50.6.1174

Sawyer, R. K. (2012). *Explaining Creativity: The Science of Human Innovation* (2nd ed.). Oxford University Press.

Seligman, M. E. P. (2011). *Flourish: A New Understanding of Happiness and Well-Being – and How to Achieve Them.* Nicholas Brealey.

Seligman, M. E. P., Reivich, K., Jaycox, L., & Gillham, J. (2007) *The Optimistic Child: A Proven Program to Safeguard Children against Depression and Build Lifelong Resilience.* Houghton Mifflin.

Simonton, D. K. (2016). Defining creativity: Don't we also need to define what is not creative? *Journal of Creative Behavior, 52,* 80–90. https://doi.org/10.1002/jocb.137

Tanggaard, L., & Juelsbo, T. (2016). Mess. In V. P. Glăveanu, L. Tanggaard & C. Wegener (Eds.), *Creativity: A New Vocabulary* (pp. 78–86). Palgrave.

Tracy, J. L., & Robins, R. W. (2004). TARGET ARTICLE: "Putting the self into self-conscious emotions: A theoretical model." *Psychological Inquiry*, *15*(2), 103–125. https://doi.org/10.1207/s15327965pli1502_01

Vecchi, V. (2010). *Art and Creativity in Reggio Emilia: Exploring the Role and Potential of Ateliers in Early Childhood Education*. Routledge.

von Thienen, J., Meinel, M., & Corazza, G. E. (2017). A short theory of failure. *Electronic Colloquium on Design Thinking Research*, *17*, 1–5.

Vygotsky, L. S. (1978). *Mind in Society: The Development of Higher Psychological Processes*. Harvard University Press.

Wood, D., Bruner, J., & Ross, G. (1976) The role of tutoring in problem solving. *Journal of Child Psychology and Psychiatry 17*, 89–100. https://doi.org/10.1111/j.1469-7610.1976.tb00381.x

Zielinska, A., & Karwowski, M. (in press). Living with uncertainty in the creative process: A self-regulatory perspective. In R. A. Beghetto & G. Jaeger, (Eds.), *Uncertainty: A Catalyst for Creativity, Learning and Development*. Springer.

27 Organizational Affective Climate and Creativity at Work

Kyle Emich and Li Lu

Many ideas grow better when transplanted into another mind than in the one where they sprang up.

- Oliver Wendell Holmes (1872)

Rational thoughts never drive people's creativity the way emotions do.

- Neil deGrasse Tyson (2009)

Initially, we wanted one quote to open this chapter. Opening with a quote helps relate material to popular culture and experience, and provides anecdotal evidence of empirically supported effects. However, as we could not choose between these quotes, we kept both. We could not choose because Mr. Holmes and Dr. Tyson are both right. Since creativity emphasizes idea generation, it naturally lends itself to collective environments as interaction with diverse others allows for a varied knowledge base from which to pull ideas. Further, as Mr. Holmes observes, the naturally diverse perspectives inherent in collectives allow for the novel reinterpretation and recombination of ideas (Emich & Vincent, 2020). Thus, creativity is often best realized as a social process leveraging collective information exchange to combine and reapply ideas into novel and useful solutions. Additionally, in line with Dr. Tyson's observation, researchers have established that affect plays a large role in individual creativity (e.g., Baas et al., 2008). Still, the relationship between affective states and collective action is much less well understood.

In this chapter, we review work on affective climate and creativity at work. We begin by reviewing the effects of positive and negative affective climate on creativity in teams and organizations. Then, we summarize emerging scholarship on the relationship between discrete emotional climate and creativity. Building on our review of the extant empirical treatment of affective climate and reflecting on a deficiency in how affective climate is theoretically considered, we then offer a new definition of affective climate. Our newly proposed definition has the advantage of encompassing both the *shared* and *unshared* components of affective climate.

Motivated by this new definition, we propose four future research directions in the hope of advancing our understanding of how affective climate influences collective creativity. First, the tendency for higher level affective states to be treated as mere manifestations of their individual-level analogs has hampered a more nuanced understanding of affective climate. As demonstrated later, affective climate, as a collective experience, can manifest distinctly from individual affective states. Related to this point, in our second future direction, we caution researchers in treating affective climate as necessarily homogeneous; instead, future work should also consider how heterogeneous affective climate might arise from the contrasting experience of a shared event or environment. Third, affective climate is a collective state subject to both bottom-up and top-down influences. The extant literature has mostly explored bottom-up processes. As such, more work on top-down processes, especially those originating above the team level, is necessary. Fourth, there is little extant work on discrete collective affect, including social-emotional climates, which are worth exploring due to their inherently relational nature. We hope these propositions spur future work aimed at delineating the complex relationship between affective climate and creativity.

Positive and Negative Affective Climate

Climate refers to a collective response to the collective experience of a given situation (Ostroff et al., 2013). Most often, it refers to people's cognitive response in terms of their perception of the collective environment. Because of this emphasis, climate is most often defined in terms of perceptions of shared practices, policies, procedures, and routines (Ostroff et al., 2013). However, shared collective experiences can also produce affective responses. These responses may be based on perceptions of the collective environment (Parke & Seo, 2017) or may arise directly from it, independent of such perceptions. Here, we chose to use the term *affective climate* instead of *emotional climate* since the term *affect* encompasses a variety of emotion-laden constructs such as mood, emotion, sentiment, and dispositional affect (González-Romá et al., 2000). Traditionally, the *shared* portion of this definition has been interpreted to mean that for an affective climate to exist, members of a collective must experience the same affective state. For instance, affective climate is often defined as "the shared affective experience of a work group or team" (Cropanzano & Dasborough, 2015, p. 845) or as "requir[ing] a shared perception of the emotion in question" (Ashkanasy & Nicholson, 2003, p. 24). However, in reality, while this shared affective experience refers to a collective affective tone, affective climate is dependent on *shared perceptions or experiences*, not necessarily *shared affective responses to those experiences* (Knight et al., 2018; Ostroff et al., 2013).

Most work considering affective climate does so in terms of the two broad underlying dimensions of positive and negative affect (Cropanzano & Dasborough, 2015; Gamero & González-Romá, 2020). In some sense, it was reasonable to begin to establish our understanding of affective climate by studying how general positive and negative affective tones influence collective behavior, since positive and negative affects represent two broad dimensions of feeling that do not necessarily stem from specific events or focus attention on themselves (Isen, 2008). Additionally, these dimensions have consistently been linked to individual creative output (Amabile et al., 2005).

Currently, most of the evidence regarding the effects of positive and negative affective climate on creativity comes from the literature on group or team affective tone. This also makes sense, since team members are more likely to engage in the frequent interactions and shared experiences that give rise to shared affect than members of broader units or organizations (de Rivera, 1992). Group or team affective tone refers to the occurrence of consistent or homogeneous state affect among group or team members (George, 1990). It is generally assessed by first calculating an agreement score among team members regarding a particular affective state. This should be done by examining ICC1 and ICC2 (Bliese, 2000). However, some researchers also use r_{wg}, despite its inability to compare within-group and between-group agreement. After an acceptable level of within-team agreement is established, researchers generally use a team mean to represent team-level affective tone.

Developing creative ideas begins with retrieving information relevant to a focal problem, and associating and combining that information to form initial ideas (Finke et al., 1992). While some ideas represent near-replications of existing phenomena, others represent incremental advances and the most creative shift conceptions of a given task or problem to a new starting point (Sternberg et al., 2002). However, such highly creative ideas are rare as people generally take the path of least resistance by generating highly accessible ideas involving habitually associated concepts (Ward, 1994). For example, when drawing alien animals, most people give them eyes and legs, and most attach the legs to the bottom of the body (Polman & Emich, 2011; Ward, 1994). To produce an idea that is truly novel and useful in meeting task demands, one must move beyond established associations to combine previously unassociated elements. This involves seeking out information related to multiple conceptual categories and combining that information (Amabile et al., 2005).

Because, as laid out in the broaden-and-build theory of positive emotions (Fredrickson, 2001), positive affect spurs the cognitive flexibility that allows people to seek out and connect disparate ideas (Isen, 2008), teams with a positive affective tone tend to come up with more creative ideas than their neutral or negative counterparts do. For example, Bramesfeld and Gasper (2008) found that positive mood helps group members move beyond initial preferences and focus on combining aspects of broader information sets, improving group information exchange. Similarly, Grawitch and colleagues (2003) found that positive group affective tone increases the originality of group ideas, and allows groups to identify important domains for improvement when autonomy is high. Kim and Shin (2015) found that positive group affective tone increases a group's confidence in its abilities (i.e., collective efficacy), allowing it to persist in the face of setbacks and set and maintain effort toward creative goals. Shin (2014) also found that positive group affective tone shifts groups to be more promotion focused and discuss a wider range of ideas, improving creativity. Finally, Kim et al. (2016) demonstrate that having a positive team affective climate allows workers with naturally positive trait affect to express that affect in the form of creativity. While most of these findings rely on a simple transformation of individual-level findings to the team level, the effect of positive affect on creativity is also enhanced in teams, where team members' subjective perspectives allow them to naturally combine others' ideas with their own experience, resulting in new unique ideas (Emich & Vincent, 2020).

Alternatively, as described in affect-as-information theory, negative affect linked to the immediate environment signals threat (Forgas, 1995). This concurrently signals the need for focused, deliberate information processing to navigate away from the threat and mobilizes energy to persist until the threat is avoided. While the former attentional narrowing often reduces creative thought, the latter persistence effect has the potential to boost creativity in certain instances (De Dreu et al., 2008). However, the important question for researchers and practitioners is: boost creativity relative to what? Before we go on, let us address the obvious comparator: does this persistence effect boost creativity over the shared experience of positive affect?

Addressing this is relatively straightforward, since most papers describing the creative benefits of negative affect cite the same three papers, which we now address briefly in turn. First, Jones and Kelly (2009) often get miscited because of their accurate, but misleading, subtitle "Negative Mood Leads to Process Gains in Idea-Generation Groups." It is true Jones and Kelly (2009) found that groups experiencing shared negative affect generate more creative ideas *than individuals experiencing negative affect*. However, in this study, groups experiencing negative and positive affect produced equally creative ideas. Later work, with a larger sample size, found that teams experiencing positive affect indeed produced more creative ideas than teams experiencing negative affect using the same experimental task (Emich & Vincent, 2020). Second, Tsai and colleagues (2012) found that negative group affective tone can increase creativity when team trust is high. However, they also found a negative trend, across conditions, of negative group affective tone on team creativity in the set of field R&D teams they studied. In other words, it is not that collective negative affect increases creativity; it is that it generally decreases creativity except in instances when trust is high. Finally, Knight (2015) found that while group positive affective tone increases early team exploratory search, it can reduce late-stage exploratory search. Conversely, group negative affective tone increases exploratory search in these later stages. However, he also found that the pattern produced by positive affect enhances team performance, stating "that for a team to score in the top 25% ... members had to engage in high levels of early search and exhibit a steep decline in search during the second half of their team's life" (p. 112). In other words, the most creative teams were those with high positive affect, who took more time early on to consider ideas.

As a result, overall, the literature strongly suggests that positive team affective tone enhances collective creativity, while negative team affective tone diminishes it. However, in certain instances, the benefits in persistence garnered by shared negative affect can improve collective creativity. The dual pathway to creativity model, which states that flexible thinking and the systematic and effortful exploration of possibilities both enhance creativity (De Dreu et al., 2008), best explains this finding. Its persistence pathway was derived from the premise that creative ideas can be produced through the extensive exploration of normative heuristic associations (Finke et al., 1992). For example, when participants are asked to think about the environment on the planet where their imagined aliens live, they are able to break out of typical animal categorizations and demonstrate greater creativity (Ward, 1994). While work on positive affect is clearly linked to the individual-level flexibility pathway, notably, both Jones and Kelly (2009) and Knight (2015) found that negative collective affect can lead to greater persistence in exploring ideas and narrowing those ideas to address a creative problem. Therefore, it appears that in certain instances, such as late in the team process or when trust is high among team members, the persistence facilitated by negative affect can allow teams to safely continue to explore and discuss ideas and thus produce more creative solutions than they would have otherwise (i.e., in a neutral affective state). However, this rarely allows them to produce ideas that are more creative than collectives experiencing positive affect.

While a dearth of research exists examining affective climate above the team level, work that does also generally focuses on broad climates of positive and negative affect. Of this work, two papers relate these climates back to creativity. In their case study of a financial services division of a German automobile company, Maimone and Sinclair (2010) found evidence that positive affective climate, including contentment, comfort, and satisfaction, increases organizational creativity. In this vein, in their study of 81 branches of a Korean insurance company, Choi and colleagues (2011) found that positive affective climate following innovation increased the effectiveness of implementing that innovation. While two studies do not constitute a body of work, this indicates that positive affective climate at least promotes collective environments conducive to the creation and adoption of novel and useful ideas.

We also see evidence to this effect from several other studies exploring the effect of positive and negative affective climate on organizational processes and outcomes related to creativity. For example, Tse et al. (2008) found that positive affective climate (defined to include acceptance, sincerity, support, warmth, and enthusiasm) allows workplace friendship to more easily develop, which in turn positively affects team member exchange, which involves willingness to help others, share ideas and feedback with them, and recognize them for their contributions. Arfara and colleagues (2018) found similar results at the Greek Independent Administrative Authorities. Because of the necessity of information exchange and idea integration to creativity, it seems that this may help explain the positive relationship between positive affective climate and collective creativity. Additionally, Ozcelik and colleagues (2008) found that entrepreneurial ventures that promote a positive affective climate perform better and can grow more quickly. Because of entrepreneurial ventures' inherent reliance on innovation (Drucker, 2014), this also supports the role of positive affective climate in collective creativity.

Discrete Emotional Climate and Creativity

While most work on affective climate has focused on general positive and negative affect, a small set of work has focused on discrete emotional climates. Discrete emotions refer to basic emotional states that evoke specific responses to experienced stimuli, which may involve different cognitive and regulatory processes (Izard, 2010). Thus far, findings from this line of work fit the activation-regulatory focus explanation of affect developed by Baas and colleagues (2008). This explanation states that the hedonic tone (positive vs. negative), activation level (high vs. low), and regulatory focus (promotion vs. prevention) of a given affective state influence the mindset it engenders and subsequent creativity. Affective states such as fear, disgust, and calmness have a prevention focus. People experiencing these states want to move away from triggering stimuli either because they find those stimuli scary or disgusting, or because they want to maintain their current state of calm. Prevention-focused states narrow attentional scope and reduce cognitive flexibility and risk-taking tendencies, reducing creativity (Friedman & Förster, 2001). Alternatively, states such as anger, disappointment, and excitement are promotion focused. They make people want to get up and do things: to seek out new stimuli to interact with. Because of this, they encourage the exploration and pursuit of new ideas and promote creativity (Friedman & Förster, 2001).

Translating this to the collective level, Tran (2010) and Vuori and Huy (2016) theorize that climates of fear may lead members to oppose innovation and change, reducing collective creativity, unless they feel they can control the cause of that fear. Low (2008) provides an example of the prevention-focused mechanism, showing that climates of fear in neighborhoods instigate social exclusion, fortification, and racialization. Alternatively, Vuori and Huy (2016) argue that a climate of pride can reduce resistance to change, increase collective learning, and thus boost collective creativity. They provide qualitative data supporting this point, finding that the organizational structures and the history of Nokia generated a climate of fear among top managers, which spread to middle managers, disrupting information exchange and innovation. This led to the smartphone giant's rapid collapse from 2005 to 2010. Similarly, Sawyer and Clair (in press) find that collective hope can motivate collectives toward goals and the pursuit of grand challenges, which involves developing creative solutions to complex societal issues.

Other work exploring the role of activation in collective creativity has found that it often has a positive effect (although again, this should theoretically depend on the valence and regulatory focus of the activated state). Knight and Baer (2014) found that nonsedentary work configurations, where employees are encouraged to stand and walk around over the course of the day, create a climate of affective arousal, which leads to greater collective information elaboration and creative idea generation. Like Vuori and Huy (2016), this study is noteworthy because of the clear collective process mechanism identified in the form of collective information elaboration. Moreover, Chiang and colleagues (2020) show that climates of low arousal, characterized by emotional exhaustion – in this case, experienced from having to deal with an authoritarian leader – reduce all types of performance, including creative performance, by reducing motivation to complete tasks and breaking communication and connection patterns among members.

Although conducted to test the role of affective diversity in teams, not necessarily affective climate, Emich and Vincent (2020) examined how various affective states influence the collective creativity process. Overall, we found strong support for the activation-regulatory focus model. Activated promotion-focused states, including happiness, anger, and excitement, increased teams' focus on idea generation, improving creative output. Alternatively, activated prevention-focused states caused teams to abandon the idea-generation process in favor of idea selection, reducing their creativity. In line with Knight and Baer (2014), deactivated states resulted in complacency and disengagement with the creative task. Finally, we also found that prevention-focused states tend to dominate promotion-focused states, such that if a particular team contains members experiencing each type of affective state (e.g., scared and happy members) at equal activation levels, teams tend to focus on idea selection and produce fewer creative ideas.

Summary of the Relationship between Affective Climate and Creativity

Thus far, scholars have tackled affective climate by examining either broad positive and negative affect or discrete emotion. Further, a burgeoning theoretical foundation has been built in this area, based on work involving the broaden-and-build, affect-as-information, and activation-regulatory focus models of affect and the dual pathway model of creativity. This foundation seems to suggest that a *valence-activation-regulatory focus model* can provide an overarching framework to understand the impact of affective climate on creativity at work. Regarding valence, work on positive and negative affective climate indicates that, in general, positive affective climate increases collective creativity by allowing members to broaden their thought–action repertoire, recognize ideas in others, and combine those ideas with their own perceptions. This may also stem from positive affective climate's ability to increase the confidence of those collectives to complete their tasks (i.e., collective efficacy) and produce a collective promotion focus (Grawitch et al., 2003; Kim & Shin, 2015).

However, evidence also indicates that negatively valenced affective climates can produce creative output if they motivate employees to seek out disparate information or persist in their creative task (Baas et al., 2008), such as when trust is high (Tsai et al., 2012). Work on discrete emotion explicates this relationship, generally showing that creativity is possible when negative affective climates are both activated and promotion focused. Most of this work focuses on how affective climates of anger have the potential to increase creative output (activated, promotion-focused climate; Emich & Vincent, 2020; Grant & Smith, 2021), while climates of fear decrease creative output (activated, prevention-focused climate; Tran, 2010; Vuori & Huy, 2016). Similarly, other work shows that affective climates of low activation, such as of exhaustion, reduce motivation and subsequent performance (Chiang et al., 2020; Knight & Baer, 2014).

Overall, the practical programmatic (see Cronin et al., 2021) takeaway is this: to increase collective creativity, try to create climates of activated positive affect when possible. If not possible, such as during the COVID-19 pandemic, try to create climates of activated promotion-focused negative affect, such as anger, focused on something outside of the collective (e.g., anger at systemic injustice; Grant & Smith, 2021). Prevention-focused affective climates or unactivated affective climates are likely to hinder creative output. Still, it is important to take this advice with a grain of salt. In all, we identified 30 studies of affective climate above the team level, only two of which deal directly with creativity. These inferences were mostly drawn from work on affective climate in teams, or made based on the observation of mechanisms that are theoretically related to creativity. This leaves ample opportunity for future work on affective climate and creativity, guided by several broad takeaways.

A New Definition, Reflections, and Future Opportunities

Despite the evidence reviewed, much more work must be done before we truly understand the relationship between affective climate and creativity. Particularly, most current work is constrained by anachronistic assumptions of homogeneity (affect that constitutes a climate is identical) and cross-level isomorphism (collective affect operates as individual affect does). To this end, we propose a new definition of affective climate that relaxes these assumptions and brings the definition of affective climate in line with other climate types (Ostroff et al., 2013). Specifically, we define affective climate as: *the affective state that forms among members of a collective in response to their shared experience*. First, this new definition shifts the focus of affective climate from the *shared affective experience* of members of a given collective to their collective response to their *shared environment*, which necessarily includes affect. Second, it thus affords researchers an opportunity to investigate the "unsharedness" or variance of affective climate in collectives. In other words, a shared experience that spawns varied affective responses among members can still create an affective climate. Importantly, this shift facilitates four future research directions, which will help to map the nuances of the relationship between affective climate and collective creativity.

The Idiosyncratic Manifestation of Affective Climate

First, in line with previous definitions of affective climate (e.g., Parke & Seo, 2017), our definition allows affective states to manifest differently at their higher collective level since collective affect is not necessarily a simple analog of its individual-level construction. Whether considering teams or broader organizations, affective climates are embedded in broader social systems and thus influence and are influenced by the interactions of those systems, including the communication and information exchange patterns that result in creativity and innovation. This is evidenced in work showing that experimental affect manipulations involving interacting groups produce stronger effects (Klep et al., 2013), and that positive affect has a stronger effect on creativity in its collective rather than its individual form (Emich & Vincent, 2020).

Consider anger. At the individual level, anger has the potential to improve creativity because it is a promotion-focused activated state, spurring the exploration and pursuit of new ideas (Friedman & Förster, 2001). However, instituting a climate of anger within a particular organization must be carefully managed due to the complexities associated with collectives. As mentioned above, while a climate of anger toward something external to the organization may allow organizational members to come together and thus exchange information and integrate ideas, a climate of anger focused on members of the collective may result in increased relationship conflict and a subsequent restriction of information sharing. Thus, considering climates of anger is not as simple as classifying their regulatory state and activation level. Such climates should also be considered in light of their social focus and influence on collective action.

While some work on affective climate has explored its unique collective effects, most simply adapts individual-level theory to the collective level. Future research will benefit from exploring the idiosyncratic manifestation of affective climate at the collective level. For instance, future work could leverage the social nature of fear in motivating people to seek safety and comfort from others, or consider the reciprocal unique information sharing and processing that may occur in climates of excitement. Examining social-emotional climates may facilitate such work, which we elaborate below.

The Potential Heterogeneity of Affective Climate

Second, in line with previous work on climate (e.g., Ostroff et al., 2013), and some previous work on collective affect (Emich, 2014; Emich & Vincent, 2020; Knight et al., 2018), our new definition of affective climate suggests that affective climate is dependent on shared experiences, but not necessarily equivalent affective responses to those experiences. This leaves open the possibility that a single affective climate may contain multiple affective states if members' responses to their shared environment differ. Remember, *climate* is defined as the "meanings people attach to interrelated bundles of experiences" (Schneider et al., 2013, p. 361). As such, our definition of affective climate refers to the affect emerging from such experiences, driven by both member interaction and collective policies, practices, and procedures. To be clear, shared experiences will often result in the manifestation of convergent affect, trending toward homogeneity, which profoundly influences collective creativity. However, broader affective climate can also manifest as heterogeneous. To examine heterogeneous affective climates, researchers could manipulate them experimentally (e.g., Emich & Vincent, 2020) or categorize them using a person-centered approach such as latent profile or faultline analysis. Or, if researchers were interested in variance in a single affective state, a variable-centered approach focused on identifying distribution properties (e.g., variance, minimum, maximum, skew) of a given affective state could be used (see Emich et al., 2021 for a review and extension). Still, this is an important distinction because, at this point in the study of affective climate, we must be careful not to fall into the trap of defining it solely in terms of affective convergence, as we did when studying team affect (Emich, 2020). This would only repeat the error of mistaking the empirical limitations of the study of collective affect with their theoretical manifestation (Emich & Lu, 2017). It would also add to the error of conflating the shared experience of a collective environment with the affect produced by that shared experience.

Consider work by McConville and colleagues (2020), who, through a series of focus-group interviews, found that the colonial oppressive roots of New Zealand's founding result in mixed affective responses to the shared experience of the holidays of Waitangi Day, celebrating the founding of the nation, and Anzac Day, celebrating fallen soldiers. Particularly, white descendants of British nationals hold these holidays in regard, feeling comfort and belonging, or alternatively view them with anger and confusion if they perceive they are being confronted for their ancestors' role as oppressors. Alternatively, native Māori often feel ashamed, disgusted, or angry at being portrayed as colonial caricatures. In this case, the experience of a shared event (a national holiday) results in a shared affective experience with two (or more) distinct affective responses based on ethnicity and perceptions of oppression.

As work on collective affect began with the study of shared team affective tone, which George (1990) originally defined as "consistent or homogeneous affective reactions within a group" (p. 77), work on climate began with Kurt Lewin (e.g., Lewin et al., 1939) in a time when multilevel theorizing was in its infancy. Because of this, it was assumed that to exist as a collective construct, team or organizational members must agree on their experienced state (George, 1990). However, we now understand that it is entirely possible for a collective property to exist configurationally (Kozlowski & Klein, 2000). As Ostroff and colleagues note (2013), "[the molar or homogeneous] view underestimates the complexity of climate in that patterns or configurations based on relative emphasis or priorities likely exist and a patterned approach may more accurately reflect climate" (p. 653). This is also consistent with data showing that in large collectives, such as many organizations, it is unlikely that every individual will experience the same emotion in response to the same event (Weiss & Cropanzano, 1996). For example, Choi and colleagues (2011) find that when companies introduce new employee programs, some employees react positively while others react negatively. Both individual reactions to the innovation and the collective affective climate (of mixed affective experiences) surrounding the innovation predict its success. Additionally, Emich (2014) and To and colleagues (2021) found that the simultaneous presence of positive and negative affect in teams can respectively facilitate team information exchange and creativity. While the concept of variation in levels of a given affective state has begun to be recognized in the adaptation of terms such as *affective climate strength* and *uniformity*, which reflect variance and patterns of affect within a collective (Gamero & González-Romá, 2020), thus far, the literature has mostly ignored the possibility that the experience of multiple affective states can constitute a singular affective climate (Emich & Lu, 2020).

As such, an opportunity exists to conduct work examining affective climates that contain multiple types of affect based on member characteristics. As McConville and colleagues' (2020) work on privilege highlights, these climates exist, although more homogeneous affective climates are likely the norm. To this point, some team-level work has begun to explore the effects of members experiencing qualitatively different emotions. Emich and Vincent (2020) provide a model of these effects on creativity. Understanding such affective climates is a necessary step in building accurate and predictive models of how actual workplace experiences influence creativity and innovation.

The Multilevel Nature of Affective Climate

Third, our definition highlights that affective climate emerges from both the dynamic interaction of its individual-level components and through environmental factors that can influence individuals' behavior and provide their collective experience a sense of shared meaning (Ostroff et al., 2013; Kozlowski & Klein, 2000). Together, these bottom-up and top-down processes produce shared (although not necessarily identical) collective states, in this case affective states, which can be said to exist at this higher level.

While both top-down and bottom-up processes explain how a particular affective state manifests at a higher collective level, currently most work has focused on bottom-up micro-processes, most likely because we consider emotions "intimate ephemeral experiences" (Menges & Kilduff, 2015, p. 847). These processes generally include the tendency for people to automatically mimic others' affective states, the tendency to consciously observe others' affective state and adjust toward similarity, the tendency to look to others and copy their response when one is unsure how to act, and the tendency to empathetically shift toward another's affective state (for a review, see Emich, 2020). Over time, as members attempt to make sense of shared events, they also tend to reappraise their initial evaluation and affective response toward the shared collective understanding (Kozlowski & Klein, 2000).

However, in larger collectives such as organizations, branches, departments, or entire industries, members do not necessarily interact on a consistent basis. The increased adoption of remote work practices has only accelerated this tendency. In these larger collectives, top-down drivers such as collective policies, practices, procedures, and routines may play an outsized role in determining people's shared affective experience (Menges & Kilduff, 2015; Ostroff et al., 2013; Parke & Seo, 2017). For example, collective emotional norms prescribe appropriate and inappropriate emotional displays (Hochschild, 1983), which are often formalized through personnel practices, such as hiring and keeping employees who follow display rules, and organizational structure, such as promoting employees who follow these rules to be more visible (Diefendorff et al., 2011; Knight et al., 2018). Collectives such as service organizations directly communicate which emotions are necessary for a particular job (Ashkanasy & Daus, 2002). For example, servers and stewards are expected to smile, while undertakers are expected to be solemn. Additionally, shared affective experiences can be manufactured through rituals, which involve gathering, greeting, and rhythmic communication and movement (Collins, 2004). For example, many religious services involve communal singing. Walmart and other organizations begin the day with a morning cheer (Menges & Kilduff, 2015). Many workplaces also orchestrate a weekly happy hour. In these ways, collectives develop a shared understanding of which affective behaviors are important and rewarded motivating members to act within that shared understanding (Parke & Seo, 2017). Future work should explore how such shared environments, and the shared experiences that occur in those environments, influence collective affect and creativity.

Social-Emotional Climates

Fourth, because the subset of emotions classified as "social emotions" necessarily depend on experiencing other people's actions or interpreting their underlying thoughts or feelings (Hareli & Parkinson, 2008), studying them provides the opportunity to build theory regarding how specific affective climates influence specific collective processes. Although there is some debate over which emotions should be classified as "social," here we follow Hareli and Parkinson (2008) in defining *social emotions* as those that necessarily include the appraisal of another person as the object of the emotion, or necessarily involve the appraisal of social rules, norms, or agency. For example, emotions such as anger or frustration, which arise out of assessments of fairness as related to another person, are considered social emotions. Classic work such as that by Ellsworth and Smith (1988), Fridja (1986), Lazarus (1991), and Weiner (1986) define a wide variety of affective experiences using these criteria, including love, pride, compassion, shame, contempt, guilt, jealousy, schadenfreude, gratitude, envy, anger, and admiration (Hareli & Parkinson, 2008).

While emotions such as happiness, sadness, and fear can be driven by others, and are generally more socially oriented than broad affective states since they manifest in response to specific stimuli, they may also be triggered by nonsocial stimuli. Similarly, although such nonsocial emotions can result in social behavior, for example, positive affect can increase helping (Levin & Isen, 1975), "social emotions have more direct and consistent effects on certain social behaviors than other nonsocial and social emotions do" (Hareli & Parkinson, 2008, p. 146). As such, the relationship between pity and helping is stronger and more consistent than that of positive affect (Hareil & Parkinson, 2008). Additionally, these social effects are the most typical consequences of social emotions; since although most emotions have some social function, only social emotions have specific reliable social functions. Because social emotions arise relative to specific social situations, and result in specific responsive behaviors, they provide opportunity for specific predictive theory to be built relating such affective climates to collective behavior, which is especially important to theory regarding collective creativity given the previously discussed benefits of collectives for pursuing creative endeavors.

The little work that focuses on social-emotional climates provides strong evidence of their importance on collective processing. Interestingly, much of this work currently sits outside the psychological and organizational sciences. For example, Grant and Smith (2021) use the example of the COVID-19 pandemic to show how a climate of anger, in this case, driven by perceptions of systematic injustice and social isolation and spread through social media, can motivate coordination and collective action. Although this work does not delve into creativity, these behaviors underlie the necessary recombination of ideas in creative problem solving. Additionally, the formation of rallies and protests represents a novel and often useful solution to perceived injustice given the social isolation and shelter-in-place directives present during the pandemic.

A second social emotion whose collective manifestation has received research attention in the organization sciences is companionate love (as opposed to romantic love). As Barsade and O'Neill (2014) write in their explication of cultures of companionate love in nursing homes, "Unlike self-focused positive emotions (such as pride or joy), which center on independence and self-orientation, companionate love is an other-focused emotion, promoting interdependence and sensitivity toward other people" (p. 552). In their work, Barsade and O'Neill (2014) found that cultures of companionate love reduce employee exhaustion (which is often high among nursing home workers); increase teamwork, importantly, by focusing employees on each other; and amplify levels of positive affect in employees with high trait positive affect. Palkovitz (2007) shed light on this point in a meta-analysis of father–son relationships, finding that affective climates including connection, attachment, and love (all components of companionate love) result in stronger relationships. Again, these findings have important implications for creativity. Although Barsade and O'Neill (2014) study affective culture and not affective climate, affective climate acts as a more proximal predictor of the effects of affective culture on collective outcomes, often acting as a key mechanism of its influence (Parke & Seo, 2017). In other words, an organization's shared deep-rooted beliefs, values, and assumptions regarding affect and affect-related behaviors (culture; Parke & Seo, 2017) influence employees' affective responses to their shared experiences (climate). Because of this, it is reasonable to assume that climates of companionate love also make collectives more other-focused and amplify trait positive affect. In turn, this should allow such collectives to be more creative than their relationally apathetic counterparts (Polman & Emich, 2011; Isen, 2008).

In summary, an opportunity exists to conduct more work on social emotions, which inherently involve collective processes and thus overcome the persistent issue of cross-level isomorphism in work on collective affect. Of the 30 studies on affect above the team level we identified, 18 involved broad positive and negative affect. Only three involved explicitly social emotions. Again, such work will not only help explicate the relationship between affective climate and creativity, but will also allow for relatively straightforward theory building as social emotions are directly related to specific social appraisals and processes.

Conclusion

Importantly, we now recognize the validity of the quotes that began this chapter. Creativity is indeed a collective phenomenon and affect plays a large role in its occurrence. However, collectives and affect are both complex. As such, perhaps exploring collective affect is doubly so. Here, we provide a summary of where we are and, more importantly, where we need to go to navigate this complexity. In response, we hope young (and old) researchers take heart. There is a lot of good research left to do.

References

Amabile, T. M., Barsade, S. G., Mueller, J. S., & Staw, B. M. (2005). Affect and creativity at work. *Administrative Science Quarterly, 50*(3), 367–403. https://doi.org/10.2189/asqu.2005.50.3.367

Arfara, C., Lamprakis, A., Tsivos, G., & Samanta, D. I. (2018). The role of work-group emotional intelligence in learning organizations: A case study of the Greek public sector. *International Journal of Organizational Leadership, 7*(3), 240–255. https://doi.org/10.33844/ijol.2018.60383

Ashkanasy, N. M., & Daus, C. S. (2002). Emotion in the workplace: The new challenge for managers. *Academy of Management Perspectives, 16*(1), 76–86. https://doi.org/10.5465/ame.2002.6640191

Ashkanasy, N. M., & Nicholson, G. J. (2003). Climate of fear in organisational settings: Construct definition, measurement and a test of theory. *Australian Journal of Psychology, 55*(1), 24–29. https://doi.org/10.1080/00049530412331312834

Baas, M., De Dreu, C. K., & Nijstad, B. A. (2008). A meta-analysis of 25 years of mood-creativity research: Hedonic tone, activation, or regulatory focus?. *Psychological Bulletin*, *134*(6), 779–806. https://doi.org/10.1037/a0012815

Baer, M. (2012). Putting creativity to work: The implementation of creative ideas in organizations. *Academy of Management Journal*, *55*(5), 1102–1119. https://doi.org/10.5465/amj.2009.0470

Barsade, S. G., & Knight, A. P. (2015). Group affect. *The Annual Review of Organizational Psychology and Organizational Behavior*, *2*, 21–46. https://doi.org/10.1146/annurev-orgpsych-032414-111316

Barsade, S. G., & O'Neill, O. A. (2014). What's love got to do with it? A longitudinal study of the culture of companionate love and employee and client outcomes in a long-term care setting. *Administrative Science Quarterly*, *59*(4), 551–598. https://doi.org/10.1177/0001839214538636

Bliese, P. D. (2000). Within-group agreement, non-independence, and reliability. In K. J. Klein & S. W. J. Kozlowski (Eds.), *Multilevel Theory, Research, and Methods in Organizations* (pp. 349–381). Jossey Bass.

Bramesfeld, K. D., & Gasper, K. (2008). Happily putting the pieces together: A test of two explanations for the effects of mood on group-level information processing. *British Journal of Social Psychology*, *47*(2), 285–309. https://doi.org/10.1348/000712607X218295

Chiang, J. T. J., Chen, X. P., Liu, H., Akutsu, S., & Wang, Z. (2020). We have emotions but can't show them! Authoritarian leadership, emotion suppression climate, and team performance. *Human Relations*, *74*(7), 1082–1111. https://doi.org/10.1177/0018726720908649

Choi, J. N., Sung, S. Y., Lee, K., & Cho, D. S. (2011). Balancing cognition and emotion: Innovation implementation as a function of cognitive appraisal and emotional reactions toward innovation. *Journal of Organizational Behavior*, *32*(1), 107–124. https://doi.org/10.1002/job.684

Collins, R. (2004). Rituals of solidarity and security in the wake of terrorist attack. *Sociological Theory*, *22*(1), 53–87. https://doi.org/10.1111/j.1467-9558.2004.00204.x

Cronin, M. A., Stouten, J., & van Knippenberg, D. (2021). The theory crisis in management research: Solving the right problem. *Academy of Management Review*, 46(4), 667–683.

Cropanzano, R., & Dasborough, M. T. (2015). Dynamic models of well-being: Implications of affective events theory for expanding current views on personality and climate. *European Journal of Work and Organizational Psychology*, *24*(6), 844–847. https://doi.org/10.1080/1359432X.2015.1072245

De Dreu, C. K. W., Baas, M., & Nijstad, B. A. (2008). Hedonic tone and activation level in the mood-creativity link: Toward a dual pathway to creativity model. *Journal of Personality and Social Psychology*, *94*(5), 739–756. https://doi.org/10.1037/0022-3514.94.5.739

de Rivera, J. (1992). Emotional climate: Social structure and emotional dynamics. In K. T. Strongman (Ed.), *International Review of Studies on Emotion* (vol. 2, pp. 197–218). John Wiley & Sons.

Diefendorff, J. M., Erickson, R. J., Grandey, A. A., & Dahling, J. J. (2011). Emotional display rules as work unit norms: A multilevel analysis of emotional labor among nurses. *Journal of Occupational Health Psychology*, *16*(2), 170–186. https://doi.org/10.1037/a0021725

Drucker, P. (2014). *Innovation and Entrepreneurship*. Routledge.

Ellsworth, P. C., & Smith, C. A. (1988). Shades of joy: Patterns of appraisal differentiating pleasant emotions. *Cognition and Emotion, 2*, 301–331. https://doi.org/10.1080/02699938808412702

Emich, K. J. (2014). Who's bringing the donuts: The role of affective patterns in group decision making. *Organizational Behavior and Human Decision Processes, 124*, 122–132. https://doi.org/10.1016/j.obhdp.2014.03.001

Emich, K. J. (2020). Well, I feel differently: The importance of considering affective patterns in teams. *Social and Personality Psychology Compass, 14*, e12523. https://doi.org/10.1111/spc3.12523

Emich, K. J., & Lu, L. (2017). He thought, she thought: The importance of subjective patterns to understanding team processes. *Journal of Organizational Behavior, 38*(1), 152–156. https://doi.org/10.1002/job.2122

Emich, K. J., & Lu, L. (2020). How shared and unshared affect impact team creative success. In A. McKay, R. Reiter-Palmon, & J. Kaufman (Eds.), *Explorations in Creativity Research: Creative Success in Teams* (pp. 146–162). Academic Press. https://doi.org/10.1016/B978-0-12-819993-0.00008-4

Emich, K. J., Lu, L., Ferguson, A., Peterson, R. S., & McCourt, M. (2021). Team composition revisited: A team member attribute alignment approach. *Organizational Research Methods*, 10944281211042388. https://doi.org/10.1177/10944281211042388

Emich, K. J., & Vincent, L. C. (2020). Shifting focus: The influence of affective diversity on team creativity. *Organizational Behavior and Human Decision Processes, 156*, 24–37. https://doi.org/10.1016/j.obhdp.2019.10.002

Finke, R. A., Ward, T. B., & Smith, S. M. (1992). *Creative Cognition: Theory, Research and Application*. MIT Press.

Forgas, J. P. (1995). Emotion in social judgments: Review and a new affect infusion model (AIM). *Psychological Bulletin, 117*, 39–66. https://doi.org/10.1037/0033-2909.117.1.39

Fredrickson, B. L. (2001). The role of positive emotions in positive psychology: The broaden-and-build theory of positive emotions. *American Psychologist, 56*(3), 218–226. https://doi.org/10.1037/0003-066X.56.3.218

Friedman, R. S., & Förster, J. (2001). The effects of promotion and prevention cues on creativity. *Journal of Personality and Social Psychology, 81*(6), 1001–1013. https://doi.org/10.1037/0022-3514.81.6.1001

Fridja, N. H. (1986). *The Emotions*. Cambridge University Press.

Gamero, N., & González-Romá, V. (2020). Affective climate in teams. In L. Yang, R. Cropanzano, C. S. Daus, & V. Martinez-Tur (Eds.), *The Cambridge Handbook of Workplace Affect* (pp. 244–256). Cambridge University Press.

George, J. M. (1990). Personality, affect, and behavior in groups. *Journal of Applied Psychology, 75*(2), 107–116. https://doi.org/10.1037/0021-9010.75.2.107

González-Romá, V., Peiró, J. M., Subirats, M., & Mañas, M. A. (2000). The validity of affective work-team climates. In M. Vartiainen, F. Avallone, & N. Anderson (Eds.), *Innovative Theories, Tools and Practices in Work and Organizational Psychology* (pp. 97–109). Hogrefe & Huber.

Grant, P. R., & Smith, H. J. (2021). Activism in the time of COVID-19. *Group Processes & Intergroup Relations, 24*(2), 297–305. https://doi.org/10.1177/1368430220985208

Grawitch, M. J., Munz, D. C., Elliott, E. K., & Mathis, A. (2003). Promoting creativity in temporary problem-solving groups: The effects of positive mood and autonomy in problem definition on idea-generating performance. *Group Dynamics: Theory, Research, and Praactice, 7*(3), 200–213. https://doi.org/10.1037/1089-2699.7.3.200

Hareli, S., & Parkinson, B. (2008). What's social about social emotions? *Journal for the Theory of Social Behaviour, 38*(2), 131–156. https://doi.org/10.1111/j.1468-5914.2008.00363.x

Hochschild, A. R. (1983). *The Managed Heart: Commercialization of Human Feeling.* University of California Press.

Holmes, O. W. (1872). The Poet at the Breakfast-Table, VIII. *The Atlantic Monthly*, 30 (178), 225–240.

Isen, A. M. (2008). Some ways in which positive affect influences decision making and problem solving. In M. Lewis, J. Haviland-Jones & L. F. Barrett (Eds.), *Handbook of Emotions* (3rd ed., pp. 548–573). Guilford Press.

Izard, C. E. (2010). The many meanings/aspects of emotion: Definitions, functions, activation, and regulation *Emotion Review, 2*, 363–370. https://doi.org/10.1177/1754073910374661

Jones, E. E., & Kelly, J. R. (2009). No pain, no gains: Negative mood leads to process gains in idea-generation groups. *Group Dynamics: Theory, Research, and Practice, 13*, 75–88. https://doi.org/10.107/a0013812

Kim, M., & Shin, Y. (2015). Collective efficacy as a mediator between cooperative group norms and group positive affect and team creativity. *Asia Pacific Journal of Management, 32*, 693–716. https://doi.org/10.1037/a0013812

Kim, M. J., Choi, J. N., & Lee, K. (2016). Trait affect and individual creativity: Moderating roles of affective climate and reflexivity. *Social Behavior and Personality: An International Journal, 44*(9), 1477–1498. https://doi.org/10.2224/sbp.2016.44.9.1477

Klep, A. H., Wisse, B., & van der Flier, H. (2013). When sad groups expect to meet again: Interactive affective sharing and future interaction expectation as determinants of work groups' analytical and creative task performance. *British Journal of Social Psychology, 52*(4), 667–685. https://doi.org/10.1111/bjso.12000

Knight, A. P. (2015). Mood at the midpoint: Affect and change in exploratory search over time in teams that face a deadline. *Organization Science, 26*(1), 99–118. https://doi.org/10.1287/orsc.2013.0866

Knight, A. P., & Baer, M. (2014). Get up, stand up: The effects of a non-sedentary workspace on information elaboration and group performance. *Social Psychological and Personality Science, 5*(8), 910–917. https://doi.org/10.1177/1948550614538463

Knight, A. P., Menges, J. I., & Bruch, H. (2018). Organizational affective tone: A meso perspective on the origins and effects of consistent affect in organizations. *Academy of Management Journal, 61*(1), 191–219. https://doi.org/10.5465/amj.2016.0671

Kozlowski, S. W. J., & Klein, K. J. (2000). A multilevel approach to theory and research in organizations: Contextual, temporal, and emergent processes. In K. J. Klein & S. W. J. Kozlowski (Eds.), *Multilevel Theory, Research, and Methods in Organizations: Foundations, Extensions, and New Directions* (pp. 3–90). Jossey-Bass.

Lazarus, R. S. (1991). *Emotion and Adaptation*. Oxford University Press.

Lewin, K., Lippitt, R., & White, R. K. (1939). Patterns of aggressive behavior in experimentally created "social climates." *The Journal of Social Psychology*, *10*(2), 269–299. https://doi.org/10.1080/00224545.1939.9713366

Levin, P. F., & Isen, A. M. (1975). Further studies on the effect of feeling good on helping. *Sociometry*, *38*(1), 141–147. https://doi.org/10.2307/2786238

Low, S. M. (2008). Fortification of residential neighbourhoods and the new emotions of home. *Housing, Theory and Society*, *25*(1), 47–65. https://doi.org/10.1080/14036090601151038

Maimone, F., & Sinclair, M. (2010). Affective climate, organizational creativity, and knowledge creation: Case study of an automotive company. In W. J. Zerbe, E. J. Charmine E. J., & M. A. Neal (Eds.), *Emotions and Organizational Dynamism*, vol. 6, *Research on Emotion in Organizations* (pp. 309–332). Emerald Group.

McConville, A., Wetherell, M., McCreanor, T., Borell, B., & Moewaka Barnes, H. (2020). "Pissed off and confused"/"Grateful and (re) moved": Affect, privilege and national commemoration in Aotearoa New Zealand. *Political Psychology*, *41*(1), 129–144. https://doi.org/10.1111/pops.12610

Menges, J. I., & Kilduff, M. (2015). Group emotions: Cutting the Gordian knots concerning terms, levels of analysis, and processes. *Academy of Management Annals*, *9*(1), 845–928. https://doi.org/10.5465/19416520.2015.1033148

Ostroff, C., Kinicki, A. J., & Muhammad, R. S. (2013). *Organizational Culture and Climate*. John Wiley & Sons.

Ozcelik, H., Langton, N., & Aldrich, H. (2008), Doing well and doing good: The relationship between leadership practices that facilitate a positive emotional climate and organizational performance. *Journal of Managerial Psychology*, *23*(2), 186–203. https://doi.org/0.1108/02683940810850817

Palkovitz, R. (2007). Challenges to modeling dynamics in developing a developmental understanding of father-child relationships. *Applied Development Science*, *11*(4), 190–195. https://doi.org/10.1080/10888690701762050

Parke, M. R., & Seo, M. G. (2017). The role of affect climate in organizational effectiveness. *Academy of Management Review*, *42*(2), 334–360. https://doi.org/10.5465/amr.2014.0424

Polman, E., & Emich, K. J. (2011). Decisions for others are more creative than decisions for the self. *Personality and Social Psychology Bulletin, 37*, 492–501. https://doi.org/10.1177/0146167211398362

Sawyer, K. B., & Clair, J. (in press). The double-edged sword of hope: A narrative ethnography of the evolution of an organization tackling the grand challenge of commercial sex exploitation. *Administrative Science Quarterly*. https://doi.org/10.1177/00018392211055506

Schneider, B., Ehrhart, M. G., & Macey, W. H. (2013). Organizational climate and culture. *Annual Review of Psychology*, *64*, 361–388. https://doi.org/10.1146/annurev-psych-113011-143809

Shin, Y. (2014). Positive group affect and team creativity: Mediation of team reflexivity and promotion focus. *Small Group Research*, *45*, 337–364. https://doi.org/10.1177/1046496414533618

Sternberg, R. J., Kaufman, J. C., & Pretz, J. E. (2002). *The Creativity Conundrum: A Propulsion Model of Kinds of Creative Contributions.* Psychology Press. https://doi.org/10.4324/9780203759615

To, M. L., Fisher, C. D., Ashkanasy, N. M., & Zhou, J. (2021). Feeling differently, creating together: Affect heterogeneity and creativity in project teams. *Journal of Organizational Behavior*, *42*(9), 1228–1243. https://doi.org/10.1002/job.2535

Tran, V. (2010). The role of emotional climates of joy and fear in team creativity and innovation (Working Paper No. 10/054). Centre Emile Bernheim Research.

Tsai, W. C., Chi, N. W., Grandey, A. A., & Fung, S. C. (2012). Positive group affective tone and team creativity: Negative group affective tone and team trust as boundary conditions. *Journal of Organizational Behavior*, *33*, 638–656. https://doi.org/10.1002/job.775

Tse, H. H. M., Dasborough, M. T., & Ashkanasy, N. M. (2008). A multi-level analysis of team climate and interpersonal exchange relationships at work. *The Leadership Quarterly*, *19*(2), 195–211. https://doi.org/10.1016/j.leaqua.2008.01.005

Tyson, N. deGrasse. (2009). *Neil deGrasse Tyson on His Books.* Big Think. https://bigthink.com/videos/neil-degrasse-tyson-on-his-books/.

Vuori, T. O., & Huy, Q. N. (2016). Distributed attention and shared emotions in the innovation process: How Nokia lost the smartphone battle. *Administrative Science Quarterly*, *61*(1), 9–51. https://doi.org/10.1177/0001839215606951

Ward, T. B. (1994). Structured imagination: The role of conceptual structure in exemplar generation. *Cognitive Psychology*, *27*, 1–40. https://doi.org/10.1006/cogp.1994.1010

Weiner, B. (1986). *An Attributional Theory of Motivation and Emotion.* Springer-Verlag.

Weiss, H. M., & Cropanzano, R. (1996). Affective events theory. *Research in Organizational Behavior*, *18*(1), 1–74.

28 Group Affect and Creativity

Hector Madrid, Malcolm Patterson, and Rodrigo Alday

Whether affect influences creativity has fascinated psychologists for decades. The diverse studies conducted in this field at the person level show that both positive and negative affect are related to the generation of novel ideas (George, 2007; Hennessey & Amabile, 2010; Madrid & Patterson, 2018; Zhou & Hoever, 2014). This means that enthused, joyful, and inspired, individuals are prone to think and behave in an unconventional way to solve problems (Amabile et al., 2005; Madrid et al., 2014), just as they do when feeling worried, tense, and anxious in a context of social support (George & Zhou, 2007; To et al., 2011). However, creativity is not only an individual endeavor; the production of novel and useful ideas can also be achieved by individuals working together in groups (Kanter, 1996; S. J. Shin & Zhou, 2007; Tsai et al., 2012). Yet, compared with individual creativity, less debate and research has focused on affect in groups. Thus, in this chapter, we first survey and discuss studies of affect and creativity in groups to provide a comprehensive review, and then we move on to build on existing knowledge in this field, arguing that our understanding of the relationship between affect and creativity in groups should include group interpersonal processes in the form of social integration. Finally, opportunities for future research are proposed.

Group Affect and Creativity

In the context of groups, the affective experience of group members is labeled as "group affective tone" (George, 1996). This construct refers to the shared and consistent experience of the same feelings among members of the same group (Collins et al., 2013). Accordingly, groups can be characterized by positive group affective tone, negative group affective tone, or both. In the following sections, we present and discuss studies examining group affective tones and creativity, which were identified using a scoping literature review. The latter provides an overview of the type, extent, quantity and quality of research available. By mapping existing research, the review can identify research gaps and future research needs.

Positive Group Affective Tone and Creativity

Most of the studies on affect in groups have focused on the influence of positive group affective tone on creativity (Table 28.1). In theoretical terms,

Table 28.1 *Summary of studies on group affect and creativity*

Reference	Group type	Theory	Method	Creativity operationalization	Main results
Grawitch, Munz, Elliott, et al. (2003)	Undergraduate college students	Broaden-and-Build theory	Laboratory experimental study	Creativity task with measures of idea fluency, originality, and usefulness	• Positive affect was positively related to creativity in a divergent thinking task.
Grawitch, Munz, & Kramer (2003)	Undergraduate college students	Broaden-and-Build theory	Laboratory experimental study	Creativity task with measures of idea fluency, originality, and usefulness	• Positive affect was positively related to creativity in a problem-solving task.
Kim & Shin (2015)	Professional teams	Social cognitive theory	Field survey study	Team leader ratings of creativity	• Positive affect was positively related to team creativity. • Collective self-efficacy mediated the positive relationship between positive affect and team creativity.
Rhee (2006)	Not specified	Broaden-and-Build theory	Laboratory experimental study	Creativity task with measures of idea generation	• Positive affect was positively related to broaden-and-build interactions. • Broaden-and-build interactions were positively related to creativity.
Jones & Kelly (2009)	Undergraduate college students	Broaden-and-Build theory, mood-as-information	Laboratory experimental study	Creativity task with measures of idea generation	• Positive affect was positively related to group creativity. • Negative affect was positively related to group creativity.

Table 28.1 (*cont.*)

Reference	Group type	Theory hypothesis	Method	Creativity operationalization	Main results
Klep et al. (2011)	Undergraduate college students	Broaden-and-Build theory, mood-as-information hypothesis	Laboratory experimental study	Creativity task with measures of idea originality	• Positive affect was positively related to creativity. • Negative affect was negatively related to creativity.
Tsai et al. (2012)	Professional teams (R&D)	Dual-tuning and group-centrism hypotheses	Field survey study	Team leader ratings of creativity	• Positive affect was negatively related to creativity when both negative affect and trust were high, but positive affect was positively related to creativity when negative affect was high and trust was low.
Klep et al. (2013)	Undergraduate college students	Mood-as-information hypothesis	Laboratory experimental study	Creativity task with measures of idea fluency	• Negative affect was negatively related to creativity when group members had future expectations for interaction, but not when there were not those expectations.
Shin (2014)	Professional teams	Broaden-and-Build theory	Field survey study	Team leader ratings of creativity	• Positive affect was positively related to creativity. • Positive affect was positively related to team reflexivity. • Team reflexivity mediated the relationship between positive affect and creativity.

Study	Sample	Theory	Method	Outcome	Findings
Shin et al. (2016)	Professional teams	Broaden-and-Build theory, social cognitive theory	Field survey study	Team leader ratings of creativity	• The indirect relationship between positive affect and team creativity via team reflexivity was positive when transformational leadership was high, but there was no such relationship when transformational leadership was low.
Chi (2019)	Professional teams (R&D)	Broaden-and-Build theory and substitution hypothesis	Field survey study	Team leader ratings of creativity	• Team information exchange mediated the positive relationship between positive affect and individual creativity. • The indirect positive relationship between positive affect and individual creativity via team information exchange was stronger when supervisory support was low rather than high.
Huang et al. (2021)	Professional teams	Broaden-and-Build theory, threat-rigidity hypothesis	Field survey study	Team leader ratings of creativity	• Positive affect was positively related to team innovation via team information elaboration. • Negative affect was negatively related to team innovation via team information elaboration.

543

Table 28.1 (*cont.*)

Reference	Group type	Theory	Method	Creativity operationalization	Main results
					• Positive affect was positively related to team innovation via team information elaboration, when transformational leadership was high rather than low. • Negative affect was negatively related to team innovation via team information elaboration, when transformational leadership was high rather than low.
Emich & Vincent (2020)	Undergraduate college students	Hedonic tone, regulatory focus, and affective activation	Laboratory experimental study	Creativity task with measures of idea generation and selection	• Promotion-focused activated positive and negative affect was positively related to creativity. • Prevention-focused activated negative affect was negatively related to creativity.

and as an extension of early research on affect and creative thinking, the hypothesis of a positive relationship between group positive affect and creativity relies on Broaden-and-Build theory (Fredrickson, 2001), which proposes that positive feelings expand cognition and build resources, such that attention is broader, and thinking is divergent. This cognitive mindset offers a wider amount of task-related information and knowledge that intertwine in a flexible and unconventional way. This was the argument adopted by Grawitch, Munz, Elliott, et al. (2003) and Grawitch, Munz, and Kramer (2003) to explain the results of their seminal experimental studies, in which positive group affect was positively related to creative performance. In these studies, affect was experimentally induced using imaginary exercises, while creativity was assessed with a series of interdependent problem solving and divergent thinking tasks, from which fluency, originality, and usefulness of solutions and ideas were evaluated. However, one limitation of these studies is that broaden-and-build processes are primarily defined as cognitive processes at the individual level of analysis (Amabile et al., 2005), which does not necessarily capture the behavioral underpinnings of the relationship of affect and creativity in groups.

To address this problem, Rhee (2007) proposes the notion of "Broaden-and-Build Interactions," which denotes a series of interpersonal behaviors that have the potential to facilitate creativity. First, *Building of Ideas* involves the process of brainstorming by which group members cross-fertilize their knowledge and ideas to produce novel solutions. Second, *Morale-Building Communication* refers to patterns of positive feedback among group members, which are supportive of their efforts to work creatively. Third, *Active Affirmation* is about building an environment of trust, where groups members feel accepted and encouraged to speak out and propose their ideas. The core proposal of this approach is that broaden-and-build interactions explain the effect of group positive affect on creativity. This was supported in an experimental study (Rhee, 2006), using a decision-making task, in which positive group affect led to increased broaden-and-build interactions, which in turn were positively related to group creativity, expressed in the fluency of novel ideas generated by each group, depicting a mediation process. Based on the same rationale, diverse experimental and field studies have supported the positive relationship between group positive affect and creativity, claiming broaden-and-build processes as the theoretical explanation for such an effect (Chi, 2019; Grawitch, Munz, & Elliott, et al., 2003; Grawitch, Munz, & Kramer, 2003; Huang et al., 2021; Jones & Kelly, 2009; Klep et al., 2011; Y. Shin, 2014; Y. Shin et al., 2016).

Moreover, other mediational processes explaining the relationship between positive group affective tone and creativity have been proposed and supported. Kim and Shin (2015), drawing on social cognitive theory (Bandura, 1986, 1997), demonstrated that collective self-efficacy is a mechanism linking positive group affect and creativity. This form of efficacy conveys beliefs about the group's skills and capabilities for coordination, communication, and collaboration (Zaccaro et al., 1995). Thus, positive affect should increase collective self-efficacy due to priming of memory with positive valenced content, denoting previous successful performance, and building optimism when executing the tasks in hand.

Also, Shin (2014) examined whether group reflexivity is another mediating mechanism in the relationship between positive group affect and creative performance. Group reflexivity is the collective behavior of monitoring and reflecting on strategies, plans, and work processes, together with generating and evaluating possible changes in the group's operations (De Jong & Elfring, 2010). Previous research showed that reflexivity is a precursor of creativity and innovation in groups (West, 2002); yet, whether this effect originated from positive affect was not established. However, Shin's field study with multiple working groups found support for this mechanism, observing that, because positive feelings infuse cognitive flexibility and build broader action repertories, positive group affective tone is positively related to reflexivity, which in turn is positively associated with group leaders' ratings of creativity. The similar construct of group information elaboration has been also proposed as a mechanism for the effect of positive group affect on creativity. This refers to a pattern of interpersonal behavior in which group members exchange information and perspectives, discussing and integrating them with a focus on group performance (Van Knippenberg et al., 2004). Huang et al. (2021), appealing to Broaden-and-Build theory, found that positive group affective tone increases the likelihood of group information elaboration and thereby creativity, expressed in group leaders' ratings of performance. Similar results were observed by Chi (2019), using group information exchange, namely, open and fluid group communication, as the mediator variable.

Studies have also examined possible moderators in the relationship between positive group affective tone and creativity in groups. Transformational leadership was supported as a boundary condition that moderates the positive relationship between group positive affect and creativity via group reflexivity, such that this effect occurs when transformational leadership is high, but not when low (Y. Shin et al., 2016). This effect was replicated in Huang et al.'s (2021) study. This synergetic influence is likely due to the inspirational and charismatic meaning of transformational leadership behavior boosting the broadened cognitive and action repertory associated with positive affect. Chi (2019) also observed that leadership plays a role in the link between affect and creativity in groups, but in the opposite direction. He proposed that contextual support from leaders is beneficial when group members lack resources to perform well, but not when resources are available, which is called the *substitution effect* (Gilmore et al., 2013). In the case of affect and creativity, if group positive affect is understood as a psychological resource, then its positive effect on creativity should occur when contextual support is low but not high. This was supported by the study of Chi (2019), which showed that the positive relationship between team members shared positive feelings and creativity performance was positive and strong when leader support was low but attenuated in the case of supportive leaders.

Negative Group Affective Tone and Creativity

The proposed relationship between group negative affective tone and creativity theoretically draws on the "affect-as-information" and the "threat rigidity" hypotheses (Schwarz & Clore, 1983; Staw et al., 1981). According to the first, affect provides important information about situations, such that when negative, feelings provide information cueing that the situation is problematic, leading people to persist in addressing the problem and find a solution (George & Zhou, 2007). As a result, narrow and convergent cognitive processes and information processing emerge to clearly delineate the issues to be dealt with and thinking is convergent based on well-established heuristics to solve the problem. The threat rigidity hypothesis is consistent with this principle, proposing that negative affect tends to be appraised as a signal of risk in the environment, increasing narrowing cognition, and making individuals less flexible in problem solving (Huang et al., 2021). Thus, negative affect has the potential to reduce creativity as this demands flexible, not rigid, cognition.

Notwithstanding the above, only few studies have observed a direct relationship between group negative affective tone and creative performance. Using an experimental design with college students, Klep et al. (2011) observed that groups characterized by group negative affect perform much better in analytical than creative tasks (operationalized as originality of drawings), which especially happens when there is an expectation among group members to meet again in the future (Klep et al., 2013). However, in another experimental study, based on a similar sample, Jones and Kelly (2009) observed that groups in the negative affect condition spend more time evaluating their novel ideas, which therefore leads to increased creative performance, using a task of advertising slogan creation for a fictitious travel agency. Thus, instead of showing a strong and consistent main effect, the influence of group negative affective tone on creativity seems to be dependent on third variables acting as boundary conditions. For example, in the study of Huang et al. (2021) mentioned earlier, the results indicate that group negative affective tone is negatively related to creativity via information elaboration when transformational leadership is high, rather than low, which may be explained by the effect of the threat rigidity. In other words, leaders' pushing for unconventional work may be counterproductive when team members, due to the experience of negative affect, deduce that the performance situation is problematic, demanding a conventional, rather than creative, problem solution.

Moreover, a recent study of Emich and Vincent (2020) argues for a finer-grained view of affect in relation to creativity in groups. They distinguish between activated and deactivated affective states, which differ in terms of their energy expenditure (Russell, 1980). Also, a distinction is made between promotion- and prevention-focused affective states, where the former is associated with the presence of rewards, whereas the latter is associated with threats in the environment (Baas et al., 2008; De Dreu et al., 2008; Higgins, 1997). Their study showed that both promotion (e.g., happiness, anger) and prevention (e.g., tension, fear) states with greater activation are involved in creativity in groups. In the first case, activated-promotion affect, whether positive (e.g., happiness) or negative (e.g., anger), exerts a positive effect on idea generation, while in the second activated-negative affect leads to decreased novelty of ideas.

Finally, using much more complex theorization, the study of Tsai et al. (2012) proposed and supported, with a sample of professional R&D teams, a three-way interaction between group positive affective tone, negative affective tone, and trust within teams for the prediction of creative performance. Accordingly, high levels of group negative affect together with high levels of trust lead to a negative relationship between positive affect and creativity (the opposite result occurs when negative affect is high, but trust is low). In other words, positive affect is negatively related to creativity when negative affect is also experienced in a context of trust among group members. This dampening effect occurs because negative affect together with trust configurate a "group centrism" process (Kruglanski et al., 2006), which involves increased rejection of deviant points of view, resistance to change, conservatism, and traditionalism, in other words, group conformity (Asch, 1955), all of which is opposed to creative thinking and cross-fertilization of ideas.

Our survey and review of the literature show that a body of theoretical and empirical literature has focused on the relationship between affect and creativity at the group level of analysis. The emerging evidence has provided a number of insights into this relationship including mediating mechanisms and boundary conditions.

Social Integration in the Relationship between Group Affect and Creativity

A limitation of the studies identified in our literature review is the almost exclusive adoption of cognitive mechanisms primarily described for the individual level of analysis to explain why and when the relationship between these variables occurs, especially broaden-and-build processes (Fredrickson, 2001). These cognitive routes can apply at the group level of analysis; however, we propose that the influence of affect on creativity in groups also unfolds by a series of interpersonal psychological processes, labeled "social integration."

Social integration is an umbrella construct that captures a series of emergent psychological states and interpersonal behavior in groups, such as cohesion, trust, and psychological safety, together with collaboration and conflict (cf., Knight & Eisenkraft, 2014; Madrid & Patterson, 2021). In the domain of group emergent states, cohesion is the sense of belonging among group members around a strong identity, and when high, cohesion involves the desire to keep working together over time (Beal et al., 2003). Trust is the state of attributing good intentions to the actions of group members, which leads to, for example, taking risks and sharing information within the group (Costa, 2003; De Jong et al., 2015; De Jong & Elfring, 2010; Sheppard & Sherman, 1998). Psychological safety is similar to the state of trust, but they are distinct as the latter is about the extent to which the benefit of the doubt is given to group members. In contrast, psychological safety denotes whether other group members give the benefit of the doubt to you. Thus, this construct captures whether the group environment is open to being oneself and expressing one's own points of view, ideas, proposals, and suggestions (Edmondson, 1999), which is an expression of a participative context, allowing the fertilization of knowledge and ideas. In turn, regarding group behavioral processes, collaboration involves the collective execution of tasks and mutual assistance between group members (Beersma et al., 2003; Tjosvold, 1984). This collaboration is conveyed in the exchange of knowledge and experience to solve problems and the provision of social and emotional support when group members work together (Drach-Zahavy, 2004; Ganster et al., 1986). In contrast, conflict describes friction in group members' relationships due to the perception of incompatibilities about interests, viewpoints, and ways of interacting (Jehn & Bendersky, 2003). Specifically, task conflict denotes disagreement about how problems should be addressed and solved and how tasks must be executed, while relationship conflict describes tension between group members linked to their personalities, values, interests, and motivations (Behfar et al., 2011; Beitler et al., 2018; DeChurch et al., 2013; Guenter et al., 2016).

Diverse studies have shown that these components of social integration are associated with creative outcomes in groups, such that creativity is greater when cohesion, trust, psychological safety, and collaboration are present (Frazier et al., 2017; Hulsheger et al., 2009; West, 2002). This effect is likely because working with novel ideas is risky due to challenging the status quo and the potential emergence of resistance to change linked to new ways of doing things in the group (Kanter, 1996; Madrid et al., 2014; Yuan & Woodman, 2010). As such, this form of social integration provides the contextual conditions for assuming risk-taking in sharing information, voicing ideas and concerns, making suggestions, and working on making novel ideas happen in practice, all of which are necessary actions to generate a creative output. On the other hand, in general, conflict denotes weaker social integration, where discrepancies separate group members, reducing the likelihood of collective and collaborative efforts (De Dreu & Weingart, 2003; De Wit et al., 2012). Nevertheless, these issues primarily apply to relationship conflict, characterized by tension between group members due to real or perceived differences. In contrast, task conflict can increase group performance when psychological safety is present within the group (Bradley et al., 2012). This synergetic effect occurs because task conflict delivers diversity in knowledge about how to solve the problems, which is cross-fertilized if the group work environment is safe; namely, groups members feel free to be themselves and express what they believe is important for group functioning and performance (Edmondson & Lei, 2014).

If social integration is important for fostering or inhibiting group creativity, knowing whether and how group affect influences social integration is salient to providing a more comprehensive account of the relationship between affect and creativity in groups. Theoretical and empirical research indicates that group affective tones exert influences on social integration (Knight & Eisenkraft, 2014). When shared feelings among group members are positive, the sense of cohesion, trust, and psychological safety increases, while collaboration ripples through group members (Barsade, 2002; Costa, 2003; Frazier et al., 2017). These effects are likely to occur because cognitive flexibility linked to positive affect facilitates the building of positive social perceptions and attitudes, together with increased flexibility in perspective-taking in the collective realm.

In contrast, the influence of negative group affective tones on social integration, and thereby on creativity, involves more complexity. The effects of negative feelings over group functioning are context-dependent, such that a negative influence occurs only when the source of affect is internal rather than external to the group (Knight & Eisenkraft, 2014). Thus, when negative group affect emerges from, for example, internal errors, failures, or poor previous performance, social integration tends to be weakened, leading to, for example, reduced cohesion, trust, and safety and limited collaboration, and even increasing intragroup conflict. This dampening effect of negative feelings on social integration occurs because of the emergence of narrowing interpersonal cognition, reduced perspective-taking, and enhanced tension, irritability, and impulsivity typically linked to emotional and interpersonal conflict (Greer & Jehn, 2007).

Taking the social integration mechanisms and the broaden-and-build processes proposed in the literature on group creativity together, we propose an initial model in which they are mediator variables that make possible the translation of group affect into group creativity (Figure 28.1). Specifically, positive and negative affective tones convey flexible and convergent cognitive

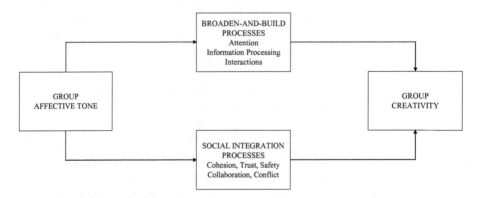

Figure 28.1 *Model of group affect and creativity.*

processes, respectively, associated with attention and information processing. At the same time, these forms of group affect influence cohesion, trust, psychological safety, collaboration, and conflict. As a result, both sets of mechanisms influence creative outcomes in groups.

Proposals for Future Research

As part of our review, we also identify a series of issues that need more attention and opportunities for further research to expand our understanding of this phenomenon, which are presented below.

1. Creativity conceptualization. In the studies reviewed here, creativity has been mainly conceptualized as the generation of novel and useful ideas, and operationalized as fluency and originality of ideas. Thus, this stream of research can be expanded to consider the process of creativity as well. This process involves problem identification, idea production, and idea selection before the creative solution is achieved. Another relevant model to account for is the process of innovation, which incorporates behavioral stages to make novel ideas happen (Amabile, 1988; Kanter, 1996). For example, group members discuss, champion, reject, and select these ideas after problem identification and idea generation and the chosen ideas are then tested and implemented in practice. From this perspective, a relevant question is whether group affect has equivalent or discrete influences on all the creative/ innovation process stages.

2. Affective valence. Most studies have concentrated on the main effects of either positive or negative affect on group creativity. Nevertheless, as with studies conducted at the individual level of analysis, the group affective experience can be described in a complex configuration, where positive and negative affects interact, having a synergetic effect on group creativity. For example, the dual-tuning model of affect and creativity at the person level indicates that higher levels of creativity occur when both positive and negative feelings are experienced in a context of social support. Following this rationale, as described earlier, the study of Tsai et al. (2012) supported the dual-tuning model in groups; however, the results were in the opposite direction. Specifically, positive group affective tone has the potential to reduce group creativity when negative group affective tone is also high under a context of within-group trust. This suggests that complex effects of affect on creativity could work in a different way depending on the level of analysis.

3. Affective diversity. Studies in the literature of group affect and creativity assume homogeneity in group affective tones; namely, group affect entails shared and consistent feelings with the same affective valence (positive or negative) among group members. Nevertheless, not all groups are characterized by this affective consistency because there is the chance that group

members differ in the intensity of their affective states. For example, in a team, some individuals might be strongly enthusiastic, while others are mildly or weakly enthusiastic. The notion of affective diversity captures this phenomenon (Barsade & Gibson, 2012). In other words, groups can differ in the strength of their affective tones. In another related phenomenon, group members differ in the feelings they are experiencing. For example, a sub-group might be feeling enthusiastic, whereas other group members are not enthusiastic but are experiencing frustration. Consequences of affective diversity have been the subject of limited investigation in general and in relation to creativity in particular (Barsade & Knight, 2015; Collins et al., 2013). However, two hypotheses can be discussed in this regard, based on the categorization-elaboration model of group diversity (Van Knippenberg et al., 2004). First, the categorization hypothesis states that differences in the strength and type of affect in groups would inform about the existence of subgroups that create the conditions for conflict, and thereby, in general, creativity might be impaired. Second, the elaboration hypothesis implies that affective diversity denotes diversity in the composition of groups in terms of, for example, abilities, knowledge, and motivations, all of which convey a broader amount of material that benefits more complete solutions to problems faced. This positive effect of affective diversity is also promoted by broadening interpersonal cognition and flexibility, which is beneficial to, for example, creativity (George & King, 2007). Thus, the study of affective diversity is another route to explore in future studies on creative performance.

4. Causality direction. Research thus far has focused on group affect as a predictor of group creativity, and has not paid attention to a possible reverse causality between these constructs. There are theoretical reasons to believe that the latter is likely because the production of a creative outcome may be an event satisfying the basic psychological needs of agency, achievement and purpose, which, when rewarded, leads to the experience of positive affect (Deci et al., 2017; Van den Broeck et al., 2016). A handful of studies at the individual level of analyses have proposed and tested these possible effects, but the evidence is mixed and far from conclusive (Amabile et al., 2005; Tavares, 2016), and, to the best of our knowledge, nonexistent in the context of groups.

5. Methods. All the above recommendations imply new challenges in the research methods adopted. Creativity operationalization in terms of a behavioral process requires adequate instrumentation to differentiate its different behavioral stages. Addressing affective valence and dual-tuning models, together with affective dispersion, involves larger samples using groups as the level of analysis and the adoption of sophisticated statistical techniques to deal with synergetic effects. Finally, causality issues imply the use of longitudinal designs to capture, beyond the experimental context in laboratories, the causal dynamics in the relationship between group affect and creativity.

Final Remarks

This chapter addressed whether, how, and when group affect is related to group creativity. The review of the relevant literature indicates that positive and negative shared affective states among group members are related to broadened and narrowed cognitive processes that expand or limit the likelihood of the production of novel and useful ideas in groups. As part of the same review, we identified that psychological mechanisms claimed to explain how group affect influences group creativity primarily pertain to the individual level of analysis, especially the broaden-and-build processes. Thus, to address this limitation and expand our understanding of the affect–creativity relationship in groups, we present theoretical and empirical research, and an initial depiction of a model, indicating that interpersonal processes, labeled social integration, also participate in the relationship between affect and creativity in groups. Finally, we highlighted that research on group affect and creativity is far from complete because there are still diverse theoretical and methodological issues to resolve to comprehensively understand this phenomenon.

References

Amabile, T. M. (1988). A model of creativity and innovation in organizations. *Research in Organizational Behavior*, *10*, 123–167.

Amabile, T. M., Barsade, S. G., Mueller, J. S., & Staw, B. M. (2005). Affect and creativity at work. *Administrative Science Quartely*, *50*(3), 367–403. http://dx .doi.org/10.2189/asqu.2005.50.3.367

Asch, S. E. (1955). Opinions and social pressure. *Scientific American*, *193*(5), 31–35. https://doi.org/10.1038/scientificamerican1155-31

Baas, M., De Dreu, C. K. W., & Nijstad, B. A. (2008). A meta-analysis of 25 years of mood-creativity research: Hedonic tone, activation, or regulatory focus? *Psychological Bulletin*, *134*(6), 779–806. https://doi.org/10.1037/a0012815

Bandura, A. (1986). *Social Foundations of Thought and Action: A Social-Cognitive View*. Prentice-Hall.

Bandura, A. (1997). *Self-Efficacy: The Exercise of Control*. W. H. Freeman.

Barsade, S. G. (2002). The ripple effect: Emotional contagion and its influence on group behavior. *Administrative Science Quarterly*, *47*(4), 644–675. http://dx.doi.org/ 10.2307/3094912

Barsade, S. G., & Gibson, D. E. (2012). Group affect: Its influence on individual and group outcomes. *Current Directions in Psychological Science*, *2*(2), 119–123. https://doi.org/10.1177/0963721412438352

Barsade, S. G., & Knight, A. P. (2015). Group affect. *Annual Review of Organizational Psychology and Organizational Behavior*, *2*(1), 21–46. http://dx.doi.org/10 .1146/annurev-orgpsych-032414-111316

Beal, D. J., Cohen, R. R., Burke, M. J., & McLendon, C. L. (2003). Cohesion and performance in groups: A meta-analytic clarification of construct relations. *Journal of Applied Psychology*, *88*(6), 989–1004. https://doi.org/10.1037/0021-9010.88.6.989

Beersma, B., Hollenbeck, J. R., Humphrey, S. E., et al. (2003). Cooperation, competition, and team performance: Toward a contingency approach. *Academy of Management Journal, 46*(5), 572–590. https://doi.org/10.2307/30040650

Behfar, K. J., Mannix, E. A., Peterson, R. S., & Trochim, W. M. (2011). Conflict in small groups: The meaning and consequences of process conflict. *Small Group Research, 42*(2), 127–176. https://doi.org/10.1177/1046496410389194

Beitler, L. A., Scherer, S., & Zapf, D. (2018). Interpersonal conflict at work: Age and emotional competence differences in conflict management. *Organizational Psychology Review, 8*(4), 195–227. https://doi.org/10.1177/2041386618808346

Bradley, B. H., Postlethwaite, B. E., Klotz, A. C., Hamdani, M. R., & Brown, K. G. (2012). Reaping the benefits of task conflict in teams: The critical role of team psychological safety climate. *Journal of Applied Psychology, 97*(1), 151–158. https://doi.org/10.1037/a0024200

Chi, N.-W. (2019). Is support always good? Exploring whether supervisory support enhances or attenuates the beneficial effect of positive group affective tone on team and individual creativity. In N. M. Ashkanasy, W. J. Zerbe & C. E. Härtel (Eds.), *Emotions and Leadership* (vol. 15, pp. 133–157). Emerald. https://doi.org/10.1108/s1746–979120190000015007

Collins, A. L., Lawrence, S. A., Troth, A. C., & Jordan, P. J. (2013). Group affective tone: A review and future research directions. *Journal of Organizational Behavior, 34*, S43–S62. https://doi.org/10.1002/job.1887

Costa, A. C. (2003). Work team trust and effectiveness. *Personnel Review, 32*(5), 605–622. https://doi.org/10.1108/00483480310488360

De Dreu, C. K. W., Baas, M., & Nijstad, B. A. (2008). Hedonic tone and activation level in the mood-creativity link: Toward a dual pathway to creativity model. *Journal of Personality and Social Psychology, 94*(5), 739–756. https://doi.org/10.1037/0022-3514.94.5.739

De Dreu, C. K. W., & Weingart, L. R. (2003). Task versus relationship conflict, team performance, and team member satisfaction: A meta-analysis. *Journal of Applied Psychology, 88(4),* 741–749. https://doi.org/10.1037/0021-9010.88.4.741

De Jong, B. A., Dirks, K., & Gillespie, N. (2015). Trust and team performance: A meta-Analysis of main effects, contingencies, and qualifiers. *75th Annual Meeting of the Academy of Management, AOM 2015, 101*(8), 744–749. https://doi.org/10.5465/AMBPP.2015.234

De Jong, B. A., & Elfring, T. (2010). How does trust affect the performance of ongoing teams? The mediating role of reflexivity, monitoring, and effort. *Academy of Management Journal, 53*(3), 535–549. http://dx.doi.org/10.5465/amj.2010.51468649

De Wit, F. R. C., Greer, L. L., & Jehn, K. A. (2012). The paradox of intragroup conflict: A meta-analysis. *Journal of Applied Psychology, 97*(2), 360–390. https://doi.org/10.1037/a0024844

DeChurch, L. A., Mesmer-Magnus, J. R., & Doty, D. (2013). Moving beyond relationship and task conflict: Toward a process-state perspective. *Journal of Applied Psychology, 98*(4), 559–578. https://doi.org/10.1037/a0032896

Deci, E. L., Olafsen, A. H., & Ryan, R. M. (2017). Self-determination theory in work organizations: The state of a science. *Annual Review of Organizational*

Psychology and Organizational Behavior, 4(1), 19–43. https://doi.org/10.1146/annurev-orgpsych-032516-113108

Drach-Zahavy, A. (2004). Toward a multidimensional construct of social support: Implications of provider's self-reliance and request characteristics. *Journal of Applied Social Psychology, 34*(7), 1395–1420.

Edmondson, A. C. (1999). Psychological safety and learning behavior in work teams. *Administrative Science Quarterly, 44*(2), 350–383. http://dx.doi.org/10.2307/2666999

Edmondson, A. C., & Lei, Z. (2014). Psychological safety: The history, renaissance, and future of an interpersonal construct. *Annual Review of Organizational Psychology and Organizational Behavior, 1*(1), 23–43. https://doi.org/10.1146/annurev-orgpsych-031413-091305

Emich, K. J., & Vincent, L. C. (2020). Shifting focus: The influence of affective diversity on team creativity. *Organizational Behavior and Human Decision Processes, 156*, 24–37. https://doi.org/10.1016/j.obhdp.2019.10.002

Frazier, M. L., Fainshmidt, S., Klinger, R. L., Pezeshkan, A., & Vracheva, V. (2017). Psychological safety: A meta-analytic review and extension. *Personnel Psychology, 70*(1), 113–165. https://doi.org/10.1111/peps.12183

Fredrickson, B. L. (2001). The role of positive emotions in positive psychology: The Broaden-and-Build theory of positive emotions. *American Psychologist, 56*, 218–226.

Ganster, D. C., Fusilier, M. R., & Mayes, B. T. (1986). Role of social support in the experience of stress at work. *Journal of Applied Psychology, 71*(1), 102–110. https://doi.org/10.1037//0021-9010.71.1.102

George, J. M. (1996). Group affective tone. In M. A. West (Ed.), *Handbook of Work Group Psychology* (pp. 77–93). John Wiley & Sons.

George, J. M. (2007). 9 Creativity in organizations. *The Academy of Management Annals, 1*(1), 439–477. https://doi.org/10.1080/078559814

George, J. M., & King, E. B. (2007). Potential pitfalls of affect convergence in teams: Functions and dysfunctions of group affective tone. In E. A. Mannix, M. A. Neale, & C. P. Anderson (Eds.), *Research on Managing Groups and Teams: Affect and Groups* (vol. 10, pp. 97–124). Elsevier.

George, J. M., & Zhou, J. (2007). Dual tuning in a supportive context: Joint contributions of positive mood, negative mood, and supervisory behaviors to employee creativity. *Academy of Management Journal, 50*, 605–622. http://dx.doi.org/10.5465/amj.2007.25525934

Gilmore, P. L., Hu, X., Wei, F., Tetrick, L. E., & Zaccaro, S. J. (2013). Positive affectivity neutralizes transformational leadership's influence on creative performance and organizational citizenship behaviors. *Journal of Organizational Behavior, 34*, 1061–1075. https://doi.org/10.1002/job.1833

Grawitch, M. J., Munz, D. C., Elliott, E. K., & Mathis, A. (2003). Promoting creativity in temporary problem-solving groups: The effects of positive mood and autonomy in problem definition on idea-generating performance. *Group Dynamics: Theory, Research, and Practice, 7*(3), 200–213. https://doi.org/10.1037/1089-2699.7.3.200

Grawitch, M. J., Munz, D. C., & Kramer, T. J. (2003). Effects of member mood states on creative performance in temporary workgroups. *Group Dynamics, 7*(1), 41–54. https://doi.org/10.1037/1089-2699.7.1.41

Greer, L. L., & Jehn, K. (2007). The pivotal role of negative affect in understanding the effects of process conflict on group performance. In E. Mannix, M. Neale, & C. Anderson (Eds.), *Affect and Groups* (pp. 21–43). Emerald.

Guenter, H., van Emmerik, H., Schreurs, B., et al. 2016). When task conflict becomes personal: The impact of perceived team performance. *Small Group Research*, *47*(5), 569–604. https://doi.org/10.1177/1046496416667816

Hennessey, B. A., & Amabile, T. M. (2010). Creativity. *Annual Review of Psychology*, *61*, 569–598. https://doi.org/10.1146/annurev.psych.093008.100416

Higgins, E. T. (1997). Beyond pleasure and pain. *American Psychologist*, *52*, 1280–1300. http://dx.doi.org/10.1037/0003-066X.52.12.1280

Huang, L. C., Liu, Y., Cheung, G. W. hung, & Sun, J. M. (2021). A multilevel study of group affective tone and team innovation: A moderated mediation model. *Group and Organization Management*, *70*. https://doi.org/10.1177/10596011211029411

Hulsheger, U., Anderson, N. R., & Salgado, J. (2009). Team-level predictors of innovation at work: A comprehensive meta-analysis spanning three decades of research. *Journal of Applied Psychology*, *94*(5), 1128–1145. https://doi.org/10.1037/a0015978

Jehn, K. A., & Bendersky, C. (2003). Intragroup conflict in organizations: A contingency perspective on the conflict-outcome relationship. *Research in Organizational Behavior*, *25*(3), 187–242. https://doi.org/10.1016/S0191-3085(03)25005-X

Jones, E. E., & Kelly, J. R. (2009). No pain, no gains: Negative mood leads to process gains in idea-generation groups. *Group Dynamics*, *13*(2), 75–88. https://doi.org/10.1037/a0013812

Kanter, R. M. (1996). When a thousand flowers bloom: Structural, collective, and social conditions for innovation in organizations. In P. Myers (Ed.), *Knowledge Management and Organisational Design* (pp. 93–131). Butterworth-Heinemann. https://doi.org/10.1016/b978-0-7506-9749-1.50010-7

Kim, M., & Shin, Y. (2015). Collective efficacy as a mediator between cooperative group norms and group positive affect and team creativity. *Asia Pacific Journal of Management*, *32*(3), 693–716. https://doi.org/10.1007/s10490-015-9413-4

Klep, A. H. M., Wisse, B., & van der Flier, H. (2011). Interactive affective sharing versus non-interactive affective sharing in work groups: Comparative effects of group affect on work group performance and dynamics. *European Journal of Social Psychology*, *41*(3), 312–323. https://doi.org/10.1002/ejsp.775

Klep, A. H. M., Wisse, B., & van der Flier, H. (2013). When sad groups expect to meet again: Interactive affective sharing and future interaction expectation as determinants of work groups' analytical and creative task performance. *British Journal of Social Psychology*, *52*(4), 667–685. https://doi.org/10.1111/bjso.12000

Knight, A. P., & Eisenkraft, N. (2014). Positive is usually good, negative is not always bad: The effects of group affect on social integration and task performance. *Journal of Applied Psychology, 100*(4), 1214–1227. https://doi.org/10.1037/apl0000006

Kruglanski, A. W., Pierro, A., Mannetti, L., & De Grada, E. (2006). Groups as epistemic providers: Need for closure and the unfolding of group-centrism.

Psychological Review, 113(1), 84–100. https://doi.org/10.1037/0033-295X.113.1 .84

Madrid, H. P., Niven, K., & Vasquez, C. A. (2019). Leader interpersonal emotion regulation and innovation in teams. *Journal of Occupational and Organizational Psychology, 92*(4). https://doi.org/10.1111/joop.12292

Madrid, H. P., & Patterson, M. G. (2018). Affect and creativity. In R. Reiter-Palmon, V. L. Kennel, & J. C. Kaufman (Eds.), *Individual Creativity in the Workplace* (pp. 245–265). Elsevier.

Madrid, H. P., & Patterson, M. (2021). Affect and proactivity in teams. In K. Z. Peng & C. Wu (Eds.), *Emotion and Proactivity at Work. Prospects and Dialogues* (pp. 215–236). Bristol University Press.

Madrid, H. P., Patterson, M. G., Birdi, K. S., Leiva, P. I., & Kausel, E. E. (2014). The role of weekly high-activated positive mood, context, and personality in innovative work behavior: A multilevel and interactional model. *Journal of Organizational Behavior, 35*(2), 234–256. https://doi.org/10.1002/job.1867

Rhee, S.-Y. (2007). Group emotions and group outcomes: The role of group-member interactions. In E. A. Mannix, M. A. Neale, & C. P. Anderson (Eds.), *Research on Managing Groups and Teams: Affect and Groups* (vol. 10, pp. 55–95). Elsevier. https://doi.org/10.1016/S1534-0856(07)10004-9

Rhee, S.-Y. (2006). Shared emotions and group effectiveness: The role of broadening-and-building interactions. In K. M. Weaver (Ed.), *Proceedings of the 65th annual meeting of the academy of management* (CD).

Russell, J. A. (1980). A circumplex model of affect. *Journal of Personality and Social Psychology, 39*(6), 1161–1178. https://doi.org/10.1037/h0077714

Schwarz, N., & Clore, G. L. (1983). Mood, misattribution, and judgments of well-being: Informative and directive functions of affective states. *Journal of Personality and Social Psychology, 45*(3), 513–523. https://doi.org/10.1037/0022-3514.45.3 .513

Sheppard, B. H., & Sherman, D. M. (1998). The grammars of trust: A model and general implications. *Academy of Management Review, 23*(3), 422–437. http:// dx.doi.org/10.5465/amr.1998.926619

Shin, S. J., & Zhou, J. (2007). When is educational specialization heterogeneity related to creativity in research and development teams? Transformational leadership as a moderator. *The Journal of Applied Psychology, 92*(6), 1709–1721. https://doi .org/10.1037/0021-9010.92.6.1709

Shin, Y. (2014). Positive group affect and team creativity: Mediation of team reflexivity and promotion focus. *Small Group Research, 45*(3), 337–364. http://dx.doi.org/ 10.1177/1046496414533618

Shin, Y., Kim, M., & Lee, S. H. (2016). Positive group affective tone and team creative performance and change-oriented organizational citizenship behavior: A moderated mediation model. *Journal of Creative Behavior, 53*(1), 52–68. https://doi.org/10.1002/jocb.166

Staw, B. M., Sandelands, L. E., & Dutton, J. E. (1981). Threat-rigidity effects in organizational behavior: A multilevel analysis. *Administrative Science Quarterly, 26*(4), 501–524. https://doi.org/10.2307/2392337

Tavares, S. M. (2016). How does creativity at work influence employee's positive affect at work? *European Journal of Work and Organizational Psychology, 25*(4), 525–539. https://doi.org/10.1080/1359432X.2016.1186012

Tjosvold, D. (1984). Cooperation theory and organizations. *Human Relations, 37*(9), 743–767. http://dx.doi.org/10.1177/001872678403700903

To, M. L., Fisher, C. D., Ashkanasy, N. M., & Rowe, P. A. (2011). Within-person relationships between mood and creativity. *Journal of Applied Psychology, 97*(3), 599–612. https://doi.org/10.1037/a0026097

Tsai, W., Chi, N., Grandey, A., & Fung, S. (2012). Positive group affective tone and team creativity: Negative group affective tone and team trust as boundary conditions. *Journal of Organizational Behavior, 33*(5), 638–656.

Van den Broeck, A., Ferris, D. L., Chang, C. H., & Rosen, C. C. (2016). A review of self-determination theory's basic psychological needs at work. *Journal of Management, 42*(5), 1195–1229. https://doi.org/10.1177/0149206316632058

Van Knippenberg, D., De Dreu, C. K. W., & Homan, A. C. (2004). Work group diversity and group performance: An integrative model and research agenda. *Journal of Applied Psychology, 89*(6), 1008–1022. https://doi.org/10.1037/0021-9010.89.6.1008

West, M. A. (2002). Sparkling fountains or stagnant ponds: An integrative model of creativity and innovation implementation in work groups. *Applied Psychology, 51*(3), 355–387. http://dx.doi.org/10.1111/1464-0597.00951

Yuan, F. R., & Woodman, R. W. (2010). Innovative behavior in the workplace: The role of performance and image outcome expectations. *Academy of Management Journal, 53*(2), 323–342. http://dx.doi.org/10.5465/amj.2010.49388995

Zaccaro, S. J., Blair, V., Peterson, C., & Zazanis, M. (1995). Collective efficacy. In J. E. Maduxx (Ed.), *Self-Efficacy, Adaptation, and Adjustment: Theory, Research, and Application* (pp. 305–328). Plenum Press.

Zhou, J., & Hoever, I. J. (2014). Research on workplace creativity: A review and redirection. *Annual Review of Organizational Psychology and Organizational Behavior, 1*(1), 333–359. https://doi.org/10.1146/annurev-orgpsych-031413-091226

29 Psychological Safety and Creativity

The Glue That Binds a Creative Team

Roni Reiter-Palmon and Meagan Millier

Research on the topic of creativity and innovation in organizations has increased steadily over the past few decades. Interest in creativity and innovation and the factors that facilitate or hinder these has developed due to the importance of these issues for organizational survival and growth (Shalley et al., 2004). In the past few decades, factors such as rapid changes in the marketplace, major advances in technology, and increased globalization have increased the need of organizations to develop creative ideas, solutions, processes, and products (Mumford et al., 2002; Shalley et al., 2004; West et al., 2004). A recent report by IBM and MIT (Fleming et al., 2019) analyzed jobs and tasks from 2010 to 2017 and found that tasks that could be conducted by machines, including AI and machine learning, were disappearing at a higher rate from job descriptions. On the other hand, tasks that required intellectual skill, knowledge, and creativity increased, and also increased in value. In addition, the World Economic Forum notes that future skills necessary for workers include critical thinking, problem solving, creativity, and innovation as four of the top five skills (Whiting, 2020). These two reports together indicate that creativity is critical for individual employees.

As problems facing organizations have become more complex, and as work has become more interdependent, it has become clear that solutions to these problems cannot be developed by a single individual (Bell & Kozlowski, 2008; Paulus & Nijstad, 2003). The use of teams in the workplace to address these complex problems has increased, and with it the interest in team creativity has also increased (Reiter-Palmon et al., 2011). The use of teams to address complex problems also indicates that it is critical to understand how teams solve problems creatively. When discussing team creativity, a number of research streams have emerged to understand how teams capitalize on individual creativity and develop creative products or ideas. Specifically, work regarding team creativity has focused on team cognition, or how team members think and develop shared cognition that leads to creative solutions (Harvey, 2014; Reiter-Palmon & Paulus, 2020). A second stream focuses on the social processes that emerge in teams during team interactions and how those facilitate or inhibit team creativity (Harvey & Kou, 2018; Reiter-Palmon, 2021).

Most team effectiveness models include team social processes as a central feature (Hackman, 1987; Mathieu et al., 2008). Further, many models distinguish between taskwork and teamwork (McIntyre & Salas, 1995). Taskwork describes the interactions with tools, tasks, and systems (Bowers et al., 1997). Teamwork, on the other hand, reflects processes associated with the social interaction of team members that ensure adaptive behavior and successful collective action to complete team taskwork (McIntyre & Salas, 1995; Salas et al., 2004). However, different models and frameworks of teamwork include different variables (Mathieu et al., 2008; Rousseau et al., 2006; Salas et al., 2005; Salas et al., 2007). That said, there are some commonalities across the different models, and one important team social process that has emerged, especially as it relates to team creativity and innovation, is that of psychological safety (Reiter-Palmon et al., 2011; Salas et al., 2005).

In this chapter, we discuss the role of psychological safety as an important social process that facilitates team creativity and innovation. We review the literature on psychological safety and its relationship with creativity, particularly team creativity. We then discuss how psychological safety can facilitate both other important team processes and cognition relevant to creative performance. Finally, we discuss potential antecedents to psychological safety and the factors that facilitate effective emergence of psychological safety in teams.

Psychological Safety and Creativity at the Individual Level

Psychological safety has been defined as the belief that it is safe to engage in interpersonal risk-taking in the workplace (Edmondson, 1999). As noted by Edmondson, "The term is meant to suggest neither a careless sense of permissiveness, nor an unrelentingly positive affect but, rather, a sense of confidence that the team will not embarrass, reject, or punish someone for speaking up. This confidence stems from mutual respect and trust among team members (Edmondson, 1999, p. 354)." As this quote suggests, psychological safety allows individuals to share information and voice opinions, even when those are uncomfortable to share. As noted in this quote, psychological safety does not mean that people are "nice" for the sake of being nice. In fact, in psychological safe teams, individuals may feel more comfortable to discuss difficult issues, raise concerns, and have disagreements with other team members.

As the definition and description of psychological safety suggests, emotions are at the core of this construct. Psychological safety allows team members to share difficult information, not only potentially eliciting a negative emotional reaction, but also allowing team members to cope with these negative emotions through positive emotions such as trust and respect (Edmondson, 1999). As such, psychological safety can be viewed as an important team emotional construct.

Much of the work on individual-level psychological safety has suggested that it is an important antecedent of creative performance at the individual level (Carmeli et al., 2014; Madjar & Ortiz-Walters, 2009). Similarly, the research on climate for creativity has found that a climate of psychological safety facilitates the creative performance of teams and individuals (Amabile & Gryskiewicz, 1989; Ekvall, 1996; Hunter et al., 2007). In this sense, psychological safety has been evaluated as a part of the team emotional context that allows the individual to be more creative. The direct effects of psychological safety on creativity and innovation are well documented. However, researchers have also been interested in the specific mechanisms by which psychological safety facilitates creativity and innovation.

One important factor that was found to mediate the relationship between psychological safety and creativity or innovation at the individual level has been engagement. Liu and Ge (2020) studied the relationship between psychological safety, work engagement, and creativity. The sample consisted of participants working in the banking industry in China. Creativity was measured using supervisory evaluations of each individual, whereas measures of psychological safety and work engagement were completed by the individual employee. The results indicated that the relationship between psychological safety and creativity were fully mediated by engagement.

Other studies have focused on the components of work engagement. Kark and Carmeli (2009) evaluated the role of vitality – a specific aspect of work engagement focusing on energy and vigor, which can be considered important emotional components of work engagement. They found that vitality mediated the relationship between psychological safety and creativity, measured as self-evaluation of creativity or engagement in the creative process. Finally, Chen et al. (2020), using a sample of R&D employees, found that the relationship between psychological safety and creativity was mediated by creative process engagement. Higher psychological safety was related to higher reported engagement in specific cognitions associated with creativity such as problem construction, idea generation, and idea evaluation (Reiter-Palmon & Illies, 2004). Higher engagement in the creative process, in turn, was associated with higher supervisory evaluations of creativity. Motivation, a construct similar to work engagement, was also found to mediate the relationship between psychological safety and creativity (Vinarski Peretz & Carmeli, 2011).

Psychological safety has been linked to team member willingness to discuss information openly, share information, and make suggestions (Burke et al., 2006; Edmondson, 2004; Salas et al., 2005). Gong et al. (2012) studied relationships among psychological safety, individual creativity, employee proactivity, and information exchange in a sample of 190 dyads of employees and their supervisors. They proposed that proactive employees seek information in exchanges with others; information exchange, in turn, fosters trusting relationships that provide psychological safety for employee creative endeavors. The results suggested that proactive employees engage in more information exchange and that the relationship between information exchange and creativity is fully mediated by trust. While psychological safety was not directly measured, trust and psychological safety share similarities, and the reasoning for the hypothesized relationship was based on the psychological safety literature. Similarly, psychological safety has been found to influence reflection regarding performance (Carmeli et al., 2014). Reflection regarding performance focuses on what can be learned from previous performance episodes, correcting deficiencies, and has been linked to learning as well as creativity (Schippers et al., 2014).

These studies have focused on measuring creativity at the individual level and viewing the team as part of the context in which individual-level creativity may occur. They have looked mainly at variables at the individual level such as engagement, motivation, and proactivity. It is important to note that team creativity, where creativity is manifested and measured as a team construct, is receiving more attention and becoming more important for organizations. As such, we will now review the literature in which team creativity and psychological safety were evaluated.

Psychological Safety and Creativity in Teams

As psychological safety is often conceptualized as a team-level phenomenon, it is not surprising that much of the research evaluating psychological safety and creativity has focused on teams and has found it to be an important predictor of creativity and innovation in teams (Burningham & West, 1995; Han et al., 2019; Hu et al., 2018; West & Anderson, 1996). Research focusing on dyads and teams has found that psychological safety has a direct influence on creativity and innovation. Choo et al. (2007) studied 206 manufacturing project teams and found that psychological safety influenced knowledge creation and creativity. Greenbaum et al. (2020) found a relationship between supervisory evaluation of team creativity and psychological safety as evaluated by the employees.

Trust and psychological safety have also been suggested to influence the interpretation of behavior of other team members, and therefore may be directly related to the interpretation of conflict (Salas et al., 2005). When trust is low, disagreements and other ambiguous information are more likely to be interpreted in a negative way, resulting in negative responses from team members. Backup and support behaviors, that is, behaviors in which one team member provides support or takes over a task, may also be more likely to be misinterpreted as micromanagement (Salas et al., 2005). It has also been suggested that psychological safety influences communication and knowledge sharing in teams. Kessel et al. (2012) studied 73 healthcare teams and found that psychological safety facilitated knowledge sharing, which in turn led to improved creativity and innovation. Similarly, Liu et al. (2021) studied R&D teams and found that psychological safety facilitated individual and team knowledge sharing, which in turn facilitated team creativity. Wilkens and London (2006) studied hospital teams and found that psychological safety was related to the creative performance of these teams. Innovation in medical care and processes are critical for improving medical care and reducing adverse effects. Further, psychological safety was positively related to learning orientation, feedback seeking, and feedback giving, and negatively related to conflict in the team.

Psychological safety in teams has been studied in relation to learning. Specifically, Edmondson's (1999) initial interest in psychological safety was due to its effect on team and organizational learning. She reasoned that the open and honest conversation resulting from an atmosphere of psychological safety allows team members to discuss concerns as well as errors. Whereas in teams in which psychological safety is low, team members will be concerned about being blamed and having conflict if errors are brought up. It is, however, important to discuss errors and mistakes so that team members can learn and not repeat those. Tucker et al. (2007) studied hospital project improvement teams that were in charge of developing and implementing new processes and practices. They found that psychological safety improved learning activities such as identifying best practices and modifying these best practices to fit with the context. These learning activities led to successful implementation of new evidence-based processes and practices in the hospital. Huang et al. (2008) studied psychological safety in R&D teams. They found that psychological safety led to improved team learning, which led to improved team performance, including creativity and innovation.

Psychological safety has also been found to be critical to team communication, which, as previously discussed, is necessary for creativity and innovation. Psychological safety ensures that team members have a sense of mutual trust and respect, which facilitates communication because team members know their contributions and opinions will be valued (Carmeli et al., 2014; Kessel et al., 2012). Therefore, team members are more willing to speak up and share ideas, provide feedback or constructive criticism, and discuss ways of improving teamwork and taskwork in the future (Edmondson, 1999). Psychological safety also aids teams in gaining the benefits of task-oriented conflict, while simultaneously reducing the risk of relational conflict (Bradley et al., 2012). Further, team members are more likely to view conflicting information and input as beneficial to the team, rather than as a criticism or a personal attack (Bradley et al., 2012). When psychological safety is developed early in teams, team members tend to experience less relational conflict over the course of the team's lifecycle (Curşeu & Schruijer, 2010). Conversely, when the team environment is not conducive to sharing knowledge, opinions, or ideas, creativity is hindered, partly due to a lack of communication (Nicholson & West, 1988; West & Richter, 2008). Further, low psychological safety leads team members to interpret the behavior of others on a team in a negative way, leading to more conflict (Curşeau & Schruijer, 2010), which in turn reduces creativity and innovation. For example, one team member may share an idea with the team during a meeting, and another team member immediately points out the shortcomings of that idea. In a climate of low psychological safety, this behavior might be interpreted negatively, such that the person proposing the idea sees the other team member as trying to ridicule or undermine their input. However, in a climate of high psychological safety, the person proposing the idea might interpret the team member's critique more positively, such that they were offering up constructive criticism to help improve the idea, or transition into something better.

One conclusion emerging from the research reviewed is that psychological safety is an overarching construct that facilitates the enactment of multiple social processes that have already been linked to creativity such as collaboration, information sharing, conflict, and communication (Edmondson & Lei, 2014; Reiter-Palmon et al., 2011). As psychological safety is such an important factor in facilitating creativity and can serve as an antecedent for multiple social processes that are important for creativity, it is essential to understand the antecedents of psychological safety.

Antecedents of Psychological Safety

Leadership

The most commonly studied antecedent of psychological safety is that of leadership. Leaders are particularly important due to their influential role and their effect on team climate, and they are viewed as a key determinant of psychological safety (Liu et al., 2016; Nembhard & Edmondson, 2006). As leadership is a very broad construct, it is not surprising the multiple studies have investigated the relationship between leadership and psychological safety using different perspectives, theories, and approaches to leadership.

Transformational Leadership

Transformational leadership is one of the most commonly studied leadership approaches. Overall, work regarding transformational leadership and creativity tends to show that transformational leadership supports creativity (Gong et al., 2009). Transformational leaders inspire and harness followers to transcend their own self-interests in pursuing collective goals and become more effective by performing beyond their perceived expectations (Bass & Avolio, 1990). Specifically, transformational leaders exhibit four types of behaviors: idealized influence, inspirational motivation, intellectual stimulation, and individualized consideration (Bass & Avolio, 1990). Leaders exhibiting idealized influence serve as role models for followers who respect and trust them and attempt to emulate their behaviors. Transformational leaders also inspire their followers by articulating an ambitious and appealing vision and motivate others to embrace and realize this vision (i.e., inspirational motivation). These two components reflect charismatic leadership behaviors. Leaders who intellectually stimulate their followers encourage them to challenge the norms and take risks by addressing problems in a novel way (Hu et al., 2012). By displaying individualized consideration, transformational leaders encourage followers by showing consideration and support that help them grow (Hoffman et al.,

2011). Transformational leaders create a climate of psychological safety by establishing an environment where employees can challenge assumptions (intellectual stimulation), provide support (inspirational motivation and individualized consideration), and encourage employees (idealized influence and inspirational motivation).

While transformational leadership has been studied extensively as a leadership style that facilitates creativity, interestingly, only a few studies have evaluated the relationship between transformational leadership and psychological safety. Similarly, the role of psychological safety as a mediator between transformational leadership and creativity as an explanatory mechanism has been neglected. Carmeli et al. (2014), using three waves of data collection, found that transformational leadership collected in time 1 predicted psychological safety and reflexivity in time 2, which in turn predicted engagement in creative processes and thinking at work measured in time 3. Zhou and Pan (2015) found that transformational leadership predicted psychological safety which in turn predicted creative process engagement (similar to Carmeli et al.). In addition, they found that creative process engagement was directly related to supervisor rated creativity.

Focusing on behaviors that are related to creativity, Yin et al. (2019) found that the intellectual stimulation dimension of transformational leadership predicted psychological safety, which, in turn predicted knowledge sharing, an important antecedent of creativity (Carmeli et al., 2010). Detert and Burris (2007), in two different studies of employees and their supervisors, found a relationship between transformational leadership and voice behavior, or being willing to be proactive and raise concerns, which is a known predictor of creativity (Zare & Flinchbaugh, 2019), and that this relationship was mediated by psychological safety.

Ethical Leadership

Ethical leadership is defined as "the demonstration of normatively appropriate conduct through personal actions and interpersonal relationships and the promotion of such conduct to followers through two-way communication, reinforcement, and decision-making" (Brown et al., 2005, p. 120). Specifically, ethical leadership is viewed as including two components – the moral person and the moral manager. The moral person includes specific moral traits such as honesty and trustworthiness, whereas the moral manager suggests that the leader displays moral managerial behaviors such as discussing ethical issues with employees and showing concern and respect for employees (Brown & Treviño, 2006). Using this definition, it is clear that ethical leaders exhibit caring, concern, trustworthiness, and respect and are being responsive to employees. These are the same characteristics that Edmondson (1999) suggested are important for the development of psychological safety. It is therefore not surprising that ethical leadership has been found to be predictive of psychological safety (Younas et al., 2020; Wadei et al., 2021).

Further, in studies examining the relationship between ethical leadership and creativity, psychological safety was found to be a mediator between the two. Younas et al. (2020) studied employees in the textile industry, and measured employee perceptions of ethical leadership in time 1, psychological safety in time 2, and creativity at time 3. Using structural equation modeling the results indicated that ethical leadership was predictive of psychological safety, which, in turn predicted creativity. Wadei et al. (2021), using employees from organizations in healthcare, finance, and telecommunication, measured ethical leadership perceptions in time 1, with a measure of psychological safety and supervisor evaluations of employee creativity being completed three weeks later. Here as well, ethical leadership was found to be predictive of psychological safety, which, in turn, predicted supervisory evaluations of creativity. Tu et al. (2019) focused on team-level creativity, and also found that psychological safety mediated the relationship between ethical leadership and team-level creativity as evaluated by the supervisor. Interestingly, the relationship between ethical leadership and psychological safety was moderated by supervisor support for creativity. When supervisor support for creativity was high, the relationship between ethical leadership and psychological safety was stronger. Finally, work by Peng et al. (2019) evaluating 107 R&D teams found that self-serving leadership, which is a form of unethical leadership, hinders team creativity through lower psychological safety.

In addition to psychological safety being a mediator between ethical leadership and creativity, other outcomes that are related to creativity have also been investigated. Knowledge hiding, which focuses on deliberate attempts to not disclose necessary information, has been studied by Men et al. (2020). They found that psychological safety mediated the relationship between ethical leadership and knowledge hiding, such that ethical leadership was related to increased psychological safety, which reduced knowledge hiding. Previous work has found that knowledge hiding was detrimental to creativity (Bogilović et al., 2017; Černe et al., 2014), and knowledge sharing (the opposite of knowledge hiding) is an important antecedent of creativity in teams (Carmeli et al., 2010). Hu et al. (2018) found that ethical leadership influences voice behavior through psychological safety.

Leader Humility

Humble leaders are open to admitting their own mistakes and learning from them. These leaders are also open to the suggestions of their subordinates, and as a result are likely to foster psychological safety. Hu et al. (2018) measured leader humility, psychological safety, and creativity in 72 teams from different information technology firms. Psychological safety was found to mediate the relationship between leader humility and team creativity. Similar findings were obtained by Gonçalves and Brandão (2017) using 73 teams from multiple organizations. Wang et al. (2018) also evaluated the relationship between humble leadership, psychological safety, and creativity using time-lagged data from 328 employees in 106 teams in which creativity was required. Employees evaluated leader humility in time 1 and psychological safety and knowledge sharing in time 2. Leaders provided evaluation of creative performance for each employee in time 3. Wang et al. (2018) found that psychological safety mediated the relationship between humble leadership and individual-level creativity. They further found that the relationship between psychological safety and creativity was moderated by knowledge sharing. Specifically, when psychological safety was high, the degree of knowledge sharing had no effect on creativity; however, when psychological safety was low, higher knowledge sharing was related to higher creativity. Further support is provided by a study on self-serving leadership. Self-serving leaders put their own interests above those of the team members and the organization. Self-serving leadership, considered the opposite of leader humility, has been found to negatively influence psychological safety and as a result hindered creative performance in teams (Peng et al., 2019).

Leader Inclusiveness

Leader inclusiveness has been defined by Nembhard and Edmondson (2006, p. 947) as "words and deeds by a leader or leaders that indicate an invitation and appreciation for others' contributions." As such, a leader who is inclusive will invite input from others, include team members in discussion and decision making, and facilitate voice. Nembhard and Edmondson studied leader inclusiveness in relation to psychological safety and engagement in quality improvement in hospitals. Hirak et al. (2012) also evaluated leader inclusiveness in hospitals. In this longitudinal study, leader inclusiveness was associated with perceptions of psychological safety. Performance was evaluated in time 2 and consisted of a measure of learning from previous episodes of performance, especially failure. Increased psychological safety led to increased learning. Bienefeld and Grote (2014) studied the effect of psychological safety on speaking up in teams within aircrews. Aircrews tend to be very hierarchical, so speaking up, even in the face of errors, can be difficult. On the other hand, not speaking up when a crew member notices an error can lead to a disaster. Bienefield and Grote suggest that inclusive leaders would facilitate feelings of psychological safety, which in turn will allow aircrew members to feel comfortable speaking up, that is, speaking to the leader, when an error is detected. Voice and speaking up have been found to be important antecedents of learning as well as of creativity and innovation (Burke et al., 2006; Edmondson, 2004).

Summary

The review of the literature regarding the relationship between various leadership approaches and psychological safety suggests that leadership can exert a strong influence on psychological safety. What all these leadership approaches have in common is that they all focus on the leader as providing some form of support to the individual employee and the team. Leaders may provide support through transformational leadership, leader inclusiveness, humility, or ethical leadership, but in all cases, the important factor is that leaders are viewed by the subordinates as welcoming of opinions, supporting, and allowing team members to participate fully in discussions and decision making.

Team and Organizational Structure

Team structure refers to issues related to hierarchy and division of labor within a team. Bunderson and Boumgarden (2010) surveyed members from 44 teams as well as their managers in a technology firm. Team structure was found to predict team learning, and this relationship was mediated by psychological safety. Further, psychological safety was related to less conflict and increased information sharing. Bresman and Zellmer-Bruhn (2013) hypothesized that organizational and team structure (i.e., hierarchy, clearly identified leader, clear roles) were important for team learning. In this study, data from R&D teams in the pharmaceutical industry were obtained. Team structure encouraged internal and external team learning behavior by promoting psychological safety.

Eisenberg and DiTomaso (2019) proposed a theoretical model of the relationship between team structure and its effect on trust and communication. They conceptualized team structure across three different dimensions: (1) Configuration, where teams may contain isolates, that is, lone team members in a location; (2) Assignment, whether team members were members of multiple teams; and (3) Geographical, focusing on physical and temporal aspects. They suggest that all three types of structure will influence trust and communication patterns, and that psychological safety would be an important characteristic in this relationship. Given the increase in use of virtual teams for creative work (Reiter-Palmon et al., 2021), understanding how these different configurations relate to psychological safety is important.

Other work has focused on the relationship between organizational policies and psychological safety. Carmeli and Zisu (2009), in a study of a large healthcare organization, found that perceived organizational support and trust in the organization were predictive of psychological safety. Singh et al. (2013) found that diversity practices in an organization was related to diversity climate and psychological safety.

Social Processes

The majority of the research on psychological safety and social processes in teams focuses on the effect that psychological safety has on processes such as communication and voice. However, some research has focused on the opposite effect, that is, to what extent to these social processes influence the development of psychological safety. Carmeli and Gittel (2009), in a series of studies, found that high-quality relationships, specified as having shared goals, shared knowledge, and mutual respect, led to enhanced psychological safety. Similar results were obtained in a longitudinal study by Carmeli et al. (2009). Gu et al. (2013) found that trust, effective information exchange, and shared goals (which they combined and termed *social capital*), were related to the development of psychological safety. Similarly, Huang and Jiang (2012) found that social capital was predictive of psychological safety in a study of 60 R&D teams. Wong et al. (2018) studied 256 employees and their leaders and found that participative decision making led to increased psychological safety, which, in turn led to team creativity.

Schulte et al. (2010) conducted a longitudinal study of 69 teams over a 10-month period. Interestingly, they found not only that social relationships within the team predicted psychological safety over time, but also that psychological safety predicted better social relationships, such as asking team members for advice and help. This finding of a reciprocal relationship is particularly important, as psychological safety has been studied as both an antecedent to effect social relationships and an outcome of it.

Conclusion

In this chapter, we have provided a review of the literature supporting the contention that psychological safety is an important predictor of individual and team creativity. Further, psychological safety has been found to be predictive of additional important antecedents of creativity and innovation such as knowledge sharing, learning, and effective communication (Reiter-Palmon et al., 2011). We further elucidated the antecedents of psychological safety, specifically the role that leadership, structure, and social processes play in facilitating the development of psychological safety. Finally, an important issue raised is whether psychological safety leads to more effective social processes or whether these effective social processes lead to the development of psychological safety. Schulte et al. (2010) provide intriguing evidence that both are occurring, and this reciprocal relationship should be studied further.

References

Amabile, T. M., & Gryskiewicz, N. D. (1989). The creative environment scales: Work environment inventory. *Creativity Research Journal, 2*(4), 231–253. https://doi.org/10.1080/10400418909534321

Bass, B. M., & Avolio, B. J. (1990). Developing transfwormational leadership: 1992 and beyond. *Journal of European Industrial Training, 14*(5), 21–27. https://doi.org/10.1108/03090599010135122

Bell, B. S., & Kozlowski, S. W. (2008). Active learning: Effects of core training design elements on self-regulatory processes, learning, and adaptability. *Journal of Applied Psychology, 93*(2), 296–316. https://doi.org/10.1037/0021-9010.93.2.296

Bienefeld, N., & Grote, G. (2014). Shared leadership in multiteam systems: How cockpit and cabin crews lead each other to safety. *Human Factors, 56*(2), 270–286. https://doi.org/10.1177%2F0018720813488137

Bogilović, S., Černe, M., & Škerlavaj, M. (2017). Hiding behind a mask? Cultural intelligence, knowledge hiding, and individual and team creativity. *European Journal of Work and Organizational Psychology, 26*(5), 710–723. https://doi.org/10.1080/1359432X.2017.1337747

Bowers, C. A., Braun, C. C., & Morgan Jr, B. B. (1997). Team workload: Its meaning and measurement. In M. T. Brannick, E. Salas, & C. W. Prince (Eds.), *Team Performance Assessment and Measurement* (pp. 97–120). Psychology Press.

Bradley, B. H., Postlethwaite, B. E., Klotz, A. C., Hamdani, M. R., & Brown, K. G. (2012). Reaping the benefits of task conflict in teams: the critical role of team psychological safety climate. *Journal of Applied Psychology, 97*(1), 151. https://psycnet.apa.org/doi/10.1037/a0024200

Bresman, H., & Zellmer-Bruhn, M. (2013). The structural context of team learning: Effects of organizational and team structure on internal and external learning. *Organization Science, 24*(4), 1120–1139. https://doi.org/10.1287/orsc.1120.0783

Brown, M. E., & Treviño, L. K. (2006). Ethical leadership: A review and future directions. *The Leadership Quarterly, 17*(6), 595–616. https://doi.org/10.1016/j.leaqua.2006.10.004

Brown, M. E., Treviño, L. K., & Harrison, D. A. (2005). Ethical leadership: A social learning perspective for construct development and testing. *Organizational Behavior and Human Decision Processes, 97*(2), 117–134. https://doi.org/10.1016/j.obhdp.2005.03.002

Bunderson, J. S., & Boumgarden, P. (2010). Structure and learning in self-managed teams: Why "bureaucratic" teams can be better learners. *Organization Science, 21*(3), 609–s624. https://doi.org/10.1287/orsc.1090.0483

Burke, C. S., Stagl, K. C., Salas, E., Pierce, L., & Kendall, D. (2006). Understanding team adaptation: A conceptual analysis and model. *Journal of Applied Psychology, 91*(6), 1189–1207. https://doi-org.leo.lib.unomaha.edu/10.1037/0021-9010.91.6.1189

Burningham, C., & West, M. A. (1995). Individual, climate, and group interaction processes as predictors of work team innovation. *Small Group Research, 26*(1), 106–117. https://doi.org/10.1177%2F1046496495261006

Carmeli, A., Brueller, D., & Dutton, J. E. (2009). Learning behaviours in the workplace: The role of high-quality interpersonal relationships and psychological safety. *Systems Research and Behavioral Science, 26*(1), 81–98. https://doi.org/10.1002/sres.932

Carmeli, A., & Gittell, J. H. (2009). High-quality relationships, psychological safety, and learning from failures in work organizations. *Journal of Organizational Behavior, 30*(6), 709–729. https://doi.org/10.1002/job.565

Carmeli, A., Reiter-Palmon, R., & Ziv, E. (2010). Inclusive leadership and employee involvement in creative tasks in the workplace: The mediating role of psychological safety. *Creativity Research Journal, 22*(3), 250-260. https://doi.org/10.1080/10400419.2010.504654

Carmeli, A., Sheaffer, Z., Binyamin, G., Reiter-Palmon, R., & Shimoni, T. (2014). Transformational leadership and creative problem-solving: The mediating role of psychological safety and reflexivity. *The Journal of Creative Behavior*, *48*(2), 115–135. https://doi.org/10.1002/jocb.43

Carmeli, A., & Zisu, M. (2009). The relational underpinnings of quality internal auditing in medical clinics in Israel. *Social Science & Medicine*, *68*(5), 894–902. https://doi.org/10.1016/j.socscimed.2008.12.031

Černe, M., Nerstad, C. G., Dysvik, A., & Škerlavaj, M. (2014). What goes around comes around: Knowledge hiding, perceived motivational climate, and creativity. *Academy of Management Journal*, *57*(1), 172–192. https://doi.org/10.5465/amj.2012.0122

Chen, L., Wadei, K. A., Bai, S., & Liu, J. (2020). Participative leadership and employee creativity: A sequential mediation model of psychological safety and creative process engagement. *Leadership & Organization Development Journal*, *41*(6), 741–759. https://doi-org.leo.lib.unomaha.edu/10.1108/LODJ-07-2019-0319

Choo, A. S., Linderman, K. W., & Schroeder, R. G. (2007). Method and psychological effects on learning behaviors and knowledge creation in quality improvement projects. *Management Science*, *53*(3), 437–450. https://doi-org.leo.lib.unomaha.edu/10.1287/mnsc.1060.0635

Curşeu, P. L., & Schruijer, S. G. (2010). Does conflict shatter trust or does trust obliterate conflict? Revisiting the relationships between team diversity, conflict, and trust. *Group Dynamics: Theory, Research, and Practice*, *14*(1), 66–79. https://psycnet.apa.org/doi/10.1037/a0017104

Detert, J. R., & Burris, E. R. (2007). Leadership behavior and employee voice: Is the door really open? *Academy of Management Journal*, *50*(4), 869–884. https://doi.org/10.5465/amj.2007.26279183

Edmondson, A. C. (1999). Psychological safety and learning behavior in work teams. *Administrative Science Quarterly*, *44*(2), 350–383. https://doi.org/10.2307%2F2666999

Edmondson, A. C. (2004). Psychological safety, trust, and learning in organizations: A group-level lens. In R. M. Kramer & K. S. Cook (Eds.), *Trust and Distrust in Organizations: Dilemmas and Approaches.* (pp. 239–272). Russell Sage Foundation.

Edmondson, A. C., & Lei, Z. (2014). Psychological safety: The history, renaissance, and future of an interpersonal construct. *Annual Review of Organizational Psychology and Organizational Behavior*, *1*(1), 23–43. https://doi.org/10.1146/annurev-orgpsych-031413-091305

Eisenberg, J., & DiTomaso, N. (2019). Structural decisions about configuration, assignments, and geographical distribution in teams: Influences on team communications and trust. *Human Resource Management Review*, 100739. https://doi.org/10.1016/j.hrmr.2019.100739

Ekvall, G. (1996). Organizational climate for creativity and innovation. *European Journal of Work and Organizational Psychology*, *5*(1), 105–123. https://doi.org/10.1080/13594329608414845

Fleming, M., Clarke, W., Das, S., Phongthiengtham, P., & Reddy, P. (2019). The future of work: How new technologies are transforming tasks [Report]. *MITIBM Watson AI Lab*.

Gonçalves, L., & Brandão, F. (2017). The relation between leader's humility and team creativity: The mediating effect of psychological safety and psychological capital. *International Journal of Organizational Analysis, 25*(4), 687–702. https://doi.org/10.1108/IJOA-06-2016-1036

Gong, Y., Cheung, S. Y., Wang, M., & Huang, J. C. (2012). Unfolding the proactive process for creativity: Integration of the employee proactivity, information exchange, and psychological safety perspectives. *Journal of Management, 38*(5), 1611–1633. https://doi-org.leo.lib.unomaha.edu/10.1177/0149206310380250

Gong, Y., Huang, J. C., & Farh, J. L. (2009). Employee learning orientation, transformational leadership, and employee creativity: The mediating role of employee creative self-efficacy. *Academy of Management Journal, 52*(4), 765–778. https://doi.org/10.5465/amj.2009.43670890

Greenbaum, R. L., Bonner, J. M., Mawritz, M. B., Butts, M. M., & Smith, M. B. (2020). It is all about the bottom line: Group bottom-line mentality, psychological safety, and group creativity. *Journal of Organizational Behavior, 41*(6), 503–517. https://doi.org/10.1002/job.2445

Gu, Q., Wang, G. G., & Wang, L. (2013). Social capital and innovation in R&D teams: the mediating roles of psychological safety and learning from mistakes. *R&D Management, 43*(2), 89–102. https://doi.org/10.1111/radm.12002

Hackman, J. R. (1987). The design of work teams. In J. W. Lorsch (Ed.), *Handbook of Organizational Behavior* (pp. 315–342). Prentice-Hall.

Han, S. J., Lee, Y., & Beyerlein, M. (2019). Developing team creativity: The influence of psychological safety and relation-oriented shared leadership. *Performance Improvement Quarterly, 32*(2), 159–182. https://doi.org/10.1002/piq.21293

Harvey, S. (2014). Creative synthesis: Exploring the process of extraordinary group creativity. *Academy of Management Review, 39*(3), 324–343. https://doi.org/10.5465/amr.2012.0224

Harvey, S., & Kou, C. (2018). Social processes and team creativity: Locating collective creativity in team interactions. In R. Reiter-Palmon (Ed.), *Team Creativity and Innovation.* (pp. 87–127). Oxford University Press.

Hirak, R., Peng, A. C., Carmeli, A., & Schaubroeck, J. M. (2012). Linking leader inclusiveness to work unit performance: The importance of psychological safety and learning from failures. *The Leadership Quarterly, 23*(1), 107–117. https://doi.org/10.1016/j.leaqua.2011.11.009

Hoffman, B. J., Bynum, B. H., Piccolo, R. F., & Sutton, A. W. (2011). Person-organization value congruence: How transformational leaders influence work group effectiveness. *Academy of Management Journal, 54*(4), 779-796. https://doi.org/10.5465/amj.2011.64870139

Hu, J., Erdogan, B., Jiang, K., Bauer, T. N., & Liu, S. (2018). Leader humility and team creativity: The role of team information sharing, psychological safety, and power distance. *Journal of Applied Psychology, 103*(3), 313–323. https://doi-org.leo.lib.unomaha.edu/10.1037/apl0000277

Hu, J., Wang, Z., Liden, R. C., & Sun, J. (2012). The influence of leader core self-evaluation on follower reports of transformational leadership. *The Leadership Quarterly, 23*(5), 860-868. https://doi.org/10.1016/j.leaqua.2012.05.004

Huang, C. C., Chu, C. Y., & Jiang, P. C. (2008, September). An empirical study of psychological safety and performance in technology R&D teams. In *2008 4th IEEE International Conference on Management of Innovation and Technology* (pp. 1423–1427). IEEE. http://doi.org/10.1109/ICMIT.2008.4654580

Huang, C. C., & Jiang, P. C. (2012). Exploring the psychological safety of R&D teams: An empirical analysis in Taiwan. *Journal of Management & Organization, 18* (2), 175–192. https://doi.org/10.5172/jmo.2012.18.2.175

Hunter, S. T., Bedell, K. E., & Mumford, M. D. (2007). Climate for creativity: A quantitative review. *Creativity Research Journal, 19*(1), 69–90. https://doi .org/10.1080/10400410709336883

Kark, R., & Carmeli, A. (2009). Alive and creating: The mediating role of vitality and aliveness in the relationship between psychological safety and creative work involvement. *Journal of Organizational Behavior, 30*(6), 785–804. https://doi .org/10.1002/job.571

Kessel, M., Kratzer, J., & Schultz, C. (2012). Psychological safety, knowledge sharing, and creative performance in healthcare teams. *Creativity and Innovation Management, 21*(2), 147–157. https://doi.org/10.1111/j.1467-8691.2012.00635.x

Liu, K., & Ge, Y. (2020). How psychological safety influences employee creativity in China: Work engagement as a mediator. *Social Behavior and Personality: An International Journal, 48*(8), 1 7. https://doi-org.leo.lib.unomaha.edu/10.2224/ sbp.9211

Liu, W., Zhang, P., Liao, J., Hao, P., & Mao, J. (2016). Abusive supervision and employee creativity: The mediating role of psychological safety and organizational identification. *Management Decision, 54*(1), 130–147. https://doi.org/10 .1108/MD-09-2013-0443

Liu, Y., Keller, R. T., & Bartlett, K. R. (2021). Initiative climate, psychological safety and knowledge sharing as predictors of team creativity: A multilevel study of research and development project teams. *Creativity and Innovation Management, 30*(3), 498–510. https://doi-org.leo.lib.unomaha.edu/10.1111/ caim.12438

Madjar, N., & Ortiz-Walters, R. (2009). Trust in supervisors and trust in customers: Their independent, relative, and joint effects on employee performance and creativity. *Human Performance, 22*(2), 128–142. https://doi.org/10.1080/ 08959280902743501

Mathieu, J., Maynard, M. T., Rapp, T., & Gilson, L. (2008). Team effectiveness 1997_2007: A review of recent advancements and a glimpse into the future. *Journal of Management, 34*(3), 410–476. https://doi.org/10.1177% 2F0149206308316061

McIntyre, R. M., & Salas, E. (1995). Measuring and managing for team performance: Emerging principles from complex environments. In R. Guzzo & E. Salas (Eds.), *Team Effectiveness and Decision Making in Organizations* (pp. 149–203). Jossey-Bass.

Men, C., Fong, P. S., Huo, W., et al. (2020). Ethical leadership and knowledge hiding: a moderated mediation model of psychological safety and mastery climate. *Journal of Business Ethics, 166*(3), 461–472. https://doi.org/10.1007/ s10551-018-4027-7

Mumford, M. D., Scott, G. M., Gaddis, B., & Strange, J. M. (2002). Leading creative people: Orchestrating expertise and relationships. *The Leadership Quarterly, 13* (6), 705–750. https://doi.org/10.1016/S1048–9843(02)00158-3

Nembhard, I. M., & Edmondson, A. C. (2006). Making it safe: The effects of leader inclusiveness and professional status on psychological safety and improvement efforts in health care teams. *Journal of Organizational Behavior*, *27*(7), 941–966. https://doi.org/10.1002/job.413

Nicholson, N., & West, M. (1988). *Managerial Job Change: Men and Women in Transition*. Cambridge University Press.

Paulus, P. B., & Nijstad, B. A. (Eds.). (2003). *Group Creativity: Innovation through Collaboration*. Oxford University Press.

Peng, J., Wang, Z., & Chen, X. (2019). Does self-serving leadership hinder team creativity? A moderated dual-path model. *Journal of Business Ethics*, *159*(2), 419–433. https://doi.org/10.1007/s10551–018-3799-0

Reiter-Palmon, R. (2021). Leading for team creativity: Managing people and processes. In A. S. McKay, R. Reiter-Palmon, & J. C. Kaufman (Eds.), *Creative success in teams* (pp. 33–54). Academic Press.

Reiter-Palmon, R., & Illies, J. J. (2004). Leadership and creativity: Understanding leadership from a creative problem-solving perspective. *The Leadership Quarterly*, *15*(1), 55–77. https://doi.org/10.1016/j.leaqua.2003.12.005

Reiter-Palmon, R., Kramer, W., Allen, J. A., Murugavel, V. R., & Leone, S. A. (2021). Creativity in virtual teams: A review and agenda for future research. *Creativity: Research, Application, Theory*, *8*(1), 165–188. https://doi.org/10.2478/ctra-2021-0011

Reiter-Palmon, R., & Paulus, P. B. (2020). Cognitive and social processes in team creativity. In M. D. Mumford (Ed.), *Creativity and Innovation in Organizations* (pp. 161–190). Routledge.

Reiter-Palmon, R., Wigert, B., & de Vreede, T. (2011). Team creativity and innovation: The effect of group composition, social processes, and cognition. In M. D. Mumford (Ed.), *Handbook of Organizational Creativity* (pp. 295–326). Academic Press. https://doi.org/10.1016/B978–0-12-374714-3.00013-6

Rousseau, V., Aubé, C., & Savoie, A. (2006). Teamwork behaviors: A review and an integration of frameworks. *Small Group Research*, *37*(5), 540–570. https://doi.org/10.1177%2F1046496406293125

Salas, E., Sims, D. E., & Klein, C. (2004). Cooperation at work. In C. Spielberger (Ed.), *Encyclopedia of Applied Psychology*, (pp. 497–505). Academic Press.

Salas, E., Sims, D. E., & Burke, C. S. (2005). Is there a "big five" in teamwork? *Small Group Research*, *36*(5), 555–599. https://doi.org/10.1177%2F1046496405277134

Salas, E., Stagl, K. C., Burke, C. S., & Goodwin, G. F. (2007). Fostering team effectiveness in organizations: Toward an integrative theoretical framework. In B. Shuart, W. Spaulding, & J. Poland (Eds.), *Modeling Complex Systems* (pp. 185–243). University of Nebraska Press.

Schippers, M. C., Edmondson, A. C., & West, M. A. (2014). Team reflexivity as an antidote to team information-processing failures. *Small Group Research*, *45*(6), 731–769. https://doi-org.leo.lib.unomaha.edu/10.1177/1046496414553473

Schulte, M., Cohen, N. A., & Klein, K. J. (2010). The coevolution of network ties and perceptions of team psychological safety. *Organization Science*, *23*(2), 564–581. https://doi.org/10.1287/orsc.1100.0582

Shalley, C. E., Zhou, J., & Oldham, G. R. (2004). The effects of personal and contextual characteristics on creativity: Where should we go from here?. *Journal of Management*, *30*(6), 933–958. https://doi.org/10.1016/j.jm.2004.06.007

Singh, B., Winkel, D. E., & Selvarajan, T. T. (2013). Managing diversity at work: Does psychological safety hold the key to racial differences in employee performance? *Journal of Occupational and Organizational Psychology*, *86*(2), 242–263. https://doi.org/10.1111/joop.12015

Tu, Y., Lu, X., Choi, J. N., & Guo, W. (2019). Ethical leadership and team-level creativity: Mediation of psychological safety climate and moderation of supervisor support for creativity. *Journal of Business Ethics*, *159*(2), 551–565. https://doi.org/10.1007/s10551-018-3839-9

Tucker, A. L., Nembhard, I. M., & Edmondson, A. C. (2007). Implementing new practices: An empirical study of organizational learning in hospital intensive care units. *Management Science*, *53*(6), 894–907. https://doi.org/10.1287/mnsc.1060.0692

Vinarski-Peretz, H., & Carmeli, A. (2011). Linking care felt to engagement in innovative behaviors in the workplace: The mediating role of psychological conditions. *Psychology of Aesthetics, Creativity, and the Arts*, *5*(1), 43. https://psycnet.apa.org/doi/10.1037/a0018241

Wadei, K. A., Chen, L., Frempong, J., & Appienti, W. A. (2021). The mediation effect of ethical leadership and creative performance: A social information processing perspective. *The Journal of Creative Behavior*, *55*(1), 241–254. https://doi.org/10.1002/jocb.449

Wang, Y., Liu, J., & Zhu, Y. (2018). Humble leadership, psychological safety, knowledge sharing, and follower creativity: A cross-level investigation. *Frontiers in Psychology*, *9*, 1727. https://doi.org/10.3389/fpsyg.2018.01727

West, M. A., & Anderson, N. R. (1996). Innovation in top management teams. *Journal of Applied Psychology*, *81*(6), 680–693. https://psycnet.apa.org/doi/10.1037/0021-9010.81.6.680

West, M. A., Hirst, G., Richter, A., & Shipton, H. (2004). Twelve steps to heaven: Successfully managing change through developing innovative teams. *European Journal of Work and Organizational Psychology*, *13*(2), 269–299. https://doi.org/10.1080/13594320444000092

West, M. A., & Richter, A. (2008). Climates and cultures for innovation and creativity at work. In J. Zhou & C. E. Shalley (Eds.), *Handbook of Organizational Creativity* (pp. 211–236). Erlbaum.

Whiting, K. (2020, October 21). *These Are the Top 10 Job Skills of Tomorrow: And How Long It Takes to Learn Them*. World Economic Forum. https://www.weforum.org/agenda/2020/10/top-10-work-skills-of-tomorrow-how-long-it-takes-to-learn-them/

Wilkens, R., & London, M. (2006). Relationships between climate, process, and performance in continuous quality improvement groups. *Journal of Vocational Behavior*, *69*(3), 510–523. https://doi.org/10.1016/j.jvb.2006.05.005

Wong, Y. Y., Chow, I. H. S., Lau, V. P., & Gong, Y. (2018). Benefits of team participative decision making and its potential to affect individual creativity. *Journal of Applied Social Psychology*, *48*(7), 369–376. https://doi.org/10.1111/jasp.12517

Yin, J., Ma, Z., Yu, H., Jia, M., & Liao, G. (2019). Transformational leadership and employee knowledge sharing: explore the mediating roles of psychological safety and team efficacy. *Journal of Knowledge Management*, *24*(2), 150–171. https://doi.org/10.1108/JKM-12-2018-0776

Younas, A., Wang, D., Javed, B., et al. (2020). Positive psychological states and employee creativity: The role of ethical leadership. *The Journal of Creative Behavior*, *54*(3), 567–581. https://doi.org/10.1002/jocb.391

Zare, M., & Flinchbaugh, C. (2019). Voice, creativity, and big five personality traits: A meta-analysis. *Human Performance*, *32*(1), 30–51. https://doi.org/10.1080/08959285.2018.1550782

Zhou, Q., & Pan, W. (2015). A cross-level examination of the process linking transformational leadership and creativity: The role of psychological safety climate. *Human Performance*, *28*(5), 405–424. https://doi.org/10.1080/08959285.2015.1021050

30 Leadership, Creativity, and Emotions

Shane Connelly and Elif Gizem Demirag Burak

When people think about creativity, its connection to leadership is not typically what first springs to mind. While design, original thinking, and the generation of novel, useful solutions are vital to many organizations, the idea that structuring creative work activities and managing creative people may seem inconsistent or incompatible with the nature of creativity. However, scholars have long recognized that creativity in organizational contexts does not arise in a vacuum. Creative ideas and the innovations essential to creative work are influenced by a variety of individual attributes, resource availability, work climate, and other organizational members, including leaders (Amabile et al., 1996; Shalley & Gilson, 2004). Organizational leadership plays a key role in fitting these pieces together to facilitate and coordinate the expertise, knowledge, creative processes, and collaboration required for creative work (Amabile et al., 2004; Mumford et al., 2002). Additionally, emotions play important roles by influencing creative processes, motivating engagement in creative work, and enabling creative people to work together.

Creativity and innovation have been defined in a variety of ways, especially in leadership studies. Many scholars associate creativity with novel idea generation and innovation with novel idea implementation, but disagreement remains regarding conceptual definitions. In Hughes et al.'s (2018) review of 195 studies of leadership, creativity, and innovation, 164 provided conceptual definitions. Most of the studies that explicitly studied creativity (96%) defined it as the generation of ideas that are new/novel and useful/applicable. Of the 68 studies that explicitly considered innovation, definitions were more variable, with 75% focusing on implementing or applying ideas and one or more additional components (e.g., creating new ideas, products, or processes). Overlap in definitions has led to a lack of clarity in conceptualizing and measuring creativity and innovation. Additionally, these authors highlight the problem of including products or outcomes as part of the definitions of these constructs, making it difficult to separate these phenomena from their effects. Here, we use the largely agreed upon definition of creativity as the generation of novel, useful ideas (Amabile, 1997; Runco & Jaeger, 2012) and innovation as the implementation of new ideas (Andersen & Kragh, 2013; Drazin et al., 1999; Hughes et al., 2018). Before considering how leaders influence creativity, it is important to first consider the nature of the demands that creativity and innovation in organizations place on individuals engaged with this work.

The Nature of Creative Work and Why Leadership Is Important

Creativity and innovation are required in organizational settings where work tasks are complex and ill defined, and can be approached and implemented in different ways. Prior research has highlighted the importance of direct and indirect leadership influences on creativity and innovation (e.g., Agars et al., 2012; Amabile et al., 2004; Carmeli et al., 2013; Mumford et al., 2002). Mumford et al. (2002) and others have identified several challenging aspects of creative work that suggest the need for leadership. First, domain expertise and knowledge serve as important foundational building blocks for the types of cognitive processes involved in creativity. Defining or constructing problems or challenges sets up a problem frame and imposes structure onto creative work (Reiter-Palmon & Illies, 2004). Technical expertise enables leaders to contribute to problem definition and to offer unique insights into what technical, organizational and industry factors are important to consider (Agars et al., 2012). Employees designing new products, processes, or ideas may benefit from consulting knowledgeable leaders in the early stages of information gathering and idea generation. McMahon and Ford (2013) found that leader heuristic transfer or the conveyance of expertise-based creative processes (e.g., pattern recognition, discovery) to employees was positively related to employee creativity, directly and through boosting intrinsic motivation. Second, creative work is time consuming and effortful, requiring persistence, motivation, and tolerance for failure (Mumford et al., 2002). Leaders can exert positive effects by setting realistic/flexible timelines, encouraging risk-taking, rewarding persistence as well as productivity, and acknowledging that failure occurs on the pathway to viable creative ideas (Howell & Boies, 2004; Mumford & McIntosh, 2017). Third, creative work in organizations often involves collaborating with other people in team settings to generate new ideas and turn them into innovative products, services, or other output (Koen et al., 2014; Zhang et al., 2011). This includes working closely with others on one's own project team and coordinating with people from other teams or organizational units. Leaders often facilitate these connections through networking capabilities and through mitigation of the communication challenges and higher stress experienced in teams composed of members from different functional areas (Keller, 2001; Mumford et al., 2014). Thus, facilitating creativity in organizations requires technical expertise and complex cognition as well as social and emotion-based capabilities (Ivcevic et al., 2021; Mumford et al., 2000; Ohly et al., 2010).

Leaders are also essential for successful innovation in organizations. With regard to implementing creative ideas, leaders often have greater access to resources, knowledge about constraints internal and external to the organization, awareness of timeframes, and understanding of the competitive landscape (Euchner & Henderson, 2011; Mumford et al., 2002). Accordingly, leaders play an important role in evaluating the viability of moving forward with ideas and in fostering innovation within and across organizations (Howell & Boies, 2004).

Creative employees often generate many more ideas and approaches than can feasibly be implemented. Leaders who consider the opportunities and constraints operating in the broader organizational and external environments will identify and support new ideas that have higher chances of successful implementation (e.g., Andersen & Kragh, 2013). Leader and employee emotions have also been shown to have positive and negative influences on innovation (Rank & Frese, 2008; Viori & Huy, 2016). Emotions impact a variety of processes involved in managing innovation in organizations such as idea evaluation (Mastria et al., 2019), conflict management (Desivilya et al., 2010), risk-taking (Braumann & DeSteno, 2012), and adapting to change (Huy, 2002). Accordingly, the next section briefly reviews research on the influence of emotions on creativity and innovation.

Why Are Emotions Important for Creativity and Innovation?

Creativity has been studied extensively in relation to positive and negative affectivity. Research has shown that positive affect broadens the scope of attention, stimulates divergent thinking (Ashby et al., 1999; Isen, 2004), and creates cognitive variation (Clore et al., 1994), which are all necessary for creativity or generating novel ideas. Empirical research has shown that positive affect is strongly associated with creativity (e.g., Baas et al., 2008). However, there are some limitations about this relationship. Results from a meta-analysis (Davis, 2009) showed that the effect of positive mood on creativity is contingent on the referent mood state (neutral and negative) and dependent on the nature of the task. For instance, Baas et al. (2008) shows that tasks that take longer than 4 minutes do not benefit from positive mood inductions.

Although the positive affect and creativity link is well established, more research is still needed to explain how negative affectivity is linked to creativity (Amabile et al., 2005). Earlier research suggests that the positive relationship between negative affectivity and creativity was mostly found for creative accomplishments in arts (Feist, 1999). More recent studies have suggested that negative affect was shown to have positive effects with analytical processes (Visser et al., 2013), but results for positive and negative affect have been mixed, suggesting more complexity in the relationship between emotion states and creativity. Baas and colleagues' (2008) meta-analysis examined the relationship between specific moods (positive, neutral, and negative) and creativity. The results showed that positive mood states that are activating and associated with an approach motivation enhance creativity more than deactivating moods with avoidance motivation and prevention regulatory focus. Positive activating emotions have been associated with increased cognitive flexibility. The study also found that creativity was not associated with negative-deactivating moods with approach motivation and a promotion focus, but lower creativity was associated with negative activating moods with an avoidance motivation and prevention focus. Interestingly, De Dreu et al. (2008) showed that negative activating emotions like anger and fear enhanced idea fluency and originality because these emotions are associated with persistence on creative tasks. However, other studies have explored the role of negative activating emotions beyond the lab studies. To et al. (2012) examined the influence of high activation positive and negative moods on creative process engagement (CPE) in postdoctoral and graduate honors students working on individual research thesis projects. They found that activating positive and negative moods are positively associated with CPE assessed at the same time. However, negative activating mood has longer lasting positive effect on CPE than positive activating mood (To et al., 2012).

More recent research has examined discrete emotions and their potential role in creative efforts. Scholars have emphasized the importance of concentrating on discrete emotions in organizational research instead of aggregating discrete emotions into positive and negative emotions (e.g., Connelly & Torrence, 2018; Gooty et al., 2009). Influences of discrete emotional states may have differential impacts on different creative processes. For instance, one study found that a higher level of curiosity correlates with greater creativity (Schutte & Malouff, 2019). Another study has shown that expression of anger results in creativity in organizations when the observers have high epistemic motivation (e.g., Van Kleef et al., 2010). For instance, same-day joy is significantly correlated with higher creativity, whereas same-day anger, sadness, and fear are significantly correlated with lower creativity (Amabile et al., 2005). A few studies have shown a positive effect of emotional ambivalence (i.e., the simultaneous experience of positive and negative emotions such as happiness and sadness) on creativity in organizations (Fong, 2006). Emotional ambivalence leads to an individual's recognition of unusual associations essential for creativity (Fong, 2006). Kung and Chao (2019) examined the role of mixed emotions (e.g., anger and happiness) in the collective creative performance. They found that mixed emotion interactions (angry – sad) were more creative than the same emotion interactions (angry – angry) in the negotiation settings.

Scholars have also investigated the relationship between emotions and innovation. In many of these studies, innovation has been treated as the same construct with creativity, and therefore, similar findings to the creativity and emotions relationship were obtained. Like creativity, an individual's emotions in the innovation processes could influence others'emotions and the likelihood of having an innovative outcome. Vuori and Huy (2016) have examined how emotional processes influenced the failure of Nokia, which has been considered one of the most innovative organizations. Their qualitative study suggests shared negative emotions at the managerial level negatively affected the innovation processes in Nokia. For instance, top-level managers' fear of rivalries and mid-level managers' fear of their superiors and peers harmed the groups' communication, which caused a failure in the smartphone innovation process. Choi et al. (2011) investigated the role of employee's emotional reactions toward the innovative processes in the organization. They found that managerial involvement and training for innovation influence employee's cognitive reappraisal of the innovation. Cognitive appraisal then predicted how employees react emotionally (positive or negative) to innovative processes and the collective use of innovation.

A few theories have explicitly considered the connection between leadership and emotions. These provide a useful context for examining relationships of emotions and leadership to creativity and innovation at different levels of analysis.

Leadership and Emotions in Organizations

Leaders and employees engaged in creativity and innovation are subject to many types of affective events capable of triggering positive or negative emotional states. Design changes, employee/team conflicts, and proposal rejections have the potential to trigger frustration, anxiety, and other negative emotional states. Approval of ideas, successful prototype tests, and new market opportunities may generate excitement, interest, or other positive emotion states. Affective Events Theory (AET) suggests that these emotional reactions shape impulsive, affectively driven reactions as well as more carefully considered judgments and decisions (Weiss & Cropanzano, 1996). Other theories articulate individual differences and various leadership and emotion processes operating at different levels of analysis in organizational settings (Ashkanasy & Humprey, 2011) and routes of influence through which emotions exert influence in leadership settings (Van Knippenberg & Van Kleef, 2016).

Drawing on Ashkanasy's (2003) multilevel theory of emotions, Ashkanasy and Humphrey (2011) outline a five-level view of leadership and emotions. Level one includes discrete emotional states such as optimism and anger as well as general positive and negative states and moods. These models emphasize the importance of within-person changes in leader or follower emotion states and how these exert influence on perceptions and behavior in the workplace. Relative to individual employee emotions, leader emotions could be more consequential if they influence decisions that have strategic consequences for an organization (Ashkanasy & Humphrey, 2011).

The second level focuses on individual differences in emotion such as the experience, expression, and regulation of discrete emotions and moods. Trait-based emotions, affect, and emotional intelligence abilities of leaders and employees are included here. This level focuses on more stable affective traits and abilities that exert influence across situations and events that influence cognition, effort, job commitment, and other important outcomes. Leaders' ability to recognize and regulate emotions in themselves and others may be critical for creativity and innovation. These emotional capacities influence leaders' ability to read reactions, motivate and encourage employees, and establish effective relationships and influence others inside and outside of their organizations (Madrid et al., 2019). Leaders often engage in emotional labor (Hochschild, 1983) by suppressing emotions or reappraising situations in ways that enable authentic emotions (Grandey, 2000; Humphrey et al., 2008). Likewise, leaders can play a role in helping others to manage their emotional reactions and expressions (Ashkanasy & Humphrey, 2011; Connelly et al., 2013; Ivcevic et al., 2021).

Level three describes the social role of emotions, emotion displays, and emotion regulation in interpersonal exchanges as they influence leader relationships with employees and others. This level highlights the importance of emotions in social exchanges that can provide information about a leader's or employee's emotions, beliefs, and intentions (Keltner & Haidt, 1999). Van Knippenberg and Van Kleef (2016) examine leadership through the lens of the Emotions as Social Information (EASI) theory (Van Kleef, 2009), offering evidence that leader displays of emotions exert influence through an affective contagion route, resulting in similar or reactionary emotions in employees and through a cognitive interpretation route, resulting in inferences about and attempts to understand leader emotional displays. Various moderating factors determine the dominance of each path and the relationships of affective contagion and cognitive interpretation to perceptions and behavior. Some moderators that have been examined include task type, relationship with the leader, interdependence with the leader, and emotion display rules in the organization.

Given such moderators, the impacts of positive and negative leader emotion displays are complex. Van Knippenberg et al. (2016) suggest that evidence to date shows positive leader emotions resulting in better outcomes when the contagion route is dominant, while negative leader emotions result in better outcomes when the cognitive interpretation route is dominant. They also note the need for more research examining the moderators influencing which route dominates and the effects of leader emotion being processed through these two different routes on workplace outcomes.

Ashkanasy and Humphrey's (2011) level four focuses on how groups are influenced by the emotional composition of group members and by the emotions related to the quality of leader–member exchange (LMX) in groups and teams. LMX aims to understand the dyadic relations between leaders and followers and the quality of this relationship (Graen & Uhl-Bien, 1995). LMX theory emphasizes the idea that leadership is based on a transaction or exchange between leaders and followers (Graen et al., 1982; Graen & Scandura, 1987; Liden et al., 1997). The emphasis of LMX theory is on how leaders and followers coexist to create high-quality workplace relationships that make it possible to create good leadership outcomes (Graen & Uhl-Bien, 1995). Emotional contagion within groups is also important at this level, especially for workgroups experiencing new opportunities, change, or crises that threaten their well-being and task performance.

Trait and state emotions of group members and leaders can have different types of effects on the group, team, and dyads. Positive and negative emotions may spread throughout the team, having different effects on team processes such as cohesion and team performance capabilities (Kelly & Barsade, 2001). Leader and team member emotions can also impact dyadic communication and exchanges in positive and negative ways. Given the salience of leaders in organizational settings, leader emotions are especially influential on group and dyadic social processes and employee emotions. Leaders play an important role in mood management, which is one of the key aspects of team leadership (Ashkanasy & Humphrey, 2011).

The fifth level suggests the importance of leaders in shaping broad contextual variables such as climate and culture. Organizational climate, or the collective feeling employees have toward their organization, its leaders, and policies, and organizational culture, or the collective beliefs, values, and assumptions employees have about an organization, both have emotional foundations. Leader emotions and behaviors linked to affective events in an organization have the potential to shape and reinforce climate and culture, which have cascading effects on employee perceptions, emotions, and performance that can be conducive to or disruptive of creativity and innovation.

A growing body of empirical research offers insights into how leader emotions and emotion capabilities influence employee emotions, cognitions, and behavior in creative work contexts. Much of this research orients around how various leadership styles and positive or negative affect relate to employee creativity, while discrete emotion displays and states have been explored more recently, as seen in the examples provided next.

Leadership, Emotions, and Individual Creativity

Transformational leadership has been one of the most researched leader behavioral styles for fostering creativity in organizations (e.g., Elenkov & Manev, 2009; Jansen et al., 2009; Reuvers et al., 2008). Transformational leaders may enhance creativity in organizations because they expand followers' interests, establish an emotionally evocative vision for followers, generate awareness among the followers of the purposes of the group, and motivate followers to focus on the good of the group (Bass & Avolio, 1990). Hughes et al. (2018) point to the remarkably consistent findings in the leadership styles research showing that positive styles like transformational, authentic, ethical, and empowering leadership show positive relationships (of similar size) with employee creativity, while negative styles such as destructive and authoritarian leadership show negative relationships with employee creativity. They suggest this positivity bias could be the results of leader style measures assessing how much employees like the leader rather than distinct styles.

Some studies have begun incorporating emotions and other moderators to better understand models of leadership and creativity. For example, Rego et al. (2014) found that authentic leadership, a form of positive, ethical, and transparent leadership, was positively related to employee creativity. This effect was mediated through employee hope and positive affect. Subsequent research has also shown positive effects of authentic leadership through its positive effect on employee affective commitment (Ribeiro et al., 2020).

Relatedly, cross-cultural research on authoritarian leadership, a leader style emphasizing leader control and authority and employee obedience, shows the detrimental effects of this leadership style on employee emotions and creativity (Guo et al., 2018). Authoritarian leadership was related to greater employee fear and defensive silence (a coping mechanism for managing fear), which detracted from creativity. The relationship between authoritarian leadership and fear was weaker in employees with higher levels of psychological capital.

Given the demanding nature of creative work, employees can experience a heavy workload and competing demands on their time. Emotional stability and leadership style can have positive effects on helping employees to deal with this. A longitudinal daily diary study over 10 days found that daily work engagement marked by vigor, dedication, and absorption in one's work mediates the relationship between employee emotional stability and creativity (Park et al., 2021). Paradoxical leadership helps employees to connect and integrate competing demands on their time and effort, and high levels of paradoxical leadership strengthened the relationship of emotional stability to work engagement.

Employees engaged in creative and innovative work activities may experience not only fluctuating emotions but also negative ones like anger and frustration. Anger has been shown to lead to greater acceptance of risk (e.g., Lerner & Tiedens, 2006), suggesting it could have benefits for creativity and innovation. Optimistic risk assessments and acceptance of risk are often a part of engaging in creative work. However, the effects of anger appear to be contingent on aspects of the context or environment emphasizing either cognitive interpretations or affective/feeling components of anger. Baumann and DeSteno (2012) showed that when features of a task highlight cognitive appraisals of controllability and certainty that are associated with anger, risk acceptance is higher. However, when the context highlights the negative valence or negative feelings aspect of anger risk acceptance was lower. The anticipated frustration or conflict aftereffects of anger influenced responses to risk. Other negative emotions like fear have been shown to have detrimental effects on creativity and innovation, as highlighted in Vuori and Huy's (2016) study of Nokia.

Leadership, Emotions, and the Social Side of Creativity

Creative and innovative work in organizations is often done in groups or teams (Mumford et al., 2014). Collaboration and group processes that promote cohesion and the ability of people to work effectively with each other is important. Interpersonal and intergroup relationships among employees and leaders are important for creativity, with leaders playing a key role in establishing the environment for creativity. Leaders may sometimes work as part of a collaborative group but also may operate outside of the group. In both cases, their leadership style, emotion displays, and emotion regulation capabilities can help or hinder creative collaborations. Although leaders need to form groups and teams, setting goals and expectations with team members, leaders' project staffing and right selection of a project's members also influences creative work that will be accomplished by the team (Mumford et al., 2014). Emotions influence interpersonal relationships and functioning and can drive important collaborative aspects of creativity.

Positive emotions in the workplace facilitate the development of trust, communication, and higher quality LMX relationships among leaders and followers, while negative emotions can send signals about needed changes in direction, quality, or team interactions. Research has shown that LMX influences emotions, creativity, and a group's ability to work well together (e.g., Atwater & Carmeli, 2009). High-quality LMX relationships between leader and team members increase mutual trust, obligation, and respect, and empower team members (Graen & Uhl-Bien, 1995).

Leader–member exchange is positively associated with employees' energetic feelings that trigger a high level of involvement in creative work (Marion, 2012). One recent study (Xie et al., 2020) found that LMX stimulates positive moods (e.g., enthusiasm, being inspired and determined) and intrinsic motivation, which enhances employee's creative performance. It is also important to note that LMX differentiation, or the situation where leaders have relationships of different quality with different followers in their team, has the potential to influence employees' work performance (Henderson et al., 2009). Differential LMX can foster positive emotions for some followers and negative ones for others or create both positive and negative emotions simultaneously.

High and low LMX employees may respond differently in terms of creative effort and working with others. Early studies have suggested that the high quality of LMX between the leader and follower correlates with high performance (e.g., Erdogan & Enders, 2007). However, studies have shown the importance of context. Olsson et al. (2012) investigated how the quality of the dyadic leader–member relationships affects individuals' creative performance in different research groups. They found that LMX has a positive association with creativity in the academic research group. However, leader- and member-rated LMX is negatively correlated with positive affect and creativity in the commercial research group, where creativity was measured as the number of publications and where performance stakes are higher.

Studies on LMX suggest that it may differ in terms of its influence on employees doing creative work. Volmer et al. (2012) examined job autonomy as the moderator of LMX and creative work involvement relationship. They found that the LMX–creative work involvement association was stronger for employees who reported high job autonomy. Pan et al. (2012) analyzed the mechanisms through which LMX influences employee creativity. They showed that alternative motivation-oriented psychological empowerment and social exchange–oriented felt obligation fully mediated the LMX and employee creativity relationship. The structure of a work unit moderated this relationship such that LMX and the employee creativity relationship was more substantial in organic structures (i.e., characterized by flexible, loose, decentralized structures) than mechanic structures (i.e., characterized by extensive departmentalization, high formalization, and high centralization). Similar research has been conducted on innovative work behavior. Schermuly et al. (2013) found that psychological empowerment fully mediates the relationship between LMX and innovative work behavior.

The emotion management strategies leaders use to regulate follower emotions can influence the quality of LMX (Little et al., 2016). Little et al. (2016) found that employees perceive their relationship with leaders as positive when leaders apply cognitive change and situation modification and negative when leaders use attention deployment.

Collaboration sometimes involves managing task-based conflict or creative differences as well as interpersonal conflicts, especially in teams where members are not operating from a shared mental model (Mohammed et al., 2010) or when team cohesion is low. Studies have shown that a significant association exists between task conflict and creativity at the employee level (Li et al., 2018) and the team level (Farh et al., 2010). Li et al. (2018) have found a curvilinear relationship between employee creativity and task conflict, and employees' growth needs strength (i.e., the desire for personal accomplishment, learning, and development) moderates this relationship. Similarly, Farh et al. (2010) also found a U-shaped relationship between task conflict and team creativity, such that creativity was highest when task conflict was at the moderate level. Zhang and Zhou (2019) examined the role of vertical task conflict (supervisor–subordinate dyad) between LMX and employee creativity. They found that in a high-quality LMX relationship, LMX impedes employee creativity by suppressing vertical task conflicts. These findings suggest that negative emotional states have some value for employees engaged in creative, innovative work, but they need to be managed.

Negative emotions can arise from task and interpersonal conflicts, and leaders can play a role in helping teams to manage those emotions. Leaders can promote shared mental models and help teams engage in problem-focused coping by interpreting the world, setting goals, crafting messages, making decisions, and interacting with followers (Griffith et al., 2014). Griffith et al. (2014) showed that distraction can be a useful emotion regulation strategy for reducing negative emotions arising from interpersonal conflict in teams. Attention deployment emotional regulation strategies may be useful in this context, despite the finding that deployment strategies may not benefit LMX relationships. If lessening interpersonal conflict in the team is critical for success of the team, leaders may prioritize that over the LMX relationship. Thus, different kinds of relational goals may be helped or harmed from attention deployment. Leaders who are skilled at recognizing the causes of negative emotions can intervene to help members regulate these emotions when needed (Madrid et al., 2019; Thiel et al., 2012).

However, research has recognized the value of negative emotions in creative contexts (Rank & Frese, 2008; Van Kleef et al., 2010). Negative emotions, especially more activating ones, can lead to more task persistence (Baas et al., 2008; George & Zhou, 2002), group effort (Sy et al., 2005), and building social connections (Gray et al., 2011). Leaders need to be able to recognize when this is the case and to create a supportive environment that enables a range of emotional experience and expression. Giving negative feedback is one domain where emotions have the potential to be beneficial or detrimental, depending on which emotions are experienced and displayed by leaders providing the feedback and employees receiving it. Anger displays when giving feedback tends to have negative effects, while other emotions such as disappointment have more positive effects (Johnson & Connelly, 2014).

Leadership, Emotions, and Climate for Creativity

The positive organizational climate promotes and fosters creativity in the organization. Leaders have a crucial role in setting a positive emotional climate in the organization and establishing a climate for creativity, which should not be confused with simply displaying and fostering positive emotions. Leaders influence followers' cognitive appraisal of events (e.g., crisis, task, or relationship conflicts) and their affective states toward the events in the organization. Leaders also provide constant support for creativity as it requires expertise and collaboration (Mumford et al., 2002).

Specific leader behaviors and characteristics enhance and facilitate a climate for creativity in an organization (Agars et al., 2012). Leaders facilitate knowledge sharing among team members, exchange of information, and motivation to work together (Mumford et al., 2002). Interpersonal skills, expertise, creative problem solving, social skills, and planning to facilitate group interactions, generating, and evaluating ideas effectively are essential when leading individuals involved in creativity (Agars et al., 2012; Mumford et al., 2002). Leadership styles are also important for establishing an organizational climate for creativity (Agars et al., 2012).

The emotional climate and climate for creativity have some overlaps. Both climates may facilitate a positive work environment that allows psychological safety, promotes proactive work behaviors, and increases employees' psychological capital and self-efficacy. Feeling psychologically safe at work is crucial for achieving creative tasks. In a psychologically safe environment, individuals can take risks, extend their boundaries, and develop alternative approaches to the issues at hand. Psychological safety at work encourages individuals to speak up and enhances proactive work behaviors such as employee voice behavior (Parker & Collins, 2010). Research has found that employee voice behavior is positively correlated with creativity (Ng & Feldman, 2012). Furthermore, employees who exhibit voice behavior are perceived as highly creative, primarily when their opinion benefits the organization (Chen & Hou, 2016). The positive organizational climate also has a crucial role in increasing an individual's self-efficacy. Self-efficacy is necessary for individuals to realize their creative potential with the belief that they can perform creative work effectively (Tierney & Farmer, 2002). A positive organizational climate also enables people to build psychological capital (Luthans, 2002). Four aspects of psychological capital – efficacy, hope, optimism, resilience – have been found to positively affect employees' creativity (Yu et al., 2019).

As the research on leadership, emotions, creativity, and innovation develops, existing findings and challenges beyond those already mentioned bear consideration for advancing research and leadership practices.

Challenges, Implications, and Future Directions

One challenge in studying leadership, creativity, and emotions is that researchers often fail to define the type of creativity being studied. Kaufman and Beghetto's Four C model of creativity (2009) suggests that different types of creativity may have different antecedents, correlates, and consequences. According to this model, four types of creativity exist: creativity in the learning process (mini-c), everyday creativity (little-c), professional creativity that requires expertise (Pro-c), and eminent creativity (Big-C). Each type of creativity can be mapped onto different types of work which may be influenced in different ways by emotion. Not all work requires creativity; therefore, individuals may not need to have Pro-c because the work does not require this. Additionally, global evaluations of an employee's work may be confounded by perceptions of overall level of job performance. Future studies could identify which of the Four Cs is most central to the jobs(s) and occupations in which leadership, creativity, and emotions are being studied. Furthermore, creativity and innovation criterion variables focusing on evaluations of specific facets of work that require novel, useful solutions, processes, products, or other outcomes would be more revealing for teasing out the complexities of leadership and emotion influences.

Relatedly, studying creativity within specific work domains may be important because norms for creativity and emotion displays may vary significantly across domains (Agars et al., 2012; Grandey et al., 2013). Research has also suggested that while creativity and innovation processes generalize across different jobs or occupations, the technical background and expertise needed for successful creative and innovate efforts in organizations are domain specific (Baer, 2015). Different climates, norms, and approaches to creativity and innovation could influence the emotional climate and emotion display rules operating for a given organization or occupation. For example, creativity and innovation in educational institution settings versus R&D, healthcare, or other types of occupational settings have domain specific requirements shaping creative efforts and also have different emotion display rules. These factors are important for leaders to consider together when figuring out how emotions fit into the management of creative individuals and teams.

In addition to these challenges, there are also challenges regarding measurement. How should creativity and innovation be measured? As the conceptualizations of these constructs vary across studies, so should their measurement.

However, creativity has most often been measured with self- and other-reports or rating scales (Hughes et al., 2018). The accuracy of self-report measures of creativity has been debated (Pretz et al., 2014), and managers providing ratings of employee creativity or innovation may not have a chance to observe the full range of an employee's behavior in this regard. Further, some leaders could be biased against individual employees or certain groups of employees. For instance, other kinds of non-performance-based motivations (e.g., favoritism, nepotism) can creep into performance evaluations (Riggio & Saggi, 2015). Study designs also influence the measurement of creativity. Many studies are conducted with student samples, potentially limiting ecological validity and generalizability of findings to organizational settings. Alternatively, field studies employing single-source survey data from one time point are subject to method/source bias effects (Podsakoff et al., 2012). There can be high fidelity in field studies, whereas there can be low fidelity in lab studies. Indeed, in a recent review by Hughes et al. (2018), scholars called for new instruments (e.g., psychometric scales) that assess all stages of creativity/innovation and different facets and types of creativity/innovation. Although beyond the scope of this chapter, similar types of challenges exist in leadership and emotions research.

Research has identified mediating mechanisms and moderators to explain the relationship between leadership, emotions, and creativity. However, there is still a need for identifying potential mediators and moderators beyond what has been done in the leadership styles literature. Although positive affect correlates to creativity positively, only a few studies investigated positive affect as a mediator of positive leadership styles (Hughes et al., 2018). Further, there can be other potential moderators such as society, culture, and gender. Earlier research has shown that leaders' emotional displays and behavior and style affect followers and their emotions differently in different cultural contexts. Research has shown that individuals require a facilitative work environment to accomplish creative tasks, and leaders play an important role in creating and facilitating this kind of environment (Mumford et al., 2002; Mumford et al., 2014). Leaders' emotional expressions have the potential to influence creative processes in different ways, depending on whether these displays are processed through affective or cognitive routes of influence. Van Knippenberg and Van Kleef (2016) called for testing dual mediation models given that emotions can operate simultaneously through these routes and different moderators could influence which one will be more dominant. For example, female and male leader emotional displays are perceived, interpreted, and responded to differently (e.g., Lewis, 2000). Finally, there is a need for greater understanding of the intersection of leadership emotions and creativity at individual, dyadic, group, and organizational levels.

Conclusion

Leader emotions and emotion regulation capabilities exert direct and indirect effects on employee creativity and innovation in organizations. The influence of emotions is complex in that both positive and negative affect and discrete emotional states have positive and negative effects and operate at multiple levels to influence the creative and innovative processes and behavior as well as the interactions and organizational environments supporting them. In highlighting important aspects of the intersection of leadership emotions and creativity research, this chapter will hopefully stimulate additional research in this area and will give organizational leaders of insights about how to foster creativity and innovation.

References

Agars, M. D., Kaufman, J. C., Deane, A., & Smith, B. (2012). Fostering individual creativity through organizational context: A review of recent research and recommendations for organizational leaders. In M. D. Mumford (Ed.), *Handbook of Organizational Creativity* (pp. 271–291). Elsevier. https://doi .org/10.1016/B978-0-12-374714-3.00012-4

Amabile, T. M. (1997). Motivating creativity in organizations: On doing what you love and loving what you do. *California Management Review, 40*(1), 39–58. https:// doi.org/10.2307/41165921

Amabile, T. M., Barsade, S. G., Mueller, J. S., & Staw, B. M. (2005). Affect and creativity at work. *Administrative Science Quarterly, 50*(3), 367–403. https:// doi.org/10.2189/asqu.2005.50.3.367

Amabile, T. M., Conti, R., Coon, H., Lazenby, J., & Herron, M. (1996). Assessing the work environment for creativity. *Academy of Management Journal, 39*(5), 1154–1184. https://doi.org/10.2307/256995

Amabile, T. M., Schatzel, E. A., Moneta, G. B., & Kramer, S. J. (2004). Leader behaviors and the work environment for creativity: Perceived leader support. *The Leadership Quarterly, 15*(1), 5–32. https://doi.org/10.1016/j.leaqua.2003.12.003

Andersen, P. H. & Kragh, H. (2013). Managing creativity in business market relation-ships. *Industrial Marketing Management, 42*(1). 82–85. https://doi.org/10.1016/j .indmarman.2012.11.007

Ashby, F. G., Isen, A. M., & Turken, A. U. (1999). A neuropsychological theory of positive affect and its influence on cognition. *Psychological Review, 106*(3), 529–50. https://doi.org/10.1037/0033-295x.106.3.529

Ashkanasy, N. M. (2003). Emotions in organizations: A multi-level perspective. In F. Dansereau & F. J. Yammarino (Eds.), *Multi-Level Issues in Organizational Behavior and Strategy (Research in Multi-Level Issues*, vol. 2, pp. 9–54). Emerald. https://doi.org/10.1016/S1475-9144(03)02002-2

Ashkanasy, N. M., & Humphrey, R. H. (2011). Current emotion research in organiza-tional behavior. *Emotion Review, 3*(2), 214–224. https://doi.org/10.1177/ 1754073910391684

Atwater, L., & Carmeli, A. (2009). Leader-member exchange, feelings of energy, and involvement in creative work. *The Leadership Quarterly, 20*(3), 264–275. https://doi.org/10.1016/j.leaqua.2007.07.009

Bass, B. M. & Avolio, B.J. (1990). Developing transformational leadership: 1992 and beyond. *Journal of European Industrial Training, 14(*5), 21–27. https://doi.org/ 10.1108/03090599010135122

Baas, M., De Dreu, C. K. W., & Nijstad, B. A. (2008). A meta-analysis of 25 years of mood-creativity research: Hedonic tone, activation, or regulatory focus? *Psychological Bulletin, 134*(6), 779–806. https://doi.org/10.1037/a0012815

Baer, J. (2015). The importance of domain-specific expertise in creativity. *Roeper Review: A Journal on Gifted Education, 37*(3), 165–178. https://doi.org/10.1080/02783193.2015.1047480

Baumann, J., & DeSteno, D. (2012). Context explains divergent effects of anger on risk taking. *Emotion, 12*(6), 1196–1199. https://doi.org/10.1037/a0029788

Carmeli, A., Gelbard, R., & Reiter-Palmon, R. (2013). Leadership, creative problem-solving capacity, and creative performance: The importance of knowledge sharing. *Human Resource Management, 52*(1), 95–121. https://doi.org/10.1002/hrm.21514

Chen, A. S. Y., & Hou, Y. H. (2016). The effects of ethical leadership, voice behavior and climates for innovation on creativity: A moderated mediation examination. *The Leadership Quarterly, 27*(1), 1–13. https://doi.org/10.1016/j.leaqua.2015.10.007

Choi, J. N., Sung, S. Y., Lee, K., & Cho, D, S (2011). Balancing cognition and emotion: Innovation implementation as a function of cognitive appraisal and emotional reactions toward innovation. *Journal of Organizational Behavior, 32*(1), 107–124. https://doi.org/10.1002/job.684

Clore, G. L., Schwarz, N., & Conway, M. (1994). Affective causes and consequences of social information processing. In R. S. Wyer, Jr. & T. K. Srull (Eds.), *Handbook of Social Cognition: Basic Processes: Applications* (pp. 323–417). Erlbaum.

Connelly, F., Friedrich, T., Vessey, W. B., et al. (2013). A conceptual framework of emotion management in leadership contexts. In R. E. Riggio & S. J. Tan (Eds.), *Leader Interpersonal and Influence Skills: The Soft Skills of Leadership* (pp. 101–137). Routledge.

Connelly, S., & Torrence, B. S. (2018). The relevance of discrete emotional experiences for human resource management: Connecting positive and negative emotions to HRM. In *Research in Personnel and Human Resources Management*. Emerald. https://doi.org/10.1108/S0742-730120180000036001

Davis, M. A. (2009). Understanding the relationship between mood and creativity: A meta-analysis. *Organizational Behavior and Human Decision Processes, 108*(1), 25–38. https://doi.org/10.1016/j.obhdp.2008.04.001

De Dreu, C. K. W., Nijstad, B. A., & van Knippenberg, D. (2008). Motivated information processing in group judgment and decision making. *Personality and Social Psychology Review, 12*(1), 22–49. https://doi.org/10.1177/1088868307304092

Desivilya, H. S., Somech, A., & Lidgoster, H. (2010). Innovation and conflict management in work teams: The effects of team identification and task and relationship conflict. *Negotiation and Conflict Management Research, 3*(1), 28–48. https://doi.org/10.1111/j.1750-4716.2009.00048.x

Drazin, R., Glynn, M. A., & Kazanjian, R. K. (1999). Multilevel theorizing about creativity in organizations: A sensemaking perspective. *The Academy of Management Review, 24*(2), 286–307. https://doi.org/10.2307/259083

Elenkov, D. S., & Manev, I. M. (2009). Senior expatriate leadership's effects on innovation and the role of cultural intelligence. *Journal of World Business, 44*(4), 357–369. https://doi.org/10.1016/j.jwb.2008.11.001

Erdogan, B., & Enders, J. (2007). Support from the top: Supervisors' perceived organizational support as a moderator of leader-member exchange to satisfaction and performance relationships. *Journal of Applied Psychology, 92*(2), 321–330. https://doi.org/10.1037/0021-9010.92.2.321

Euchner, J., & Henderson, A. (2011). The practice of innovation: Innovation as the management of constraints. *Research-Technology Management, 54*(2), 47–54. https://doi.org/10.5437/08953608X5402009

Farh J. L., Lee C., & Farh, C. I. (2010). Task conflict and team creativity: A question of how much and when. *Journal of Applied Psychology, 95*(6), 1173–1180. https://doi.org/10.1037/a0020015

Feist, G. J. (1999). The influence of personality on artistic and scientific creativity. In R. J. Sternberg (Ed.), *Handbook of Creativity* (pp. 273–296). Cambridge University Press.

Fong, C. T. (2006). The effects of emotional ambivalence on creativity. *The Academy of Management Journal, 49*(5), 1016–1030. https://doi.org/10.5465/amj.2006.22798182

George, J. M., & Zhou, J. (2002). Understanding when bad moods foster creativity and good ones don't: The role of context and clarity of feelings. *Journal of Applied Psychology, 87*(4), 687–697. https://doi.org/10.1037/0021-9010.87.4.687

Gooty, J., Gavin, M., & Ashkanasy, N. M. (2009). Emotions research in OB: The challenges that lie ahead. *Journal of Organizational Behavior, 30*(6), 833–838. https://doi.org/10.1002/job.v30:610.1002/job.619

Graen, G., Novak, M. A., & Sommerkamp, P. (1982). The effects of leader–member exchange and job design on productivity and satisfaction: Testing a dual attachment model. *Organizational Behavior and Human Performance, 30*(1), 109–131. https://doi.org/10.1016/0030-5073(82)90236-7

Graen, G. B., & Scandura, T. A. (1987). Toward a psychology of dyadic organizing. *Research in Organizational Behavior, 9*, 175–208.

Graen, G. B., & Uhl-Bien, M. (1995). Relationship-based approach to leadership: Development of leader-member exchange (LMX) theory of leadership over 25 years: Applying a multi-level multi-domain perspective. *The Leadership Quarterly, 6*(2), 219–247. https://doi.org/10.1016/1048-9843(95)90036-5

Grandey, A. A. (2000). Emotional regulation in the workplace: A new way to conceptualize emotional labor. *Journal of Occupational Health Psychology, 5*(1), 95–110. https://doi.org/10.1037/1076-8998.5.1.95

Grandey, A. A., Diefendorff, J. M., & Rupp, D. E. (2013). *Emotional Labor in the 21st Century: Diverse Perspectives on Emotion Regulation at Work*. Routledge, Taylor & Francis Group.

Gray, H. M., Ishii, K., & Ambady, N. (2011). Misery loves company: When sadness increases the desire for social connectedness. *Personality and Social Psychology Bulletin, 37*(11), 1438–1448. http://doi.org/10.1177/0146167211420167

Griffith, J. A., Connelly, S., & Thiel, C. E. (2014). Emotion regulation and intragroup conflict: When more distracted minds prevail. *International Journal of Conflict Management, 25*(2), 148–170. https://doi.org/10.1108/IJCMA-04-2012-0036

Guo, L., Decoster, S., Babalola, M. T., et al. (2018). Authoritarian leadership and employee creativity: The moderating role of psychological capital and the mediating role of fear and defensive silence. *Journal of Business Research, 92*, 219–230. https://doi.org/10.1016/j.jbusres.2018.07.03

Henderson, D. F., Liden, R. C., Glibkowski, B. C., & Chaudhry, A. (2009). LMX differentiation: A multilevel review and examination of its antecedents and outcomes. *The Leadership Quarterly, 20*(4), 517–534. https://doi.org/10.1016/j .leaqua.2009.04.003

Hochschild, A. R. (1983). *The Managed Heart Commercialization of Human Feeling*. University of California Press.

Howell, J. & Boies, K. (2004). Champions of technological innovation: The influence of contextual knowledge, role orientation, idea generation, and idea promotion on champion emergence. *The Leadership Quarterly, 15*(1), 123–143. https://doi .org/10.1016/j.leaqua.2003.12.008

Hughes, D. J., Lee, A., Tian, A. W., Newman, A., & Legood, A. (2018). Leadership, creativity, and innovation: A critical review and practical recommendations. *The Leadership Quarterly, 29*(5), 549–569. https://doi.org/10.1016/j.leaqua .2018.03.001

Humphrey, R. H., Pollack, J. M., & Hawver, T. (2008). Leading with emotional labor. *Journal of Managerial Psychology, 23*(2), 151–168. https://doi.org/10.1108/ 02683940810850790

Huy, Q. N. (2002). Emotional balancing of organizational continuity and radical change: The contribution of middle managers. *Administrative Science Quarterly, 47*(1), 31–69. https://doi.org/10.2307/3094890

Isen, A. M. (2004). Some perspectives on positive feelings and emotions: Positive affect facilitates thinking and problem solving. In A. S. R. Manstead, N. Frijda, & A. Fischer (Eds.), *Feelings and Emotions: The Amsterdam Symposium* (pp. 263–281). Cambridge University Press. https://doi.org/10.1017/ CBO9780511806582.016

Ivcevic, Z., Moeller, J., Menges, J., & Brackett, M. (2021). Supervisor emotionally intelligent behavior and employee creativity. *The Journal of Creative Behavior, 55*(1), 79–91. https://doi.org/10.1002/jocb.436

Jansen, J. J. P., Vera, D., & Crossan, M. (2009). Strategic leadership for exploration and exploitation: The moderating role of environmental dynamism. *The Leadership Quarterly, 20*(1), 5–18. https://doi.org/10.1016/j.leaqua.2008.11.008

Johnson, G., & Connelly, S. (2014). Negative emotions in informal feedback: The benefits of disappointment and drawbacks of anger. *Human Relations, 67*(10), 1265–1290. https://doi.org/10.1177/0018726714532856

Kaufman, J. C., & Beghetto, R. A. (2009). Beyond big and little: The Four C model of creativity. *Review of General Psychology, 13*(1), 1–12. https://doi.org/10.1037/ a0013688

Keller, R. T. (2001). Cross-functional project groups in research and new product development: Diversity, communications, job stress and outcomes. *Academy of Management Journal, 44*(3), 547–555. https://doi.org/10.2307/3069369

Kelly, J. R., & Barsade, S. G. (2001). Mood and emotions in small groups and work teams. *Organizational Behavior and Human Decision Processes, 86*(1), 99–130. https://doi.org/10.1006/obhd.2001.2974

Keltner, D., & Haidt, J. (1999). Social functions of emotions at four levels of analysis. *Cognition and Emotion, 13*(5), 505–521. https://doi.org/10.1080/026999399379168

Koen, P. A., Bertels, H. M. J., & Kleinschmidt, E. J. (2014). Managing the front-end of innovation – Part I: Results from a three-year study. *Research-Technology Management, 57*(2), 34–43. https://doi.org/10.5437/08956308X5702145

Kung, F. Y. H., & Chao, M. M. (2019). The impact of mixed emotions on creativity in negotiation: An interpersonal perspective. *Frontiers in Psychology, 9*(2660), 1–14. https://doi.org/10.3389/fpsyg.2018.02660

Lerner, J. S., & Tiedens, L. Z. (2006). Portrait of the angry decision maker: How appraisal tendencies shape anger's influence on cognition. *Journal of Behavioral Decision Making, 19*(2), 115–137. https://doi.org/10.1002/bdm.515

Lewis, K. M. (2000). When leaders display emotion: How followers respond to negative emotional expression of male and female leaders. *Journal of Organizational Behavior, 21*(2), 221–234. https://doi.org/10.1002/(SICI)1099-1379(200003) 21:2<221::AID-JOB36>3.0.CO;2-0

Li, Y., Yang, B., & Ma, L. (2018). When is task conflict translated into employee creativity? The moderating role of growth need strength. *Journal of Personnel Psychology, 17*(1), 22–32. https://doi.org/10.1027/1866-5888/a000192

Liden, R. C., Sparrowe, R. T., & Wayne, S. J. (1997). Leader-member exchange theory: The past and potential for the future. In G. R. Ferris (Ed.), *Research in Personnel and Human Resources Management* (vol. 15, pp. 47–119). Elsevier Science/JAI Press. https://doi.org/10.1037/0021-9010.86.4.697

Little, L. M., Gooty, J., & Williams, M. (2016). The role of leader emotion management in leader–member exchange and follower outcomes. *The Leadership Quarterly, 27*(1), 85–97. https://doi.org/10.1016/j.leaqua.2015.08.007

Luthans, F. (2002). The need for and meaning of positive organizational behavior. *Journal of Organizational Behavior, 23*(6), 695–706. https://doi.org/10.1002/ job.165

Madrid, H. P., Niven, K., & Vasquez, C. A. (2019). Leader interpersonal emotion regulation and innovation in teams. *Journal of Occupational and Organizational Psychology, 92*(4), 787–905. https://doi.org/10.1111/joop.12292

Marion, R. (2012). Leadership of creativity: Entity-based, relational, and complexity perspectives. In M. D. Mumford (Ed.), *Handbook of Organizational Creativity* (pp. 457–479). Elsevier Academic Press. https://doi.org/10.1016/B978-0-12-374714-3.00018-5

Mastria, S., Agnoli, S., & Corazza, G. E. (2019). How does emotion influence the creativity evaluation of exogenous alternative ideas? *PloS ONE, 14*(7). https://doi.org/10.1371/journal.pone.0219298

McMahon, S. R., & Ford, C. M. (2013). Heuristic transfer in the relationship between leadership and employee creativity. *Journal of Leadership & Organizational Studies, 20*(1), 69–83. https://doi.org/10.1177/1548051812465894

Mohammed, S., Ferzandi, L., & Hamilton, K. (2010). Metaphor no more: A 15-year review of the team mental model construct. *Journal of Management, 36*(4), 876–910. https://doi.org/10.1177/0149206309356804

Mumford, M. D., Gibson, C., Giorgini, V., & Mecca, J. (2014). Leading for creativity: People, products, and systems. In D. V. Day (Ed.), *The Oxford Handbook of Leadership and Organizations* (pp. 757–782). Oxford University Press.

Mumford, M. D., & McIntosh, T. (2017). Creative thinking processes: The past and the future. *Journal of Creative Behavior, 51*(4), 317–322. https://doi.org/10.1002/ jocb.197

Mumford, M. D., Scott, G. M., Gaddis, B., & Strange, J. M. (2002). Leading creative people: Orchestrating expertise and relationships. *The Leadership Quarterly, 13* (6), 705–750. https://doi.org/10.1016/S1048-9843(02)00158-3

Mumford, M. D., Zaccaro, S. J., Harding, F. D., Jacobs, T. O., & Fleishman, E. A. (2000). Leadership skills for a changing world: Solving complex social problems. *The Leadership Quarterly, 11*(1), 11–35. https://doi.org/10.1016/S1048-9843(99)00041-7

Ng, T. W. H., & Feldman, D. C. (2012). The effects of organizational and community embeddedness on work-to-family and family-to-work conflict. *Journal of Applied Psychology, 97*(6), 1233–1251. https://doi.org/10.1037/a0029089

Ohly, S., Kase, R., & Skerlavaj, M. (2010). Networks for generating and for validating ideas: The social side of creativity. *Innovation, 12*(1), 41–52. https://doi.org/10.5172/impp.12.1.41

Olsson, L., Hemlin, S., & Pousette, A. (2012). A multi-level analysis of leader-member exchange and creative performance in research groups. *The Leadership Quarterly, 23*(3), 604–619. https://doi.org/10.1016/j.leaqua.2011.12.011

Pan, W., Sun, L.Y., & Chow, I. H. S. (2012). Leader-member exchange and employee creativity: Test of a multilevel moderated mediation model. *Human Performance, 25*(5), 432–451. https://doi.org/10.1080/08959285.2012.721833

Park I. J, Shim, S., Hai, S., Kwon, S., & Kim, T. G. (2021). Cool down emotion, don't be fickle! The role of paradoxical leadership in the relationship between emotional stability and creativity. *The International Journal of Human Resource Management*, 1–31. https://doi.org/10.1080/09585192.2021.1891115

Parker, S. K., & Collins, C. G. (2010). Taking stock: Integrating and differentiating multiple proactive behaviors. *Journal of Management, 36*(3), 633–662. https://doi.org/10.1177/0149206308321554

Podsakoff, P. M., MacKenzie, S. B., & Podsakoff, N. P. (2012). Sources of method bias in social science research and recommendations on how to control it. *Annual Review of Psychology, 63*, 539–569. https://doi.org/10.1146/annurev-psych-120710-100452

Pretz, J. E., & McCollum, V. A. (2014). Self-perceptions of creativity do not always reflect actual creative performance. *Psychology of Aesthetics, Creativity, and the Arts, 8*(2), 227. https://doi.org/10.1037/a0035597

Rank, J., & Frese, M. (2008). The impact of emotions, moods and other affect-related variables on creativity, innovation, and initiative. In N. M. Ashkanasy & C. L. Cooper (Eds.), *Research Companion to Emotion in Organizations* (pp. 103–119*)*. Edward Elgar. https://doi.org/10.4337/9781848443778.00015

Rego, A., Sousa, F., Marques, C., & Pina e Cunha, M. P. (2014). Hope and positive affect mediating the authentic leadership and creativity relationship. *Journal of Business Research, 67*(2), 200–210. https://doi.org/10.1016/j.jbusres.2012.10.003

Reiter-Palmon, R., & Illies, J. J. (2004). Leadership and creativity: Understanding leadership from a creative problem-solving perspective. *The Leadership Quarterly, 15*(1), 55–77. https://doi.org/10.1016/j.leaqua.2003.12.005

Reuvers, M., Van Engen, M. L., Vinkenburg, C. J., &Wilson-Evered, E. (2008). Transformational leadership and innovative work behaviour: Exploring the relevance of gender differences. *Creativity and Innovation Management, 17*(3), 227–244. https://doi.org/10.1111/j.1467-8691.2008.00487.x

Ribeiro, N., Duarte, A., Filipe, R., & Torres de Oliveira, R. (2020). How authentic leadership promotes individual creativity: The mediating role of affective commitment. *Journal of Leadership and Organizational Studies, 27*(2), 189–202. https://doi.org/10.1177/1548051819842796

Riggio, R. E., & Saggi, K. (2015). If we do our job correctly, nobody gets hurt by nepotism. *Industrial and Organizational Psychology, 8*, 19–21. https://doi.org/10.1017/iop.2014.5

Runco, M. A., & Jaeger, G. J. (2012). The standard definition of creativity. *Creativity Research Journal, 24*(1), 92–96. https://doi.org/10.1080/10400419.2012.650092

Schermuly, C. C., Meyer, B., & Dämmer, L. (2013). LMX and innovative behavior: The mediating role of psychological empowerment. *Journal of Personnel Psychology, 12*(3), 132–142. https://doi.org/10.1027/1866-5888/a000093

Schutte, N. S., & Malouff, J. M. (2019). The impact of signature character strengths interventions: A meta-analysis. *Journal of Happiness Studies: An Interdisciplinary Forum on Subjective Well-Being, 20*(4), 1179–1196. https://doi.org/10.1007/s10902-018-9990-2

Shalley, C. E., & Gilson, L. L. (2004). What leaders need to know: A review of social and contextual factors that can foster or hinder creativity. *The Leadership Quarterly, 15*(1), 33–53. https://doi.org/10.1016/j.leaqua.2003.12.004

Sy, T., Côté, S., & Saavedra, R. (2005). The contagious leader: Impact of the leader's mood on the mood of group members, group affective tone, and group processes. *Journal of Applied Psychology, 90*(2), 295–305. https://doi.org/10.1037/0021-9010.90.2.295

Thiel, C. E., Connelly, S., & Griffith, J. A. (2012). Leadership and emotion management for complex tasks: Different emotions, different strategies. *The Leadership Quarterly, 23*(3), 517–533. https://doi.org/10.1016/j.leaqua.2011.12.005

Tierney, P., & Farmer, S. M. (2002). Creative self-efficacy: Its potential antecedents and relationship to creative performance. *The Academy of Management Journal, 45*(6), 1137–1148. https://doi.org/10.5465/3069429

To, M. L., Fisher, C. D., Ashkanasy, N. M., & Rowe, P. A. (2012). Within-person relationships between mood and creativity. *Journal of Applied Psychology, 97*(3), 599–612. https://doi.org/10.1037/a0026097

Van Kleef, G. A. (2009). How emotions regulate social life: The emotions as social information (EASI) model. *Current Directions in Psychological Science, 18*(3), 184–188. https://doi.org/10.1111/j.1467-8721.2009.01633.x

Van Kleef, G. A., Anastasopoulou, C., & Nijstad, B. A. (2010). Can expressions of anger enhance creativity? A test of the emotions as social information (EASI) model. *Journal of Experimental Social Psychology, 46*(6), 1042–1048. https://doi.org/10.1016/j.jesp.2010.05.015

Van Knippenberg, D., & Van Kleef, G. A. (2016). Leadership and affect: Moving the hearts and minds of followers. *The Academy of Management Annals, 10*(1), 799–840. https://doi.org/10.1080/19416520.2016.1160515

Visser, V. A., van Knippenberg, D., van Kleef, G. A., & Wisse, B. (2013). How leader displays of happiness and sadness influence follower performance: Emotional contagion and creative versus analytical performance. *The Leadership Quarterly, 24*(1), 172–188. https://doi.org/10.1016/j.leaqua.2012.09.003

Volmer, J., Spurk, D., & Niessen, C. (2012). Leader–member exchange (LMX), job autonomy, and creative work involvement. *The Leadership Quarterly, 23*(3), 456–465. https://doi.org/10.1016/j.leaqua.2011.10.005

Vuori, T. O., & Huy, Q. N. (2016). Distributed attention and shared emotions in the innovation process: How Nokia lost the smartphone battle. *Administrative Science Quarterly, 61*(1), 9–51. https://doi.org/10.1177/0001839215606951

Weiss, H. M., & Cropanzano, R. (1996). Affective Events Theory: A theoretical discussion of the structure, causes and consequences of affective experiences at work. In B. M. Staw & L. L. Cummings (Eds.), *Research in Organizational Behavior: An Annual Series of Analytical Essays and Critical Reviews* (pp. 1–74). Elsevier Science/JAI Press.

Xie, Z., Wu, N., Yue, T., et al. (2020). How leader-member exchange affects creative performance: An examination from the perspective of self-determination theory. *Frontiers in Psychology*, *11*(573793), 1–10. https://doi.org/10.3389/fpsyg.2020.573793

Yu, X., Li, D., Tsai, C. H. & Wang, C. (2019). The role of psychological capital in employee creativity. *Career Development International, 24*(5), 420–437. https://doi.org/10.1108/CDI-04-2018-0103

Zhang, A. Y., Tsui, A. S., & Wang, D. X. (2011). Leadership behaviors and group creativity in Chinese organizations: the role of group processes. *Leadership Quarterly, 22*(5), 851–862. https://doi.org/10.1016/j.leaqua.2011.07.007

Zhang, X., & Zhou, K. (2019). Close relationship with the supervisor may impede employee creativity by suppressing vertical task conflict. *R&D Management, 49*(5), 789–802. https://doi.org/10.1111/radm.12375

31 A Multilevel Model of Emotions and Creativity in Organizations

Neal M. Ashkanasy and March L. To

In this chapter, we seek to apply Ashkanasy's (2003a) Five-Level Model of Emotions in the Workplace (FLMEW; see also Ashkanasy & Dorris, 2017; Ashkanasy & Humphrey, 2011a), which we argue provides a broad framework to enable a deep understanding of how human emotions underpin their creativity at five different levels of organizational analysis. In line with Rank and Frese (2008), we define creativity broadly as "the development of novel and useful ideas, products, or problem solutions" (p. 104). This is a broad definition, however, and covers a range of different forms of creativity and creative behaviors in workplace settings that we argue can occur at every level of organizational analysis. Thus, a creative employee might seek to manage the work context so it is more conducive to creativity (Cummings & Oldham, 1997; Luksyte & Spitzmueller, 2016). This is because a leader would be expected to strive to encourage creative self-efficacy (Huang et al., 2016) or would reach out to fellow team members to help them to become more creative by, for example, reducing the effects of work overload (De Clercq & Belausteguigoitia, 2019).

Mumford and his associates (2012) were the first to outline the multilevel nature and effects of creativity and creative behavior and identified three levels of analysis: (1) individual differences in creative behavior, (2) creative groups and teams, and (3) creative organizational culture. More recently, To and Fisher (2019) addressed creativity at three levels: (1) within-person over time, (2) between persons in dyads, and (3) at the team level of analysis (see also To, Tse et al., 2015). In this chapter, we address the topic of creativity across the five levels of analysis as set out by Ashkanasy (2003a). In the following sections, we begin by introducing the Five-Level Model, and then discuss the relationship of emotion and creativity at each of its levels. We conclude by outlining how the different parts of the model enable the development of a more comprehensive and integrated multilevel model of emotions and creativity in organizations; and provide some suggestions for future research on the nexus of emotions and organizational creativity.

The Five-Level Model of Emotion in the Workplace (FLMEW)

The Ashkanasy (2003a) Five-Level Model includes five distinct but overlapping levels of analysis: (1) temporal varying emotions and creativity at

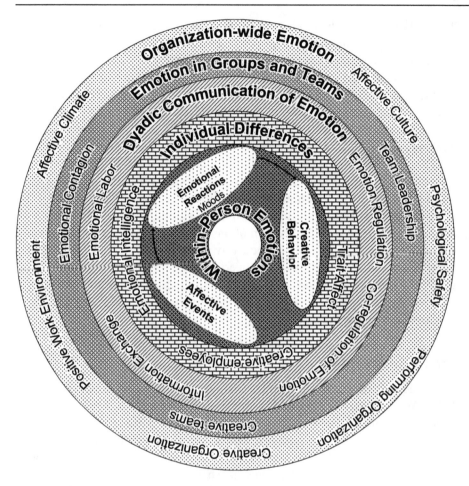

Figure 31.1 *A Five-Level Model of emotions and creativity in organizations.*

the "within-person" level, (2) individual differences in emotions and creativity at the "between-persons" level, (3) how emotions and creativity are expressed and communicated at the interpersonal level of analysis, (4) emotions and creativity as collective phenomena at the level of groups and teams, and (5) emotions and creativity as organization-wide phenomena. We illustrate the model in Figure 31.1, where we represent the levels as concentric circles (and where each lower level is embedded in the next higher level).

The first level of the model refers to employees' momentary experiences of, and reactions to, affect and emotion in their environment (Clark et al., 1989). This level is based in the idea of "affective events" that are constantly occurring in the workplace (Weiss & Cropanzano, 1996) and result in emotional reactions that in turn determine employees' transient attitudes and behavior. The emphasis at Level 2 is on the way that emotions are expressed and experienced by employees who share different personality traits and abilities such as trait affectivity (Watson et al., 1985) or emotional intelligence (Mayer & Salovey,

1997). At Level 3 of the model, the focus shifts to interpersonal exchanges and how employees communicate and perceive emotions in relationships, typically conceptualized as interpersonal emotional regulation (Troth et al., 2018), emotional expressions (Van Kleef, 2014), or emotional labor (Grandey, 2000; Hochschild, 1983/2012). Key concepts at Level 4 in the model include group affective tone (George & Zhou, 2002), emotional contagion (Hatfield et al., 1993), and emotional leadership (Humphrey, 2002). At the top level, Level 5, key concepts include emotional climate (de Rivera, 1992) and organizational culture (Ashkanasy & Härtel, 2014).

Ashkanasy (2003b) argues further that, although emotional behaviors and attitudes at the five levels are distinct conceptually, their effects cross all five levels of analysis. This means that the effects of emotions at each level cannot be considered in isolation. In effect, emotions at each of the five levels "cascade throughout the organization, subsequently impacting key organizational variables that underpin organizational performance" (Ashkanasy et al, 2020, p. 375). In the next sections of this chapter, we discuss emotions at each of the five levels of analysis with a view to drawing out their connections to employee creativity and creative behavior.

Level 1: Within-Person

In considering Level 1 (temporal variations in affect and creativity) in the FLMEW, we refer to Affective Events Theory (AET; Weiss & Cropanzano, 1996), which models how "affective events" that derive from the organizational environment (e.g., new technology, leader behavior) affect employees' subsequent attitudes and behavior. At the core of the model is the idea that employees experience *object-oriented emotions* (such as anger, sadness, fear, disgust, or happiness). For example, an employee might experience fear when told to expect layoffs as a result of new technology; or anger when they see a less-qualified colleague promoted. When such experiences become endemic, the result might then become *moods*, which are longer lasting than emotions and are generally not object oriented (cf. Frijda, 1986).

According to AET, such emotional reactions (which can include either emotions or moods) lead in turn to one of two distinct forms of behavior: (1) "affect-driven" or (2) "judgment-driven." The former tends to be an impulsive and immediate response to a singular event, while the latter tends to emerge in the longer term as a result of (positive or negative) attitudes derived from repeated instances of the event. Depending on the emotion driving the behavior, they can be either positive or negative. Examples of negative behavior can include verbally assaulting a colleague who has made a mistake (affect-driven) or engaging in deviant behavior (judgment-driven) as a form of retaliation to an organization perceived to be toxic (cf. Khattak et al., 2020). Examples of positive behavior can include suggesting innovative ideas to a helpful colleague (affect-driven) or resolving to commit to a supportive organization (judgment-driven).

Turning now to consider how this relates to creativity, we see numerous examples where researchers using diary and/or experience-sampling methods (e.g., see Binnewies & Wornlein, 2011; Bledow et al., 2013; Fisher et al., 2013; To et al., 2012) report that affect and creativity both fluctuate over short periods of time within a person. The question as to whether creativity is associated with positive versus negative affect, however, remains controversial. On the one hand and based on Fredrickson's (2001) "broaden-and-build" model, researchers have tended to assume that positive affect facilitates creativity and innovation (since such affect leads to optimistic appraisals). When people are experiencing negative affect, on the other hand, they tend to become more pessimistic (Seo et al., 2004), and therefore "drill down" to try to discover what went wrong, rather than to try and think of new ideas. Isen and her associates (Isen, 1999; Isen et al., 1987) came to a similar conclusion based in the results of lab studies – showing positive moods facilitate increased cognitive flexibility, leading to more creative ideas.

While conventional understanding in the creativity and affect literature seems to reinforce the (widespread) view that positive affect links to creativity, we note the existence of research (see Baas et al., 2008; To, Fisher et al., 2015) showing that negative moods may sometimes also serve to facilitate increased creativity. In this view, authors (such as George & Zhou, 2007) refer to "dual tuning theory," where both positive and negative affect can foster creativity (depending on "information signals"). Grounded in Schwarz and Clore's (2003) mood-as-information model, the dual tuning theory posits that, on the one hand, positive moods may be seen to signal a problem-free situation, and therefore enhance cognitive flexibility for novel attempts (see Isen, 1999; Isen et al., 1987). Negative affect, on the other hand, may serve to signal that the employee needs to search for higher quality solutions to solve a difficult problem or status quo (George & Zhou, 2002; To et al., 2012; To, Fisher et al., 2015).

In a related vein, De Dreu et al. (2008) and Nijstad et al. (2010) pose a similar model to dual tuning: the "dual pathway" model. These authors argue that creativity can be facilitated either via positive affect (leading to increased cognitive flexibility) or negative affect (leading to increased persistence). A critical difference between this model and dual tuning theory is the inclusion of *activation*, which is a factor in both pathways; this is because activation represents the "cognitive energy" needed for creative thought. In the case of positive affect, creative energy acts as a precursor for the flexibility employees need to think up creative ideas. According to this theory, flexibility energizes creativity by opening access to remote knowledge and wider categorizations that, in turn, enables employees to find heretofore undiscovered connections among seemingly unrelated sources of information (see also Friedman & Förster, 2010).

In the instance of negative affect, activation may be via *effortful persistence*. In this view, an individual who is experiencing negative affect can achieve creativity through a process of effortful and prolonged search for new solutions to a problem. In a meta-analysis to investigate apparent inconsistencies in relationships between positive and negative affect and creativity, Baas et al. (2008) found that that, while positive affect does generally engender creativity though the activating effects of flexible thinking, negative affect can also lead to creativity consistent with the activating effects of persistence (although the latter effects tend to depend more strongly on context).

The idea that both positive and negative affect can link to creativity under different circumstances has been supported in field-based experience-sampling research conducted by Amabile et al. (2005) and Binnewies and Wörnlein (2011). More recently, To and his colleagues (To et al., 2012; To, Fisher, et al., 2015) studied affect and creativity among employees engaged in a long-term project and found that, rather than positive versus negative affect, the key to employees' engagement in momentary creative behavior is *activation*. Thus, To et al. (2012) found that both positive and negative activating affect link to participants' engagement in creativity, while deactivating positive and negative effect link to reduced creative engagement. In a follow-up study, To, Fisher, et al. (2015) found that, while the link between activating positive affect and creative engagement holds across the board, activating negative mood links to creative engagement only in specific combination of trait and context.

The defining feature of Level 1 effects is that they vary across time. In this regard, Bledow and his associates (2011; 2013) found that temporal changes in affect (or an "affective shift") can result in variation in creativity across the working day. Specifically, these authors found that individual creativity at work increases as mood improves during the working day. Especially, early in the workday, negative moods serve to draw employees' attention to goal discrepancies and the need for them to take corrective action. As the day progresses and the employee's positive affect improves, then the employee is likely to become more energized and motivated to look for more creative solutions to the problems they have encountered earlier in the day.

Level 2: Between-Persons

So far in this chapter, we have discussed the effect of affective states on creativity and creative behavior at Level 1 in the Ashkanasy (2003a) model, concluding that the evidence appears to show that both positive and negative activated affect can engender creativity in different circumstances, via either flexible or systematic cognitive processes. As Ashkanasy (2003b) argues, however, the various levels of analysis should not be considered in isolation. In this regard, Baas and his coauthors (2008) deduced from their meta-analysis results that "there is more to the mood-creativity relationship than hedonic tone [valence], and activation, or their interaction" (p. 797). This brings us to Level 2 in the FLMEW, which concerns the effects of individual differences on creativity and creative behavior. One important variable in this regard is trait goal orientation (VandeWalle et al., 2001), which To and his colleagues (2012, see also To, Fisher, et al., 2015) found to determine the effects of both employee affect as well as their creative process engagement.

In this chapter, however, we focus on the two individual difference variables identified by Ashkanasy (2003a; see also Ashkanasy & Dorris, 2017; Ashkanasy & Humphrey, 2011a): (1) emotional intelligence (Mayer & Salovey, 1997) and (2) trait affect (Watson & Tellegen, 1985; Watson et al., 1988). In line with the tenets of AET (Weiss & Cropanzano, 1996), individual differences such as these moderate the effect of affective events on employees' subsequent behaviors and attitudes. We discuss the effects of each of these individual difference variables on creativity next.

Emotional Intelligence

In this view (and consistent with the Mayer and Salovey, 1997, definition of emotional intelligence), high emotional intelligence employees should be better able than their low emotional intelligence compatriots to perceive, to assimilate, to understand, and ultimately to manage their emotions. Based on this theory, Jordan et al. (2002) argue that high emotional intelligence employees would tend to react less negatively to negative affective events (e.g., impending job losses) than their low emotional intelligence coworkers (see also Jordan et al., in press; Lopes et al., 2006).

More recently, Sánchez-Ruiz and colleagues (2011) found a positive relationship between trait emotional intelligence (Petrides et al., 2007) and creative behavior. In another study, Geher and colleagues (2017) related an ability measure of emotional intelligence (the Baron-Cohen et al., 2001, "Reading the Mind in the Eyes" test) to an other-rated measure of creativity and found a consistently positive relationship across nine measures of spontaneous creativity. Along similar lines, Parke et al. (2015) found in a multimethod field study that both emotion regulation and emotional facilitation ability enhance managers' ability to "use their PA to enhance their creativity" (p. 917). Finally, while Ivcevic et al. (2007) failed to find a link between an ability measure of emotional intelligence (the MSCEIT, Mayer at al., 2002) and creative behavior, they did find a relationship between a self-report measure of "emotional creativity" (Averill, 1999) and artistic creativity. In support of the interactive effects of emotional intelligence moreover, Ivcevic and Brackett (2015) later found in a study (of high school students' creative behavior) that, while emotion regulation ability predicts creativity, this effect only holds for students who are high in trait openness to experience.

Trait Positive and Negative Affect (PA vs. NA)

In terms of the moderating effects of trait positive and negative affect (PA vs. NA): high PA individuals should, by definition, be expected to experience more positive affect in response to positive affective events than their low trait PA peers; and the opposite should hold for high trait NA individuals. This effect is apparent in a study of employee engagement and attitudes conducted by Dalal and his associates (2012). It is also supported in a study by Gilmore et al. (2013), the authors report on a field study of transformational leadership and employee creative behavior. Gilmore and his associates found that, while transform-ational leadership relates to creative behavior in low trait PA employees, this effect was not apparent for high trait PA employees, who were in general more creative and therefore did not need to be encouraged by their (transform-ational leaders) to be more creative. In another study, Kim et al. (2016) found that trait PA relates to employee creativity, especially when accompanied by group-level positive affective climate and group reflexivity. This finding con-firms that the trait affect–creativity relationship, even for positive trait PA, is context dependent.

In summary, while the empirical evidence for a relationship between trait and other self-report measures of emotional intelligence and creative behavior is strong and consistent, the results for ability-based measures of emotional intelli-gence are mixed.

Level 3: Interpersonal Relationships

How organizational employees communicate emotions to others both inside and outside the organization is the focus at Level 3 in the FLMEW. Traditionally, this level of analysis is encapsulated in the idea of *emotional labor*, which Hochschild (1983/2012) defines as "management of feeling to create a publicly observable facial and bodily display" (p. 7). As such, the construct was originally intended to model frontline service encounters with external stakeholders such as customers and clients. Grandey (2000) subse-quently argued that labor is essentially a type of impersonal emotional regula-tion, where employees adjust their displays of emotions in response to organizational display rules (cf. Diefendorff & Richard, 2003).

More recently, based on the work of Zaki and Williams (2013), Troth et al. (2018) proposed that emotional labor is an example of *organizational interper-sonal emotion regulation*. In this view, emotional regulation can take four different forms, based on dimensions of focus (self- vs. other-focused) and locus (response-independent vs. response-dependent). Troth and her coauthors argue that interpersonal emotion regulation can be: (1) entirely other-focused (as in emotional labor); (2) different depending on focus (self- vs. other); (3) co-occurring (i.e., when two parties try to regulate their emotions in a two-way interaction); or (4) a coregulation process (where the two parties help each other to regulate their emotions).

Such interpersonal regulatory episodes became important when, in order to seek creative solutions to problems, organizational members engage in social exchanges with coworkers to obtain information and feedback that will help them to develop and then to refine creative ideas (cf. Hargadon & Bechky, 2006; Hennessey & Amabile, 2010). In this view, creativity can be seen to be more than a process that takes place solely at the individual or within-person level, but as a process of interpersonal communication enacted at the dyadic (Van Kleef et al., 2010; Van Kleef, 2014) or group (Barade & Knight, 2015) level of analysis.

We focus here on interpersonal dyadic interactions where, according to the Van Kleef et al. (2010) "emotions as social information" (EASI) model, emotions should play a critical role in the creativity process (see also Van Kleef, 2014). In his EASI theory, Van Kleef argues that emotions inform the behavior of interaction partners via two distinct processes, where observers of another party's emotional expressions can: (1) experience the same feelings directly as a result of emotional contagion (Hatfield et al., 1993); or (2) cognitively process the other's emotional cues to deduce their feelings and thoughts (cf. Forgas, 2002).

Under this scenario, a coworker's expressions of positive emotion (e.g., happiness or excitement) can be seen on the one hand to communicate positive feelings and energy, which should lead in turn to a flexible and optimistic mindset associated with creativity (Isen, 1999; Fredrickson, 2001). On the other hand, expression of negative emotions (e.g., anger or frustration) can lead to negative feelings in other employees and therefore serve to inhibit creativity. For instance, Miron-Spektor et al. (2011) found in a laboratory study that observers' perceptions of angry expressions tended to inhibit observers' creative thinking. Other researchers (e.g., Lelieveld et al., 2012; Wubben et al., 2009) report that observers' perceptions of negative emotions such as anger trigger retaliation against the expresser and thus negate collaborative creativity.

As we discussed earlier, however, the effects of negative emotions on creativity and creative behavior can be more equivocal, especially when observers engage in the second (more complex and thoughtful) of the two EASI processes. In this instance, an observer's perception of positive emotions by their partner might be seen to signal on the one hand that additional creative effort is not necessary because the current solution is satisfactory (cf. George & Zhou, 2002, 2007; Martin & Stoner, 1996). On the other hand, observers may be motivated to engage in greater creative effort when they infer from struggling coworkers that a problem can only be solved after persistent attention. This motivating effect (of an observer's perceptions of negative affect) was demonstrated by Miron-Spektor and her colleagues (2011), who found across four laboratory studies that "paradoxical frames" (where individuals "recognize and embrace contradictions," p. 229) can lead to creative behavior following observation of others' negative (e.g., anger) emotions. In a similar vein, Van Kleef and his colleagues (2010) found that angry (rather than neutral) feedback tends to spur individuals to seek additional information that, in turn, increases their engagement and subsequent creativity. Based on these findings, it looks like negative expressions may convey dissatisfaction with a current solution and therefore boost observers' creativity (but only for those who consider the cues deliberately, Van Kleef et al., 2010).

Level 4: Groups and Teams

At the fourth level of the FLMEW, the focus turns to analysis at the level of groups and teams, where emotions are typically spread via emotional contagion, which can be horizontal (i.e., among group members, see Barsade, 2002; Hatfield et al., 1993), vertically downward (i.e., from leaders to group members, see Sy et al., 2005), or vertically upward (i.e., from group members to the leader, see Tee et al., 2013). In this regard, George (2000) argues that leaders play a key role in setting the *affective tone* of the group. Moreover, and as Sy and his colleagues found, a leader's role can be pivotal in setting a positive affective tone in a group. In turn, and as Gooty et al. (2010) show, groups whose leaders foster a positive emotional tone become both more cohesive and more effective (see also Humphrey, 2002).

The interplay of group affect and team-level creativity has been attracting increasing research attention (e.g., see Jones & Kelly, 2009; Tsai et al., 2012), often from the perspective of affective convergence theory. According to this view, individual positive or negative affective experiences are shared with teammates and result in a positive or negative *group affective tone* (Barsade & Knight, 2015; George, 1990). Similar to the effects of positive and negative affective states on creativity at lower levels of the FLMEW, research findings at the group level have been mixed, however. In the following paragraphs, we discuss first positive, then negative effective tone effects.

Positive Group Affective Tone

As we discussed earlier, Fredrickson's (2001) broaden-and-build theory holds that positive affect should foster creativity, including in groups. Support for this view comes from lab studies by Grawitch and Munz and their colleagues (Grawitch, Munz, Elliott, et al., 2003; Grawitch, Munz, & Kramer, 2003) and Klep et al. (2011), who found that groups whose members were induced to feel positive tended to complete tasks more creatively. While Hu et al. (2018), Shin (2014), and Tang and Naumann (2016) later found field study support for this effect, Tsai and his colleagues (2012) were unable to replicate this effect in a field study involving R&D teams. Moreover, other scholars (e.g., see George & King, 2007) go so far as to argue that positive group mood may not only not be the best way to engender team creativity; it might even be detrimental. The argument here is that a positive affective tone might serve to lull members into a sense of "hedonistic complacency" (Wegener & Petty, 1994, p. 1034) and therefore to suppress contrary opinions that would help make group decisions more robust.

Concerning the effects of negative group affect, research findings are again mixed. The notion that negative group mood might sometimes promote creativity in groups was supported in lab studies conducted by Jones and her associates (Jones & Kelly, 2009; Jones & Spoor, 2007). These authors argue that their findings suggest group members are more likely to search for better solutions when they challenge the status quo by expressing their negative feelings. Jones and Kelly argue in particular that the beneficial effects of expressed negative mood applies more to the context of groups (rather than individuals) because a diversity of views constitutes an expanded information resource. A counterargument to this view can be found in research by Cole et al. (2008), who found in a field study of 61 work teams that the negative effects of dysfunctional team behavior and team performance tend to be facilitated by the group's perceptions of high negative affective expressivity. In this regard, Kelly and Spoor (2007) found further that negative group affect can increase inter-personal conflict, leading to reduced information exchange and cooperation, and ultimately team creativity.

Finally, we note that a defining feature at the group level of analysis is that it opens the possibility of intragroup diversity effects. In the context of group affect, this implies that different group members may share different levels of positive or negative affect (cf. Barsade & Knight, 2015; Collins et al., 2013). Such diversity may be in terms of affective traits over the longer term (see Barsade et al., 2000; Kaplan et al., 2013) or shorter-lived differences in state affect experienced in teams over time.

Early research (e.g., Barsade et al., 2000; Kaplan et al., 2013) suggests that diversity in trait affectivity among members plays a negative role by decreasing team cooperation and group performance. In a recent study, To et al. (2021) found that shorter-lived diversity in members' state affect produces fewer of these social liabilities and can instead facilitate team creativity through infor-mation exchange and elaboration. To and his team also found, however, that such creative benefit of state affect diversity occurs only for teams with a well-developed transactive memory system to legitimize and coordinate the differ-ences flowing from members' diverse feelings (To et al., 2021).

Level 5: The Organization as a Whole

At the outer level of the FLMEW sits Level 5 (see Figure 31.1), which takes in affect as an organization-wide phenomenon, typically operationalized in terms of an organization's affective climate or culture. It is, however, important to distinguish culture from organizational climate. In this regard, the former represents employees' immediate collective conscious perceptions of their work environment (Schneider et al., 2011). In the specific context of affect, de Rivera (1992, p. 197) refers to *affective climate* as "an objective (emotional) phenom-enon that can be palpably sensed." Referring to an organization's culture, Ashkanasy and Härtel (2014) note that it derives from the collective experiences of organizational members, often based on unstated assumptions (cf. Schein, 1992). Regarding affect, culture is embodied in an organization's *emotional display rules* (Diefendorff & Richard, 2003) that, in turn, are manifested in the organization's climate (see also Pizer & Härtel, 2005).

From the perspective of organization-wide affect, Härtel (2008) notes that a *positive work environment* (PWE) is the key to enabling employee flourishing (including creativity) (see also Härtel & Ashkanasy, 2011). According to Härtel (2008), employees in a PWE view their organization as "respectful, inclusive and psychologically safe; leaders and coworkers as trustworthy, fair and open to diversity; and characterized by ethical policies and decision-making" (p. 584). Ashkanasy et al. (2020, p. 379) note that a PWE is achieved via "facilitating positive workplace relationships [Krzeminska et al., 2018], constructive conflict management [Ayoko & Härtel, 2016], trust [Kimberley & Härtel, 2007], diversity openness [Härtel & Fujimoto, 2000], and organizational justice [Kimberley & Härtel, 2007]." Hu and her colleagues (2018) found in particular that psychological safety is a precursor for employee creativity.

The foregoing characteristics of a PWE also establish the climate and culture needed to "guide and shape individual creativity by creating a climate that communicates both the organization's goals regarding creativity and the means to achieve those goals" (Tesluk et al., 1997, p. 27). This idea has been supported in empirical studies by Gouthier and Rhein (2011), who found a positive relationship between "pride in service" and creativity, and Man and Yue (2019), who found that "an emotional culture of joy, companionate love, pride, and gratitude fostered organizational citizenship behavior," including creativity (p. 5). In another study, Matos (2017) found in a field study of the cork industry that a positive relationship between "an emotional culture of joviality" (p. 7) and team leaders' ratings of individual and team creativity. Matos also found that this relationship was mediated by an association between joy and a "cognitive culture of innovation" (p. 16).

The Dynamic and Interactive Nature of Emotions and Creativity across the Five Levels

In this chapter so far, we have discussed how emotions relate to creativity and creative behavior across the five levels set out by Ashkanasy (2003a) in the FLMEW, which we represent in Figure 31.1 as five concentric enclosing layers. Ashkanasy and Dorris (2017) emphasize, however, that the levels in the FLMEW should not be considered as static and isolated. Instead, they are both interrelated and dynamic. In this regard, the authors note that emotions and affect in organizations are constantly changing. In the following, we discuss the dynamic and interactive nature of emotions in the FLMEW model.

Creativity as a Dynamic Feature of the FLMEW Model

As we noted earlier in this chapter, creativity in organizations is not a static concept. Moreover, this dynamism is present at all levels in the model, beginning with Level 1 where, according to the tenets of AET (Weiss & Cropanzano, 1996), emotions and affect are continuously varying. Indeed, this is the main reason researchers prior to the 1990s tended to steer clear of this field (see Ashforth & Humphrey, 1995).

In effect, just as creativity can vary at the individual level, it can also do so at the level of teams or even the organization overall. In this regard, Ashkanasy and Härtel (2014) argue that, even when an organization exhibits a generally healthy PWE, organizational members and teams still have to deal with the usual disappointments and setbacks; and that these experiences are likely to result in (state) negativity and stress. Thus, while a positive culture and PWE provide a level of resilience, it is still incumbent on organizational leaders to show their positive support to organizational members (Härtel & Ganegoda, 2008).

Moreover, and as we also noted earlier, creativity is not necessarily associated with positive affect. In this regard, employees often need to act creatively to turn a difficult situation around, especially when the usual approaches are not working. In two field studies, To and his colleagues (To et al., 2012; To, Fisher et al., 2015) reported finding that, although positive affect is normally a driver of creative effort (cf. Isen et al., 1987), difficult (i.e., negative affect) situations can result in the highest levels of creative effort, especially when a problem is especially difficult to solve.

Cross-Level Effects in the FLMEW

As a final point, and consistent with Ashkanasy and his colleagues (Ashkanasy, 2003a, 2003b; Ashkanasy & Dorris, 2017; Ashkanasy & Humphrey, 2011a, 2011b), it is important to emphasize that effects at each of the levels in the model cross over to affect processes at other levels in a complex, interacting web (see also To, Tse et al., 2015). For example, the dynamic processes at Level 1 of the model are determined in part by employees' individual differences (at Level 2 of the model), the way that employees communicate their affect and creative ideas (Level 3), as well as what is going on at the level of teams (Level 4) and the organization as a whole (Level 5). For example, Sung and Choi (2021) found that leadership (a Level 4 phenomenon) affects creative behavior of team members via supportive versus dominant communication behaviors (at Level 3). Similarly, To et al. (2021) reported finding that "affect heterogeneity" across different team members (at Level 4) affects the level of creativity of the whole team (at Level 4). At the organizational level (Level 5), Maimone and Sinclair (2010) concluded from a case study of creativity (in an automotive manufacturing plant) that affective climate emerges from social interactions (at Level 3) and ultimately serves as the source of processes "fostering or inhibiting organizational creativity" (p. 309).

Future Research

By framing creativity and creative behavior in organizations as effects that can emerge at five levels of analysis suggests some intriguing ideas for future research, especially in view of the dynamic and cross-level effects that we discussed earlier. One facet in particular that creativity researchers have yet to explore is how perceiving and communicating emotion in interpersonal relationships can facilitate or inhibit organizational members' creativity. While Maimone and Sinclair (2010) have identified these processes in their case study analysis, we still need researchers to investigate these effects using more focused methods and measures (cf. Dasborough et al., 2008), especially as they relate to the idea of co-occurring emotional regulation and interpersonal coregulation introduced by Troth and her coauthors (2018). For example, this may be a situation where the ability emotional intelligence of one or both parties might play an important role (cf. Ivcevic & Brackett, 2015; Parke et al., 2015).

More research is also needed to study the dynamic and interactive nature of the processes in the FLMEW as they relate to creativity and creative behavior. The recent study of leadership (Level 4), communication (Level 3), and individual creativity (Levels 1 and 2) conducted by Sung and Choi (2021) provides a useful template for how such research can be conducted.

One area that has yet to be studied empirically is Ashkanasy and Härtel's (2014) notion of fluctuating organizational affective climate. This notion is especially relevant in the context of the 2020–21 COVID-19 pandemic, where organizations across the world have been subject to unexpected and affect-inducing environmental conditions. The rapid emergence of COVID-19 vaccines attests (see Diamond & Pierson, 2020) to the creative energy generated via adversity and the consequential negative affect.

Conclusion

In this chapter, we sought to provide an overview of the literature on emotions and creativity (and creative behavior) in terms of the FLMEW (Ashkanasy, 2003a). According to this model, employees respond to their environment via their experience of fluctuations in their affective states over time (i.e., at the within-person level). Depending in part on employees' individual differences (e.g., trait affect, emotional intelligence), these affective experiences determine their attitudes and behavior, including their level of creativity that then carry across to affect team creativity and the level of creativity of the organization as a whole. A feature of the FLMEW is that it is not static, and processes do not occur in isolation; instead, they fluctuate across the five levels, and vary moment by moment and day by day. Understanding these highly dynamic and interactive processes clearly represents a challenge for scholars seeking to understand the drivers of creativity and creative behavior in today's organizations.

In conclusion, while creative behaviors are often seen to stem from positivity and a positive work environment (PWE, Härtel, 2008), we argue that the reality is much more complex than this. Creativity can sometimes result from negative emotions, and especially those that emerge in difficult situations. Over the long haul, however, we argue that creative behavior and creativity in organizations are generally an outcome of positive organizational cultures, positive leadership practices, and positive HRM (human resource management) policies.

References

Amabile, T. M., Barsade, S. G., Mueller, J. S., & Staw, B. M. (2005). Affect and creativity at work. *Administrative Science Quarterly*, *50*, 367–403. https://doi.org/10.2189/asqu.2005.50.3.367

Ashforth, B. E., & Humphrey, R. H. (1995). Emotion in the workplace: A reappraisal. *Human Relations*, *48*, 97–125. https://doi.org/10.1177/001872679504800201

Ashkanasy, N. M. (2003a). Emotions in organizations: A multi-level perspective. In F. Dansereau, F. J. Yammarino (Eds.), *Research in Multi-Level Issues in Strategy and Methods* (vol. 2, pp. 9–54). Emerald Group. https://doi.org/10.1016/s1475-9144(03)02002-2

Ashkanasy, N. M. (2003b). Emotions at multiple levels: An integration. In F. Dansereau and F. J. Yammarino (Eds.), *Research in Multi-Level Issues in Strategy and Methods* (vol. 2, pp. 71–81. Emerald Group. https://doi.org/10.1016/s1475-9144(03)02005-8

Ashkanasy, N. M., & Dorris, A. D. (2017). Emotion in the workplace. *Annual Review of Organizational Psychology and Organizational Behavior*, *4*, 67–90. https://doi.org/10.1146/annurev-orgpsych-032516-113231

Ashkanasy, N. M., & Härtel, C. E. (2014). Positive and negative affective climate and culture: The good, the bad, and the ugly. In B. Schneider, & K. Barbera (Eds.), *Oxford Handbook of Organizational Climate and Culture* (pp. 136–152). Oxford University Press. https://doi.org/10.1093/oxfordhb/9780199860715.013.0008

Ashkanasy, N. M., Härtel, C. E. J., & Bialkowski, A. (2020). Affective climate and organization-level emotion management. In Yang, L-Q., Cropanzano, R. S., Martinez-Tur, V., & Daus, C. A. (Eds). *The Cambridge Handbook of Workplace Affect* (pp. 375–385). Cambridge University Press. https://doi.org/10.1017/9781108573887.029

Ashkanasy, N. M., & Humphrey, R. H. (2011a). Current emotion research in organizational behavior. *Emotion Review*, *3*, 214–224. https://doi.org/10.1177/1754073910391684

Ashkanasy, N. M., & Humphrey, R. H. (2011b). A multi-level view of leadership and emotions: Leading with emotional labor. In A. Bryman, D. Collinson, K. Grint, B. Jackson, & M. Uhl-Bien (eds.), *Sage Handbook of Leadership* (pp. 363–377). Sage.

Averill, J. R. (1999). Individual differences in emotional creativity: Structure and correlates. *Journal of Personality*, *67*, 331–371. https://doi.org/10.1111/1467-6494.00058

Ayoko, O. B., & Härtel, C. E. J. (2016). The role of emotions and emotion management in destructive and productive conflict in culturally heterogeneous workgroups. In N. M. Ashkanasy, W. J. Zerbe, & C. E. J. Härtel (Eds.), *Managing Emotions in the Workplace* (pp. 77–97). ME Sharpe. https://doi.org/10.4324/9781315290812-14

Baas, M., De Dreu, C. K., & Nijstad, B. A. (2008). A meta-analysis of 25 years of mood-creativity research: Hedonic tone, activation, or regulatory focus? *Psychological Bulletin*, *134*, 779–806. ttps://doi.org/10.1037/a0012815

Baron-Cohen, S., Wheelwright, S., Hill, J., Raste, Y., & Plumb, I. (2001). The "Reading the Mind in the Eyes" test revised version: A study with normal adults, and adults with Asperger syndrome or high-functioning autism. *Journal Of Child Psychology and Psychiatry, 42*, 241–251. https://doi.org/10.1111/1469-7610 .00715

Barsade, S. G. (2002). The ripple effect: Emotional contagion and its influence on group behavior. *Administrative Science Quarterly, 47*(4), 644–675. https://doi.org/10 .2307/3094912

Barsade, S. G. & Knight, A. P. (2015). Group affect. *The Annual Review of Organizational Psychology and Organizational Behavior, 2*, 21–46. https://doi .org/10.1146/annurev-orgpsych-032414-111316

Barsade, S. G., Ward, A. J., Turner, J. D., & Sonnenfeld, J. A. (2000). To your heart's content: A model of affective diversity in top management teams. *Administrative Science Quarterly, 45*, 802–836. https://doi.org/10.2307/2667020

Binnewies, C., & Wörnlein, S. C. (2011). What makes a creative day? A diary study on the interplay between affect, job stressors, and job control. *Journal of Organizational Behavior, 32*, 589–607. https://doi.org/10.1002/job.731

Bledow, R., Rosing, K., & Frese, M. (2013). A dynamic perspective on affect and creativity. *Academy of Management Journal, 56*, 432–450. https://doi.org/10 .1037/e518392013-355

Bledow, R., Schmitt, A., Frese, M., & Kuehnel, J. (2011). The affective shift model of work engagement. *Journal of Applied Psychology, 96*, 1246–1257. https://doi .org/10.1037/a0024532

Clark, L. A., Watson, D., & Leeka, J. (1989). Diurnal variation in the positive affects. *Motivation and Emotion, 13*, 205–234. https://doi.org/10.1007/bf00995536

Cole, M. S., Walter, F., & Bruch, H. (2008). Affective mechanisms linking dysfunctional behavior to performance in work teams: A moderated mediation study. *Journal of Applied Psychology, 93*, 945–958. https://doi.org/10.1037/0021-9010.93.5.945

Collins, A. L., Lawrence, S. A., Troth, A. C., & Jordan, P. J. (2013). Group affective tone: A review and future research directions. *Journal of Organizational Behavior, 34*, 43–62. https://doi.org/10.1002/job.1887

Collins, B. J., Munyon, T. P., Ashkanasy, N. M., et al. (2013, November). Positive affective asymmetry, process quality, and team decision-making effectiveness. Paper presented at the Annual Meeting of the Southern Management Association, New Orleans, Louisiana, USA.

Cummings, A., & Oldham, G. R. (1997). Enhancing creativity: Managing work contexts for the high potential employee. *California Management Review, 40*(1), 22–38. https://doi.org/10.2307/41165920

Dalal, R. S., Baysinger, M., Brummel, B. J., & LeBreton, J. M. (2012). The relative importance of employee engagement, other job attitudes, and trait affect as predictors of job performance. *Journal of Applied Social Psychology, 42*, E295–E325. https://doi.org/10.1111/j.1559-1816.2012.01017.x

Dasborough, M. T., Sinclair, M., Russell-Bennett, R., & Tombs, A. (2008). Measuring emotion: Methodological issues and alternatives. In N. M. Ashkanasy & C. L. Cooper (Eds.), *Research Companion to Emotions in Organizations* (pp 197–210). Edwin Elgar. https://doi.org/10.4337/9781848443778.00021

De Clercq, D., & Belausteguigoitia, I. (2019). Reducing the harmful effect of work overload on creative behavior: Buffering roles of energy-enhancing resources. *Creativity and Innovation Management, 28*, 5–18. https://doi.org/10.1111/caim .12278

De Dreu, C. K. W., Baas, M., & Nijstad, B. A. (2008). Hedonic tone and activation level in the mood–creativity link: Toward a dual pathway to creativity model. *Journal of Personality and Social Psychology, 94*, 739–756. https://doi.org/10.1037/0022-3514.94.5.739

de Rivera J. (1992). Emotional climate: Social structure and emotional dynamics. *International Review of Studies on Emotions, 2*, 197–218.

Diamond, M. S., & Pierson, T. C. (2020). The challenges of vaccine development against a new virus during a pandemic. *Cell Host & Microbe, 27*, 699–703. https://doi.org/10.1016/j.chom.2020.04.021

Diefendorff, J. M., & Richard, E. M. (2003). Antecedents and consequences of emotional display rule perceptions. *Journal of Applied Psychology, 88*, 284–294. https://doi.org/10.1037/0021-9010.88.2.284

Fisher, C.D., Minbashian, A., Beckmann, N., & Wood, R.E. (2013). Task appraisals, emotions, and performance goal orientation. *Journal of Applied Psychology, 98*, 364–373. https://doi.org/10.1037/a0031260

Forgas, J. P. (2002). Feeling and doing· Affective influences on interpersonal behavior. *Psychological Inquiry, 13*, 1–28. https://doi.org/10.1207/s15327965pli1301_01

Fredrickson, B. L. (2001). The role of positive emotions in positive psychology: The broaden-and-build theory of positive emotions. *American Psychologist, 56*, 218–226. https://doi.org/10.1037/0003-066x.56.3.218

Friedman, R. S., & Förster, J. (2010). Implicit affective cues and attentional tuning: An integrative review. *Psychological Bulletin, 136*, 875–893. https://doi.org/10.1037/a0020495

Frijda, N. H. (1986). *The Emotions*. Cambridge University Press.

Geher, G., Betancourt, K., & Jewell, O. (2017). The link between emotional intelligence and creativity. *Imagination, Cognition and Personality, 37*, 5–22. https://doi.org/10.1177/0276236617710029

George, J. M. (1990). Personality, affect, and behavior in groups. *Journal of Applied Psychology, 75*, 107–116. https://doi.org/10.1037/0021-9010.75.2.107

George, J. M. (2000). Emotions and leadership: The role of emotional intelligence. *Human Relations, 53*, 1027-1055. https://doi.org/10.1177/0018726700538001

George, J. M., & King, E. B. (2007). Potential pitfalls of affect convergence in teams: Functions and dysfunctions of group affective tone. In E. A. Mannix, M. A. Neale, & C. P. Anderson (Eds.), *Research on Managing Groups and Teams* (vol. 10, pp. 97–123). Elsevier. https://doi.org/10.1016/s1534–0856(07)10005-0

George, J. M., & Zhou, J. (2002). Understanding when bad moods foster creativity and good ones don't: The role of context and clarity and feeling. *Journal of Applied Psychology, 87*, 687–697. https://doi.org/10.1037/0021-9010.87.4.687

George, J. M., & Zhou, J. (2007). Dual Tuning in a supportive context: Joint contribution of positive mood, negative mood, and supervisory behaviors to employee creativity. *Academy of Management Journal, 50*, 605–622. https://doi.org/10.5465/amj.2007.25525934

Gilmore, P. L., Hu, X., Wei, F., Tetrick, L. E., & Zaccaro, S. J. (2013). Positive affectivity neutralizes transformational leadership's influence on creative performance and organizational citizenship behaviors. *Journal of Organizational Behavior, 34*, 1061–1075. https://doi.org/10.1002/job.1833

Gooty, J., Connelly, S., Griffith, J., & Gupta, A. (2010). Leadership, affect and emotions: A state of the science review. *The Leadership Quarterly*, *21*(6), 979–1004. https://doi.org/10.1016/j.leaqua.2010.10.005

Gouthier, M. H., & Rhein, M. (2011). Organizational pride and its positive effects on employee behavior. *Journal of Service Management*, *22*, 633–649. https://doi.org/10.1108/09564231111174988

Grandey, A. A. (2000). Emotional regulation in the workplace: A new way to conceptualize emotional labor. *Journal of Occupational Health Psychology*, *5*, 59–100. https://doi.org/10.1037/1076-8998.5.1.95

Grawitch, M. J., Munz, D. C., Elliott, E. K., & Mathis, A. (2003). Promoting creativity in temporary problem-solving groups: The effects of positive mood and autonomy in problem definition on idea-generating performance. *Group Dynamics: Theory, Research, and Practice*, *7*, 200–213. https://doi.org/10.1037/1089-2699.7.3.200

Grawitch, M. J., Munz, D. C., & Kramer, T. J. (2003). Effects of member mood states on creative performance in temporary workgroups. *Group Dynamics: Theory, Research, and Practice*, *7*, 41–54. https://doi.org/10.1037/1089-2699.7.1.41

Härtel, C. E., & Ashkanasy, N. M. (2011). Healthy human cultures as positive work environments. In N. M. Ashkanasy, C. E. P. Wilderom, & M. F. Peterson (Eds.), *The SAGE Handbook of Organizational Culture and Climate* (pp. 85–100). Sage. https://doi.org/10.4135/9781483307961.n6

Härtel, C. E., & Fujimoto, Y. (2000). Diversity is not the problem. Openness to perceived dissimilarity is. *Journal of Management & Organization*, *6*, 14-27. https://doi.org/10.1017/s1833367200005484

Härtel, C. E. J. (2008). How to build a healthy emotional culture and avoid a toxic culture. In C. L. Cooper & N. M. Ashkanasy (Eds.), *Research Companion to Emotion in Organizations* (pp. 575–588). Edwin Elgar. https://doi.org/10.4337/9781848443778.00049

Härtel, C. E. J., & Ganegoda, D. B. (2008). Role of affect and interactional justice in moral leadership. In W. J. Zerbe, C. E. J. Härtel, & N. M. Ashkanasy (Eds.), *Research on Emotion in Organizations* (vol. 4, pp. 155–180). Emerald. https://doi.org/10.1016/s1746–9791(08)04007-8

Hatfield, E., Cacioppo, J. T., & Rapson, R. L. (1993). Emotional contagion. *Current Directions in Psychological Science*, *2*, 96–100. https://doi.org/10.1111/1467-8721.ep10770953

Hargadon, A. B., & Bechky, B. A. (2006). When collections of creatives become creative collectives: A field study of problem solving at work. *Organization Science*, *17*, 484–500. https://doi.org/10.1287/orsc.1060.0200

Hennessey, B. A., & Amabile, T. A. (2010). Creativity. *Annual Review of Psychology*, *61*, 569–598. https://doi.org/10.1146/annurev.psych.093008.100416

Hochschild, A. R. (1983/2012). *The Managed Heart: Commercialization of Human Feeling*. University of California Press. https://doi.org/10.1525/9780520951853

Hu, J., Erdogan, B., Jiang, K., Bauer, T. N., & Liu, S. (2018). Leader humility and team creativity: the role of team information sharing, psychological safety, and power distance. *Journal of Applied Psychology*, *103*, 313–323. https://doi.org/10.1037/apl0000277

Huang, L., Krasikova, D. V., & Liu, D. (2016). I can do it, so can you: The role of leader creative self-efficacy in facilitating follower creativity. *Organizational Behavior and Human Decision Processes*, *132*, 49–62. https://doi.org/10.1016/j.obhdp .2015.12.002

Humphrey, R. H. (2002). The many faces of emotional leadership. *The Leadership Quarterly*, *13* 493–504. https://doi.org/10.1016/s1048–9843(02)00140-6

Ivcevic, Z., & Brackett, M. (2015). Predicting creativity: Interactive effects of openness to experience and emotion regulation ability. *Psychology of Aesthetics, Creativity, and the Arts*, *9*, 480–487. https://doi.org/10.1037/a0039826

Ivcevic, Z., Brackett, M. A., & Mayer, J. D. (2007). Emotional intelligence and emotional creativity. *Journal of Personality*, *75*, 199–236. https://doi.org/10.1111/j .1467-6494.2007.00437.x

Isen, A. (1999). On the relationship between affect and creative problem solving. In S. W. Russ (Ed.), *Affect, Creative Experience and Psychological Adjustment* (pp. 3–18). Brunner/Mazel. https://doi.org/10.4324/9781315784557

Isen, A. M., Daubman, K. A., & Nowicki, G. P. (1987). Positive affect facilitates creative problem solving. *Journal of Personality and Social Psychology*, *52*, 1122–1131. https://doi.org/10.1037/0022-3514.52.6.1122

Jones, E. E., & Kelly, J. R. (2009). No pain, no gains: Negative mood leads to process gains in idea-generation groups. *Group Dynamics: Theory, Research and Practice*, *13*, 75–88. https://doi.org/10.1037/a0013812

Jordan, P. J., Ashkanasy, N. M., & Härtel, C. E. J. (2002). Emotional intelligence as a moderator of emotional and behavioral reactions to job insecurity. *The Academy of Management Review*, *27*, 361–372. https://doi.org/10.5465/amr .2002.7389905

Jordan, P. J., Ashkanasy, N. M., & Lawrence, S. A. (in press). Job insecurity, emotional skills, workplace emotional reactions, and decision-making behaviors. In R. H. Humphrey, N. M. Ashkanasy, & A. C. Troth (Eds.), *Research on Emotion in Organizations* (vol. 17). Emerald Group.

Kaplan, S., LaPort, K., & Waller, M. J. (2013). The role of positive affectivity in team effectiveness during crises. *Journal of Organizational Behavior*, *34*, 473–491. https://doi.org/10.1002/job.1817

Kelly, J. R., & Spoor, J. R. (2007). Naïve theories about the effects of mood in groups: A preliminary investigation. *Group Processes and Intergroup Relations*, *10*, 203–222. https://doi.org/10.1177/1368430207074727

Khattak, M. N., Zolin, R., & Muhammad, N. (2020). The combined effect of perceived organizational injustice and perceived politics on deviant behaviors. *International Journal of Conflict Management*, *32*, 62–87. https://doi.org/10 .1108/ijcma-12-2019-0220

Kim, M. J., Choi, J. N., & Lee, K. (2016). Trait affect and individual creativity: Moderating roles of affective climate and reflexivity. *Social Behavior and Personality: An International Journal*, *44*, 1477–1498. https://doi.org/10.2224/ sbp.2016.44.9.1477

Kimberley, N. & Härtel, C. E. J. (2007). Building a climate of trust during organizational change: The mediating role of justice perceptions and emotion. In C. E. J Härtel, N. M. Ashkanasy & W. J. Zerbe (Eds.). *Research on Emotion in Organizations: Functionality, Intentionality and Morality* (pp. 237–264). Elsevier Science. https://doi.org/10.1016/s1746–9791(07)03010-6

Klep, A., Wisse, B., & Van der Flier, H. (2011). Interactive affective sharing versus non-interactive affective sharing in work groups: Comparative effects of group affect on work group performance and dynamics. *European Journal of Social Psychology*, *41*, 312–323. https://doi.org/10.1002/ejsp.775

Krzeminska, A., Lim, J., & Härtel, C. E. J. (2018). Psychological capital and occupational stress in emergency services teams: empowering effects of servant leadership and workgroup emotional climate. In L. Petitta, C. E. J. Härtel, N. M. Ashkanasy, & W. Zerbe (Eds.), *Research on Emotion in Organizations* (vol. 14, pp. 189–215). Emerald Group. https://doi.org/10.1108/s1746–979120180000014017

Lelieveld, G. J., Van Dijk, E., Van Beest, I., & Van Kleef, G. A. (2012). Why anger and disappointment affect other's bargaining behavior differently: The moderating role of power and the mediating role of reciprocal and complementary emotions. *Personality and Social Psychology Bulletin*, *38*(9), 1209–1221. https://doi.org/10.1177/0146167212446938

Lopes, P. N., Grewal, D., Kadis, J., Gall, M., & Salovey, P. (2006). Evidence that emotional intelligence is related to job performance and affect and attitudes at work. *Psicothema*, *18*(Supplement), 132–138. https://doi.org/10.1037/e514412014–138

Luksyte, A., & Spitzmueller, C. (2016). When are overqualified employees creative? It depends on contextual factors. *Journal of Organizational Behavior*, *37*, 635–653. https://doi.org/10.1002/job.2054

Maimone, F., & Sinclair, M. (2010). Affective climate, organizational creativity, and knowledge creation: Case study of an automotive company. In W. J. Zerbe, C. E. J. Härtel, & N. M. Ashkanasy (Eds.), *Research on Emotion in Organizations* (vol. 6, pp. 309–332). Emerald. https://doi.org/10.1108/s1746–9791(2010)0000006016

Martin, L. L., & Stoner, P. (1996). Mood as input: What we think about how we feel determines how we think. In L. L. Martin & A. Tesser (Eds.), *Striving and Feelings: Interactions among Goals, Affect, and Self-Regulation* (pp. 279–301). Erlbaum.

Matos, F. (2017). Foundations of *Creativity* in the *Workplace*: The *Impact* of *Cognitive* and *Emotional Culture* on *Creativity*. Unpublished doctoral dissertation. Católica-Lisbon School of Business & Econmics.

Mayer, J. D., & Salovey, P. (1997). What is emotional intelligence? In P. Salovey & D. Sluyter (Eds.), *Emotional Development and Emotional Intelligence: Implications for Educators* (pp. 3–31). Basic Books.

Mayer, J. D., Salovey, P., & Caruso, D. (2002). *MSCEIT Item Booklet Version 2.0*. Multi-Health Systems.

Miron-Spektor, E., Gino, F., & Argote, L. (2011). Paradoxical frames and creative sparks: Enhancing individual creativity through conflict and integration. *Organizational Behavior and Human Decision Processes*, *116*, 229–240. https://doi.org/10.1016/j.obhdp.2011.03.006

Mumford, M. D., Hester, K. S., & Robledo, I. C. (2012). Creativity in organizations: Importance and approaches. In M. D. Mumford (Ed.), *Handbook of Organizational Creativity* (pp. 3–16). Academic Press. https://doi.org/10.1016/b978–0-12-374714-3.00001-x

Nijstad, B. A., De Dreu, C. K. W., Rietzschel, E. F., & Baas, M. (2010). The dual pathway to creativity model: Creative ideation as a function of flexibility and persistence. *European Review of Social Psychology*, *21*, 34-77. https://doi.org/10.1080/10463281003765323

Parke, M. R., Seo, M.-G., & Sherf, E. N. (2015). Regulating and facilitating: The role of emotional intelligence in maintaining and using positive affect for creativity. *Journal of Applied Psychology, 100*, 917–934. https://doi.org/10.1037/a0038452

Petrides, K. V., Pérez-González, J. C., & Furnham, A. (2007). On the criterion and incremental validity of trait emotional intelligence. *Cognition and Emotion, 21*, 26–55. https://doi.org/10.1080/02699930601038912

Pizer, M. K., & Härtel, C. E. J. (2005). For better or for worse: Organizational culture and emotions. In C. E. J. Härtel, W. J. Zerbe & N. M. Ashkanasy (Eds.), *Emotions in Organizational Behavior* (pp. 342–361). Erlbaum. https://doi.org/10.4324/9781410611895-30

Rank, J., & Frese, M. (2008). The impact of emotions, moods, and other affect-related variables on creativity, innovation and initiative in organizations. In N. M. Ashkanasy & C. P. Cooper (Eds.), *Research Companion to Emotion in Organizations* (pp. 103–119). Edward Elgar. https://doi.org/10.4337/9781848443778.00014

Sánchez-Ruiz, M. J., Hernández-Torrano, D., Pérez-González, J. C., Batey, M., & Petrides, K. V. (2011). The relationship between trait emotional intelligence and creativity across subject domains. *Motivation and Emotion, 35*, 461–473. https://doi.org/10.1007/s11031-011-9227-8

Schein, E. (1992). *Organizational Culture and Leadership*. Jossey-Bass.

Schneider, B., Ehrhart, M. G., & Macey, W. H. (2011). Organizational climate research: Achievements and the road ahead. In N. M. Ashkanasy, C. E. P. Wilderom, & M. F. Peterson (Eds.), *The SAGE Handbook of Organizational Culture and Climate* (2nd ed., pp. 29–49). Sage. https://doi.org/10.4135/9781483307961.n3

Schwarz, N., & Clore, G. (2003). Mood as information: 20 years later. *Psychological Inquiry, 14*, 296–303. https://doi.org/10.1080/1047840x.2003.9682896

Seo, M., Barrett, L. F., & Bartunek, J. M. (2004). The role of affective experience in work motivation. *Academy of Management Review, 29*, 423–439. https://doi.org/10.5465/amr.2004.13670972

Shin, Y. (2014). Positive group affect and team creativity: Mediation of team reflexivity and promotion focus. *Small Group Research, 45*, 337–364. https://doi.org/10.1177/1046496414533618

Sung, S. Y., & Choi, J. N. (2021). Leader status behaviors and team creativity: The role of collective interactions and status conflict among members. *Journal of Organizational Behavior, 42*, 1120–1133. https://doi.org/10.1002/job.2551

Sy, T., Côté, S., & Saavedra, R. (2005). The contagious leader: Impact of the leader's mood on the mood of group members, group affective tone, and group processes. *Journal of Applied Psychology, 90*, 295–305. https://doi.org/10.1037/0021-9010.90.2.295

Tang, C., & Naumann, S. E. (2016). Team diversity, mood, and team creativity: The role of team knowledge sharing in Chinese R & D teams. *Journal of Management & Organization, 22*(3), 420–434. https://doi.org/10.1017/jmo.2015.43

Tee, E. Y. J., Ashkanasy, N. M., & Paulsen, N. (2013). The influence of follower mood on leader mood and task performance: An affective, follower-centric perspective of leadership. *The Leadership Quarterly, 24*, 496–515. https://doi.org/10.1016/j.leaqua.2013.03.005

Tesluk, P. E., Farr, J. L., & Klein, S. R. (1997). Influences of organizational culture and climate on individual creativity. *The Journal of Creative Behavior, 31*, 27–41.

To, M. L., & Fisher, C. D. (2019). Affective influences on creativity in teams. In P. B. Paulus & B. A. Nijstad (Eds.), *The Oxford Handbook of Group Creativity and Innovation* (pp. 102–117). Oxford University Press. https://doi.org/10.1093/oxfordhb/9780190648077.013.7

To, M. L., Fisher, C. D., & Ashkanasy, N. M. (2015). Unleashing angst: Negative mood, learning goal orientation, psychological empowerment and creative behavior. *Human relations, 68,* 1601–1622. https://doi.org/10.1177/0018726714562235

To, M. L., Fisher, C. D., Ashkanasy, N. M., & Rowe, P. A. (2012). Within-person relationships between mood and creativity. *Journal of Applied Psychology, 97,* 519–612. https://doi.org/10.1037/a0026097

To, M. L., Fisher, C. D., Ashkanasy, N. M., & Zhou, J. (2021). Feeling differently, creating together: Affect heterogeneity and creativity in project teams. *Journal of Organizational Behavior.* https://doi.org/10.1002/job.2535

To, M. L., Tse, H. M., & Ashkanasy, N. M. (2015). A multilevel model of transformational leadership, affect, and creative process behavior in work teams. *Leadership Quarterly, 26,* 543–556. https://doi.org/10.1016/j.leaqua.2015.05.005

Troth, A. C., Lawrence, S. A., Jordan, P. J., & Ashkanasy, N. M. (2018). Interpersonal emotion regulation in the workplace: A conceptual and operational review and future research agenda. *International Journal of Management Reviews, 20,* 523–543. https://doi.org/10.1111/ijmr.12144

Tsai, W. C., Chi, N. W., Grandey, A. A., & Fung, S. C. (2012). Positive group affective tone and team creativity: Negative group affective tone and team trust as boundary conditions. *Journal of Organizational Behavior, 33,* 638–656. https://doi.org/10.1002/job.775

Van Kleef, G. A. (2014). Understanding the positive and negative effects of emotional expressions in organizations: EASI does it. *Human Relations, 67(9),* 1145–1164. https://doi.org/10.1177/0018726713510329

Van Kleef, G. A., De Dreu, C. K., & Manstead, A. S. (2010). An interpersonal approach to emotion in social decision making: The emotions as social information model. In P. Zanna (Ed.), *Advances in Experimental Social Psychology* (vol. 42, pp. 45–96). Academic Press.

VandeWalle, D., Cron, W. L., & Slocum Jr, J. W. (2001). The role of goal orientation following performance feedback. *Journal of Applied Psychology, 86,* 629–640. https://doi.org/10.1037/0021-9010.86.4.629

Watson, D., Clark. L. A., & Tellegen, A. (1988). Development and validation of brief measures of positive and negative affect: The PANAS scales. *Journal of Personality and Social Psychology, 54,* 1063–1070. https://doi.org/10.1037/0022-3514.54.6.1063

Watson, D., & Tellegen, A. (1985). Toward a consensual structure of mood. *Psychological Bulletin, 98,* 219–235. https://doi.org/10.1037/0033-2909.98.2.219

Wegener, D., & Petty, R. (1994). Mood management across affective states: The hedonic contingency hypothesis. *Journal of Personality and Social Psychology, 66,* 1034–1048. https://doi.org/10.1037/0022-3514.66.6.1034

Weiss, H. M., & Cropanzano, R. (1996). Affective Events Theory: A theoretical discussion of the structure, causes and consequences of affective experiences at work. In B. M. Staw & L. L. Cummings (Eds.), *Research in Organizational Behavior* (vol. 18, pp. 1–74). Elsevier Science.

Wubben, M. J., De Cremer, D., & Van Dijk, E. (2009). How emotion communication guides reciprocity: Establishing cooperation through disappointment and anger. *Journal of Experimental Social Psychology*, *45*, 987–990. https://doi.org/10.1016/j.jesp.2009.04.010

Zaki, J., & Williams, W. C. (2013). Interpersonal emotion regulation. *Emotion*, *13*(5), 803–810. https://doi.org/10.1037/a0033839

32 Creativity and Emotion

Connecting the Dots

Zorana Ivcevic, Shengjie Lin, James C. Kaufman, and
Jessica D. Hoffmann

What is the role of emotions in creativity? This volume suggests that the question, as posed in this way, might not be useful. Rather, the question needs to be specified. The chapters in this Handbook address different aspects of this umbrella question, examining various aspects of creativity and affective processes. Asking good questions is part of the creative process – problem identification and construction – and each chapter poses multiple questions. In systematizing them, we employ the common distinction among creative process, person, product, and press (defined as contexts for creativity). In this chapter, we aim to provide an overview of the questions asked across the Handbook, delineate key areas for future research, and offer an integrative model of affective processes across different aspects of creativity.

The first question asked in the domain of this volume was which emotion states facilitate and which emotion states hinder creative thinking (Isen, 1999; Isen & Daubman, 1984). This now-classic research used experimental methods of mood induction (see Baas, Chapter 1) to manipulate emotion states, followed by creative thinking tasks (associative thinking, divergent thinking, and insight problem solving). These research questions were at first considered in terms of the dichotomy valence between positive and negative moods, which was subsequently redefined to add the dimension of activation and examine positive/negative activated/deactivated states (Madrid et al., Chapter 5). Problem definition influences answers to research questions. Thus, what seemed to be a benefit of positive moods for creative thinking turned out to be only a benefit of positive activated moods. This research also revealed the importance of negative activated moods on creative thinking and creative process engagement.

Although experimental research has its benefits (drawing causal conclusions being the chief one), it has major drawbacks as well. Experimental methods have been useful in neuroscientific studies, offering clues about neuroanatomical and functional correlates of emotion states and creative thinking (Chrysikou et al.,

This chapter was made possible with the support by the Botin Foundation (Emotions, Creativity and the Arts grant to Zorana Ivcevic).

Chapter 6) and the intersection of emotion and attention in creative thinking (Kane et al., Chapter 7). However, experimental methods cannot address questions about how affective processes impact long-term creative work. Because much real-life creativity requires engagement lasting days to months or even longer, rather than minutes, experimental methods need to be supplemented.

Case study and observational methods are key for generating hypotheses to understand creativity in real-life contexts. Case studies (Hanson et al., Chapter 2) offer an opportunity for in-depth analysis of creative work embedded in the specific sociocultural context. This research can provide rich material for theory building that is grounded in recognized creative contributions. For this approach to be maximally useful, scholars should be purposefully choosing who is studied and include individuals across different levels of creativity (mini-c to Big-C) and individuals of diverse social backgrounds (in terms of their gender, socioeconomic status, racial, ethnic, and cultural background). Katz-Buonincontro (Chapter 3) illustrates the need to specify affective processes and what aspects of creativity are observed. Consequently, conclusions should be made only about those specific aspects and not about creativity and emotion in general.

Qualitative studies are still relatively rare in creativity and emotion research. Their expanded use can enrich creativity studies by pointing to new questions. Botella (Chapter 11) reviewed research that used interview methods to study affective processes across domains. Such research illustrated the broad range of emotions experienced during the course of creative work (which could not be captured in experimental research) and suggests that the traditional questions about which emotions are beneficial and which are detrimental to creativity might not be the best ways to define the problem of the role affective processes play across different aspects of creativity. A new direction for research could examine emotion abilities and processes of using and regulating emotions to facilitate creative work.

Specification in the study of creativity and affective processes is crucial across research questions and methods used. Specification is necessary to start building an understanding of which affective processes predict which aspects of creativity. Ivcevic (Chapter 12) shows that emotion traits, such as extraversion, neuroticism, or trait emotional intelligence, predict self-perceptions of creativity and creative behavior that are accumulated over time better than they predict creative idea generation (e.g., performance on divergent thinking tests). This difference in prediction is not a sign of poor consistency of findings; rather, it is pointing to the fact that different psychological processes are relevant for some but not other aspects of creativity. A useful framework to guide research in connecting affective processes on one hand and aspects of creativity on the other hand is that of Brunswik symmetry, which posits that the most relevant predictors will be those of similar breadth and generality to the outcomes of interest. This framework explains why divergent thinking is less well predicted by emotion traits than self-perceptions of creativity are predicted by the same traits; divergent thinking scores are based on performance on brief tasks assessed at one point in time and emotion traits refer to typical ways of feeling (across time and situations).

The study of creativity and emotions needs more longitudinal studies, both relatively short-term longitudinal studies of individuals working on specific creative projects (e.g., To et al., 2012) and long-term studies that can examine questions such as the role of emotion traits and emotion abilities in regulating and sustaining effort, as well as in forming and maintaining relationships that influence individual or team creativity (Connelly & Demirag Burak, Chapter 30; Karwowski, Chapter 25; Lebuda et al., Chapter 16; Reiter-Palmon & Millier, Chapter 29). Ashkanasy and To (Chapter 31) explicitly point to the changes in affective processes relevant to creativity over time, but these changes are insufficiently studied.

Emotion and the Creative Process

The creative process is an umbrella term for a set of processes, including problem finding and definition, idea generation, idea evaluation and selection, and implementation or verification (Mumford & McIntosh, 2017). Yet, much of what we know about the role of affective processes in creativity is limited to idea generation, usually assessed by tests of divergent thinking or problem solving. We have learned much about this aspect of the creative process (Madrid et al., Chapter 5). Both positive activated moods and negative activated moods help idea generation, and it seems that they do so through different pathways, either by supporting flexibility or persistence (De Dreu et al., 2008). Kane and colleagues (Chapter 7) discuss specifically how affective processes influence attention during the creative process. Although there is reliable support for affective processes (positive activated moods, open-monitoring meditation and mind-wandering as emotion regulation processes) in broadening attention and facilitating divergent thinking, the mechanisms of affect and attention in convergent creative thinking, such as selection and evaluation, are less clear.

The role of affective processes in problem finding, evaluation, implementation, and verification remains largely unexamined. Similar to idea generation, we can hypothesize that problem finding would benefit from either positive activated or negative activated moods. In addition to the emotions, a relevant variable is also likely to be the emotion source. Negative energized emotions could be more beneficial to problem finding when they are relevant to the creative task than if they are unrelated to the task. For instance, problem finding aimed at identifying potential new features for smartphones might be more successful if emotion is induced by recalling frustrating experiences with a smartphone than if frustration is induced by a neutral task of working on impossible puzzles. Hoffmann and McFarland (Chapter 10) describe how emotional intelligence abilities can help the creative process. Task-relevant activated negative emotions can provide information about problems and draw attention to that which could be an object of either incremental change or radical innovation.

Qualitative studies examining the creative process across domains point to diversity of emotions and obstacles during the development of ideas into products or performances (Glăveanu et al., 2013). This process requires much problem solving that influences creativity – not by facilitating idea generation, but by (a) building environments and relationships that support creativity and (b) enabling persistence of effort toward creative goals. It can be hypothesized that affective processes most relevant to the implementation aspect of the creative process would be those pertaining to emotion abilities. These abilities will not directly help idea generation (and thus not be related to divergent thinking; for instance, Xu et al., 2019), but they will enable individuals to successfully address interpersonal conflict and build psychological safety (Reiter-Palmon & Millier, Chapter 29) and contribute to creative climate and culture (Ashkanasy & To, Chapter 31). Liu and Damian (Chapter 9) present a model that proposed three sets of strategies relevant for managing emotions in the creative process: managing intensity (so it is kept at a moderate level), managing appraisals (so that situations are interpreted as challenges and not threats), and managing adaptive resources (which moderates the effects of experience on the creative outcomes).

Several lines of emotion research are emerging as potentially relevant to the creative process, including work on specific emotions (e.g., boredom), epistemic emotions (e.g., curiosity), other-oriented emotions (e.g., empathic concern), social emotions (e.g., respect), and achievement emotions (e.g., hope). Experience-sampling studies show that deactivated negative mood (including boredom) is negatively related to creative process engagement (To et al., 2012). While the experience of boredom in itself might not help creativity, boredom can trigger regulatory actions that seek creativity as a way to reduce or change the aversive state of boredom (Gasper & Middlewood, 2014; Mann & Cadman, 2014).

Similarly, epistemic and other-oriented emotions can provide new perspectives in problem finding and idea generation, as well as support emotion regulation during implementation (e.g., by providing strategies of putting difficulties in the context of a broader purpose). A meta-analysis shows that both exploration and deprivation sensitivity aspects of curiosity are positively related to self-reported and rated creativity (Schutte & Malouff, 2020). Gross and colleagues (2020) proposed exploratory tendencies and complex information-seeking behavior as potential explanatory mechanisms in the relationship between curiosity and creativity.

Several chapters in this volume are relevant to social emotions. Lebuda and colleagues (Chapter 16) show that social emotions (e.g., embarrassment, pride, shame) may play a regulatory role in the creative process. For instance, when the results of creative activity are ready to be revealed, how individuals feel about what they have achieved (e.g., whether they anticipate social acceptance) may influence their intentions to engage in similar creative attempts in the future. Karwowski (Chapter 25) discusses social acceptance and feelings of belonging in the context of peer relationships as they relate to the creativity of children and adolescents at school. Reiter-Palmon and Millier (Chapter 29) describe psychological safety and related social emotions of trust and respect as forming a basis for creativity at work. Emich and Lu (Chapter 27) and Madrid et al. (Chapter 28) show the role that social emotions, such as fear and anger, play in the climate for creativity in the workplace. Anger is commonly experienced in the workplace when employees' performance is not fairly recognized or rewarded. Because anger is promotion focused (i.e., it moves individuals to action), it encourages exploration of new ideas. The source of anger might be important to consider; if internal to one's work environment, anger may enhance dark creativity (e.g., do harmful things to colleagues or the team; Kapoor & Mange, Chapter 18), whereas anger external to work (e.g., systemic injustice) can bring people together and enhance creativity (Emich & Lu, Chapter 27). These social emotions are based on others' reactions to an individual – whether one is accepted or in danger of being harshly criticized, how colleagues or leaders react to one's work and ideas. Although much research in this area exists in disparate literatures, we still lack a model of social emotions and their role in and across the creative process.

Other-oriented emotions (such as empathic concern) have not been systematically examined in relation to creativity, but several lines of research suggest that they can motivate engagement in the creative process, open up creators to new perspectives when generating ideas, and support persistence through implementation. Forgeard (Chapter 8) describes prosocial motivation as one of the specific motives emerging across studies with different populations. Prosocial motives for creativity are a desire to meaningfully contribute to others' lives through creative work. Social psychological research shows that prosocial motivation is associated with other-oriented emotions, such as empathy (Eisenberg & Miller, 1987). Reflecting this association, the design thinking approach explicitly incorporates empathy as an early step in the creative process that guides problem definition and frames idea generation (Henriksen et al., 2017).

Pekrun (2006) proposed a theory of achievement emotions (including enjoyment, hope, pride, relief, anger, anxiety, shame, hopelessness, and boredom), which argues that individuals' appraisals of control and values give rise to different emotions in academic settings (e.g., test, class, learning). This model has largely been applied to understanding academic achievement, but can be extended to creative achievement (Liu et al., 2021). Future research would benefit from using a framework of achievement emotions to examine concurrent and longitudinal associations with creative process engagement (e.g., employing experience-sampling methods, Cotter, Chapter 4). Such research can complement work on emotion states based on the general models of affect that examine categories of affective experience at the intersection of valence and activation (e.g., positive/negative activated or deactivated affect; Madrid et al., Chapter 5).

Emotion and the Creative Person

Traditionally, the study of the creative person has tended to focus on personality. In this tradition, Ivcevic (Chapter 12) discusses the role of emotion-related traits across different aspects of creativity. Because emotion traits describe typical ways of feeling across situations and time, they are most relevant in predicting aspects of creativity that are also accumulated through time and across situations, such as frequency of creative behavior over a year or creative achievement over a lifetime. The dominance of the Big Five model of personality traits contributed to less emphasis in recent decades on narrower personality traits, such as those specifically concerning emotions. Thus, many questions about emotion traits and creativity remain unanswered. Beyond tendencies toward positive or negative emotionality, which emotion-related traits play a role in the decision to engage in creativity, creative behavior across domains, and domain-specific creativity? Candidate domain-general traits include curiosity (Schutte & Malouff, 2020), hope (Bernardo, 2010), passion (Vallerand et al., 2003), and trait emotional intelligence (Xu et al., 2019). Research remains scarce about emotion traits predicting domain-specific creativity.

In addition to personality traits, person-level attributes relevant to understanding the role of affective processes across different aspects of creativity can be either psychological (self-concept and identity) or social-demographic. Although we know that creative self-efficacy and creative identity are related to positive emotionality, curiosity, and trait emotional intelligence in cross-sectional studies (Bang & Reio, 2017; Karwowski, 2012; Karwowski et al., 2018), longitudinal studies are needed to connect these attributes of the creative person to the extended course of the creative process. Beghetto and Schmidt (Chapter 26) propose a model of this process in the context of creative curricular experiences. According to this model, creative curricular experiences present situations of uncertainty (which are themselves emotion filled). Responding to uncertainty with strong creative self-efficacy engenders feelings of interest, curiosity, enjoyment, and challenge, and in turn creative expression and development. However, responding to the uncertainty with low self-efficacy beliefs results in self-conscious emotions (embarrassment, shame, self-doubt) and suspended creative expression and development.

The influence of social group membership in the relationship between affective processes and creativity has thus far received insufficient attention. Taylor (Chapter 13) discusses gender difference in creativity and emotion. Although the gender differences in creative thinking abilities are not significant (or might even favor girls and women), women show less creative behavior at work and are underrepresented in high levels of socially recognized creative achievement. Emerging evidence suggests that this might be at least in part due to differences in emotional experiences of work and support for creativity at work.

Other social group differences also affect emotional experiences, which could have consequences for creativity. Socioeconomic status (SES) limits knowledge acquisition, restricts social opportunities, and hurts emotional well-being (Brooks-Gunn & Duncan, 1997; Evans, 2004; Kraus et al., 2012). Emotional experiences at school are less positive and more negative for students who are of lower SES than their higher SES peers (Moeller et al., 2020). Also, SES is associated with lower creative idea generation abilities (Castillo-Vergara et al., 2018; Dudek et al., 1993), creative self-efficacy (Karwowski, 2011), and self-perceived creativity (Ivcevic & Kaufman, 2013). Emerging research suggests that SES and emotions might have a sequential effect on creativity. For example, Yang and colleagues (2020) showed support for a model where higher SES predicts hope, which in turn predicts higher creative self-efficacy and ideational behavior.

The creative person should also be considered across the life span. Russ (Chapter 14) discusses play as both the developmental context of childhood and a typical avenue for expression of childhood creativity. Affect motivates play and is expressed in pretend play directly and indirectly. Moreover, longitudinal studies show that these processes predict later creative thinking and creative production (e.g., storytelling). However, it remains unclear how developmental changes in emotion understanding influence affective and imaginative qualities in play and to what extent gains in understanding emotions contribute to later creativity. At the other end of the life span, Ermoshkina and Kahana (Chapter 15) examine the role of creativity and emotional intelligence in responding to everyday challenges of aging and identify them as resources for successful aging.

Emotions in Creative Products, Emotions as Creative Products

The connection between affective processes and creative products is twofold. First, there are creative aspects of emotions or emotional processes, such as in the case of emotional creativity or dark creativity. Second, creative behavior or products elicit emotions, have emotional benefits, and can help develop emotion abilities.

The most direct connection between creative products and emotions is the case of creativity in the domain of emotions. Trnka (Chapter 17) reviews research on emotional creativity, which is both an ability and a trait describing the experience of authentic and original, yet effective emotions (or combinations of emotions). Recently, interest in creative products in the domain of emotions has grown to include creative emotion regulation (Ivcevic et al., 2017). For example, reappraisal inventiveness has been defined as fluency and flexibility in generating different ways to reappraise an emotion-eliciting event (Weber et al., 2014). Reappraisal inventiveness of anger-evoking situations is related to performance on divergent thinking tasks and openness to experiences, but not to trait anger or frequency of using reappraisal as a regulation strategy in everyday life (Weber et al., 2014). Brain activity studies (using EEG) suggest that reappraisal inventiveness is distinct from cognitive creative ideation (such as when working on an alternate uses task) and that it includes more cognitive control and less spontaneous imagination than the cognitive task (Fink et al., 2017). These studies are opening a new avenue for research on creative emotion regulation that supports responding to life challenges and enhances well-being.

Much research on affective processes in creativity assumes its neutral or benevolent nature (e.g., creativity as a means of solving social problems and improving lives). However, recent research of negative creativity (dark or malevolent creativity) poses the question of whether these creative products are related to distinct affective processes. Kapoor and Mange (Chapter 18) describe dark creativity as using original ideas or behaviors whose end results are harmful, either intentionally or not. They draw on the dark personality traits and their affective features, as well as affective states associated with dark creativity.

Creative outcomes – products, behaviors, achievements – elicit emotions both in their audience and the creator. Although research shows that creative and innovative products (e.g., consumer products) elicit emotional reactions and that these emotional reactions have important consequences (e.g., willingness to purchase; Horn & Salvendy, 2009), emotional effects of creative products have been most systematically studied in aesthetics research. Tinio and Specker (Chapter 19) review research based on the theory that posits a mirror image correspondence between viewing art and art creation. The mirror theory describes viewing art as starting with perceiving surface features, moving to memory-based processing, and ending with aesthetic judgments and aesthetic emotional experience based on identifying underlying meaning and/or personal relevance of the art. Supporting the theory, research shows a correspondence between feelings intended by the artist and those perceived by the audience.

Engagement in everyday creative activities has emotional effects on creators. Grossman and Drake (Chapter 20) review the affective benefits of participation in everyday creative activities showing that different emotion regulation strategies are associated with participation in different creative activities. Overall, research points to artistic creative activities (e.g., music, dance, visual arts, expressive writing) as beneficial for reducing negative affect, whereas nonartistic creative activities (e.g., cooking, gardening, science) appear to be promoting or maintaining positive affect. Holinger and Kaufman (Chapter 21) examine well-being-related outcomes of everyday creative activities. They identify key features in theoretical models of well-being and describe the benefits of creativity in terms of socialization, personal growth, meaning/legacy, and flow. Orkibi and Keisari (Chapter 22) present research showing the effectiveness of creative arts therapies and propose a model to describe the role of creativity in improving mental health outcomes. This model promises to inspire future research on the processes and mechanisms by which creativity contributes to greater personal resources and positive health.

Participation in creative activities can also have implications for learning emotion abilities. As with the study of affective outcomes of engaging in everyday creative activities, much research has focused on the arts. Stutesman and Goldstein (Chapter 23) review empirical research showing that engaging in different types of arts (e.g., visual art, theatre, dance, music, multimodal art) is beneficial for social and emotional development (e.g., developing emotion regulation, theory of mind). Research on how art-based activities can help development of emotion abilities is an area where much progress has been made in recent years. However, a lot remains to be answered, especially using randomized controlled methods and examining mechanisms of influence. Future research should also address potential effects on social and emotional abilities of creative work in nonartistic domains. It could be hypothesized that at least a somewhat distinct set of abilities can be built in different domains. For instance, in domains based on teamwork (e.g., theatre), abilities related to perceiving emotions in others might be most likely to develop.

Emotion and the Context for Creativity

In this Handbook, the context for creativity was discussed in relation to school and work environments. Anderson (Chapter 24) examines anxiety (rooted in uncertainty) and fear of failure in relation to creativity and points to the importance of creative metacognition. Mechanisms of cognitive meta-cognition can enable students to cope with uncertainty and related anxiety in the course of the creative process. The challenge of education for creativity thus importantly involves teaching creative metacognition and self-regulation. Emerging research is starting to address student attitudes toward creativity at school (Ivcevic & Hoffmann, 2021) and skills and processes students can employ toward successful creative action and development (Zielińska et al., 2022).

Beghetto and Schmidt (Chapter 26) stress that affective processes influencing creativity are embedded in the sociocultural context. They discuss both socio-psychological factors (e.g., structures and behaviors that affect the nature of student motivation, such as monitoring, focus on evaluation and social comparison) and factors pertaining to the physical environment of education (e.g., taking learning beyond the confines of the school building into natural environments or cultural settings such as museums and art galleries). The common threads in settings supportive of creativity are that they stimulate flexibility and openness. Karwowski (Chapter 25) adds to this consideration of contextual factors coming from students' most immediate social environment – their peers. Here again, the lack of concern about social acceptance emerges as relevant for creativity.

In the context of work, emotional climate supportive of creativity is characterized by psychological safety (Reiter-Palmon & Millier, Chapter 29). Emich and Lu (Chapter 27) redefine affective climate as the affective state that forms among members of a collective in response to their shared experience. Madrid and colleagues (Chapter 28) add that the impact of group affective tone on creativity occurs via two distinct mechanisms – broaden-and-build processes and social integration processes (cohesion, trust, collaboration). Connelly and Demirag Burak (Chapter 30) emphasize the key role of leaders in establishing a climate beneficial to both individual creativity and social aspects of creativity. Finally, Ashkanasy and To (Chapter 31) develop an integrative model describing the role of emotions in creativity at work across five levels: (1) intraindividual level describing within-person variation through time; (2) between-person differences (especially relating to trait affect and emotional intelligence); (3) level of interpersonal relationships; (4) team or group level; and (5) the level of organizations as a whole (attributes of culture or climate). Processes across these levels are dynamic – both in terms of cross-level interactions and variations through time. Although individual and group creativity can be inspired or motivated by both positive and negative emotions, creative outcomes tend to result in environments that are characterized by positive affective qualities that facilitate coping with task challenges.

A major context influencing affective processes across different aspects of creativity that this Handbook did not tackle is culture. Culture has been examined in relation to creativity and culture has been examined in relation to emotions, but studies at the intersection of culture, emotions, and creativity remain scarce. Existing research has largely focused on the differences between the East (such as China or Korea) and West (such as the United States or Western Europe). Cultural differences have been documented in lay conceptions of creativity (Niu & Kaufman, 2013; Niu & Sternberg, 2002; Paletz & Peng, 2008), suggesting that other creativity-relevant variables could differ across cultures and thus bring forth the question of whether we are measuring the same thing when assessing creativity across cultures.

Katz-Buonincontro and colleagues (2021) tested measurement invariance of beliefs about teaching for creativity between U.S. and Chinese educators and found that creative self-efficacy, fixed creativity mindset, growth creativity mindset, and desirability of creativity for teaching success, and value of creativity for student academic and workplace success have similar latent structures across two cultures. However, Guo and colleagues (2021) found less support for measurement invariance for fluency and originality scores on two divergent thinking tests (Line Meanings and Real-World Problems) among American and Chinese college students. For the Real-World Problems test, measurement invariance was supported for fluency, but not originality, and for the Line Meanings, measurement invariance was not supported for either of the two performance criteria.

Culture also influences affective processes. For instance, there are cultural differences in ideal affect – preferred affective states or states toward which people strive – which are based on cultural values and behavioral norms about appropriate emotion expression. Tsai (2007, 2017) shows that ideal affect in the American cultural context tends to be positive and activated (e.g., being enthusiastic, excited, energized), while in the East Asian cultural context it tends to be positive and deactivated (e.g., being calm, peaceful, serene). Studies of the relationship between affective experiences and creativity outcomes have been overwhelmingly conducted in the Western cultural context. The finding that positive activated moods facilitate creative idea generation points to the correspondence between actual affect and ideal affect. Are positive activated moods equally beneficial for creative thinking in cultural contexts where people tend to aspire to experience deactivated positive affect? Or might the beneficial ingredient for creative thinking be the similarity between the actual and ideal affective states?

Toward a Model of the Role of Affective Processes across Aspects of Creativity

Where do we go from here? This Handbook brought together scholars in multiple disciplines – from psychology and neuroscience to organizational behavior to education to sociology and art therapies – who synthesized the latest research and developed models describing specific aspects of the relationship between emotions and creativity, broadly construed. In this final section we take an integrative approach and propose a model that can stimulate the next generation of research (to be reviewed in the next edition of the *Cambridge Handbook of Creativity and Emotion*).

The first step in formulating the model is to be clear about the definitions of terms. This definition is easier in the domain of emotions than in the domain of creativity. Although there is no shortage of debates about the nature of emotions (Ekman, 2016), three broad groups of emotion-related attributes can be distinguished: affective states (relatively short-term feelings, emotions, and moods), emotion-related traits (typical ways of feeling), and emotion abilities (reasoning about and with emotions, such as in the case of emotional intelligence).

Table 32.1 presents two sets of considerations in the study of emotions and creativity, with the first pertaining to the nature of creativity itself and the second pertaining to the nature of the emotion–creativity relationship. Scholars have reached consensus on the definition of creativity as involving originality and task appropriateness (usefulness or meaningfulness; Runco & Jaeger, 2012). The next task for creativity science is to specify the nature of creativity under consideration. Researchers have long distinguished the study of the creative process, creative person, creative products, and the creative press (Rhodes, 1961). Yet, research studies oftentimes refer to their findings as reflecting "creativity" as opposed to specific aspects of creativity. Theoretically, there is no reason to believe that performance on 3-minute-long creative thinking tasks, for instance, should be influenced by the same affective traits or processes as lifetime creative achievement. Thus, it is crucial for scholars to specify the nature of creativity under consideration.

Table 32.1 *Levels of analysis in the relationship between affective processes and creativity*

Specification aspect	Description	Key variables/processes
Creativity		
Time	Short term	Performance on brief laboratory tasks, reports on in-the-moment creative thinking and activity
	Long term	Frequency of creative behavior or achievement
Potential vs. actualization	Creative potential	Creative abilities, self-concept
	Behavior	Creative process engagement
	Achievement	Level of socially recognized creative achievement
Locus of judgment	Self-judgment	Self-perceived creativity
		Self-reported creative behavior
	Other-judgment	Ratings by relevant others (e.g., supervisors)
		Consensual assessment of ideas or products
Emotion–creativity relationship		
Individual	Intra-individual dynamics of performance	Affective states
	Inter-individual differences in performance and behavior	Emotion traits and abilities
Dyadic	Horizontal relationships	Affect in relationships with peers or coworkers
	Vertical relationships	Affect in relationships with teachers or leaders
Groups	Team emotional climate	Development and maintenance of psychological safety
		Emotional dynamics of conflict
Institutional	Demands and resources	Organizational norms and values affecting motivation, opportunities, and constraints for creativity
		Organization-wide affect, positive work environment
		Emotion display rules
Cultural	Societal norms and values	Lay theories of creativity
		Actual and ideal affect

The nature of creativity can be specified in relation to three criteria: time, potential versus actualization, and locus of judgment. Creativity exists and can be studied on a continuum from short term to (very) long term. Experimental studies often measure creative performance on tasks that take no more than 3 or 4 minutes to complete. This research design decision is necessary because of the short effects of mood manipulations. Also, performance on short tasks can be practically meaningful and have ecological validity in some contexts (e.g., quick idea generation in educational or workplace settings). On the opposite end of the continuum are measures of lifetime creativity, whether in everyday (Richards et al., 1988) or occupational domains (Helson et al., 1995). Depending on where on this continuum a creativity outcome measure falls, different predictors will be of (relatively) lower or greater importance.

Creativity measures (and therefore conclusions) should further be specified as measures of potential or its actualization in everyday behavior and achievement. Tests of creative thinking are theoretically conceived as measuring creative potential (Barbot et al., 2016; Torrance, 1966), as are measures of creative personality (Gough, 1979) and creative self-perceptions of creativity (Kaufman, 2012; McKay et al., 2017). By contrast, measures of behavior can assess the frequency and type of creative activities (Batey, 2007; Ivcevic & Mayer, 2009) or the level of socially recognized creative achievement (Carson et al., 2005; Simonton, 2009).

Finally, creativity measures differ in the locus of judgment – whether ideas, performances, or actions are identified as creative by the self or external judges/raters. Self-reports are used when measuring creative personality and self-perceptions of creativity, as well as in identifying creative behavior in experience-sampling or diary studies and on inventories of creative behavior and achievement (Silvia et al., 2012). External judgments of creativity are used when evaluating performance on measures of creative thinking and problem solving and evaluating products (often using the consensual assessment technique, Amabile, 1996), as well as in studies in specific contexts such as schools (e.g., peer ratings: Ivcevic & Brackett, 2015; teacher ratings: Beghetto et al., 2011) and workplaces (e.g., supervisor ratings, George & Zhou, 2007). This distinction between self-reported and externally rated creativity has been used in moderation analyses of several recent meta-analyses clearly demonstrating its importance (e.g., Puryear et al., 2017; Xu et al., 2019). We argue that it should be further specified whether the self-ratings pertain to creative potential or behavior because self-reported creative achievement is substantively different from self-reported creative personality, for instance. There is also the suggested third distinction of collaborative efforts (the concept of "We" creativity; Glăveanu, 2010).

After defining the nature of creativity under consideration, we propose that scholars need to define the level on which they examine the role of affective processes across different aspects of creativity. These levels of analysis are often implicit in empirical studies. Acknowledging them explicitly can draw attention to the need to understand creativity-relevant processes across levels. Ashkanasy and To (Chapter 31) defined multiple levels in the study of emotions and creativity in the workplace. Integrating their multi-level model with contributions of scholars who discussed specific levels of analysis (e.g., Anderson, Chapter 24; Connelly & Demirag Burak, Chapter 30; Emich & Lu, Chapter 27; Karwowski, Chapter 25; Lebuda et al., Chapter 16; Madrid et al., Chapter 28; Reiter-Palmon & Millier, Chapter 29), we describe creativity

Model of Affective Processes across Different Aspects of Creativity

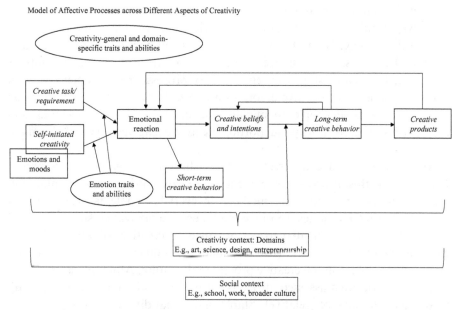

Figure 32.1 *Model of affective processes across different aspects of creativity.*

as meaningfully existing on each level from individual, to dyadic, group or team level, to institutional level, to cultural level. Table 32.1 defines features of these levels along with examples applicable in different contexts. Each lower level is embedded into the higher levels, and eventual comprehensive understanding of affective processes will require mapping of affective processes relevant at specific levels, as well as cross-level processes.

Figure 32.1 depicts an integrative model of affective processes across different aspects of creativity. Creativity depends in large part on creativity-general and domain-specific traits and abilities (Amabile & Pratt, 2016). For example, in the past three decades, research has accumulated about the personality dimension of openness to experience as predictive of creative behavior and achievement across domains (Feist, 1998; Ivcevic & Mayer, 2009; Puryear et al., 2017). Creative thinking skills are best described as domain specific (Barbot et al., 2016) and can be expected to be relevant in predicting domain-specific behavior.

Emotions and moods can be an inspiration for creative activity. This is especially the case for self-initiated creativity. Examples include artists expressing emotions in their art (Tinio & Gartus, 2018) and entrepreneurs being inspired by often frustrating social needs or failures (Zahra et al., 2009). On the other hand, creativity that is a demand in a certain context – as a school assignment or a work task – starts with the encounter with the task. Whether self-initiated or required, the start of the creative process evokes emotional reactions – affective states and moods triggered by the encounter with an open-ended problem. These reactions might be different in the case of self-initiated (and thus largely intrinsically motivated) versus required creative tasks (which might or might not be intrinsically motivated; Unsworth, 2001; Unsworth & Clegg, 2010). Emotional reactions will be moderated by emotion traits and abilities. For instance, the ability to effectively manage emotions moderates the relationship between creativity processing requirement at work and the experience of positive emotions at work (Parke et al., 2015). Emotion abilities can enable people to manage the intensity of their reactions and reappraise situations in ways supporting creative engagement (Liu & Damian, Chapter 9).

Affective states have a direct effect on short-term creative performance. Examples of this process are evident in research using experimental and experience-sampling and diary methods in everyday contexts. These studies show that affective states (positive and negative activated states, Madrid et al., Chapter 5) are related to performance on creative thinking tasks and creative engagement at work. Affective states also influence creative beliefs and intentions to engage in the creative process in the future. Although creative self-efficacy is most often assessed at one point in time and implicitly or explicitly treated as a variable of (relatively stable) individual difference, it is subject to dynamic changes, with frustrations or failures triggering self-doubt and lowering (at least temporarily) creative self-efficacy and successes boosting it (Beghetto & Karwowski, 2019).

Creative beliefs and intentions predict creative behavior and creativity of products or creative achievement. Emotion traits and abilities play a role in transforming intentions into action and in maintaining effort and persistence in long-term creative problems or projects. For individuals of average or high creative potential, the ability to successfully regulate emotions helps maintain passion for one's interests and persistence in the face of obstacles (Ivcevic & Brackett, 2015).

Importantly, emotion–creativity processes do not flow in a single direction only. Rather, creative behavior in itself evokes feelings, either diminishing negative or enhancing positive affect (Grossman & Drake, Chapter 20), and creative products evoke affective reactions (e.g., Tinio & Specker, Chapter 19).

Affective processes in creativity are embedded in different contexts and can vary according to these contexts. One type of context pertains to creativity itself – the context of creativity domains: everyday life activities and relationships, the arts, sciences, design, technology, entrepreneurship, and others. The Amusement Park Theory posits that macrodomains, or general thematic areas (e.g., the arts) can be further divided into more specific domains (e.g., visual arts) and microdomains (e.g., abstract painting; Baer & Kaufman, 2017). To the extent that creativity is domain specific, it can be expected that some differences among domains will emerge in relation to affective processes facilitating creative engagement, behavior, and achievement. Another type of context in which creativity is embedded is the social context, ranging from immediate environments, such as school and work, to the broader cultural context. Each of these contexts is characterized by its relational, institutional, and normative structures that are likely to influence affective processes. For instance, in the context of education, relevant relationships are those among peers (Karwowski, Chapter 25) and between mentors and mentees (Lebuda et al., Chapter 16); institutional influences can include exposure to creative curricular experiences (Beghetto & Schmidt, Chapter 26); and normative influences refer to culturally appropriate ways to interact with teachers or mentors (e.g., the extent to which it is socially appropriate to question teachers in class and share unconventional ideas).

This process model offers directions for future research on affective processes relevant for different aspects of creativity. For instance, although some existing research points to the moderating role of emotion abilities in transforming creative potential into creative behavior, more research is needed across samples and contexts. Perhaps the biggest avenue for future research will consider the role of contexts – creative domains and social contexts – on both affective processes and their role in creativity. In this research, what is usually implicit (e.g., industry when studying creativity in the workplace) or what is not commonly addressed (e.g., cultural differences) should become explicit and subject to systematic investigation.

References

Amabile, T. M. (1996). *Creativity in Context: Update to the Social Psychology of Creativity*. Westview Press.

Amabile, T. M., & Pratt, M. G. (2016). The dynamic componential model of creativity and innovation in organizations: Making progress, making meaning. *Research in Organizational Behavior, 36*, 157–183. https://doi.org/10.1016/j.riob.2016.10.001

Baer, J., & Kaufman, J. C. (2017). The Amusement Park Theoretical Model of Creativity: An attempt to bridge the domain specificity/generality gap. In J. C. Kaufman, V. P. Glăveanu, & J. Baer (Eds.), *Cambridge Handbook of Creativity across Domains* (pp. 8–17). Cambridge University Press.

Bang, H., & Reio Jr, T. G. (2017). Personal accomplishment, mentoring, and creative self-efficacy as predictors of creative work involvement: The moderating role of positive and negative affect. *The Journal of Psychology, 151*(2), 148–170. https://doi.org/10.1080/00223980.2016.1248808

Barbot, B., Besançon, M., & Lubart, T. (2016). The generality-specificity of creativity: Exploring the structure of creative potential with EPoC. *Learning and Individual Differences, 52*, 178–187. https://doi.org/10.1016/j.lindif.2016.06.005

Batey, M. D. (2007). A *Psychometric Investigation* of *Everyday Creativity* (Order No. U591819). Doctoral dissertation, University College, London. ProQuest Dissertations & Theses Global. (1427280692). www.proquest.com/dissertations-theses/psychometric-investigation-everyday-creativity/docview/1427280692/se-2?accountid=15172

Beghetto, R. A., Kaufman, J. C., & Baxter, J. (2011). Answering the unexpected questions: Exploring the relationship between students' creative self-efficacy and teacher ratings of creativity. *Psychology of Aesthetics, Creativity, and the Arts, 5*(4), 342–349. https://doi.org/10.1037/a0022834

Beghetto, R. A., & Karwowski, M. (2019). Unfreezing creativity: A dynamic, micro-longitudinal approach. In R. A. Beghetto & G. Corazza (Eds.). *Dynamic Perspectives on Creativity* (pp. 7–25). Springer. https://doi.org/10.1007/978-3-319-99163-4_2

Beghetto, R. A., Kaufman, J. C., & Baxter, J. (2011). Answering the unexpected questions: Exploring the relationship between students' creative self-efficacy and teacher ratings of creativity. *Psychology of Aesthetics, Creativity, and the Arts, 5*(4), 342–349. https://doi.org/10.1037/a0022834

Bernardo, A. B. (2010). Extending hope theory: Internal and external locus of trait hope. *Personality and Individual Differences, 49*(8), 944–949. https://doi.org/10.1016/j.paid.2010.07.036

Brooks-Gunn, J., & Duncan, G. J. (1997). The effects of poverty on children. *The Future of Children, 7*(2), 55–71. https://doi.org/10.2307/1602387

Carson, S. H., Peterson, J. B., & Higgins, D. M. (2005). Reliability, validity, and factor structure of the Creative Achievement Questionnaire. *Creativity Research Journal, 17*(1), 37–50. https://doi.org/10.1207/s15326934crj1701_4

Castillo-Vergara, M., Galleguillos, N. B., Cuello, L. J., Alvarez-Marin, A., & Acuña-Opazo, M. (2018). Does socioeconomic status influence student creativity? *Thinking Skills and Creativity, 29*, 142–152. https://doi.org/10.1016/j.tsc.2018.07.005

De Dreu, C. K. W., Baas, M., & Nijstad, B. A. (2008). Hedonic tone and activation level in the mood-creativity link: Toward a dual pathway to creativity model. *Journal of Personality and Social Psychology, 94*(5), 739–756. https://doi.org/10.1037/0022-3514.94.5.739

Dudek, S. Z., Strobel, M. G., & Runco, M. A. (1993). Cumulative and proximal influences on the social environment and children's creative potential. *The Journal of Genetic Psychology: Research and Theory on Human Development, 154*(4), 487–499. https://doi.org/10.1080/00221325.1993.9914747

Eisenberg, N., & Miller, P. A. (1987). The relation of empathy to prosocial and related behaviors. *Psychological Bulletin, 101*(1), 91–119. https://doi.org/10.1037/0033-2909.101.1.91

Ekman, P. (2016). What scientists who study emotion agree about. *Perspectives on Psychological Science, 11*(1), 31–34. https://doi.org/10.1177/1745691615596992

Evans, G. W. (2004). The environment of childhood poverty. *American Psychologist, 59*(2), 77–92. https://doi.org/10.1037/0003-066X.59.2.77

Fink, A., Weiss, E. M., Schwarzl, U., et al. (2017). Creative ways to well-being: Reappraisal inventiveness in the context of anger-evoking situations. *Cognitive, Affective & Behavioral Neuroscience, 17*(1), 94–105. https://doi.org/10.3758/s13415-016-0465-9

Feist, G. J. (1998). A meta-analysis of personality in scientific and artistic creativity. *Personality and Social Psychology Review, 2*(4), 290–309. https://doi.org/10.1207/s15327957pspr0204_5

Gasper, K., & Middlewood, B. L. (2014). Approaching novel thoughts: Understanding why elation and boredom promote associative thought more than distress and relaxation. *Journal of Experimental Social Psychology, 52*, 50–57. https://doi.org/10.1016/j.jesp.2013.12.007

George, J. M., & Zhou, J. (2007). Dual tuning in a supportive context: Joint contributions of positive mood, negative mood, and supervisory behaviors to employee creativity. *Academy of Management Journal, 50*(3), 605–622. https://doi.org/10.5465/AMJ.2007.25525934

Glăveanu, V. P. (2010). Paradigms in the study of creativity: Introducing the perspective of cultural psychology. *New Ideas in Psychology*, *28*(1), 79–93. https://doi-org / 10.1016/j.newideapsych.2009.07.007

Glăveanu, V. P., Lubart, T., Bonnardel, N., et al. (2013) Creativity as action: Findings from five creative domains. *Frontiers in Psychology*, *4*(176), 1–14. https://doi.org/10.3389/fpsyg.2013.00176

Gough, H. G. (1979). A creative personality scale for the Adjective Check List. *Journal of Personality and Social Psychology, 37*(8), 1398–1405. https://doi.org/10.1037/0022-3514.37.8.1398

Gross, M. E., Zedelius, C. M., & Schooler, J. W. (2020). Cultivating an understanding of curiosity as a seed for creativity. *Current Opinion in Behavioral Sciences, 35*, 77–82. https://doi.org/10.1016/j.cobeha.2020.07.015

Guo, Y., Lin, S., Guo, J., Lu, Z. L., & Shangguan, C. (2021). Cross-cultural measurement invariance of divergent thinking measures. *Thinking Skills and Creativity, 41*, 100852. https://doi.org/10.1016/j.tsc.2021.100852

Helson, R., Roberts, B., & Agronick, G. (1995). Enduringness and change in creative personality and the prediction of occupational creativity. *Journal of Personality and Social Psychology, 69*(6), 1173–1183. https://doi.org/10.1037/0022-3514.69.6.1173

Henriksen, D., Richardson, C., & Mehta, R. (2017). Design thinking: A creative approach to educational problems of practice. *Thinking Skills and Creativity*, *26*, 140-153. https://doi.org/10.1016/j.tsc.2017.10.001

Horn, D., & Salvendy, G. (2009). Measuring consumer perception of product creativity: Impact on satisfaction and purchasability. *Human Factors and Ergonomics in Manufacturing, 19*(3), 223–240. https://doi.org/10.1002/hfm.20150

Isen, A. M. (1999). On the relationship between affect and creative problem solving. In S. W. Russ (Ed.), *Affect, Creative Experience, and Psychological Adjustment* (pp. 3–17). Taylor & Francis.

Isen, A. M., & Daubman, K. A. (1984). The influence of affect on categorization. *Journal of Personality and Social Psychology, 47*(6), 1206–1217. https://doi.org/10.1037/0022-3514.47.6.1206

Ivcevic, Z., Bazhydai, M., Hoffmann, J. D., & Brackett, M. A. (2017). Creativity in the domain of emotions. In J. C. Kaufman, V. P. Glăveanu, & J. Baer (Eds.), *The Cambridge Handbook of Creativity across Domains* (pp. 525–548). Cambridge University Press. https://doi.org/10.1017/9781316274385.029

Ivcevic, Z., & Brackett, M. A. (2015). Predicting creativity: Interactive effects of openness to experience and emotion regulation ability. *Psychology of Aesthetics, Creativity, and the Arts, 9*(4), 480–487. https://doi.org/10.1037/a0039826

Ivcevic, Z., & Hoffmann, J. D. (2021). The creativity dare: Attitudes toward creativity and prediction of creative behavior in school. *The Journal of Creative Behavior*. https://doi.org/10.1002/jocb.527

Ivcevic, Z., & Kaufman, J. C. (2013). The can and cannot do attitude: How self-estimates of ability vary across ethnic and socioeconomic groups. *Learning and Individual Differences, 27*, 144–148. https://doi.org/10.1016/j.lindif.2013.07.011

Ivcevic, Z., & Mayer, J. D. (2009). Mapping dimensions of creativity in the life-space. *Creativity Research Journal, 21*(2–3), 152–165. https://doi.org/10.1080/10400410902855259

Karwowski, M. (2011). It doesn't hurt to ask . . . But sometimes it hurts to believe: Polish students' creative self-efficacy and its predictors. *Psychology of Aesthetics, Creativity, and the Arts, 5*(2), 154–164. https://doi.org/10.1037/a0021427

Karwowski, M. (2012). Did curiosity kill the cat? Relationship between trait curiosity, creative self-efficacy and creative personal identity. *Europe's Journal of Psychology, 8*(4), 547–558. https://doi.org/10.5964/ejop.v8i4.513

Karwowski, M., Lebuda, I., & Wiśniewska, E. (2018). Measuring creative self-efficacy and creative personal identity. *The International Journal of Creativity & Problem Solving, 28*(1), 45–57.

Katz-Buonincontro, J., Hass, R., Kettler, T., Tang, L. M., & Hu, W. (2021). Partial measurement invariance of beliefs about teaching for creativity across U.S. and Chinese educators. *British Journal of Educational Psychology, 91*(2), 563–583. https://doi.org/10.1111/bjep.12379

Kaufman, J. C. (2012). Counting the muses: Development of the Kaufman Domains of Creativity Scale (K-DOCS). *Psychology of Aesthetics, Creativity, and the Arts, 6*(4), 298–308. https://doi.org/10.1037/a0029751

Kraus, M. W., Piff, P. K., Mendoza-Denton, R., Rheinschmidt, M. L., & Keltner, D. (2012). Social class, solipsism, and contextualism: How the rich are different from the poor. *Psychological Review, 119*(3), 546–572. https://doi.org/10.1037/a0028756

Liu, X. X., Gong, S. Y., Zhang, H. P., Yu, Q. L., & Zhou, Z. J. (2021). Perceived teacher support and creative self-efficacy: The mediating roles of autonomous motivation and achievement emotions in Chinese junior high school students. *Thinking Skills and Creativity, 39*, Article 100752. https://doi.org/10.1016/j.tsc.2020.100752

Mann, S., & Cadman, R. (2014). Does being bored make us more creative? *Creativity Research Journal, 26*(2), 165-173. https://doi.org/10.1080/10400419.2014.901073

McKay, A. S., Karwowski, M., & Kaufman, J. C. (2017). Measuring the muses: Validating the Kaufman Domains of Creativity Scale (K-DOCS). *Psychology of Aesthetics, Creativity, and the Arts, 11*(2), 216–230. https://doi.org/10.1037/aca0000074

Moeller, J., Brackett, M. A., Ivcevic, Z., & White, A. E. (2020). High school students' feelings: Discoveries from a large national survey and an experience sampling study. *Learning and Instruction, 66*, 101301. https://doi.org/10.1016/j.learninstruc.2019.101301

Mumford, M. D., & McIntosh, T. (2017). Creative thinking processes: The past and the future. *The Journal of Creative Behavior, 51*(4), 317–322. https://doi.org/10.1002/jocb.197

Niu, W., & Kaufman, J. C. (2013). Creativity of Chinese and American cultures: A synthetic analysis. *The Journal of Creative Behavior, 47*(1), 77–87. https://doi.org/10.1002/jocb.25

Niu, W., & Sternberg, R. (2002). Contemporary studies on the concept of creativity: The East and the West. *The Journal of Creative Behavior, 36*(4), 269–288. https://doi.org/10.1002/j.2162-6057.2002.tb01069.x

Paletz, S. B. F., & Peng, K. (2008). Implicit theories of creativity across cultures: Novelty and appropriateness in two product domains. *Journal of Cross-Cultural Psychology, 39*(3), 286–302. https://doi.org/10.1177/0022022108315112

Parke, M. R., Seo, M. G., & Sherf, E. N. (2015). Regulating and facilitating: The role of emotional intelligence in maintaining and using positive affect for creativity. *Journal of Applied Psychology, 100*(3), 917–934. https://doi.org/10.1037/a0038452

Pekrun, R. (2006). The control-value theory of achievement emotions: Assumptions, corollaries, and implications for educational research and practice. *Educational Psychology Review, 18*(4), 315–341. https://doi.org/10.1007/s10648-006-9029-9

Puryear, J. S., Kettler, T., & Rinn, A. N. (2017). Relationships of personality to differential conceptions of creativity: A systematic review. *Psychology of Aesthetics, Creativity, and the Arts, 11*(1), 59–68. https://doi.org/10.1037/aca0000079

Rhodes, M. (1961). An analysis of creativity. *The Phi Delta Kappan, 42*(7), 305-310.

Richards, R., Kinney, D. K., Benet, M., & Merzel, A. P. (1988). Assessing everyday creativity: Characteristics of the Lifetime Creativity Scales and validation with three large samples. *Journal of Personality and Social Psychology, 54*(3), 476–485. https://doi.org/10.1037/0022-3514.54.3.476

Runco, M. A., & Jaeger, G. J. (2012). The standard definition of creativity. *Creativity Research Journal, 24*(1), 92–96. https://doi.org/10.1080/10400419.2012.650092

Schutte, N. S., & Malouff, J. M. (2020). Connections between curiosity, flow and creativity. *Personality and Individual Differences, 152*, (109555). https://doi.org/10.1016/j.paid.2019.109555

Silvia, P. J., Wigert, B., Reiter-Palmon, R., & Kaufman, J. C. (2012). Assessing creativity with self-report scales: A review and empirical evaluation. *Psychology of Aesthetics, Creativity, and the Arts, 6*(1), 19–34. https://doi.org/10.1037/a0024071

Simonton, D. K. (2009). *Genius 101*. Springer.

Tinio, P. P. L., & Gartus, A. (2018). Characterizing the emotional response to art beyond pleasure: Correspondence between the emotional characteristics of artworks and viewers' emotional responses. *Progress in Brain Research. 237*, 319–342. https://doi.org/10.1016/bs.pbr.2018.03.005

To, M. L., Fisher, C. D., Ashkanasy, N. M., & Rowe, P. A. (2012). Within-person relationships between mood and creativity. *Journal of Applied Psychology, 97*(3), 599–612. https://doi.org/10.1037/a0026097

Torrance, E. P. (1966). *Torrance Tests of Creative Thinking: Norms Technical Manual* (Research ed.). Personnel Press.

Tsai, J. L. (2007). Ideal affect: Cultural causes and behavioral consequences. *Perspectives on Psychological Science, 2*(3), 242–259. https://doi.org/10.1111/j.1745-6916.2007.00043.x

Tsai, J. L. (2017). Ideal affect in daily life: Implications for affective experience, health, and social behavior. *Current Opinion in Psychology, 17*, 118–128. https://doi.org/10.1016/j.copsyc.2017.07.004

Unsworth, K. (2001). Unpacking creativity. *Academy of Management Review, 26*, 289–297.

Unsworth, K. L., & Clegg, C. W. (2010). Why do employees undertake creative action? *Journal of Occupational and Organizational Psychology, 83*, 77–99.

Vallerand, R. J., Blanchard, C., Mageau, G. A., et al. (2003). Les passions de l'âme: On obsessive and harmonious passion. *Journal of Personality and Social Psychology, 85*(4), 756–767. https://doi.org/10.1037/0022-3514.85.4.756

Weber, H., de Assunção, V. L., Martin, C., Westmeyer, H., & Geisler, F. C. (2014). Reappraisal inventiveness: The ability to create different reappraisals of critical situations. *Cognition and Emotion, 28*(2), 345–360. https://doi.org/10.1080/02699931.2013.832152

Xu, X., Liu, W., & Pang, W. (2019). Are emotionally intelligent people more creative? A meta-analysis of the emotional intelligence–creativity link. *Sustainability, 11*(21), 6123. http://dx.doi.org/10.3390/su11216123

Yang, Y., Xiaobo, X., Wenling, L., & Weiguo, P. (2020). Hope and creative self-efficacy as sequential mediators in the relationship between family socioeconomic status and creativity. *Frontiers in Psychology, 11*, https://doi.org/10.3389/fpsyg.2020.00438

Zahra, S. A., Gedajlovic, E., Neubaum, D. O., & Shulman, J. M. (2009). Motives, search processes and ethical challenges. *Journal of Business Venturing, 24*(5), 519–532. https://doi.org/10.1016/j.jbusvent.2008.04.007

Zielińska, A., Lebuda, I., Ivcevic, Z., & Karwowski, M. (2022). How adolescents develop and implement their ideas? On self-regulation of creative action. *Thinking Skills and Creativity, 43*, 100998. https://doi.org/10.1016/j.tsc.2022.100998

Index

Printed in the USA
CPSIA information can be obtained
at www.ICGtesting.com
LVHW081031281023
762436LV00013B/1424